/1500

GUSTAV HOLST

GUSTAV HOLST

The Man and his Music

MICHAEL SHORT

Oxford   New York
OXFORD UNIVERSITY PRESS
1990

Oxford University Press, Walton Street, Oxford ox2 6DP

Oxford New York Toronto
Delhi Bombay Calcutta Madras Karachi
Petaling Jaya Singapore Hong Kong Tokyo
Nairobi Dar es Salaam Cape Town
Melbourne Auckland
and associated companies in
Berlin Ibadan

Oxford is a trade mark of Oxford University Press

Published in the United States
by Oxford University Press, New York

British Library Cataloguing in Publication Data
Short, Michael, 1937–
Gustav Holst: the man and his music.
1. English music. Holst, Gustav, 1874–1934
I. Title
780'. 92'4
ISBN 0–19–314154–X

Library of Congress Cataloging-in-Publication Data
Short, Michael, 1937–
Gustav Holst: the man and his music/Michael Short.
Includes bibliographical references.
1. Holst, Gustav, 1874–1934. 2. Composers-England-Biography.
I. Title.
ML410. H748S5 1990 780'. 92--dc20 89–22260
ISBN 0–19–314154–X

Typeset by Pentacor PLC, High Wycombe, Bucks
Printed in Great Britain by
Courier International Ltd., Tiptree, Essex

Preface

As Gustav Holst died before I was born, my knowledge of him is derived not from personal acquaintance but from letters, diaries, published books and articles, personal reminiscences by his pupils, friends, and colleagues, listening to and studying his music, and above all from his daughter Miss Imogen Holst. I first met her in 1969, when, at an age at which many professionals would have already begun their retirement, she was embarking on an intensive programme of work which was to culminate in the Holst centenary of 1974, and continue, despite periods of illness, until her death in 1984.

From the start of our association, she offered full exchange of information about her father's life and music, and this largely one-way traffic resulted in her exemplary *Thematic Catalogue of Gustav Holst's Music* and my own *Gustav Holst: a centenary documentation*. Her capacity for work was insatiable; her diminutive and apparently frail physique concealing an iron-willed determination to attain her objectives. Late in the evening of our first day's work, I enquired what time I should return the following morning. 'Any time you like, Dear,' was the reply. 'Would nine o'clock be all right?'—'Yes, of course, but I shall have done three hours' work by then!'

By way of respite from our labours, she would occasionally don raincoat and sou'wester to stride out into the bitterly cold wind along the Aldeburgh sea-front, coming back glowing with health and energy. She would then insist that I should do the same, from which I would return gasping, eyes streaming, and be obliged to rest for half an hour before continuing work.

She was always kind, thoughtful, and attentive to the needs of other people, and although in later years could have lived in comfort on the royalties produced by Gustav Holst's music, she chose instead to devote this income to promulgation of her father's work, while she herself lived in almost frugal austerity. Her personal generosity was therefore not based on wealth, but often involved skimping her own needs so that someone else should have what she regarded as their proper comforts.

As a musician her work was precise yet sensitive, as a lecturer she was entertaining and informative, as a teacher she was inspiring, as a writer her clear and individual style was immediately recognizable, and as a scholar her attention to detail and accuracy was beyond reproach. She was also a composer, an aspect of her talents which she did little to promote, and those of her works which have been performed and published reveal a sensitive and individual musical nature. When asked why she had not followed up her promising début as a composer (was it because of having a famous father, or the difficulties of being a woman composer, or the necessity of earning a living by teaching?) she parried the question with the brusque retort: 'Wasn't good enough!'[1] But a cursory examination of her works reveals the falsity of this remark; she had the ability to be a successful composer, but chose instead to devote her life to other matters which she considered to be more immediately important, such as working as amanuensis to Benjamin Britten, and acting as keeper of the flame of Gustav Holst's music during the dark years of neglect.

Imogen Holst intended to write a Foreword to this book, but in the event she died before the text was completed. She did however see some of the earlier drafts, and her comments would be on the lines of: 'Dear Michael, VERY many thanks for your Chapter 1. I was thrilled to read it, and enjoyed the 2nd half very much . . .',[2] followed by several pages of detailed notes and comments in her bold, characteristic handwriting, closely questioning the evidence for practically every assertion. In her own writings she became extremely meticulous, and would not let anything pass without checking and double-checking, and I hope that I have been able to apply something of the same method to my own text.

Rather than base my work on Imogen Holst's biography of her father, which was written from her own personal point of view, I have written a completely new life based on the available source materials, including contemporary criticism, although there will naturally be a certain amount of factual overlap with Miss Holst's books. This is followed by a discussion of aspects of Holst's musical style, which may be read separately from the biographical chapters, although repetition of material has been avoided as it is assumed that readers of the musical section will have also read the biography.

Whether Holst himself would have approved of books being written about his life and work is doubtful, as he derided analytical programme notes as offering scope for 'poisonous piffle',[3] and once remarked that 'Talking about music always seems to me like keeping small boys outside a sweet shop explaining to them how the sweets are made.'[4] Despite this, I offer the present book in the hope that it will be of some use to listeners who are interested in Holst's music and would like to know more about it and the circumstances in which it was written.

Besides the enormous debt of gratitude which I owe to Imogen Holst, many other people have given indispensable help with my research into the life and work of Gustav Holst. In particular, I am most grateful to Miss Rosamund Strode, Mrs Helen Lilley and Dr Colin Matthews of the Holst Foundation, and especially to Mr Lowinger Maddison, Honorary Curator of the Holst Birthplace Museum, Cheltenham, who has given much detailed information on the Holst family from his own researches. I am also grateful to Dr Eric Roseberry for his comments and advice on the technical matters dealt with in Chapter 21.

Thanks are also due to the following, all of whom have helped me at one time or another by providing information, personal reminiscences, or otherwise assisting in my work:

Argo Record Co. Ltd., Dr J. E. Arnold, Avon County Library, Bath and Wells Diocesan Choral Association, Bath Municipal Libraries, Mrs E. Behr, Mr A. Bell, Miss Helen Bidder, Blackburn Public Libraries, Blackwell's Music Shop, Bodleian Library, Boosey & Hawkes Ltd., Bristol University Library, British Broadcasting Corporation, British Institute of Recorded Sound, British Library, Bromley Public Libraries, Mr E. T. Bryant, Miss Dorothy Callard, Cambridge University Library, Capitol Records Inc., Carnegie United Kingdom Trust, Mr Arthur Caton, Central Music Library, Cheltenham Art Gallery and Museum, Cheltenham Public Library, Composers' Guild of Great Britain, Mr Roger Crudge, Mr Charles Cudworth, Daily Telegraph, Miss Nora Day, Decca Record Co. Ltd., Electric & Musical Industries Ltd., English Folk Dance and Song Society, Eothen School, Faber Music Ltd., Fitzwilliam Museum Library, Mr Lewis Foreman, Mr Frank Forty, Mr Anthony Gilbert, Glasgow University Library, Mr Jim Glover, Mrs Amy Hammond-Davies, Miss Joan Harris, Mr Martin R. Holmes, Mr W. J. Hough, Miss Jane Humfrey, Mr J. C. Iles, Imperial College, Dr Gordon Jacob, James Allen's Girls' School, Jupiter Recordings Ltd., Lambeth Palace Library, Lambeth Public Libraries, Miss Vally Lasker, Leeds City Libraries, Liverpool Record Office, London University Library, Lyrita Recorded Edition, Miss Clare Mackail, Miss Elizabeth Maconchy, Maryland University Library, Canon Lancelot Mason, Robert Mayer Concerts Society Ltd., Mr Kenneth Mobbs, Morecambe Divisional Libraries, Morley College Library, William Morris Gallery, Mr Harry Mortimer, National Museum of Labour History, Mr William Neve, New York Public Library, Newcastle-upon-Tyne City Libraries, Newcastle University Library, Mr Gerald Norris, Novello & Co. Ltd., Mrs Diana Oldridge, Oxford University Press, Mr Derek Parker, Miss F. L. Partridge, Mrs M. Pollitzer, Polydor Records Ltd., Dowager Lady Elizabeth Ponsonby, Miss Dorothy Pybus, Reading University Library, Roberton Publications, Rowe Music Library, Royal Academy of Music, Royal College of Music, Royal Military School of Music, Royal Opera House, Rural Music Schools Association, St Paul's Girls' School, Mr W. Sanderson, School of Oriental and African Studies, W. Schwann Inc., Scottish Record Office, Dr Watkins Shaw, Mrs Mary Ann Spencer, Mrs Irene Swann, Sydney Public Library, Mr Richard Telfer, Mr Kenneth Thompson, Tower Hamlets Public Libraries, Trinity College of Music, Twickenham Film Studios Ltd., Henry Watson Music Library, Westminster Public Libraries, Miss Christine Wild, Mr David H. Wilkins, Miss Pamela Willetts, Wiltshire County Library, Wycombe Abbey School.

Permission for the use of quotations in the text and the reproduction of music examples and illustrations has kindly been given by: BBC Written Archives Centre, Benslow Music

Trust, Lady Bliss, Lord Bridges, British Library, Faber Music Ltd., Trustees of the Thomas Hardy Memorial Collection in the Dorset County Museum, Dorchester, Dorset, Holst Birthplace Museum, Holst Foundation, Lambeth Palace Library, Mr Nigel Luckhurst, Royal College of Music, Royal Philharmonic Society, Society of Authors (© 1990 The Trustees of the Estate of John Masefield), Mr Sven Sternfeldt, Mrs Ursula Vaughan Williams, Westminster Central Music Library, and York University Libraries, Ontario, Canada.

I am also most grateful to the Holst Foundation for the provision of a research grant to enable this book to be completed.

Finally, I would like to thank my wife Elaine for her constant support and invaluable help in the considerable amount of research assistance and clerical work which she has carried out, and also Mrs Elizabeth Gilbert for her help in typing earlier drafts of this book.

MICHAEL SHORT

Contents

List of Illustrations

Introduction

At this stage in the late twentieth century, the name of Gustav Holst remains internationally known and respected in many areas of music-making, including orchestral, choral, wind band, brass band, and church music, at both amateur and professional levels, and his contribution to the development of music education in schools and adult education is also widely acknowledged.

From the perspective of our own time, Holst's career is distant enough to be considered as history, yet sufficiently close to be regarded as modern. He was in fact an important transitional figure, whose career overlapped the musical and social worlds of the nineteenth and twentieth centuries. Born into a family of professional musicians serving the leisured classes of Victorian England, he died at a time when technological innovations such as radio and the gramophone were bringing 'art' music to all levels of society. During his lifetime traumatic world events and social changes took place, having an inevitable effect on the arts, and the activities of radical composers called into question previous conceptions of what music should be like and what function it should perform in society. Alienation from such experiments was leading towards stagnation of the concert repertoire; the impact of the industrial revolution had all but obliterated the native folk-song tradition in England, and the rise of recording and broadcasting had begun to have a debilitating effect on amateur music-making.

Amidst these changes, Holst faced many of the difficulties which beset composers of the present day: how to earn a living, how to find time to compose, what kind of music to write and for what resources, and how to evolve an artistic philosophy which would establish a relationship between his own work and the world in which he lived. The days of the old-style court or church musician were long gone; private patronage was dwindling, but large-scale state support for the arts had not yet arrived. In such a situation a composer might easily withdraw into his own private creative world to write in an idiom which could be meaningless to the general public, but such an approach would have been anathema to Holst, who believed very strongly in music as a means of human communication. According to his friend and colleague Ralph Vaughan Williams: 'He loved his fellow creatures too much to allow his message to them to appear in vague or incomprehensible terms.'[1] And the substance of Holst's message was the expression of emotion, which he declared to be 'The fundamental necessity in all art'.[2] This emotion was not egotistical self-expression, nor aimless wallowing in sentimentality for its own sake (which Holst regarded as 'the supreme crime in art'[3]) but the expression of a communality of feeling and experience, which he believed it is the composer's special task to convey: 'Musicians express in sound what all men feel', he declared[4].

Despite his initial training at the Royal College of Music, Holst was largely self taught as a composer, learning by experience, which led him to think deeply about the principles of his art. Preconceived systems or academic theories of composition were of no use to him; he had to find his own way, not only stylistically in the long term, but also when beginning each new work. He was constantly searching for the 'right' notes; for ways in which his inner vision could be converted into practical reality. Sometimes his attempts were brilliantly successful, and at other times fumbling and clumsy, but this did not worry Holst, for he considered that a composer must be prepared 'to turn out a lot of stuff which isn't really of any value. Every fourth production will probably be the best he can achieve.'[5] This refusal to abide by safe solutions was the approach he recommended to his students, and in this respect he has been apty described as 'his own best pupil'.[6] For Holst the main attraction of composition lay in the unforeseen and the unsuspected—as he once remarked: 'The fact is, I don't like any music very much if it is highly polished and sounds fluent. I like to have a sense of struggle which an artist has had with his material.'[7]

Holst was impervious to the whims of fashion, but was always willing to try something new, to satisfy his own curiosity. He found this stimulating, and when at a loss for inspiration his motto was: 'Do something you have never done before!'[8] Into this philosophy, the concept of worldly success or failure never entered. Although he was naturally pleased when his music was performed and appreciated, he did not go out of his way to attract public attention. In fact, he went to the opposite extreme in declaring that failure, rather than success, was the best thing for an artist: 'If nobody likes your work, you have to go on just for the sake of the work. And you're in no danger of letting the public make you repeat yourself.'[9] And to a pupil he wrote: 'Failure is a most important part of an artist's training and one you cannot afford to do without.'[10] Even at the height of his fame, Holst was wary of success and its associated trappings. As Havergal Brian recalled of his own musical journalism: 'Holst shrank from the least whisper of personal publicity, and feared lest he should override any of his fellows. I know this is so, for more than once he has asked me to forbear mentioning his name.'[11]

How then did this reticent schoolteacher come to write in his spare time a work such as *The Planets*, which has become a standard item in the repertoire of the world's symphony orchestras, and which sounds as fresh and meaningful in the late twentieth century as it did when first performed in 1918? What was the motivation which led him to devote his free time to composition when he could have been simply relaxing from his teaching duties? His friend and colleague Vally Lasker declared: 'A composer is not a person who can compose, but someone who can't help composing,'[12] and it was this subconscious momentum which drove Holst onwards, especially through the earlier part of his career. His collaborator Clifford Bax described this period: 'Year by year he composed his music in the late hours or during brief holidays—at, in short, times when most men are complacently idle. No young artist would despair or would haul down his flag if he knew, as I know it, that record of hard work and neglect during thirty years.'[13] Holst believed that all a composer can do is to carry on writing, committed to his own ideals, in the belief that one day his work will come to be appreciated by listeners, and it was in this spirit that he started work on *The Planets* just before the First World War, when the whole fabric of European culture seemed to be on the verge of degeneration into barbarism.

The source of Holst's inner strength can be found by examining his personality, which was a remarkable combination of opposing characteristics, maintained in a subtle balance which protected him from extremism. He was at once friendly, gregarious, jolly, and rumbustious, but at the same time solitary, remote, and seemingly aloof. He was concerned with the warmth of human relationships, but also with mystical speculation. He was perceptive and business-like, but often quite naïve in his attitudes, both in life and in his music. He was both a practical realist and also a dreamer and visionary. His thought could be simultaneously simple and complex; the logical clarity of expression which he ceaselessly advocated being set against the irrational products of a strongly creative imagination; the straightforward schoolmaster was also a restless, introspective artist.

Many of his friends noticed the contrast between his vigorous, outgoing, open-hearted, cheerful nature, and his other-worldliness; as if he had access to some special knowledge of the universe which they had not. Perhaps this was an ultimate realization that in spite of all human activites and relationships, the external physical world will continue with or without the human race, a philosophical theme which appears in several of Holst's works. These contrasts in his personality are apparent in his music, sometimes even within a single work. The mind which produced much mild, inoffensive music was also the creator of some of the most violent sounds the musical world had yet heard, reflecting both the light and dark sides of man's nature. *The Planets*, for example, contains moments of genuine passion and overwhelming emotion, demonstrating that Holst had such feelings within himself, but he was also capable of writing totally innocuous music. As he wrote to Edwin Evans in 1911: 'I have something within me that prompts me to write quite light music now and then. For instance my Suite in E flat . . . Two songs without words for small orchestra . . . a Suite in E flat for military band: and King Estmere . . . All these are as genuinely part of me as the Veda hymns. The question of their ultimate value rests with the critic—with you. But they are not pot-boilers and I shall probably continue to do this sort of thing.'[14] To all these works Holst brought the same degree of artistic concentration and integrity; in the words of Ralph Vaughan Williams: 'There was no compromise about Holst, either in his music or in his character. He was thorough; he did not know what it was to do things by half.'[15] Although such total honesty and directness could often be disconcerting to his friends and colleagues, they eventually came to accept this outlook as an integral part of his nature.

Because of the dichotomy in Holst's character, it was perhaps only through music that he was able to reveal his deepest feelings, using his lighter style as a screen for more profound emotions. In opera particularly he resorted to trite or facetious subjects, as if fearing that the medium might be too open and direct to provide sufficient camouflage. He was fond of the whimsical, quirky scherzo (*Uranus* being a magnificent example), and it is no accident that his first performed orchestral work and also his last composition were both in this form.

The steadfast side of his character is most evident in his lifelong devotion to teaching, while his artistic restlessness was often sublimated in the solitary walking tours through the English countryside which he undertook with increasing frequency during his later years. His outgoing personality therefore perhaps concealed an inner solitude, which he struggled to transcend through his music. On a more mundane level, it is possible that Holst's chronic short-sightedness contributed to his feelings of isolation. Imogen Holst recalled that her father was incapable of recognizing his own family 'at a distance of more than six yards',[16] and at a Promenade concert in the early 1920s Holst was observed by an American critic who commented on 'that half puzzled, half shy expression of his, looking like a learned librarian disturbed among his books'.[17]

Whatever the reasons for the disparities of Holst's character, he certainly turned them to good advantage in the composition of music, where the ability to divide the mind into separate compartments is a most useful attribute. Vaughan Williams considered that 'It is the blend of visionary with the realist that gives Holst's music its distinctive character,' and although he was a dreamer, he 'never allowed his dreams to become incoherent or meandering ... Holst's music is sometimes described as mystical, and rightly so, but we must not imagine from this something precious or vague. His texture, his form, his melody is always clear cut and definite.'[18] (The exact nature of Holst's mysticism remains unclear. Although not conventionally religious, he believed strongly in supra-human forces, and besides dabbling in astrology was much influenced by Eastern thought, particularly the doctrines of Dharma and reincarnation.)

Towards the end of his career there were signs that Holst might have been able to reconcile these opposing tendencies, had he lived into old age and a final 'third period' of composition. Many composers become milder in outlook as they progress through their careers, abandoning their youthful iconoclasm as they accept the inevitability of old age, but in Holst's case he turned to a mood of pervasive melancholy, as exemplified by *Egdon Heath*, punctuated by lightweight works such as *The Wandering Scholar*. Only at the very end of his life was there a suggestion of a possible reconciliation between the remoteness of some of his 'serious' works with the straightforward unselfconsciousness of his lighter vein, as is evident in the *Lyric Movement* of 1933, and had he lived longer it is possible that such a fusion may have led him to new achievements in his art.

This might have been possible during his lifetime had he not devoted so much time and energy to teaching, but although he first took up teaching as a means of earning a living, it soon became of such importance to him that he came to believe that this must have been his pre-ordained path in life. He accepted the limitations on his time which it imposed, and although this did not prevent him from composing his works, it did impede the consolidation and development of both style and material, as he would often turn to something new rather than fully explore the territory which he had already opened up, or make use of ready-made devices from previous works instead of developing their inherent possibilities. Sometimes his music took a considerable time to come to fruition, which at least provided a useful gestation period; he was already planning his opera *The Perfect Fool* in 1908 but it was not until 1920 that he was able to start work on it, and the result would doubtless have been quite different had he been able to compose it straight away. In consequence of this lack of time, many of his later works are quite short, thus precluding him from focusing his abilities on the problems of large-scale musical form. Holst's feelings about teaching were expressed in a letter to W. G. Whittaker, written soon after the completion of *The Planets*, and just as he was beginning work on *The Hymn of Jesus*: 'Oh my friend,' he exclaimed, 'Why do we waste our lives trying to teach! (Don't trouble to answer—I've already thought of several answers.)'[19] Armed with this philosophy, Holst was able to create works which were to bring him international fame and lasting recognition as one of the most significant composers of his generation.

1

Early Years
(1874–1893)

Gustavus Theodore von Holst was born on Monday 21 September 1874 at 4 Pittville Terrace (now Clarence Road) Cheltenham, the first child of Clara and Adolph von Holst. The house has been restored by Cheltenham Borough Council, and was opened to the public in 1975 as the Holst Birthplace Museum.

Although the Holst family probably originated in Scandinavia, by the late seventeenth century branches were established in Poland, Germany, and subsequently Russia when in 1703 Christian Lorenz moved his family home from Rostock to Riga in Latvia. By the end of the eighteenth century, Gustav Holst's great-grandfather Matthias was well established as a pianist, composer, and harp teacher to the Imperial Russian court at St Petersburg, and married a Russian, Katharina Rogge, their first child Gustavus Valentine being born in 1799. Despite its strong connections with the Imperial court, the family was obliged to flee from Russia a few years later, apparently for political reasons, and in common with many other European exiles Matthias sought refuge in England. He settled in London, installing his family in fashionable Fitzroy Square, and soon built up a respectable practice as music teacher to the middle-class residents of the neighbourhood. He also began to acquire a reputation as a composer, providing incidental music for plays such as the 1807 production of *Ulthona the Sorceress* at the Sans Pareil Theatre in the Strand, and publishing many compositions, including several rondos for the harp and a work entitled *Gustavus*, a 'grand military piece in the Swedish stile'.[1] In 1810 Katharina gave birth to a second son, Theodore, who was destined to establish a reputation as an accomplished painter of scenes of legend and mythology. By 1827 a more relaxed political climate in Russia enabled Matthias to return to Riga for a short period, but by 1830 he was back in London, where he remained until his death in 1854.

Gustavus Valentine followed in his father's footsteps as a musician, and after a short period in Scotland, by 1832 was established in Cheltenham where he taught the harp and piano to the society of the town. During the 1820s he began to add the prefix 'von' to his surname in emulation of the German branch of the family, doubtless with the intention of enhancing his status in the eyes of prospective pupils. One of his specialities was to present his pupils' accomplishments at public concerts *en masse*: twenty-four young ladies would play twelve grand pianos in programmes of classical overtures and operatic selections, arranged and conducted by himself. This professional success provided sufficient security for contemplation of marriage, and he chose as his wife Honoria Goodrich of Norwich, who thus became the first English member of the Holst family. Honoria gave birth to five children: Gustavus Matthias, Catherine, Lorenz, Adolph, and Benigna, several of whom were destined for musical careers. Gustavus Matthias became a pianist and composer who had considerable success in Scotland, Lorenz emigrated to Australia, Benigna (known as 'Nina') also became a pianist, and Adolph became a pianist and music teacher like his father. After a period of study in Hamburg where his aunt Caroline was harpist to the Prussian court, Adolph returned to Cheltenham where he soon became well known as an exceptional pianist, teacher, conductor, and organist of All Saints' Church. He also gave regular recitals at the Assembly Rooms, and directed chamber orchestra concerts at the Montpellier Rotunda.

In July 1871 Adolph married one of his pupils, Clara Cox Lediard, the fifth child of Mary Croft Lediard and Samuel Lediard, a solicitor of Cirencester, who allowed the newly-wed couple to live in 4 Pittville Terrace, a house which he owned in Cheltenham. Soon after the marriage, however, Adolph was obliged to obtain a silent keyboard for practice at home as his wife began to suffer from nerves, especially during her first pregnancy. She was herself a singer and talented pianist, having given recitals in Cheltenham and played the harmonium in church before her marriage, but was too sensitive to endure the sound of her husband's routine daily practice of scales, arpeggios, and studies.

When their first child was born, he was christened Gustavus Theodore, after his grandfather and great-uncle, the ceremony taking place at All Saints' Church on 21 October 1874. Two years later a second son, Emil Gottfried, was born, but these were to be the only living children of Clara, for on 12 February 1882 she died of heart disease and dropsy, following a still birth a few months previously.

Adolph could no longer remain in the same house after this tragedy, and on 1 April 1882 moved to 1 Vittoria Walk, Cheltenham, asking his sister Nina to help him bring up the two motherless boys. This arrangement continued until August 1885, when Adolph married another of his pupils, Mary Thorley Stone, daughter of the Reverend Edward Stone, Rector of Queenhill, Upton-on-Severn. Mary was herself a competent pianist, but allowed her passionate interests in philosophy and religion to override all other matters, to the detriment of her own musical development and also the well-being of her stepsons, whose health began to suffer in consequence. Gustav was particularly badly affected, suffering from bouts of asthma and deterioration of the eyesight, although Emil's more robust constitution saved him from the worst consequences of their stepmother's neglect. Mary subsequently gave birth to two sons of her own; Matthias Ralph and Evelyn Thorley, and all four boys were brought up in the same offhand fashion.

Adolph turned a blind eye to such domestic matters and concentrated on his profession, which included introducing his sons to the basic principles of music. Gustav was encouraged to play the piano as soon as he could reach the keyboard, and at the age of four was taken to church where he heard his father play on the organ a tune which he himself had learnt on the piano, at which he loudly cried out: 'That's *my* tune!'.[2] Another childhood experience was of looking out of the window at Pittville Terrace and seeing a group of Morris men with blackened faces dancing in the street outside; this incident frightened him considerably, and he remembered it for the rest of his life. In the intimate atmosphere of family

musical evenings, the young Gustav made his first acquaintance with Scottish and Irish folk-songs, and in the streets of
Cheltenham he was fascinated by a hurdy-gurdy man whose
instrument could only play one tune, and each time he heard it
there were fewer notes than before, so that eventually the
melody was barely recognizable. This was the Northumbrian
pipe-tune *Newburn Lads*, which in later life Holst was to use
as the basis of his *Toccata* for piano. As a child, he also had the
opportunity of playing on an old Egyptian flute, and was
intrigued by 'the very curious melodic effects which could be
produced thereon'.[3] Such free melodic declamation without
the constraints of conventional harmony may have influenced
his later settings for solo voice, and could also have sown the
seeds of his subsequent interest in oriental scales and melodic
intervals.

Besides the piano, Holst was also made to study the violin
and the trombone, which his father thought would be an
effective antidote for the boy's asthma. But the piano was his
principal instrument, and Adolph taught him technique and
repertoire with the intention that he should eventually
become a concert pianist, despite the rather worrying appearance of neuritis in his son's right hand. Although Gustav
shared his father's enthusiasm for Mendelssohn, his own tastes
leaned more towards the style of Grieg, whom Adolph regarded
as something of a modernist, so that Gustav had to wait until
his father was out of the house before trying out the *Lyric
Pieces* at the piano.

After a short time at a local preparatory school, in the
autumn of 1886 Holst entered the Cheltenham Grammar
School, which was then undergoing radical changes. The
ancient buildings which had previously housed the school
were in the process of being demolished, to be replaced by
purpose-built accommodation on the same site. During these
building operations, classes were held in a former Presbyterian
chapel on the opposite side of the High Street, and this was
where Holst received his education; he had left the school by
the time the new premises were completed.

Perhaps because of the difficulties of this makeshift accommodation, in which the pupils had to study as best they could
while squeezed into the cramped chapel pews, Holst was not

happy during these schoolboy years, but nevertheless managed to do quite well academically; in 1888 coming first in Form 4, first in French and German (the latter without much difficulty, as he was the only boy to study that language) and second in English and Divinity. In 1889 he took the Oxford Local Examination, First Division, and passed in English, History, Shakespeare, French, German, and Music. To his fellow pupils he was known as 'Sausage', doubtless because of his short-sightedness and asthmatic tendencies which rendered him unsuitable for the more boisterous schoolboy pursuits, but he was able to make an impressive display of his musical talents when he appeared in a school concert on 18 December 1890, playing Mayer's *La Fontaine* as a piano solo, Grieg's *Goblin's Dance* in a piano duet, and the solo part in two movements from a Piano Quintet by A. Burnett. This concert was probably Holst's first public appearance as a musician.

In addition to his skills as a performer, Gustav was also developing an interest in composition, although he had never had any lessons in the subject, and was unacquainted with the rudiments of harmony and counterpoint. In 1887 he had been given Macaulay's *Lays of Ancient Rome* to study for school-work, and conceived the idea of setting the story of Horatius as a cantata for chorus and orchestra. Saying nothing to his father, he worked secretly on this composition in his bedroom, while studying a copy of Berlioz's *Treatise on Instrumentation* to initiate himself into the mysteries of orchestration. One day, when the work was still incomplete but the family was out of the house, he took the score downstairs to try it through on the piano. He was so shocked and disappointed by what he heard that he never wrote another note of the music; his rudimentary technique had completely failed to capture the sounds which he had imagined in his head.

But this unnerving experience did not deter him from following his natural urge to compose, and he was soon trying his hand at other, less pretentious pieces. As a regular reader of the *Boy's Own Paper*, his attention was caught by the November 1888 issue, which offered 'TWO PRIZES, of *Two Guineas* and *One Guinea* respectively, for the best musical setting, with organ or piano accompaniment, of any of the verses appearing in our last volume . . . or in the Summer and

Christmas parts of 1888. There will be two classes only . . . the Junior embracing all ages up to 18, and the Senior from 18 to 24.' The announcement went on to state that a winning composition from the previous competition would be published in the forthcoming Christmas number of the magazine.

Spurred on by thought of the cash prizes and the added incentive of possible publication, the young Holst composed a piece which was duly submitted before the deadline date of 28 February 1889. After an agonizing wait of several months, the issue of 28 September announced the prize-winners: Holst's name appeared sixth in order of merit in a list of twenty-nine competitors awarded certificates in the Junior Division. This tantalizing proximity of success inspired him to participate in the following three annual competitions. From the issue of 29 December 1888, he chose a poem by P. Shaw Jeffrey entitled *Nowell*, setting it for mixed voices and piano under the title *A Christmas Carol*. For this work, Holst was awarded First Prize in the Junior Division, coming fourth in overall order irrespective of age in a total field of seventy-three competitors. Flushed with success, he went on to win the Junior First Prize in each of the following two years, after which he seems to have magnanimously retired from the competition in order to allow others a chance of winning. In the event, the magazine did not publish his prize-winning works, and apart from *A Christmas Carol* and a *New Year Chorus* the other pieces which he submitted remain unidentified, although they probably still survive among the manuscripts dating from his schoolboy years.

During this time, Holst was taking his first steps towards a musical career in his native town. His father gave regular concerts as a piano soloist at the Montpellier Rotunda, and it was probably there that Gustav heard a chamber orchestra for the first time. Adolph encouraged the boy's interest by allowing him to attend rehearsals and to help with checking parts and cueing in missing instruments (a skill which Holst was to put to good use in later life). Adolph also employed his son's talents at All Saints' Church, where Gustav sang in the choir and sometimes played violin or trombone in the small orchestra which was assembled for concerts and festive occasions.

One great advantage of his father's position at All Saints' was that Gustav had virtually unlimited access to the organ, ostensibly for practice, but also for surreptitiously trying out his own compositions. In 1891 he wrote *Four Voluntaries* for the organ, comprising a March, Allegretto Pastorale, Postlude, and Funeral March, the whole group being dedicated 'without any permission whatever' to his aunt Nina von Holst. The score contains directions for organ registration, revealing a detailed knowledge of such matters, and at the end of the manuscript he added a note: 'I know this is atrociously written out, but I am so sick of it that I cannot copy it any more. The stops are meant for our large organ and will not do for yours. I am thinking of writing a piano duet for you and Miss Scott. It will be very difficult and therefore will just suit you.'[4] Whether this projected duet ever materialized is not known, as none of his surviving duets date from this period, but Holst did write several other pieces that year, including songs and orchestral works, and also began an anthem entitled *The Listening Angels* which includes the first example of his use of a hidden choir, prompted by the lines: 'Solemnly from distant voices rose a vesper hymn'.

December 1891 was a busy time for the young composer, for during that month no fewer than three of his compositions were performed at public concerts in Cheltenham. On Wednesday 16 December, the première of a *Scherzo* for small orchestra was given at a Musical Afternoon at the Montpellier Rotunda, while on the following Saturday the Rotunda Orchestral Band included an *Intermezzo* in its sixth Saturday Afternoon Popular Concert of the winter season. The local newspaper subsequently reported to its readers that the latter work consisted of an 'opening movement with muted first violin, with pizzicato accompaniment, and a tuneful melody in second part for clarionet and flutes'. Moreover, 'The work was well received, and the youthful composer bowed his acknowledgements.'[5] On Boxing Day, the Rotunda was once again the scene of a Holst première, this time of a song entitled *Die Spröde*, sung by Gertrude Bendall. This setting of lines by Goethe probably stemmed from his German studies at school, but on this occasion the singer chose to perform the song in an English translation under the title *The Coquette*.

Perhaps in the belief that he had now firmly established himself as a promising composer, Holst threw himself into the composition of a Symphony in C minor, the score of which bears the inscription: 'Begun Jan: 11th Finished Feb: 5th'. These dates belie the fact that he was normally a slow and painstaking worker, but it is probable that the work had to be completed during one of his father's absences from the house, when the piano would have been available for a short period.

Despite the local success of some of his compositions, the time was now approaching when realistic plans would have to be made for Gustav's future after leaving the Grammar School. He applied unsuccessfully for a scholarship to Trinity College of Music, London, whereupon his father decided to improve the boy's basic theoretical knowledge by sending him to Oxford to study counterpoint with George Frederick Sims, organist of Merton College. Although failure to obtain the scholarship must have been a disappointment to Holst (and Trinity College officials were chagrined to be reminded of it in later years), he subsequently wrote to his friend W. G. Whittaker on his failure to obtain an appointment at the college: 'If TCL is what it was 30 years ago I fear I congratulate you on your escape!'.[6]

In Oxford, Holst stayed with his grandmother Mary Croft Lediard, and worked hard at strict counterpoint, so that in a few months he had acquired a good grounding in the subject. At the end of his stay he gave a solo piano recital at the Constitutional Hall, Cowley Road, in which he gave the first performance of his new *Arpeggio Study* (under the title *Study in E minor*) and also played Gottschalk's *Mazurka de Concert*, afterwards noting: 'Both pieces twice encored'.[7] Other compositions of this period include anthems, songs, and a setting of Charles Kingsley's *Ode to the North East Wind* for male voices and orchestra.

On his return from Oxford, Holst obtained an appointment as organist and choirmaster at the Cotswold village of Wyck Rissington, which included the conductorship of a fifty-strong choral society at nearby Bourton-on-the-Water. The salary was low (£4 per annum at Wyck Rissington; nothing at all at Bourton) but the practical experience was invaluable for an aspiring composer, and Holst undertook the work with enthusiasm, even going so far as to construct the platform himself for his first concert. He arranged accompaniments for such instruments as were available locally and conducted performances of works such as John Farmer's oratorio *Christ and His Soldiers*, besides giving a few individual lessons on piano and organ. Although Bourton-on-the-Water was then on the railway, the Saturday service was restricted and there were no trains at all on Sundays, so that Holst had to stop over two nights before returning to Cheltenham on the Monday. He stayed with one of his singers, John Wilkins, whose brothers Cecil and Edgar also sang in the choir. When returning to his lodgings in Bourton after an evening service at Wyck Rissington, he would walk the two miles back across the fields in the dark, lighting his way with a lantern. Many years later, when he had become a successful composer, Holst still remembered his friends in these villages, and would often call in at Bourton-on-the-Water if he got a chance when visiting the Cotswolds.

The railway provided the young Holst with another kind of musical experience which was to have a devastating effect on him. On 13 July 1892 he took an excursion train to London to hear a performance of *Die Götterdämmerung* at Covent Garden, conducted by Gustav Mahler. The performance began at 7 p.m., and although some cuts had been made, lasted until midnight, the *Musical Times* later reporting that despite the length of the performance 'very few persons left the house before Brünhilde's thrilling act of Suttee'.[8] Holst was stunned, partly by the scale of the drama, but principally by the passionate expression of the music, which amazed him by its technical audacity. The young country organist returned to Cheltenham dazed and confused, his musical values having been seriously shaken by this overwhelming experience.

But this opening of new vistas was not sufficient to dislodge the strongest influence on his own musical style; that of Arthur Sullivan, a composer admired by both Gustav and his father. This influence is evident throughout Holst's main composition of 1892; a two-act operetta entitled *Lansdown Castle, or The Sorcerer of Tewkesbury*, for which a local resident, Major A. C. Cunningham, wrote the libretto: 'a slender stringing together, in a whimsical way, of various incidents, more or less improbable', according to the *Gloucester Chronicle*.[9] On 22 December 1892 some selections from the work were performed at a Grand Orchestral Concert at the Assembly Rooms in Cheltenham, conducted by the composer, but it was not until the following year that it was performed in full. On 7 February 1893 a cast of amateurs, 'assisted by Miss Ida Webb, Medallist, RAM'[10] gave the first complete performance at the Cheltenham Corn Exhange under the direction of local musician D'Arcy de Ferrars, with Holst himself as piano accompanist, the performance being repeated on the following two days.

The audience was surprised at the composer's youth, which one critic remarked 'was suggestive either of unusual talent or of precocious mediocrity',[11] but was soon won over by his musical ingenuity and gift for writing pleasing melodies. Several numbers were encored, including a 'Nagging Trio', and his newly-won contrapuntal skill was much admired, particularly in a four-part laughing fugue and the quartet 'Beef and Beer'. But the society of Cheltenham were not amused by one number which used a distorted form of an Anglican chant as a magical incantation; this, they thought, was going too far. As to the plot, it is difficult to discern any coherent dramatic thread running through the work. The time is the reign of King Henry VII, and the action takes place in the hall of Lansdown Castle and in the Sorcerer's den at Tewkesbury. A full description of the plot would be tedious and pointless, as Holst clearly regarded the libretto as simply an excuse for music rather than as a dramatic entity in its own right, but it is interesting to note that sorcery and a magic mirror are important factors in the operetta; themes which were to reappear more than once in his later work.

On the whole, the press was enthusiastic, although one review began with the laconic remark that 'Since all comic operas of recent date have more or less followed the lines of the Gilbert and Sullivan collaboration, this can hardly claim to be an exception.' But the writer did allow that 'much of the music is bright and tuneful, and does great credit to the young composer, as well as gives promise of future achievements'.[12] The *Gloucester Chronicle* reported that 'The music is remarkable, and not unworthy of a trained and experienced musician.

Throughout it gives proof of the possession of very great and available talent . . . Mr Gustav von Holst's melodies are always flowing, tuneful, expressive, and free from conventionality,'[13] while the *Echo* commented: 'Young Mr Gustav von Holst gives evidence not only of genius, but of careful laborious study.'[14]

As Gustav pasted these reviews into his first press-cutting scrap-book (now preserved in the Birthplace Museum) his father decided that the boy was perhaps indeed destined for a successful career as a composer, and urged him to apply for a scholarship at the Royal College of Music. The score of *Lansdown Castle* was submitted with his application as evidence of the young composer's talents, but the College authorities were not impressed, and the scholarship was refused.

Undeterred, Adolf borrowed £100 from one of his relatives (probably his sister Nina) to cover a couple of years' maintenance and tuition, and entered his son's name for the ordinary entrance examination. Gustav duly travelled to London for the examination, which was held in the building which now houses the Royal College of Organists, and found himself sitting next to a boy of the same age called Fritz Hart, who was later to become one of his closest friends. When the examination was over, they walked together in Kensington Gardens and introduced themselves, Holst pedantically insisting that the 'von' in his name should always be observed. Fritz Hart, who had been a chorister at Westminster Abbey, was alarmed to discover serious deficiencies in Holst's musical knowledge during this conversation, but none the less realized that his fellow candidate had a deep intuitive understanding of the essentials of music. A few weeks later, both applicants learnt that they had successfully passed the examination, and they entered the College in May 1893 at the beginning of the Summer term.

2

The Student
(1893–1898)

On his arrival in London, Holst found himself in a completely different world. He made many new friends and immersed himself in a busy round of music-making and concert-going. At first there were some problems with his studies: besides his poor eyesight, the neuritis in his right arm was worsening (as can be seen from his manuscripts of the period), making his piano studies with Frederick Sharpe increasingly difficult. This affliction was to remain with him for the rest of his life, and years later he vividly described the feeling when symptoms were at their worst: 'My arm is like a jelly overcharged with electricity.'[1] Eventually he was obliged to abandon his intention of becoming a concert pianist, and concentrated on the trombone, which he studied under George Case. He did however keep up keyboard work on the organ, under William Stephenson Hoyte, who besides being a professor at the College was also organist of All Saints' Church, Margaret Street. It may have been through Hoyte that Holst first became acquainted with plainsong (later to bear fruit in *The Hymn of Jesus*) as it was often used in the services at All Saints' at that time.

Another difficulty was that despite his months of study at Oxford, Holst's knowledge of harmony and counterpoint was still not up to the standard required by the College, and Charles Stanford refused to accept him as a composition pupil until he had taken a special course in theory. This was not quite so humiliating as it may appear, as Stanford had himself recently undergone a refresher course in modal counterpoint under W. S. Rockstro, and evidently believed that a dose of the same sort of thing would do his pupils no harm. Holst therefore studied theory with with Rockstro and Frederick Bridge, eventually gaining admission to Stanford's composition class, where his teacher found him to be 'enthusiastic, and happily not devoid of humour'.[2] Holst's other studies were with Georg Jacobi for instrumentation, and Hubert Parry (Director of the College) for history of music; Holst later recalled that Parry's classes had given him 'a vision, which I learned to call History'.[3]

Whether these various teachers had much influence on him as a composer is doubtful, for it was to be some years before he began to develop a distinctive style of his own. He later recalled that as a student he had devoted a large amount of time and effort to the study of academic counterpoint, and was encouraged to do so by being told that if he persevered he would recover a sense of choral writing which had died out since Elizabethan times. Some time later, when he came to study the works of the English madrigalists, he realized that academic counterpoint had little connection with their art, and declared that he could not think of a couple of pages of Tudor music which would pass a music degree examination when he was a student. He considered that in later years he had learnt more about counterpoint from Byrd and Weelkes than he had ever done from his college teachers.

Among his fellow students, Holst quickly made friends with Fritz Hart and Evlyn Howard-Jones, and became part of a group which frequented Wilkins' tea-shop in Kensington, where Fritz Hart, at that time a fanatical Wagnerian, would expound the virtues of his hero with the aim of converting Holst to the cause. Other contemporaries at the College included William Hurlstone, Samuel Coleridge-Taylor, Thomas Dunhill, and later, John Ireland.

Holst found lodgings in Hammersmith, a district of London with which he was to have close connections for the rest of his life. He had a small bed-sitting room which although sparsely furnished was kept clean and tidy by the landlady. When Fritz Hart visited him there he was surprised to find that Holst had no piano—his modest weekly allowance would not stretch to hiring one—and he was therefore obliged to write his exercises and compositions without the aid of a keyboard. Before each lesson with Stanford, Holst would arrive early at the College to search for a piano on which to try out his work. Sometimes he was disappointed at the results, recalling the *Horatius* episode of a few years before, but Fritz Hart declared that on the whole Holst did better without a piano than most of his fellow students did with one. Adolph sent a regular weekly allowance of £1, with the occasional complaint: 'Do you require so much every week?'[4]

At the end of term Holst returned to Cheltenham, alleviating the pressure on his finances by walking part of the way. This was to become a regular habit, and he would sometimes walk or cycle the 97 miles from London to Cheltenham, with his trombone slung on his back. Occasionally he would take the opportunity of practising the instrument while resting during the journey, to the astonishment of the farmers on whose land he sat. As his attacks of asthma had by now abated, Holst enjoyed these journeys, and remained a keen walker throughout his life. His interest in cycling may have been stimulated by the Cheltenham musical magazine *The Minim*, which carried articles discussing its virtues during this period.

During his first vacation Holst looked up old friends, including the dedicatee of an *Introduction and Bolero* for piano duet, to which he had added the inscription: 'This was written expressly for and dedicated to My adored Beloved Sweet-Heart.'[5] The young lady in question was probably the eighteen-year-old Mabel Forty, whose strong personality and lively sense of humour would doubtless have made her attractive to Holst. They often played piano duets together, including arrangements of Haydn symphonies, works for which Holst subsequently held a life-long admiration, perhaps instigated by this early practical acquaintance with them. Mabel's father, Frank Forty, was an enthusiastic amateur musician and co-founder of the Cheltenham music firm of Dale, Forty & Co., which existed until 1961. He was a close friend of Adolph von Holst (whom he referred to as 'Old Von') and sang bass in the choir of All Saints Church. Frank was convinced that Gustav would become a successful composer, and gave him every encouragement.

Just before returning to London for the autumn term of 1893, Holst visited Worcester Cathedral to hear a performance of Bach's Mass in B Minor during the Three Choirs Festival. This was his first acquaintance with the work and he was overwhelmed by its exultant choruses. In the Sanctus he suddenly experienced a feeling of floating above the heads of the audience, and found himself taking a firm grip on his chair to prevent his head from hitting the cathedral roof.

Back in London, Holst returned to his studies and continued to compose, although none of his works were ever deemed worthy of inclusion in official College concerts during his time there. (He later parcelled up all his schoolboy and student compositions, labelled them 'Early Horrors', and consigned them to the depths of his music cupboard.) Despite this, during his student years several of his pieces were performed outside the College, and some were even considered good enough to be accepted by well-known publishers.

His aunt Anna Newman ran a school at Barnes with the assistance of her daughter May who had a flair for drama, and when she heard Holst was studying in London she asked him to compose a musical play for her pupils to perform. Holst responded with enthusiasm, persuading Fritz Hart to write the libretto, and between them they concocted *Ianthe*, a 'romantic operetta for children'. The plot of this work was based on an idea provided by Mrs Newman, who reserved the right to edit the libretto, with the result that at the first performance Fritz Hart could hardly recognize his own lines. He described Holst's music 'as something between *Ruddigore* and *Walküre*, with a dash of himself and something of the *Erl King*'.[6] The project seems to have been a resounding success, and the following year the authors were asked to collaborate on another production. This time they produced *The Idea*, a much more workmanlike piece, which was destined to feature in Novello's children's music catalogue for more than half a century.

In these pieces, the main musical influence remained that of Arthur Sullivan, but other factors were beginning to have an effect on Holst's creative work. During his first term at College he attended a season of Wagner operas at Covent Garden, and Fritz Hart's enthusiastic advocation of Wagner's music was beginning to have an inevitable effect on him. Holst later recalled that he had had 'the shock of his life' on hearing the first bars of *Tristan und Isolde* played by an orchestra, as his previous knowledge of the work had been based entirely on the piano reduction of the vocal score.[7] Literary influences also began to affect his music, and he read widely, discovering authors such as George Macdonald, Walt Whitman, and William Morris, thus planting the seeds of several later musical works in his mind. He was also reading the novels of Sir Walter Scott, and used Scott's words for song settings such as *Anna-Marie* (from *Ivanhoe*) and *The White Lady's Farewell* (from *The Monastery*). The compositions he wrote for his College classes during this period include a *Theme and Variations* for string quartet, a *First String Quartet*, and a *Bolero* for orchestra. The labour involved in writing out these scores was intensified by the pain of his neuritis, and he sometimes had to tie a pen-nib to his finger in order to write at all, thus slowing down his writing speed considerably. At the end of his song *There Sits a Bird on Yonder Tree* he added a note to the singer: 'Please take great care of all these songs and return them as soon as you can. I have no copies and no time to copy them.'[8] He tried various remedies to cure his neuritis, including becoming a strict vegetarian for a time, but all to no avail.

In the summer of 1894 Holst returned to Cheltenham, and again took the opportunity to revisit some of his Cotswold haunts. In September he gave an organ recital at Middleton Parish Church, Oxfordshire, playing works by Bach, Mendelssohn, and Guilmant, as well as accompanying other performers. Two weeks later he returned to take part in a Saturday evening entertainment consisting of a concert followed by a farce entitled *Içi on parle français* in which the performers, including Holst, 'entered with great spirit into the acting, much to the delight of the audience, who were constantly convulsed with laughter'.[9]

Returning to College in the autumn, he continued to produce student works including an *Air and Variations* for piano and string quartet, a *Short Trio* for piano and strings, and a *String Trio* in G minor; songs to words by Walter Scott and Thomas Hood, and a number of unaccompanied part-songs, including *Fathoms Deep Beneath the Wave*, (Walter Scott)

Summer's Welcome and *Winter and the Birds* (Fritz Hart), and *Now Winter's Winds are Banished* (English translation from Meleager) for female voices, and *Love Wakes and Weeps* (Scott) for mixed voices.

Towards the end of term, a crisis began to loom on the horizon: the money which his father had borrowed to support his musical education was almost at an end, and there was no prospect of his being either willing or able to negotiate another loan. Faced with the possibility of an abrupt termination of his studies, Holst redoubled his efforts to obtain a scholarship, at which he had already made several unsuccessful attempts. Finally, in February 1895, at his eighth attempt and a short time before reaching the age limit, he was informed that he had been awarded a scholarship for composition, providing free tuition together with a maintenance grant of £30 per annum. This must have been welcome news for Adolph, who had recently retired as organist of All Saints' Church and whose income must have been considerably reduced in consequence. By way of celebration, Adolph arranged a performance of his son's *Duet* for organ and trombone on 8 May at Highbury Congregational Church, Cheltenham, in which he himself played the organ, and John Boyce, a local musician, was the trombonist. For his part, Gustav must have been pleased at his success, and resolved to make the best use of his remaining time as a student.

He continued to write pieces for his lessons with Stanford, who suggested that Fritz Hart should write a one-act libretto based on Beau Brummel for Holst to set to music. Stanford proposed that the main feature of the plot should be a game of whist, and took a personal interest in the progress of the opera, making many suggestions for alterations, to the annoyance of Holst as he laboured over his score. When complete, *The Revoke* was submitted to Stanford, who was enthusiastic despite its lack of stylistic originality, and he very nearly succeeded in getting it staged at the Opéra Comique in Paris, where his own *Shamus O'Brien* was playing at the time. Instead, Holst had to be satisfied with a try-through by his fellow students, conducted by Stanford, and although they performed well, Holst was disappointed by the sound of his orchestration, and subsequently rescored parts of the work under Stanford's supervision. Eventually the opera was put into rehearsal by a group of friends, including Harry Dearth, Edith Bristow, Morfydd Williams and Eaton Cooter, but despite this preparation it was never performed in public, and the only practical result, according to Fritz Hart, was the marriage of two of the cast. However, Holst felt that he had achieved something worth while, and entered the works as 'Op. 1' in a notebook in which he intended to list the titles of all his compostions as they were completed.

Other pieces written during 1895 included part-songs to words by Thomas Hood, an uncompleted *Children's Suite* for small orchestra, and two *Dances* for piano duet, the first of which is in a five-beat metre, later to become a hallmark of many of his compositions.

After spending the summer vacation in Cheltenham, Holst returned to London in September, celebrating his twenty-first birthday by walking most of the way. When he arrived back at College, an encounter took place which was to have a great effect on his life and work, and also on the entire development of English music in the early twentieth century. Ralph Vaughan Williams had returned to College as a full-time student after an absence of three years, and there met Holst, who opened the conversation by quoting an extract from Sheridan's *The Critic*. This caught Vaughan Williams's fancy, and on discovering that they were both Gloucestershire lads, they immediately struck up a friendship which was to endure until Holst's death. Vaughan Williams had already been at the College from 1890 to 1892, but had left to study history at Cambridge, although during his time there he had visited London regularly for composition lessons with Parry and had also studied with Charles Wood and other teachers. Now he was back to study composition under Stanford, and found himself in the company of Holst, Fritz Hart, Evlyn Howard-Jones, Thomas Dunhill, and John Ireland. Vaughan Williams joined the tea-shop set, and later recalled that they would discuss 'every subject under the sun from the lowest note of the double bassoon to the philosophy of *Jude the Obscure*'.[10]

Although Fritz Hart had been Holst's closest friend during his first years at college, from the autumn of 1895 Vaughan

Williams assumed this role, and he and Holst started to hold regular 'field days' during which they would play through and discuss each other's compositions. They kept up this practice long after leaving college, even when each had become a composer of international reputation. Vaughan Williams later referred to his 'cribbing' from Holst, but it is clear that the influence was a two-way process: Holst's objective approach to the problems of composition helped Vaughan Williams tame his rather unruly musical inspiration, while something of Vaughan Williams's wider education and experience rubbed off on Holst.

In addition to their routine studies, they both took part in a performance of *Dido and Aeneas* given by the College students at the Lyceum Theatre on 20 November as part of the Purcell bicentenary celebrations. This first performance in modern times was conducted by Stanford, with expanded orchestration especially provided for the occasion by Charles Wood, 'with well-intentioned but mistaken zeal', according to the *Musical Times*.[11] But the magazine did concede that the students could 'scarcely have failed to have benefited by the study necessitated by the preparation of the work', and this performance was probably the beginning of Holst's lifelong admiration for Purcell's music.

It was at about this time that Holst started to supplement his scholarship by playing the trombone in theatre orchestras and seaside bands. In the winter he played for pantomime in London (often at Drury Lane), and in the summer would join a band playing selections on the pier at various resorts. When the students returned to college at the end of the summer vacation, impressing each other with stories of the international music festivals they had attended, Holst would chip in with lively accounts of playing the trombone on the sea-front at Blackpool, Brighton, or Folkestone. During these summer seasons he was at first paid at the rate of two guineas per week for playing three times daily and twice on Sundays, with no expenses for travelling. This particular band was made up of two-thirds Englishmen and one third foreigners, with an English conductor. On another occasion, however, Holst joined a similar band having roughly the same proportion of English and foreign musicians, but this time they were all dressed in gold-braided uniforms, described as the 'White Viennese Band', and instructed to speak with foreign accents when conversing within earshot of the public. This enhanced their status to such an extent that although they only played twice daily during the week and not at all on Sundays, their pay was now three guineas per week plus their train fares from London. This was one of Holst's earliest experiences of the curious prejudice which the English public has against its own musicians. He later remarked: 'It was understood that if you were a good musician you must be a foreigner. And if you were a foreign musician it followed that you must be a better one than an English one.'[12] The conductor of the band, a certain Stanislaus Wurm, may or may not have been a foreigner, as the English practice of assuming a foreign name in order to gain added status was as common then as it is now. As a student, Holst was assured that he was destined for success, because people would assume from his name that he was a German, and it was therefore ironical that he was later obliged to drop the 'von' from his name as a result of virulent anti-German feeling during the First World War.

On the whole, Holst tried to carry out his duties in these bands to the best of his abilities, but found them boring and time-wasting. He referred to this work as 'Worming', after the band's conductor, and later wrote: 'I am certain that Worming is very bad for one—it makes me so sick of everything so that I cannot settle down to work properly.'[13] He would rather have been composing his own music, and although he did manage to get some writing done when he was playing at one of the London theatres, he found it much more difficult at the seaside.

Back at college, he continued to write student exercises for his teachers, and also tried his hand at another one-act opera, *The Magic Mirror*, which was to be his last collaboration with Fritz Hart. The libretto was based on a story from George Macdonald's *Phantastes: a faerie romance*, one of Holst's favourite books (and which was later to inspire an orchestral work). But *The Magic Mirror* was destined never to be completed. While Holst was working on the score, Fritz Hart left the College to go on tour in the Midlands, so that further discussion of the project had to be carried on by post. After sketching the music for the opening scenes, Holst sent a copy to Hart, asking for his comments, but when Hart replied making some criticisms of the music, Holst stopped work and wrote no more. According to Hart, the original sketches were destroyed by the composer, and his own copies subsequently lost, but this account cannot be true as the British Library now holds a set of sketch pages in Holst's own hand.

Holst also wrote a number of student chamber works, which may have been tried through by his friends as some of the scores bear rehearsal numbers in red ink. They include an incomplete *Fantasiestücke* for oboe and strings, a *Sextet* for oboe, clarinet, bassoon, violin, viola, and cello, some *Variations* for the same instrumentation, and a *Quintet* for piano, oboe, clarinet, horn, and bassoon. He also continued to write part-songs, including a set of three for female voices to words by Heine, and several for mixed voices, to words by various authors. Among his surviving manuscripts from this period there are also sketches for several orchestral pieces, some of which are marked 'Jacobi', indicating that they were written for his orchestration classes at the College.

Besides his studies, Holst also played an active part in the social side of student life, and the minutes of the Literary and Debating Society record that during the 1896–7 session Holst spoke on 'The Future of English Music', proposing that 'Academic Training Should be Abolished', while Vaughan Williams read papers on Purcell and Bayreuth and opened a debate on the motion that 'The Moderate Man is Contemptible'. In fact, Holst had been interested in philosophical matters since his boyhood days, when he had listened to his stepmother discussing theosophy with her circle of friends. But now his interests began to take a more political turn, and he joined the Hammersmith Socialist Society, where he heard lectures given by such formidable figures as William Morris and George Bernard Shaw in the meeting room at Kelmscott House, Morris's home in Hammersmith. It is interesting to speculate on Holst's political views during his student years, particularly in view of his great-grandfather's sudden departure from Russia for allegedly political reasons, but it is likely that his interest stemmed more from sources such as the musical magazine *The*

Minim, which sometimes included articles discussing socialism, than from study of theoretical Marxism. In any case, his
only true vocation was for music, and when he was asked to
form a Hammersmith Socialist Choir he accepted with
enthusiasm and immediately began the work of training the
singers and organizing concerts. He was also occasionally to be
seen perched on a cart playing a harmonium, while being
dragged round the streets of Hammersmith by a group of
enthusiastic distributors of socialist propaganda.

This early experience of socialism did not seem to influence
the course of Holst's actions in later life: in 1910, when asked
what he was doing to aid the emergent suffragette movement,
he replied: 'I'm afraid I only give them my moral support,'[14]
and when the First World War broke out he immediately
volunteered for service, in common with many other socialists
who pragmatically abandoned their idealistic internationalism,
although in the event he was rejected for medical reasons.
During the General Strike of 1926 he found himself unable to
decide on the rights and wrongs of the situation, and wrote to
Vaughan Williams: 'I find that I am a hopeless half-hogger and
am prepared to sit on the fence for as long as possible, partly
through laziness and through force of habit, but chiefly
through discovering that if I am a fool in music I am the
damnedest of fools in everything else.' He went on to say that
he believed in 'the Hindu doctrine of Dharma, which is one's
path in life', and that one should stick to this path without
worrying whether it is successful or not.[15] Accordingly, the
young Holst concentrated on his musical work, leaving
politics to the more militant members of the Hammersmith
Socialist Society.

Among the first recruits to his new choir was Harry
Harrison, who brought along his fair-haired sister Emily
(generally known by her second name of Isobel) with whom
Holst promptly fell in love. They subsequently became
engaged and were married a few years later, much to the
disappointment of Holst's fellow student Thomas Dunhill,
who had also been captivated by her charms. The most
immediate result of Holst's engagement to Isobel was that she
made him shave off the beard which he had grown to make
himself look older when applying for jobs as a trombonist, and

insisted that he should improve his clothing to a more presentable standard.

It seems that Holst had persuaded most of his immediate circle of friends to join him in his new socialist venture, for on 26 March 1897 the choir held a 'Glee Concert and Dramatic Entertainment' consisting of part-songs by Holst (including the first performance of *Clear and Cool* to words by Charles Kingsley) with Dunhill accompanying at the piano, followed by a performance of *The Anarchist*, 'an original Comedy in One Act' by Fritz Hart, in which Holst was cast in the role of Benjamin Beechcroft, Dunhill as Beechcroft's son, and Isobel as the Lodging House Keeper's daughter. The play apparently centred on a plot to blow up the Albert Memorial, and ended with the singing of the 'Marseillaise'. A few months later, another farcical one-act play was given, this time written by Holst himself, consisting, according to Fritz Hart, of 'an ingenuous mixture of all the out-worn farces he had ever seen or read',[16] although Holst apparently considered it to be quite original. In this play, which turned on the situation resulting from an intercepted letter, Holst played the part of the hero (a Curate) and Isobel was his wife. The only other character was an Italian who at a critical moment in the drama had to sing the intermezzo from Mascagni's *Cavalleria Rusticana*. Holst also tried his hand at writing a serious play on a Nordic subject, but this was never performed. According to Vaughan Williams, these youthful attempts at dramatic writing were regarded by Holst as an apprenticeship for writing opera libretti, for which he felt he should be adequately prepared.

In the autumn of 1896, an announcement of two prizes was made by the Magpie Madrigal Society for the best part-songs submitted by students of the Royal College and the Royal Academy of Music. The Society had been founded in 1886 by Lionel Benson with the object of giving concerts for charitable purposes, and the prizes were intended to encourage good choral writing by composition students. Holst submitted a setting of words by Fritz Hart entitled *Light Leaves Whisper*, and was awarded the prize designated for the Royal College of Music. The successful works were duly performed by the Magpie Madrigal Society on 25 May 1897 at Stafford House (subsequently Lancaster House), and this first major public performance of one of Holst's works in London was reviewed by *The Times*,[17] whose critic described the piece as 'a moderately elaborate composition in six parts, with a good deal of expression and poetic feeling'. The writer went on to commend the choir for giving such a good performance despite the circumstances; apparently the singers were deployed on the staircase of Stafford House, and as they numbered 63 sopranos, 50 altos, 26 tenors, and 41 basses, it is a wonder that they had room to breathe, let alone sing. On 3 June the programme was repeated by the same performers at St James's Hall, Piccadilly (on the site of the later Piccadilly Hotel), which at that time was the most important concert hall in London, with excellent acoustics, affording perfect hearing from each of its 2,500 seats. *Light Leaves Whisper* was published later that year by Laudy & Co., becoming the first of Holst's works to appear in print, and bore a dedication to the composer's aunt Nina von Holst.

Other works of 1897 included a *Scherzo* for string sextet, and his first substantial work for full orchestra: *A Winter Idyll*, whose earnest attempts at drama and contrasting liveliness fail to alleviate its inherent tedium. He also wrote several songs for voice and piano; of these, it is interesting to note that *Airly Beacon*, *Sing Heigh-ho*, and *Slumber-Song (Soft, Soft Wind)* are settings of words by Charles Kingsley which Holst's teacher Stanford had himself previously set as Nos.1–3 of his *Four Part-Songs*, published by Novello in 1892. In addition to *Light Leaves Whisper*, Holst's *Slumber-Song* and a song to words by Ibsen entitled *Margrete's Cradle-Song* were also published by Laudy in 1897, so that his career as a published composer got off to a good start that year.

In July 1897, Vaughan Williams wrote to Holst to ask whether he would be interested in taking over from him the post of organist and choirmaster of St Barnabas' Church, South Lambeth, at a salary of £50 per annum. Vaughan Williams had been there for two years (his 'first and last organist post'[18]), and although he had left college in 1896 had no need to earn a living as he had a private income. He found the work irksome, describing the choirmen as 'louts', the vicar 'quite mad', and the church itself as 'this damned place'.[19] He was planning to spend some time in Berlin after his marriage in October and wanted to be released from the job as quickly as possible. Holst had already deputized at St Barnabas' occasionally (the vicar being 'rather struck by the way you took that choir practice', according to Vaughan Williams[20]) but in any case was asked to stand in for his friend until a permanent replacement could be found. Besides the normal duties, the post included giving occasional organ recitals and conducting the choral society 'whenever it intermittently exists'. Holst was in two minds about taking on the permanent position, and although he did deputize for Vaughan Williams on several occasions in August 1897, the post eventually went to his fellow student John Ireland. At this time Holst had responsibility for another choir, of which Vaughan Williams later recalled: 'I remember a certain choral society which in his youthful enthusiasm he over-dosed with Bach's cantatas, with the result that he was asked to retire in favour of some other conductor and the society returned to its wallowing in the mire.'[21]

Holst continued to write songs and part-songs, to texts by such writers as Thomas Hood, George Macdonald, Francis Thompson, and William Morris. One song for voice and piano, *Awake, My Heart*, was a setting of words by Robert Bridges, and in later years when Holst and Bridges had become close friends, the author suggested that Holst might set this poem to music, being apparently unaware of this early song which was published in 1908. It seems that Bridges had had a musical setting in mind when he had originally conceived the poem, as he wrote to Holst in 1925: 'I wish that one day you would look at a poem of mine which I wrote deliberately for a cello obligato: for if it should appear to you to possess the peculiar cello suggestion which I intended, it is possible that you might like to supply it: the poem is "Awake my heart to be loved"—I wrote it after hearing Piatti lavishing his wonderful passion on some quite paltry words.'[22] When he learnt that Holst had already set the poem during his student days but was later dissatisfied with this early work, Bridges replied: 'I was interested to hear that you had once tried my cello piece: and ashamed of myself for having failed you. It was definitely the cello I had in mind, and I imagined its obbligato passion to be quite free of the singer's particular preoccupation.'[23]

In addition to his trombone playing in the vacations, Holst

occasionally took on engagements during term time: on 7 December 1897 he played in the Queen's Hall Orchestra under Richard Strauss, who was making his first appearance before a British audience. The programme consisted of works by Wagner, Mozart, and the conductor's own *Tod und Verklärung* and *Till Eulenspiegel*, both of which were superbly played, according to the *Musical Times*, 'excepting a few uncouth-sounding passages for the brass'.[24] Holst was probably blameless for these lapses, as on another occasion he was one of two players singled out for praise by Hans Richter when conducting in London.

On Saturday 5 February 1898, a 'Grand Evening Concert' was given by the Hammersmith Socialist Choir at 29 The Grove, London W. Holst conducted and played the piano, and also accompanied Isobel in a performance of his song *Two Brown Eyes*. Two weeks later one of Holst's compositions was included in a charity drama performance on 18 February at the Matinée Theatre, London, during the interval of which the 'programme of music' included an orchestral version of the *Ländler* from his children's operetta *Ianthe*; a movement which was to resurface in several guises in his work during the next few years.

Apart from a few songs, his only substantial work of 1898 was *Örnulf's Drapa*, a 'scena' for baritone and orchestra based on a translation of Ibsen's *Vikings at Helgeland*. There is no record of any performance of this work, and it was never published. But Holst did have some success in publication that year, after writing to A. J. Jaeger (Elgar's 'Nimrod') of Novello, to ask about having some songs privately printed as he had been unable to find a publisher willing to accept them. Jaeger dissuaded Holst from this idea (fortunately as it turned out, as these youthful efforts were subsequently disowned by their composer), but did accept on behalf of Novello a mixed-voice part-song entitled *Love is Enough*, and so began a long association with the firm which was subsequently to publish many of Holst's major works.

Although his composition scholarship was due to come to an end in 1898, Holst was offered an extension for a further year, but after giving the matter serious consideration he decided against it. He had now been at the College for five years, and felt that it was time to make his own way in the world of music, so during the summer vacation he successfully applied for a post as trombonist and répétiteur with the Carl Rosa Opera Company, and wrote to Hubert Parry to explain his reasons for leaving. On 10 September Parry replied: 'My dear Von Holst, You are not at all likely to "give offence" to any authorities at the RCM; they have much too good an opinion of you. I am very sorry we shall not have the benefit of your presence at the RCM this next term, but you are quite right to take an opportunity of the kind you tell me of.'[25] Accordingly, Holst packed his bags and his trombone and set off to join the Carl Rosa company at the Lancashire seaside resort of Southport.

3

The Orchestral Musician
(1898–1903)

Writing a few years earlier, George Bernard Shaw described the Carl Rosa Opera Company as a 'fortuitous assemblage of middle-class amateurs competing with one another for applause'. According to Shaw, the singers played shamelessly to the gallery, introduced alterations and interpolations into their parts, assumed false Italian names and sang in broken English. He hoped that the company would receive severe criticism, and plenty of it: 'The diction and deportment of the Carl Rosa artists leave everything to be desired,' he declared.[1]

When Holst joined the company in the autumn of 1898, things had apparently not changed much. As répétiteur, his duties were to make an early start at the piano each morning, hammering out the notes for the cast to learn, for although some of them had beautiful voices, many were not adept at reading music. The repertoire at that time consisted of established foreign works such as *La Bohème*, *Carmen*, and *Cavalleria Rusticana*, with a sprinkling of home-produced material such as Balfe's *The Bohemian Girl*, Wallace's *Maritana*, and MacCunn's *Diarmid*. When Holst joined the company, Stanford's *Shamus O'Brien* was also in the repertoire, conducted by the young Henry Wood. Apparently Wood showed great kindness to Holst, and on one occasion even went so far as to pay for a deputy when Holst was suffering from influenza.

Holst's natural aversion to pretentiousness must have been strengthened during his time with the Carl Rosa company, but he was able to obtain a practical insight into the problems of operatic composition, although it would be some years before this was to bear fruit in his own work. Of the operas he wrote later in his career, several are comic operas, suggesting that at heart he was unable to take this genre seriously, perhaps as a result of his early experiences.

During his absence on tour, Holst managed to keep in touch with Vaughan Williams by sending him postcards from the places in which he happened to find himself. In response to one such card, Vaughan Williams replied, enquiring about the publication of one of Holst's part-songs: 'Thanks awfully for your post card . . . have you heard from Francis Thompson, tell me when you do—and when it will be coming out. Will it do for my choral society? or is it too hard? How is Deptford appreciating your efforts? Where do you go after Deptford? Do you stop about and is there any chance of your coming to see us?'[2] The work referred to was probably Holst's four-part setting of Francis Thompson's poem *To Sylvia*, published by Novello the following year.

Although conditions were not ideal, Holst continued to compose as best he could while on tour, and by way of relaxation and mental stimulation took up the study of Sanskrit literature, which was to have an important influence on his later work. His interest in the subject began when the company was at Scarborough and he found himself at a loose end: a friend lent him one of Friedrich Max Müller's books (probably one of the volumes of *The Sacred Books of the East*) which captured his interest and prompted his curiosity to know more about the subject. On his return to London, he visited the Department of Oriental Languages at the British Museum, but was dismayed to find that the books there were mostly in the original Sanskrit. So, with characteristic determination, he enrolled at the London School of Oriental Languages to take a course in Sanskrit. His teacher was Mabel Bode, first wife of Milton Bode, manager of the County Theatre, Reading, an Irishwoman with a strong sense of humour, known to all as 'Patsy'. Holst was her first Sanskrit pupil and they quickly struck up a friendship. In spite of his touring commitments he devoted as much time as he could to his studies, and later remarked: 'I believe . . . that if you really want passionately to do something, you will find time. I used to study Sanskrit in the train—I learned the alphabet, at least. Much good it did me, but I learnt it'.[3] He soon found that he could make his own versions of Sanskrit texts by studying the original together with a published translation, and then putting both on one side and reproducing the meaning as nearly as possible in English: not a literal translation, but one which would serve the purpose he had in mind—that of setting the texts to music. For he had discovered in Sanskrit literature a rich untapped source of inspiration which was to provide the basis for many of his musical works.

Having achieved a working ability as a translator, Holst began the task of writing a libretto for a large-scale opera in three acts entitled *Sita*, which was to occupy him for several years; the score not being completed until 1906. The work is based on a story from Valmiki's *Ramayana* of c.500 BC, Sita being the Hindu god of both destruction and creation, and is scored for a large orchestra with a cast of seven soloists, choruses of Mortals and Rakshas (evil spirits), and a hidden chorus of Voices of the Earth. Holst worked painstakingly on the libretto in his spare time, occasionally seeking the advice of his friends. In 1901, Vaughan Williams wrote to say that he admired the libretto of *Sita* very much, and that although he had a few criticisms they were not important. But as late as 1903, Holst wrote to Vaughan Williams: 'I am certainly going to rewrite the words of Sita as you suggest. They are disgraceful and that was largely due to Worming etc. I used to write them at odd moments, often in the orchestra.'[4]

Meanwhile he was continuing to compose despite the difficulties of touring, and completed two orchestral works during 1899: a *Suite de Ballet*, consisting of a *Danse Rustique*, *Valse*, *Scène de Nuit*, and *Carnival*, and the overture *Walt Whitman*, in tribute to a poet whose words he was to set in several of his later works. These two compositions show little evidence of Holst's mature style, but he was becoming more assured in his handling of orchestral resources, as a consequence of his growing experience as an orchestral musician. The Suite in particular is an attractive work, with well-contrasted movements and orchestration appropriate to the musical material: bright and jaunty in the livelier movements, and subtle and sensitive in the slower ones. Although the style is typical of late nineteenth-century ballet music, the chromaticism is not distasteful, and occasional touches such as a Ravellian lightness in the *Valse* and a repetitive scale figure in the barcarolle-like *Scène de Nuit* give the music an individual character. *Walt Whitman*, on the other hand, is heavy with noble idealism, exhibiting a rather close acquaintance with the works of Wagner, Strauss, and Mendelssohn. He also began work on a 'Cotswolds' symphony, and continued to write songs and part-songs.

Occasionally there were performances of his works in London and Cheltenham. On 9 May 1899 at St George's Hall, Langham Place (adjacent to the Queen's Hall), a play entitled *His Majesty's Musketeers*, adapted from Dumas's novel, was presented 'Under the Patronage and support of the Ladies' Kennel Association'. Fritz Hart composed some incidental music, the orchestra being under the direction of 'Herr von Holst'. Included in the musical selections were two pieces by Holst: the *Ländler* from *Ianthe*, and a *Minuet and Jig* (possibly from the *Suite in G minor* mentioned below). On the following Saturday, 13 May, Holst was in Cheltenham, where he appeared at 'Herr Lortzing's Ladies Choir "At Home" ' at the Montpellier Rotunda, giving with his father the first performance of his *Duet in D* for two pianos. On 8 July, another Cheltenham performance took place in a concert given at the Ladies' College by pupils of Miss Sawyer and Lewis Hann, including a Berceuse and Dance from a *Suite in G minor* by Holst. At the end of the year, Holst stayed in London, playing the trombone for the pantomime season; two daily performances of four hours each in the pit of the Coronet Theatre. He accepted the customary tedium, but found that he was unable to think of composition or work on the libretto of *Sita*, and so he settled down to read all the novels of Turgenev, borrowed from Vaughan Williams volume by volume. In addition to playing the trombone in theatre orchestras and touring with the Carl Rosa Opera Company, Holst was also organist at the Royal Opera House, Covent Garden for several seasons.

In January 1900 he rescored *Örnulf's Drapa*, and for the next few months continued to work on the *Cotswolds Symphony*, which he eventually completed on 24 July at Skegness while on tour with the Carl Rosa company. The work consists of four movements, the second of which is an Elegy in memory of William Morris (who had died on 3 October 1896), containing moments of passionately intense expression. As with his other works of this period, this symphony bears little evidence of Holst's later style, except for some use of melodic fourths in the Scherzo, and a pedal-point in the Elegy.

Despite his growing experience as an orchestral composer, Holst's most successful work of 1900 was in fact for unaccompanied voices; an *Ave Maria* for eight-part female chorus. Rooted in the harmonic language of the nineteenth century, this overtly romantic piece demonstrates Holst's considerable skill and assurance in handling the intricate part-writing of the double chorus. It was published towards the end of the year by Laudy and immediately attracted favourable reviews. Holst sent a copy to the distinguished pedagogue Ebenezer Prout, who replied: 'It is very ingeniously written, and I do *not* think the counterpoint too free. Nobody would expect such a piece to be written in *Strict* Counterpoint. I am afraid that the fact of its being written for 8-part female chorus will prevent its having a large sale; there are very few female choirs good enough to divide into eight parts without coming to grief.'[5] *The Minim* described it as a 'clever work' in which 'the composer has produced good results, and has, evidently, studied the compositions of the old writers, such as Tallis and Palestrina, to great advantage',[6] while J. A. Fuller Maitland wrote that Holst's composition 'is so deftly worked and so massively designed that he is certain to go far'.[7] Vaughan Williams was very impressed, and showed the piece to his cousin Diana Massingberd, who sang in the Magpie Madrigal Society, in the hope that she would persuade the choir to take an interest in it. Writing some years later, Holst's friend W. G. Whittaker said that the *Ave Maria* was 'obviously suggested by the old "a capella" schools, but yet quite distinctive and not in the slightest degree an anachronism',[8] while later still Michael Tippett described it as 'Verdi-like'.[9]

In the autumn of 1900, Holst ceased to tour regularly with the Carl Rosa company and took a job as second trombonist with the Scottish Orchestra, based in Glasgow. At that time the orchestra was conducted by Frederick H. Cowen and the concerts usually given in the St Andrew's Hall (destroyed by fire in 1962). Although the orchestra's programmes consisted of the usual repertoire such as Beethoven symphonies and Wagner overtures, the standard of musicianship was much higher than in the Carl Rosa company, and Holst was able to extend his knowledge of orchestral technique. He later said that he had been fortunate in having had the opportunity to learn orchestration 'from the inside out',[10] and towards the end of his life he spoke of his gratitude for 'having known the impersonality of orchestral playing'.[11] His work left little time for composition, as the orchestra gave four concerts a week during the season, including visits to towns outside Glasgow which involved travelling as well as the usual rehearsals, but he made the best use of any moments of free time to carry on with his creative work.

On 22 November 1900, Holst's boyhood musical hero Arthur Sullivan died in London, marking the end of an era in the English musical theatre. Whether Holst was particularly moved by this event is doubtful, however, for he was now in the throes of Wagner-worship, and was working on the score of his large-scale opera *Sita*, which was to be one of the most Wagnerian of all his compositions. As he knew nothing of authentic Indian music, and had discounted the notion of a pseudo-oriental pastiche, he indulged himself in the chromatic idiom in which he now felt thoroughly at home. He was simultaneously working on *The Youth's Choice*, a 'musical idyll in one act', also strongly Wagnerian in style. Vaughan Williams wrote to say that he liked the music of this work, but that the words were not up to the same standard, in fact: 'I think the whole scheme of the verses is bad.' After making some criticisms of particular points in the libretto, he went on to say that the style was 'much too loose', advising Holst to say what he meant and no more, and to avoid the use of archaic words which had lost their meaning, 'otherwise it will read like Corder's translation of Wagner'.[12] Apparently Holst's method of writing was first to contrive the rhymes and then concoct the lines leading up to them, which accounts for the awkwardness of the resulting verse.

On 23 May 1901 the *Ave Maria* was given its first performance at St James's Hall, London, by the Magpie Madrigal Society conducted by Lionel S. Benson; the work being commended as 'scholarly' by the critic of *The Times*. It was performed again on 11 July by the Choral class of the Royal College of Music as part of their end-of-term concert.

Now that Holst had a regular job as a trombonist and was beginning to establish himself as a composer, he and Isobel decided that they were at last able to get married. The ceremony took place at Fulham Registrar's Office on Saturday 22 June 1901, and the couple moved into their new home: two furnished rooms above a shop at 162 Shepherd's Bush Road, Brook Green. Their first visitor was Fritz Hart, who brought with him the depressing news that Thomas Dunhill had discovered a pair of parallel fifths in Holst's much-admired *Ave Maria*, but now that the work was in print there was little that could be done about it.

After only a few weeks of married life, news arrived from Cheltenham that Adolph von Holst had died suddenly on 17 August at the age of fifty-six. He was buried in Cheltenham Cemetery on 21 August, and in an obituary notice, *The Minim* described him as 'A fine pianist, well known in musical circles. He was organist of All Saints Church for 26 years . . . and was a local examiner for the Royal College of Music. His son, Gustav, late student of that institution, is a promising musician, and has produced some excellent compositions.'[13]

Readjusting after this shock, Holst packed his suitcase, said his farewells to Isobel, and travelled north again for the autumn season of the Scottish Orchestra. Although he was glad of regular employment, he was hoping eventually to be able to give up trombone playing, which was keeping him away from home for long periods of time, so that he could devote as much time as possible to composition. In an attempt to generate an independent income, he tried writing pot-boilers such as songs and short instrumental pieces, but these did not find much favour with publishers, and he once again toyed with the idea of having his music printed at his own expense. He was dissuaded from this by Vaughan Williams on the grounds that the words 'Author's Property' on the title-page of a score immediately branded the composer as second-rate, regardless of the quality of the music. Instead, Vaughan Williams offered more positive help by persuading the proprietors of the musical magazine *The Vocalist* to publish one of Holst's salon pieces for violin and piano, *Song Without Words*, in the issue of December 1902. The editorial column drew attention to the piece in glowing terms:

'We are able to give a most effective and very charming solo for violin and piano, written by that talented and rising composer, Mr Gustave

Von Holst, whose promise when a student at the Royal College of Music bids fair to be amply fulfilled . . . It may interest our readers to know that this particular piece has been most cordially received by several of our leading violinists, two of whom have already added it to their *répertoire*, both for public performances and for academical purposes . . . It may be noticed that we have not selected a piece which ambles about only in the first position, for our purpose was not merely to endeavour to please the beginner, we preferred rather to provide a piece which was really melodious and at the same time distinctly meritorious, without involving such technical difficulties as would prove unnecessarily irksome to violinists of moderate ability, and we do not hesitate to say that as providing a means for displaying the technical abilty, and for bringing out the fervour of a musical soul (if there be any) of the performer, the present piece amply provides both, and will doubtless find many friends.'

This blatantly commercial eulogy was doubtless written by Vaughan Williams himself, who was on the staff of the magazine at that time. To this brief composition Holst added several other violin and piano pieces, including *A Spring Song* (published in *The Vocalist* of April 1903), *Greeting, Maya,* and *Valse Etude,* and also arranged the *Ländler* from *Ianthe* for two violins and piano (published in the September 1903 issue of *The Vocalist*). Several of these pieces were produced in alternative versions for cello instead of violin, and arrangements were made for piano solo, organ, and small orchestra. They were subsequently published by various firms, including Novello, Ashdown and Willocks. Holst also wrote two pot-boilers for piano: *Fancine* and *Lucille,* which were published by Weekes in 1902 under the title *Deux Pièces.*

On 14 and 15 April 1902, another children's operetta was presented at St Mary's School: entitled *Fairy Pantomime of Cinderella,* it seems to have been as successful as its predecessors. The *Parish Gazette* reported that 'Mr Gustav von Holst was energetic in front of the stage accompanying all the music composed and set to the libretto by himself. Pretty and taking was that music, too!'[14] None of this music seems to have survived, but it was doubtless in much the same vein as *Ianthe* and *The Idea.*

A week later, on 22 April, Holst presented a concert of his own at the Cleveland Hall in Barnes, including the first public performances of five of his songs: *Margrete's Cradle-Song, Soft, Soft Wind* (both dedicated to Anna Newman), *Awake, My Heart*, and *The Ballade of Prince Eric*, all sung by Eva Hart, together with *Hymn to the Dawn* sung by J. Campbell McInnes. Holst played the accompaniments himself, and also performed some piano solos and duets with his aunt Nina. This must have been quite a taxing occasion, as his neuritis showed no signs of abating. Of the songs, none are particularly outstanding, but it is interesting to note that the *Hymn to the Dawn* (also known as *Invocation to the Dawn*) was the first of the settings which Holst made of his own translations from Sanskrit literature. He later wrote: 'The old Invocation to the Dawn was pretty bad but bears a family likeness to the first of the Veda songs [*Vedic Hymns*] which was written long after.'[15] *The Herald* published a review of the concert, referring to Holst as 'this talented young gentleman', and going on to say that 'of the many capital concerts given in Barnes, few have come within the category of "high-class" to which that provided by Mr Gustav von Holst must be assigned.'[16]

But the high point of the month was the first performance of the *Cotswolds Symphony*, given on 24 April at the Bournemouth Winter Gardens by the Bournemouth Municipal Orchestra conducted by Dan Godfrey; the first time an orchestral work of Holst's had been played professionally. Gustav, Isobel, and Vaughan Williams left London early in the morning to reach Bournemouth in time for the rehearsal, and as the day progressed Holst became nervous and anxious because of errors in the parts and uncertainty over queries which Godfrey kept raising. But in the event the performance went well. The *Bournemouth Visitor's Directory*[17] commented that 'Without being remarkable, the symphony evidenced sound workmanship, and the elegy and scherzo were particularly effective', while *The Times* cavilled about the title: 'What the composer exactly means us to understand by this is not very clear. There is evidence of much musicianly writing and considerable talent for melody, and this is more noticeable in the slow movement, the best thing in the work. The first movement is very weak and lacking in originality. The audience seemed pleased with the symphony, and gave it a good reception.'[18]

On 1 May, Holst's part-song *Love is Enough* was performed

by the Watford Choral Union conducted by a friend from student days, Evlyn Howard-Jones, and three of his mixed-voice part-songs were published during the year: *A Love Song* (dedicated to Isobel), *Dream Tryst* (dedicated to Vaughan Williams's wife Adeline), and *Ye Little Birds*, a lively and effective piece which demonstrates considerable command of choral writing.

Since the previous summer Holst had been working sporadically on his two operas, but in August 1902 an incentive appeared in the form of an international competition for a one-act opera organized by the Milan publisher Sonzogno, similar to the 1890 contest which had produced Mascagni's *Cavalleria Rusticana*. The proffered cash prize of £2,000 seems very large in comparison with income levels at that time, but Signor Sonzogno was clearly hoping that the prize-winning work would prove to be another money-spinner for his firm. Holst decided to submit *The Youth's Choice*, and threw himself into a frenzy of work to complete the score by the deadline of 31 January 1903. He travelled up to Glasgow once again, where he devoted every spare moment to work on the opera, writing to Linetta Palamidessi da Castelvecchio in Cheltenham to ask her to make an Italian translation of the words. By December Holst was close to panic, and wrote to his translator: 'I am sorry to say it is very doubtful whether I shall get it finished in time. I am doing my best but I have four concerts a week and endless rehearsals and travelling besides which my old enemy writer's cramp has turned up.'[19] The autumn season ended with a concert conducted by Richard Strauss on 23 December, including his *Serenade* for wind instruments and the tone-poems *Don Juan* and *Tod und Verklärung*, in which Holst played as best he could despite a feverish cold brought on by the Glasgow weather. Nevertheless he battled on with *The Youth's Choice*, and by mid-January the work was complete. He chose as his pseudonym the motto: 'Search deep enough, there is music everywhere' (an adaptation of a quotation from Carlyle which appeared on the cover of each issue of *The Minim* magazine), and sent off the score, writing in triumph to Signorina Castelvecchio: 'It has gone!! My life is now a blank!!'[20]

The end of the winter season was now approaching, and as Holst had heard that his father's estate had at last been settled and that he was to receive a small inheritance, he and Isobel decided to spend it on a spring holiday in Germany as a kind of deferred honeymoon, or 'study and holiday combined', as Holst put it.[21] They left at the beginning of March, visiting Berlin, Dresden and Munich, and sampling the musical life, art galleries, and museums wherever they went (including the National Gallery in Berlin, where they were particularly impressed by the Arnold Böcklin room). They also met members of the German branch of the Holst family, including Holst's second cousin Matthias, and some German musicians to whom Holst showed the scores of his recent compositions. It was while they were in Berlin that Holst completed his orchestral work *Indra*, which was the first major work to be written as a result of his Sanskrit studies. Indra was the Hindu god of Rain and Storm, and Holst added a note to his score describing the scenes the music was meant to portray: a drought parches the land because the rain-clouds have been seized by a dragon; men pray for salvation to Indra, who overcomes the dragon and rain falls while men give praise to the god. Later in the year this work was tried through by Royal College of Music students conducted by Parry, but it was never performed in public. Fritz Hart recalled that Parry's sarcastic remarks during the rehearsal offended Holst, who withdrew the work as a result of this experience.

But he was still working on the gigantic opera *Sita*, and wrote from Germany to Vaughan Williams: 'I feel sometimes inclined to chuck *Sita* in case it is only bad Richard I [Wagner]. Unless one ought to follow the latter until he leads you to fresh things. What I feel is that there is *nothing* else but Wagner excepting Italian one act horrors.' He was worried about the influence of foreign composers on his work, and considered that continental musicians were unable to comprehend what he was getting at in his music, concluding that 'Seeing foreigners is a mistake as a rule. Don't you think we ought to victimize Elgar? Write to him first and then bicycle to Worcester and see him *a lot*? . . . Or else make a list of musicians in London whom we think worthy of the honour of being bothered by us and *who have time and inclination to be bothered* and then bother them.'[22]

During this holiday, Holst corresponded regularly with Vaughan Williams, for whom he and Isobel also did some copying work, including the parts for Vaughan Williams's *Symphonic Rhapsody*. This supplemented their finances, and they also saved money by cycling to Munich instead of going by train. The holiday was a great success, relaxing and invigorating, and it gave Holst an opportunity to think about the problems of being a composer and of his own future in particular. Summer was approaching, and with it the annual necessity of taking a job with a seaside band to make ends meet until the beginning of the Scottish Orchestra's autumn season. But Isobel suggested that they should curtail their holiday so that they would have enough money left to see them through the summer, and Holst could devote his whole time to composition. If they were unable to get by, there was always an offer of a loan from Vaughan Williams to fall back on. In fact Holst would have liked to remain in London all the year round, and wrote to Vaughan Williams: 'I feel more and more that my mode of living is very unsatisfactory. It is not so bad in London say during the "French Milliner" when I did a fair amount of writing every day but the Worm is a wicked and loathesome waste of time . . . I think it would be a great thing for me if I could always live in London and say goodbye to the Worm and all seaside bands. I should be sorry to leave the Scottish for some things but it really would be better on the whole.'[23]

On their return from Germany, Holst learnt that *The Youth's Choice* had not succeeded in reaching the final of the Sonzogno competition. Of the 234 scores which had been submitted by composers from various countries, three had been short-listed for performance, but Holst's work was not among them. In the course of its deliberations, the jury had rejected all works which were not based on a good libretto, however good the music, so that *The Youth's Choice* may have failed simply because of its words, without a note of the score being examined by the judges.

Holst and Isobel must have been greatly disappointed, as the prize money would have provided sufficient security for him to give up his work as a trombonist. But he was not deterred from his aim of becoming a composer, and during the summer months Holst stayed at home concentrating on his own work, while Isobel supplemented their income by taking on dressmaking for their friends. They had moved from their flat at Brook Green and were now living south of the Thames, at 31 Grena Road, Richmond, close to Sheen Common and within walking distance of Kew Gardens. The music which Holst produced at this time is not outstanding; mainly pot-boilers written in the hope of finding a ready market among publishers. He wrote a number of soprano and baritone songs, including three settings of poems by Thomas Hardy. One song, *A Prayer for Light* (to words by Eric Mackay) was submitted for a prize offered by the baritone Charles Phillips, and although it did not win the award, Phillips performed it during his concert at the Bechstein Hall on 12 December 1903.

Novello published one of Holst's violin solos (*Greeting*), a canon for children's voices entitled *Clouds o'er the Summer Sky*, and the part-song *Now is the Month of Maying*, a lively setting of the words of Morley's ballett, of which the original music was doubtless quite unknown to Holst. The *Musical Times* commented: 'It is always pleasant to think about May, especially when April winds blow, and those who sing Mr Gustav von Holst's part-song should have a very pleasant time indeed, for the music is blithesome and gay. There is a good deal about "Fa, la, la," in the text, but then it was written in the sixteenth century, when fal lals were *de rigeur*.'[24] He also composed an 'old English ballad' for chorus and orchestra entitled *King Estmere*, to words from Percy's *Reliques of Ancient Poetry*; a tale of knightly chivalry set in a rather conventional style, clearly intended to appeal to amateur choral societies. There is little evidence of the mature Holst in this work, although it does contain fragments of ideas which were subsequently to reappear in a more developed form in *The Planets*, and the melodic style leans more towards traditional English song than Teutonic sources, although the harmony remains rooted in the nineteenth century. Sorcery crops up again in this work, as the means by which the heroes overcome their foe, and may have been one of the factors which attracted Holst to the text.

He also completed a wind quintet, which he sent to the flautist Albert Fransella a few years later, and never saw again. The score remained lost until the 1950s when it turned up in a pile of music purchased in Derbyshire by a London flautist. When Edwin Evans was preparing material for *Cobbett's Cyclopedia of Chamber Music* in 1925, Holst told him that he did not want the quintet to be mentioned; perhaps because the score was missing, but possibly because he did not consider it good enough to stand beside his more mature compositions. But on eventual publication in 1983, the quintet was recognized as a musicianly and attractive composition, well written for the ensemble, with a good understanding of instrumental texures. Although the editors decided to delete some of the 'padding' which Holst later came to detest, the quintet in its revised form is a worthwhile contribution to the wind repertoire, and not at all deserving of its composer's condemnation. The style is once again typical of the late nineteenth century, although fleeting hints of other things appear, such as a folk-like version of the variation theme, and a melodic snippet reminiscent of Ravel's famous *Pavane*.

4

The Teacher
(1903–1908)

In November 1903 Holst rejoined the Scottish Orchestra for the winter season, but did not remain long because of a turn of events which was to change the whole direction of his musical career. That autumn, Vaughan Williams took up a post as music teacher at James Allen's Girls' School in West Dulwich, South London, and on a couple of occasions asked Holst to deputize for him. When Vaughan Williams decided to leave the job in 1904, Holst was asked to become his successor, and so began his career as a teacher, which was to occupy him for the rest of his life and which was to become as important to him as composition itself. His duties were to teach singing and to organize and conduct the school orchestra; tasks which he carried out with enthusiasm and an ingenuous disregard for the formalities of school life. At that time it was customary for male teachers to be chaperoned by a schoolmistress who would keep strict watch from the platform during classes, but Holst insisted on dispensing with this antiquated practice, to no apparently detrimental effect.

One of his pupils, Dorothy Callard, had vivid memories of him at the school: 'I first came to his notice when he turned me out of class for misbehaving. I had a stormy interview with the Head Mistress who said that in future I should do maths during the music period. He sent for me afterwards, and said that he was sorry that she had interfered in a purely private row, and would I do something for him. He had been told that I had a marvellous memory, so would I come to him after school every Friday afternoon and make him turn out his pockets to see what letters he ought to have posted, and write a card to remind him of what he ought to be doing. I did this for the rest of my school life, and he often gave me music to copy or transpose.'[1] According to another ex-pupil, Dorothy Nutting, the headmistress was something of a killjoy who regarded music as a waste of time and who was only interested in the examination successes of her pupils, so that Holst's classes must have come low on her list of priorities. However, one of the things which Holst liked about the school was its proximity to Dulwich Art Gallery, which he often visited and described as '*adorable . . .* also *small . . .* also *free*'.[2]

His teaching duties allowed a certain amount of time each week in which to compose, and he started work on a scena for soprano and orchestra entitled *The Mystic Trumpeter*, a setting of Walt Whitman's poem 'From noon to Starry Night' from the collection *Leaves of Grass*. These same words were also later set for chorus and orchestra by Hamilton Harty, who knew Holst in 1904, and it is possible that the two composers may have discussed the possibilities and problems of setting the text. Writing some years later, Basil Hogarth considered Harty's version to be 'without a doubt far superior to that of Holst',[3] while in the year of Holst's death the *British Musician*, apparently unaware of either setting, exclaimed: 'One craves a Bach to deal with "The Mystic Trumpeter".'[4] Although there are inevitable points of similarity between the two versions, the most telling difference is in the way in which the final ecstatic words: 'Joy! Joy! all over Joy' are dealt with. Harty takes the obvious course, setting them for full chorus, *fff*, whereas Holst ends his setting with the orchestra playing *pppp*, his ectasy being one of restraint and spiritual transcendence. This ending characteristically reveals Holst's individual approach to the problem of expressing emotion in music without recourse to banalities.

Although his musical language was still steeped in chromaticism, a number of melodic and harmonic fragments provide glimpses of the mature Holst. The horn and trumpet calls with which the work begins contain suggestions of the polytonality which was to enrich many of his later works, and foreshadow the freely repeated calls in the *Pageant of London* and *The Perfect Fool*, the tauter tenor tuba and trumpet stretto in *Mars*, even re-emerging as late as the *Choral Fantasia* of 1930. There are alternating chordal effects similar to those in *The Planets*, some fragments of typically Holstian melody, and a pulsating triadic figure for three flutes, which subsequently reappears in *The Hymn of Jesus* and also in the *First Choral Symphony*. *The Mystic Trumpeter* is the first of Holst's works in which such individual stylistic features begin to make their appearance.

A big event for Holst in 1904 was the first performance of his *Suite de Ballet*, which he conducted himself at the first Royal College of Music Patron's Fund concert in the St James's Hall on 20 May. The Fund had been set up the previous year by Samuel Palmer, a director of the Reading biscuit firm of Huntley & Palmer and member of the College Council, who had given the sum of £20,000 to finance performances of works by younger British composers. From the works submitted, fourteen scores by eleven composers were selected, including Holst's *Suite de Ballet* and *Örnulf's Drapa*; the other successful composers including Henry Geehl, Frank Bridge, York Bowen, and William Hurlstone. There were the inevitable murmurs of discontent: a letter to *The Times* complained that although the Fund had been set up to encourage British musicians, of the eleven composers chosen, three had 'distinctly foreign names'.[5] The writer also claimed that the establishment of the Fund put the Royal College of Music in the position of being able to control the future of British music, and that the College 'experts' were academic in outlook and blind to innovation.

Despite such carping, the first concert seems to have been a success, and Holst's *Suite de Ballet*, together with Hurlstone's *Fantasie-Variations*, stood out from the rest of the programme. The critic of *The Times* disapproved of the lugubrious atmosphere of most of the works performed, and declared that 'For the reason that a cheerful ray of sunshine is worth all the finest black effects, Mr Hurlstone's superb, even masterly, "Fantasie-variations on a Swedish air", and Mr von Holst's orchestral suite in E♭, which have health and happiness written all over them, towered, to our thinking, over the rest of the programme, and carried one a substantial step further in the conviction of the real abilities of these composers.'[6] Although Holst went on to justify these expectations, Hurlstone's career was cut short by his untimely death at the age of twenty-nine the following year.

On 8 June 1904, four recent songs by Holst were given their first performance at the Bechstein Hall by Maja Kjöhler, accompanied by Muriel Davenport. These were *Calm is the Morn, My True Love Hath My Heart, Weep You No More, Sad Fountains,* and *Lovely Kind and Kindly Loving;* only two of which were eventually published, the last not until twenty years after its composition. Several short pieces were published during 1904 however, including *Maya* and *Valse Etude* for violin and piano, two songs entitled *Dewy Roses* and *Song of the Woods,* and a part-song for mixed voices, *Thou Didst Delight My Eyes,* of which the *Musical Times* declared: 'His setting of the lines by Mr Robert Bridges bears witness to the young composer's talent, for the music combines simplicity with effectiveness to a degree that sets forth with peculiar significance the diffident spirit underlying the words.'[7]

In the autumn of 1904, Holst began teaching evening classes at the Passmore Edwards Settlement (subsequently Mary Ward Centre) in Bloomsbury, in addition to his daytime work at James Allen's Girls' School, and thus embarked on the second strand of his teaching career, in adult education, which was to give him as much enjoyment and sense of achievement as did his daytime school-teaching. Vaughan Williams had played the viola in a string quartet at the Settlement during Richard Walthew's musical directorship from 1900 to 1904, and it was probably at his suggestion that Holst applied for the post when Walthew left. The first concert of the Settlement Choral Society under their new conductor was given on 11 December 1904, and Holst included in the programme his own part-song *Dream Tryst;* probably its first public performance. He remained Director of Music at the Settlement until 1908, and during his time there conducted many concerts, including performances of cantatas by J. S. Bach which had never been heard before in England. Isobel sang in the choir and sometimes played cello or bass in the orchestra, while Vaughan Williams occasionally played viola or sang bass in the choir, with his wife Adeline assisting on cello.

Vaughan Williams also helped Holst in another way at this time by putting on at his own expense a concert of works by Holst and himself. This took place on 2 December 1904 at the Bechstein Hall, and was given by the singers Edith Clegg,

Beatrice Spencer, Walter Creighton, and Foxton Ferguson, with
Harriet Solly (violin), Hamilton Harty (piano), and Holst
playing the accompaniments of his own songs. It included the
first public performances of five of Holst's songs: *Soft and
Gently* (words by Heine), *In a Wood* (Hardy), *I Will Not Let
Thee Go* (Robert Bridges), *Cradle Song* (Blake), *Peace* (Alfred
Hyatt), and a second performance of *Calm is the Morn*, which
had been premièred by Maja Kjöhler the previous June. The
Daily Telegraph reported that the concert was well attended,
and described Holst's songs as 'refined and graceful'.[8]

At about this time a committee was formed by a group of
clergymen for the purpose of compiling a supplement to the
hymn-book *Hymns Ancient and Modern*, which many users
considered to be unsatisfactory and out of date. Percy Dearmer
was elected chairman and the group set to work, but it soon
became clear that the amount of material proposed for
inclusion was so great that the supplement would be almost as
large as the original, and they therefore decided to produce a
completely new hymn-book under the title *The English
Hymnal*. Dearmer asked Cecil Sharp's advice as to the choice
of Music Editor, and they decided on Vaughan Williams, who
at first protested that he knew little about hymns, but
subsequently agreed to accept the task on condition that it
would take up only about two months of his time (in the event,
it occupied him for nearly two years). For the new hymnal, he
resolved to look for 'the finest hymn tunes in the world',[9]
including traditional songs and folk-songs, as well as early
hymn tunes which he gathered from the published psalters of
Day, East, and Playford, together with tunes by Tallis, Lawes,
and Gibbons. Besides contributing anonymously a few tunes
himself he invited several contemporary composers to write
tunes especially for the new book. Holst helped with this
editing work, and thus became familiar with many tunes,
including the plainsong melodies which he was later to use in
The Hymn of Jesus. Holst also composed three new hymns of
his own: *From Glory to Glory Advancing* (words from the
Liturgy of St James), *Holy Ghost, Come Down Upon Thy
Children* (words by F. W. Faber), and *In the Bleak Mid-winter*
to words by Christina Rossetti, a simple setting which was to

become one of his best-known compositions. The tunes were named after places with which he had connections at that time: *Sheen*, after the locality of his new home in Richmond; *Bossiney* after a village in Cornwall which he visited on holiday; and *Cranham* after the Cotswolds village where the Lediard family owned a cottage and where his mother had played the harmonium in church. In Cranham itself there is a strong tradition that Holst actually composed *In the Bleak Mid-winter* while staying in the village; a cottage there now bears the name Midwinter Cottage.

Despite the composition of these hymns, the intensive editorial work on *The English Hymnal* seems to have dulled the creativity of both Holst and Vaughan Williams, as they both found themselves at a loss for musical ideas at about this time and were unable to compose anything at all. Vaughan Williams therefore suggested that they should both set the same text for voice and piano: Walt Whitman's 'Darest Thou Now, O Soul' from *Whispers of Heavenly Death* (in *Leaves of Grass*). When the songs were completed and compared, as he later recalled, Vaughan Williams declared that 'The prize was awarded by us to me'.[10]

A more tangible and substantial prize was offered at the beginning of 1905 when the Milan music publisher Tito Ricordi announced a competition for an opera by an English composer, with a cash prize of £500 plus a 40 per cent share of performing fees. The judges were to be Charles Stanford, Joseph Bennett, Percy Pitt, and Ricordi himself. Although the closing date was not until 31 December 1906, a summary of the libretto had to be submitted first for approval, so Holst sent in the libretto of his still unfinished opera *Sita*, subsequently learning that it was among the 52 libretti which had been selected by the judges from a total entry of 191. Holst set to work to finish his score, but after completing the first act found that his recurrent neuritis was inhibiting progress. Several of his friends rallied round to help him with the remaining two acts: Sidney Goldsmith and Fritz Hart wrote down some of the music from dictation, sitting at a table beside Holst as he worked from sketches at the piano, while Vaughan Williams lent a hand and also gave £20 so that Fritz

Hart could be employed to work on the full score. When the opera was complete, Sidney Waddington played it through on the piano for the benefit of the group of friends who had worked so hard on the score, and Holst duly submitted the work, although he had to wait until the beginning of 1908 for the decision of the judges.

Meanwhile, occasional performances of his compositions were taking place, although too infrequently for his liking. On 5 January 1905 Dan Godfrey conducted the *Suite de Ballet* at the Bournemouth Winter Gardens, and on 16 April Holst gave a concert at the Passmore Edwards Settlement which included the first performance of his setting of *The Sergeant's Song* from Thomas Hardy's *The Trumpet Major*.

As part of the celebrations for the anniversary of Shakespeare's birthday at Stratford-on-Avon that year, a revival was planned of Ben Jonson's masque *Pan's Anniversary, or The Shepherd's Holyday*, which had been performed on New Year's Day 1625 for the entertainment of King James I and had apparently not been performed since. Vaughan Williams was asked by the organizers to compose some music for the production, and he in turn asked Holst to help him by providing orchestral arrangements of some keyboard music and traditional English tunes. Holst's contribution, under the title *Stratford Revels*, included settings of *Sellinger's Round*, *The Lost Lady Found*, *Maria Marten*, and *All on Spurn Point*, a Galliard (*La Spagnoletta*), a Pavan (*Mal Sims*), and *Rogero*. The masque was sucessfully performed in Bancroft Gardens, Stratford-on-Avon, on 24 April 1905, by the chorus and orchestra of the Choral Union, with a Stratford soloist and two professional singers from Frank Benson's Shakespeare Company, conducted by Vaughan Williams.

On 29 June the fourth Royal College of Music Patron's Fund concert included the first performance of *The Mystic Trumpeter*, with Cicely Gleeson-White as soloist and Holst conducting. This concert took place in London at the Queen's Hall, the orchestra consisting partly of students and partly of members of the London Symphony Orchestra. The work had a mixed reception, one reviewer drily commenting that 'Mr Gustav von Holst showed that he took modern composers rather than old masters as his models, the result being, as might be expected, not altogether satisfactory.'[11] The concert did have one beneficial result however: he was offered a further performance of the work in the following season of the Royal Philharmonic Society's concerts.

In the autumn of 1905, Holst took on an additional teaching post, through which he was to make one of his most important contributions to musical education, and which he was to hold for the rest of his life. Two years before, St Paul's School, the boys' public school founded by John Colet in 1509, had sprung an offshoot when St Paul's Girls' School was founded, with Frances Ralph Gray as its first Head (subsequently High) Mistress. In her previous post as headmistress of a school at St Andrews, she had attended a recital given by Adine O'Neill (wife of the composer Norman O'Neill), a fine concert pianist who had studied with Clara Schumann, and was so impressed that she had asked her to take on the job of Music Mistress in the new school. By 1905, St Paul's had grown to accommodate 157 girls, and it was clear that another music teacher was needed to teach singing, enabling Mrs O'Neill to concentrate on the piano. The post of Singing Mistress was duly advertised, but having interviewed several candidates Miss Gray concluded that none were really suitable as they all seemed to be more interested in technique than true musicianship. She then sought further advice from Adine O'Neill, who told her that Gustav Holst was beginning to make a name for himself as a composer, and as he was already teaching music in a girls' school, he might be prepared to teach at St Paul's as well. Accordingly, Miss Gray wrote straight away to Holst, who came to see her the next day, and it was immediately agreed that he would take on the responsibility for teaching singing in the school.

Singing was held in low regard at that time, both by parents and also some members of the staff, who placed it well down on their scale of educational priorities. The High Mistress was constantly faced with requests for girls to be excused from singing in order to concentrate on 'more important' work, but as she seldom approved such requests, being convinced of the therapeutic value of singing, they gradually declined as time went on, particularly as Holst and the Gymnasium Mistress were in agreement about the importance of good breathing and had obtained the support of the school's Medical Officer, who declared that from her point of view singing lessons were of great value to health. Moreover, the girls soon found that they actually enjoyed singing under Holst's direction, and their parents liked to come to the school concerts to hear their daughters' musical accomplishments. Every girl was expected to sing, even if she claimed that she could not. In the Singing Class, the pupils would stand in a long line in front of Holst in the Lecture Room, and were taught correct breathing, clear diction, rhythm by means of clapping exercises, and to hold their music up so that they could see the conductor simply by moving their eyes, instead of nodding their heads up and down in the 'pecking' movements seen in many choirs. Although not a singer himself, Holst was meticulous in attention to details of voice production, and often gave individual pupils instruction in vocal technique, with special exercises designed to overcome particular problems.

He was fond of teaching clear pronunciation by using pieces of music which presented special problems, such as a round to the words 'My Jane hath a lame, tame, crane', which forced a distinction between 'n' and 'm'. He would often divide the class into two groups, to sing in turn phrases which he would write on the blackboard, and each group would listen for mistakes in the other's performance. He also sometimes tested their attention to the conductor by giving them a deliberately erratic beat. They were taught to keep their voices well under control—Irene Bonnett was cautioned: 'If you keep on singing so loudly now you will have no voice when you are older.'[12] At first they sang unison and two-part songs and then went on to rounds and more difficult music. Holst's favourite material for class singing was Donald Tovey's *Laudate Pueri*, a collection of unaccompanied Latin motets by composers such as Vittoria, Palestrina, and Lassus, which he used as his 'bread-and-butter' music, describing the collection as 'the most wonderful thing published for women's voices'.[13]

But he had difficulty in finding other suitable material and wrote in frustration: 'I find the question of getting music for girls' schools perfectly hopeless. I get reams of twaddle sent me periodically, and that is all the publishers seem to think is suitable for girls.'[14] He was to discover that 'arrangements for giving people bad music are more competent and extensive than those for giving them good music',[15] and therefore arranged and composed music himself for female voices. He adapted mixed-voice works such as Bach cantatas, in which the tenor parts would be sung by the senior girls, with notes transposed up an octave where necessary. If the soprano line rose too high he would transpose the notes down an octave for the sake of less able singers. The girls themselves thoroughly enjoyed the singing classes and looked forward to Holst's visits with eager anticipation. When he arrived to play for morning prayers a ripple of excitement would run through the assembly. As Irene Bonnett later wrote: 'There is no doubt about the fact that he made all music interesting and alive and that we were caught up in this spirit and were inspired to do our best'.[16] Another pupil, Nancy Gotch, recalled: 'He always said what he thought, and was firm but never, never unkind.'[17] His influence was summed up by Diana Lucas, one of his pupils in his early years at the school: 'The values in our day were moral (Miss Gray) and musical and gently humane (Gustav Holst). He was so kind and full of deep feeling that he improved everyone who knew him.'[18] So infectious was Holst's enthusiasm that the girls would often be found in *ad hoc* groups singing rounds and part-songs when they ought to have been devoting themselves to other activities, even at times when they could have been letting off steam in the playground. As Holst himself recalled: 'It was one of the great moments of my career when I came in early one morning on a dark winter's day, to fetch my letters before school hours. I found several of the girls had come earlier still, without saying a word to me, and were sitting round the class room fire singing Palestrina for sheer love of the music.'[19]

For school concerts, Holst would persuade some of the girls' fathers to join the choir, so that full mixed-voice music could be performed, especially Bach cantatas such as *Sleepers Wake*, in which the whole of the school would take part, crowded into the Main Hall, with the audience squeezed into the gallery. He was lucky that many of his pupils came from talented families: occasionally Henry Wood (whose daughter Averil was at the school) could be seen among the basses, and Steuart Wilson would sometimes sing the tenor solos.

In addition to the singing classes, Holst was also later asked to teach conducting, which he did by making his pupils direct a piano duet and try to control erratic tempi and spot the mistakes which the performers deliberately introduced into their parts; and also music theory, to which he brought the same individual approach characteristic of his other teaching. He invented his own terminology, describing counterpoint as 'streaky bacon', and harmony as 'layer-cake in chunks, with different layers in each chunk', claiming that 'the best book for composers is the textbook in composition we use in this school—Walter de la Mare's *Peacock Pie*.'[20] But above all he was practical, insisting that no girl should study counterpoint until she had first sung it. Instead of dry academic exercises, he would use well-known hymn tunes such as *St Anne* and *Hanover* as the basis of counterpoint lessons, and would insist on the importance of rhythm: 'That's what music is all about,' he would say, declaring that the early composers such as Byrd and Tallis knew this most of all.[21] He was keen on developing keyboard skills, and would make his pupils improvise accompaniments to songs (allowing a little time for preparation) and gave them Bach's Trio Sonatas to play on two pianos, telling them that the six organ sonatas were among the greatest music ever written and that this was the best way to get to know them. He was however wary of overemphasis on the piano, which he thought was in danger of becoming 'an institution instead of an instrument'; if a girl wanted to study the piano, she was encouraged to do so, but Holst himself placed greater value on group performance such as choral singing and orchestral playing.

His pupils' own compositions were often performed in the school, as he believed that this should be done as a matter of course: 'All children have an instinct for it', he said, 'and it ought not to be considered an esoteric mystery. There ought to be more writing and performing in a small way—pieces written for the joy of self expression . . . Compare learning the piano: there's no fuss made about that. Why should one make a fuss about composing?'[22] He would often play such pieces, particularly canons with organ pedal lines, before morning prayers, being most pleased by those compositions which produced maximum effectiveness by the simplest of means.

Although he conveyed to his pupils his enthusiasm for his own favourite composers, Holst was always conscious of the dangers of being too partisan, realizing that his own outlook might not be entirely objective. 'I have three feelings about works of art,' he explained; 'Interest, romance and love. I'd never say that the works I love most are necessarily the best.'[23] To counteract the effect of too much Byrd and Palestrina, he would sometimes give the girls popular songs such as *Tipperary* and *Little Grey Home in the West*, but despite this, some of his pupils found that on leaving school it was to be some years before they could listen to or perform Romantic music with any real enjoyment. Holst's own attitudes were expressed in a 1924 letter to Edwin Evans: 'Surely you don't consider Schumann, Liszt, Brahms or Rubenstein "models of purity". All four of them get near the border line of incoherence at times and at least one of them goes over it. And another of them certainly "tried" to be original which is as fatal as trying to be funny. Models of purity exist in every age—surely Ravel is as much one as Haydn . . . Weakness is ugliness—weakness in rhythm whether of the bar or the movement. Therefore Liszt and Rubenstein are usually ugly and Schumann and Brahms occasionally. And Haydn and Ravel never. Both the latter are sometimes dull but not so dull as an ugly composer when he is dull as well as ugly.'[24]

Holst tried to make the study of music enjoyable, rather than something to be studied simply for academic purposes. 'Some of us give children music as we give them medicine and tell them it will be good for them,' he complained.[25] The enthusiasm of his pupils is evidence that his approach was eminently successful, and many Paulinas remembered with pleasure their time in Holst's music classes. As at James Allen's Girls' School, he had no time for bureaucracy or pomposity, and would join in entertainments and social events as if he were one of a family; on one occasion conducting the orchestra while dressed as an Arab in flowing white robes. At meal-times he would tell jokes to the girls sitting near him, and the resulting hilarity would dispel the contrived formality of such occasions. The girls' nickname for him was 'Gussie', and some of them were concerned that he looked so harassed, but his expression may have been the result of his short-sightedness rather than any deficiencies in the behaviour of his pupils.

His method of teaching was always to try to draw out his pupils' natural ability instead of trying to force knowledge into them, and he seemed to have an instinctive aptitude for accomplishing this. He once declared that 'A free hand to get the best out of the available material, both human and otherwise, is all that one is entitled to expect in this life',[26] and that 'The ideal of a teacher should be to make oneself unnecessary.'[27] He was not a trained teacher, and had to discover how to go about it as he went along, often extending his own musical knowledge and understanding of human nature in the process. His compositions for female voices stem directly from this experience, and he later wrote to Edwin Evans: 'It has been a natural predilection fostered by having to teach 600 girls per week for some years. In spite of obvious drawbacks, I consider that I have learnt as much through my school teaching as I did previously as a trombone player in the Carl Rosa and Scottish Orchestra.'[28]

This additional teaching commitment at St Paul's Girls' School prevented Holst from composing as much as he would have liked during 1905, but he did manage to complete a work for violin and orchestra entitled *A Song of the Night*, and set some of the songs in Tennyson's *The Princess* for his pupils at James Allen's Girls' School. Two of these part-songs call for an additional 'echo' choir, to be located in an adjoining room or corridor, and the intervening door would be gradually closed as the words 'dying, dying. . . ' faded into silence at the end of *The Splendour Falls*; a device he later used to great effect at the end of *The Planets*.

As he developed his work at the Passmore Edwards Settlement, the concerts there began to include items of considerable musical interest. On 5 November 1905 he gave the first complete performance in England of Bach's *Peasant Cantata*, while on 10 December the programme included the cantatas *Soul Array Thyself (Schmücke dich)* and *There is no more Soundness (Es ist nichts Gesundes)*. Soloists in these concerts included Lucy Broadwood, Betty Booker, Edith Clegg,

J. Campbell McInnes, Merlin Davies, and Francis Harford, the orchestra being led by Isidore Schwiller and Madame de Bobinsky. The choir was supplemented by boys from the Board School in nearby Cromer Street, and the orchestra also included some professional players in the wind section. As many as fifteen rehearsals were devoted to the December concert, and in the event all the work was worth while, the cantatas being well received by 'a democratic audience—well-to-do people and poor folks sitting side by side most happily and all equally appreciative of the music'. For those unfamiliar with concert etiquette, a large notice was fixed to the back of the conductor's chair, requesting silence during the music. The Warden of the Settlement also stipulated that the audience should reserve its applause until the end of each cantata, but in vain, as 'Several times they showed a desire to applaud after movements they specially liked, but the Conductor waved his hands at them and they subsided.' These performances were so successful that there was a demand for more on similar lines, and although the Warden explained that the concerts had only been possible through the generosity of several well-known musicians (probably including Vaughan Williams), he was urged by Holst to 'solicit funds for the continuance of the work'.[29]

At about this time an important new influence began to have its effect on Holst's own compositions: that of English folk-music. Although for centuries composers had been interested in folk-songs and dances, often incorporating them into their own work, very little systematic collecting had been done. Then in the early years of the twentieth century, several musicians in different countries realized that the heritage of folk-music was in danger of being obliterated by modern industrial life, and set out to record as much of it as they could find for the benefit of posterity. In Hungary, Béla Bartók first became conscious of folk-music in 1904; although he had been born in a peasant village, he realised that he had never listened properly to the music of such communities, so with his friend Kodály he set out on expeditions to isolated parts of Hungary and Romania with the intention of collecting as many folk-songs as possible. In England, several composers also became interested in folk-music at this time, often by chance contact with traditional singers, and musicians such as Vaughan Williams, Cecil Sharp, and Percy Grainger began to tour the country in the hope of saving the traditional music of England from oblivion.

Holst followed the progress of his friends' collecting expeditions with great interest, but had no time to collect songs himself. But he responded to the simplicity and metrical freedom of the songs which were replayed to him, and these qualities eventually enabled him to develop a characteristic style of his own. He was in no way opposed to outside influences as such, provided they were relevant to his purpose, and later wrote: 'I believe very strongly that we are largely the result of our surroundings and that we never do anything alone. Everything that is worth doing is the result of several minds playing on each other',[30] a principle which is the very essence, if not a definition of folk-music.

Holst was astonished at the beauty of melody and expressive power of many of the traditional English songs, and began to think of using them in his own creative work. In 1905–6 Vaughan Williams was writing his first *Norfolk Rhapsody*, following a collecting trip to that county, and Cecil Sharp suggested to Holst that he also should try his own hand at the art of setting folk-songs in an orchestral context, which resulted in the *Two Selections of Folksongs*, later revised and retitled *A Somerset Rhapsody* and *Songs of the West*. Holst used as his source material the songs which had been collected and edited by Sharp and published in the collection *Folksongs from Somerset*, together with Baring Gould's *Songs of the West*, and in the *Somerset Rhapsody* he tried to give the assembly of tunes some narrative coherence by arranging them according to an imaginary scenario. As he later wrote to Edwin Evans: 'There is no definite programme but the form grew out of a suggestion of pastoral country becoming filled with human activities but surviving them all'[31] (a notion similar to that expressed in *Egdon Heath* more than twenty years later). A more detailed programme note explained that the composer had imagined a quiet pastoral country (the 'Sheep-shearing Song') across which come the sounds of an approaching group of soldiers ('High Germany'). A young man is courting his girl but is persuaded to join up with the soldiers and go away to war

('The True Lover's Farewell'). The soldiers pass on, receding into the distance, and the quiet atmosphere of the opening returns.

The *Two Selections* were first performed on 3 February 1906 at the Pump Room, Bath, by the City of Bath Pump Room Orchestra conducted by the composer, as part of a lecture programme on Somerset folk-songs given by Cecil Sharp. Holst's music was loudly applauded and was described as 'a charming selection of songs of Somerset' by the critic of the *Bath Chronicle*, 'the audience being delighted with the fine manner in which the charming old airs were presented.'[32] In the light of this performance Holst revised both scores the following year, omitting some of the original tunes, but it was to be some time before a further performance took place. However, the *Somerset Rhapsody* eventually became one of his first widely-performed compositions, although *Songs of the West* slipped into obscurity and was never published.

This experience of setting folk-songs was to convince Holst of the virtues of simple modal melodies and helped him dispense with the paraphernalia of chromaticism. His enthusiasm was based mainly on the music rather than the words, however—as he explained to Edwin Evans: 'I consider the English tunes magnificent but their words often unworthy of them.'[33] Despite this reservation, he was to set many folk-songs (including their words) for various musical forces during the ensuing few years.

The first of his original compositions to show this new influence were the *Two Songs Without Words* for small orchestra, whose melodies sound like folk-tunes but are in fact the composer's own, demonstrating the extent to which he had absorbed the spirit of folk-music. But he soon abandoned the practice of writing 'pseudo-folk' melodies, allowing the essential features of folk-song, such as clarity, simplicity, modality and rhythmic flexibility to permeate his own personal musical style.

On 31 May 1906 the second performance of *The Mystic Trumpeter* was given at the sixth Philharmonic Society concert of the season, the soloist being once again Cicely Gleeson-White and the conductor Frederick Cowen. This first appearance of a work by Holst in the programmes of the Philharmonic Society was accorded a mixed reception by the press. Several critics praised the work, the *Daily News* going so far as to predict that 'Mr Gustav von Holst is a man who should rise very high',[34] but others were quick to detect disturbing signs of modernism. 'There were some painful dissonances', reported the *Musical Standard*, but 'whether intended by the composer or due to inaccuracies in the orchestra it is hard to say'.[35] Some members of the audience expressed their disapproval at the end of the performance, but most were sympathetic and applauded both composer and soloist, although one suspects that much of this was for Miss Gleeson-White's tackling of the 'difficult and rather thankless voice part',[36] having had to battle against Holst's rather heavy orchestration (he later revised the work as a result of this performance). The last word must however go to the *Clarion*, whose critic declared that 'If the work was not a success it was at least a splendid failure'.[37] Holst himself seemed pleased, and wrote to the Secretary of the Philharmonic Society a few days later: 'Would you please thank the Council of the Philharmonic Society very heartily from me for the great honour they have done me. I have never before had any composition of mine so beautifully performed and I am most grateful to all concerned in it.'[38]

On 19 July Holst conducted the first performance of *Two Songs Without Words* at a Royal College of Music concert, and this work was accepted for publication by Novello, the printed score bearing the dedication: 'To R.V.W.'. Another work published at this time was the cantata *King Estmere* which he had written in 1903 and dedicated to his teacher Charles Stanford, being issued by Charles Avison Ltd with the aid of a grant from the Royal College of Music Patron's Fund.

In the first months of 1907, Holst began work on the first of several settings of his own translations from the *Rig Veda*; the *Vedic Hymns* for voice and piano. Unlike the *Ramayana*, which he had used as a source for his opera *Sita*, the *Rig Veda* dates from a much earlier period, and is in fact the oldest known work of Sanskrit literature. The hymns of which it consists are simple invocations of the gods, including Agni (god of fire), Ushas (the dawn), Surjya (the sun), Vayu (the wind), and the Maruts (Indra's attendant storm-cloud gods). with prominence given to Indra, the storm-god, bringer of the all-important rain, whose beneficial influence has been the object of prayer throughout Indian history. These atmospheric invocations are clearly ideal material for declamatory musical treatment, and Holst used the possibilities to good effect. Although he had never heard any Indian music, in his search for the most suitable notes to express the feeling of the words he came to use some scales which bear a resemblance to the ragas of Indian music. He wrote twelve of these songs altogether, but later reduced the number to nine, arranging them into three groups of three, in which form they were published some years later.

At this time, Holst also wrote *Four Old English Carols* for mixed voices and piano (also arranged for female voices) of which W. G. Wittaker wrote: 'They have so much the odour of folk-tunes, that the writer imagined for some years that the melodies were traditional and was much astonished to find that they were the composer's own.'[39] These simple settings include tonal contrast between soloists and choral response, and have a modal, medieval atmosphere and folk-like character which was to come to fruition several years later in the part-song *This Have I Done for My True Love.*

In the spring of 1907, a further facet of Holst's teaching career fell into place when he began to teach evening classes at Morley College for Working Men and Women, in South London. The College had originated from the desire of the philanthropist Emma Cons to help the poorer classes of the capital by providing entertainment dissociated from the customary evil of alchohol. In 1880 she took over the Royal Victoria Hall (the 'Old Vic') with the aid of the wealthy benefactor Samuel Morley, and by the end of the decade the venture had developed to include educational classes provided in response to popular demand. In due course it was decided to separate such classes from the theatrical entertainment, and Morley College was therefore opened in September 1889 in premises adjoining the theatre in the Waterloo Road. A wide range of subjects was covered, including music classes which began in 1890, and in 1892 an orchestra had been formed

under the direction of the theatre's bandmaster Alfred Dove
and flourished throughout the 1890s. By the early 1900s a
choir had been formed under the direction of the singing
teacher Seemer Betts, and violin classes were given by Paul
Stoeving, but music at Morley seems to have been an uphill
struggle at that time, so that in June 1904 Betts tendered his
resignation, giving as his reason 'the want of opportunities of
giving concerts'. After being persuaded to continue for a while,
he was made redundant two years later when the Borough
Polytechnic music classes were transferred to Morley together
with their teacher H. J. B. Dart.

Early in 1907 Dart died, and the Executive Committee was
faced with the problem of finding a successor. Ralph Vaughan
Williams had occasionally lectured at the College so the
Committee initially approached him, but he replied that he
had too many existing commitments, and suggested that they
should ask Holst instead. Although Holst was already teaching
during the daytime at James Allen's Girls' School and St Paul's
Girls' School, and on certain evenings at the Passmore Edwards
Settlement, he was now faced with new financial respons-
ibilties because of his wife's pregnancy, and he therefore
decided to apply for the post. Interviews were held at the end of
March, as a result of which Holst was selected from a short-list
of three, and at a Committee meeting on 8 April his
testimonials were read and his appointment confirmed, the
hours of duty being left to be arranged as far as possible to suit
both students and teacher. It was also decided that 'the fee for
Harmony should be increased to 10/- if necessary, Mr von
Holst having asked for a higher fee and that the time should be
extended to 1½ hours.'[40] This uncharacteristically mercenary
demand by Holst was doubtless prompted by the impending
arrival of the new member of his family, and concern at the
prospect of having another mouth to feed. The baby was
causing Isobel so much pain and discomfort that she thought
she might be carrying twins, which would have made their
financial situation even more precarious. Eventually, on 12
April the baby arrived: a daughter who was baptized Imogen
Clare a few weeks later at Barnes Church, with Fritz Hart as
godfather and Mabel Dalby as godmother. The child cried
continually during her first months of life, reducing Holst's

nervous state to a low ebb ('Imogen is practising coloratura—the sort that foghorns usually perform—and my brain feels pulpy whenever she lets fly,' he wrote[41]) and he was driven out of the house to walk over Sheen Common in the early hours of the morning to obtain some peace of mind before starting his day's teaching.

At the beginning of the summer term Holst took up his new Morley College appointment, and was welcomed by the college magazine with the words: 'Mr von Holst is in the front rank of modern English composers and his connection with the College augurs well for its musical future.'[42] He immediately set about making improvements, persuading the Principal to arrange for a new piano to be hired for the autumn term, and for the old 'worn-out' one to be disposed of. He began to instil new life into the choir and orchestra, deleting dross from the repertoire and aiming for a higher standard of performance; this provoked murmurs of discontent from those students who were set in their ways, and some began to drop out, to the dismay of the college authorities who wondered whether they had done the right thing in appointing Holst. But things soon improved, as the classes began to attract a new kind of student with enthusiasm and willingness to learn, so that the College started to acquire the basis of its later reputation as a centre for adult music-making. In those early days, however, conditions were primitive and facilities virtually non-existent, so that the classes were carried on mainly by sheer enthusiasm. Most of the students had left school at an early age and worked at humdrum jobs in London, so that Morley often became for them the main centre of their existence; one of them describing the College as 'a sort of heaven we go to on Mondays and Wednesdays'.[43]

Holst soon became dedicated to the ideals of amateur music-making, and admired the values of the Elizabethan period when music-making was widespread among the middle and upper classes, believing that participation in performance is essential to civilized living. In his lectures on 'England and her Music', he would quote a foreigner's remark that the English like music but can do without it; a situation which would have been unthinkable in the sixteenth century. He followed

Tolstoy's maxim that 'Art is a means of communication', and considered that musical communication takes place not just between composer and listener, but also among the performers themselves. He once declared: 'We all begin our education by being amateurs, and in the real sense of the word, we must remain amateurs,'[44] even going so far as to claim that the only difference between Mozart's music and that of the average British soldier was one of degree.

He quickly established a rapport with his students, strongly disapproving of the way some musicians 'talked-down' to amateur performers, and insisted that everyone who wished to do so should take part in music-making, regardless of their own particular level of ability. He once said that there were plenty of other choirs and orchestras in London for people who *could* sing and play, but Morley College was the only place which catered for those who couldn't. Despite this, all students were expected to work towards a high standard, as far as their individual abilities would permit. As one of his successors in the post, Michael Tippett, put it: 'Holst brought something quite new into music in the sphere of adult education—his insistence on an uncompromising standard of artistry.'[45] As in his school-teaching, Holst had the knack of drawing out the student's own latent abilities, often revealing talents which they themselves had not realized they possessed. One of his Morley College students later recalled that he was regarded with mingled feelings of affection and respect, 'And a conviction rooted in experience that what he wanted us to do was the right and proper thing for us . . . we put aside at once the least thought of anything that might have been displeasing to him.'[46]

Holst was always conscious of the financial problems facing his students, who came mainly from lower income groups, and he would often give free tuition to promising students, or the lessons would sometimes be paid for by Vaughan Williams, who also gave practical help by giving tuition himself from time to time. Holst was responsible for the choir and orchestra, and harmony, counterpoint, composition, and solo singing classes. The choir turned out to be of a fairly high standard, and he immediately set them to learn the works of his favourite composers: Palestrina, Vittoria, the Elizabethans, and J. S. Bach (giving the student's Bach's motto: 'The aim of music is the glory of God and pleasant recreation'). But the orchestra was not up to the same standard, as there was difficulty in attracting sufficient numbers of proficient wind players. He began the practice of giving regular college concerts, at first twice a year in June and December, so that the students would have a definite aim to work towards. Theory students were encouraged to write and arrange music for the practical resources available to them, and students' own compositions were included in the college concerts . To supplement the wavering strength of the choir and orchestra on such occasions, Holst often drafted in some of his pupils from James Allen's and St Paul's Girls' schools and sometimes their mothers and fathers too, together with members of the teaching staff. The final rehearsal for a concert would consist of a run-through of the works to be performed, with an explanatory talk about the music, illustrated by examples played by the assembled performers. In this way education and pleasure were combined in the same event. To encourage his students further, Holst would invite musicians from outside the College to appraise their work; many distinguished musicians visited the College in this capacity over the years, including Edwin Evans, Hugh Allen, Herbert Howells, and Adrian Boult. He also occasionally gave special lectures himself, and on 3 November 1907 spoke on 'The Beginnings of Modern Music', which included a reference to the origins of dancing in religion and primitive rites, an idea which was later to be a major factor in the composition of *The Hymn of Jesus*.

Despite his increased teaching responsibilities, Holst managed to do a certain amount of creative work during 1907. Besides composing the *Vedic Hymns* and *Four Old English Carols*, he revised *Songs of the West* and *A Somerset Rhapsody*, and arranged folk-songs for various combinations of voices and instruments, but apart from this he wrote only a song, *The Heart Worships*, to words by Alice M. Buckton. The first performance of this was given by Edith Clegg on 16 November at the Aeolian Hall in London, together with three of the *Vedic Hymns*. The *Daily Telegraph* reported that 'The new songs of Mr Gustav von Holst, however, were more interesting; this young English composer has shown before now that he has something to express, and no small power of expression.'[47]

Among Holst's surviving manuscripts there is also some incidental music which he wrote for a play by Alice Buckton entitled *Nabou, or Kings in Babylon*, which was probably composed at about this time. The play was published by Methuen in 1906, but no information regarding any performance of Holst's music has yet come to light.

The new year began with depressing news. On 9 January 1908 the *Morning Post* carried an announcement of the result of the Ricordi opera competition: of the 52 libretti which had originally been approved, 29 had actually been set to music, and the prize had been awarded to Edward Woodall Naylor, the Cambridge organist and musicologist, for his opera *The Angelus*. The announcement went on to say that two other operas had been placed second in order of merit: *Helen*, and *Sita*, from which Holst realized that he had failed to win the prize by only a narrow margin. Fritz Hart recalled that Stanford had 'disliked *Sita* intensely and unreasonably',[48] and as it emerged that another of the judges had cast his vote in favour of *Sita*, it is possible that the prize-winner had been chosen as a compromise in the face of irreconcilable opinions. In the event, when *The Angelus* was duly performed at Covent Garden in 1909 it turned out to be disappointing, though musically well made, and despite a revival by the Carl Rosa company it never entered the general operatic repertoire. *The Times* wrote: 'Like so many other compositions of the present day, it has many good points, yet scarcely enough unity or individuality to excuse the many short-comings. Of these last, the frequent lapses into commonplace are the worst.'[49]

This was small consolation for Holst, who had not only failed to win the cash prize, but whose labour of composition and scoring had been in vain. Vaughan Williams wrote in sympathy: 'I'm sorry (a) that you haven't got £500, (b) that you are not promised a performance,' but went on to appeal to his distrust of musical academicism: 'The real, important thing is that you have *not* been put in the awful position when "all men speak well of you" [Luke 6:26]—Think, the awful stigma to have gone through life with a prize opera on your back— almost as damning as a mus: doc . . . I don't know that even my faith in you would have been quite strong enough to have stood the shock of approval by J. Bennet ... after all the *most* important thing is that you've written a big work and that you aren't in the awful position of being continually praised by those whose opinions and methods you despise in every way.'[50] All was not entirely lost however, as Holst was asked to send the score of *Sita* to Ricordi's Milan office for possible publication, although it was to be some time before a decision would be reached.

But Holst had learnt his lesson. His love affair with Romantic megalomania was over; he had simplified his musical style as a result of his contact with English folk-song, and he knew that he must now also simplify the dramatic construction of any future operatic works. In spite of his years with the Carl Rosa company, he still knew little about practical stagecraft, largely because he had been unable to see much of the stage action from the depths of the orchestra pit, but also because of that company's idiosyncratic methods. He resolved to compose a work which would be simple, clear, and effective, using a minimum of resources and thus be fairly easy to produce.

But first there were more immediate problems. His teaching work had to go on, but he was feeling tired and depressed and unable to cope with the strain of teaching hundreds of schoolgirls by day and then having to instil encouragement into amateurs in the evenings. He felt as if he needed a holiday, and Vaughan Williams offered him £50 to make this possible, writing from Paris, where he was studying with Ravel: 'It is most important—to my mind—that this should be a real holiday to make up for all your past years of strain. If you compose during it all the better—but if you have an idea all the time that you must have something to show for it—then you will spoil your holiday and effectually prevent yourself from composing. If—even—you only come back teaching very well it would mean that it came easier and left you more energy for other work.'[51]

Holst and Isobel decided that he should use the money to go abroad alone after Easter, as his doctor had recommended a warm climate for the worsening neuritis in his right hand. He was granted leave of absence from his schools and colleges for the first few weeks of the summer term, and the knowledge that he was to have a holiday gave him fresh energy and enabled him to survive a strenuous Spring term of teaching and music-making. On 21 February two of the *Vedic Hymns* were performed at a Dunhill Chamber Concert at the Steinway Hall, together with *The Heart Worships* and *Soft and Gently*, and towards the end of term there was a students' tea and social at Morley College at which Holst conducted some of his own music. On 11 March he wrote to a colleague: 'I pray hourly for my holiday. My latest idea is to go to Algiers!'[52] Near the end of term, Holst wrote in the college magazine: 'Although I shall be with you a fortnight longer, I take this opportunity of thanking you for all the hard work and enthusiasm you have shown during the last year. The classes and lessons will continue after Easter as usual. Miss von Holst [his aunt Nina] will take the piano pupils. Having been one of her pupils myself years ago, I know you will enjoy her lessons. Miss Newbiggen, a pupil of William Shakespeare at the Royal Academy of Music, will take the private singing lessons; while the harmony, choral and orchestral classes will be taken by our good friend Mr Cecil Coles, who has so often helped me in the past. I ask you to show all three the same diligence and goodwill that you have always shown me. And, finally, I shall look forward to seeing you all again in September.'[53] On 4 April the first performance of *King Estmere* was given at the Queen's Hall by the New Symphony Orchestra and the Edward Mason Choir, and on 11 April Holst conducted the final concert of the term at Morley College. On Good Friday, some members of the Morley College choir took part in Charles Corri's performance of Rossini's *Stabat Mater* at the Old Vic, but in the absence of Holst, who had already left for Algeria.

He spent his holiday wandering through the streets of Algerian towns and exploring the surrounding countryside by bicycle. He was particularly attracted by the Arab quarter of Algiers, which fascinated him with its sights, sounds, and smells. Although he did not attempt any actual composition during the holiday, he jotted down in a notebook some musical fragments, which were later to appear in some of his compositions. In this book there is a phrase marked 'Arabe (girl singing to two birds—they reply)', a 'Chanson des femmes Arabes -not like it!', a tune marked 'Beduin Nomad—fairly correct', and an 'oboe tune in procession 5am (they had been at it all night!)'.[54] The first of these entries is marked 'PF', showing that at this early date he was already planning his opera *The Perfect Fool*, and a version of this phrase appears in the 'Dance of the Spirits of Fire' in the ballet music with which the opera begins. It is interesting that Béla Bartók was to visit the same region five years later, and like Holst, found much inspiration in the fascinating native folk-music which he heard there.

5

From Sanskrit to Folk-Music
(1908–1911)

On his return from Algeria, Holst felt refreshed and full of energy for both teaching and composition. He immediately began work on what was to be his first characteristically mature composition, the chamber opera *Savitri*. For the libretto, he once again turned to Sanskrit literature, selecting an incident from the *Maha-Bharata*, which, like the *Ramayana* on which he had drawn for *Sita*, dates from the later phase of Sanskrit when it had ceased to be vernacular and had become the stylized language of the educated classes. The stories related in this work may well have their origins in legends of a much earlier period, although it is doubtful if any are as old as the *Rig Veda* hymns. The *Maha-Bharata*, which is said to be eight times as long as the *Iliad* and *Odyssey* combined, is an account of a three-week-long battle between two cousins descended from the legendary king Bharata. From this gigantic work, Holst selected an incident in which Savitri, wife of Satyavan, is visited by Death, who tells her that he has come to take away her husband. Instead of reviling Death, she praises him, then passionately implores him to grant her one wish for herself—her own life in all its fullness. She then claims that Satyavan's life is essential to the fulfilment of her own, and thus outwits Death, who is forced to retire defeated. In the original story, Satyavan was a noble prince whose father had taken refuge in a forest after being robbed of his kingdom, but Holst ignores this royal connection, making Satyavan an ordinary woodcutter, and turning the story into a simple allegory of the triumph of Love over Death. He wrote the libretto himself, using his usual method of translating from the Sanskrit, and as he worked he found that the music and words 'really grew together'.[1]

Having studied Sanskrit for some years, he found that he had begun to assimilate the philosophy embodied in the literature and realized that his own personal outlook had much in common with it. He clearly felt a sympathy for the story of Savitri, and produced a unique work which is a subtle and imaginative expression of a philosophical idea. Although Holst described *Savitri* as an 'opera da camera', it was really intended for performance in the open air, the only scenery specified being a long path leading from the distance up to a foreground clearing in which the action takes place. The idea for the setting came from his walks on Sheen Common near his home, and he once showed his friend Isidore Schwiller an avenue of trees on the common which he thought would be an ideal setting for the work.

There are only three characters in the opera, accompanied by an instrumental ensemble consisting of two string quartets, a double-bass, two flutes, and cor anglais, together with a hidden wordless chorus. When the work was eventually performed some years later, the conductor Hermann Grunebaum suggested that female voices would be more effective than mixed voices for this chorus, and Holst hurriedly rewrote the parts in time for the first performance (and gave the manuscript vocal score to Grunebaum in gratitude for his advice). The economy of these resources makes a striking contrast to the massive forces required for *Sita*, and shows Holst in a more practical frame of mind; realizing the enormous difficulties of staging a large-scale opera he pruned everything down to the essentials, thus achieving the highest degree of simplicity and purity of expression. The subtlety of this work is an antithesis to some of the bombastic methods of the nineteenth century; the same reaction as that experienced by Debussy, but it is worth noting that *Pelléas et Mélisande* was not performed in England until May 1909, when *Savitri* had already been completed (although Holst may have heard Debussy conduct *La Mer* and *Prélude à l'Après Midi d'un Faune* at the Queen's Hall in February 1908). At a time when composers such as Strauss, Mahler, and Schoenberg were indulging in works of gargantuan proportions, Holst's economy of means anticipated the smaller ensembles which were to come into vogue, for musical as well as economic reasons, after the First World War.

Although he did not attempt to write in a pseudo-oriental style, something of the feeling of Indian music comes through, by what must have been an intuitive process on Holst's part (as in the *Vedic Hymns*). He was still feeling his way stylistically; intriguing new sounds appear beside conventionally harmonized passages, and there is a strong modal influence, deriving from his study of English folk-song. In fact, many of the motifs are neither fully modal nor tonal, but represent a musically heightened expression of the natural speaking human voice, making free use of characteristic intervals such as the minor second and minor third. This often results in an impression of bitonality, but in a consecutive, rather than a simultaneous manner. A degree of formal cohesion is produced by the use of Death's opening recitative as a kind of leitmotif, and the instrumental ensemble is used to emphasize certain points; for instance, the dark tone-colour of the cor anglais when Satyavan is smitten by Death, and the sustained choral chord and string tremolo at the mention of Maya (illusion). Throughout the work, the instruments are used with subtlety and restraint, although the most effective section of all is perhaps the opening, which has no accompaniment at all. In *Savitri*, Holst created one of the most refined works in the history of opera. Although there are moments of passionate expression, the vocal exhibitionism which he had witnessed in the Carl Rosa company is rejected in favour of a simple and lyrical expression of human emotion. His success in this work was doubtless due to his sympathy with oriental thought and his distaste for the improbable plots and sub-plots of conventional opera, which often serve merely as vehicles for vocal display.

The composition of *Savitri* made considerable demands on his time during 1908, so he decided to give up his teaching at the Passmore Edwards Settlement, and during the summer holidays moved house from Grena Road to 10 The Terrace, Barnes, next door to his aunt's school. In this elegant Regency house he was able to find sufficient peace for composition in his first-floor music room overlooking the Thames, and he and Isobel had also rented a tiny cottage on the Isle of Sheppey where they could escape from London at weekends. Of this setting, Isobel wrote: 'It is just lovely at Whitsun with all the little lambs, and the trees and fields covered with blossom . . .'[2]

In these new surroundings he was able to put the finishing touches to *Savitri* and to start work on a series of compositions which were to be the culmination of his Sanskrit period. Although he had already set some of his translations from the *Rig Veda* as songs for voice and piano in the *Vedic Hymns*, he now felt the need for a stronger and more versatile medium of expression, and therefore embarked on a series of *Choral Hymns from the Rig Veda* which were to occupy him over the next few years. The First Group is scored for mixed chorus and orchestra, and consists of three hymns: *Battle Hymn, To the Unknown God*, and *Funeral Hymn*. Once again, Holst avoided any pseudo-oriental effects, and as Richard Capell remarked many years later: 'So far as the spirit of the music went, the hymns might almost as well have belonged to prehistoric Gloucestershire as to the valley of the Indus. It was a misapprehension of 25 years ago to put the strangeness of the musical style down to Oriental influences. Strange it certainly was then . . .'[3] According to the *Musical Times*, the Hymns were 'Sound, firm impressions of the East from a sane Western perspective',[4] and Holst's friend W. G. Whittaker declared that the composer had 'allowed the imagery of Sanskrit literature to permeate his mind so strongly that he is able to attain the desired end without any artificial means'.[5] The critic Edwin Evans wrote: 'The Hindu theology may supply the titles, but it is Nature herself who is the subject of each in turn, and, with all due regard to Mr Holst's Sanskrit studies, it is permissible to suspect that the inspiration of the text as well as the music owes more to a personal conception of the elements than to the actual language of the Rig Veda.'[6]

It was in these works that Holst was able to develop his ideas on asymmetrical metres (e.g. five or seven beats in the bar), which he considered to be more suitable for setting the rhythms of the English language than the more usual duple or triple time, but despite such technical innovations, it was the spiritual vision and philosophical basis of the works which made them seem so different at that time (Whittaker described them as 'ultra-modern' when his choir performed the First Group in 1912,[7] although to later ears they may seem rather bland, even insipid in places). Holst submitted the Hymns to various publishers, but without success, and a few years later went against all advice and had them published at his own expense. It was not until 1920 that any publisher could be persuaded to accept the earlier *Vedic Hymns* for voice and piano.

However, 1908 saw the commercial publication of several smaller pieces, including the songs *Awake, My Heart* and *She Who is Dear to Me*, the *Four Old English Carols*, and an arrangement of *Seven Scottish Airs* for strings and piano ('written for school purposes and published because I was hard up', as Holst later admitted[8]). This last piece, dedicated to his friend Harriet Solly who had often played in his concerts at the Passmore Edwards Settlement and Morley College, consists of a sequence of traditional Scottish melodies. It was first performed at Leighton House by the Israfil Sextette under the German title *Schottische Skizze*, and was described by one newspaper as 'curious and eccentric'.[9] Holst later wrote to his pupil Irene Bonnett, suggesting that a chorus could be added to the ensemble: 'You can get the words of the 7 Scot: Airs from almost any book of Scottish tunes. It just depends on how many you want to use. A good way is to begin with the Stu mo run (Red is the path) then do "We will take the good old way" *without* chorus: bring the latter in on "O Gin I were" and then let them wait until the final entry of Auld Lang Syne. But probably you'll hit on a better way.'[10] Other pot-boilers which appeared in the same series were Holst's arrangements for piano and strings of a *Bourée* by W. C. MacFarren, *Dreaming* and *March* by Berthold Tours, and *Minuet d'Amour* by Frederick Cowen, the conductor under whom he had served during his time in the Scottish Orchestra.

Although he had given up his work at the Passmore Edwards Settlement, Holst continued his activities at Morley College with enthusiasm. On 7 October he conducted the choir and orchestra at a prize-giving ceremony in the Royal Victoria Hall (including a performance of Percy Grainger's arrangement of *I'm Seventeen come Sunday*) and on 19 December directed a students' concert in the library of Morley College. This concert included the first performance of three of his own folk-song arrangements for chorus and orchestra: *On the Banks of the Nile*, *The Willow Tree*, and *Our Ship She lies in Harbour*, with Alice Haselgrove as soloist. The college magazine's reviewer seems to have been quite overcome by the proceedings, reporting that 'Climax upon climax followed with such startling dramatic effect that we were amazed at the stupendous results which Von Holst was able to obtain from his orchestral forces ... Miss Haselgrove on this occasion surpassed all that she has ever done in the College. The pure simplicity of the folk-songs, and the charm and graceful unobtrusiveness of the singer, stood in correct ratio to each other. She sang with perfect confidence and grace.'[11]

It was at about this time that Holst took his eighteen-month-old daughter with him to one of his classes at James Allen's Girls' School. While Holst directed the class, Imogen sat on a side table and mimicked his conducting. He encouraged her musicality, and at home would sit her on his lap at the piano, letting her play pentatonic tunes on the black notes, while he would improvise suitable accompaniments.

At the beginning of 1909, Holst started work on two sets of incidental music, for a children's pageant at Stepney, and a masque at St Paul's Girls' School. *The Vision of Dame Christian* formed part of the celebrations of the four-hundredth anniversary of the foundation of St Paul's School, from which the Girls' School was derived, and was intended to be performed only every ten years and never outside the school. Holst was alarmed to discover that he was expected to be author as well as composer: 'Miss Gray has ordered me to write the music *and words* of a masque for St Paul's', he wrote. 'This and my Parsifal [*The Perfect Fool*] ought to ensure an early grave for someone—I don't quite know who!'[12] But in the event the words were written by the High Mistress herself, and tell the story of Dame Christian, mother of John Colet (Dean of St Paul's and founder of St Paul's School) and her vision of the great future which awaited her son's school and the subsequent foundation of the Girls' School several centuries later. The music begins with an introduction featuring an oboe solo, followed by a lament for the shortness of life and the ruthlessness of death. Then there is a 'Hymn of Praise to God' for the life of John Colet and a 'Solemn Music' in which unseen spirits sing to his memory, followed by a chorus of rejoicing for the victory of life over death. Holst was pleased with his music, later writing to Edwin Evans: 'Personally I value this very highly—all the performers were my own pupils (choir and orchestra of about 120) and the music is quite elaborate—not a bit the ordinary school girl stuff. Finally it contains my best tune—a solemn dance.'[13] By way of involving as many pupils as possible in the production, two girls were chosen to learn each part, so that they could perform on alternate days.

It was during rehearsals for the masque that Holst first met Vally Lasker, then a piano teacher at the school, who was to become one of his closest associates. She had in fact been teaching at the school since 1907, but only for two days a week, which had never yet coincided with Holst's own two days per week. When she first saw him he was standing on a chair, conducting without a baton, which she thought rather odd, but they soon became friends, and she subsequently assisted him in the preparation of many of his scores, besides giving two-piano performances and 'try-throughs' of his new works with her colleague Nora Day.

In early 1909 Holst also composed his *Suite No.1* for military band, a remarkable departure from the usual transcriptions and operatic selections which pervaded the band repertoire at that time, and a precursor of the serious works for wind band which were to proliferate later in the century. Each of the three movements is based on a motif derived from the opening Chaconne, an economical method of construction giving the whole Suite a considerable degree of thematic coherence. Bandsmen who took part in early performances spoke of their excitement on being confronted with such an interesting and challenging work, and the Suite has now become a classic of the band repertoire. It is possible that Holst wrote the work for the prize competition organized at that time by the Worshipful Company of Musicians, but his name does not appear in the list of prize-winners, and the earliest performance which can be traced dates from 1920.

Besides composing this work and the sets of incidental music, Holst also organized a performance of Purcell's *King Arthur* at Morley College during the spring term of 1909, writing in the College magazine: 'I can only find mention of one performance of the complete work in modern days. It was done a few years ago at the Birmingham Festival under Hans Richter.'[14] Once again, Vaughan Williams lent a hand with the preparation and also with the actual performance. At the end of term there was a Morley 'Music Students' Social Tea' at which Alice Haselgrove sang some of Holst's folk-song settings with chorus and orchestra, all the performers being members of the College music classes.

At the beginning of April, Holst received a reply from Ricordi, regretting that they had at last decided against publication of *Sita*, despite its high commendation in their competition. This final rebuff of his earlier work may have spurred Holst towards the completion of his new opera *Savitri*, the full score of which was finished on 27 April.

The beginning of the summer term was taken up with performances of the *Stepney Children's Pageant*, which took place at Whitechapel Art Gallery from 4 to 20 May. The incidental music consisted of various choruses and dances, several of which were based on traditional tunes collected by G. B. Gardiner, Fuller Maitland, and Cecil Sharp. The task of orchestration and copying the parts was shared with Isidore Schwiller, whom Holst had first met as leader of the Carl Rosa Opera Company orchestra. Children from various schools in Stepney took part, together with buglers from the Jewish Lads' Brigade and the Aeolian Orchestra led by Rosabel Watson.

Besides all this practical activity, Holst found time to devise a scheme for scholarships to provide tuition for poorer students at Morley College, which he submitted to the Executive Committee on 17 May. The Committee decided against a formal system of scholarships however, but that 'in special cases of pupils recommended by Mr von Holst the Council should consider favourably the remission of fees'.[15] A few weeks later the College music classes demonstrated their achievements in a concert under Holst's direction, which included two duets from Purcell's *King Arthur* arranged by Holst: *Shepherd, Shepherd, Leave Your Labours* and *The Stream Daughters* (both later published by Novello).

On 22 July 1909 the first performance of *The Vision of Dame Christian* was given at St Paul's Girls' School, with several students from Morley College playing in the orchestra alongside the girls. But hardly any fraternization was possible as the performance took place under the rigorous supervision of Miss Gray, who imposed a strict code of conduct on performers and audience alike. One pupil, Charis Frankenburg, recalled that even her own brother was prohibited from watching the performance in which she took part, despite his position as Captain of St Paul's School, the High Mistress having ruled that no girl with a brother at St Paul's be allowed to appear on the days the boys were invited, 'because she might know some of his friends'.[16] The performance of the masque subsequently became an institution at the school, and every girl had one opportunity of seeing or taking part in it during her time there. Miss Gray later recalled that whenever ex-pupils returned to spend an evening with current pupils, 'they very seldom separate without having sung through the Masque music'.[17]

When the term had ended, Holst was able to relax and get down to composition during the holidays. A dancer then working in London had asked him to write a new work suitable for ballet, and he produced an *Oriental Dance* for orchestra, influenced by memories of his holiday in Algeria, and dedicated to his friend Edwin Evans, whose initials are incorporated in the musical material. The dance project eventually fell through, but Holst kept his score and the following year incorporated it into his suite *Beni Mora*. Another abortive project was a proposed collaboration between Holst and Norman O'Neill to provide incidental music for Maeterlinck's play *The Blue Bird*. O'Neill had been appointed Musical Director of London's Haymarket Theatre and was expected to provide music for those productions which required it. He was busy writing music for *King Lear* and felt unable to cope with any further work, so he asked Holst to help him with the Maeterlinck play. For the summer of 1909, Norman and Adine O'Neill had rented some rooms in a farmhouse near Steyning in Sussex, and they invited Holst there for a discussion of the project. On a swelteringly hot day, Holst set off from London by bicycle, without any headgear to protect himself from the sun, and on arrival promptly fainted from heat exhaustion. When he had recovered, he sat with the O'Neill's under a shady tree where they took their meals, and when the time came to return to London they persuaded him to take his bicycle on the train instead of cycling all the way. In the event, the proposed collaboration never took place, and O'Neill composed all the music for *The Blue Bird* himself.

Holst did however complete the Second Group of *Choral Hymns from the Rig Veda*, scoring them for female voices and orchestra or piano with violins ad lib. Like the first, this group consists of three hymns, *To Varuna* (God of the Waters), *To Agni* (God of Fire), and *Funeral Chant*. In these hymns, Holst further explored the possibilities of unusual metres, cross-rhythms, and scales, employing contrapuntal devices of imitation and canon. The second hymn contains varying divisions of a five-beat metre, and a rhythm of repeated triads which he was later to use to good effect in *The Hymn of Jesus*. He also started work on another Sanskrit composition, *The Cloud Messenger* for chorus and orchestra, using a text selected from the *Meghaduta*, a lengthy poem by Kalidasa, of the fifth century AD. Holst had already spent considerable time on his translation, based on R. W. Frazer's adaptation in his book *Silent Gods and Sun-steeped Lands*, and later recalled of the work that 'Including translation it took me seven years—7 *happy* years of course'.[18] The story is of a poet who sends a cloud towards the Himalayas to take a message of love to his wife, from whom he is separated. The cloud passes a holy city on the way, giving the composer an opportunity to include dances of the temples, and when these have been passed and all is quiet, the cloud delivers its message by whispering in the ear of the sleeping woman. *The Cloud Messenger* is the largest choral work of Holst's Sanskrit period, but its musical language is excessively steeped in Wagnerian chromaticism, and shows none of the inventive diversity of the *Choral Hymns from the Rig Veda*, of which he was to write two more groups during the period of its composition.

In brief moments of relaxation, Holst occasionally found time to join in social activities and to meet other musicians: during this period he was sometimes to be seen at 31a King's Road, Chelsea, where Percy Grainger and his mother held regular gatherings during which new works by young composers would be tried out. Holst's name was also appearing further afield: on 8 October the revised version of *Songs of the West* was performed at Government House, Bombay, by the Governor's Band under the direction of its bandmaster Edward Behr, a fellow graduate of the Royal College of Music. Although this performance was described as 'from Composers' Manuscript',[19] the material was probably copied, as Holst himself conducted the first European performance on 11 December at the Excelsior Hall, Bethnal Green, given by the Oxford House Music Association.

At the beginning of 1910, Holst looked again at the *Oriental Dance* which he had written the previous year, and decided that as it had not been used for its original purpose, he would add two further movements to form an Oriental Suite, entitled *Beni Mora* after the setting of Robert Hichens's popular novel *The Garden of Allah*. Of the two additional movements, the Second Dance bears a passing resemblance to the Arab Dance in Tchaikovsky's *Nutcracker*, but it is the Finale which is the most remarkable, being based on the four-note oboe tune which Holst had noted during his holiday in Algeria. It had been played over and over again for hours on end during a street procession, and Holst re-created this experience by repeating the tune for no less than 163 bars in the third movement of the suite. This finale is entitled 'In the Street of the Ouled Naïls', after the street in Biskra in which Bedouin dancing girls (Ouled Naïls) perform each night in dance halls and cafés. In a programme note, Holst asked the listener to imagine himself approaching a village at an oasis, in the still, dry air of the desert at night. The music here is mysterious, veiled and atmospheric. Drawing nearer, the traveller sees the dim outline of a white-robed Arab procession wending its way through the streets, and hears a flute playing a repetitious melody which continues throughout the movement. On entering the village and joining the procession, fragments of other tunes are heard, gradually growing louder until in the Street of the Ouled Naïls the bewildering variety of music from the open doors mingles with the tune of the procession, producing an ever-changing interplay of melodies, keys, and rhythms. Eventually, the traveller passes through the village and out again into the empty night of the desert.

This simple programmatic scheme is interesting in several respects. Firstly, the idea of a procession is a feature of many of

Holst's compositions, and as this is the first work in which it appears, it seems that the idea originated during his Algerian holiday of 1908, when he heard the repeated melody and saw the procession passing beneath his window. The idea of hypnotic repetition clearly came from the same source, and was to be subsequently used to great effect in *Mars*. Thirdly, the concept of strands of diverse music combining together and then separating is paralleled in *Putnam's Camp*, the second of Charles Ives's *Three Places in New England*, in which the sounds of two bands coming together at a village fête are combined, although they are playing quite independent music in different keys, rhythms and tempi. Ives (who was born a month after Holst) wrote this piece at about the same time as *Beni Mora*, but the two composers had probably never even heard of each other, let alone have had any knowledge of what the other was doing. *Beni Mora* is not authentic Arab music, but neither is it pastiche, as it has a distinctive and evocative character of its own, making it one of Holst's few unjustifiably neglected works.

Another task which occupied Holst during the first months of 1910 was the composition of incidental music for a Pageant of London, to be given as part of the first Festival of Empire held at the Crystal Palace in South London. Various composers were to provide music for sections of the pageant, and the musical director, W. H. Bell, asked Holst to be responsible for the scenes depicting the Danish attack on London in 1016. This episode tells the story of the siege of London by the Danes, and of their defeat by the combined English and Norse forces, who pulled down London Bridge with ropes from their boats, thus forcing the invaders to retreat from the capital. Holst's music included the inevitable battle music and trumpet calls (which involve four unsynchronized motifs freely repeated by spatially separated players), a *Raven Song*, the Norse battle song *Biarkamal*, and a choral song *The Praise of King Olaf* to words from the Norse poem *Olaf's Drapa*. It was to be performed by a wind band of 50 players together with a choir of 500, and Holst worked hard on his score to have it ready in time, helped by Isobel who copied in some of the words. They must both have been considerably disappointed, therefore, when the Festival was suddenly cancelled on the death of King Edward VII, just as the celebrations were about to take place (it was revived the following year as a coronation tribute to the new King, George V).

But Holst was basically in good spirits: on 6 April, the revised version of *A Somerset Rhapsody* had been performed at the Queen's Hall by the New Symphony Orchestra conducted by Edward Mason, and received critical acclaim; Holst later describing the performance as 'my first real success'.[20] It was an auspicious occasion, with a distinguished audience which included the Queen and many well-known musicians. The programme included works by several young British composers, but *The Standard* reported that 'By far the best thing of the concert was Gustav von Holst's *Somerset Rhapsody* for orchestra, which is built upon a couple of folk-like melodies. It is full of delightful little touches of orchestral colour, and the treatment generally is masterly.'[21] The *Daily Telegraph* went further; after describing the whole programme as 'an embarrassment of riches', their reviewer continued: 'At length the climax was reached in Mr Gustav von Holst's *Somerset Rhapsody* ... a piece of music that stamped the concert indelibly, since no more distinguished a piece has issued from a British pen for many a day. Mr von Holst is clearly quite young—he, like his comrades, had to bow his acknowledgments from the platform—but he has something of the master's grasp of the orchestra as of composition, and a command of colour without detriment to his knowledge of form that is quite uncommon. There is real charm in his utterance of what presumably are Somerset folk-tunes—very lovely and characteristic they are—and the cleverness and wit in his union of the two themes, and his harmonisation, more especially when he adopts the modern manner after emphasising the tunes themselves, is exquisite in its fancy, delicacy and point. Indeed Mr von Holst's combination of acquired musicianship of a high order with innate artistry is so unusual that it is easy to believe that he is only at the outset of a career that may lead to heights unnapproachable by his comrades.'[22] Among the audience was the conductor Landon Ronald, who was so impressed with the work that he conducted it himself at the Queen's Hall in June and in Birmingham in October, and in various other places during the next couple of years, including the Hallé Orchestra season of 1912. The reception of the work by press, public, and musicians alike is perhaps best summed up in the words of Richard Capell: 'It had only to be heard to be liked by all.'[23]

Another success came the following month, when on 4 May Holst conducted the Handel Society in a performance of *King Estmere* at the Queen's Hall. The critics seemed to like the work, which had been given its première in the same hall two years before, although Holst's performance came in for some criticism. The *Birmingham Daily Post* reported that 'Mr Gustav von Holst's *King Estmere* is a very charming work. He has caught the spirit of the quaint old ballad very neatly, and he contrives to give the right, remote medieval atmosphere without any uncomfortable experiments in archaic harmony. His work was not very well sung or played, though he was conducting it in person, but nevertheless its grace and beauty made themselves felt in an unmistakable manner.'[24]

Later in the month the *Seven Scottish Airs* were performed in a students' concert at Morley College, and in July a special ceremony was held at St Paul's Girls' School to mark the inauguration of the new organ which had been installed in the main hall. Frances Ralph Gray wrote a paraphrase of the words of Psalm 148 under the title *A Hymn to God the Creator* (which Holst was later to use in the second of his settings of *Two Psalms*) and Frederick Bridge gave a recital demonstrating the capabilities of the new instrument.

By this time Holst had completed a third group of *Choral Hymns from the Rig Veda*, differing from the first two in having an accompaniment for harp instead of orchestra. As he later recalled: 'The 3rd Vedas were written in 1910 for Frank Duckworth and his ladies' choir at Blackburn who were the first musical executants to take me seriously as a composer. I never saw them until 1913 when I went to conduct a programme of my own things but for about 12 years FD has always written and asked if I had anything for him to do and in the old days it used to buck me more than a little. So Veda no.III is an attempt at making a little return.'[25] This group also differs from its predecessors in consisting of four hymns instead of three: *Hymn to the Dawn*, *Hymn to the Waters*, *Hymn to Vena*, and *Hymn of the Travellers*.

Other works completed in 1910 were mainly arrangements of existing material, rather than original compositions. He orchestrated a set of Morris dance tunes which had been collected and harmonized by Cecil Sharp, arranged some *Sacred Rounds and Canons* for equal voices for use in school classes, and concocted a fantasy on Christmas carols entitled *Christmas Day*, in which several well-known tunes appear.

On 17 November, Holst directed performances of *Songs of the West* and *A Somerset Rhapsody* at the Pump Room in Bath, where his mode of conducting caught the attention of the local critic: 'A striking feature of Mr von Holst's reading was that he dispensed altogether with the use of the baton, a practice which, while of course not unusual in musical circles, is very seldom in evidence at the Pump Room Annexe,'[26] while on 15 December he acted as accompanist for several of his own folk-song settings which were performed by the New Chamber Music Club at St George's Vestry Hall, Mount Street, London. On Christmas Eve he completed the full score of *The Cloud Messenger*, but was apparently dissatisfied with the work, and revised it substantially over the next two years.

The first performance of *Christmas Day* was given at Morley College on 28 January 1911, and was so successful that it was repeated on 18 February at a music students' 'Tea and Social' (an annual event, initiated by Holst). Although the College magazine described the work as a 'delightful composition',[27] the composer himself dismissed it merely as a mundane arrangement, later writing to W. G. Whittaker: 'Xmas Day can be done pf and str or any other combination but it's poor stuff anyhow and not worth doing.'[28] In spite of the success of these concerts, there was apparently some doubt as to the continuation of music classes at Morley, but a meeting of the General Purposes Committee on 27 February decided that the classes should continue until the end of June on condition that the attendance was satisfactory.

The following month saw the first performance of two groups of *Choral Hymns from the Rig Veda*. On 16 March Frank Duckworth conducted the Third Group with his Blackburn Ladies' Choir at Blackburn Town Hall, and on 22 March the Second Group was performed by the Edward Mason Choir and orchestra at the Queen's Hall, for which Holst thoughtfully arranged for his Morley students to obtain tickets at reduced prices (sometimes he even provided free tickets for those who could not afford to pay).

Browsing through some of his earlier manuscripts, Holst reassessed the incomplete *Fantasiestücke* for oboe and string quartet which he had written as a student in 1896, and decided to revise it, discarding the opening Air and Variations, and completing the work as a suite of three movements: March, Minuet, and Scherzo. The result was a rather unsatisfactory mixture, in which nineteenth-century textbook harmonies rub shoulders with expressive folk-like melodies, demonstrating the extent to which his thought and technique had moved on in the intervening period. The first performance of this new version was given at a meeting of the Oxford and Cambridge Musical Club on 6 April 1911 (under the title *Three Pieces*) and the piece was repeated at the end of the month at the People's Palace, Mile End Road (under the title *Suite*) but was thereafter virtually ignored. The very conventionality of the music mitigates against it, as there are neither hints of Holst's mature style, nor any of the explorativeness of the Sanskrit hymns which he was working on at the time. After these two performances, he realized that resuscitation of student compositions is not necessarily a good idea, and did not bother to promote the work any further.

On 28 April Holst accompanied Leila Duart in a performance of four of the *Vedic Hymns* at the Bechstein Hall, including the first performance of *Ratri* which was eventually discarded from the final set. He was still trying to secure publication of these songs, but without success, and in March 1911 the critic Edwin Evans complained that 'in any musical country save England the Vedic Hymns would have been published long ago'.[29]

During the first months of 1911, Holst was working on a composition for cello and orchestra at first entitled *A Song of the Evening* (alluding to the earlier *A Song of the Night* for violin and orchestra), but changed this to *Invocation* before the first performance, which was given at the Queen's Hall on 2 May 1911 by May Mukle with the New Symphony Orchestra conducted by Landon Ronald. May Mukle had performed Vaughan Williams's *Symphonic Rhapsody* in 1904, and it was probably through her acquaintance with Vaughan Williams that Holst had got to know her. The work begins with an improvisatory solo, leading into quietly evocative music which is atmospheric and sensitive, without making any undue demands of orchestra or soloist. But the embryonic ideas presented here were later to re-emerge in a more developed form in *Venus*: melodic fragments, textures, and pulsating chords all give an appetizing foretaste of the later work.

Other music which occupied Holst during the first part of 1911 included the *Two Eastern Pictures* for female voices and harp (again for Frank Duckworth's choir) based on the Spring and Summer cantos of Kalidasa's poem *Ritsusamhara* which describes the six seasons of the Indian year, and an orchestral suite entitled *Phantastes* (originally *Fantastic Suite*) inspired by George Macdonald's book of that name; the four movements, Prelude, March, Sleep, and Dance, being preceded by quotations from the writings of Lewis Carroll, Samuel Foote, Beethoven, and Macdonald himself. In this work Holst indulged his skill as an orchestrator and exploited every opportunity offered by the texts for musical illustration, sometimes to the point of over-stating the obvious. To the bizarre march illustrating the progress of Carroll's Jabberwock, he added a sentence from an academic examination paper: 'We strongly advise the student to use only the natural horns,'[30] providing an opportunity to write an open-note theme which diverges uncomfortably from its supporting harmony.

For the forthcoming coronation of King George V he wrote a unison song entitled *In Loyal Bonds United*, and for the Festival of Empire which had been postponed from the previous year Cecil Sharp asked him to make military band arrangements of the morris dance tunes which Holst had previously scored for small orchestra. He also found time to compose one of his finest wind band works, the *Suite No. 2 in F*, whose movements are based on traditional folk-tunes, culminating in a Finale in which the Dargason and Greensleeves are combined in a simultaneous counterpoint, which also appears in the Finale of the *St Paul's Suite*. Holst had previously used the idea of combining folk-tunes in *A Somerset Rhapsody*, but this happy fusion of disparate elements is a contrapuntal *tour de force*. The manuscript score contains evidence of considerable revision, perhaps as a result of performance: although the earliest traceable performance dates from 1922, the Suite may well have been intended for the 1911 Festival of Empire and played during one of the daily band concerts whose complete programmes were not printed in the official brochure. The Festival took place at the Crystal Palace from 12 May to 27 October, and during those months Guards bands played daily from 11.30 a.m. to 10.30 p.m., in addition to performances given by the Festival of Empire Military Band and the Crystal Palace Band, so there was ample opportunity for the Suite to be played at some time during the Festival. Cecil Sharp used Holst's band arrangements of his morris dance tunes for his own Festival series of lectures and demonstrations of folk-dancing and singing-games performed by children from Brompton Oratory School, and the Pageant of London, including the music contributed by Holst, was performed several times by massed voices and bands under the direction of the 'Master of the Music', W. H. Bell.

On 22 June 1911, King George V and Queen Mary were crowned, and the following day the royal couple made a progress through South London. Soon afterwards they passed through Dulwich on their way to the Crystal Palace, and a pupil of James Allen's Girls' School later remembered Holst being among the crowd in the village street, and that he hoisted her on to his shoulders so that she could get a better view.

Despite the pressures of these demanding activities, Holst devoted the major proportion of his energies to an even more ambitious project during the first half of 1911. This was no less than the first performance in modern times of Henry Purcell's *The Fairy Queen* by the music students of Morley College. The work had been first produced at the Queen's Theatre in London in 1692, but after the composer's death in 1695 the score was lost, and despite an appeal in 1701 when a reward was offered for its recovery, remained missing for over 200 years. At the end of the nineteenth century, J. S. Shedlock was asked by the Purcell Society to compile an edition of the work for publication in their series of Purcell's works, and by carefully piecing together fragments from various sources, both manuscript and published editions such as the *Select Songs in the Fairy Queen* of 1692, he managed to produce a version which although incomplete, was as near to the original as could be achieved in the circumstances. When his work was engraved and ready to be printed, Shedlock happened to be in the library of the Royal Academy of Music one day, and on taking down a volume at random from the shelves was astonished to find that he was holding the long-lost manuscript full score of *The Fairy Queen*. The Purcell Society was thus able to publish the original score in full, and when Holst outlined his plan to produce a concert performance of the work, the Society readily gave permission for a set of manuscript parts to be prepared.

The performance was planned for June 1911, and from the previous November the music students at Morley College were hard at work copying out parts. In all, some 1500 pages of parts were copied: an enormous task in which some of Holst's colleagues such as Vally Lasker lent a hand, and a chastening reminder of the amount of labour involved in producing performance materials before the advent of photocopying. In several of the choruses the soprano parts were found to lie too high for untrained voices, and whole sections had to be tranposed down a tone, with the alto parts adjusted where necessary, thus adding to the labour. However, as Holst's pupil Jane Joseph later recalled, the students who helped in this monumental task did not feel as if they were wasting their free time or being exploited; instead, they felt privileged to be working at Holst's side: 'He is indisputably master, and no less indisputably comrade.'[31]

Finally, the big day of the performance arrived on Saturday 10 June. For the occasion, the College hired the adjacent Royal Victoria Hall; boxes were priced at one guinea, reserved balcony stalls 2*s*.6*d*., unreserved seats 1*s*.6*d*.,1*s*., and 6*d*., and programmes 1*d*. each. Messages of support were received from distinguished musicians such as Parry, Alexander MacKenzie, and Henry Wood, and although the College had invited both the King and senior politicians, hardly expecting them to accept, they did at least send encouraging replies, Balfour expressing his 'profound interest' and his 'deepest regret' that he would not be able to be present because of a visit abroad.[32]

A large audience assembled, consisting mainly of outsiders who had heard of the preparations and were keen to hear the result (there was disappointingly little interest among the College's own non-music students), and before the performance began, Vaughan Williams appeared in front of the curtain to give a short introduction, explaining that it was not in fact an opera, but incidental music to Shakespeare's *A Midsummer Night's Dream*, and that although a few cuts had been made, the work was substantially the same as when it had last been performed at the end of the seventeenth century. In the following performance, all the participants acquitted themselves well, the soloists including such Morley College stalwarts as Alice Haselgrove, Percival Poole, Helen Greig, Beatrice Payne, Ernest Raggett, and Ernest Hoare. The orchestra was led by Isidore Schwiller, who played the violin obbligato in 'The Plaint' in Act III, and among the violas was Vally Lasker, who later claimed that she had been obliged to learn the instrument for the occasion in only four lessons. The performance received long notices in national newspapers such as *The Times* and the *Daily Telegraph*, and everyone concerned with the event felt that they had accomplished something worthwhile under Holst's direction and encouragement. In fact, the example of this performance did a great deal to motivate subsequent productions of the work, such as the staged version conducted by Cyril Rootham at the New Theatre, Cambridge, in February 1920, and so great was Holst's advocacy of the music of Purcell that one critic was later moved to declare that at that time Morley College and St Paul's Girls' School together constituted 'the Purcellian centre of the world'.[33]

6

From School to Queen's Hall
(1911–1913)

The intense concentration and energy demanded by his various activities during the first half of 1911 were beginning to have an adverse effect on Holst's health. He frequently lost his voice through tiredness and would call in at the Vaughan Williams's house at 13 Cheyne Walk after a day's teaching and immediately fall asleep from sheer exhaustion. The housekeeper, Mrs Mott, used to prepared boiled eggs for tea whenever Holst came, as Vaughan Williams's wife Adeline believed strongly in their reviving power. But as the term came to an end it was clear that what Holst needed was a refreshing holiday, so with the money which Cecil Sharp had paid him for scoring the morris dance tunes he set off for a walking tour in Switzerland with the young composer Cecil Coles. Holst was keen to use bicycles as their transport within that country, being apparently oblivious to their incongruity to the terrain, but there is no evidence that they actually did so. It was of necessity a fairly short holiday because of overlapping terms at his schools and Morley College, but it was what he needed and he returned refreshed, relaxed, and ready for work.

At Morley he was able to reduce his teaching burden by arranging for some of his classes to be taken by colleagues: his aunt Nina was to teach the piano, and the singers would be taught by Mabel Dalby, thus leaving him free to concentrate on the more advanced pupils in these subjects. This arrangement enabled him to devote more time to composition, and he started work on a setting of *Hecuba's Lament* from Euripides' *The Trojan Women*, using Gilbert Murray's English translation. The work is scored for contralto solo, three-part female chorus, and orchestra, and with characteristic attention to practicalities Holst arranged the orchestration so that the work could be played with reduced instrumentation; even so, he had to wait several years for its first public performance.

In November *A Somerset Rhapsody* was performed in Bournemouth by the Municipal Orchestra (whose last performance of a Holst work had been the première of the *Cotswolds Symphony* in 1902), and on 6 December Edgar Bainton conducted the première performance of the First Group of *Choral Hymns from the Rig Veda* at Newcastle Town Hall, with the Newcastle-upon-Tyne Musical Union. Another first performance was that of the mixed-voice version of *Four Old English Carols*, given in London at the Bechstein Hall by the Oriana Madrigal Society conducted by Charles Kennedy Scott; the last important event in what had been a busy year for Holst.

At the beginning of 1912, Holst added another girls' school to his schedule of teaching; Wycombe Abbey School at High Wycombe, Buckinghamshire, which had links with St Paul's Girls' School, and which he visited once a week until 1917. At first he was rather uncertain of his new pupils, and they of him; one girl later recalled that at lunch on Wednesdays the door would open and their stern headmistress would appear, followed by Holst peering anxiously over the top of his thick-lensed spectacles. She would lead him through the assembled girls to a seat at the high table, where a specially selected pupil would be delegated to sit next to him and engage in intelligent conversation. These occasions were never a success; Holst was much more at ease in the classroom, where everyone could relax and enjoy making music. As at his other schools, he quickly secured the interest and affection of his pupils, who came to refer to him as 'Von Slosh', a name which later appeared in an examination paper on twentieth-century composers, to the puzzlement of the examiner. However, his classes at Wycombe did not go entirely smoothly: on his arrival at the school, Holst had continued to use the *National Song Book* which had been the mainstay of his predecessor, and he gave the girls a diet of *John Peel*, *Annie Laurie*, *Scots wa'hae*, and *The Ash Grove*, 'until we were heartily sick of them', as one pupil recalled.[1] A mutiny broke out, with a demand for authentic English folk-songs (led by one agitator who was a member of the English Folk Dance Society) and a chance to sing more part-songs so that they could pit their musical abilities against the girls of St Paul's. But this brief strike failed to produce any result, as Holst was unable to persuade the school to supply a replacement for the song book, and as he had to play all the piano accompaniments himself he was unable to coach the singers in the finer points of choral technique. He did, however, teach the girls to the best of his abilities in the circumstances, as was the case with all his teaching.

Neither did he neglect his girls at St Paul's Girls' School. At the beginning of the year he wrote for them a special *Playground Song* to complement the official school song. The idea had been proposed in the school magazine, when a pupil appealed for a song which could be sung by teams returning from victorious sporting occasions. The High Mistress took up the idea, encouraging the girls to write suitable verses, but stipulating that the author of the successful contribution must be prepared to allow it to be altered in the interests of editorial expediency. The final text was an amalgam of one contribution with several others, so that according to Miss Gray the original writer 'will, perhaps, hardly recognise her own production',[2] and Holst set the resulting verse to music for unison voices and piano. The words reflect the cheerful vigour which was quite acceptable in those days but to later ears sounds uncomfortably reminiscent of life at Ronald Searle's St Trinian's:

> With joyful hearts our song we raise,
> For many a jocund scene
> In swimming-bath, gymnasium,
> And playground cool and green
>
> . . . .
> Come victory or failure
> St Paul's will play the game!

Although the song was sung on various school occasions, it was never published, and the original manuscript is now preserved in the school's archives.

A more important work, completed during the first months of 1912, was the fourth and last group of *Choral Hymns from the Rig Veda*, scored for male voices and strings, with brass ad lib. Like the Third Group, it consists of four hymns, to Agni,

Soma, Manas, and Indra, in the last of which a later critic found 'surprising heartiness quite out of character'.[3] Perhaps the compositional experience of the *Playground Song* had more than a passing influence on Holst's more serious work.

He also composed settings of *Two Psalms* for mixed voices, string orchestra, and organ or brass instruments, making alternative arrangements for female voices for his school pupils. The first, *To My Humble Supplication* (Psalm 86), is a setting of the authorized version text for tenor solo, with a metrical version by Joseph Bryan for the chorus; the second being the paraphrase of Psalm 148, *Lord, Who Hast Made Us for Thine Own*, which Frances Ralph Gray had written for the inauguration of the organ at St Paul's Girls' School in 1910. The melodies were taken from the Genevan Psalter of 1543 and *Geistliche Kirkengesänge* of 1623; the second tune being already well-known to users of the *English Hymnal* from its use in *Ye Watchers and Ye Holy Ones* to words by Athelstan Riley. But Holst's settings, though simple, are much more than mere hymn harmonizations; they are interesting and effective textures which remain within the capabilities of amateur singers. In both Psalms there is variety of tonal contrast; in the first between phrases given to the tenor solo and divided female voices in alternation, and in the second between imitative choral phrases and the straightforward presentation of the melody by the orchestra. There are even moments of drama, as at the end of the first Psalm, where a Neapolitan chord clashes semitonally against a tonic pedal point; an effect which was to be taken to extreme lengths two years later at the end of *Mars*. In these Psalms, Holst provided accessible music in which technique is used for simple expressive purposes, and the temptation to indulge in clever elaboration for its own sake is avoided.

Besides composition, there was an increasingly busy round of concerts. On 11 January Holst travelled to Bournemouth for another performance of *A Somerset Rhapsody*, this time conducting the work himself, while on 21 March Frank Duckworth directed the first performance of *Two Eastern Pictures* by the Blackburn Ladies' Choir in a charity concert at

Blackburn Town Hall. On 25 March the first London performance of the First Group of *Choral Hymns from the Rig Veda*
was given by the Edward Mason Choir and Orchestra at the
Queen's Hall, and on 1 May Holst conducted the first
performance of *Beni Mora* in the same hall in a concert
organized by Henry Balfour Gardiner. This was the last of four
concerts which Gardiner had put on at his own expense in
1912, with the aim of promoting music by younger British
composers, including Cyril Scott, Percy Grainger, Hamilton
Harty, Norman O'Neill, Arnold Bax, Arthur Fagge, and Charles
Kennedy Scott. At the first concert of the series, Percy
Grainger's *Father and Daughter*, scored for an orchestra of 30
mandolins and guitars, caused a sensation, but *Beni Mora* did
not make the same kind of impression, receiving an diverse
reaction from both press and audience. The *Musical Times*
commented favourably, commending Holst for his skill in the
Finale: 'Its clever mingling of dance music, such as might issue
from the cafés, with the music of an Arab procession passing
from the desert through the town and out into the desert again,
was an interesting feat of imagination and technique,'[4] but
other critics were less kind, one brusquely commenting: 'We
do not ask for Biskra dancing girls in Langham Place.'[5] Holst's
friend W. G. Whittaker later wrote of the Finale: 'On first
hearing, this movement appears wholly bizarre, but a better
acquaintance with it reveals great power and much striking
beauty.'[6] The audience's reaction was as mixed as that of the
critics; while some applauded, others hissed this composer
who dared to combine various Arab tunes without bothering to
integrate them into a scheme of conventional harmony.
Writing in 1938, R. W. Wood wondered what all the fuss had
been about: from his perspective *Beni Mora* seemed 'harmless
enough . . . scarcely more than hack-work'.[7] Hack-work or not,
this performance helped to bring Holst's name before a wider
musical public, and was one further step towards establishing a
reputation as an up-and-coming composer whose future career
would be well worth watching.

At Morley College, there had been a big advance in the
orchestral classes, and on 8 June the students presented a
concert including Bach's cantata *Halt im Gedächtnis Jesum
Christ*, sung in German as no English translation existed at

that time, together with Holst's arrangements of the folk-songs *Young Herchard* and *Beautiful Nancy*, sung by Percival Poole. To round off the term, the Morley students went to St Paul's Girls' School for a garden party and concert, during which 'Mr Percival Poole gave his inimitable rendering of Mr von Holst's arrangement of "Herchard of Taunton Dene".'[8] These visits took place in a more relaxed atmosphere than the Masque performances of 1909, and were to become regular annual events, providing a means of contact between the predominantly working-class Morley students and the middle-class girls of St Paul's. The visits were eagerly anticipated by all, and sometimes included musical competitions between the two groups. Paulinas and their teachers would act as hostesses and sing and perform with the guests, and the day usually ended with a simple meal. For her part, Miss Gray never quite forgot the fierce handshake bestowed upon her by an over-zealous banjo player from Morley College.

During the summer months, London was once again witness to the brilliant performances of Diaghilev's Ballets Russes, who had made their first visit to Britain the previous year, when they had given two seasons at Covent Garden. For these 1911 appearances, Diaghilev had kept to the standard repertoire, believing that the English public was not yet ready for the music of more advanced composers such as Stravinsky, but in 1912 he took the plunge, and *The Firebird* was given its British première at Covent Garden on 18 June. Stravinsky himself came to London for this performance (his first visit to England), where he met Thomas Beecham and the critic Edwin Evans. As Evans was a friend of Holst and often gave him press tickets for concerts, it is likely that Holst heard *The Firebird* during this season, and may even have met its composer. The music had a great effect on him, as indeed it did on all who heard it, and Stravinsky's influence was to become apparent in several of Holst's subsequent works.

On 23 July an important première of one of Holst's own works took place in London, when he conducted the New Symphony Orchestra in the first performance of the *Phantastes Suite* at the Queen's Hall, in the presence of the King and Queen.

Composed the previous year, the work is dedicated to Holst's family friend Frank Forty, and calls for a large orchestra including alto flute and celesta, but despite these touches of orchestral colour Holst was dissatisfied with the work and withdrew it after this first performance. He probably realized that he had overdone certain bizarre effects and that some of his musical jokes had outstayed their welcome, or perhaps hearing Stravinsky's music had made him aware of a wider musical world beyond his own immediate experience and this had forced him to see his own work in a new light. Either way, he did not revise the Suite and it was never played again.

Although Holst concluded that the work had serious faults, the critics were divided in their opinion. The *Morning Post* reported that it was 'A work of so much picturesqueness that some of the effects won a smile from the King', going on to say back-handedly that 'The work reveals a keen sense of humour and orchestral imagination, if no striking quality as music,'[9] while the *Yorkshire Post* agreed that it 'proved more remarkable for the cleverness of its scoring than for originality'.[10] The *Musical Times* thought it 'well repaid the performing' and that the programmatic intentions were 'interesting, entertaining, and musically attractive',[11] while the *Manchester Guardian* said that it 'boasts of many clever orchestral effects and a good deal of unpretentious melody'.[12] But several strong influences on Holst's music did not go unremarked: the *Daily Mail* commented that 'The little pieces are full of the quaint orchestral pranks to which the Russians and French have accustomed us in recent years',[13] while the *Birmingham Post* thought it to be 'an ingenious and cleverly scored piece of fairy music something in the manner of Tchaikovsky'.[14] A most remarkable accolade came from *The Bystander*, which described Holst as the 'English Stravinsky',[15] claiming to discern more logic in his music than in that of the Russian master, and chiding the English public for its failure to elevate Holst to an honoured position. Despite this eulogy, Holst realized that *Phantastes* was not worthy of his talents, and deleted the title from his list of compositions.

Besides the influence of Stravinsky, a further cultural shock lay in store for Holst, when on 3 September Henry Wood conducted the world première of Schoenberg's *Five Pieces for*

Orchestra at the Queen's Hall. Once again, it is not entirely clear whether Holst was actually present on this occasion, but as the event aroused considerable interest among musicians he would undoubtedly have made an effort to be there. A second performance which took place in January 1914 is noted in his appointments diary, so it seems likely that he attended at least one, if not both, of these concerts.

The critics, who had gingerly ventured into the realms of modern music via *The Firebird* a few months before, were stunned and confused by Schoenberg's music, even though the organizers had taken the precaution of describing the work as 'experiments in dissonance'. *The Times* reported that 'It was like a poem in Tibetan; not one single soul in the room could possibly have understood it at a first hearing,'[16] while the *Musical Times* called the pieces 'distracting fancies of delirium' and described the audience as 'bewildered and shocked'.[17] At first a few ripples of laughter went round the hall, but when it was realized that the music was meant to be taken seriously, tedium set in, and 'the want of ideas and continued vagueness became wearisome, and developed into absolute boredom in the Finale', according to *The Referee*.[18] Some members of the audience were severely affected by this unexpected attack on their senses; Percy Scholes found that a lady sitting next to him was in tears, suffering fron effects similar to those of physical assault. Although doubtless not quite so overcome, Holst was intrigued by this strange new music, which he described as 'like Wagner, but without the tunes',[19] and the seeds of one of his own greatest works were sown in his mind.

But meanwhile there were day-to-day matters to be dealt with. Mental adjustment from the giddy heights of a Schoenberg world première to the mundane world of evening classes at Morley College was a transition which Holst was able to make with ease, and was doubtless one of the factors which prevented him from becoming an 'ivory-tower' composer. He was always attentive to the practical problems faced by the students attending evening classes, and on 15 September attended a meeting of the Executive Committee of Morley College to explain the insecure financial basis of the music classes, which had outgrown their resources and could not be kept going at their existing level. Solo performers could not always afford to pay for individual lessons, and extra players had to be engaged for the orchestra to make up the necessary instrumental balance. Obtaining sufficient suitable music was also a problem, and Holst described his efforts to borrow material from various sources and his students' diligence in helping to copy out parts. He cited the successful production of *The Fairy Queen* as an example of what could be achieved despite these limited resources and asked for greater support for the musical activities of the College. The Committee however was not impressed, and although they were shamed into approving a scholarship for one particular student by Holst's offer to teach him for nothing if necessary, on the question of obtaining music they advised Holst to continue to borrow it.

On 24 October Holst visited Newcastle to conduct the Newcastle Philharmonic Orchestra in a performance of *Beni Mora*, which had not been heard before in that city, and on 12 November Edith Clegg included Holst's setting of *Beautiful Nancy* in her recital at the Bechstein Hall. The following month another Holst work was heard for the first time in the Newcastle area: the First Group of *Choral Hymns from the Rig Veda* was performed on 17 December by the Tynemouth, Whitley and District Choral Union, conducted by W. G. Whittaker, who was to become one of Holst's closest friends. Holst was unable to be present because of his teaching commitments, but Whittaker wrote to him describing the concert: 'Those members of the audience who think Handel the final word in art were greatly puzzled by your works, but all the enlightened souls were very much impressed, and expressed, in no hesitant terms, their admiration of the originality and beauty of your compositions.'[20]

During the second half of 1912 Holst completed no new works, but carried out considerable revision of *The Cloud Messenger*, *The Mystic Trumpeter*, and the *Suite de Ballet*. He also began work on a suite for string orchestra which was to become the *St Paul's Suite*. The previous year he had taken over responsibility for the St Paul's Girls' School orchestra, which had been started by the violin mistress, Dorothea Walenn. It consisted of a few violins, viola, cello, and double-bass, to which a tambourine, two toy drums, and some tin whistles were sometimes added. A piano was used to support the strings, and after the installation of the organ in 1910, this was used to fill in woodwind parts. Three players sat on the organ bench, sometimes including Miss Gray herself, who would rely on the two schoolgirls to give clear cues for her entries. She also later experimented with a 'wheezy old harmonium' to provide a bassoon part, but concluded that 'by that time the orchestra had improved so much that I felt I was too obviously out of place'.[21] From the start, Holst encouraged orchestral playing by the pupils, believing that every pupil with enthusiasm should be allowed to play in the orchestra, regardless of ability, and by his inspirational leadership managed to draw hidden talents from even the most unlikely pupils.

He provided them with a diet of Haydn, Purcell, and Bach, including the Rondeau from *The Fairy Queen*, the *Air on the G string* and Boccherini's *Minuet*, and by way of light relief, Strauss waltzes, which he conducted with gusto, having learnt them well during his 'Worming' days. This is basically the same fare which he gave his orchestra at Morley College, and of all the music played, his favourite instrumental composer was clearly Joseph Haydn. Many years later he recalled: 'Haydn . . . is the friend of all instrumentalists, of orchestral players, and above all, of string quartet players. A few years ago when I was conducting several amateur orchestras each week I realised that there were two recurring problems in my life. The pleasant one being: Which Haydn symphony shall I do next term? The difficult one being: "What orchestral work can I do that is not written by Haydn?"'[22] Holst derived much pleasure from conducting the school orchestra; perhaps even more than those unruly pupils who would sit at the back out of range of the conductor's poor eyesight and use the rehearsal as an opportunity for misbehaviour. In directing an orchestra containing players of various levels of ability, Holst clearly saw himself in the same tradition as Purcell, who wrote music for a girls' school; Bach, who composed functional music according to the requirements of his employers; and Haydn, who was able to mould his music to take account of the technical abilities of his players.

As he had yet to write an original work for school orchestra, he decided to compose the *St Paul's Suite* especially for the school. This was to consist of four movements: Jig, Ostinato, Intermezzo, and Finale. Although a Jig is often found in suites, it rarely appears as the first movement, and Holst used it here to establish the light-hearted, folk-like mood of the entire work. The Ostinato combines a waltz theme with a recurring duple pattern of quavers, while the Intermezzo has something of an oriental atmosphere, including a vivace tune based on a melody noted during his Algerian holiday of 1908. The Finale is a transcription of the fourth movement of the *Suite No. 2* for military band, with the insertion of five further variations, and the combination of 'Greensleeves' and the 'Dargason' has the same exhilarating effect as in the wind band version; school performances sometimes being enlivened by the pupils singing the traditional words of 'Greensleeves', with tambourines brought in at the climax and 'Ha!' shouted loudly on the last chord. The use of words meant that the movement could not be performed at too fast a tempo, and Imogen Holst considered that the correct speed is the one which is most suitable for dancing. Holst himself liked the two heavy accents of the 6/8 bars to continue against the 3/4 on the appearance of 'Greensleeves', to emphasize the rhythmic contrast between the two tunes ('Kinsey and the LSO second violins once gave it to me in grand style,' he recalled; 'The effect was intoxicating'[23]).

In this work, Holst created music which is playable by schoolgirls or professionals, yet is musically effective, while presenting interesting and challenging problems of performance. While he was working on the suite, the Governors were able to secure the presentation of a set of wind instruments to the school, and Holst therefore wrote some optional parts for those pupils who could play the new instruments, but these remained in manuscript and the work was subsequently published for strings alone. Holst would allow his pupils to try several wind instruments until they found one that suited them, and they were then assigned to the percussion section to accustom themselves to counting bars and coming in in the right place. Then, when they had mastered the basic notes of their instrument, they would join the appropriate section with a special part written by Holst to match their particular level of ability. This policy resulted in occasional imbalance: at one time the orchestra had as many as six oboes but no clarinets, and at another six flutes, but it later settled down to a more conventional distribution of parts. Sometimes girls were made to study another instrument to widen their orchestral experience. One pupil, Nancy Gotch, recalled her days in the orchestra: 'I was told . . . that as I had played the violin I would from now on be a viola and sit with Miss Vally Lasker. So I got hold of an instrument from my sister and set about to learn the clef as best I could . . . Vally and I sawed away happily together. Our Director of Music was referred to affectionately as "Gussie", and what an inspiring conductor he was. We could have played anything if he had willed it so. His fair-haired wife played the double-bass and she sometimes argued with him; we listened in silent awe when this happened. It never lasted long.'[24]

Although the majority of his players had no thought of becoming professional musicians, Holst's methods allowed those with talent and determination to go as far as they wished, and he was particularly pleased when one of his pupils, Helen Gaskell, went on to become a professional oboist (unusual for a woman at that time) becoming the first woman to join the woodwind section of the Queen's Hall Orchestra, later joining the BBC Symphony Orchestra where her cor anglais playing was particularly admired.

1913 began with an important performance: on 3 January Holst conducted *Beni Mora* at a joint conference and festival of the Musical League and the Incorporated Society of Musicians, held in Birmingham Town Hall. Part of the audience was intrigued by the unusual atmosphere of Holst's work, but the remainder were indignant that the rules of academic composition, of which they considered themselves the arbiters, had been so blatantly flouted and began to laugh openly at the music. The *Musical Times* reported that the protesters 'seemed shocked at the naughtiness of some of the harmonies, which probably would not parse according to, say, Goss'.[25] However, this performance was an important milestone on Holst's path towards recognition, and whether the assembled musicians and pedagogues liked *Beni Mora* or not, it clearly stood out from the other music in the concert which included works by Arnold Bax, Edgar Bainton, Henry Balfour Gardiner, and the first performance of Havergal Brian's overture *Doctor Merryheart*.

As in the previous year, Henry Balfour Gardiner presented a further series of concerts at the Queen's Hall, including three of Holst's compositions: on 11 February the *Two Eastern Pictures* were given their first London performance by the Oriana Madrigal Society conducted by Charles Kennedy Scott; on 25 February the revised version of *The Mystic Trumpeter* was sung by Cicely Gleeson White with the New Symphony Orchestra conducted by Holst himself; and on 4 March Holst conducted the London Choral Society and the New Symphony Orchestra in the first performance of *The Cloud Messenger*. In a separate concert at the Queen's Hall on 27 February, the Edward Mason Choir gave the first London performance of the Third Group of *Choral Hymns from the Rig Veda*, in a programme which included Balfour Gardiner's cantata *News from Whydah*, whose accompaniment Holst had rescored for small orchestra at about this time.

Once again, the reception given to Holst's works was mixed. The *Musical Times* was impressed by the Edward Mason concert ('the most enterprising and altruistic concert of the season'), declaring that 'Mr von Holst's new "Rig Veda" music is a fitting sequel to the first and second sets, which have earned a well-deserved reputation. It is fancy-free, and yet well thought-out. The design of it for female voices with harp accompaniment does not promote variety, but Mr von Holst has made it a natural medium, and his independence of thought fully sustains the interest.' But the same journal was not so impressed by the revised version of *The Mystic Trumpeter*, remarking that 'This composer always displays fancy, but it cannot be said that in this long piece he is at his best.' After describing *The Cloud Messenger* as 'the most important work in the programme' it recorded laconically that 'it took 42 minutes to perform, and proved not to be particularly interesting'. The critic did however allow that 'There are some fine climaxes, a female voice chorus to the words "Behold, the sacred city", that has real beauty', but concluded that 'there is not sufficient continuous inspiration in the composition to maintain interest throughout.'[26] The *Morning Post* found 'ability, not to say genius, revealed in the music',[27] but other critics were divided, and although the vocal score was published by Stainer & Bell, the work failed to catch the attention of either musicians or audiences, and fell into an oblivion from which it has never recovered.

When Holst was revising the work for publication, Vaughan Williams wrote to say that he had looked through it again, and found that 'most of it is beautiful and there are only one or two places I don't care for which I shall not bother you with as they are merely matters of opinion'.[28] W. G. Whittaker wrote: 'There is an envigorating strength about the address to the Cloud with which the choral portion begins, and the short description of village life which follows is charming in its naivity ... The description of the sacred city, with its glittering roofs, its tinkling bells and its solemn temple dances is Oriental without being fantastically so, and the exquisitely tender message which closes the Ode, is an expression of real and intense emotion.'[29] Later writers have been uncertain about the work; Havergal Brian found that it 'has a Wagnerian tinge: striking melodic basses: a forecast of the processional march style, found in later works and in the symphonies of Gustav Mahler',[30] while Edmund Rubbra in comparing it with the *Choral Hymns from the Rig Veda* found that 'it is curiously lacking in the pointed significance of the earlier hymns: it sprawls rather formlessly, is unadventurous, and what orientalism there is in the music is of an obvious kind— whole-tone scales and augmented seconds.'[31]

Holst himself thought that *The Cloud Messenger* was one of the best things he had written, and its lack of success was therefore particularly disappointing. As he wrote to Frank Duckworth: 'The "Cloud" did not go well, and the whole thing has been a blow to me. I'm fed up with music, especially my own.'[32] Despite the loyal support of his friends, these performances had made Holst realize that there were still some serious defects in his music. He was grateful to Balfour Gardiner for enabling his works to be brought before the public, but there would be no further opportunities of this kind as Gardiner was exasperated by the surly behaviour of the musicians of the New Symphony Orchestra and their overt opposition to new music, and was dubious about continuing the series; the advent of war eventually deciding the matter.

Holst expressed his thanks to Gardiner by dedicating to him the *Hymn to Dionysus* for female voices and orchestra, on which he had been working during the early months of 1913. The words are from Gilbert Murray's translation of the opening chorus of Euripides' *Bacchae*, consisting of a hymn of praise to the 'Giver of Wine' sung by his followers the Asiatic Bacchae women, who invite the people of Thebes to join in their celebrations with dancing, singing, and musical instruments. What suddenly motivated Holst to take an interest in ancient Greek drama is not quite clear, except that at this time Vaughan Williams was working on some incidental music for the *Bacchae*, using the same translation, for a project in collaboration with Isadora Duncan. This production never actually materialized, but Vaughan Williams may have shown Holst some of his music during one of their 'field days'. Holst's setting of the Hymn does not attempt to reproduce authentic Greek music, but evokes an atmosphere of religious frenzy, using technical devices such as modal and pentatonic scales and quasi-oriental chromatic harmonies, to produce a work which contains anticipations of motifs later used successfully in *The Planets* and *The Hymn of Jesus*.

At this time Vaughan Williams was also preparing the music for the annual Shakespeare festival at Stratford-on-Avon, of which he was musical director. Amongst other music, he used Holst's *Two Songs Without Words* as entr'acte music for *Richard II*, *The Merry Wives of Windsor*, and *Henry IV*, Part 2: this event may have been Holst's first acquaintance with the texts he was to use in his opera *At the Boar's Head* several years later.

In contrast to the disappointments of the London concerts, Frank Duckworth's Blackburn Ladies' Choir gave a successful concert on 10 March, which he declared 'will be remembered by Holst as long as he remembers anything'.[33] The first half of the programme was conducted by Duckworth, while the whole of the second half was devoted to music by Holst, conducted by the composer. The works performed included the *Two Eastern*

Pictures, the Third Group of *Choral Hymns from the Rig Veda*, some songs and folk-song settings for voice and piano, and several of the *Songs from 'The Princess'*. Although this event doubtless gave Holst's morale a welcome boost, he was still tired and suffering from nervous exhaustion as a result of his arduous teaching schedules, so it was with some relief that he accepted an invitation from Balfour Gardiner to join him on an expenses-paid holiday trip to Mallorca, in the company of Clifford and Arnold Bax.

Holst arranged for his Morley College classes to be taken over by Denis Browne, with Vally Lasker deputizing for him at St Paul's, and on 27 March set off for Victoria station, where for the first time he met Clifford Bax, who was later to collaborate with him on several projects. Bax already knew of Holst, partly via his brother Arnold, and partly through being present at the recent performance of *The Cloud Messenger*. When Holst told him of his interest in astrology, Clifford expounded on that subject at some length, much to the disapproval of Balfour Gardiner who was a vehement rationalist and who derided all the mystical and religious ideas discussed by his companions during the holiday. None of the party had visited Spain before, but Gardiner had taken the trouble to learn a little Spanish, and with this they hoped to get by. During the journey, the three composers discussed musical matters, while Clifford Bax eavesdropped on the conversation while browsing through a Spanish phrase-book. According to him, the three musicians discussed technique, and 'with irreproachable courtesy they demonstrated misjudgements of orchestration by quoting from each other's works'.[34] Holst was obliged to defend the works of Bach against the criticisms of Arnold Bax, who claimed that his music lacked emotion.

Arriving in Gerona in the late afternoon, they decided to explore the city before dinner. When the time came for the meal, Holst could not be found, so the others set off without him. He met them a little while later when they were standing listening to a group of folk musicians, explaining that he had been 'losing himself', which was the only real way to explore a city. During the meal the main topic of conversation was 'fogginess' in the arts. The next morning they found a fair in progress in Gerona, and wandered round the market-place which was crowded with stalls. In the afternoon they travelled to Barcelona, and during the journey Holst and Clifford Bax discussed the expressive qualities of words, compared with realities. Bax pointed out that memory enhances experience, to which Holst replied that he would rather hear *Parsifal* than remember it, while Balfour Gardiner sat in the corner of the compartment, scowling at all this metaphysical speculation. They spent several days in Barcelona, visiting all the tourist spots, and one rainy afternoon went to a bullfight: Clifford Bax and Gardiner were keen to see it, but Arnold and Holst were only persuaded to go against their will.

Before embarking for Mallorca, they decided to spend a night at the Benedictine monastery of Montserrat, taking a train to the village of Monistrol at the foot of the mountain on which it stands. Holst immediately set off on foot up the slopes while the others took the mountain railway, and after reaching the monastery and arranging their rooms, they went out to admire the view. A bell summoned them to dinner and when they returned to the monastery there was Holst, 'weary but enthusiastic'. After supper Holst and Arnold Bax went outside for some more exploration, while the others joined them after having looked in at a concert in the chapel and departed hastily after hearing some of the music.

The following day they returned to Barcelona, and embarked for Mallorca in the evening. Arnold Bax and Gardiner retired early to their cabins, while Holst and Clifford promenaded the deck, watching the lights of Barcelona recede into the distance, and philosophically discussing artistic success and failure. On arrival at Palma, they explored the town together and became acquainted with the local liqueur *verdad*, which immediately found favour with all members of the party. Clifford Bax recalled that 'rarely have I seen a man look more blessed than Gustav Holst as he fondled his evening glass', although on one occasion Holst refused some verdad, and in reply to Clifford's remark 'You've turned ascetic, Gustav?', replied: 'My dear boy, your true sybarite is always ascetic. The sensation of drinking verdad is worth saving up.'[35] After dinner they would take their drinks to their rooms where they would discuss various matters, from music to women: Holst astonishing the others by declaring that he had taught women for years and did not regard them as at all inferior to men.

After spending ten days in Palma, they travelled by the new railway to Soller and Miramar for a further week, after which they returned to Palma for a few days. Clifford Bax had to return to England before the others, and on his last evening the four friends gathered in Gardiner's room for drinks and a discussion which centred on the subject of the immortality of the soul, a topic which attracted the scorn of Gardiner and on which Holst refused to be drawn. The conversation then turned inevitably to the subject which was at the back of everyone's mind: the possibility of a war between Britain and Germany.

One result of this holiday was that Holst's interest in astrology developed rapidly, and according to his mentor Clifford Bax, he became 'a remarkably skilled interpreter of horoscopes';[36] an interest which was to bear fruit in *The Planets* suite a year or so later. After their return, Bax gave Holst a copy of the *Notebooks* of Samuel Butler, which was to become one of his favourite sources of quotations.

On resuming work at St Paul's, Holst found that the new music wing was almost complete, and arrangements were being made for the opening ceremony. The wing had been designed by Gerald Horsley, uncle of Holst's pupil Nancy Gotch, and one of its features was that its rooms would be sound-proofed against noise from the outside (and passers-by isolated from the sounds made within). One day Holst asked his pupil Irene Bonnett to bring her violin and join himself and the High Mistress in a taxi trip to a factory in South London. On arrival, the party was taken to the firm's warehouse, where Irene was shut in a small room fitted with the proposed sound-proofing system, and told to play as loudly as she could, while Holst and Miss Gray listened outside. The experiment seems to have been a success, and the sound-proofing was soon installed in the new wing, ensuring that the new rooms would be a peaceful environment in which to work.

The inauguration of the new wing took place on 1 July 1913, the opening ceremony being conducted by the Revd E. S. Palmer, Chairman of the school's Governors. By way of testing the acoustics, the girls sang the 'Old Hundredth' Psalm, followed by several repetitions of the school song, after which the guests proceeded to the hall, where Holst conducted a performance of *The Vision of Dame Christian*. Although the Masque had been first performed only four years previously and was originally intended to be repeated once every ten years, it was felt that an exception should be made for this important occasion as the opening of the new wing was such a significant event in the musical life of the school. After the Revd Palmer's speech, in which he exhorted the girls not to neglect the English 'old masters' in their study of music, the Principal of the Royal Academy of Music, Alexander Mackenzie, spoke of Holst's achievements as a composer, and urged that all music study should be directed towards the goal of correct interpretation of the composer's intentions. He concluded with a call for patriotism in all the arts and in music in particular, 'for we have composers in England of whom we have every right to be proud'.[37] This was received with much applause, and in her reply Miss Gray expressed her thanks to all concerned in the new project, but above all to Adine O'Neill and Gustav Holst for their fine work at the school, without which the building would be of no use at all.

For his part, Holst was delighted with his sound-proof room in the new wing, which would for the first time enable him to compose music in peace and quiet, isolated from the distractions of the outside world. He came to regard his key to the room as one of his most precious possessions, and would go there to compose on Sundays and during the school holidays. He often spoke of the 'spell' which the room had for him, and would save up musical ideas which occurred to him during his teaching hours, knowing that he would have no difficulty in writing them down when the time came. The first work to be completed there was the *St Paul's Suite*, which he had been working on since the previous year and which he named after the school in gratitude for the new facilities. Many of his later works were written in the tranquillity of this room, and in 1931 Frances Ralph Gray said that it 'is now and I think always will be known as Mr Holst's room'.[38]

7

Astrology and the War
(1913–1916)

All in all, the year 1913 was an important one for events affecting Holst's life and career. In addition to the Balfour Gardiner concerts, which provided invaluable contact between the composer and his prospective public, the year saw the publication of Edmund Fellowes's edition of Thomas Morley's madrigals, of which Holst later declared: 'I think I can say that since this event I have never been quite the same man.'[1] His own interest in early music had begun just as he was emerging from the shades of Wagnerism, and the contrast of objective values of proportion and harmony against the Romantic obsession with the whims of the individual artist provided a refreshing stimulus for his own work. He realized that music had not made steady 'progress' over the centuries (in fact, he did not believe that *anything* in art had steadily progressed[2]), and therefore regarded earlier music not as a fossilized ritual or as simple escapism, but as a means of rediscovering an English heritage which had been obscured by European influences since the death of Purcell, to provide that vital element of regeneration essential to the healthy development of any art. He was however not averse to Germanic influences as such, and was always ready to learn from any composer of the past, once remarking to the critic Sydney Grew, apropos of Beethoven: 'I can always learn something fresh from the Fourth Symphony'.[3] Although he himself had edited some sixteenth-century pieces for publication, including *How Merrily We Live* by Michael Este and Byrd's *Benedictus*, Holst regarded himself as an amateur in the field of musicological research, and was glad to be able to leave such work in the hands of experts such as Fellowes, who devoted his entire career to this task.

Another influential factor was the return to London of

Diaghilev's Ballets Russes for two seasons: the first from 4 February to 7 March 1913 at Covent Garden, and the second from 25 June to 25 July at the Theatre Royal, Drury Lane—the last performance there marking the 100th appearance of the company in London. For the opening night of the February season, Diaghilev had decided that the British public was now ready for more advanced music, and therefore programmed *Petrushka*, which had received its première in Paris in June 1911. At this time, the company was also hard at work on the choreography for *The Rite of Spring*, which was to receive its première in Paris at the end of May. The Ballets Russes arrived in London six weeks early for their first London season of the year, and spent this time rehearsing *The Rite of Spring* at the Aldwych Theatre, which had been placed at their disposal by Thomas Beecham. As Holst's friend Edwin Evans was in close contact with the Diaghilev company during its visits to London, it is more than likely that Holst knew about these rehearsals, and may well have looked in at the theatre, where the dancers could be seen rehearsing to piano accompaniment. In due course the work received its notorious first performance in Paris on 29 May, and was given in England for the first time on 11 July.

The London audience had heard all about the scandal of the Paris première and was eager to hear the new work; Diaghilev asked Edwin Evans to give an introductory talk before the performance, but the audience became restive and Evans was obliged to withdraw so that the ballet could begin. Although the English audience naturally did not emulate the French by staging a riot in the theatre, it was none the less baffled and disconcerted by the music. Richard Capell wrote: 'Its savagery is horrific ... the most outlandish cries and groans ... To hear this *Festival of Spring* is the most curious of experiences; but one cannot believe one would ever get it to yield a moment's actual pleasure,'[4] while the *Musical Times* commented: 'The music baffles verbal description. To say that much of it is hideous as sound is a mild description. There is certainly an impelling rhythm traceable. Practically it has no relation to music at all as most of us understand the word.'[5] For Holst, however, Stravinsky's music opened up a whole new world of sound; particularly the rhythms of *The Rite of Spring* and the orchestral colour of *The Firebird* and *Petrushka*, and these performances were doubtless a major influence in his decision to compose a large-scale orchestral work of his own.

During the summer of 1913, Holst moved home to 10 Luxemburg Gardens, Brook Green, just round the corner from St Paul's Girls' School, and thus very close to his sound-proof room. The house on the Barnes riverfront was given up with reluctance, as Isobel had become fond of it, but the river air had affected Holst's throat so much that he had experienced difficulty in speaking, and they therefore regretfully decided to move to a more healthy spot.

In the autumn the usual round of daytime teaching and evening classes began once again; the Morley College choir and orchestral classes being larger than ever, 'and also moderately punctual'.[6] W. G. Whittaker wrote from Newcastle to tell Holst about his choir's performance of the First Group of *Choral Hymns from the Rig Veda* and that the Armstrong College choir had started to learn *The Cloud Messenger*. There were professional performances, too: on 17 November *A Somerset Rhapsody* was performed at the Queen's Hall, and three days later Holst conducted the Finale of *Beni Mora* in a Royal Philharmonic Society concert in the same hall. On 15 December he was in Birmingham, where he conducted *Beni Mora* at the Birmingham and Midland Institute, and on the following day was back in London for a concert of carols and Christmas music in Westminster Cathedral Hall, where he conducted the cathedral choir in the third and fourth of the *Four Old English Carols*.

At the end of this busy term he decided to refresh his mind by going on a five-day walking tour in Essex just after Christmas, despite the wintry weather. He took a train to Colchester, and then set out on foot in a north-westerly direction, eventually arriving at Thaxted, a place which was subsequently to have an important influence on his life and work. He was impressed by the peaceful atmosphere and astonished at the fifteenth-century Guildhall and other old buildings clustered along the main street, but above all by the magnificent medieval church, towering above the houses at the top of the hill, more like a cathedral than a humble parish church; a public demonstration of the town's medieval prosperity based on a flourishing cutlery trade. He stayed overnight at the Enterprise in Town Street, and after looking round once again concluded that he liked the place so much that he would like to live there. A few months later, he heard that a cottage belonging to the writer S. L. Bensusan was to let at Monk Street, two miles south of Thaxted at the top of a hill on the Dunmow road. Holst and Isobel went to see it, arriving in the middle of a rainstorm, and knew immediately that it was the right place for them and decided to rent it straight away. Built in the seventeenth century, the cottage had a thatched roof, old beams, open fireplaces, and a view across the fields towards the spire of Thaxted Church in the distance. Water had to be drawn from a hand-pump in the garden, at which all three members of the family took their turn. Imogen Holst recalled that as a child she saw the farmer in a nearby field sowing the seeds broadcast, and she remembered the farm horses moving leisurely along the lanes and the carrier's cart which called every Wednesday afternoon. It was in these peaceful surroundings that Holst was to begin work on *The Planets*, although most of the suite was composed in his sound-proof room at St Paul's Girls' School. The cottage was the Holst's family home until 1917, but no trace of it now remains, as it was burnt down some years later, and road-widening works have obliterated all traces of the garden.

On 17 January 1914 Schoenberg's *Five Pieces for Orchestra* were once again performed at the Queen's Hall, this time conducted by the composer himself, who was making his first appearance in London. Perhaps mindful of the laughter which had greeted the work at its London première in 1912, he insisted that the programme should carry the statement: 'Herr Arnold Schoenberg has promised his co-operation at today's concert on condition that during the performance of his orchestral pieces perfect silence is maintained.'[7] An 'immense audience' turned out, doubtless attracted by the notoriety of the first performance, and the concert was described by the musical press as a 'great sensation'.[8] Among the critics, some sensed that genuine creativity lurked behind the unfamiliarity of the style; Ernest Newman wrote that 'There are some strangely beautiful things in these Five Orchestral Pieces ... some fumbling, with ideas only half realised ...'[9] When the performance was over, Schoenberg received polite applause, but the audience demonstrated its true feelings by giving Henry Wood an ovation when he returned to the platform to conduct the remainder of the programme.

There is no doubt that the *Five Pieces* made a great impression on Holst, and provided one of the impulses that were to spark off the creation of *The Planets*, but he was never one to take things too seriously, and soon had an opportunity to lampoon the modernist school in a production at Morley College. On 21 March, the music students held their annual 'Tea and Social', for which Holst concocted a *Futuristic Tone-Poem in H* for two voices and orchestra. The work was introduced by James Brown (later to become a violin teacher at the College) who explained that the composer's intention was to express the 'somethingness of something', and that the instruments called for included a 'Contrabass macaroon', a 'Babyphone (appealling specially to mothers)', a 'Tubular Pneumatic Buzzaphone', together with 'a quartet of muted scoops' and a pair of 'Te(a)tra(y) Chords especially imported from Lyons in the South of France'. A special feature of the work would be the use of the seventeenth inversion of the Metropolitan and District Sixth, and Holst would be obliged to conduct with two batons, one for the strings and one for the wind, as one section would be playing in seven and the other in nine beats to the bar. Later on the time would be $\frac{9.666}{16}$ and $\frac{X-Y}{\text{n-th}}$ for the two sections respectively.

The performance lasted twelve and a half minutes, 'during which all the changes were rung on, musical and otherwise, mostly otherwise ... it was *fff*, *ppp*, and *mmm*, ad lib ...', according to the *Morley College Magazine*.[10] In the Grand Finale, Percival Poole led the singing with the aid of a gramophone trumpet, the audience joining in with 'Everybody's doing it, doing it, doing it', bringing the work to a grand climax. The audience clamoured for the composer, but in vain. Eventually attribution of authorship was decided by ballot, and Norman Ramsden stepped forward to acknowledge the applause. Besides the innovative two-baton technique, this work seems to have anticipated various twentieth-century trends, including Da-Daism, Expressionism, the Darmstadt school, and Maoist communal composition, but to the great regret of musicologists no written material for the *Futuristic Tone-Poem* now survives (if indeed there ever was any).

On a more serious level, two important first performances of Holst's works took place during the month; the *Hymn to Dionysus* was performed at the Queen's Hall on 10 March by the Oriana Madrigal Society and the Queen's Hall Orchestra conducted by Holst himself, and in the same hall on 18 March the Edward Mason Choir and New Symphony Orchestra gave the first performance of the Fourth Group of *Choral Hymns from the Rig Veda*.

During the first few months of 1914 Holst had been working on *A Dirge for Two Veterans* for male voices, brass and percussion; a setting of words by Walt Whitman, which he may have come across through Vaughan Williams, who had set them himself in 1911, later using this setting as a movement of his cantata *Dona Nobis Pacem* (Vaughan Williams may in turn have discovered the words through a setting by his Cambridge teacher Charles Wood, performed at the Leeds Festival in 1902). But Holst's version is in his own characteristic style, with restrained intensity of feeling—the 'sad procession' was to feature in several of his later works, and the trumpet calls are a foretaste of the violence which was to erupt in *Mars*. The contract for publication of the *Dirge* is dated 27 June 1914, showing that the work was composed before the outbreak of the First World War, but a premonition of war was in the air; a gigantic arms race was reaching its climax, and it was clear that it would only be a matter of time before Europe exploded into violence.

Holst now decided that the time had come to begin work on his large-scale orchestral suite, to which he subsequently gave the title *The Planets* (at first it was called *Seven Pieces for Large Orchestra*, in emulation of Schoenberg's title). In this suite many different strands of Holst's style, interests and influences were drawn together, to produce a work which though described by one critic as the 'English *Sacre du Printemps*',[11] might just as well have been called the 'English

Five Pieces for Orchestra', for there is as much evidence of Schoenberg as there is of Stravinsky in the music. It was natural that Stravinsky's rhythmic verve and brilliant orchestration should have an immediate effect on a fellow composer, but at first sight Holst and Schoenberg would seem to belong to completely different worlds. Although born within a few days of each other, their careers had followed quite different paths; the European intellectual seemingly having little in common with the English schoolmaster. Both composers were dedicated to high standards of music-making, but Holst was also the champion of the amateur performer, declaring: 'If something is worth doing, it is worth doing badly!',[12] an attitude which would doubtless have been anathema to Schoenberg, the founder of the élitist Society for Private Musical Performances. Schoenberg's attitudes may have been anathema to Holst, but the high level of practical musicianship and strong creative imagination evident in his music impressed Holst, who responded to these qualities in Schoenberg's work. He realized that Schoenberg's themes would never be whistled by the man-in-the-street, but he incorporated some of Schoenberg's ideas into his own work, adding his individual capacity for direct communication, and thus produced in *The Planets* a far more accessible work than the *Five Pieces*, transmuting the influence so that the result is immediately recognizable as English in character and individually Holstian in style.

The idea of *The Planets* had been gestating for a while, and Holst later recalled: 'That work, whether it's good or bad, grew in my mind slowly—like a baby in a woman's womb ... For two years I had the intention of composing that cycle, and during those two years it seemed of itself more and more definitely to be taking form.'[13] Although astrology was his starting point, he arranged the order of movements to suit himself, ignoring some important astrological factors such as the influence of the sun and the moon, and attributing certain non-astrological qualities to each planet. Nor is the order of movements the same as that of the planets' orbits round the sun; his only criterion being that of maximum musical effectiveness. Holst himself described the work as 'a series of mood pictures', acting as 'foils to one another', with 'very little contrast in any one of them',[14] implying that the expressive mood of each is complete, without the development and conflict of themes of different character as may be found in conventional sonata form. In fact Holst used the astrological connotations of the planets simply to give the mood of each movement, and then structured the resulting musical material according to his own principles. Just before commencing work on the suite he wrote: 'As a rule I only study things which suggest music to me. That's why I worried at Sanskrit. Then recently the character of each planet suggested lots to me, and I have been studying astrology fairly closely. It's a pity we make such a fuss about these things. On one side there is nothing but abuse and ridicule, with the natural result that when one is brought face to face with over-whelming proofs there is a danger of going to the other extreme. Whereas, of course, everything in this world . . . is just one big miracle. Or rather, the universe itself is one'.[15]

Some of the characteristics attributed to the planets by Holst may have been suggested by Alan Leo's booklet *What is a Horoscope?*,[16] which he was reading at this time. Leo describes those born under the influence of Mars as being independent, confident, ambitious, and enterprising, skilful in action, 'headstrong and at times too forceful', while Venus awakens the 'affectional and emotional side of her subjects, giving them a keen appreciation of art and beauty'. Mercury, the 'winged messenger of the gods' gives 'adaptability, fertility of resource, and the ability to use the mind in various ways'; Jupiter brings 'an abundance of life and vitality—those born under its influence are cheery and hopeful in disposition, and possess a noble and generous spirit', while Saturn 'makes the progress through life slow and steady—those under its influence will be more plodding and persevering than brilliant and active . . .'. 'Uranus will incline its subjects towards the metaphysical and occult side of life, producing 'eccentric, strange, and erratic' reactions: 'Sudden and unexpected events will enter into their lives, and they should always be prepared for the unexpected.' Lastly, Neptune has a great influence over psychic tendencies, helping mediums and other sensitive people to transcend mundane distractions and 'tune-in' to vibrations from another world.

Holst began work on *Mars* around May 1914, working partly in the rural peace of the cottage near Thaxted, and partly in the sound-proof room at St Paul's Girls' School, neither location giving any indication of the intensity of violence to be found in the music. The most striking feature of this first movement is of course its rhythm, or rather, its metre; by using five beats to a bar Holst achieved a feeling of relentless impetus, as if a 6/4 metre had been cut short by one beat in order to hurry on impatiently from one bar to the next. He had used the same metre for similar reasons in the *Battle Hymn* of the First Group of *Choral Hymns from the Rig Veda* with a rhythm based mainly on crotchet beats, and in *To Agni* in the Second Group he enhanced the effect by incorporating quavers into the rhythm. But in *Mars* this idea is considerably intensified by the use of triplets, deriving from a phrase in *King Estmere* which also appears in a developed five-beat form in this movement. The rhythmic 'col legno' effect of the opening was first heard in *Beni Mora*, from which work some of the appoggiatura harmonies also derive, and trumpet calls echo those previously heard in *The Mystic Trumpeter*, *A Somerset Rhapsody*, and *The Pageant of London*. Harmonic dissonances abound, often resulting from clashes between moving chords and static pedal-points, recalling a similar effect at the end of Stravinsky's *Firebird*. Although battle music had been written before, notably by Richard Strauss in *Ein Heldenleben*, it had never expressed such violence and sheer terror; Holst's intention being to portray the reality of warfare rather than glorify deeds of heroism. The quiet music at the beginning of the movement is tense with apprehensive menace, whose expression becomes more and more urgent, finally exploding into the colossal chords of the coda. He thus succeeded in evoking a feeling of horror as must seize any soldier on realizing the overwhelming nature of the forces advancing against him, and the probability of his own imminent death. Holst was insistent that *Mars* should be performed at a quick tempo, faster than a normal march,[17] to give an enhanced impression of inhuman and mechanical forces, lurching forward relentlessly and unstoppable; an uncanny premonition of the mechanized warfare of the later twentieth century.

At the time that *Mars*, which has been called 'the most ferocious piece of music in existence',[18] was emerging from the mind of its creator, Holst's day-to-day life went on much as usual. On 6 May his part-song *The Homecoming* was performed by male-voice choirs competing in the Morecambe Festival, and on 13 June Morley College students gave a performance of Charles Burke's cantata *St Patrick's Breastplate* under Holst's direction. Burke was an Irishman domiciled in London who had taken up music late in life as a student at Morley College, and had become a well-known figure in the College's musical activities. The performance of his composition must have given him a special thrill, especially as repeat performances were called for, including one given by the Bach Choir at the Queen's Hall, and the work was also subsequently published at Holst's instigation.

On 10 July Holst conducted *Carnival* from his *Suite de Ballet* in a Patron's Fund concert at the Queen's Hall, and on 18 July the Morley College students once more visited St Paul's Girls' School for an end-of-term garden party and concert evening, during which the *Futuristic Tone-Poem in H* received its second and final performance, being played for the most part in total darkness.

And then, just as Holst was finishing the first sketch of *Mars*, the inevitable became reality and Europe was plunged into war. At first the effect on music in Britain was considerable, and in retrospect, ludicrous. All Germanic music was immediately banned: at the Queen's Hall Promenade concert on 15 August the national anthems of Britain and her allies were played, followed by a programme in which Tchaikovsky's *Capriccio Italien* had been hastily substituted for Strauss's *Don Juan*, and an all-Wagner evening was replaced at the last moment by a Franco-Russian programme, the management fearing a riot by patriotic audiences. Thomas Beecham and Landon Ronald drew up a programme of promenade concerts at the Albert Hall 'from which there would be a complete absence of Teutonic music',[19] and large numbers of German musicians vanished from orchestras overnight, to be replaced by their British counterparts who rapidly claimed the places they considered rightfully theirs. Various silly schemes were proposed, such as banning all German music written after the formation of the Empire in 1870 (thus dividing Brahms's works into admirable and reprehensible), and there was an outcry against choral societies performing works by German composers until it was realized that *The Messiah* and *Elijah* would no longer be heard. The French evaded the *Messiah* problem by claiming that Handel should really be regarded as an English musician.

The effect of all this on Holst was less immediate. Like Vaughan Williams, who had enlisted in the Royal Army Medical Corps, he volunteered for military service, but was rejected after a cursory medical inspection revealed his shortsightedness, neuritic right hand, and bad digestion. Disappointed by this rebuff, he continued with his usual routine, composing at weekends and in the holidays, often in the cottage in Essex. Even here he was not left entirely untouched by the prevailing war fever, for the people of Thaxted soon became suspicious of this 'Von Holst' in their midst, and rumours began to circulate that he was in fact a German agent, using his musical activities as a cover for espionage. At the outbreak of war, spy hysteria swept through all the belligerent countries: in Britain anyone with German connections was suspected of treachery, and sometimes feelings got out of hand with mobs of rioters breaking the windows of shopkeepers of German origin or thought to be sympathetic to the enemy. German grocers were suspected of poisoning food, and barbers of cutting throats; it is said that even Dachshund dogs were kicked in the streets.

In such an atmosphere it is no wonder that suspicion fell upon Holst, and in due course he was reported to the Thaxted police as being someone whose activities were worthy of investigation. The police, however, could find no evidence against him, and he was therefore allowed to continue his peaceful life and soon became friendly with many of the villagers, who overcame their prejudices sufficiently as to refer to him as 'our Mr Von'.[20] Holst himself considered that 'the only German thing about me is my upspringing hair',[21] and later recalled that 'the time I was writing *The Planets* and the *Hymn of Jesus* was the happiest period of composition that I've had',[22] so that these allegations could not have worried him unduly.

One of the first friends he made in Thaxted was the vicar, Conrad Noel (son of the Victorian poet Roden Noel), a socialist and neo-medievalist, who had held the living there since 1910. Noel was gifted with limitless energy; his sermons were brilliant, and with infectious enthusiasm he encouraged the restoration of ancient buildings and the revival of folk-dancing and of music in church ceremonies. One Sunday morning Holst went to church, where he saw the people's procession, led by a small child holding a bunch of flowers on which perched a large bumble-bee. He was much intrigued by this sight, by the procession, and the singing, and after the service spoke to Noel and offered to help with training the choir. Noel already knew of Holst, and had been hoping that he might help with the church music, so that the offer was quickly accepted and it was agreed that Holst would assist by playing the organ and conducting the choir. To this voluntary task he brought his usual enthusiasm and insistence on the highest standards, even going so far as to arrange professional training in London for one of the singers, Lily Harvey, who worked at the sweet factory and was gifted with a voice of exceptional quality.

According to Clifford Bax, at this time Holst was feeling rather tired of life, having struggled at composition for years with little encouragement. But Holst was in fact in the midst of one of his greatest creations, which was to bring him success far beyond what he himself might have dreamed possible, bearing in mind his belief that success was one of the worst things that could happen to a creative artist. In the autumn of 1914, in an atmosphere of depressing news from the battle-fronts, and uncertainty and worry uppermost in many people's minds, he began work on *Venus* and *Jupiter*; the former one of the most sublime evocations of peace in music, and the latter a robust expression of unselfconcious jollity.

The opening bars of *Venus* are identical to the beginning of Holst's song *A Vigil of Pentecost* to words by Alice M. Buckton, which he wrote at about this time. Composers have often used smaller forms such as songs and piano pieces to experiment with ideas before using them in larger works, and Holst was no exception. He also thought nothing of making use of other composers' ideas if they could be turned to his own purposes, and in *Venus* there is some affinity with the 'Ronde des Princesses' in Stravinsky's *Firebird*, an adaptation of the celesta passage from the second of Schoenberg's *Five Pieces for Orchestra*, and a characteristic pulsating chordal effect deriving from the end of Vaughan Williams's *Sea Symphony*. There are also echoes of some of Holst's own earlier works, such as alternating chords from *The Mystic Trumpeter* of 1904 and material from the more recent *Invocation* for cello and orchestra. Apart from the horns, the brass remain silent during this movement, but Holst used all the remaining colours of his orchestral palette to convey a mood of resigned peacefulness, tinged with languid sensuality and sweet nostalgia.

Although *Jupiter* was to become the fourth movement of *The Planets*, it was in fact written immediately after *Venus*. It opens with vigorous figuration reminiscent of the bustling activity of the opening of *Petrushka*, with a theme whose syncopated rhythms are similar to those of the 'Infernal Dance' in *The Firebird*, and a linking phrase in rising fourths derived from the discarded *Phantastes Suite*. For the middle section, Holst retained the motivic shapes of his opening material, but changed the mood from jollity to relaxed self-satisfaction, producing a feeling similar to that of 'Nimrod' in Elgar's *Variations*, a work which had affected him deeply. He later wrote: '1880 is usually given as the date of the "modern Renaissance" in English music. For me it began about twenty years later when I first knew Elgar's *Enigma Variations*. I felt that here was music the like of which had not appeared in this country since Purcell's death.'[23] This section of *Jupiter* might therefore be considered as Holst's repayment of his musical debt to Elgar.

Because of the exigencies of life in wartime London, there was little in the way of professional performance of Holst's music at this time. Life continued at school, Thaxted, and Morley College much as before, except that an increasing number of his adult pupils were volunteering for the services. Holst made a small contribution of his own to the war effort by writing some incidental music for a production of John Masefield's *Philip the King*, performed on 5 November 1914 at the Royal Opera House, Covent Garden, in aid of 'The Arts Fund for the

Relief of Members of the Artistic Professions in Distress owing to the War'. The play was produced by Granville Barker, with Holst conducting his own music, but the score and parts of this seem to have disappeared, and all that remains are a few remarks jotted in his pocket notebook for the period.

1915 opened in an atmosphere of gloom and despondency. The war which everyone thought would be 'over by Christmas' was still dragging on, and it was becoming apparent that there would be a long and bitter struggle before the outcome would be resolved. Although, like everyone else, Holst was considerably worried by these international events, he still managed to devote himself to mundane matters such as the replacement of a faulty piano at Morley College.

The first work which he wrote that year was a setting of the *Nunc Dimittis* for unaccompanied eight-part mixed chorus, performed in Westminster Cathedral on Easter Sunday (4 April) by the cathedral choir conducted by Richard R. Terry. Although the work begins with a typically Holstian build-up of intervals, producing a sustained, resonant chord, the music suddenly changes to Renaissance style, with chordal, unison, and imitative passages; a *tour de force* of pastiche, with occasional idiosyncratic melodic and harmonic touches. The original manuscript was lost after the first performance, but a part-autograph copy survived and was used as the basis of the first published edition issued by Novello in 1979, sixty-four years after the work's completion.

After this short piece, Holst returned to *The Planets*, completing *Saturn*, *Uranus*, and *Neptune* during the year. For the basic material of *Saturn*, he again turned to a previous work, this time the female-voice part-song *Dirge and Hymeneal* to words by Thomas Lovell Beddoes, which he had written earlier in the year. (Having used the *Dirge* in this way, he then discarded it, but it is in fact a worthwhile composition in its own right, and a characteristic example of his choral style.) Taking the original chords of the part-song, Holst made a much more effective and evocative version for *Saturn* by changing their modality and shifting their rhythmic placing, to produce a syncopated 'breathing' effect. Another phrase from the part-song is given added character by emphasizing its off-beats (melodically altered to contrary motion) and starting it halfway through the bar, a violent disorientation which contrasts vividly with the measured progress of the slow procession which it interrupts. A one-bar phrase derived from *King Estmere* also appears, as a contrast to the opening material. The ostinato alternation of two unresolved chords, which Holst uses here to suggest the inevitable passage of time and the process of ageing, also appears in the sixth of Schoenberg's *Kleine Klavierstücke*, which Holst may have heard before writing this music, and it is interesting that Schoenberg's chords were later used unaltered by Matyas Seiber in his cantata *Ulysses* to suggest the immensity of space; infinity of time and space being ultimately the same in the language of relativity.

An alternative explanation of the origin of the ostinato chords came from Holst's pupil Dorothy Callard, who recalled his insistence that she should visit Durham Cathedral while on holiday, as he had done himself, where she heard two bells being tolled before services by 'two very old men in black gowns, very slow and solemn', the sound echoing down the narrow streets near the cathedral, from which she believed Holst may have got the idea of old age associated with tolling chords.[24]

While Holst was putting the finishing touches to *Saturn* in his sound-proof room at St Paul's, two pupils, Irene Bonnett and Nancy Gotch, arrived for a harmony lesson. Beckoning them in, he suggested that instead of doing harmony, they should all sit at the grand piano and read through the large pencilled score. The girls felt honoured to have participated in this first-ever performance of *Saturn*, but Holst himself seemed unconcerned by the importance of the occasion: 'The composer sat between us and talked about it now and again; he never spoke of it as his Creation but more as if it were something that he had happened to write down.'[25] On another occasion in the same room, Nancy Gotch and Dorothy Ramsbottom turned the pages for Nora Day and Vally Lasker, while Holst conducted them in the first try-through of the two-piano version of *Mars*.

Holst considereded *Saturn* to be the best movement of *The Planets*, and there is no doubt that it is a powerful expression of desolate and piercing emotion, carefully controlled at first,

building up to a climax of violent intensity. Although subtitled
'The Bringer of Old Age', the feelings of panic and fear
expressed in this movement may have originated in Holst's
childhood experiences of asthmatic attacks, during which each
breath might well have been his last. Writing to Adrian Boult
after the first performance, Holst explained: 'In the opening
some intruments are quite "dead". Others have$<>$. Make
the latter as emotional as possible . . . The 4 flute tune (Tempo
I) was soft enough but try and get the timp, harps, and basses
also down to nothing. This part must begin from another world
and gradually overwhelm this one. That is the nearest verbal
suggestion I can give you.'[26] So successful was he in evoking
emotion in this movement, that according to R. O. Morris, at
an early performance at the Queen's Hall, 'Quite a number of
old ladies in our neighbourhood were seen to rise from their
seat, stagger for an instant, and then feel their way, feebly but
with evident determination, towards the exit.'[27] If these ladies
had managed to sit through the movement, they might well
have been reassured by the peace and tranquility of its ending
(which despite its affinity with the 'dawn' music in *Daphnis et
Chloé* is a transformed presentation of thematic material from
earlier in the movement).

One Sunday evening towards the end of August, after an
entire day composing alone in his room at St Paul's, Holst
wrote to Valley Lasker: 'I've nearly done a rough sketch of
The Rough Sketch for ♅ [*Uranus*]. ♆ [*Neptune*] is still in the
clouds . . . It is 9 PM and I've been at school 12 hours having a
heavenly time getting all my meals and making a hell of a mess
generally.'[28] *Uranus* begins with a tremendous four-note brass
motif, reminiscent of the chords announcing the fearsome
appearance of Pân in Ravel's *Daphnis et Chloé*, but despite
this, and a passing resemblance to the Berlioz of the *Symphonie
fantastique*, the main influence on the movement is clearly
that of Dukas's *The Sorcerer's Apprentice*, which was first
performed in London in 1899 and was doubtless well known to
Holst. After a series of merry pranks, the spell is undone by a
'magic' chord following a loud climax, probably deriving from
the similar effect at the end of the Infernal Dance in
Stravinsky's *Firebird* (also appearing in Percy Grainger's
setting of the folk-song *Lord Melbourne*), and the magician

disappears in a whiff of smoke as the sonic impetus of the movement diminishes from *fff* to *ppp* in the space of a few bars.

In the final movement, *Neptune*, the absence of definite thematic material and the reliance on shifting tone-colours recall the changing textures of *Farben*, the third of Schoenberg's *Five Pieces*, while its opening owes something to the ebb and flow of the beginning of the second part of *The Rite of Spring*; a detail such as the sustained open-position minor triad for trombones would have caught Holst's trombonist's ear and lodged in his subconscious until he was ready to to use it. Although this movement undoubtedly demonstrates the influence of Schoenberg and Stravinsky, the falling minor third motif for flutes had in fact appeared long before in Holst's work, notably in *The Mystic Trumpeter* of 1904 (and was also to recur in other later compositions, such as *The Hymn of Jesus* and the *First Choral Symphony*). To his already large orchestral forces, Holst added a female voice choir for this movement, providing an unusual and unexpected tone-colour unobtainable from the orchestral instruments alone. Although Debussy had included a wordless female chorus in his *Sirènes* (and Ravel a mixed chorus in *Daphnis et Chloé*), the use of such a choir was still unusual in symphonic music, but was a natural device to someone who spent his days teaching in a girls' school. Holst's years of experience of the capabilities of girls' voices enabled him to write the choral parts with assurance, even though the notation of the chords may seem at first sight to be rather complex (writing in 1920, Alfred Kalisch described them as presenting 'almost superhuman difficulty to the female chorus'[29]). At the end of the movement the sound fades gradually into the distance, either by a door being closed between the choir and the hall, or by the singers walking slowly away down a corridor; a 'fade-out' effect which Holst had previously used in the *Songs from 'The Princess'*, and nowadays often heard in broadcasts and recordings, but totally original in those pre-electronic days.

In *Neptune*, Holst's aim was to depict in music the mystery and wonder of outer space, Neptune then being the furthest known planet of the Solar system. He conveyed its remoteness by keeping the dynamics *pp* throughout, ending in total silence; a silence which is as much part of the music as the preceding notes. This transcendental evocation of the vastness of space is an evocative example of the power which music has to express concepts beyond the comprehension of the rational mind, and in later years, when he read James Jean's book *The Mysterious Universe,* Holst realized with excitement that the ideas which were put forward in scientific terms were exactly the same as those which he had been trying to express in music many years before.

Having completed six movements of *The Planets,* Holst turned to another work before composing the remaining movement, *Mercury.* The Japanese dancer Michio Ito was working at London's Coliseum Theatre at this time, and had asked Holst to write a work based on ancient Japanese themes. The result was the *Japanese Suite;* four brief dances with a prelude and interlude, founded on tunes whistled to Holst by the dancer. Despite its provenance, the Suite has little in common with traditional Japanese music, and is more reminiscent of the Mendelssohn of the *Hebrides* overture, with occasional idiosyncratic touches of harmony. In the *Dance of the Marionette* there is much use of the glockenspiel and interplay between 6/8 and 3/4 metres, similar to those subsequently used in *Mercury* (although here in a slower, more laboured form) and it is clear that Holst used the *Japanese Suite* as a proving-ground for these ideas. It is uncertain whether the Suite was actually used for its intended purpose in the theatre, but it subsequently became the first of Holst's works to be heard at a Promenade concert, although it was not widely performed thereafter.

The composition of a 'Japanese' suite by an English composer (who had previously written the 'Oriental' suite *Beni Mora*) prompts a definition of genuine nationalism in music, a matter which was discussed by *The Times* of 10 July 1915 in a review of Elgar's *Polonia.* As a result of this article, the *Musical Herald* sounded out the opinions of several composers by asking the question: 'Do you, as a British composer, think that our wide sympathies check our national spirit in composition?' Holst replied evasively: 'It is useless to approach the question without an entire absence of prejudice and a delicate balance of artistic values.' He declared that 'In art everthing matters except the subject,' and suggested that composers show their own nationality more when their range of subject matter is broader: 'When this breadth of outlook is most apparent in English history—as in the 16th century—English music flourishes. Contrast the Elizabethan, a brilliant linguist, poet and musician, with the Englishman of the 18th century. No wonder there is so much difference between the madrigal and the glee.'[30] (Ironically, the same issue of the magazine carried advertisements for some of the most narrow-minded children's songs, such as *Knit, Knit, Knit* for girls, and *Our Khaki Daddy* for infants, described as 'a certain success at school concerts'.)

In addition to composing and arranging, Holst had been busy as usual with teaching, and also found time to attend a Christmas vacation conference on musical education, to which he contributed an illustrated talk on 'Certain possibilities of the School orchestra'. He was as yet inexperienced as a lecturer, and wrote to Whittaker: 'I'm down to speak on school orchestras and I wish I wasn't. It will probably do *me* good but I'm doubtful about the audience. Besides which I object to things doing me good in the Xmas holidays.'[31] In the middle of the conference he wrote: 'I'm going to every meeting of this conference and feel ill in consequence!'.[32]

During the first few months of 1916, Holst returned to *The Planets*, finishing *Mercury* and thus completing the suite. This movement, subtitled 'The Winged Messenger', was described by R. O. Morris as 'a mere activity, whose character is not defined; we know nothing of him except the swiftness of his movement'.[33] And although Morris then went on to denigrate the movement by claiming that such a simple concept was 'not worth while putting into music, because (given a technique like Mr Holst's) it is too easy', there is no doubt that the piece succeeds because of its sheer panache in expressing the god's fleet-footedness in purely musical terms. The bitonal side-slipping of E major and B flat major triads, coupled with alternating metres of 3/4 and 6/8 produce an ever-changing image of movement, sometimes hurrying, sometimes relaxed and free-wheeling, but always moving swiftly forwards towards an ever-receding horizon. The idea of alternating metres may have stemmed from Holst's acquaintance with Fellowes's editions of English madrigals, which abound in cross-rhythms and other more complex relationships, but he took this basic technique and via his experimentation in the *Japanese Suite*, transformed it into a much faster, fleeting context, in keeping with the character he wished to portray in music.

The work on which Holst had laboured for nearly two years had now outgrown the normal dimensions of a suite, and had become a cycle of seven tone-poems in which conventional symphonic procedures had been replaced by his own individual methods of dealing with the problems of large-scale musical form. According to Clifford Bax, Holst immediately lost interest in astrology once *The Planets* had been completed, but he was referring to inspiration for musical composition, as Holst continued to cast horoscopes for his friends; a 'weakness' from which he derived considerable pleasure.

8

Music at Thaxted
(1916–1917)

Having put an enormous amount of creative energy into the composition of one of the great masterpieces of twentieth-century orchestral music, Holst turned to smaller forms such as part-songs and folk-song arrangements, but in the very first work of this kind written in 1916 he demonstrated that masterpieces can be written on a small scale as well as for large forces. In Thaxted one Sunday, instead of preaching a sermon, Conrad Noel read out from the pulpit a medieval poem taken from William Sandy's collection *Christmas Carols, Ancient and Modern*, published in 1833. The book had been bought at a second-hand stall in a London street market by Robert Woodifield and brought to Thaxted, whereupon Conrad Noel copied out the words of this poem and pinned them up in the church porch. On finding that the traditional tune associated with the words was rather dull, Holst decided to set the poem himself for unaccompanied mixed voices, and the result was *This Have I Done for My True Love* ('Tomorrow Shall Be My Dancing Day') which he considered to be his best part-song. The poem evokes the primitive association between dancing and religious rites (which was to bear further fruit the following year in *The Hymn of Jesus*), and in order to emphasize the folk-origins of this idea, Holst wrote a modal melody of such effective simplicity that many people assumed that he had simply arranged an existing folk-tune. When the piece was subsequently published, Holst sent a copy to Edwin Evans, with a letter saying: 'Please accept this—it's only a partsong but probably the best I've done. The tune is mine.'[1] Holst dedicated the piece to Conrad Noel, who was interested in the primitive origins of religion, and it is commemorated at Thaxted by an inscription on one of the church bells, which reads: 'I ring for the general dance'.

But not everyone shared Noel's enthusiasm for seeking the origins of Christianity in the religious rites of ancient times. Some time later, on hearing that the words of a poem about dancing were displayed in the porch of Thaxted Church, the diocesan bishop wrote to demand that they should be removed, and was only dissuaded by Noel pointing out that Holst's musical setting was sung throughout the land, including several of the great cathedrals. As late as 1951, when the Dorking Oriana Choir was preparing for the Leith Hill Festival, some of the singers complained about the words of Holst's part-song, objecting to the mention of dancing in association with religion. Vaughan Williams wrote to them: 'I am amazed . . . I had hoped that the killjoy and lugubrious view of religion which once obtained was now happily dead.' After citing several references to dancing in the Bible, he offered a compromise: 'I should advise all those who do not feel themselves worthy to sing the beautiful words of this carol to vocalise and to leave the words to those singers who have not this inhibition. But if they do this they will miss a great spiritual experience.'[2] For Holst and Noel, the attraction of the words was the forthright expression of joy through dancing and religious worship free from Puritanism; the word 'carol' itself originating in dancing and only later becoming specifically associated with Christmas.

W. G. Whittaker had assumed that the melody was a folk-song when he wrote to ask if he could include the part-song in a forthcoming concert, and Holst replied that as it was not in fact a traditional melody, he would arrange a real folk-song especially for the occasion. On 24 April he sent Whittaker his arrangement of 'The Seeds of Love' for unaccompanied chorus, explaining: 'I had given up all hope of writing anything for yr concert when this "came" all at once just 24 hours ago along with some more ideas for arranging folk songs.'[3] He was able to arrange some more songs during the Easter holidays, so that when Whittaker wrote to say that he was pleased with the first arrangement, Holst replied: 'So glad you like the folk song. And am also glad I did it because I went on and did 4½ more. The ½ being hung up until August.'[4] The remaining song was finished during the summer holiday, completing the set of *Six Choral Folksongs*, of which Holst dedicated the first three to

Whittaker and his singers and the remainder to Charles Kennedy Scott and the Oriana Madrigal Society. Of the melodies used, five had been collected by George B. Gardiner, the remaining one being taken from Baring Gould's *Songs of the West*.

The first performance of *The Seeds of Love* was given in Newcastle on Saturday 27 May 1916 by the Newcastle-upon-Tyne Bach Choir conducted by W. G. Whittaker, the programme proudly announcing: 'Specially arranged by Mr Von Holst for this concert'. The *Six Choral Folksongs* are practicable but undistinguished arrangements, and Holst subsequently remarked: 'It's a limited form of art . . . when one works so long in a small form mannerisms are almost inevitable.'[5] Other arrangements which he made at this time included several for unaccompanied female voices, published under the title *Old Airs and Glees*. Holst chose as his literary collaborator Clifford Bax, who later recalled: 'He brought me two or three oblong old volumes of eighteenth-century "airs and glees", asking me to write new words for the old tunes. The existing words were inane or bawdy or in some foreign language.' Bax went on to describe his method of working: as he had no knowledge of music, he would scribble down nonsense words which fitted the musical phrases which Holst played. 'By this device we could make sure, for instance, of not placing a short or a thin vowel upon a high note. Then, with the nonsense to guide me, and feebly singing the air a dozen times (but to myself alone), I did my best to write words that should catch the mood of the music. Gustav . . . was enthusiastic about the results.'[6]

During the Spring term, both *The Cloud Messenger* and the Third Group of *Choral Hymns from the Rig Veda* had been performed in Newcastle at Armstrong College, and Whittaker reported to Holst: 'After another term's rehearsing of the Rig Veda set (it is the second time now that I have prepared them for performance) I feel that every word I said to you about them two or three years ago requires only to be underlined. The choir made faces over them at the beginning, but came to love them, and sang them tonight with tremendous enthusiasm. We had about 110 women in the choir, and a very sympathetic pianist, and we all thoroughly enjoyed them.'[7] The College magazine declared: 'One feels strongly that Von Holst follows his own bent in his own way; there is nothing in music like his particular utterance, and the sincerity and truth of it makes us feel that it can endure both time and criticism'.[8]

And then, at Whitsun, came the high spot of the year. The previous Christmas, Holst had invited a few of his Morley College pupils, including Lilian Twiselton and Christine Ratcliffe, to visit Thaxted to sing in the church, and he then had the idea of organizing a kind of festival in which a whole group of his pupils would participate. Conrad Noel seized upon this idea with enthusiasm, and together they set about making arrangements for the Morley music students and girls from St Paul's to visit Thaxted for the Whitsun weekend of 10–12 June, to make music and relax in the Essex countryside. For the Morley College students, this was a wonderful opportunity to escape from the pressures of wartime life in the capital, and for many of them it would be their only chance to get away from London. For the schoolgirls too, the opportunity to go away for a weekend of music making was an exciting prospect, although some of their parents were apprehensive about allowing their daughters to go on such a jaunt, especially as they had heard tales of 'high church' goings-on at Thaxted. Eventually, however, a sizeable group set off from London, arriving in Thaxted on the Friday evening and Saturday morning, loaded down with instrument cases of various shapes and sizes. Among the Morleyites was twenty-four-year-old Jack Putterill, who was later to become a curate and subsequently himself vicar of Thaxted, continuing the work begun by Conrad Noel.

The Morleyites lodged with families in the village, while the Paulinas were accommodated at the Vicarage, where they slept on the floor of a large room. The sounds of musical instruments and singing voices could be heard all over the village, and on the Saturday evening everyone assembled in the church to join the local singers in a long rehearsal of the music which was to be performed the following day. The visitors were surprised by the size and lightness of the building, and were even more pleased when they discovered that the acoustics were excellent for choral music.

Whit Sunday dawned grey and showery; by 9.45 a.m. the choir

and orchestra were in their places in the Becket chapel, almost hidden from the congregation by a carved screen. Although the sky was cloudy, occasional shafts of sunlight shone down through the windows into the large airy spaces of the church, casting golden patches of light on to the pillars and hangings. Here and there on the stone floor stood large earthenware jars filled with larkspurs, peonies and beech boughs, and high up under the timber roof swallows darted in and out of clouds of blue incense. It was a scene which made a strong impression on all present, and remained in their memories for many years to come. The music was performed as part of the church service, and included works by Purcell, Vittoria, Lassus, and Palestrina, together with the Bach Mass in A which the Morley students had performed in London the previous week. As applause in church was disapproved of in those days, the congregation was denied the opportunity of expressing its appreciation, but the *Morley College Magazine* later reported that 'Both choir and orchestra felt satisfied when at the end they saw their conductor's face.'[9] The afternoon was free time, devoted to spontaneous music-making; then at 7 p.m., after Evensong, the whole programme of music was repeated in the church before a large congregation. On the Whit Monday it rained all day, but this did not dampen the enthusiasm of the participants. At 11 a.m. there was an exact repetition of the previous day's service, and in the afternoon Isobel kept open house at the Monk Street cottage where dozens of people were served with tea while sheltering from the rain. They immediately resorted to impromptu music-making: Elizabethan songs, rounds and part-songs, accompanied by violin, penny whistles, piano, and mouth organ.

At 6.30 a garden party was scheduled at the Vicarage, but because of the rain it had to be held indoors, and the house soon vibrated to the sounds of music and morris dancing. After supper, a melodrama was presented in the barn, followed by more dancing. The following day, Holst and Conrad Noel took a well-earned rest while others made music in the church, and at four o'clock the performers presented a brief concert especially for Holst's benefit. By 5.30 the last of the visitors were on their way back to London. A few days later Holst wrote to Whittaker:

I would have written before but I was so tied up with our music festival (or rather feast) at Thaxted last week.

It *was* a feast—an orgy. Four whole days of perpetual singing and playing either properly arranged in the church or impromptu in various houses or still more impromptu in ploughed fields during thunderstorms or in the trains. It has been a revelation to me. And what it has revealed to me and what I shall never be able to persuade you is that quantity is more important than quality. We don't get enough. We practise stuff for a concert at which we do a thing once and get excited over it and then go off and do something else. Whereas on this occasion things were different. Take the Missa Brevis for instance. The Morleyites had practised it since January. On June 3rd they did it *twice through* at their concert. On June 10th they rehearsed it and other things for three hours in Thaxted Church. On Whitsunday we did it during service in the morning, again in the evening, again on Monday morning. And some enthusiasts went through it again on Tuesday morning with violin and piano. The same applies to the other things we did. Some of the motets were learnt over a year ago.

In the intervals between services people drifted into church and sang more motets or played violin or cello etc. And between all this others caught bad colds through going long walks in the pouring rain singing folksongs and rounds the whole time. The effect on us was indescribable. We weren't merely excited—we were quite normal only rather more alive than usual. Most people are overcome by mountain air at first. In the same way others are excited by certain big music. The remedy in both cases is to have more and more and More! What a mercy it is that we cannot meet otherwise I'd jaw your head off. I enclose the programme. There were about 15 Morleyites, 10 St Paul's girls, 10 outsiders and 10 Thaxted singers. The latter did grandly. Most of them work at a factory here and I have been asked to give them quicker music next year. It seems that they sang all day every day at their work for months and the slow notes of the Bach corals seriously affected their output![10]

Thaxted was to be the stimulus for several works which Holst composed at this time. One evening he went into the church at dusk and saw his Morley pupil Christine Ratcliffe sauntering in the shadows, playing her violin while softly improvising a wordless song. This incident gave him the idea of writing the *Four Songs* for voice and violin, using texts selected from Mary Segar's *A Mediaeval Anthology*, his interest in medieval poetry having begun during his student days when as a

member of the Hammersmith Socialist Society he had heard
William Morris lecture on the art and literature of the Middle
Ages. In these songs, Holst gave a new rhythmic freedom to the
musical expression of the words (deriving from the metrical
flexibility of English folk-song) and concluded that this was the
best way to set the English language to music. As a student he
had been brought up on English translations of texts set by
foreign composers, and as such translations were often of poor
quality, the problem of finding an exact musical counterpart
for the rhythms of English poetry rarely arose. As Edwin Evans
remarked: 'So far from learning how to set an English text
adequately, he and his fellow-students were not even made
aware of the difficulties of the problem.'[11] Holst later wrote: 'I
find that *unconsciously* I have been drawn for years towards
discovering the (or *a*) musical idiom of the English language.
Never having managed to learn a foreign language, songs
always meant to me a peg of words on which to hang a tune.
The great awakening came on hearing the recits in Purcell's
Dido ... In the CM [*The Cloud Messenger*] and Savitri,
especially the latter, the words and music really grew together.
Since then I've managed now and then to do the same thing
with other people's words especially in the violin songs ("My
Leman" is a good instance of a tune at one with the words). But
in all this there is no conscious principle, no "ideal", no axe to
grind.'[12]

Having written three songs with Christine Ratcliffe's mellow
mezzo-soprano voice in mind, Holst was disappointed to find
that she was unable to articulate the words properly with the
violin under her chin, and so the idea of vocal part and violin
accompaniment being performed by the same person had to be
abandoned. Dulcie Nutting was called in to sing the songs,
although the range was rather low for her higher soprano voice.
A few months later Holst composed a further setting (*I Sing of
a Maiden*) in a higher register more suited to her own voice,
but the first three songs were never transposed from their
original pitch.

He also wrote some part-songs especially for the Thaxted
singers, using medieval texts selected mainly from Mary
Segar's *A Mediaeval Anthology*. *Of One That Is So Fair and
Bright* is a simple carol of great beauty, with an unforced

varying metre and an alternation of solo with choral response recalling the *Four Old English Carols* of 1907. *Lullay My Liking* is another unaccompanied carol which has subsequently become well known, while *Terly Terlow* is accompanied by oboe and cello, like the *Welcome Song* of 1907–8. The part-song *Bring Us In Good Ale* always reminded Imogen Holst that on certain Sundays Conrad Noel would invite his parishoners to a meal at the Vicarage, for which everyone had to bring something to eat and drink: 'I can remember one occasion when a breathless tenor arrived at our home:—would my mother please lend them a loaf and some butter because no-one had brought anything except beer! I always think of it when this carol gets to the verse: "Bring us in good ale and bring us *nothing else*".'[13] Holst also arranged three old melodies for chorus and orchestra under the titles *Let All Mortal Flesh Keep Silence, Turn Back, O Man,* and *A Festival Chime* (originally entitled *Our Church-bells at Thaxted*), which became known as the *Three Festival Choruses.* Once again, Clifford Bax provided English versions for two of these hymns and tried to find the nearest equivalent open vowels in English to match the Latin originals: 'While trying to write sense, I had to construct a poem from the longest monosyllables which I could assemble.'[14] According to Bax, Vaughan Williams declared that *Turn Back, O Man* should be sung at the beginning of every marriage service!

One composition of this period was not entirely successful: a *Phantasy* for string quartet, based on folk-songs collected in Hampshire by G. B. Gardiner. Perhaps because players and listeners alike expect something more sophisticated from a quartet than mere stringing together of tunes, this idea did not work very well, and although there were some clever contrapuntal combinations of melodies, the result seemed rather artificial and contrived, and Holst decided to wait until he had heard the work in performance before passing judgement.

Although he had involved himself in a lot of amateur music-making, little had happened to advance Holst's professional career as a composer during 1916. On 19 August, *The Times* published a letter from D. Marblacy Jones, complaining that no works by Parry, Bantock, Boughton, Scott, Wallace, Vaughan

Williams, or Holst were to be included in the forthcoming Promenade concert season at the Queen's Hall: 'Is it too much to ask that, in common decency, we should honour these composers who are serving their country on active service [i.e. Wallace and Vaughan Williams] by giving their music an occasional performance? I do not think a Promenade audience would consider it a hardship to have closer acquaintance with the work of these composers, even if some German works have to be sacrificed.'

Anti-German prejudice was clearly still lurking beneath the surface of English musical life, but on a more practical level the war was having a serious effect on amateur music-making. As the British Expeditionary Force had suffered appalling casualties in the battles of Flanders, and the supply of eager volunteers was drying up, Lloyd George introduced conscription for all unmarried men between the ages of eighteen and forty-one. In various walks of life women took over jobs previously done by men, to release greater numbers for service in the armed forces, but in choral singing such an expedient was impossible, and in October 1916 Holst complained to Whittaker: 'Morley choir started last month with 50 women and 2 men, and 50 per cent of the men could not sing!'[15]

In spite of the wartime difficulties of communication, Holst made a point of trying to keep in touch with his Morley students at the front, some of whom actually managed to keep up their musical interests amid the dreadful conditions of the trenches. Cecil Coles, who had been a member of the Morley orchestra and also a teacher of elementary harmony and sight-singing at the College, had joined the Queen Victoria's rifles, and while in the trenches started to write a suite for small orchestra. He sent the first movement to Holst, but soon afterwards died of wounds received during a volunteer expedition to rescue some wounded comrades from no man's land. Most of Coles's private papers were subsequently destroyed by a shell, including his sketches for the remainder of the suite. Another Morley student, Sydney Bressey, visited Holst in the autumn of 1916 after being sent home to recover from a wound received in France, where he had been awarded the Military Medal. On reaching Victoria Station, he made several telephone calls and eventually located Holst at St Paul's Girls'

School, to which he was immediately invited. He produced a setting of Shelley's lines 'Music, when soft voices die' which he had written in the trenches in a small pocket notebook, using makeshift music staves drawn in pencil, and on seeing this, Holst immediately sent for his pupil Megan Foster, who tried through the song in the school Singing Hall, while Holst and the High Mistress sat beside the young composer as he listened to his work for the first time. Holst was so impressed by the song that he promised to arrange its first public performance in a forthcoming Morley College concert.

On 5 December the first performance of *Savitri* was given by students of the London School of Opera at the Wellington Hall, St John's Wood, sharing the bill with Holbrooke's *Pierrot and Pierrette*. T. C. Fairbairn was stage director, and the work was conducted by Herman Grunebaum, whose suggestion for giving the chorus to female instead of mixed voices has already been mentioned. It is possible that this stemmed as much from lack of male singers as from purely artistic reasons, but in any event Holst thought the work was much improved by the change, and Imogen Holst considered that 'it was impossible to imagine it sounding otherwise'.[16] The soloists were George Pawlo as Satyavan, Mabel Corran as Savitri, and Harrison Cook as Death; the orchestra being led by Dorothy Bridson.

The opera seems to have been well received by those who heard it, including the press, which generally commented very favourably. Holst considered submitting the score to the Carnegie Trust for publication in their scheme to aid British composers; whether he did so or not is not known, but the work did not receive an award that year and publication was delayed until 1923 when it was accepted by F. & B. Goodwin Ltd. Two other first performances of works by Holst took place on 19 December, when *Terly Terlow* and *Lullay My Liking* were sung at the Aeolian Hall by the Oriana Madrigal Society conducted by Charles Kennedy Scott.

By the end of 1916 the orchestration of *The Planets* was virtually complete. He had decided to use a very large orchestra, including quadruple woodwind, six horns, and two timpanists, in complete contrast to the subtle economy of

Savitri. Only a gigantic orchestra would do for the portrayal of colossal forces, but it would also provide a wide palette of tone-colours on which to draw for the more subtly orchestrated movements. Various assistants helped him with the task of preparing the full score, particularly his colleagues Vally Lasker and Nora Day and his pupil Jane Joseph (whom he referred to as 'my three right arms'[17]). Holst originally composed the work in a version for two pianos, on which he marked indications for the instrumentation in red ink. When his neuritis was too bad for him to do the scoring himself, the amanuenses would work from this annotated manuscript, while Holst worked nearby, ready to be consulted on any problems which might arise. Describing her part in this work, Nora Day recalled: 'We used to get the scoring paper ready, clefs, bar-lines, instruments, etc., the length of the bars taken from the piano score—occasionally to put passages into the full score.'[18] When he was short of time he would leave the assistants to carry on with the work by themselves, writing an occasional note to explain what he wanted: 'If you are pining for a job there is no reason why the bars should not be ruled so I enclose a list of instruments. Use the very big MS paper and make the bars fairly small until the 3/2 fff—stop just before there. Also . . . you might begin scoring. Besides the bass Fl requiring his notes written a 4th up and the bass ob an 8° up the harmonics of the harp sound an 8° above what is played and so you have to write the notes an 8° too low!'[19] Occasionally the amanuenses would write notes outside the normal range of a particular instrument, so Holst would regularly check their work to ensure its practicability. Vally Lasker and Nora Day were already familiar with the two-piano version, as they had played it to him movement-by-movement in the sound-proof room as it was composed, and even after scoring had been completed they continued to play this version in concerts and recitals in various parts of the country, and occasionally to visiting conductors on Saturday mornings at St Paul's, when a few Paulinas were sometimes privileged to be present. Nora Day recalled that Holst was insistent that the pianists should try to reproduce the orchestral sound as closely as possible: 'During the first war when orchestral performance was impossible, Miss Lasker and I played *The Planets* on two pianos. The scoring was marked—and we had to observe it! It irritates me now to hear transcriptions played like piano pieces.'[20] Some of the sustained orchestral effects were not at all suited to piano transcription, and Holst wrote to Whittaker: 'The last one Neptune is so ridiculous on the piano that I have arranged it for organ duet.[21] Even then it isn't quite successful.'[22] Besides relying on the help of Nora Day and Vally Lasker in preparing his scores and performing two-piano versions of his works, Holst would often play them excerpts from his work-in-progress to seek their opinion, a process which he called 'trying it out on the dog'.[23]

9

Wartime in London
(1917–1918)

With this task completed, Holst immediately began to think of writing another major work. *The Hymn of Jesus* was beginning to take shape in his mind, but would have to wait until the summer holidays when sufficient time would be available for serious work on the music. Meanwhile, he started to prepare the text, making a translation from the Greek by the same methods as he had used when studying Sanskrit. He had chosen a text from *The Apocryphal Acts of St John* by G. R. S. Mead, a Theosophist whom Holst may have first heard about via his stepmother. The words are supposedly those sung by Christ and his disciples after supper on the evening before the Crucifixion, as described by St Matthew (26: 30): 'And when they had sung an hymn, they went out into the mount of Olives.' The apocryphal text adds more detail to the description: 'He commanded us to make as it were a ring, holding one another's hands, and Himself standing in the middle. He said: Respond Amen to me. He began then to sing a hymn and to say: Glory to thee, Father! And we, going about in a ring, said Amen, Amen . . . So then, my beloved, after this dance with us, the Lord went out: and we men gone astray or awakened out of sleep fled all ways.'[1] Holst knew very little Greek, but Jane Joseph taught him the elements of the language, and armed with this grounding he set to work. He would copy out each word separately, and underneath write its phonetic pronunciation, together with the nearest equivalent English word. Then he would read through the sentence a few times and write down his own version, keeping as closely to the meaning of the original as possible. Clifford Bax was able to give him some help by suggesting suitable phrases for use in the English version.

Holst worked on this translation during the early months of 1917 in moments of spare time amid his normal teaching activities. On 17 January there was a concert at Morley College which included the first performance of Sydney Bressey's *Music When Soft Voices Die*, sung by Dulcie Nutting with piano accompaniment. A few days later Holst sent a copy of the programme to W. G. Whittaker: 'I enclose Morley's latest effort. Bressey's song caused a sensation. He wrote it in his soldier's pocket book in a dug out in the firing line. He was able to get leave for the concert being in England wounded.'[2] Soon after this concert Bressey rejoined his unit in France, but this time did not return.

On Friday 9 March Holst travelled to Newcastle to visit W. G. Whittaker and rehearse the choir of Armstrong College for a concert on 12 March in which he conducted the Second Group of *Choral Hymns from the Rig Veda*, *Tears, Idle Tears*, *Pastoral*, and the *Ave Maria*. On his return to London, Holst wrote to Whittaker: 'I have never heard the Ave Maria and "Tears" so well sung before and as I had not heard the "Ave" for sixteen years you can guess what a joy it was to me. I always enjoy rehearsals more than concerts but I have rarely enjoyed a rehearsal as much as I did on Sunday morning.'[3] On Tuesday 13 March, Holst's *Invocation* was performed by Thelma Bentwich and Myra Hess at a Wigmore Hall recital, while on 24 March there was the usual music students' Social at Morley College, to which Holst invited his Sanskrit teacher Mabel Bode, now Professor of Pali at London University and lecturer in the new School of Oriental Studies, to talk about Sanskrit literature before a performance of the Second Group of *Choral Hymns from the Rig Veda* given by the College students.

After the Easter holiday, Holst's main preoccupation was the forthcoming second Whitsun festival to be held at Thaxted. During the spring term he had been working hard on the arrangements (on 17 February he wrote: 'A little time ago I felt that it was my duty to the country to abandon the festival. But now I don't!'[4]), and gave close attention to details such as accommodation for the visitors whom Irene Bonnett was bringing: 'As your friends are not coming for Saturday's rehearsal I suppose they don't want to sing or play. Tell them to write for rooms at the "Cock" (small and cheap) or "Swan" (large and expensive). They *must* secure rooms beforehand.'[5] At last the Morleyites and Paulinas set off for Thaxted on Friday and Saturday 25 and 26 May, undeterred by reports of a German bomber force being sighted over the Essex coast. On their arrival they set about turning the village once again into one large music festival: 'We kept it up at Thaxted about 14 hours a day,' Holst later wrote.[6] As in the previous year, the music was performed as part of the normal church services, rather than in the form of concerts. There was a three-hour rehearsal in the church on the Saturday evening, and the music was performed the following morning as part of the Whit Sunday High Mass; there was a large congregation and the brightly coloured veils worn by the women and the blossoming branches and candles carried during the people's procession round the church again made a striking impression. The programme included the first performance of the *Three Festival Choruses*, which Holst had written especially for Thaxted ('The whole district is singing "The Church bells in Thaxted" now,' he wrote a few days later[7]) and three of the *Four Songs* for voice and violin, performed by Dulcie Nutting and Christine Ratcliffe. This was the ideal setting for the performance of these songs, with their simplicity and flexibility of rhythm; as a later reviewer wrote: 'Mr Holst . . . has caught to perfection the intimate devotion of the text—so much so, in fact, that the settings call for surroundings other than the concert room. One hates to think of applause or bouquets after such things. The songs need the atmosphere of the home or the church.'[8]

The musical programme was repeated in an extended version during the Evensong service, and again on Whit Monday morning, while on both afternoons there was 'a sort of sacred sing-song'.[9] Holst recalled: 'We did odds and ends in church, Morleyite compositions, rounds, canons (the 8 part one in my 3d series with the 8 groups placed right round the church!) and also went round the village and serenaded people . . . They filled in the intervals by singing and playing in church (where "Sumer is icumen in" simply *grew* up from a group of people) in the houses, in gardens, on doorsteps (where I found 3 girls trying to sing the 8 pt round!) in the streets (the local policeman shut them up about 11 PM) and once on the church tower from whence they sang the Byrd Mass.' The performers consisted of 'about 20 trebles, eight altos, two tenors, three basses, four first violins, four seconds, two violas, three cellos, one bass, two flutes, two oboes, one horn, one local cornet and organ'.[10] One wit invented compound names for the mixtures of Morleyites, Paulinas and Thaxted locals: 'Morthaxes' (Morley and Thaxted) and 'Paumorthaxes' (St Paul's, Morley, and Thaxted), a convoluted terminology which mercifully did not survive the weekend. As in the previous year, the performers sang and played for the sheer enjoyment of it, with scant reward except the approval of their conductor—as one of them put it: 'When he beamed on us and said, "I'm proud of you all", it was handsome payment for our efforts.'[11] On the Whit Monday evening a number of the Morleyites had to return to London in order to start work first thing the following morning, but as the train was crowded they were all put into a horse-box in which they sang sixteenth-century motets throughout the journey.

Although the Whitsun festivals continued to be held in later years in various places, none seem to have matched the levels of enthusiasm and enjoyment which were achieved at Thaxted in 1916 and 1917. The tradition of those days is still maintained there: the Kyrie from Byrd's three-part Mass is often sung in church services, and Holst's arrangements of the carols *On this Day*, *I Saw Three Ships*, and *Masters in This Hall* are performed on Christmas morning. Students from Morley College visit the town at Whitsun, and the 1917 banner still hangs in the church and is carried round in procession, bearing the words of J. S. Bach which Holst chose for it: 'The aim of music is the glory of God and pleasant recreation.' Holst's work at Thaxted did a great deal to foster the liberalization of church music and to persuade church authorities to allow the performance of non-liturgical and secular music in places of worship, nowadays generally taken for granted.

During 1917 Holst moved from Monk Street into Thaxted itself, renting a house in Town Street called The Steps (subsequently The Manse), which now bears a commemorative plaque near the window of his music room. Although this was a peaceful spot in which to work, he continued to use his sound-proof room at St Paul's during term-time, working at Thaxted in the school holidays.

At last the summer term came to an end, and Holst was able to settle down to compose the music for *The Hymn of Jesus*. The forces he chose consisted of two mixed choirs, a semi-chorus of female voices, and, in his own words: 'An orchestra of rather more than a dozen, in other words, a damned big one'.[12] The opening plainsong melody is given to the trombones, a device which Rimsky-Korsakov had used in his *Russian Easter Overture*, in which trombones imitate the chanting of Orthodox priests. Holst may have played this work during his time as an orchestral musician, or perhaps the idea may go back as far as his schoolboy study of Berlioz's *Treatise Upon Modern Instrumentation*, which contains the passage: 'In *mezzo-forte* in the medium register in unison or in harmony with a slow movement, trombones assume a religious character. Mozart in his choruses of the *priests of Isis* in the Zauberflöte, has produced admirable models of the manner of giving these instruments a sacerdotal voice and attribute. In forte . . . they chaunt, instead of roar.'[13]

The use of plainsong in a non-liturgical work can be traced at least as far back as Berlioz's use of the Dies Irae melody in the *Symphonie fantastique*, but Holst's use of it is an interesting antecedent of later twentieth-century composers who have used plainsong themes as the basis of their works. Although Holst's interest in plainsong may have begun when he was an organ pupil of W. S. Hoyte, it was through his work on the *English Hymnal* (used for services in Thaxted Church) that he had acquired a closer knowledge of several plainsong melodies, including the two hymns which he used for the introduction to *The Hymn of Jesus*: 'Vexilla Regis Prodeunt' (The Royal Banners Forward Go) and 'Pange Lingua Gloriosi Proelium Certaminis' (Sing My Tongue, the Glorious Battle). Both are Easter hymns, with words by Bishop Venantius Fortunatus (530–609 AD), from manuscript versions in the Sarum Antiphoner.

According to Richard Capell,[14] Holst stated that *The Hymn*

of Jesus had been written under the influence of Weelkes'
madrigals published in Fellowes's edition of 1916, but little
evidence of this can be heard in the music. One of the most
characteristic features of the work is the use of harmony as an
expression of intense religious experience: massive conglom-
erations of sound produced by the double chorus and orchestra
contrast dramatically with the simple 'Amens' sung by the
semi-chorus in parallel triads, interspersed between phrases of
the Hymn. To later ears the level of harmonic dissonance does
not perhaps seem as striking as it must have done to the work's
first hearers, many of whom were used to the more comfortable harmonizations of nineteenth-century oratorio. Although
the vertical sonorities may appear daunting on paper, Holst
had in fact paid detailed attention to their practical feasibility.
Many of the sharpest dissonances arise from the movement of
chords whose notes clash against one another to produce a
scintillating effect, but such moments are carefully aproached
and quitted logically according to the principles of counterpoint. The second striking feature of the work is its association
of religion with dancing, a notion which Holst had previously
encountered in the text of the part-song *This Have I Done for
My True Love*. In fact dancing has long played an important
part in religious ritual; the ancient Egyptians and Greeks
believed that the gods themselves danced, and there are several
references to dancing in the Old Testament. Examples of this
practice still survive in Christian worship, as in the ceremonies
in Seville and of the Shakers of America, but it is most
widespread in the culture of primitive non-Christian peoples,
particularly in initiation ceremonies, to which the text of *The
Hymn of Jesus* bears a marked resemblance. As the words
state: 'Ye who dance not, know not what we are knowing.'
Holst set this dance to a five-beat rhythm similar to that in *To
Agni* of the Second Group of *Choral Hymns from the Rig Veda*,
forming a kind of central development section before returning
to the mood of the opening. Although there is a contrast
between this dancing movement and the contemplative plainsong hymns and static choral phrases, during the Hymn itself
the plainsong tunes of the opening reappear, to form a coherent
link between the sections. Echoes of *Venus* appear in the
alternating chords of the harmony, and brass calls hark back to

The Mystic Trumpeter of 1904. Holst himself thought that *The Hymn of Jesus* was the best thing he had written up to that time, although he subsequently realized that the sequential passages at the words 'Beholding what I suffer' were rather commonplace, but by that time the work was in print and it was too late to alter it. Although more of a mystic than an orthodox believer, Holst was nevertheless interested in religion, and Sydney Grew recalled that in 1932 he was 'divining the spiritual impulses that realised themselves in Beethoven's D major setting of the Mass'. In *The Hymn of Jesus* Holst created one of the most important Christian choral works of the twentieth century, drawing a parallel with his friend Vaughan Williams, who wrote effective religious music despite his own agnosticism. Perhaps their lack of conventional faith enabled them to observe with detachment; to capture the essence of sacred music, which might not have been so apparent had they been more closely involved in their own personal beliefs.

The task of preparing the full score of *The Hymn of Jesus* was undertaken by Dulcie Nutting, who had joined the orchestra and choir at Morley College after leaving school, and who was to remain a stalwart of the College for the rest of her long life. Wartime circumstances still restricted the number of men available for musical activities, but occasionally a few could be mustered for particular occasions—as Holst wrote to Whittaker on 18 December: 'Last night the choir actually amounted to 52 including 12 men, 5 of whom were tenors.'[15] The proximity of Morley College to Waterloo Station placed it in a prime target area for Zeppelin bombers, and several attempts to hit the station had been made from 1916 onwards. In September 1917 a major air raid occurred on the first night of term, after which classes were transferred to the basement gymnasium whenever attacks took place (usually on clear, moonlit nights). This basement was also designated as a public air-raid shelter, and people hurrying down from the street would often find themselves in the midst of a Morley choir rehearsal. Many locals were surprised to find that instead of music-hall songs in the shelter, the entertainment was more likely to consist of motets by Palestrina or a Mass by William Byrd. But it was a strain on everyone, and Holst complained: 'I am fed up with raids—in the day time the children are worn out and nervy and at night the cellar concerts are a great success but they last *hours* without any interval and leave one limp for tomorrow's work.'[16]

On 29 November a War Emergency Entertainments concert of British music was given at the Steinway Hall, which included the first performance of Holst's *Phantasy on British Folksongs* for string quartet. This performance confirmed his doubts about the work, and he decided to withdraw it from his list of compositions, later writing to Edwin Evans: 'I also tried to write a string quartet . . . and I don't want that to be more than a "guilty secret".'[17] (Imogen Holst eventually arranged the work for string orchestra under the title *Fantasia on Hampshire Folksongs*.) In Newcastle on 15 December, W. G. Whittaker gave the first performance of Holst's carol *Of One That Is So Fair and Bright* with his Newcastle-upon-Tyne Bach Choir in a concert of British Christmas music. During the war years Holst was involved in many similar concerts in aid of charities concerned with the effects of the war, and Isobel also worked as a part-time volunteer driver for the Green Cross organization.

1918 began without any prospect of cessation of hostilities, although all the belligerents were dreaming of a great offensive leading to a major breakthrough which would end it all. Life at home, however, still had to go on regardless, especially in the capital, where it was important to keep up morale despite the constant bombing raids.

In January Holst invited Whittaker to London for a few days, and besides conducting some of his own folk-song arrangements at a Morley College concert, Whittaker gave a public lecture at the Old Vic on 'The Work of Gustav Holst', with musical illustrations provided by Morley students and the Oriana Madrigal Society. On the following day two of Holst's *Four Songs* for voice and violin were performed at Morley College by Dulcie Nutting and May Blair; this was apparently the first public performance of *I Sing of a Maiden* as it had been omitted from the performance in Thaxted Church the previous Whitsun.

At the beginning of the war, Holst had received a letter from a young conductor named Adrian Boult, enquiring whether he had written anything for small orchestra. Holst had sent him the scores of *Two Songs Without Words* and *A Somerset Rhapsody*, but no performance had resulted and the two musicians did not meet until 1916, when Holst took Boult for a long walk through Kew Gardens, Sheen Common, and Richmond Park, and arranged for him to hear *The Planets* played on two pianos by Vally Lasker and Nora Day at St Paul's Girls' School. Then in February and March 1918 Boult gave a series of four concerts at the Queen's Hall with the London Symphony Orchestra (then reduced to some fifty players) which established his reputation as one of Britain's outstanding conductors. The concert on 4 February included the *Country Song* from *Two Songs Without Words*, and the following day Holst wrote to Boult: 'Everybody is wild with enthusiasm over your beautiful rendering of the Country Song. Please accept my (a) thanks (b) blessing (c) congratulations. I hope you were satisfied. It's a splendidly plucky enterprise of yours and I do hope you'll get adequate support.'[18] Thus began a close and enduring musical association during which Boult was to demonstrate his skill in interpreting many of Holst's major works, particularly *The Planets*, which he was to conduct in concerts, recordings and broadcasts throughout his long career. Before his 1918 Queen's Hall concerts Boult was so little known that the Board of the London Symphony Orchestra asked him to provide references before they would allow him to conduct the orchestra, but as soon as they heard his performances they realized that they were dealing with a musician of exceptional capabilities. Because of the bombing raids the audiences for these concerts were rather depleted, but word soon went round that Adrian Boult was a conductor whose future career would be well worth watching.

By way of relieving the tedium of life under the stress of war, Holst decided to produce another extravaganza on the lines of the *Futuristic Tone-Poem* of a few years before. This time it was to be an operatic production, under the title *Opera as She is Wrote*, described as being in 'six acts and five languages (including tonic sol-fa)'.[19] The work was rehearsed during the air raids, and performed at Morley College on 9 March 1918.

The first five acts consisted of an English ballad opera by 'Balface', an Italianate offering entitled *Il Inspettore* by 'Verdi-zetti', a Wagnerian concoction involving the heroine Screim-hild, impressionism in the style of 'Depussy', featuring 'Paliasse', and a Finale by 'Horriddinsky-Kantakoff'; the whole accompanied by 'a vast orchestra', with 'five hidden choirs of mermaids, and a chorus of Italian brigands disguised as fir trees and food inspectors'. The sixth and final act, 'before which the mind reels and staggers', was to portray the Opera of the Future, and an advance announcement promised that 'the scenery and lighting effects will be beyond words, even those of an N.C.O.'.[20]

Each act had its own remarkable characteristics, but several items stood out, including an Early Victorian version of *The Keel Row*—'adagio con molto espressione con molto coloratura con molto modulations', according to Holst.[21] The Italian scene included 'banditti, condottieri, carabinieri, all delightful things in "i", including the "occhiali", those basses in 5ths, which on paper look like "spectacles", beloved by Rossini',[22] and rose to a climax with 'three soloists singing tonic solfa and the brigands shouting "Away away she shall be mine" for 15 minutes'[23] (this phrase was to re-emerge in Holst's comic opera *The Perfect Fool* a few years later). For the Depussy scene, Dulcie Nutting 'repeatedly assured us how unhappy she felt sitting, as she did, like Maeterlinck's heroine in the tower, on the unstable equilibrium of various superposed chairs and tables', while Holst instructed the orchestra to play whole-tone scales. As Adrian Boult remarked, it sounded just like Debussy. For the Wagnerian scene, lest there be any misunder-standing, the *Morley College Magazine* published a full explanation:

Hear the composer's own words: 'The music is built out of an indefinite number of motives, light and dark. There is one for every mood of every character; thus there is Scriemhild sleepy, Scriemhild very sleepy, Scriemhild just on the point of going to sleep, Scriemhild asleep—the last motiv consisting solely of a low C throbbed out by the basses . . .' As to the philosophical purport of 'Scriemhild's Awakening', he says—'The essence of life is that entity has no substance. Conceive then a soul seeking to combine pure ineffable mind with gross material substance, and at once we are confronted with an impossible task. But what is the nature of the Impossible? The Possible partakes of the nature of indispensable illumination, and can be attained at the cost of Free Will only with an infinite amount of subconscious effort. It is the idea of Infinity that I wish to show by my drama; effort must be brought out by the brass, the impossible by the strings. The relation of Time to Eternity is obvious, for I have disregarded the former, and the whole drama suggests the latter.'[24]

The assembled instrumental forces turned out to consist of no more than half a dozen players, but the sonorous effect of a massive orchestra was achieved by 'a remarkable feat of orchestration'.[25] Although this kind of thing can be dismissed as mere adolescent humour, it did in fact give Holst some ideas for his later satirical opera *The Perfect Fool*. For example, the trombone theme at the beginning of *The Perfect Fool* came from the burlesque Wagner scene of *Opera as She is Wrote* (and originally from the *Phantastes* suite of 1911 which he had withdrawn from his list of compositions). This same theme was also used in another work which Holst was writing at this time, the incidental music to a play by Clifford Bax entitled *The Sneezing Charm* ('An Arabian Nights Phantasy in Rhyme') which was produced at the Royal Court Theatre, Sloane Square, in 1918. In fact the whole of the ballet music in *The Perfect Fool* is based on this incidental music, and its invocations of the Spirits of Earth, Water, and Fire, scored in attractive instrumental colours, form a brilliant orchestral work which has become a standard item in its own right in the English repertoire.

There were occasional performances of Holst's music at concerts in the London area. On 18 March George Pawlo sang three of the *Vedic Hymns* in his concert at the Wigmore Hall (including the first public performance of *Creation*), while on 4 April Ethel Waddington and Mollie Livermore performed the *Four Songs* for voice and violin at a recital at Blackheath. On 13 April there was an 'Easter Soirée' at Morley College, which included a repeat performance of *Opera as She is Wrote* (Holst wrote to his pupil Irene Bonnett: 'If you want a good laugh come to Morley tomorrow'[26]); on 16 April the first public performance of the last three of the *Six Choral Folksongs* was given by their dedicatees Charles Kennedy Scott and the

Oriana Madrigal Society at the Old Vic Theatre; and on 4 May there was another Saturday Group Concert at Blackheath which included several of Holst's works besides a repeat performance of the *Four Songs* for voice and violin.

Then came the third Whitsun festival at Thaxted. The events followed the same pattern as in previous years, including orchestral music by Purcell and Lawes, and choral works by Morley, Wilbye, and Palestrina. Before the Sunday morning service, a female-voice choir climbed to the church roof, where they sang Vittoria's *Come Holy Ghost*, while the service itself included movements from Byrd's three-part Mass and Holst's festival choruses *Let All Mortal Flesh Keep Silence* and *Turn Back, O Man*. There were also compositions by his pupils Wilfred Palmer and Jane Joseph, and the first public performance of two of Holst's own works, *This Have I Done for My True Love* and *Diverus and Lazarus*, an arrangement of the traditional carol collected by Lucy Broadwood. But despite the enthusiasm of the performers, the mood was not the same as in previous years, and this was in fact the last Whitsun festival to be held at Thaxted. In the heady atmosphere following the Bolshevik revolution in Russia the previous autumn, Conrad Noel had begun to demand a more committed attitude from those who took part in church activities, and started to expound the principles of Communism from the pulpit. He offended some of Holst's pupils by calling them 'camp followers' because they did not live up to the Christian ideals in which they claimed to believe, with the result that the visitors felt that they could not come to Thaxted again. Holst himself took Noel's views with a pinch of salt, referring to 'Conrad's comic gospel of hate',[27] and continued to help with the music in the church, often playing the organ for services, especially at Christmas time.

Back in London, there was a Morley College concert on 1 June, which included the first performance of a *May Day Carol* which Holst had arranged for voice and two violins, and some rounds composed by his pupils. On 9 June *The Sneezing Charm* opened at the Royal Court Theatre, and at the beginning of July the Morley students went to St Paul's Girls' for their annual joint garden party, which included a repeat performance of *Opera as She is Wrote*. Once again, this was a great success, and Holst wrote to Whittaker: 'At the end came the most wonderful moment of my life. Everyone had been rolling about with laughter for over an hour and we were all dressed as brigands mermaids etc (I had just been Pelleas in a blue robe, a cork moustache and a yellow turban). As if it were the normal ending (probably it was) they all stood up as they were and sang the Byrd Kyrie as if their hearts were breaking.'[28]

Despite the acute shortage of male voices, Holst continued his teaching work at Morley College until the end of the summer term, and was then given a year's leave of absence to undertake educational work for the YMCA. Throughout the war he had applied to do emergency work of various kinds, and had always been turned down for reasons of health, but he now had an opportunity to volunteer for work among the troops stationed in Europe. The Music Section of the YMCA Education Department had been formed 'to develop musical activities in YMCA huts and centres throughout the field of war, amongst the training camps and hospitals in this country, and the internment camps in neutral and enemy countries', and its Organizing Secretary, the music critic Percy Scholes, had put out an appeal for assistance from musicians who were 'either over age or obviously unfit for service'.[29] When Holst offered his services, Scholes at first thought of sending him to Holland, where Edgar Bainton (who had been a civil prisoner in Germany for nearly four years) had been appointed YMCA Music Organizer for the internment camps, and whose assistants Benjamin Dale and Percy Hull had been repatriated, leaving a gap to be filled. All seemed to go well at first; Holst attended a medical examination on 14 June and succeeded in fulfilling the minimal requirements, but then came a snag. It was felt by the YMCA authorities that the 'von' in Holst's name would not go down too well with the Allied internees, who might think that he was a German, and he was therefore rejected for the appointment in Holland.

Scholes then suggested to Holst that he might consider dropping the 'von' from his name, thus making it easier for him to obtain a YMCA appointment. After some consideration, Holst decided to accept this advice, and duly changed his name to Gustav Theodore Holst by deed poll dated 18 September

1918. He subsequently discovered that a deed poll was not in fact a legal necessity for change of name, and that his family seemed to have little claim to use the 'von' in any case, but the way was now clear for him to be sent abroad as a YMCA Music Organizer. At St Paul's, Miss Gray solemnly informed the assembled girls that 'We must all give up something in the War', and that consequently Mr Holst had volunteered to give up his 'von'.[30] Holst must have ironically recalled his student days when a well-known composer had remarked that he envied him his foreign-sounding name as it would be a great help in establishing a reputation in the eyes of the British public. But times had changed; even the Royal family had changed its name as a consequence of the war, and Holst probably felt no regrets as he was generally opposed to pretentiousness of all kinds.

As a first step towards his new work he had to attend a preliminary training course at Welbeck Camp in Nottinghamshire, from where he wrote: 'I'm here under canvas and in mud learning my job.'[31] In a letter to Frances Ralph Gray he expanded a little: 'I am writing this in the driest part of the camp—the YMCA cookhouse, of which only ¾ of the ground is flooded so far . . . Would you object if I came home next September a raging Bolshevik? If I had a clear field with the lads here I could do some good work. But their superiors! Especially those in charge of their minds!! By the time you get this I presume there will be very little mud left—the camp will be a lake.'[32] The course lasted a few weeks, during which he was informed that he was to be sent to work among the troops at Salonica; and then he was back in London, waiting to be notified of his date of departure. Although he had been granted leave of absence from his teaching commitments, the Morley College authorities could not guarantee to keep his job open beyond the end of the current session, but meanwhile would make do with temporary teachers. Holst suggested either Richard Terry of Westminster Cathedral, or Dr Harris, organist of Lichfield Cathedral; the College decided on Terry, and at St Paul's Girls' School Norman O'Neill took over the orchestra during Holst's absence.

But the uncertainty of wondering when he was to leave Britain was eclipsed by a far more exciting event. Henry Balfour

Gardiner, who had already helped Holst financially on several occasions, now decided to give him a very special farewell gift, in the form of a private professional performance of *The Planets* at the end of September. Holst hurried to see Adrian Boult, who was doing war work as a government official, bursting into his office and exclaiming: 'Balfour Gardiner has given me a wonderful parting present. It consists of Queen's Hall, full of the Queen's Hall Orchestra, for the whole morning on Sunday week. We're going to do *The Planets* and you're going to conduct.'[33] Boult received this sudden announcement with characteristic equanimity and immediately set himself to the task of learning the score, assisted by Vally Lasker and Nora Day, who played the two-piano version for him several times so that he could become familiar with the work as quickly as possible. Meanwhile, frantic preparations were going on, involving Holst's friends, colleagues, and pupils, who were engaged in the mammoth task of preparing a full set of orchestral parts. Luckily, the score consisted of separate sections for the individual movements, so that several groups of copyists could work on it simultaneously.

The choir of St Paul's Girls' School was coached for the choral part in *Neptune*, and as Sunday 29 September approached it seemed as if the whole school was involved in the performance in one way or another (Adrian Boult doubted whether any other work at all was done at the school at this time). Finally, all was ready, and on the evening before the concert Holst dined with Gardiner, Boult, and a few friends at Gardiner's club, the Savile. They discussed various points in the score and Geoffrey Toye pointed out a passage in *Neptune* where the brass play chords of E minor and G sharp minor together, saying: 'I'm sorry Gustav, but I can't help thinking that's going to sound frightful.' To which Holst replied: 'Yes I know; it made me shudder when I wrote it down, but what are you to do when they come like that?'[34] (As with many similar examples, the actual sound turned out to be much less dissonant than it appeared on paper. Edward Dent was surprised that the work sounded 'much less modern' than he had expected from reading the score.)

The Queen's Hall had been booked for three hours on the Sunday morning from 10.30 a.m. to 1.30 p.m., and the private concert was to consist of a rehearsal followed by a performance of the entire work. The choir was positioned in the stalls, while the invited audience took its place in the circle, including many of Holst's friends, colleagues, and pupils, well-known musicians such as Henry Wood, and the entire staff and pupils of St Paul's Girls' School. Among the audience were Isobel and eleven-year-old Imogen, who vividly remembered sitting in the darkened auditorium, looking down on the performers from her seat in the circle. The orchestra was led by Maurice Sons, a distinguished professor at the Royal College of Music, and the twenty-nine-year-old Adrian Boult calmly and competently directed the players as they sight-read the music movement by movement until 11.40, when they took a break. Then at twelve o'clock the whole suite was performed straight through, the choir slowly walking away from their seats and out of the hall at the end to achieve the required diminuendo in *Neptune*. The audience was overwhelmed—such music had never been heard before, and Holst received an ovation. Legend has it that even the charladies cleaning an adjacent corridor were moved to dance when they heard the music of *Jupiter*. Henry Wood was very impressed, as were Norman O'Neill and other officials of the Philharmonic Society, who immediately offered Boult an engagement to conduct two of their concerts during the coming season, to include the first public performance of *The Planets*. Holst was surrounded by friends and admirers, but eventually managed to slip away with his family to join Conrad Noel in a nearby basement tea-shop. The following day Holst wrote to Boult: 'I have discovered that there is no need for me to thank you or to congratulate you. It would be as ridiculous as for you to tell the Queen's Hall Orchestra that you didn't know the scores! You covered yourself with glory and the players are tremendously impressed . . . and your success is so certain that anything I could say or write would be impertinent.'[35] Later, he wrote about *Mars*: 'You made it wonderfully clear—in fact *everything* came out clearly that wonderful morning.'[36]

When all the congratulations had died down, there was a brief hiatus while Holst waited for notification of his departure date for Salonica. He filled in the time by taking a short course in piano tuning and repairing with J. Alfred Murdoch of Messrs Allison's Pianos Ltd, so that he would be well prepared to deal with practical mechanical problems as well as strictly musical ones. Then at the end of October he suddenly heard that he was to proceed to Salonica at thirty-six hours' notice. He hurriedly made final arrangements for his departure and said his farewells;—to Clifford Bax he remarked: 'Thank heaven, they've found some use for my music. It's all I can do.'[37]

10

Barrack-Room and University
(1918–1920)

On 1 November 1918 Holst arrived in France, where he was subjected to lengthy bureaucratic delays before he could proceed further. Eventually he joined a party of British personnel on a train bound for Rome, a journey which took some forty hours, and on arrival had to endure even more delays and form-filling. By 10 November he was *en route* for Brindisi, and he watched the Italian landscape becoming more barren as the train crawled slowly southwards ('Algeria was Bond St compared to this', he wrote home to Isobel[1]). Then the following day came the announcement of the Armistice, which was greeted with jubilation and much mutual congratulation and embracing between the Italians and British. But the news of peace made no difference to Holst's journey; demobilization of the large numbers of troops in various parts of Europe would take many months, and YMCA educational work would be essential to keep up their morale until they could be sent home. Holst wrote to Isobel: 'It has been wonderful beyond words, but all along I have felt that there will be deep disappointment for most of us if we expect the mere signing of peace to reform the world.'[2] On 14 November he wrote from Brindisi that he was still waiting for a boat to Salonica: 'I have been writing this while serving at the canteen with intervals for playing to the men. We have about 60 British sailors here also this place has been inundated with 300 Serbian refugees ... One of the Serbians was a musician. He got a piece of YMCA paper like this one and ruled some lines and wrote out the Serbian national anthem and two dances for me and I played them and they all sang.'[3]

Five days later Holst was on Corfu (which he described as a

'rather jolly island'[4]), waiting for another boat to take him on the final stage of his journey to Salonica. He found that his YMCA badge was a passport to friendship with the many Allied troops on the island, and was taken on sightseeing tours by eager volunteers. He finally arrived in Salonica on 1 December, finding himself disorientated in 'a nightmare of organisation, co-ordination, schemes, army forms, etc.'.[5] He had been dispatched to what had in effect become a forgotten corner of the war, where the British public thought the troops were simply idling away their time; music-hall songs were written about taking holidays there ('If you don't want to fight, go to Salonica'). But in fact conditions in the Balkans bore little resemblance to a holiday. Allied troops had arrived in Salonica at the end of 1915, and the following year had been joined by soldiers from the unsuccessful Gallipoli expedition; these were disorganized and lacked proper winter clothing, with the result that many suffered from frostbite during the ensuing winter. Few ordinary soldiers had been granted local leave during those three years, let alone leave in Britain. Although most people at home imagined that the troops were encamped just outside the town and spent most of their free time in it, the front was in fact 60 miles away, and leave passes for the journey to Salonica were virtually unobtainable. The great fire of August 1917 had destroyed a large section of the town, but few British troops were ever given an opportunity to visit what remained of it. These restrictions did not apply to officers, who could easily obtain periods of leave in Salonica, and many generated resentment by organizing events such as hunting with fox-hounds, from which ordinary soldiers were excluded.

To make matters worse, the British troops had been demoralized by the disastrous failure of their offensive on the Doiran front, plus widespread malaria, fever, and an influenza epidemic during which 10,000 soldiers were admitted to hospital. Large quantities of poison gas had been released by the British, to which the enemy (Germans and Bulgarians) had replied by firing gas shells into the British trenches with debilitating results. At the end of September the Bulgarians had requested an armistice, but instead of rejoicing, the British troops received the news with war-weary indifference.

Such was the disorganized and demoralized situation in which Holst found himself. From Salonica, which he described as 'a ramshackle, muddled affair',[6] he was sent to Summer Hill Camp, where Vaughan Williams had been posted for a few months in the Autumn of 1916. Vaughan Williams wrote to Holst: 'I wonder how you are getting on and whether you are arrived at your job yet—I hope for your sake it's not that god-forsaken place Summer Hill Camp.'[7] Apparently Vaughan Williams's main duties with the Royal Army Medical Corps had been to fill in puddles to prevent mosquitos breeding, and to wash down red bricks laid on the ground in the form of a cross as a signal to enemy aeroplanes; in between these tasks he had found time to organize and train the unit's band.

In the absence of precise instructions, Holst decided to go about the job by trial and error, and wrote to Vally Lasker: 'I'm going round in a friendly way, helping people when they want me and clearing out when they don't. I've done so for three days already with complete and most surprising success.'[8] He made contact with a Captain William Vowles, who had been trying to organize some musical activites; Holst walked in while Vowles was practising the piano in preparation for a talk, and insisted on helping out by acting as chairman. Vowles later recalled meeting Holst a few days after the talk: 'He had a bandage round his head and various pieces of plaster on his face and nose. "This is your fault", he said, "I was so excited after your talk that on my way back I was gazing up at the stars and humming the themes of the pieces you played and did not see a big hole in the road!" '[9]

Having spent most of his teaching career in middle-class girls' schools, the prospect of coping with large groups of toughened cynical soldiery might have deterred Holst, but in fact he achieved instant and unqualified success. His activites aroused tremendous enthusiasm among the troops, who volunteerd to join in all kinds of music-making; they seemed to be surprised and gratified that anyone was bothering to do anything for them at all. Nowadays, when so much music of all kinds is instantly available at the turn of a switch, it is difficult to imagine what it must have been like at that time to receive a visit from someone who was able to play and conduct music, and the soldiers responded whole-heartedly to Holst's efforts. Because of the constantly changing situation he had to be ready to adjust to any set of circumstances: demobilization was being carried out in a sporadic and haphazard way; sometimes Holst would arrive at a camp to organize an orchestra or give a lecture, only to find that most of the troops had left the previous day. He later recalled: 'The best bit of inventing I ever did was an impromptu History of Music one night. It was in the dark; we were waiting for the lorries with nothing to do while we waited, so I started talking a History of Music. I couldn't *see* anybody, you know—only the ends of lighted cigarettes. I just went on talking to the cigarette ends. I don't know whether anybody listened . . .'[10] He wrote home: 'The thing promises to be a great success, and I am overwhelmed by the quantity and the quality of the men who want music here. Occasionally, but not often, I am also overwhelmed—or partly so—by the difficulties.'[11] He had been given a room near the GHQ hut where he would be available each afternoon on an informal basis to teach music to anyone who cared to come along—an arrangement which found great favour with the soldiers, who were more accustomed to the rigours of a military timetable. Holst discovered that the level of musical knowledge and accomplishment varied enormously; some of his pupils were immature but were much encouraged by his efforts. To beginners he taught the elements of the tonic sol-fa system, while others considered that singing a simple tune was beneath them and wanted something 'better'. On one occasion sixteen men turned up for tuition, of whom fourteen were keen to learn the piano, and two wanted to learn how to sing. After a 'heart to heart' talk with Holst these numbers were reversed and he thus had a choir of fourteen voices which later went on to win first prize in a musical competition. One of his pupils was an aspiring composer, who brought a composition called *Vox Populi* for criticism. After looking through it, Holst pointed to a long passage of 'bare' writing, asking the pupil the reason for it. 'It is intended to be elemental' was the reply, to which Holst remarked, 'Yes, I understand, but you must not confuse "elemental" with "elementary"!'[12] Holst found it quite easy to get soldiers interested in any subject during a single lecture but to get them to work at it for week after week was another matter. He did however have several very keen pupils, and managed to enlist some new recruits for the Morley College orchestra, who promised to join when they returned to London on demobilization.

By the beginning of 1919 things had improved somewhat at Summer Hill Camp, and Holst wrote: 'We live sumptuously—food overwhelming in quantity and quite good in quality, wine cheap and the average YM worker here is a really fine fellow. When I go up into Bulgaria I shall probably have a rough time for a night or two but in Salonica I have a warm bed and lately we can have as much charcoal for braziers as we like. And above all, I have the fifth part of an orderly who cleans my boots, bless him. And all this time we get brilliant sunshine each day. Finally I've found a really good piano in a camp at which I lectured . . .'[13] When a set of tools arrived from YMCA headquarters, Holst wrote in dismay to Isobel: 'Scholes has sent a complete piano repairing outfit . . . I am bewildered each time I look at it,'[14] and later recalled: 'Except when a note was more than ½ tone out I always did more harm than good in my efforts. People should *never* experiment—it loosens the pins and makes the instrument infinitely worse in the long run.'[15]

At the end of January Holst went on a weekend car trip into Bulgaria, where he found the army scattered over a vast area with camps breaking up as men were dispersed to demobilization points. He crossed the Struma valley, where heavy fighting had taken place, and reported 'The greatest sight I have ever seen—I saw Greek peasants and their oxen ploughing the battlefield for the first time since the fighting ceased!'[16] On his return to Salonica he toured camps in the area, arranging lectures and concerts, including trying to project the words of songs on to a cinema screen in the absence of suitable music books. He conducted Schubert's 'Unfinished' Symphony and Mendelssohn's Violin Concerto with the Artillery School orchestra which had been founded by Henry C. Colles (music critic of *The Times*), who had been an artillery captain at Salonica before Holst's arrival. But he was still uncertain of the value of his work, writing to Whittaker: 'Probably some effect is produced but it doesn't show on the surface because one gets a fresh lot of pupils every few weeks—sometimes days.'[17]

By way of making his efforts more accessible to the majority of the troops, Holst decided to organize a concert of British music, fixing the date for 24 February. As a preliminary event he gave a lecture on British music in the Church Hall at Summer Hill Camp, followed by a rehearsal of the band and soloists. An audience of over 500 turned up, and Holst wrote: 'It was packed with a jolly, keen rowdy audience who hardly breathed during the music, who kindly laughed noisily at my jokes (I spouted mildly before each item) and then bellowed and stamped by way of applause.'[18] This preliminary lecture/rehearsal was so successful that Holst was concerned lest the actual concert might turn out to be an anticlimax. On Sunday 23 February a full rehearsal was held at the 52nd General Hospital, Salonica, in which all the music for the concert was tried through in front of an uninvited audience of between four and five hundred men, and the following day there was an afternoon rehearsal (attracting an audience of 300) preceding the concert. The programme was to consist of *Hiawatha's Wedding Feast* followed by various choral, vocal, instrumental, and orchestral items by Purcell, Stanford, Elgar, Collins, Lawes, German, and Grainger. The choir was made up of soldiers and nurses from the 43rd General Hospital and the orchestra was the Artillery Training School Band, consisting of flute, piccolo, oboe, clarinets, horns, cornets, trombones, piano, percussion, and fifteen strings. The choir had been trained by Captain Vowles, who conducted *Hiawatha's Wedding Feast*, while Holst conducted the remainder of the programme. Despite Holst's misgivings, the concert was an overwhelming success; an enormous audience turned up, sitting and standing in any space which would accommodate them inside and outside the 52nd General Hospital's large theatre marquee, while hundreds more (including senior staff officers) had to be turned away. The standard of performance was high, and the only complaint to be heard among the audience was that this kind of thing should have been put on long before. Because of the great demand from those unable to get in, the organizers agreed to repeat the concert on the following evening ('in order to prevent a free fight'[19]), and this again was a tremendous success.

After the first concert an oboe player helped Holst find his way through the dark to the main road, but hardly had they parted than Holst fell into a ditch and sprained his ankle. He was immediately taken to a hospital in the suburb of Kalamaria, where his foot was heavily swathed in bandages, but this did not prevent him from appearing in front of the orchestra for the repeat performance the following evening: 'So there was a more freakish conductor than ever last night'.[20] The next morning his ankle was X-rayed, revealing a suspected fracture, and he was ordered not to walk without using crutches. However, further scrutiny of the X-ray photographs failed to confirm this diagnosis, and Holst was allowed to return to his quarters.

A few days later, on 27 February 1919, the first public performance of *The Planets* suite conducted by Adrian Boult took place in London at the Queen's Hall, in the absence of its composer. Perhaps this was just as well, because it was an incomplete performance, omitting *Venus* and *Neptune*, and Holst was not in favour of the work being performed in such a truncated form. When preparing the programme, Adrian Boult had written to Vally Lasker: 'Gustav told me he would like to have all seven planets done at the first performance, and of course there is no question that it would be best for *musicians*, but the general public is a different matter, & I do most strongly feel that when they are being given a totally new language like that, 30 minutes of it is as much as they can take in, & I am quite sure that 90% if not 95% of people only listen to one *moment* after another, & never think of music as a whole at all.'[21]

The previous November Holst had written to Boult making various suggestions regarding his interpretation, asking that *Mars* should sound 'more unpleasant and far more terrifying' and that *Saturn* should be 'as emotional as possible' with the climax 'big and overwhelming'.[22] But the only way Holst had of knowing how well the performance had gone was by means of the press-cuttings sent to him by his friends, which reached him several weeks after the event. His only comment was: 'It's all quite nice, except that people seem to dislike Saturn which is my favourite.'[23]

As a result of a chance remark which he had made to the YMCA authorities while he was in hospital in Kalamaria,

Holst was unexpectedly granted a special leave permit to take a week off to visit Athens. He went during March, and the visit made a great impression on him. He admired the modern buildings as well as the ancient monuments, but was particularly impressed by the Parthenon, which he described as a building which 'sings and dances through sheer joy of existence', a phrase which embodied Holst's interpretation of the term Classical.[24] 'It is impossible to talk or write about Athens,' he wrote to Isobel, 'The whole trip was Revelation and Inspiration and one cannot talk about these . . .'[25]

On his return to Salonica he continued with his musical activities, on one occasion being obliged to join the second violins in the orchestra. He wrote home: 'I have not practised the violin since I was 13! . . . It was great fun, but I fear I was not of much use, especially when I had to go out of the first position. I got into 3rd all right, but I could not get back to the first again gracefully!'[26] (This statement is not entirely accurate, as Holst had occasionally played second violin in an *ad hoc* quartet at Vaughan Williams's home in Cowley Street, Westminster, where he lived from July 1898 to early 1899, which apparently persisted for some years, as Holst refers to the 'Cowley Str Wobblers' in a letter from Munich in 1903.[27] However, it was probably true that he had not practised the violin seriously since his schoolboy days.) During March his personal books and music arrived in Salonica, having taken five months to get there, and thus made his teaching work much easier. Also from home came news that on 19 March W. G. Whittaker had given a performance of the *Hymn to Dionysus* in Newcastle with the Armstrong College Choir, and that the first concert performance of the *Japanese Suite* had been given on 22 March by the Bradford Permanent Orchestra.

Holst had known for some time that he was likely to be transferred to Constantinople in the wake of the Headquarters of the British army, and at the end of March was told that he was to leave within a few days. The night before his departure his kitbag was stolen, containing all his personal possessions, letters, and diaries. Among the missing items which he never saw again was his musical notebook, in which he had noted down sketches for works in progress.

On arrival in Constantinople he immediately set about exploring the city on foot, and walked so much that his sprained ankle began to give trouble. At first his teaching duties were light, allowing sufficient time for exploration, but soon his time was taken up in making arrangements for musical activities and lectures in the army camp at Feneraki. On 14 April he attended an education conference at GHQ at which the idea of a competitive music festival was put forward; a proposal which Holst took up with enthusiasm. On Good Friday he attended a Greek Orthodox service, and the following day went first to an Armenian church at Kum Kapon and then to a Greek church in the evening, where the service lasted from 11.30 p.m. until 3 a.m. on Easter Sunday morning. After a brief sleep, he went to another Armenian church in Pera, followed by a special YMCA service for the Allied troops later in the morning.

More music and instruments arrived from home, and on 24 April he held his first violin class, for which too many pupils turned up for him to be able to give more than rudimentary tuition, and on the same day he conducted the first meetings of the YMCA orchestra and choir. On 25 April the musical competition was announced, and entries were invited from choirs and orchestras from all the British troops in the area. The following day Holst worked on scoring the folk-song *Spanish Ladies* for unison voices and orchestra, but from then on had little time for such activities as his days were filled by a continual round of lecturing, teaching individual pupils, and conducting, including a performance of madrigals on a house-top overlooking the Sea of Marmora, with the sun setting in the distance. Holst found his work in Constantinople 'much more thrilling than in Salonica, chiefly, I suppose, because I've now got some music to work with. It *does* make a difference.'[28]

He had been asked by the YMCA and the army to continue his work for a further year, but he was doubtful about doing so. He wrote to Miss Gray explaining his quandary: 'I feel that the work at home is the more important of the two as it is the more permanent and certain in the results. The work here is that of a pioneer and it *might* be that at the end of a year I *might* lay the foundations for someone else to carry on with.'[29] Isobel went to see his employers, who were mostly agreeable to his continued absence—at Morley College Richard Terry agreed to continue to take Holst's classes, provided that he could send a deputy when he was too busy to come himself, and it was arranged that Percy Scholes would take the University Extension classes there. Holst however was still unsure as to exactly when he would return and what sort of work he would do when he got back. He had a fear of becoming involved in administrative work, and felt that his real vocation was to continue with his teaching work among amateurs and schoolgirls, declaring that: 'An artist should do creative work and anything that brings him into contact with people, characters and souls, such as teaching. And he should avoid all routine, organisation or questions of mechancial efficiency.'[30] When the post of Director of the Royal College of Music had become vacant on the death of Parry in October 1918, he wrote to Vally Lasker: 'The Directorship of the RCM is an excellent example of the sort of big job that kills an artist. Parry sacrificed himself to save an awkward situation but I still feel that the sacrifice was too great. I don't mind Allen taking it on but I dread RVW being offered something of the sort. I suppose he would decline. But he would accept if the question of self-sacrifice and duty came in as it did with Parry. The whole matter is too complicated for a letter but I have very definite ideas on it and some day I'll inflict them on you.'[31]

On 10 May Holst received a telegram informing him that *The Hymn of Jesus* had been selected by the Carnegie United Kingdom Trust as one of five works to receive an award that year, out of sixty-four compositions submitted by British composers. The adjudicators described the work as 'a notable addition to the choral music of this country. It is strikingly original in plan and conception, and expresses with an impressive fidelity the mysticism and the power of the words.'[32] The award consisted of subsidized publication under the imprint of Stainer & Bell Ltd., who immediately put the vocal and full scores into production.

For Holst in Constantinople however, things were not going too well. The weather had suddenly deteriorated and there was unrest among the civilian population; camp pickets had to be doubled and the soldiers stood on guard in the cold and wet for hours on end. On 19 May Holst had only one pupil and found himself without an orchestra or choir. He occupied himself with scoring his own music and odd jobs such as mending a piano in the camp. But the situation rapidly improved and he was soon busy with preparations for the forthcoming musical competition, for which he had specified music by Byrd, Purcell, Henry Lawes, Weelkes, and Morley, together with some English folk-songs, so that 'it may convince people here that there's something in British music after all'.[33] He persuaded the YMCA to publish a version of Byrd's three-part Mass which he and Jane Joseph had edited with English words for use in Thaxted Church, 'in the belief that our soldiers and sailors will learn to love singing and listening to this masterpiece of English music'.[34]

The competition was to take place on 7 June, to be followed by a massed concert of choirs and orchestras on Whit Monday, which would be repeated every night of the week. Holst had decided to include in the concert a version of *A Festival Chime* under the title *A Chime for the Home-Coming*, with words specially written for the occasion by Lieut A. Redford of the Manchester Regiment, and he spent the few days before the concert in a desperate search for the necessary bells. Other music scheduled for the concert included works by Purcell, German, Vaughan Williams, Elgar, Grainger, and a setting of *Dashing Away with the Smoothing Iron* by Holst's pupil Irene Bonnett. The music by Purcell included several movements from incidental music for *The Gordian Knot Untied*, *The Married Beau*, *The Old Bachelor*, and *The Virtuous Wife*, which Holst had previously arranged as string suites with ad lib wind parts for use at St Paul's Girls' School and for which he was unable to find a publisher until some years after the war had ended. (On publication, the *Musical Times* commented: 'It was a happy thought to rescue such delightful music . . . now that the interest in Purcell is so keen it is to be hoped that this salvage work will be carried on with vigour . . . Nothing could be better for school orchestras and amateur bands than these Suites.'[35])

The festival concerts were held in the YMCA Théatre Petits Champs and were open to all Allied troops of the Army of the Black Sea without payment; the competition adjudicator being Captain Vowles, with whom Holst had worked in Salonica. Entries had been received from a wide area; some from as far as a thousand miles away, and the competitors included bands, choirs, violinists, pianists, singers, and composers. When Vowles arrived, he discovered that he was expected to play the viola, sing in the choir, and also lecture on music, in addition to adjudicating the festival. When he protested that he had not prepared any lecture material, Holst simply pushed him through the curtains on to the stage and let him get on with it. Holst also persuaded Vowles to conduct a separate choir to sing *Sumer is Icumen In* while walking down the aisle towards the main choir and away again at the end. The competition got off to an uncertain start when the French contingent and its orchestra failed to appear, but the event went ahead in spite of this setback, and was a great success. Afterwards Holst got some of the performers to try through *A Chime for the Home-Coming*, which he then took away to copy out the orchestral parts for use in the forthcoming evening concerts. On Whit Monday there was a successful morning rehearsal; the choir numbering about 30 and the orchestra 20 players, but in spite of this the evening concert turned out to be rather dull, and afterwards Holst felt exhausted. Throughout the week the standard of performance at the evening concerts varied erratically, as did the size of the audiences, which were sometimes quite small. The Tuesday concert was attended by the Commander-in-Chief, while on the morning of Saturday 14 June there was a comic song competition by way of light relief, and after the evening concert prizes were presented to the competition winners. Holst wrote to Isobel that 'on the whole our musical competition has been a success, although not a brilliant one. But it has left a deep impression on many, especially the choir, and that is the main point.'[36] He was glad that the festival was over, as he felt that he had done some good work, but also because he had finally decided not to accept the YMCA's offer of another year's duty and was looking forward to being able to return home as soon as the festival was over.

On the Sunday after the week of concerts the weather was very hot, so Holst did nothing but 'loll about all day' in his quarters and in the gardens at Bomonti Park, and in the evening he had a farewell get-together with William Vowles and other friends at the Petits Champs.[37] The following morning he went shopping for gifts to take home, and bought some embroidery for Isobel. By 3 p.m. he was on board ship, and at 7.30 sailed for Italy. On 17 and 18 June the ship stopped to take on more troops and arrived at Taranto on 21 June, where Holst had to spend the night in a rowdy hut in 'terrific heat'.[38] The next day he rose at 4.20 a.m. to walk and swim, and joined his train for departure at 11.15 a.m. The accommodation was not entirely up to standard, however, as the passengers occupied themselves for most of the afternoon in a 'bug hunt'. The train crawled lethargically through Italy, with two-hour meal-breaks at Bari, Termino, and Castelmaria, finally arriving at Faenza at 9 a.m. two days later. Having all day to spare, Holst visited the cathedral and other sights before rejoining the train for the journey through the Alps. The weather now turned cold and wet and the travellers soon discovered that the roof of their compartment was not entirely waterproof. At midday the train stopped at St Germaine, where Holst went for a walk alone, and on 27 June arrived at the outskirts of Paris, which was circumnavigated with many stops, finally arriving at Boulogne the following afternoon. After some confusion, Holst managed to board a boat for England, arriving at Folkestone at 7.30, where he joined the London train and arrived exhausted at Vally Lasker's flat in Talgarth Road at 11 p.m. The next day (Sunday) he met his stepbrother Max and visited Imogen at her school in Caterham in the afternoon, and the following day, after playing the organ for prayers at St Paul's Girls' School, calling at the Royal College of Music and the YMCA offices, took the train to Thaxted to rejoin his wife.

After resting for a week or so he began to resume his teaching duties, and received a tremendous welcome from his pupils. On 12 July he reported to Whittaker: 'I'm having a wild time. My clothes were nearly torn off by 350 small people at my Dulwich school yesterday.'[39] He arranged to teach at St Paul's for only three days a week, spending Thursday to Sunday at Thaxted and catching the early train to London on Monday mornings. On 4 July he conducted the *Two Songs Without Words* and *Carnival* from the *Suite de Ballet* at a Royal College of Music concert which was attended by the Prince of Wales, and on 29 July there was a special end-of-term concert at St Paul's, after which he returned to Thaxted for a few days.

Then, to refresh his mind, he set out on a walking tour in the Cotswolds and nearby areas, including a visit to Balfour Gardiner at Ashampsted, Berkshire. In Hampshire he was caught in a rainstorm and sheltered at the Grosvenor Hotel, Stockbridge, where he had to get into bed while the staff dried his clothes, but his enthusiasm for the English countryside was undiminished: 'The walk today has been splendid and the Teste Valley is beautiful,' he wrote.[40]

After visiting Cirencester and Oxford, he returned to Thaxted about the middle of August and settled down to compose a work which was motivated by the waste of life and futility of the war, the *Ode to Death*, in memory of the musicians and friends, particularly the young composer Cecil Coles, who had been killed in the trenches. For the words, he turned once again to Walt Whitman's *Leaves of Grass*, this time choosing the elegy 'When lilacs last in the Dooryard Bloom'd' from 'Memories of President Lincoln', invoking 'lovely, soothing death' with sequences of parallel fifths in an atmosphere of quiet resignation at the beginning and end of the work (although juxtaposed against more conventional material in the central part). Such calmness in the face of the inevitable recalls the attitude of Savitri, a feature of Hindu literature and philosophy which can be traced in Holst's music throughout his career.

By the end of the summer of 1919 he had almost finished writing the libretto of his satirical opera *The Perfect Fool*. At first he had asked Jane Joseph if she would undertake the task ('being my old pupil she won't take offence if I tell her that it won't do', he confided to Isobel[41]), but it is not clear whether she actually started work on the project. 'After trying for a long time, I have taught myself to feel what is wanted in a libretto,' Holst remarked; 'You have two distinct jobs in the words:-1) to make the situation clear, as simply as possible, 2) having done so, to rub it in. But the libretto of the Fool wants a light touch, and I find I haven't one.'[42] He next turned to Clifford Bax, who declined on the grounds that he was unable to find the plot as amusing as the composer evidently imagined it to be, and at this stage Holst decided to write the words himself, undeterred by his own earlier efforts or by the example of certain composers whose literary abilities have not matched their musical gifts. He was well aware that a bad libretto could spoil a work, but knew that music could rise above even the most banal words: 'What a pity that Beethoven should have had such drivelling libretti,' Holst once remarked; 'Of course, most people say that the libretto of *The Magic Flute* is contemptible, but it isn't—to me!'[43]

As the autumn season began, he found himself much in demand as a conductor of his own works. On 1 September he conducted the first London concert performance of the *Japanese Suite* at a Queen's Hall Promenade concert with the New Queen's Hall Orchestra, and on 22 November directed the same orchestra at the Queen's Hall in a performance of *Venus, Mercury,* and *Jupiter.* Holst disliked incomplete performances of *The Planets,* objecting particularly to ending the suite with *Jupiter* to provide a 'happy ending', but sometimes had to accede to the requests of conductors. He once remarked that such performances were better than no performance at all. This particular occasion was the first public performance of *Venus,* which Boult had omitted from his Philharmonic Society concert earlier in the year, and Alfred Kalisch commented: 'The "Venus" movement . . . bears the sub-title "The Bringer of Peace"—which, however, seems an inconclusive peace, with no League of Nations to give it stability. It is the least powerful, in point of imagination, of the series, but like the rest shows a fine sense of rich orchestral colour. The composer made the other two movements sound considerably less dramatic and elemental than did Mr Boult when he conducted them, but a little more intellectual. In any event, it is a notable work.'[44] On 14 December Holst conducted the same three movements at the Queen's Hall as part of a Sunday Musical Union concert, while on 23 December the Oriana Madrigal Society conducted by Charles Kennedy Scott gave the first London performance of *This Have I Done for My True Love* in their concert in the Aeolian Hall. Not everything was a success for Holst that autumn however: he submitted *Hecuba's Lament* to Novello for publication, but much to his disappointment it was rejected (the work was eventually published a few years later by Stainer & Bell).

During the term he occasionally visited Eothen School at Caterham (at which Imogen had been a pupil from 1917 to 1919) to lecture on music at the invitation of Jane Joseph who taught there, and for whom he also deputized from time to time. Then, towards the end of term, a new factor came into his teaching commitments. Hugh P. Allen, now Director of the Royal College of Music, asked Holst to join the staff to teach theory and composition, and a few weeks later a similar request came from University College, Reading. Adrian Boult had been conductor of the choral society and orchestra at Reading, but had resigned owing to pressure of work. The Music Committee had then decided to combine the conductor-ship with a teaching appointment in harmony and com-position, which would incorporate the existing classes in the theory of music. Two names were suggested for the appoint-ment; those of Holst and Thomas Dunhill, and after taking the advice of Hugh Allen, the Committee decided to offer the post to Holst. The acceptance of these two appointments meant resigning from his teaching at James Allen's Girls' School (although he did return occasionally to mgive lectures and conduct carol-singing), but he retained his posts at St Paul's Girls' School and Morley College.

At Reading, Holst was responsible for individual composi-tion tutorials and for taking classes in harmony and counter-point (which all full-time music students were expected to attend), in addition to conducting the orchestra and choral society. This teaching of music specialists was a different matter from coping with schoolgirls and amateur musicians in adult evening classes, but as usual Holst managed to find a way of approaching the problem and became just as successful as a professor of composition as he had been in his other teaching activities. As with other composers who have taught composi-tion for a living, the lessons made him think more deeply about his own beliefs and forced him to articulate ideas which had previously existed only instinctively in his mind and which he had never before had to put into words. He regarded his teaching not as a master imparting knowledge to a pupil, but as a process of mutual discovery in which both could share. As he wrote in 1921: 'In the Middle Ages a great painter had several pupils working in close comradeship with him in his studio. This is one of the best ways of fostering the artistic impulse and the power of artistic expression. And one of its best features is the continual comradeship with the master.

This ensures education in the deeper sense: the unfolding of the pupil's mind—largely unconsciously.'[45]

He also wrote of 'The wonderful feeling of unity with one's pupils when teaching, a feeling of contact with their minds other than the contact occasioned by speech'.[46] He believed that the teacher's work should be confined to watching over his pupil's efforts and offering guidance when necessary, and as with his school-teaching work, he thought that the prime objective of a teacher was to make himself unnecessary. This was even more pertinent in the case of composition students, for he doubted whether composition can be taught at all; the most a teacher can do is to try to draw out talents which the pupil may or may not possess and help him find his own way. As he told his pupil W. Probert-Jones: 'If you have no ideas, I can't do anything for you; I can only try to bring out what is already inside, I cannot put music *into* you.'[47] He was not patronizing, and always made his pupils feel that their own work was worth taking seriously; although he would make suggestions for improvements, he would not insist that these should be followed, and would leave it to the pupil to make the final decision.

Holst never expected his pupils to follow his own style, preferring them to develop their own individuality, but even so, a few of them did imitate some of his own mannerisms such as ostinato chords, descending bass lines and asymetrical metres, although this gave him no particular pleasure. His real interest was in pupils with ideas (undisciplined as they may be) and an urge to compose, rather than those who had acquired academic ability but were lacking in any real creativity. His lessons would consist partly of analysis of works by the masters, and partly of criticism of the pupil's own work. He would insist on clarity and conciseness of musical thought, cutting out any padding or unnecessary complications which did not add anything to the basic musical concept. Note-spinning and empty rhetorical gestures were anathema to him, and he made his pupils question the value of every note. Although he regarded clarity in thinking, hearing, and feeling as prime aims in composition, he was also aware of the danger of concentrating on craftsmanship simply for its own sake: 'This clarity is to me the ideal in training the composer, but we must remember that training is only a small part of education; and we must take care that a blind worship does not lead us into cheap formalism. This will never happen if the student is really educated—if his powers of feeling and expressing emotion are drawn out.'[48]

By way of widening his pupils horizons, he would constantly refer to the works of creative artists in other fields, drawing parallels between their work and the problems of the aspiring composer. His views on literature were conveyed in such a way that his pupils immediately became caught up in his own enthusiasms: after one such talk about Conrad's *Lord Jim*, Edmund Rubbra immediately rushed out to read all the books by Conrad which he could find.

If the weather were fine, Holst would take his pupils for a walk, during which all manner of subjects would be discussed, from Conrad to William Morris, including the work of composers such as Palestrina and Vittoria. This informal approach to study was the same as he had used successfully with the troops in Macedonia. Holst recalled an incident from that period: 'I was speaking on Music to some soldiers for about an hour and a half, and afterwards while a few of us were talking together I happened to refer to the lecture I had just given. "Lecture?—you call that a lecture? That wasn't a lecture—that was a chat!" '[49] As with the troops, his main ingredient for success with his composition pupils was his own love of music which he was able to convey to those who studied with him, generating an enthusiasm of their own which would carry them through the problems of later years as they struggled to make their own careers as composers. In his article 'The Education of a Composer', Holst firmly stated that it is love of music, not mere admiration, which is the real education of a composer, and in a lecture which he gave at Yale University in 1929 he declared:

In the teaching of art we aim at the production of artists, of exceptional people, of aristocrats, in whatever department of life they may happen to be, whether builders of cathedrals or good cooks in village inns. The best definition of what I call an aristocrat is Gilbert Murray's: 'Every man who counts is a child of tradition and a rebel from it'. The production of such a man is the aim of the teaching of art. If we are teachers our first duty is to make our pupil a child of tradition. We can only do that if we are ourselves its children. Not merely students but children, steeped in the love of our tradition— that unconscious love that children possess and which is the most contagious emotion in the world. Our influence on our pupil is assured if we have this.[50]

This love of music is well illustrated by an incident which a Morley College student recalled some years later: 'In the composition class we seldom had technical details without the vivifying warmth of musical appreciation. I remember, for example, the night when Schubert's songs were brought out to illustrate some point under discussion. We had our illustration but the whole song was sung by one of the students, and the lesson finished by Holst remarking in a reverent whisper: "But that's the sort of music that should be listened to and not talked about".'[51]

But this love of music must be backed up by competent musicianship, which Holst encouraged his pupils to acquire through experience, avoiding formal theoretical learning as much as possible, in accordance with his favourite paraphrase of Samuel Butler: 'Never learn to do; learn by doing.'[52] Imogen Holst, who studied at the Royal College of Music, later recalled: 'I can remember that when I was about 14 he said to me: "There's one thing I want you to promise me. Don't ever read a textbook on harmony".'[53] He followed no rigid methods in his teaching—each problem was treated on its own merits and related to the abilities and style of the pupil. But neither did he believe in total freedom; rather, that all artistic endeavours are governed by laws of proportion which remain constant throughout changes of style and fashion, and which can only be assimilated by experience. Above all, he would insist that his pupils' compositions should be practical, and that they should be capable of writing for amateurs as well as for professionals; often organizing ad hoc ensembles to try through their work. He even encouraged them to write for players of limited ability if that was all they had available. He advised them to make their instrumentation as flexible as possible (as he himself did in many of his own works) and to score their compositions for small ensembles before attempting to write for larger forces.

Such students were fortunate to have had Holst as a teacher.

Few composers make successful teachers, and many out-standing teachers of composition do not achieve success as composers themselves. If given the choice, most pupils would probably prefer to study with a creator, rather than with a theoretician, but to find a good teacher and creative artist combined in one person is a happy chance, and Holst's pupils were quick to realize their good fortune and to take full advantage of it. As Arthur Bliss remarked: 'I had heard movements from his gigantic suite *The Planets*, and to have a lesson from a man who could make an orchestra sound so magnificently vivid as he could was a wonderful opportunity . . .' Bliss had written two studies for orchestra which had been accepted for performance in the Patron's Fund concerts, but wanted some advice on them before the parts were copied. He took them along to Holst, who looked ‹through them with interest. 'He pounced on a tune that I had rather weakly given to the cellos,' Bliss recalled; ' "But this is a trombone tune", Holst said, "it *can't* be anything else!" How right he was, when I heard it! In my second and rather lengthy "Study" he looked at the first and second page and then suddenly turning to me said, "But *when* is it going to begin?"'—a devastating criticism but accurate. It hadn't really begun. I knew that instinctively.'[54]

Another pupil with a subsequently distinguished career was Edmund Rubbra, who studied with Holst both at Reading and at the Royal College of Music. Rubbra later wrote that 'Holst's over-riding characteristic as a teacher was his deep identification with what a struggling young composer was trying to say. Not many teachers would carry his pupil's problems away with him and worry over them between lessons and to send a solution on a post-card: or, when genuinely pleased with something a pupil had written, organise a performance *and* a small audience for the next lesson. Nothing could give a young composer more confidence in himself than this unself-conscious sharing of the problems of music-making between master and pupil.'[55] Holst conducted a performance of a one-movement work for piano and orchestra by Rubbra, with the composer as soloist, and encouraged him to simplify his style and resources by writing songs for voice with accompaniment other than the piano. Holst was particularly intrigued by one such song, entitled *Rosa Mundi*, which made Rubbra realize that he had discovered a new lyrical direction for his music, having its roots in his own musical nature rather than being imposed from outside. But Holst did not approve of one of Rubbra's fugues on an ultra-chromatic subject, which had been suggested by R. O. Morris as an antidote to excessive diatonicism. Another pupil said of Holst's methods: 'If you do anything really dreadful, he says "Yes. This is quite bad. We all do this sort of thing". He rarely tells you a thing as a fact, but illustrates the point from essays and books and poems. If you are doing well he makes you go on—draws out what you have.'[56]

Besides detailed practical comments, Holst also gave his students general advice and guidelines for their efforts. To a pupil who had left college, he wrote: 'I'm glad you're composing, but don't indulge in the waste paper basket. Put things in cold storage on a shelf for six months, and then see how they are keeping. If they look fresh and wholesome, send them to me.' To Whittaker he remarked: 'Never write music when you feel excited,'[57] and: 'I think a good rule is—"never compose anything unless the not composing of it becomes a positive nuisance to you." Which is a paraphrase of what Samuel Butler said of learning.'[58] One ex-pupil who had gone on to university wrote to him to say that she was worried about her musical prospects, and Holst replied: 'Your present state of mind is *absolutely ideal* for a student—you could not better it if you tried. So go on doing things VWI [Very Well Indeed] and go on being depressed about yourself and as long as you don't overdo either one person, at least, will feel happy about you. And—as the young composer said when they asked who was the greatest living musician—That's Me! Having had more experience in failing at exams than anyone else I know I don't feel quite certain that it is really the best of luck to always pass.'[59]

Holst did not expect his pupils to bring new compositions every week, for he believed that music could not be forced out of them—the work had to go through a natural gestation process until it developed sufficient identity and impetus to emerge of its own accord. When there were no student compositions to look at he would analyse scores ranging from the classics to twentieth-century music—he was particularly fond of *Petrushka* as an example of brilliant orchestration, and was excited by Vaughan Williams's Mass in G minor, which he brought to his classes as soon as it was published. He did not use his own works as examples, much to the regret of his students, but they nevertheless studied them privately and his latest publications were awaited with eager anticipation. In a discussion of various composers' works, one pupil condemned a composition by one of Holst's contemporaries, thinking that it would not appeal to him, but was surprised to find that he did in fact like it (his tastes were wide-ranging and unpredictable) and was therefore dismayed when Holst pressed him for his reasons, exposing the lack of evidence for his remark. Holst always preferred sincere disagreement to insincere agreement, and Edmund Rubbra recalled that 'This preference led in my case to many wordy battles about the respective merits of his contemporaries.'[60] None of Holst's successful pupils imitated his style in their subsequent careers (although traces of his influence are widespread), but all were greatly influenced by his teaching, expressed best by Edmund Rubbra: 'In Holst's presence one felt one's own musical stature heightened and one's powers strangely augmented.'[61]

11

Growing Fame
(1920–1922)

Holst's big event of early 1920 was the first performance of *The Hymn of Jesus*. Or rather, there were two first performances: the choral class at the Royal College of Music learnt the work during the spring term and gave a performance at the College under Holst's direction on 10 March, while on 25 March he conducted the first public performance at a Royal Philharmonic Society concert at the Queen's Hall with the newly-formed Philharmonic Choir and orchestra. The work was dedicated to Vaughan Williams, who after hearing it 'wanted to get up and embrace everyone and then get drunk'.[1] This enthusiasm was shared by the rest of the Queen's Hall audience who clamoured for a repetition, but despite the pleas of several musicians who went behind the scenes to demand a repeat, this was denied to them. Such a choral work had never before been heard in Britain, and the music made a deep impression on the audience.

A student who took part later recalled: 'I shall never forget the rehearsals at the Royal College of Music for one of the first performances ... To us who were young then and eager for something that would lift us out of the rut of common experience this very new music which, for all its novelty of expression seemed firmly rooted in the great tradition of English choral writing, came first as a shock, then as a revelation. To many the work was like a trumpet call in the renaissance of English creative music. To some of us it seemed something even more, a vindication of the right of the English composer to be considered as a potential contributor to the general musical culture of the world at large.'[2] Donald Tovey wrote: 'It completely bowls me over. If anybody doesn't like it, he doesn't like life. It is obviously inspired by the profoundest emotional sense of the Eucharist. The words seem to shine in the light and depth of a vast atmosphere created by the music.'[3] Writing of a later performance, the *Musical Times* described the work as a 'strange but not incongruous blend of archaism and modernism',[4] and Edmund Rubbra considered that it is the symbolism of the pagan initiation ceremony which 'gives the work its fascinating blend of earthly activity and heavenly serenity'.[5]

At all events the work was a great success and was performed many times in various places during the next few years. In April 1920 Holst wrote to Whittaker: 'The 1st ed is exhausted, the Phil is repeating it on June 2nd, the RCM and Oxford are doing it this summer and most other people in the autumn!'[6] By 1923 the Carnegie edition of the vocal score had passed through several editions, numbering 8,500 copies in all, demonstrating the enormous popularity of choral singing at that time and the eagerness of choral societies to perform new works by British composers.

As the summer approached, Holst decided to revive the idea of the Whitsun festivals, although they could no longer be held at Thaxted because of the friction with Conrad Noel (whose views had become so notorious that some Cambridge under-graduates had gone to Thaxted and cut a hole in the medieval church door in order to break in and tear down the Red Flag and Sinn Fein banner which hung inside). So in 1920 it was decided to hold the festival at Dulwich, and permission was obtained to use the quadrangle and chapel of Alleyn's College. This festival included the usual favourite music of Holst and his pupils, together with the first performance of a *Short Festival Te Deum* which he had written for his Morley College students the previous year. The programme was rehearsed in the quadrangle on Saturday 22 May, and performed as part of a service the following morning. Because the Chapel was not large enough to accommodate choir, orchestra, and congregation, the service was held in the open air, and the resulting scene was as colourful as at Thaxted, with each girl wearing a brightly-coloured veil. In the afternoon the performers went in procession to the Infirmary where they played and sang for the old people there, and in the evening there was another open-air service, followed by informal music-making. On the Monday there was a similar morning service, the afternoon being spent in the Chaplain's garden and looking round the art gallery, with more informal music in the evening. According to the *Morley College Magazine*: 'Two features of particular interest during the evening were a Mystery Play, "The Adoration of the Shepherds", and the delightful dancing of Mr Holst's gifted little daughter with her troop of nymphs and swains, the orchestral music for which was composed by the little dancer herself.'[7] The final session was held in the Chapel, and included another first performance: the Kyrie from Vaughan Williams's Mass in G minor, of which Dorothy Callard later recalled: 'The most exciting thing that happened was, that whilst we were eating our lunch in the chaplain's garden, Mr Holst came to me and said Uncle Ralph is writing us a Communion service for our festivals. He has brought the Kyrie with him this morning. Now you borrow my fountain pen and go into the vestry and make eight single voice copies and we'll try it through. So I did. Twelve of us went up into the chapel gallery, with Mr Holst perched on the corner of the balustrade, and Ralph Vaughan Williams on the organ seat . . .'[8]

For some time W. G. Whittaker had been planning to give the first public performance of Holst's *Two Psalms*, which dated from 1912. This was eventually fixed for 18 July 1920, and Holst was invited to Newcastle to conduct. The Psalms were scored for mixed voices, strings, and organ, but as the performance was to take place in the open air, the organ part was rearranged for brass band and last-minute scoring was done to give the voices and strings some extra support from wind instruments. The performance took place in the interval of a football match at St James's Park Ground, Newcastle, before a crowd of twenty thousand people; the Newcastle and District Festival Choir numbered 800, the orchestra 100 and the St Hilda Brass Band 30 players.

At last term was over, and Holst wrote to Whittaker: 'Just off to a Benedictine Monastery for a week where I am going to learn plainsong and write a comic opera.'[9] The monastery was Quarr Abbey near Ryde in the Isle of Wight, where the Benedictines had settled in 1901 after their enforced departure from Solesmes for non-compliance with the Law of Associations; the comic opera was *The Perfect Fool*, whose synopsis he had drafted the previous year. On 20 August he wrote to Vally Lasker: 'I've nearly finished the first sketch of the libretto ... I simply wrote any drivel that came into my head ...',[10] and later to Whittaker: 'I've been longing to do my Perfect Fool opera for 14 years and at last it's begun. (N.B. It is *meant* to be funny).'[11] Of the monastery, he remarked: 'As a place for writing the libretto of a comic opera it leaves much— most everything in fact—to be desired. The Monks are dears ... and I got housemaid's knee through attending so many services ...'[12] Later in the summer he drafted the music for the whole work, and made a 'complete sketch' the following year, but it was not until 1922 that the opera was completed in its final form.

One work which he did complete during 1920 was the *Seven Choruses from the Alcestis of Euripides*, written for a perform-ance of the play at St Paul's Girls' School, and dedicated to the High Mistress, Frances Ralph Gray. The choruses are scored for voices in unison, harp, and three flutes, although they were sometimes performed with pizzicato strings instead of harp. The words were taken from Gilbert Murray's translation of the *Alcestis* and are set in an economical but effective way, well within the capabilities of undeveloped voices.

On 19 September Holst conducted the City of Birmingham Symphony Orchestra at the Theatre Royal, Birmingham, in performances of the *Japanese Suite*, the *Jig* from the *St Paul's Suite*, and a dance entitled *The Djinn* from the incidental music to *The Sneezing Charm*. A few weeks later a ballet called *A Magic Hour* was performed at the Old Vic by members of the Morley College music and gymnastic classes under Holst's direction; the music for this was probably taken from *The Sneezing Charm*, which eventually also provided the ballet music with which *The Perfect Fool* begins.

At the beginning of October, Holst wrote to Whittaker: 'We are doing some of the choruses from the B minor at Morley ... We have 40 rough sopranos who try and play follow my leader without a leader, ten altos who are really mezzos, ten good musical chaps who try and sing tenor (and who usually succeed!) and ten inefficient basses. Next Sunday I am going to try and conduct some of the Planets at Birmingham with a band mostly composed of Cinema players. So you see, life is not dull.'[13] This latter performance was put in the shade the following month by the first public performance of the entire suite, given at the Queen's Hall on 15 November by the London Symphony Orchestra conducted by Albert Coates. The work was enormously enhanced by being performed complete, and even the critic Alfred Kalisch, whose response had previously been lukewarm, was moved to write: 'The whole gains immensely when rounded off by the last number, "Neptune the Mystic" (heard for the first time), with its ethereal ending . . . The performance was remarkably fine.'[14] The work received a tremendous ovation, and when Coates beckoned Holst to the platform to acknowledge the applause, he came forward 'like a schoolboy summoned by the head', according to one eyewitness.[15] An ex-pupil of his, Nancy Gotch, also saw him at this time: 'I sat near him in the Queen's Hall . . . Holst might have been anyone up from the country, staring at the orchestra with a hand on each knee—completely absorbed, but with a "this is none of me" expression. The applause and the singling of him out at the end to acknowledge it seemed to mystify and embarrass him.'[16]

This successful performance confirmed the stature of the work in the view of both public and musicians, and conductors were soon vying with each other to give performances even though Holst had as yet been unable to find a publisher willing to accept it. In particular, there was some friendly rivalry between the Chicago and New York Symphony Orchestras for the privilege of giving the first American performance; as Albert Coates had already conducted it in London, he wanted to give it with the New York orchestra, but Frederick Stock had heard a performance of the two-piano version and wanted the work for Chicago. A compromise was eventually agreed: the performances would take place on the same day in each city, but because of the time zone difference, New York would just have the edge.

As a result of these performances, Holst's name began to be known to a wider public, and he found himself increasingly pestered by journalists and gossip-column writers. He detested all such interviewers and the photographers they brought with them, and his replies would become briefer until eventually he would withdraw into silence, making it clear that the interview was at an end. By refusing to submit to the public's demand for sensational information about well-known 'personalities' he was to set the seal on his eventual fall from favour, but he insisted on leading an ordinary life, and as Arthur Bliss later remarked:

> One is far too apt to take for granted the exceptional artist who can be seen living daily in our midst. There he is, just like us, getting on a bus, or sitting and eating in a tea-shop! If we miss an opportunity to meet and talk with his—well, there will surely be other chances. And then he dies, and there is *no* second chance. I now feel this deeply about Holst. I was with him only a few times, but each is indelibly engraved on my memory by some short pithy statement that he made. He had the utter honesty of opinion that riveted attention: there was no possibility of misunderstanding what he thought or what he felt.[17]

Holst sensed the fickleness of the public, who expect their idols to burn themselves out and be replaced by other newer gods, and therefore failed to provide the required journalistic copy. He was much more at ease making music, either with professionals or with amateurs and schoolchildren, and his new-found success did not prevent him from appearing in public with amateur performers; on 9 December 1920 he conducted the Strolling Players Amateur Orchestral Concert Society in a performance of his *Two Songs Without Words* at the Queen's Hall. On 21 November the first London performance of the *Two Psalms* (intended for amateur singers) had been given at the Temple Church, and he was also pleased that his *Ave Maria* had been chosen as a test-piece for the Blackpool Festival, some twenty years after its date of composition; the success of *The Planets* was clearly beginning to have some beneficial side-effects.

At Christmas a festival was organized at Glastonbury by Rutland Boughton, which was to include a performance of the *Four Songs* for voice and violin, and Holst and his family were invited by the authoress Alice Buckton, who ran the Chalice Well Hostel in the town, to stay with her from 31 December to 5 January. Holst in turn asked his ex-pupil Irene Bonnett and two of her friends to come along as a string trio to take part in a performance of Miss Buckton's mystery play *Eager Heart*. Alice Buckton was 'an old acquaintance' of Holst's, and besides writing incidental music for her play *Nabou, or Kings in*

Babylon, he had set her words in the songs *The Heart Worships* and *A Vigil of Pentecost* (which subsequently became absorbed into the music of *Venus*). Irene Bonnett was advised that the stay *'may* be rather nice',[18] Holst's uncertainty arising from their hostess's disconcerting eccentricities, such as suddenly telling her guests to stop eating while she read aloud a passage from some book she happened to have with her at dinner-time.

The new term got off to a good start at Morley College after Christmas, the orchestra numbering about 50, the choir about 60, and the sight-singing class 40 students. Although the orchestra was lacking in bassoons and trombones, some promising bassoonists were taking lessons at the College, 'and the trombones we don't want', according to Holst.[19] Some of his ex-students, such as Lilian Twiselton, were now themselves teaching at the College, but even with this assistance, many pupils had to be turned away because of pressure of numbers. College concerts were attracting large audiences, and the overflow often had to be accommodated in a room adjoining the concert hall.

At the beginning of April the first South-East London Musical Festival was held at Manor Place Baths in the Walworth Road; the adjudicators being Harold Darke and Harvey Grace for the vocal classes, and Thomas Dunhill for the instrumental events. Holst entered his Morley College students for most of the categories, and they distinguished themselves by making a clean sweep of the prizes. In the string orchestra class the Morleyites, conducted by Holst, won with 89 marks, roundly defeating the Borough Polytechnic, and in the full orchestra category, the Morley orchestra found itself to be the only competitor, therefore winning by default of opposition, but its performance of the Entr'acte music from Schubert's *Rosamunde* was good enough to earn 81 marks from the adjudicator. In the choral category, Holst conducted the Morley choir in the two test-pieces: Purcell's *With Drooping Wings* and Pearsall's *Who Shall Win My Lady Fair*, earning 90 and 93 marks respectively, easily defeating the other four contending choirs.

The 1921 Whitsun festival was held at Isleworth in Middlesex. After rehearsals in Isleworth Church on Saturday 14 May, the performances were given in church the following day as part of the morning and evening services, and on the Whit Monday there was a performance of Purcell's music for *Dioclesian* at Bute House, Brook Green. For this occasion, which was apparently the first time the music had been heard in public since its performance at Covent Garden in 1784, Holst dissociated the score from its original dramatic setting, and reassembled it to a story specially written by Jane Joseph. This performance was repeated at Morley College on 4 June as part of a students' concert conducted by Holst, and also in Hyde Park on 7 July as part of a League of Arts pageant.

In addition to his commitments as a conductor, Holst was increasingly in demand as a lecturer: on 20 May he lectured at the Goold Hall in Edinburgh on 'The Education of the Composer' at the invitation of the Incorporated Society of Musicians, and on 14 June his presence was required in two places at once: he was to conduct a choral and orchestral concert at University College, Reading (including a performance of *This Have I Done for My True Love*), while on the same evening Adrian Boult directed *The Planets* at the Queen's Hall as part of the 1921 British Music Society Congress. But perhaps the most exciting event of the year was the first professional performance of *Savitri*, for which he had waited so long. The work was performed at the Lyric Theatre, Hammersmith, on 23 and 24 June, and was conducted by Arthur Bliss, who later said that he was thus able to repay some of Holst's kindness when giving him lessons in composition. The soloists were Dorothy Silk (later to be involved in many performances of Holst's music), Steuart Wilson, and Clive Carey, and the designs were by Claude Lovat Fraser, who created a memorable set by using richly coloured costumes against a sombre background of trees and a darkening sky. Bliss conducted from the wings, where the musicians were hidden with the chorus so that the soloists' contact with the audience would be unimpeded. As an overture, the *Hymn of the Travellers* from the Third Group of *Choral Hymns from the Rig Veda* was used to set the mood before the opera began. The performances were a great success, and on the first night Holst was called to the stage many times to acknowledge the applause. *The Times* reported that the work was 'a perfect little masterpiece of its kind, and we can think of nothing else which belongs to the same kind',[20] while the *Musical Times* dismissed the plot ('there is nothing here to stir more than a languid interest') but declared: 'The music was everything. It was a new flavour in modernism—delicate, only half earthly, recalling nothing else, and mixed with no bitter spices. Perhaps it suggested a vegetarian diet; but that was better than bad meat. Mr Holst can be daring as any experimentalist, but his efforts are certain, and they make music.'[21]

On 30 June the ballet music from *The Perfect Fool* was performed at a Royal College of Music Patron's Fund public orchestral rehearsal in the College concert hall, with Holst conducting. Or rather, Holst started to conduct, but when he came to the passage where seven-beat bars are grouped in pairs to produce a cross-rhythm, the performance fell apart and he had to ask Adrian Boult to come up and take over the baton.

At this time the Russian ballerina Tamara Karsavina was in London to give a summer season at the Coliseum, supported by Laurent Novikoff and an English *corps de ballet*. She asked Holst, Arthur Bliss, and Arnold Bax to contribute music for her choreography, and on 4 July an ensemble dance to Holst's music was performed under the title *Jack in the Green*. No such title appears in his own list of compositions, and it is probable that the music used was the Finale of the *St Paul's Suite*, whose orchestration may have been expanded by Holst for this occasion.

After this performance, Holst made a preliminary visit to Hereford, where he was to conduct *The Hymn of Jesus* at the Three Choirs Festival in the autumn, and then returned to London for the summer holiday, during which he conducted three movements from *The Planets* at the Queen's Hall on 17 August.

Because of the disruption caused by the war, the Three Choirs Festival had not been held at Hereford since 1912, and the performance of *The Hymn of Jesus* in the cathedral on 8 September 1921 marked its return with a special success. The *Musical Times* reported: 'His *Hymn of Jesus*, whether we like it or not, is one of the boldest and most original choral works that have been produced for many years past. It has now been heard on several occasions, but never under such favourable conditions. In the spacious Norman nave, with its massive grey pillars and ancient history, this mystical, archaic-sounding music, which so fits the quaint text, had its fitting environment.'[22] A later writer on the Three Choirs festivals described the work as 'written in the ultra modern idiom which Mr Holst is known to favour', and that although the music was difficult for the chorus, the performance was 'an effective and brilliant rendering'.[23]

Although Holst had been defeated by the seven-beat metre in *The Perfect Fool* ballet music two months previously, this performance of *The Hymn of Jesus* confirmed his stature as a conductor of his own music. He had the ability to inspire amateur performers to give of their best, and had an easy relationship with professionals, who regarded him as one of themselves rather than as another of the succession of career conductors foisted upon them. Before beginning a rehearsal, Holst would clamber about among the orchestra, greeting old friends and discussing details of the parts with various players, often leaving a trail of overturned music stands in his wake. His conducting was calm and efficient, with a clear sense of rhythm, and he dealt with all problems from a practical point of view, based on his own experience as an orchestral musician. He claimed that his own music did not require much in the way of conducting technique to produce its effects —the score contained all necessary information, and the performers only had to play or sing the notes exactly as they were written. He was intolerant of slapdash playing, in later years becoming particularly exacting in this respect, but would sometimes stop a rehearsal in order to congratulate an individual musician on an especially fine piece of playing. He would not hesitate to criticize an orchestra if he felt it was justified, but was able to put his point of view in a polite and constructive manner which could cause offence to no one. Although only of medium height (about 5ft. 6in.), he had the ability to dominate an orchestra simply by the strength of his personality. Sometimes, when his neuritis was bad, he would conduct with his left hand instead of his right, and in large buildings such as cathedrals where his short-sightedness was a handicap, he would ask someone to stand nearby to relay the signals of the officiating clergy so that he could commence the performance at the right moment. According to Harvey Grace, who himself acted in this capacity, Holst had a magnetic influence over his performers, describing him as an 'interpretative and evocative genius', and that 'though physically he was not demonstrative . . . there was, instead, a degree of nervous tension that was probably more exhausting, as it was certainly far more effective.'[24] Perhaps the best assessment of his qualities as a conductor was given by Dulcie Nutting in describing his work with the students of Morley College: 'Holst's conducting was so expressive, they felt the beauty of the music, and it showed in their performances.'[25]

It was at this time that the Persymphans Orchestra from the Soviet Union visited Britain; an ensemble which played without a conductor at all. Holst was interested in this venture, but unlike some other musicians, decided not to pass judgement until he had actually heard the orchestra perform. He readily gave permission for them to perform his own music, as did Arthur Bliss and Vaughan Williams, but Elgar was reported to be 'not very enthusiastic' about the idea.[26]

After the success of *The Hymn of Jesus* at the Three Choirs Festival, Holst, Vaughan Williams, and W. G. Whittaker set off from Hereford on a walking tour through the surrounding countryside. Whittaker had brought his camera and took several photographs of the two composers in relaxed mood, clad in informal hiking clothes.

For some time Whittaker had been editing and arranging his *North Countrie Ballads, Songs and Pipe-Tunes*, and when these were published by Curwen later in the month, Holst immediately thought of using some of the tunes in his current work. He had received a commission from an American named Alice Barney to compose a ballet to her own scenario, and planned to include some of the folk-tunes in it. He wrote to Whittaker: 'The books of songs make a feast indeed . . . Would you allow me to murder two or three of them in a ballet for Chicago? It sounds mixed but I got the books and a little commission from the USA about the same time and your tunes ran through my head when I thought of the ballet. But I shall ill-treat them disgracefully.'[27] Holst composed the work in the autumn of 1921, giving it the title *The Lure, or, The Moth and the Flame*, but in the event did not use any of Whittaker's tunes, although at one point there is a suggestion of a light-footed clog dance. The score contains fragmentary echoes of several of Holst's previous works, including *Beni Mora*, *Mars*, and *The Perfect Fool*, and there are also textures reminiscent of *Petrushka* and *The Rite of Spring*, with an English country-dance tune thrown in for good measure. All this indicates haste of composition, as does the condition of the manuscript, but despite Holst's efforts to have the score ready in time, the ballet was apparently never performed, and Holst's music remained neglected and unpublished for many years. However, 1921 was a good year for publication of several of his other works; besides *The Planets* being accepted by Goodwin & Tabb, the same firm agreed to publish *Beni Mora* (written eleven years before), and Stainer & Bell accepted the ten-year-old *Hecuba's Lament* which had previously been turned down by Novello. Augener published the *Seven Choruses from the Alcestis of Euripides*, and Boosey & Hawkes accepted the *Suite No.1* for military band.

Now that he was becoming more widely known as a composer, Holst found it much easier to persuade publishers to accept works which they had previously rejected for publication. As one journalist discovered: 'On asking Mr Holst what other unheard music he had in store for us, it is found that his new works are largely old ones that publishers and concert-givers have not previously permitted us to hear.'[28] The pressures of his success forced him to agree to such things as the publication of the *maestoso* theme from *Jupiter* as a unison song under the title *I Vow to Thee, My Country*. It was Vaughan Williams who had suggested that the theme should be provided with words for public singing, and when Holst was asked to set to music Sir Cecil Spring Rice's patriotic poem *The Two Fatherlands*, he was relieved to find that the words fitted the *Jupiter* theme, as he had no time to undertake an entirely new composition.

On his return to London, Holst was involved in a busy round of music-making besides his usual teaching, together with the work of composing *The Lure* and the incidental music for a pageant to be performed at the Church of St Martin-in-the-Fields. On 18 September he conducted movements from *The Planets* at the Queen's Hall, and again on 8 October; while on

14 October he gave a speech at the Forum Club, entitled 'Mr Holst on Modern Tendencies'. On 4 October a performance of Purcell's *Dioclesian* music was given by Morley students at the Old Vic; a performance which owed much to the hard work and enthusiasm of his pupil Jane M. Joseph. Holst wrote to Whittaker on 6 October: 'Besides starting term I've had Dioclesian (thanks to JMJ it was splendid—the girl really has ideas), the Chicago ballet and the music for a big pageant. I've got through most of it at the expense of my hand . . .'.[29] The pageant was given every evening from Monday to Saturday 7–12 November, at Church House, Westminster, to raise funds towards the cost of restoration of the Church of St Martin-in-the-Fields. The crypt of the church served as a night refuge for the down-and-outs of London, where they received soup and a bed for the night, and Holst so admired the Reverend Dick Sheppard who carried out this work, that he readily agreed to provide the music for the pageant. The words were by Laurence Housman, and the theme was 'The working of the spirit of Christ throughout the ages'. Most of the music consisted of arrangements of works by other composers, including Vittoria, Tallis, Allegri, Bach, and his own pupil Charles Burke, together with settings of old English tunes such as *Rogero* and *Lord Willoughby*, melodies from *Piae Cantiones*, and his own *Turn Back, O Man*, performed by students from Morley College. On the whole, the performances were successful, although Holst spoke of the difficulty of maintaining the standard of amateur performance night after night. Another difficulty was that Holst was unable to see any of the stage action from his conductor's podium, so that Dulcie Nutting had to be stationed nearby to signal to him when the music was due to begin or end. The whole pageant was so well received that it was decided to repeat it in March the following year, and the Executive Committee of Morley College readily gave permission for the music students to devote extra class time to the project. When all the performances were over, Holst was presented with a silver cigarette box especially inscribed as a memento from the performers in appreciation of all the hard work he had devoted to the pageant. As a non-smoker, he was unable to use the box for its intended purpose, but he kept it until his death and it is now displayed in the Holst Birthplace Museum in Cheltenham.

Another gift which he received at this time was of much greater interest to him; an admirer presented him with a tuning-fork which had once belonged to Beethoven. It had originally been given to the violinist George Bridgetower, and had subsequently been passed on from 'one decent musician to another'. Although he normally had little regard for material possessions, Holst treasured this tuning-fork, and on his death left it to his closest musical colleague, Ralph Vaughan Williams.

At the beginning of December, Albert Coates conducted the ballet music from *The Perfect Fool* in a Royal Philharmonic Society concert at the Queen's Hall. Although this music had been performed by students at the Royal College of Music a few months before at a Patron's Fund rehearsal, this was the first time that it had been heard by the general public. The intention was to whet the appetite for the première of the complete opera (which was not to take place until 1923) and audience and critics alike found much to admire in the ballet music.

1922 opened with an important performance in Toronto: Albert Coates gave the first Canadian performance of *The Planets* with the New York Symphony Orchestra at Massey Hall on 11 January, to the by now customary critical acclaim. Back at home, Holst was occupied with student concerts at Morley College and at Reading, and with lecturing on music education to a group of teachers in Newcastle. On 9 February he conducted *A Somerset Rhapsody* at the Queen's Hall, and two days later he was in Bristol to conduct movements from *The Planets* at the Colston Hall.

At the beginning of March there was an afternoon performance of *The Hymn of Jesus* at the Albert Hall, given by the Royal Choral Society conducted by Hugh Allen (of which one critic reported that the audience which had sat through *The Dream of Gerontius* began to slip away as Holst's unfamiliar music filled the hall), and another performance on the same evening in Edinburgh, where it was given by the Edinburgh Royal Choral Union conducted by Donald Tovey. Holst was in Manchester that evening, conducting movements from *The Planets* at the Free Trade Hall, and two days later the second series of performances of the St Martin's Pageant began at Church House, Westminster. At the end of the month he once again led his Morley students to victory in the South-East London Music Festival at the Conway Hall, New Kent Road, in which his unison song *O England, My Country* (from the Stepney Children's Pageant of 1909) was sung by the combined choirs, and he also journeyed to Eastbourne to direct a performance of *The Hymn of Jesus*.

On 8 April, Holst gave a lecture on Purcell to the London Section of the Incorporated Society of Musicians in the Botanical Theatre at University College. Richard R. Terry acted as chairman, and excerpts from *Dioclesian* were performed by students from Morley College. In his talk, Holst drew a parallel between Purcell and himself, as both had written music for performance in girls' schools, and both had worked in the theatre (although in Holst's case his experience was mainly confined to playing the trombone in the pit). Holst's manner of lecturing was informal and conversational, and one reporter noted that 'Mr Holst . . . was by no means at his least interesting when he digressed from his notes. These digressions were frequent.'[30] When it came to the musical illustrations, 'He placed a tattered volume of the Purcell Society edition on a precarious music-stand, where everyone foresaw it would fall to pieces at the first fortissimo. It did, and the performance went on quite unperturbed with some of the pages inside-out or upside-down.'[31]

A music festival was to be held in Bournemouth at Easter, and the organizers invited Holst to conduct the Bournemouth Municipal Orchestra in movements from *The Planets* at the Winter Gardens. He decided to combine the trip with a short holiday, and cycled to Bournemouth where he called on the orchestra's director, Dan Godfrey. Arriving on Easter Sunday morning, he rang the bell of Godfrey's flat, whereupon Mrs Godfrey leaned out of the window to see a dishevelled cyclist with a dirty haversack on his back. Assuming him to be the newspaper man, she told him to leave the papers in the service lift. 'I am Gustav Holst; I want to see Mr Godfrey,' Holst replied, whereupon he was admitted and shown into the bedroom where Godfrey was resting after a heavy week's work. 'I've brought the papers!' he cried as he entered the room.[32]

Another confusion of identity awaited Holst a few days later.

He set off on a two-day walking tour into Dorset to visit Thomas Hardy, whose work he had long admired, and who had invited him to visit him in Dorchester. To shield his eyes from the sun, Holst had donned an old panama hat, from under which he peered through his usual pair of thick-lensed spectacles, and on presenting himself at Max Gate, Hardy's wife exclaimed: 'Oh, Mr Hardy never sees photographers.'[33] Fortunately, Holst had brought his invitation with him and was admitted to meet the distinguished writer, an encounter which was eventually to lead to the composition of *Egdon Heath*. Hardy got out some old music books which had been used by his father in his days as a church musician, but Holst was apparently disappointed to find that Hardy seemed to know little about music. (According to Clifford Bax, Holst reported that Hardy's favourite compositions were *Drink To Me Only With Thine Eyes* and *Gaily the Troubador*, but perhaps he was having his leg gently pulled, as Hardy had in fact played the violin quite well in his youth.)

By the end of May, preparations were almost complete for the annual Whitsun festival, which that year was to be held at Blackheath in All Saints' Church. This building provided more room than previous locations, so that the performers were able to see the conductor without undue strain. Moreover, the acoustics offered a good balance of sound, so that the Whit Sunday performances passed off to everyone's satisfaction. On the Monday there a 'Whit Monday Musical Picnic' in the garden of a nearby house at Blackheath, including a performance of Euripides' *Alcestis* in Gilbert Murray's translation, for which Holst was to conduct his *Seven Choruses* as incidental music. The daughter of the house, Madeleine Smith, recalled the rehearsals: 'Our tennis court made a perfect open-air theatre surrounded by trees with ample audience space ... It was a hot day and they rehearsed all morning. Sitting on the bank watching I noticed the conductor constantly stroking the top of his head. So I went into the vegetable garden and picked a large rhubarb leaf, and in a pause in the proceedings offered it to him. He accepted it graciously and conducted the rest of the rehearsal with it on his head.'[34] (Miss Smith's father claimed that Holst also wore the rhubarb leaf at the subsequent performance.) The play was produced by the Morley College

Dramatic Society, with musicians from Morley, St Paul's, and an additional contingent from the British Music Society. Holst's music had been originally scored for unison voices, harp, and three flutes, but for this occasion he seems to have rearranged the accompaniment for larger forces, as the *Morley College Magazine* reported: 'Mr Holst's happy amplification of his original scoring of the music gave everyone in the orchestra something to do.'[35] Unfortunately, neither score nor parts of this expanded orchestration can now be traced.

Towards the end of the summer term, Holst received a copy of the published score of Vaughan Williams's Mass in G minor, which was dedicated to Holst and his Whitsuntide Singers. Although they had tried through the Kyrie during the 1920 Whitsun festival, the singers were now faced with the task of learning the entire work. 'How on earth Morleyites are ever going to learn the Mass I don't know', Holst wrote to the composer; 'It is quite beyond us but still further beyond us is the idea that we are not going to do it. I've suggested that they buy copies now and then when we meet in September I'll sack anyone who does not know it by heart! ... We are all tremendously proud of the dedication.'[36] Holst admired the Mass very much, and never tired of pointing out that its harmony was based entirely on triads, without a single discord: 'No foreigner would dare to commit such outrages,'he declared.[37] Although Holst's choir sang the Mass on many occasions, the first public performance was in fact given by the City of Birmingham Choir conducted by Joseph Lewis, on 6 December 1922.

As soon as term had ended, Holst went away on a short holiday to visit his Reading student W. Probert-Jones at Ashbourne in Derbyshire. At the same time, the Registrar of University College Reading wrote to Holst to tell him that a grant of £100 was to be made available for the purchase of instruments for the orchestra, with a further £50 subsidy for the session's concerts, a proposal with which Holst 'heartily concurred'.[38] This provision doubtless resulted from persistent lobbying of the College authorities by Probert-Jones.

On his return from Derbyshire, Holst began work on what was to become the *Fugal Overture* for orchestra. He wrote to Probert-Jones: 'As soon as I got to work after my visit I unexpectedly wrote a thing that was meant for an overture and even now is in strict sonata form: but it happens to be a Fugue! Also it is a Dance! At present I am calling it Bally Fugue, although perhaps Fugal Ballet would be more correct.'[39] Although fugal techniques are used in the work, the texture is not as academic as the title might imply, the mood being one of vitality and gaiety, made all the more so by the inclusion of a brief poignant interlude of bleakness which gives a foretaste of *Egdon Heath*. The rhythmic liveliness of the Overture stems mainly from division of the four-beat bar into irregular groupings instead of the more usual patterns, producing syncopations and cross-rhythms which have an almost joyous effect. Such techniques are similar to those found in Ravel's Piano Trio of 1914, but the *Fugal Overture* is distinctively Holstian in sound and concept, and served him well as an exercise in linear composition, paving the way for some of his later more substantial works.

The Overture was mostly composed in the sound-proof room at St Paul's Girls' School. Although Holst had recently rented a flat (with financial help from Vaughan Williams) at 32 Gunterstone Road, Baron's Court, to reduce the amount of travelling between Thaxted and London, this was so close to the school that he wrote very little music in the flat itself, finding it much more convenient to work in his sound-proof room at weekends and at Thaxted during the holidays.

During August that year the first International Festival of Modern Music was held in Salzburg, and included a performance of Holst's *Four Songs* for voice and violin, which were well received despite insufficient rehearsal. As one correspondent reported: 'Dorothy Moulton's interpretations of the British songs were throughout adequate, but the subtleties of Bax's two songs and of Holst's songs with violin were, on the whole passed by. The distinction of expression of these songs had no counterpart in any of the foreign works, and the Holst group made a remarkable impression on all sides, in spite of the fact that the violinist seemed unable to grasp the composer's purpose.'[40] Holst's music was beginning to be heard more widely in Europe; besides a performance of movements from *The Planets* in the Vienna Konzerthaus conducted by Adrian

Boult, *Beni Mora* became the first of his works to be heard in Paris when it was performed at the Salle Gaveau on 31 October 1922 by the City of Birmingham Orchestra conducted by Appleby Matthews, and the same work was performed at Łódź in Poland and introduced to Swiss audiences via a performance in Geneva by the Suisse Romande Orchestra conducted by Ernest Ansermet.

In England, Holst was in demand at many performances of his own music. On 7 September the *Two Psalms* were performed at a Three Choirs Festival concert in Gloucester Cathedral, in the same programme as the première of Arthur Bliss's *Colour Symphony*, and on 21 September Holst conducted the ballet music from *The Perfect Fool* at a Queen's Hall Promenade concert. At the beginning of October the whole opera was tried through in Holst's room at St Paul's Girls' School with Clive Carey, Steuart Wilson, and Mrs Southam singing and Vally Lasker at the piano. 'I think it will be good fun,' Holst wrote,[41] not suspecting the bafflement the work would provoke at its first performance. He had completed only a sketch, and had yet to produce a vocal score and full score, so he asked Nora Day and Vally Lasker to give him all their spare time for a period of six weeks, and with assistance from Jane Joseph, they set to work. Holst would go through the sketch, indicating the instrumentation to Nora Day, who produced pages of full score, passing them down in batches of four to the room below, where Vally Lasker would convert them into vocal score. In this way the scores were produced on time, and in gratitude for the help he had received Holst dedicated the finished opera to his two colleagues.

Holst now faced a completely new experience in music-making. He had been approached by the Columbia Graphophone Company to make a recording of *The Planets*, the idea having come from the company's chairman, Louis Sterling, who knew Holst's music although he had never met the composer. It was agreed that Holst would conduct the suite, and the first session was held on 15 September 1922, when *Jupiter* was recorded with the London Symphony Orchestra. He quickly adapted himself to the unfamiliar environment of the studio, and the session was successful, despite the problems of recording such a large orchestra by acoustic means (the string basses had to be replaced by a tuba to obtain an effective bass sound). Although recording of the remainder of the suite was postponed for several months, *Jupiter* was released as a single disc in March 1923 as a preliminary to the complete set.

The Planets was also included in the opening concert on 4 October of the Leeds Triennial Festival, revived in 1922 for the first time after the war, the London Symphony Orchestra being augmented to 114 players (including 66 strings) for the occasion. Holst did not hear this performance as he arrived in the city the following day, but was guest speaker at a dinner organized by the Association of Leeds Professional Musicians and attended the first performance of the *Ode to Death*, given in Leeds Town Hall on 6 October by the Festival Chorus and London Symphony Orchestra conducted by Albert Coates. Holst was astonished to find that he was now regarded as a celebrity, and after the concert had to be escorted to the police station until mobs of admirers and autograph-hunters had dispersed.

Further excitement followed the next week, when Holst was a principal participant in a surprise planned for Vaughan Williams on his fiftieth birthday. Early in the morning of 12 October, Holst and a group of friends crept silently into the garden of 13 Cheyne Walk and suddenly burst into song with a performance of a part-song specially written for the occasion by Jane Joseph. Vaughan Williams was naturally amazed to be awakened in such a manner, and invited the singers indoors for an impromptu party.

12

International Acclaim
(1922–1924)

A busy round of activity now followed. Holst travelled to Monmouthshire to lecture to the Newport Music Club on 'Music in England', and on his return visited the Columbia studios to hear a playback of the finished disc of *Jupiter*. On 28 October he conducted the *St Paul's Suite* at the Queen's Hall with the New Queen's Hall Orchestra, and in the next few weeks undertook a series of journeys taking him to Cambridge, York, and Newcastle, where he conducted the Newcastle-upon-Tyne Bach Choir in a performance of the *Ode to Death* on the fourth anniversary of Armistice Day.

The physical and mental strain of such intense activity was beginning to have a detrimental effect, as these engagements had to be fitted into his normal teaching routine, and his appointments diary was becoming dangerously overcrowded. In mid-November he wrote to Whittaker: 'I am feeling rather tired and have the *Planets* at Birmingham facing me as well as many other little trifles.'[1] The Birmingham performance took place on 29 November, and the following day Holst lectured on 'Musical Education' to the Birmingham branch of the British Music Society. On 1 December, he was back in London to give a more curiously-titled lecture, 'Stunted Choirs', to the Girls' Secondary School Branch of the British Music Society. Other lectures followed, involving rapid travel from one part of the country to another, and on several occasions he was unable to attend important performances of his own music because of conflicting dates. One such concert took place on 2 December when the first public performance of *Hecuba's Lament* was given at the Colston Hall, Bristol, by Edith Clegg and the female chorus and orchestra of the Bristol Philharmonic Society conducted by Arnold Barter. This work had had to wait several years for its première, following the abandonment of

Balfour Gardiner's 1914 concert series for which it had been originally scheduled. After the concert, the performers sent Holst an inscribed inkstand to commemorate the occasion, although he had been unable to be present himself.

At the end of such an exhausting term, it was a relief to get back to Thaxted for the Christmas holidays and to enjoy the company of family and friends. The festivities included charades in which Conrad Noel played a performing lion and Holst the roles of a curate holding a dancing class in a teetotal night club and a 'simple lifer' who makes his own clothes. Besides such relaxing activities, he took advantage of some free time in the holidays to finish writing out the full score of the *Fugal Overture*, which he completed on 4 January 1923.

The new year was to be full of activity for Holst, for besides his increasing commitments in conducting performances of his own works, it was also the tercentenary of the deaths of William Byrd and Thomas Weelkes, both of whom he much admired, and he consequently found himself much in demand to speak about their music. On 9 January he lectured on 'The Tercentenary of William Byrd and Thomas Weelkes' to a meeting of the Musical Association at the London Academy of Music, with musical illustrations provided by the Morley College choir. This lecture was repeated at Morley the following Saturday, and was so successful that Holst was asked to repeat it again on 17 April. There was also a special Morley College concert on 27 January, attracting such a large audience that many people had to be turned away, so that it too had to be repeated the following week.

During February he lectured in Manchester, Burnley, Leeds, Glasgow, and York, and was himself was the subject of lectures given by Vaughan Williams in Blackpool and Arnold Bax in Bristol. And then on 20 February an incident ocurred which was to have a serious effect on him for the rest of his life. While conducting a rehearsal for a Byrd and Weelkes commemorative concert at Reading, he slipped off the rostrum and struck the back of his head. He was able to go ahead with the evening concert, but as he had already decided to give up his work there, this was in fact his last appearance. After the perform-ance his pupils and members of the orchestra and Choral

Society presented him with some Purcell Society volumes in appreciation of his work at the College. Although his teaching at Reading came to an end, he did not lose interest in the work of the music department there, and would always ask Probert-Jones for news of current activities whenever he saw him.

Following the accident, Holst's doctor allowed him to continue work on condition that he should regard himself as an invalid, and treat himself accordingly. This sensible advice was immediately ignored by the patient, who threw himself back into his usual routine, with the result that he quickly suffered a nervous breakdown and was ordered by a specialist to take a complete rest for several weeks. His work at Morley College was taken over by Philip Collis and Vaughan Williams, and Balfour Gardiner taught at Reading until Holst's successor was appointed. At the end of March Holst wrote to Whittaker: 'I'm getting on but feel strongly disinclined for work (Not that I do any!).'[2] He was unable to attend the first London performance of *Hecuba's Lament*, given at the Queen's Hall on 14 March by the Philharmonic Choir conducted by Charles Kennedy Scott, of which the *Musical Times* reported: 'Miss Clara Serena . . . was quite a detached Hecuba. Perhaps that is why the work, all good Holst, sounded as if it had been composed easily.'[3] In fact, the composer did not hear the work performed in public until March 1929, although he may have heard a try-through in 1912.

The need for rest was all the more important because he had accepted an invitation from the University of Michigan to lecture and conduct at a music festival at Ann Arbor, and needed to conserve his energy for the journey. He set out with Isobel at the end of April on board the liner *Aquitania*, and during the voyage sketched out a draft of the *Fugal Concerto* for flute, oboe and strings ('The World's Shortest Concerto', as he called it[4]). The style of this work is overtly neo-classical, which he seems to have arrived at by following his own inclinations rather than through the influence of any particular models. Although he may have heard *Pulcinella* when it was performed in London by the Diaghilev company in 1920, neo-classicism was not yet fully established as a major idiom of twentieth-century music; Stravinsky did not write his *Octet* until late 1922, and his *Concerto* for piano and wind instruments dates from 1923–4. Holst's version of the style is light and elegant, with typically individual touches such as displacement of rhythmic motifs and unexpected harmonizations. The Concerto's second movement is almost Bachian in character, while in the Finale he introduced the English country-dance tune *If All the World Were Paper* as an effective counterpoint to his thematic material. Strangely, Holst's penchant for neoclassicism did not lead him to admire one of the archetypal examples of the style, Stravinsky's *Apollon Musagète*, which he described as 'amazingly dreary'.[5]

The tedium of the voyage was relieved by conversation with their fellow-passenger Arthur Bliss, and on arrival at Ann Arbor Holst completed the *Fugal Concerto* in the library of the University of Michigan. The first performance was given on 17 May 1923 at a private concert in the house of the University's President Burton, by players from the Chicago Symphony Orchestra conducted by Frederick Stock, and in gratitude for the hospitality which he and Isobel received during their stay, Holst presented his manuscript full score to the University.

The main purpose of his visit was to conduct some of his own works at the Ann Arbor May Festival, particularly *The Hymn of Jesus*, together with *Beni Mora*, *A Dirge for Two Veterans*, *A Fugal Concerto*, and the ballet music from *The Perfect Fool*. Duncan McKenzie recalled an incident during the Festival, during which Holst was conducting the *Dirge for Two Veterans* (which he had in fact never heard before) in front of an audience of some 4,000 people, when he suddenly put down his baton, and announced in a 'bland afternoon-tea voice' that there was an error in one of the parts and that he would take the opportunity to correct it. 'He then made his way to the third trombone desk, had a *sotte voce* but evidently warm argument with the player, produced a telescoping gold pencil, and made some alterations. The work started again and ended in tumultuous applause.'[6] Eric De Lamarter (associate conductor of the Chicago Symphony Orchestra) went to the artist's room to congratulate Holst at the end of his part of the programme and the two went for a stroll, during which Holst confided that while conducting the *Dirge* for the second time he had realized that he had been mistaken in amending the trombone part; it had been correct in the first place. Ought he to have stopped the performance again and recorrected the mistake? De Lamarter replied that one stoppage was dramatic, but a second would have produced the opposite effect.

Holst liked his surroundings, and declared: 'A week or so in Ann Arbor is worth a month of rushing about. The people are not only kind but intelligently kind and without fussing you in the least they will give you one of the happiest times of your life.'[7] During his stay he was invited to accept the vacant post of Professor of Music at the University, but after due consideration decided to decline the offer, partly because he felt that he no longer had the energy for such a task ('10 years ago I'd have jumped at it,' he explained wistfully[8]), and partly because 'I am very happy in my work in England and am not at all anxious to change.'[9] He was also concerned about possible disruption of his daughter's education: Imogen was now at St Paul's Girls' School, but 'not old enough either to be transplanted or left alone in England'.[10] For the same reasons he also declined the Directorship of the Eastman School of Music at Rochester, New York, which was offered to him at this time.

During his visit, Holst was able to meet his erstwhile YMCA colleague William Vowles, who came over from Chicago to stay a night at Ann Arbor, and at the beginning of June, Holst and Isobel went to Chicago themselves, to visit Holst's stepbrother Thorley, who practised law in that city, and meet other members of the family. Holst and Isobel made many new friends in the USA, particularly Austin Lidbury, who was manager of a chemical works at Niagara: 'His family come from Lancashire and he has kept the real feeling for music,' Holst wrote; 'However busy he may be at times he makes time to see musicians and to entertain them. He's the greatest thing in Niagara—the Rapids are second, the power stations third, Lidbury's cellar fourth, the country around fifth and the Falls the twentieth.' The only thing which did not receive Holst's approval was the lack of mixed-voice choirs in the area, 'as people prefer men's glee clubs and women's choirs'.[11]

Besides missing the 1923 Whitsun festival, Holst's visit to the USA also prevented him from attending the première performance of *The Perfect Fool*, which was given on 14 May at the Royal Opera House, Covent Garden, by the British National Opera Company conducted by Eugene Goossens. The company, which was the successor of Thomas Beecham's opera company, had made its first appearance in Bradford in February 1923, and the production of such a work so early in its existence was due to the initiative of its artistic director Percy Pitt, who also included works by Rutland Boughton and Ethel Smyth in the same season.

The work's reception by public and critics was confused, mainly because of their surprise and bewilderment at the plot, or lack of it; the *Musical News & Herald* complained that 'Mr Gustav Holst, with all his unquestionable modesty, made an excellent advertisement for his opera in keeping the plot and details a secret...'[12] As far as could be gathered, Holst's intention had been to produce a parody or satire on the whole art of opera as performed on the British stage. This idea clearly stems from his Morley College entertainment *Opera as She is Wrote*, and its origins may even go back as far as the rejection of *Sita* by the Ricordi adjudicators and Holst's subsequent discovery of a different kind of opera in *Savitri*. The action, such as it is, turns on the inability or unwillingness of the Fool to take any interest in wooing a Princess, despite the prompting of his Mother and competition from a Wizard, and in the final scene the Fool yawns and falls asleep from sheer apathy, to the consternation of everyone, not least the audience. Freed from the constraints of a more detailed synopsis, this sketchy outline enabled Holst to introduce parodies in the style of Wagner, Verdi, and Debussy, and to include in his libretto banalities which make an audience feel uneasy as to whether they are to be taken seriously or not. Holst himself insisted that the opera was intended to be funny, but refused to be drawn as to the significance of the characters or the plot, merely asking that 'the spirit of high comedy shall be maintained throughout'.[13]

A fortuitous clue as to the meaning of the work was perhaps given by a musical magazine which published a critique together with a photograph of Holst over the caption 'The Perfect Fool'. Although this was regarded as an unfortunate gaffe, it is possible that Holst actually intended the work to be an expression of the relationship between himself and the art of opera. The various characters in the work can be interpreted in this light; with the Fool representing Holst himself, the other contenders for the favours of the Princess (or the Spirit of Opera) include a Wizard with great magical powers (Strauss?), a Troubador who sings an Italian pastiche in the style of Verdi, and a Wanderer who does the same for Wagner. In spite of the talents of these three, none of them is successful in wooing the Princess: only the Fool is capable of winning her, but shows no inclination to do so. In fact he utters only one word during the entire work: when told that the Princess loves him and asked if he will have her, he manages to gasp the word 'No!' before falling asleep. Holst may have felt that he possessed the necessary technical ability and imagination to become a successful operatic composer, but when confronted with the conventions of the genre, he was content to leave it to the Wizards, Wanderers, and Troubadors of this world and to go his own way.

Despite the yawns of the Fool, the audience showed little sign of boredom, and after the performance heated discussion broke out as to what it all meant. Donald Tovey suggested that the Princess was intended to represent 'Opera', while the Fool was supposed to be 'The British Public'.[14] According to Alfred Kalisch, 'Two very poetical young gentlemen pretended to see in it an allegory of the state of British music, but they could not agree ... whether the Perfect Fool was Native Art, which remained asleep and deaf to the blandishments of the public (the Princess), or whether he was the British public, which is wooed in vain by Native Art.'[15] Some critics were offended by Holst's flippant attitude to operatic tradition, as Francis Toye later remarked: 'It seems scarcely fitting for a composer who belongs to a nation that has never produced a successful music drama or serious opera to parody the particular media of his choice.'[16] Alfred Einstein proclaimed: 'For us Germans, English opera is an almost unimaginable idea,'[17] and even some English critics questioned the concept of a native art of opera—as the critic of the *Musical News & Herald* wrote: 'I cannot see that grand or romantic opera will ever be one of England's greatest musical ornaments, for I do not think that it is, or ever can be, a part and parcel of universal life in this country ...

One cannot picture a number of railway gangers waiting outside Covent Garden for the doors to open on *The Perfect Fool*; the German workman goes as a matter of course to hear Wagner.'[18] W. J. Turner complained: 'It is impossible to maintain a spirit of high comedy when there is no high comedy, and I can find none in the *Perfect Fool*,'[19] while Arnold Bennett remarked that Holst had 'the general intelligence of a fine creative artist, but when it comes to the point, he is a mere amateur at libretto writing (He is worse even than Wagner who committed the libretto of the *Twilight of the Gods*)'. Bennett noticed that even the performers seemed to be puzzled and uncertain as to what was required of them, but did concede that Holst had 'a certain scenic sense, which only failed him in one or two important details of construction', going on to say that '*The Perfect Fool* is incomparably the best modern British opera,' although considering the competition at that time, this may have been something of a back-handed compliment.[20]

Despite criticism of the plot and libretto, most people seem to have liked the music, although W. J. Turner found the opening ballet music 'reminiscent of Saint-Saëns in its commonplace Oriental colouring'.[21] Herbert Antcliffe was enthusiastic: 'Before long one expects to hear Mr Holst's melodies being hummed and shouted and whistled all over London',[22] while Edwin Evans found that 'The final impression left by this work is of energy in the domain of rhythm and of simplicity in that of tune. But for the experience that lies behind it one might describe it as boyish music. Perhaps it is this aspect of it that makes it peculiarly English, for most foreigners have remarked that an Englishman remains a boy for the greater part of his life.'[23] Particular commendation was given to the round in praise of water, sung by three girls at a well, and a fanfare for eight trumpeters who are instructed to repeat their phrases ad lib. One listener tackled Holst about the cliché-ridden words he had given to the Shepherd, but his facetious reply was: 'Well, isn't that the sort of thing they *do* sing?'[24] A much-admired achievement was that Holst had enabled the words to be heard by the audience throughout the work (except in the Wagnerian parody, where the sound of the orchestra deliberately overwhelms the singers); Edwin Evans remarked that 'In opera, such a thing has not been known for a considerable time.'[25] However, it was generally felt that spoken dialogue sounded artificial in a context where singing was the norm; the mixture of speech and song (sometimes changing from one to the other halfway through a phrase) made both sound unnatural, forcing the audience to make constant mental adjustments. On the whole though, despite its stylized characterizations and schoolboy humour the majority of the audience and critics were willing to give the benefit of the doubt to this 'mixture of opéra comique and opéra bouffe',[26] and as one critic pointed out, although the work contained naïveties, 'it could hardly contain a tenth of the naïveties in almost every opera ever written.'[27]

Although Holst had intended the ballet music to introduce the opera proper, for the performances at Covent Garden his *Fugal Overture* was used as an opening item, to set the mood. This was the first public performance of the Overture, which also received mixed reactions. Writing some time later, R. W. S. Mendl remarked: 'We all know what wonders Bach could work with the fugal form, but even he did not use it for the purpose of cracking a joke: this is what Holst did in his *Fugal Overture*—an exhilarating piece of fun from beginning to end,'[28] whereas Dyneley Hussey dismissed both the *Fugal Overture* and *Fugal Concerto* as 'Perverse exercises in the contrapuntal style, devoid of any warmth and with none of the real vitality which appears in the earlier *St Paul's Suite* for strings'.[29] Although it was Holst's own suggestion that the *Fugal Overture* should be used to introduce the opera, this must have been motivated by expediency, as he certainly did not regard the composition of an operatic overture as a trivial matter. He particularly admired Beethoven's *Leonora* No. 3 overture, describing it as 'the best theatre-music that exists, or at least the best overture'.[30]

Safely isolated in America, far from the excitements and factionalizing of a London first night, Holst read the newspaper cuttings which were sent to him with detached interest. He had done his bit by composing the opera; now it was up to others to make of it what they would.

After completing the remainder of his engagement at Ann Arbor, Holst and Isobel sailed for England in June aboard the Red Star liner *Belgenland*. They arrived in time to attend a performance of *The Perfect Fool* on 28 June, when it was coupled with the first Covent Garden production of *Savitri*. The delicate chamber opera did not fare at all well in the grandiose setting of the Royal Opera House; Richard Capell described the production as 'A performance so ill-considered that no-one without previous acquaintance could have seen its bearings. It was over-weighted with ponderous scenery, it was played nearly all the time in darkness. Dorothy Silk (the faultless heroine of the earlier production) was new to Covent Garden and had not properly gauged the house.'[31] A few days later Holst wrote to the conductor, Percy Pitt: 'Many thanks for your conducting of "Savitri". It was a pity that the chorus and orchestra were separated but otherwise I thought the performance musically was very good and for this I have to thank you first.'[32] This coupling of *Savitri* and *The Perfect Fool* (using the *Hymn of the Travellers* as a prelude to the chamber opera) was repeated three times the following January, after which *The Perfect Fool* was not revived.

In the summer and autumn of 1923, Holst returned to the studios of the Columbia Graphophone Company to complete the recording of *The Planets* which he had begun the previous year. *Venus* and *Mercury* were recorded on 23 August, *Uranus* on 24 August, *Mars* and *Saturn* on 30 October, and *Neptune* on 6 November. Conditions were difficult in the cramped recording studios of those days, putting considerable strain on the performers, and Imogen Holst recalled that after one session her father came home so tired that he was unable to walk up the stairs to bed. As there was no possibility of editing recordings at that time, each side of a disc had to be completed without error. The exposed horn solo at the beginning of *Venus* was recorded no less than thirteen times before the renowned Aubrey Brain could play it without flaw, simply because of the cramped, stuffy conditions.

In a letter to Harold Brooke dated 'Sept.12' (no year is given), Holst told him: 'I hope to record the *Fugal Overture* at Columbia next Tuesday,'[33] but there is no evidence that such a session took place.

During that autumn Holst's music was widely and frequently performed, bringing his name before a larger musical public than ever before. The *Two Psalms* were performed at the Three Choirs Festival on 5 September; on 16 September he conducted *Beni Mora* and the *Perfect Fool* ballet music at the Margate Festival, and on the same day the British National Opera Company gave the *Savitri/Perfect Fool* double bill at the Prince of Wales Theatre, Birmingham. On 4 October the two operas were performed for the first time at Leeds, and on 11 October at the Opera House, Manchester. Holst conducted the first concert performance of *A Fugal Overture* and the first public performance of *A Fugal Concerto* at the Queen's Hall on 11 October, with Robert Murchie (flute) and Leon Goossens (oboe) as soloists, together with two of his part-songs sung by the Halifax Madrigal Society. Two days later, Holst was again at the Queen's Hall, this time to conduct *The Planets*, a performance which the press described as surpassing all previous performances: 'Mr Holst seems to be forging ahead as a conductor.'[34] On 14 November he conducted the *Fugal Overture* and *Fugal Concerto* at the Eastbourne Festival, and from 18 November to 16 December conducted several performances on Sunday evenings of a revival of the *St Martin's Pageant*, which this time was given at the Lyceum Theatre. Holst conducted again at the Queen's Hall on 1 and 2 December, while the British National Opera Company gave the *Savitri/Perfect Fool* double bill in Glasgow on 14 November, and in Newcastle on 6 December.

Then on 19 December it was Vaughan Williams's turn to conduct Holst's music at the Queen's Hall, when he directed the London Bach Choir in the *Short Festival Te Deum* and the first London performance of the *Ode to Death*. As the latter work was unfamiliar to the audience, Vaughan Williams insisted that it should be performed twice, being separated in the programme by a Bach concerto. Holst was enthusiastic over the performance, and wrote to Vaughan Williams: 'It's what I've been waiting for for 47½ years . . . You are teaching those people to sing!'[35] (Vaughan Williams had been a member of the choir since 1903 and had taken over the conductorship from Hugh Allen in 1920.) Vaughan Williams replied: 'What a wonderful experience it was for me and all of us learning your wonderful music—which got better & better as we went on. It was a tussle I admit—but from the first they loved it—& I know of no other work which I shd have dared to make a choir slog so at . . .'[36]

As might be expected, at the end of such a term Holst was suffering from exhaustion, for in addition to the strenuous demands of conducting so many performances of his own music, his teaching routine had gone on as before, except for a proportion of his work at Morley College which he had relinquished on medical advice to lighten the load. 'What a term it's been!' he wrote to Whittaker from St Paul's; 'I've had 5 shows at QH, a lot of teaching at the RCM and huge classes here, Dulwich and Morley.'[37] The strain of being a figure in the public eye was also beginning to tell on him; he was constantly harassed by journalists and autograph-hunters, whom he treated with ill-concealed irritation. He was offered honorary degrees and awards of various kinds, together with invitations to become chairman or president of musical organizations, but he refused them all, believing that such free time as he had left should be spent in composing music rather than attending official functions. Also, he had never fully recovered from his accident at Reading, and since his return from Ann Arbor had been suffering from bouts of insomnia, making it difficult for him to sustain the energies needed for his various activities. When Clifford Bax greeted him one day, Holst replied: 'How am I? Well, I think I am looking forward to Devachan' (the heavenly afterlife of Sanskrit literature).[38]

It was at this point that relief came in the form of a gift from Claude Johnson, a director of Rolls Royce Ltd. After seeing a performance of *The Perfect Fool*, Johnson offered to cover the expenses of a festival of Holst's music, but as his works were already being frequently performed, Holst accepted instead a monetary gift of £1,500, enabling him to concentrate on composition for a substantial period of time. He decided to remain in Thaxted and go to London for only one day's teaching per week. At the end of January 1924 he wrote to Whittaker: 'I have cut down my teaching by half and now lead a wonderfully lazy life—probably I spend as much time in bed or on the sofa in a week as you do in a month.'[39] He was glad to be able to get away from the attention and responsibilities which fame had thrust upon him: 'I have a longing to be by myself or with not more than one or two people at a time and I dread parties or business meetings etc.,'[40] but was worried that such isolation might be open to misinterpretation: 'I have a fear lest people shall imagine that success has spoilt me and that old acquaintances and old surroundings are not good enough for me.'[41] As he wrote to Maja Köhler: 'Above all please don't think that I'm getting "swell head".'[42]

But the most important reason for seeking solitude was to be able to get on with his creative work in peace and quiet. During the autumn he had sketched the first draft of a Choral Symphony, which he was now able to revise and complete without interruption. He had chosen the words from the poems of John Keats, disregarding their original contexts and juxtaposing the excerpts in a manner which served his own musical purposes but which drew disapproval from literary purists (and even from some of his friends, such as Clifford Bax). The overall plan is that of a four-movement symphony: Allegro, Adagio, Scherzo, and Finale, preceded by an introductory section. The choral parts are an integral element of the work, rather than being subsidiary to the orchestra as in many previous choral symphonies. For the introduction and first movement, entitled *Invocation to Pan* and *Song and Bacchanale*, he chose stanzas from the chorus of shepherds in *Endymion* and from the Roundelay in Book IV of the poem. The slow movement is a setting of the entire *Ode on a Grecian Urn*, the Scherzo makes use of most of 'Fancy' and 'Folly's Song' (one of the short pieces grouped under the title *Extracts from an Opera*), and the Finale begins with the first stanza of the lines which Keats wrote in a copy of Beaumont and Fletcher's plays ('Spirit here that reignest'), continuing with lines from the *Hymn to Apollo*, the main part of the *Ode to Apollo*, and the Ode *Bards of Passion and of Mirth*.

The idea of composing a choral symphony based on extracts from the work of a single poet had been used by Vaughan Williams in his *Sea Symphony* of 1910 (based on poems by Walt Whitman), but in that case unity was achieved by selecting verses about the sea; in Holst's case there is no such unity of subject, the poems being used solely for their evocative possibilities.

Instead of a declamatory invocation, the work begins in a hushed, atmospheric way, with the chorus chanting in unison *sotto voce* (recalling the invocations of the gods in the *Choral Hymns from the Rig Veda* and the opening of the *Hymn to Dionysus*), while the strings provide a subdued fugal background over a sustained bass pedal note. This leads to a lyrical improvisatory viola solo preceding the 'Song', which is in turn introductory to the 'Bacchanal', the symphonic first movement Allegro proper. Then follows the *Ode on a Grecian Urn*, in which Holst captured the stylized nature of the scenes depicted on the urn by using the archaic sound of open perfect fifths together with pulsating woodwind figures. These perfect fifths are the obverse of the perfect fourths with which the work otherwise abounds; the cool, bland quality of the fifths contrasting with the vigorous, assertive character of the fourths. Here also is an echo of the slow-stepping 'sad procession' heard in the *Dirge for Two Veterans* of 1914. At first glance, the ensuing frenetic Scherzo may appear difficult to perform with singers of average ability, but is within the capabilities of the more accomplished choirs which Holst had in mind when writing the work. The music is light and capricious, with a dynamic energy and fleetness reminiscent of *Mercury*. To assist the voices, the choral lines are all doubled in the orchestra (except for a brief passage of a few bars), which gave him the idea of suggesting that this movement could be performed separately as an orchestral piece without the chorus. In the Finale, further use is made of the ubiquitous perfect fourth, and besides an echo of the procession in *Saturn* there is also an unashamedly straightforward tune with a touch of *nobilmente*, demonstrating Holst's continued ability to write simply and directly, as he had done in his settings for use in Thaxted Church. However, this movement is perhaps the least effective of the four, being rather episodic in construction and thus lacking the linear continuity needed for successful culmination of a substantial symphony.

He worked hard on the score, completing it in time to send his original draft sketch to Jane Joseph as a present for her birthday on 31 May in gratitude for all the practical help which she had given him. 'When it is published, you can compare your sketch with the finished article', he wrote, 'and learn either one or other of the following lessons in composition: a) The virtue and advantage of careful and prolonged study and rewriting, b) The vice and futility of careful and prolonged study and rewriting. I wonder which it will be!'[43] He also wrote to Vally Lasker, describing his solitary life in Thaxted: 'It has been wonderful to sit all day in the garden and to watch the symphony grow up alongside of the flowers and vegetables, and then to find that it is done!'[44] (While actually composing the work he had written: 'It makes me quite delirious to work at the symphony for long.'[45]) He invited various friends, including Harold Brooke of Novello, to come to Thaxted to hear the work played through at the piano, with the intention of collecting their opinions and perhaps making some final revisions before performance. When he had listened to a try-through and heard their comments, he wrote: 'I don't think I shall make any radical change, but I have already simplified two or three bars in the end of the first movement, and also the harmonies of the "Nightingale" verse of "Bards of Passion", which were too mild and luscious for my taste.'[46] Holst often referred to the work as his 'Keats Symphony', and in his list of works he described it as his First Choral Symphony, implying that he was already thinking of writing a second, but it was to be some years before he would be able to work on it, and apart from a few fragmentary sketches the Second Choral Symphony was in fact never written. During this time in Thaxted, Holst was looked after by Hubert Adams, an ex-serviceman who cooked, cleaned, and ensured that the composer did not suffer any undue disturbance to his creative work. Despite his poor health, this was clearly a peaceful and contented time for Holst, during which he could get on with his work of composition, which he regarded as the principal purpose of his existence.

But it was not an entirely isolated life: he travelled to London once a week to teach, and also fulfilled various engagements as a conductor and lecturer. On 19 January 1924 he was at the Queen's Hall to conduct *Beni Mora* (which had been performed in San Francisco for the first time a few days before), and returned the following day to conduct two movements from *The Planets*. In February there were concerts at Morley

College, Southwark Cathedral, and Brighton, and lecturing engagements at Malvern, Birmingham, and Sheffield. On 14 February he recorded *Beni Mora* for Columbia with the London Symphony Orchestra, and may also have attended the sessions during which Dora Labette and W. H. Reed recorded the *Four Songs* for voice and violin, and Marie Hall the early *Valse Etude*. The *Two Psalms* and *The Hymn of Jesus* also received their first broadcasts during the month, as the Southwark Cathedral concert on 9 February was relayed by the BBC.

At the end of February Holst was due to visit Newcastle for a weekend, for a performance of *The Cloud Messenger*, but he suddenly felt ill and had to cancel the visit. He wrote to Whittaker: 'This is a horrible blow. My head got queer on Monday and worse on Tuesday. In order to get fit for tomorrow I sent a deputy to the RCM yesterday and spent most of the day dozing by the fire and lying in bed. But it was of no use and I realise now that my presence in Newcastle would be a greater disappointment and inconvenience than my absence . . . What I feel most is not hearing the CM. I had looked forward to it so much and you have done so much for the work that I look on it as your property. And I do hate letting you down like this after all you've done and been to me.'[47] On medical advice, Holst cancelled all his engagements for the rest of the year and remained in Thaxted, where he planned to indulge in 'Silence, Solitude and Heat (not mere warmth)'.[48]

It was at this time that Holst was elected to Fellowship of the Royal College of Music; the only honorary academic award he ever accepted. His illness had impeded the normal consultation process, and he was consequently very surprised when the Fellowship was announced, as he was under the impression that he had refused it. As he confided to Vally Lasker in April: 'When the FRCM was offered me a month ago I declined it as gently and politely as I could—a little too gently as it happened!'[49]

13

'Real Composer and Tame Cat'
(1924–1925)

Holst's fame had grown so much that he had become an object of attention of the national newspapers; *The Times* of 24 March reported that 'Mr Gustav Holst has been ordered a complete rest for at least six months, and during that time he will be unable to deal with any correspondence.' During this enforced idleness, Holst saw occasional visitors ('RVW and I have had a lovely, easy going, middle-aged, weekend together,' he wrote on 7 April[1]), but was mainly alone, and had an opportunity to think over his position. He realized that even when he had fully recovered, he would not be able to sustain such a heavy teaching load as before, and therefore decided to resign from his post as Director of Music at Morley College which he had held since 1907. His resignation came into effect from the end of the 1924 summer term, although deputies were already carrying out his work there during his illness. He was succeeded by Arnold Goldsborough, then organist of St Martin-in-the-Fields, who held the post until 1928 when he in turn was succeeded by Arnold Foster, who had played in the College orchestra for some years. Both of these successors carried on the tradition of the Whitsun festivals, and all subsequent Directors of Music strove to maintain Holst's high ideals of amateur music-making. Later holders of the post have included such distinguished musicians as Michael Tippett, Matyas Seiber, and Peter Racine Fricker, all of whom built on Holst's work, sometimes in difficult circumstances.

Although he had resigned from his post, Holst kept in touch with his colleagues and pupils at Morley, and tried to attend the Whitsun festivals whenever he could. In 1924 the festival was held at All Hallows Church, Barking, and he made a special effort to attend the Sunday service, to hear the music conducted by Arnold Goldsborough. On the Whit Monday there was dancing and more music in the garden of Bute House (adjacent to St Paul's Girls' School), and although Isobel and Imogen were present, Holst himself was not well enough to attend. Another special event was a Morley College concert devoted entirely to the works of Vaughan Williams, given at the King George's Hall, Tottenham Court Road, on 14 June, again conducted by Arnold Goldsborough; Holst made sure of attending this, to be able to sit beside his old friend and listen to his music.

But patterns of music-making were beginning to change, largely because of the widening influence of broadcasting. It was no longer necessary to make long journeys to attend performances, which could now be heard by switching on a radio set and perhaps adjusting a 'cat's whisker'. There was an atmosphere of adventure and exploration in those early years of radio, and the BBC was eager to broadcast all types of material, including much contemporary music, in a way which later became more difficult when the organization grew larger and its bureaucracy congealed. In the first few months of 1924, many works by Holst were broadcast, including the *Suite No. 2* for military band, *The Planets*, the *St Paul's Suite*, the *Perfect Fool* ballet music, the *Fugal Overture, Savitri*, some of the *Vedic Hymns*, three of the *Four Songs* for voice and violin, and besides the relay from Southwark Cathedral of the *Two Psalms* and *The Hymn of Jesus*, there was a broadcast of the complete *Perfect Fool* by the British National Opera Company from His Majesty's Theatre, London, on 2 July.

Holst would occasionally call in at the BBC studios to hear what music was being performed, even though the style might be quite different from his own. According to Gordon Jacob, Holst was 'much fascinated by the eerie hints and whispers of the music of Anton Webern',[2] but there is little evidence of such a fascination in any of Holst's own work. Although he was curious and had an open mind regarding contemporary developments, his approach was similar to his attitude to advice: 'Always ask for advice, but never take it.'[3] He was against following fashion for its own sake, and wrote in 1920: 'The Philistine spirit now-a-days shows itself in acceptance rather than in refusal—in cheap, blind acceptance of any imitation of Art or Religion that happens to be popular for the moment.'[4] He also refused to take things too seriously, and once remarked: 'To go into a concert hall where modern music is being played is like being invited into a gymnasium for five minutes with the gloves,'[5] and to a friend he wrote facetiously: 'Modern music is neither modern, nor music.'[6]

By the summer, Holst felt strong enough to fulfil his agreement with Columbia for further gramophone recordings; on 22 August 1924 he recorded the *St Paul's Suite* and on 1 September the *Country Song* from *Two Songs Without Words* as a 'filler' for the remainder of two twelve-inch discs. This experience seems to have been rather exhausting, and he wrote to Whittaker: 'After recording St Paul's Suite last week I have decided not to appear in public this winter and, if possible, do no teaching. When I start work again (or if I do) I want it to be really good which it certainly is not at present. Meanwhile . . . I look to my gramophone royalties to keep me from bankruptcy.'[7] Since completing the score of the Choral Symphony in May he had composed nothing new: 'This has been the only blank August as regards composing that I can remember,' he wrote, 'but it does not matter after my wonderful Spring and although I haven't really begun anything fresh I feel that it is just waiting round the corner.'[8]

By this he must have meant large-scale compositions, for he was in fact working on several smaller pieces, and in the same letter confessed that he was 'spoiling music paper to a vast extent'. He was making use of the time to catch up on some projects which had been shelved during the composition of other works. *A Piece for Yvonne* is a short piano piece which he wrote for Yvonne O'Neill, the eight-year-old daughter of Adine and Norman O'Neill. Holst wrote to her mother: 'Dear Adine, I started Yvonne's piece about two years ago but gave it up because I felt sure she would not approve of the time signature [7/4] and I could not find a way of altering it. However, your letter has inspired me to finish it so here it is with my Respects to the young lady and her mother.'[9]

He had also been planning to compose a piece for Adine herself, and wrote to Whittaker: 'For many years I have tried to write a piano piece for Mrs O'Neill and this summer I have at last succeeded. And I finished it just in time to send it with an appropriate dedication to her on her silver wedding. But from another point of view it would have been more fitting to have dedicated it to you for it is a Toccata based on "Newburn Lads" [from *North Countrie Ballads, Songs and Pipe-Tunes*]...'[10] Holst sent the manuscript to his pupil Amy Kemp, with a request to make a copy and then present the original to Adine O'Neill after playing it to her on her wedding anniversary. This was to be preceded by a private try-through in the presence of Nora Day and Vally Lasker, who were to be asked to guess the name of the composer. Holst wrote to Amy Kemp: 'I hope to have your advice on any points that occur to you. I've only just finished it and am sure there are many things that should be altered but I am glad to get it out of the house as the temptation to dish my arm trying to play it is overwhelming.'[11]

The small number of compositions which Holst wrote for piano solo was doubtless due mainly to his neuritis and consequent difficulty of playing them himself, but perhaps also because of his aversion from the instrument as the prime vehicle of musical expression. According to Basil Hogarth in the early 1930s, Holst 'candidly confesses that he regards the piano as scarcely being a musical instrument at all',[12] but Edwin Evans reported that Holst considered it a limitation that he had 'never succeeded, to his own satisfaction, in writing a piano piece'.[13] The composition of the *Toccata* was motivated by his admiration of Adine O'Neill's playing, and he would look forward to her broadcasts with eager anticipation, particularly enjoying her playing of Scarlatti. Towards the end of his life he wrote to her from St Paul's Girls' School: 'Amongst all that you have done for me the two things I am most grateful for are, firstly, introducing me to Scarlatti and then bringing me here. And it is high time I had more of the former...'[14] The *Toccata* is a lightweight piece, bearing a stylistic resemblance to the Scherzo of the *First Choral Symphony*, and was well received by pianists when it was published, despite a few passages of rather unidiomatic writing. In its final bars, Holst's childhood memory of the Cheltenham hurdy-gurdy man's disintegrating instrument is recalled in the gradual fragmentation of the thematic material.

Holst's neuritis also prevented him from arranging some music for brass band at this time. Whittaker had written to ask permission to arrange selections from *The Perfect Fool*, and Holst responded: 'I'm sorry it's to be a selection which I loathe —having played more than a few in my days—such things hang like a curse round brass band music ... A brass band publisher came to see me last year and I begged him to consider arranging some Purcell since when I've not seen either him or my Purcell volume I lent him. If my hand were only stronger I'd do the Purcell and perhaps even the PF myself but as things are I think I'd better keep off everything but original work. (I've longed for years to arrange certain JSB fugues for both brass and military bands.) Barring my hand I'm having a lovely time. I lead the combined lives of a Real Composer and a Tame Cat!'[15]

He was however able to arrange some of his own music that summer, making male voice versions of five of the *Six Choral Folksongs* (the remaining one, *There Was a Tree*, was omitted because it 'won't go'[16]). These were published by Curwen, and Holst also persuaded the Oxford University Press to publish two collections of rounds by his Morley College pupils, under the title *Morley Rounds*. A choral work which he had more difficulty in publishing was his setting of Henry Vaughan's *The Evening Watch* for eight-part unaccompanied chorus. Holst described the setting as a motet, but its atmospheric progressions of extended fourth-chords owe nothing to the contrapuntal techniques of earlier centuries. The piece would have a limited appeal for audiences, and only the more accomplished choirs would be able to realize its full resonant effect, so that after due consideration Harold Brooke of Novello decided against publication (Holst used to call Brooke's office 'The Judgement Seat'[17]). This part-song was intended to be the first of a series of motets for unaccompanied chorus, but in fact only two were written (the second was *Sing Me the Men*, composed the following year). Both were published by Curwen in 1925, whereupon *The Times* described *The Evening Watch* as 'a piece of barren construction',[18] and Holst later commented: 'I wrote them while I was ill and cannot make up my mind about them.'[19] Curwen eventually allowed the motets to go out of print, and it was not until 1965 when *The Evening Watch* was reissued by Faber that it was recognized as a characteristic example of Holst's mature art, more in keeping with the mood of the later twentieth century than that of the 1920s.

One work which he had few doubts about was his new opera *At the Boar's Head*, which he had been sketching during the summer. While recuperating at Thaxted, Holst had been reading Shakespeare's *Henry IV*, and glancing through some volumes of country-dance tunes left in the house by Imogen (who had recently joined the English Folk Dance Society) he suddenly realized that the words he had been reading fitted some of the tunes. 'As the weather was very bad,' he wrote, 'just for something to do I wrote down all the Falstaff speeches and all the Pistol speeches that went to the tunes.'[20] He then had the idea of writing an entire opera using the traditional tunes in this way, and immediately set to work to select the words for the libretto ('as critics have decided that I can't write a libretto,' he remarked, 'the words of my new opera have been written by Shakespeare'[21]). He chose extracts from the tavern scenes in both parts of *Henry IV* and added two sonnets together with the words of three traditional songs. The forty-one traditional melodies were taken from Chappell's *Popular Music of the Olden Time*, Cecil Sharp's *Country Dance Tunes* and *Morris Dance Tunes*, and some unpublished folk-songs collected by G. B. Gardiner, to which were added three original tunes by Holst himself.

The task of combining these elements into a musical and dramatic entity gave him much satisfaction, and he revelled as much in the musical problems he had set himself as in the vivid personalities of Shakespeare's characters. Holst described the work as 'an opera which wrote itself',[22] but in fact he demonstrated considerable skill in his use of the tunes, and the work must be regarded as an original composition in its own right. Folksongs had been used in opera before, notably in the English ballad operas, Humperdinck's *Hansel and Gretel*, Stanford's *Shamus O'Brien* (in which Holst had coached singers during his days with the Carl Rosa Opera Company), and Vaughan Williams's *Hugh the Drover*, but they had never been woven together so closely that it was scarcely possible to tell where one ended and the next began. Although the words seemed to Holst to fit the tunes quite naturally, the process of forcing free dialogue into the metrical patterns of pre-existing tunes involves disruption of the interplay of verbal rhythms and also slows down the speed of delivery, thus impeding the creation of an atmosphere of quick wit and repartee. Neither can the lyricism of English folk-song convey the tension of dramatic situations or do full justice to the richness and subtlety of Shakespeare's language. Clifford Bax tried unsuccessfully on several occasions to persuade Holst to abandon the project on these grounds, but 'gently and firmly, he assured me that I was wrong.'[23]

While this work was going on, Jane Joseph had been secretly planning a surprise for Holst's fiftieth birthday. She had written to all his friends and pupils, asking if they would like to contribute towards a gift of money which would enable him to have a holiday abroad, and eventually collected the sum of £350. On the morning of 21 September the cheque arrived at Thaxted, with a list of signatures of everyone who had contributed, including Vaughan Williams, Balfour Gardiner, W. G. Whittaker, Arnold and Clifford Bax, Benjamin Dale, Thomas Dunhill, Herbert Howells, Geoffrey Shaw, Martin Shaw, Richard Terry, Adrian Boult, John Somerville, Frank Duckworth, George Gardiner, and others who although perhaps less well known, still ranked highly as friends in Holst's estimation. He was overwhelmed by this gift, not so much by the money, but by the expression of friendship from so many of his pupils and colleagues. It was reassuring to know that he had retained his friends, despite his fears that his success might have alienated them, and he must have been conscious of the fact that having reached the age of fifty, his friends of the older generation would begin to diminish in number; his teacher Charles Stanford and his friend and colleague Cecil Sharp having both died during the year.

The following month he received another unexpected gift when he was awarded the Henry Elias Howland Memorial Prize by Yale University. The prize medal was accompanied by a cheque for $1,350 and a letter which explained: 'We hope you will accept these as a testimonial of the high esteem in which your work as a composer is held by the University and an earnest of our hope that you may secure the conditions necessary for uninterrupted creative work.' The prize had been established by the University in 1915, and was awarded to 'a citizen of any country in recognition of some achievement of marked distinction in the field of literature or fine arts or the science of government', an important factor in the selection being 'the idealistic element in the recipient's work'.[24]

By the autumn of 1924 the sketch of *At the Boar's Head* was almost complete, and Holst had already started work on the full score. In mid-October he wrote to Harold Brooke: 'There is another opera sketched and I am tempted to hurry up scoring and offer it to the BNOC for the New Year.'[25] When the British National Opera Company heard about the new work, they immediately offered to produce it during their forthcoming season beginning in January 1925, despite the mixed reactions which had greeted their production of *The Perfect Fool*. The main problem for Holst was how to get the work finished in time for the first rehearsals, and after discussing the matter with Isobel, he decided to try to complete the score as soon as possible, as he felt there was little more he could do on the actual composition of the work. He wrote to Vally Lasker: 'The Symphony required endless hard thinking—the finale was the biggest problem in form I've ever tackled. Whereas having carefully revised the opera I feel that it is about as good as I can make it and I'm longing to get it off my chest.'[26] But because of his illness he felt unable to cope with the physical labour of writing out the vocal and full scores, and had to call once again on Vally Lasker, Nora Day, and Jane Joseph to help him with the task. He asked them to try to fit in with his normal working hours of 10 a.m. to 1 p.m., 2.15–3.15 p.m., or 5–7.30 p.m., but would be 'agreeable to anything barring 3.30–4.30'. In gratitude for this assistance, he dedicated the opera 'To my Scribes'.[27]

Working on *At the Boar's Head* had tired Holst considerably, despite the assistance of these amanuenses. At the end of October he wrote to Whittaker to tell him that he hoped to attend his forthcoming performance with the Newcastle Bach Choir of Byrd's Great Service in St Margaret's Church, Westminster, on 25 November, but that he would like to meet Whittaker alone afterwards: 'Parties and crowds take it out of me horribly.'[28] On 20 November he wrote again from Thaxted to say that he would not be coming after all: 'I'm very sorry but I find it impossible to come to town this weekend and so I must miss both you and Byrd. My head has been bad for the last four days and I'm only fit for solitary walking, reading by the fire or bed. I hope to be fit again in a week but until then I must be here and alone.'[29] Two weeks later he wrote: 'Barring occasional twinges and a flabby arm I'm all right now,'[30] and by the year's end he felt well enough to return to his normal routine, if not with renewed vigour, at least without the constant threat of illness.

In January 1925 he resumed his teaching duties at St Paul's Girls' School, and as the year progressed his various activities increased until his timetable became just as full as before. There were frequent and widespread performances of his music: on 18 February the *Japanese Suite* was broadcast for the first time, and on 19 February Edward Behr conducted the Bombay Symphony Orchestra in the first Indian performance of the *Two Songs Without Words*. By the end of February rehearsals had started for *At the Boar's Head*, and Holst tried to attend as many as he could, even though this meant travelling to cities such as Leeds and Birmingham where the British National Opera Company happened to be during their tour (the première was scheduled to take place in Manchester in April). On 6 March Holst was in Liverpool, to deliver the inaugural James W. Alsop lecture at the University, choosing as his subject 'The Education of a Composer', a topic on which he had often lectured, and on which he had also written an article on one of the few occasions when he had set down his views in print.

At the end of March, Holst wrote from Manchester: 'We are rehearsing every day,'[31] and the première of *At the Boar's Head* was duly given at the Manchester Opera House on 3 April, conducted by Malcolm Sargent. The performance was not a success, mainly because of the illness of Walter Hyde who was to have sung the part of Prince Hal, and as no understudy had been trained, Tudor Davies was called in at four days' notice to sing the part from a copy of the vocal score. Although elaborate steps were taken to disguise this score with an ornamental cover its presence was rather obvious, and one member of the audience remarked that it 'looked suspiciously like a set of proof-sheets strung together at one corner'.[32] Clifford Bax's warnings about the wisdom of setting Shakespeare to music were justified in the event; the audience had difficulty in following the words as well as the tunes, which succeeded each other with bewildering rapidity, while the cast were unable to act with conviction while having to concentrate so hard on their music. One critic suggested that Holst had overestimated the education and intelligence of his audience, mistakenly assuming that they would have a detailed knowledge of the original plays and would therefore easily be able to follow the opera regardless of the musical treatment of the words. In fact the audience was rather disconcerted, as the work did not seem to fit readily into any conventional category of opera (Holst described it as a 'musical interlude in one act', rather than an opera as such). Both the words and the music were too concentrated for easy assimilation, and the juxtaposition of the tavern scenes without sufficient contrast and the continual appearance of tunes which were often whisked away before the audience had a chance to savour them produced a certain monotony of effect, with little of the active drama which is essential to successful opera. Although the example of English folk-song had originally enabled Holst to distance himself from the excesses of Wagnerism, this forcing of words into a strait-jacket of traditional country-dance tunes lacked the flexibility necessary for effective word-setting. In fact, the most effective places in the score are those in which Holst composed his own music for the words, thus proving the point. In spite of the fact that tunes and words came at the audience in rapid succession, the main effect of the music was to slow down the stage action, as musical declamation of words is inevitably slower than spoken dialogue, and a great deal of Shakespeare's wit and humour were lost. By setting himself this artificial task, Holst denied himself the opportunity to create an original and effective work, which would doubtless have been the case had he written all the music himself.

The critics immediately seized upon these deficiences, which had apparently been offered to them on an open plate. The *Musical News & Herald* complained: 'For the whole hour which the performance occupied, nothing happened that was of the slightest dramatic consequence', and went on to remark that 'the tension of waiting for something to happen grew so overpowering that a simple knocking at the Inn door assumed the proportions of a big event.' The writer declared that action should not be confused with mere movement (of which there was plenty); action should lead the drama from one situation to another—simply shuffling the participants about on the stage is not enough. He pointed out that many of the characters often did nothing for long periods of time, 'and did it in the busiest and most painstaking fashion'. Comparing the opera to a film of the Derby in slow motion, he went on: 'Holst sets this crisp and bustling dialogue to music, and spins out for a whole hour a scene which Shakespeare (with his unerring instinct for what an audience will stand) gets through in less than a quarter of the time.' Although he believed that as a musician Holst could 'run rings round Mascagni and Leoncavallo', in terms of stagecraft the position was reversed. It should be possible to act an opera, the critic claimed, rather than simply to sing it while dressed in costume (this problem was cleverly evaded by Stravinsky in his 'opera-oratorio' Oedipus Rex, composed a year or so later, by keeping his singers virtually immobile, and treating them in a stylized way, almost as statues). The singers were commended for their efforts to cope with their parts, which were described as 'all but impossible (from the dramatic standpoint)'.[33]

Holst was praised by the critics for his technical ingenuity, but as the opera was found to be 'entirely lacking in the robust atmosphere of its tavern setting', 'the ingenuity must be dubbed perverse'.[34] During rehearsals the cast called the work by the irreverent title 'In the Whore's Bed', but Shakespeare's bawdier passages had in fact been eliminated from the libretto, so that the result was quite lacking in any salacious content. Some critics commented on the disparity between the modal, folk-type melodies, and those deriving from eighteenth-century ballad opera, while others found Holst's orchestration almost too sparse to support the voices. The passage of time often modifies such judgements: writing some forty years later, Winton Dean declared that Holst's use of traditional tunes was much more successful than that of Vaughan Williams in his Sir John in Love (written in 1924–8), mainly because of these sparse textures. Dean also wrote that 'Few composers have come closer than Holst to matching the authentic bite of Shakespeare's language. The moments of sentiment in particular ... are admirably judged. Although the score is full of contrapuntal ingenuities ... its impact is fresh and exhilarating.'[35] Critics of the first performance begrudgingly allowed credit to Holst for his musical skill (particularly the linking of parts of two melodies in succession so that they seem to be one), but on the whole the work was given a firm 'thumbs down', and has rarely been performed since the first British National Opera Company season of 1925–6.

Coupled with *At the Boar's Head* as a double bill was Puccini's *Gianni Schicchi*, which Holst regarded as a 'superb theatre-work',[36] as Clifford Bax recalled, remarking that Holst had much more appreciation of Puccini than was usual among composers at that time. It is hard to discover what Holst thought of his own opera, as he often had mixed feelings about his works. He also seemed to be in two minds about the quality of the performance; according to Clifford Bax, who met the composer in the street when *At the Boar's Head* was being performed in London, Holst called out to him: 'Go and hear that thing, Monday, Golders Green. They do it well,'[37] but later in the year he wrote to an acquaintance: 'My opera, *At the Boar's Head*, has just been ruined by the British National Opera Company . . .'[38] When Steuart Wilson took over the role of Prince Hal the standard of performance seems to have improved considerably, and in October Holst remarked that he had heard that 'The BH is another thing altogether thanks to Steuart. Norman Allin confirms this and adds that he never felt he could do his best before.'[39]

From large-scale works, Holst once again turned to smaller forms. On 15 April 1925 he wrote to Edwin Evans: 'I am working on something that will probably be either chamber music or waste paper.'[40] This was the *Terzetto* for flute, oboe, and viola, and the reason for the composer's doubt was that he was experimenting with bitonality and polytonality, and was uncertain whether the resulting sound would conform with the musical concept of his imagination. To emphasize the separate tonalities, he wrote each part with its own key signature, but Vaughan Williams later remarked that the three keys were 'more seen by the eye than felt by the ear'.[41] The *Terzetto* may have been influenced by the sparse, hard-edged textures and uncompromising bitonality of Ravel's Sonata for violin and cello, which was written in 1920–2 and performed in London during one of the composer's visits in the early 1920s. Whether or not Holst had heard this work when he came to compose the *Terzetto*, his own attitude to polytonality was rather different; he used it to produce an ambiguity of key centre rather than for the generation of harmonic clashes (and for his pains was taken to task by critics who found insufficient dissonance in his three-key writing). Even when he had finished the work he was unsure whether he liked it, and had to listen to it several times before he could make up his mind. He eventually came down in the work's favour, but it had little success with performers or audiences, and was not published until ten years after his death.

Another small form which Holst tackled at this time was that of the hymn-tune. He was asked to contribute to a new hymnal called *Songs of Praise*, with an editorial team similar to that of the *English Hymnal*; Percy Dearmer as general Editor, and Vaughan Williams as Music Editor, in association with Martin Shaw. The editors had decided to include several previous hymns by Holst, some of which had already become well known: *From Glory to Glory Advancing* and *In the Bleak Mid-winter* (from the *English Hymnal* of 1906), *What Heroes Thou Hast Bred* (from the 1909 Stepney Children's Pageant), the *Christmas Song* (No.1 of *Three Carols*) and a hymn version of *I Vow to Thee, my Country*. To these, Holst added four more hymns especially composed for the new publication: *O Valiant Hearts* to words by J. S. Arkwright, *In This World, the Isle of Dreams* (words by Herrick), *Onward, Christian Soldiers!* (words by Sabine Baring-Gould), and *I Sought Thee Round About, O Thou My God* (words by Thomas Heywood, adapted by Percy Dearmer). He called his tunes *Valiant Hearts*, *Brookend* (after the Tudor farmhouse near Thaxted which became his country home after giving up The Steps in 1925), *Prince Rupert* (after the Seventeenth-century tune on which the hymn is based), and *Monk Street* (after the location of his first cottage in the Thaxted area). Holst also composed another hymn entitled *Christ Hath a Garden*, but Vaughan Williams eventually decided to keep the original tune for which the words had been written. *Songs of Praise* was intended to appeal to 'the forward-looking people of every communion',[42] and included hymns by writers of various denominations. When it was published, Vaughan Williams declared that there was not a single tune in it that he was ashamed of. A revised and enlarged edition was published in 1931, containing an additional hymn by Holst: *By Weary Stages*, from *The Coming of Christ*.

Holst also found time during 1925 to complete his second 'motet' for unaccompanied voices: *Sing Me the Men*, to words by Digby Mackworth Dolben. Unlike the poem used for the first motet, these words were still in copyright, and the owner's permission was necessary before the work could be published. Accordingly, Holst wrote to the Poet Laureate, Robert Bridges, and received the reply that Bridges had assigned the rights to Herbert Paul, but did not think that permission would be refused. Writing from his home at Boar's Hill, near Oxford, Bridges went on: 'If you ever want to get a few days quiet, I wish you would come and spend them here. Your muse would be quite undisturbed, and there is no knowing what you might compose. Just now everything is very beautiful. Nothing to be heard of Oxford but its distant bells . . . but the city with all its towers and spires lying sunlit in the valley beneath us makes ‹a wonder of our lovely landscape.'[43] When Holst sent Bridges a copy of the published motet a few weeks later, Bridges replied that he longed to hear it performed, and on looking through the score commented: 'I am altogether delighted by your dealing with the mood—the music was full of satisfying impressions to me . . . it seemed to me that Dolben's spirit must have been with you.'[44] The first performance of *Sing Me the Men* was conducted by the composer on Whit-Sunday 1925 in the church of All Hallows, Barking-by-the-Tower, as part of the annual Whitsun festival given by the students of Morley College.

This contact with Robert Bridges prompted Holst to look once again at the poet's work, and he began to compose a set of seven part-song settings for female voices and strings. Holst later wrote: 'I did the first of the Bridges poems the moment I caught sight of the words. Since when I've been wondering what they mean.'[45] He wrote *Assemble, All Ye Maidens* and *Love on My Heart from Heaven Fell* in 1925, and the remainder of the set during the following year. Another choral work written in the spring of 1925 was the *Ode to C.K.S. and the Oriana*, in honour of Charles Kennedy Scott, who had directed the Oriana Madrigal Society since its inception in 1904 (when it had included Thomas Beecham among the basses). Holst had the idea of writing a short piece to celebrate the choir's twenty-first birthday, in gratitude for the many occasions on which it had performed his music; Jane Joseph wrote the words, which were a clever parody of Scott's idiosyncratic rehearsal methods, and the work gave much amusement to the singers when it was performed at their celebratory party on 29 June.

After term had ended, Holst set out on a visit to Switzerland and Germany, partly for a holiday but also to lecture on British music. At the beginning of August he was in Mürren in the Bernese Oberland, where he stayed for a week, and after a day in Lucerne and a day in Menaggio, he arrived in Maloja in the Engadine, where he also stayed a week. He wrote home: 'The pass was all pine woods with snow mountains on either side and it's easily the most dazzling travelling experience of my life.'[46] He then went on to Freiburg, where he met Vally Lasker and stayed at Clara Lasker's 'Das Rebhaus', a group of houses set in an estate on the side of a hill. From here he reported: 'The Black Forest is a new and great event in my life . . . Vally shows me her favourite spots during the day and in the evening I wander about alone in the woods and dream.'[47] But this comfortable accommodation was exceptional; he did not care for the atmosphere of the large hotels in which he was otherwise obliged to stay, and he was eventually glad to board the train for home on 17 August.

At the beginning of September the Three Choirs Festival was held in Gloucester Cathedral, where Holst conducted the first performance of his motet *The Evening Watch*. Although the work was given a polite reception by the audience, its austere and transcendental atmosphere was far removed from the kind of music normally to be heard at the festival, and many listeners were disconcerted. One reviewer found Holst's modernistic harmonies too much to take: 'The new motet . . . finds Holst carrying the use of unresolved dissonances to a degree within which the very nature of all we have hitherto understood by the word "music" seems to be consumed,' and dismissed the piece with the curt remark: 'Nobody liked

Holst's music, so far as could be discovered, and there seemed no reason why anybody should like it.'[48]

But the biggest event of the autumn was to be the première performance of the *First Choral Symphony* at the Leeds Triennial Festival. Holst travelled to Leeds on 2 October to supervise the rehearsals, and spoke at an 'Eve-of-Festival' dinner given by the Association of Leeds Professional Musicians. He stayed in the home of Professor Julius Cohen, and wrote to Vally Lasker: 'Every day in every way the Cohens grow nicer and nicer. The Festival is only camouflage. I am really here on a rest cure. Saturday: bed and breakfast, Sunday: breakfast in bed, Today: bed in afternoon. Und so weiter.'[49] He was pleased with the 'wonderfully detailed rehearsal',[50] and the Symphony was given a successful first performance on 7 October in the Town Hall, with Dorothy Silk as soprano soloist, and the London Symphony Orchestra and Festival Chorus, conducted by Albert Coates. It was repeated in London by the same performers at a Royal Philharmonic Society concert on 29 October (commemorating the centenary of their first performance of Beethoven's Ninth Symphony in 1825), but for some reason this did not go well. Vaughan Williams heard this latter performance, and commented on the choir's insensitivity to dynamic shading and the meaning of the words; he felt that the singers had not really understood the work and lacked sympathy with what Holst was trying to express in his music.

The critics, however, ignored the quality of both performances and pounced upon the more obvious aspects of Holst's work; particularly the juxtaposition of extracts from Keats's poems and his musical treatment of them. Comments ranged from the facetious (' "Spirit here that reignest" no longer says what Keats meant by it, for Keats' "here" was the leaves of Beaumont and Fletcher and Holst's "here" is presumably the Leeds Town Hall'[51]) to open hostility ('Holst presents the melancholy spectacle of a continuous and unrelieved decline . . . If *Flos Campi* is Vaughan Williams's best work, the *Choral Symphony* is probably Holst's worst'[52]). As in the case of *At the Boar's Head*, Holst was praised for his technical skill in putting the music together, but criticized for a lack of convincing expression in the result. Cecil Gray wrote: 'The music has no logic or coherence of its own, and depends almost entirely on the poems of Keats for any impression it may make ... The note of ecstasy, the wealth of imagery, the atmosphere of sensuous luxuriance, which are so characteristic of the poetry of Keats, are completely foreign to the music of Holst.'[53] W. J. Turner wondered why Holst had chosen these particular texts: 'The passages selected have no special affinity one with another—except that all are by Keats.'[54] After remarking that Holst did not express in his music what Keats had expressed in the words, Turner went on to raise a difficult philosophical problem by pointing out that if the music did express the words, then the words would be superfluous and there would be no need to sing them. If this were true, there would be no need for words in any choral or vocal music, and indeed Turner went on to question why Holst had decided to make this a choral symphony, extrapolating this to ask why he should have written the work at all (in reply to which, Holst would doubtless have quoted his version of a remark by Samuel Butler: 'Never compose anything unless the not composing of it becomes a positive nuisance to you'). Writing some years after the first performance, Ernest Newman drew attention to the difficulty of setting words for a chorus rather than for a soloist; he commended Holst for following the rhythms of the original poems, but pointed out that musical notation can never reproduce the rhythmic subtlety of spoken words; although a soloist can take liberties with musical notation in order to achieve a more natural effect, a chorus is constrained by the necessity of keeping together.[55] Edwin Evans doubted the wisdom of setting texts by major poets, asserting that 'The sheer phonetic beauty of Keats' verse is music in itself.'[56]

Much fun was had at Holst's expense over his 'Bacchanale', which Cecil Gray declared 'would be more suited to a procession of Prohibition agents' than of Bacchus and his drunken followers.[57] At the subsequent London performance, Vaughan Williams blamed the chorus for this failure of verve: 'I've come to the conclusion that the Leeds Chorus CANNOT SING—the Bacchus Chorus sounded like an Oratorio.'[58] Gray, however, reserved his most biting invective for the Finale: 'The last movement in which he takes four poems of Keats, cuts them up into pieces, puts them together again in such a way that a stanza from one poem is followed by one from another, and then proceeds to pour over these mutilated corpses, which were once poetical masterpieces, some of the dullest, most pretentious and bombastic music which has ever been written.' Gray was only willing to allow Holst credit for vulgarity: 'The only section of the work in which the music corresponds at all to the spirit of the poetry consists in the setting of Folly's song, probably the most inane and vulgar trifle Keats ever wrote.'[59] W. J. Turner later summed up the adverse criticism by proclaiming that 'There is no true creative impulse behind this composition . . . it is just an ambitious task which Mr Holst set himself.'[60]

A few critics were sympathetic; the *Musical News & Herald* was tolerant of Holst's manipulation of the poems: 'The dovetailings and omissions (amongst the latter the famous couplet of "intense surprise") leave one confident of the composer's literary taste,' going on to remark that 'In a symphony one expects something of the interior life of a man . . . But Holst's is one magnificent illustration, like a Veronese.'[61] The movement which drew most favourable comment was the *Ode on a Grecian Urn*, in which Holst's power of evoking static atmospheric moods was ideally suited to the limpid stillness of the subject matter. The *Musical News & Herald* again: 'This subtle and unfailing fidelity to the words was one of the great secrets of our polyphonic school; and it is manifest how Holst has striven, with the curious material at his disposal, so to adjust the harmony of words and music that his setting shall be, if the nature of things will permit it, as durable as the Ode—a sort of third vessel enclosing the timeless Grecian Urn.'[62] Harvey Grace wrote that 'although the vocal writing is mainly diatonic, often slight in texture and simple to the eye, it is of great rhythmic variety and interest.' He thought that the selected texts were 'well-contrasted, singable, under-standable, and very apt for musical setting'.[63] Comparisons were inevitably made with Vaughan Williams's *Sea Symphony*, which had been performed at Leeds fifteen years before, and Edwin Evans later wrote: 'Vaughan Williams's work has the advantage over Holst's that his selections from Whitman are made cohesive by a central theme—the sea; Holst's unity of purpose is at the mercy of Keats' elusive spirit . . . It has been suggested that Holst tended to be too deferential towards his poets. He would expend endless effort in devising subtle rhythms which would express them, sometimes at the expense of music which expressed himself.'[64]

Praise was given to the performers for their efforts: the *Birmingham Post* described Dorothy Silk's singing of the words as 'perfect', but gloomily predicted that 'we shall hear them murdered by some soprano or other in the years to come'.[65] The chorus was commended for its singing, particularly in the Scherzo, which according to Edwin Evans 'at first seemed to be beyond the powers of this highly accomplished choir'.[66] But the general reaction of critics and audiences was unfavourable; even Vaughan Williams felt only 'cold admiration',[67] but hoped that he would like it more after repeated hearings (he did in fact, but it took some years; after a broadcast performance in early 1934 he wrote to Holst: 'I *wholly* liked the Urn for the first time. I'm not sure that it is the Urn—but it's *you*, which is all I know & all I need to know'[68]). Vaughan Williams approved of the 'big tune' in the Finale, but the critic Dyneley Hussey found that this was 'not sufficient to compensate for the dullness and bathos of the rest'.[69]

Although Holst himself thought that 'The work as a whole is the best thing I have written'[70] (a remark which he often made about his most recent compositions), it was clear that the symphony had not been a success, and it did not enter the repertoire of choral societies' favourite works. In fact, from this point onwards, Holst's popularity started to decline, as audiences began to realize that he was not going to repeat the manner of past successes, but intended to follow any path along which his imagination and curiosity might lead him, regardless of whether his public was ready or willing to follow. His most persistent detractor was Cecil Gray, who assessed Holst's work as a mere 'compendium or *pastiche* of the styles of nearly all representative modern composers'. After denigrating the work of most of his British contemporaries, Gray went on to remark that Holst 'has no more originality of outlook than any of the composers mentioned . . . if anything he has less . . . It is largely on account of his undoubted earnestness and sincerity that his art seems the more definitely pernicious. The faults of the others are negative, his are positive. . . Mediocrities can make even the greatest virtues detestable, and Holst is an example of this. Like so many mediocre minds he is attracted by the largest and most grandiose conceptions; nothing but the greatest themes of all art will satisfy him, such as *The Planets*, *Hymns from the Rig Veda*, *The Hymn of Jesus* and so forth. In Heine's phrase, he perpetually feeds on the fixed stars and drinks the Milky Way.'[71]

This harsh criticism is refuted not only by the fact that Holst was an undoubted master of smaller forms, particularly part-songs and hymn-tunes, but also by his characteristic style, which is stamped as a fingerprint on all his works, making them immediately recognizable as his own. Few composers manage to achieve as much, and to accuse Holst of lack of originality is to ignore the individual personality evident throughout his work. He was subject to many influences, but absorbed them all and used the resulting synthesis for his own expressive purposes. Although he was a contemporary of many outstanding composers, such as Schoenberg, Stravinsky, Ravel, and Bartok, and was undoubtedly influenced by their work, his own personality was strong enough to prevent his individuality from being submerged, as happened in the case of many lesser talents exposed to the influence of such powerful figures. But Gray seemed only to be looking for glib comparisons: he thought that Stanford and Parry were 'second-hand' Brahms, Cyril Scott was imitation Debussy, Holbrook and Bantock imitation Strauss, Goossens imitation Ravel, Bliss imitation Stravinsky, and Berners conterfeit Satie. While there is substance in some of these assertions, the mere fact that Holst cannot be described as the imitator of any other single composer is sufficient to establish his individuality. But the musical public was not concerned with such niceties; if a new work bored or disconcerted them, further investigation would be inhibited, and when audiences realized that there would be no more works like *The Planets*, Holst's fortunes began to wane.

14

Lectures and Festivities
(1925–1927)

But this decline took place over a period of several years, and Holst himself would have been oblivious to it. He carried on with his usual life of composing and teaching, fitting the demands of fame into his routine as best he could. On 13 October he conducted some of his works in a concert at the Birmingham Town Hall which was broadcast by the BBC: he directed the *Fugal Overture* and *Beni Mora* (its first broadcast performance), while the Scherzo from the *First Choral Symphony* was entrusted to Adrian Boult (as Holst explained to Vally Lasker: ' "Fancy" is too much for me so dear Adrian is conducting it tonight . . . Adrian is an Angel with Brains'[1]).

On 16 October 1925 Holst was at Liverpool University to give the first series of six weekly lectures on 'England and her Music', with music examples provided by the Choral Circle of the Liverpool Centre of the British Music Society, conducted by Holst himself. A large audience turned out, and Holst was welcomed by the Vice Chancellor, Dr Adami, who described him as coming 'fresh from his great triumph at the Leeds Music Festival'.[2] After the second lecture on 23 October, the astonished audience was told to learn Morley's *Sing We and Chant It* in time to sing it the following week, copies being on sale at the exit. When they subsequently attempted to do so, Holst sharply criticized their tentative beginning and made them start again, and also found the balance between the parts unsatisfactory, urging his listeners to give close attention to these points.

Other engagements had to be fitted in: on 5 November he lectured on Purcell at University College, Bangor, and the following day was again in Liverpool for the fourth lecture of his series, also on Purcell. Holst's partisan enthusiasm perhaps

1. *Above left*, Adolph von Holst, Gustav's father.
2. *Above right*, Clara, née Lediard, Gustav's mother.
3. Holst's birthplace, 4 Clarence Road, Cheltenham.

4. Holst as a child.

5. Holst, about eleven years old.

6. Holst as a student.

7. Gustav and Isobel on holiday in Berlin, 1903.

8. Holst's first married home: a flat, 162 Shepherd's Bush Road.

10, 10 The Terrace, Barnes, Holst's home

11. Holst in his late twenties.

12. The 'Old Vic' and Morley College at the turn of the century.

13. Holst and Henry Balfour Gardiner.

. Town Street, Thaxted.

Holst and his perfomers in Thaxted church.

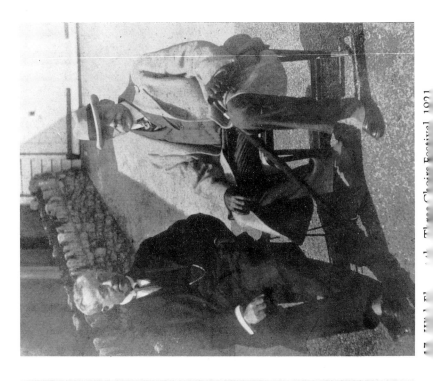

9. Isobel in the cottage at Monk Street, Thaxted

. Holst conducting *The Planets*,
20

20. Holst arrives in the USA, 1923

21. With Vaughan Williams on a walking tour, Sept. 1921.

22. Gustav and Isobel at Ann Arbor, 1923.

Holst conducting at St Paul's, 1923: Imogen is one of the horn players.

Ralph and Adeline Vaughan Williams, Holst, Mrs Longman, Vally Lasker
Nora Day, 20 Dec. 1923.

26. With students at Reading:

25. Outside the Queen's Hall, 1920s.

. Holst conducting at St Paul's: silhouette by K. M. Roberts.

At table on a visit to Scotland, *c.* 1925.

30. Holst at his desk in St Paul's Girls' School, late

On a walking tour, 1920s

Holst in the last year of his life.

32. Imogen Holst, 1933.

33. Imogen Holst, 1982.

went a little too far when he claimed in these lectures that Purcell was a finer stage composer than Wagner and was excelled in melody only by Mozart, but his performance with J. E. Wallace's choir of the Lament and chorus 'With Drooping Wings' from *Dido and Aeneas* went a long way towards convincing the audience of the justice of his cause.

In his fifth lecture he reminisced about his early days as a trombonist, recalling that he had visited Liverpool with the Carl Rosa company in 1897, and commented on the curious habit British musicians have of calling themselves by false foreign names (Holst remarked that from 1837 to 1914 the most musically effective names were German, but since 1914 French or Russian would be better; singers, of course, could always rely on the exotic value of a false Italian name). On 18 November he was in Eastbourne to conduct four movements from *The Planets*, and on 20 November returned to Liverpool for his final visit, giving two lectures on the same evening: at the University he spoke on 'England and her Music', in which he examined the future prospects for the development of English music, dismissing jazz and popular music as a mere passing phase, and at the Picton Hall he lectured on the works of Vaughan Williams to members of the British Music Society. J. E. Wallace's choir sang the Kyrie from Vaughan Williams's Mass in G minor, and Vally Lasker and Nora Day played a two-piano arrangement of his *Pastoral Symphony*. The chairman remarked that during his series of lectures at the University, Holst had not once mentioned his own music, and to remedy this there would be a concert the following week devoted entirely to works by Holst, including *Savitri*, the *Fugal Concerto*, and movements from the *St Paul's Suite*. The idea of the concert had come from A. K. Holland, music critic of the *Liverpool Daily Post*, who had suggested it to Fred Wilkinson, a Liverpool schoolmaster with a penchant for producing plays. Wilkinson had never heard of Holst, but responded to the idea with enthusiasm, and together with Holland persuaded the Sandon Studios Society and British Music Society to put on the concert under their joint auspices on 28 November 1925. By way of thanks for this performance, Wilkinson received a letter from Holst, saying that there was only one way of expressing gratitude to such a man, and that was by giving him more work to do. Holst asked if Wilkinson would be interested in producing *At the Boar's Head* in Liverpool, and a further presentation was therefore arranged for 24 April 1926, to include *Savitri*, *At the Boar's Head*, and a ballet based on movements from the *St Paul's Suite*, the conductors being J. E. Wallace and Malcolm Sargent (the programme was to be repeated by the same performers in the Parry Theatre of the Royal College of Music on 29 May). Fred Wilkinson later became headmaster of Wallasey Grammar School and subsequently of the Polytechnic Secondary School (later Quintin School) in London. His most vivid memory of Holst was of being with him in the audience for a performance of *The Planets* at the Queen's Hall; both joined in the enthusiastic applause at the end, but Holst did not reveal himself as the composer, and they both slipped quietly away without Holst being recognized.

1926 began with another series of lectures, this time in Glasgow, where Holst had been invited to give the Cramb lectures at the University. There were to be ten lectures, from 15 January to 13 February, and he decided to devote them mainly to orchestral music, although there would opportunities for discussing various other topics which interested him. Besides dealing with the development of the orchestra and its music over the centuries, Holst considered particular composers and their works, fastidiously avoiding any mention of his own music until the eighth lecture, in which he talked about *The Planets*, as there was to be a performance of three movements from the suite in Glasgow on 9 February. The final lecture was devoted to a review of the current state of British orchestral music, after which the chairman, in thanking Holst, hoped that the success of his lectures would further the cause of the establishment of a Music Department in the University. This idea eventually came to fruition in 1929 when Holst's friend W. G. Whittaker was appointed first Gardiner Professor of Music at Glasgow University.

Within this tight schedule of ten lectures in four weeks, Holst managed to find time for engagements elsewhere: on 28 January he lectured on Purcell to the York branch of the British Music Society, besides carrying on with his normal teaching duties ('Vaughan Williams tells me that I ought to leave St

Paul's', he remarked to Imogen; 'I don't feel that I could, *now.* The thing has become too much of a habit'[3]. After a lecture on Vaughan Williams's music at Malvern on 27 February, he took a refreshing walk over the Malvern Hills with Nora Day and Valley Lasker, who had played the musical examples for him.

On 2 March the first performance of the *Terzetto* was given at the Faculty of Arts Gallery, Golden Square, London, by Albert Fransella (flute), Leon Goossens (oboe), and Henry Berly (viola), a trio which also gave the first broadcast performance on 18 June in a concert relayed from Seaford House, Belgrave Square. Any lingering doubts which Holst may have had about this piece were pushed to the back of his mind by work on his current composition, the choral ballet *The Golden Goose,* based on an adaptation by Jane Joseph of a story from Grimm's *Fairy Tales* about a princess who was unable to laugh. Holst intended this work for performance during the 1926 Whitsun festival, and on 9 March wrote to Harold Brooke: 'I hope to finish the sketch in a week and the full score by Easter and Miss Lasker is working hard at the piano score.'[4] The term 'choral ballet' seems to have been coined by Holst, and aptly describes this cantata in which the singers also dance and act out the story. The music is simple but effective, much of it derived from English country-dance music, with some sweet, nostalgic 6/8 tunes and some brief moments of tender lyricism quite rare in Holst's work of any period. Particularly effective is the Human Organ, in which the singers stand immobile, waiting to be 'played' by a Showman assisted by two Gnomes who pump the air. Although originally intended for performance with action, Holst later wrote: 'I have conducted the "GG" three times, only one of which was with action, and am quite convinced that it makes a good concert piece.'[5]

At the beginning of April Holst spent the Easter weekend putting the final touches to the score of *The Golden Goose,* and then travelled to Bournemouth where he was to conduct the ballet music from *The Perfect Fool* with the Bournemouth Municipal Orchestra on 9 April. After the concert he set out on a walking tour through Dorset and Wiltshire, passing over Wareham Heath (called Egdon Heath in Thomas Hardy's novels) and finishing up on 13 April in Salisbury, from where he took a train home. 'I've had The perfect walk', he wrote to

Whittaker; 'Four days in Dorset and Wilts; 2 miles per hour with 30 min rest for each 60 walking when fresh and the reverse when not; only 4 miles main road to 50 on grass and about 12 lanes and woodland paths: no collar, lots of cider and cheese and only one blister!'[6] Although Hardy probably derived the name Egdon from Eggardun Hill in West Dorset, it was the heathland in the eastern part of the county which was so vividly evoked in his novel *The Return of the Native*, a region described by Holst as 'the partly wild, partly cultivated stretch of country that lies east of Dorchester',[7] and it was the effect of this walk, combined with reading the novel, which was to result in the composition of *Egdon Heath* the following year.

At the end of April Holst went again to Liverpool for the performance of *Savitri* and *At the Boar's Head* by the Sandon Studios Society, and then returned to London, where, despite news of the impending General Strike, plans were going ahead for the usual Whitsun festival, to be held this year at Emmanuel Church, Camberwell. The Sunday events took place successfully, and on the Whit Monday *The Golden Goose* was performed in the gardens of Bute House by students of Morley College and girls from the school. Imogen Holst, who took part in the performance, recalled that everyone enjoyed themselves immensely, the Human Organ being particularly effective, but that she found difficulty in dancing to one of the tunes: 'It was the only time I have ever found his music difficult to dance to.'[8] This production was a private performance for pupils and parents, and the first complete public performance was given in a BBC broadcast later in the year.

On 29 May a repeat performance of *Savitri* and *At the Boar's Head* was given by the Sandon Studios Society at the Royal College of Music, after which Holst got down to work on an important project which was to occupy him for the next few months: rerecording *The Planets* for the Columbia Graphophone Company. His 1923 recording of the suite had been a success, and had even been chosen by *The Gramophone* magazine as a test recording for the comparison of different types of reproducing machine, but now that electrical recording techniques had been introduced, companies were keen to rerecord their repertoire to take advantage of the improved sound quality offered by the new technology. The sessions took place between June and October 1926, and although conditions in the studio were relatively spacious compared with the discomfort associated with acoustic recording, a tense atmosphere still prevailed because of the necessity of recording each side of a disc in one 'take'. Another worry for musicians in early recording sessions was the need to limit the duration of an item to the time permissible for one side of a record. If the grooves ventured too near the centre of the disc, the sound was liable to be distorted, and the conductor was therefore inclined to hurry the tempo in order to avoid over-running the specified time. This was particularly important in the case of electrical recording, which involved a wider spacing of the grooves, thus reducing the available playing time per side. The noticeable tempo differences between the recordings Holst made of *The Planets* in 1923 and 1926 may be due to this: his 1926 *Venus* is considerably faster than his 1923 version for instance, but although *Mars* is also taken at a faster tempo in the later version, this was how Holst insisted that it should be performed, and his slower 1923 tempo may have resulted from his inexperience in the recording studio at that time. When the 1926 electrical recording was reissued as a long-playing disc in 1972, Imogen Holst said that she was disappointed only by the end of *Neptune*, whose fade-out could not be recorded properly by the equipment available in 1923, and by *Mercury*, which she found 'over-cautious', but thought that the other movements, particularly *Mars* and *Uranus*, sounded much as they did when Holst conducted them at the Queen's Hall during the 1920s.[9]

During the first half of 1926 Holst completed three more of the *Seven Part Songs* to words by Robert Bridges, and invited Harold Brooke to hear a try-through at St Paul's Girls' School at the end of the summer term. Holst wanted Brooke to make a choice for a première performance with his own choir, and despite the fact that Brooke was invited to be 'as stern as you were over the *Evening Watch*', he seems to have liked the songs, and Holst therefore dedicated three of them to him when they were subsequently published. At the beginning of September, Holst wrote to Bridges for permission to publish the words of the five completed songs, and added: 'I had intended asking you if you would care to hear them tried over before they were published but the girls who sang them to me have now left the school. We might be able to get a few singers and players in Oxford but it would be simpler to wait until after publication although I have vocal and orchestral parts of most of them. I have written them at odd moments and it has been difficult to decide the order. I hope you approve of my present arrangement.'[10] The remaining two part-songs were completed during the autumn, and Holst wrote again to Bridges suggesting an Oxford performance, explaining that 'At present I am hoping to set "Angel spirits of sleep" and "O love I complain". I am thinking of setting some others . . . and I wonder if you would object to my taking parts only of your Ode to Music written for the Purcell bicentenary particularly the dirge "Man born of desire" '[11] (in the event Holst did not set these words until 1930, when he used them for *A Choral Fantasia*).

The Three Choirs Festival was held in Worcester that year, Holst's music being represented by the *Short Festival Te Deum* of 1919, after which the BBC invited him to conduct a special programme on his birthday on 21 September. The works performed were *The Perfect Fool* ballet music, the First Group of *Choral Hymns from the Rig Veda*, the *Fugal Concerto*, *Ave Maria*, *Beni Mora*, and *The Golden Goose* (its first broadcast performance and first complete public performance). The following month another of Holst's works had its première in a radio programme when the *Toccata* was broadcast from the BBC Liverpool station as part of a piano recital given by Joseph Greene on 20 October 1926.

November was a busy month for Holst, with visits to Bristol, Manchester, and Edinburgh, where he conducted a University concert in the Usher Hall. Despite these strenuous activities, his health remained good, as is evident from a letter to Harold Brooke, declining a dinner invitation: 'I am at present flourishing in health owing to a strict regime of early to bed and late to rise.'[12]

He also managed to find time for composition: his notebooks for this period contain fragmentary sketches for the projected *Second Choral Symphony*, which was in fact never to be completed. He intended to set some poems by George Meredith, and marked various sections of a copy of Meredith's works, but apart from drafting a general plan of the symphony, this is as far as he got. One small piece which he did complete was *Chrissemas Day in the Morning* for piano solo, based on a tune from Whittaker's *North Countrie Ballads, Songs and Pipe-Tunes*. Whittaker himself had used the melody in his own compositions, and had originally obtained it from an eighteenth-century manuscript volume of tunes in the possession of the Newcastle Society of Antiquarians. Holst also started work on *The Morning of the Year*, another 'choral ballet', which was the first work to be commissioned by the music department of the BBC (of which Percy Pitt was now Musical Director). Despite this, the completed work was dedicated to the English Folk Dance Society, being based on a scenario by Douglas Kennedy, with words by Steuart Wilson. It was intended to portray mating rituals in the spring of the year, and begins with a summoning horn melody followed by a mysterious, atavistic evocation of ancient rituals; a concept which was soon to be more fully developed in the orchestral *Egdon Heath*. The music of the dances again stems from traditional English sources (via his own earlier works such as the *Jig* of the *St Paul's Suite*), but makes no claims to authenticity, being given a individual character of its own, sometimes to the point of querkiness. There are moments of simple rhythmic vigour (similar to the manner of the later populist style of Aaron Copland), but the crucial Mating Dance is rather too bland and folksy, quite lacking in any sense of pursuit or sexual urgency.

At Christmas, Holst played the organ in Thaxted Church as usual, and then set out on a four-day walk through Essex and Suffolk. On 28 December he was at Castle Hedingham, and the following day arrived in Lavenham, from where he wrote to Robert Bridges: 'As soon as school begins I will try and fix a date for our expedition to Boar's Hill ... I have restarted my pre-war habit of a short walking tour between Xmas and the New Year and so far it has been a great success. I got to Lavenham at twilight and it looked one of the loveliest villages I have ever seen outside the Cotswolds ...'[13] After going on to Bury St Edmunds and Ipswich, Holst returned to London, where he received a reply from Bridges suggesting that the copyright fee which he had been paid for the use of his words could be used to finance a trip by the performers to Boar's Hill to sing the *Seven Part-Songs*. Consideration of travel cost was not normally of concern to his Paulinas, so Holst assured him that this would not be necessary, as the 'singers and players are mostly well to do people and all will be greatly excited at the honour of coming to perform to you'.[14]

At the end of January 1927 Holst was ill for a few days with 'Flue', but was back in circulation for performances of two of his piano works: on 11 February Adine O'Neill gave the first concert performance of the *Toccata* at St Paul's, and on 18 February Helen Bidder gave the first performance of a *First Folksong Sketch* at the Aeolian Hall in London. This 'sketch' was one of two piano pieces which Holst was writing at the time, based on tunes from Whittaker's *North Countrie Ballads, Songs and Pipe-Tunes*: *O! I Hae Seen the Roses Blaw*, and *The Shoemakker* (sung on St Crispin's Day by north-country shoemakers, who would parade around the town accompanied by an *ad hoc* band of instruments). These pieces were composed for Holst's friend and colleague Nora Day, and were published the following year under the title *Two Folksong Fragments*, later reissued as *Two Northumbrian Folk Tunes*. When the publishers submitted a copy to the BBC with a view to obtaining a broadcast performance, Victor Hely-Hutchinson looked through the score and reported laconically to the Head of the Music Department: 'These little piano pieces are technically quite effective. Like most of Holst's other works, they appear to have absolutely nothing in them, but that nothing is done rather well.'[15]

On 23 February Holst and Vaughan Williams attended a Fellows' Dinner at the Royal College of Music to mark the opening of the new Inner Hall by the Prince of Wales, after which Holst embarked on a series of rehearsals for the first performance of *The Morning of the Year*, which he conducted at a BBC concert in the Royal Albert Hall on 17 March, broadcast on the National wavelengths. Holst was somewhat annoyed by a report which appeared in the press after this concert, and wrote to Percy Pitt: 'I was sorry to read in the Evening News that I consider the new ballet my best thing since the Planets. I certainly don't and if I did I would keep it to myself. I did tell one or two men privately that I thought it the best thing I had written during the last two years which is a very different matter.'[16]

A few days later, Holst's attendance was requested at what he subsequently described as 'the most overwhelming event of my life'.[17] Some months previously, a few Cheltenham musicians had met together with a view to arranging some kind of celebratory event to honour Holst, who had now become one of the town's most famous sons. The idea had originated with Dorothy Treseder and W. Lock Mellersh, who invited Lewis Hann, director of music at Cheltenham Ladies' College, to become chairman of an organizing committee. The original proposal was to present Holst with a portrait of himself, but when the idea was put to him he replied that the money would be better spent on a concert in Cheltenham so that the citizens would have an opportunity of hearing some of his larger works adequately performed. The Committee therefore approached the Mayor with a proposal to hold a Holst Festival in the town, and it was agreed to hold the event in March 1927. A subscription list was opened to subsidize direct ticket sales, and eventually sufficient funds were raised to provide for nine hours of orchestral rehearsal time for a two-hour concert. Holst was invited to conduct, and agreed to do so provided he could share the duties with Adrian Boult, who would also be prepared to take over the whole concert in case Holst's health proved unequal to the task. The City of Birmingham Symphony Orchestra (augmented to 75 players) was engaged, together with a female voice choir of 20 singers, and the municipality set about making preparations for the event. Holst travelled to Birmingham to begin rehearsals on the day after the London première of *The Morning of the Year*, and arrived in Cheltenham on 21 March after having rehearsed the whole programme, which was to consist of *A Somerset Rhapsody*, *The Perfect Fool* ballet music, *A Fugal Concerto*, *Two Songs Without Words*, and *The Planets*. The work of the rehearsal was made considerably easier by the fact that Adrian Boult had thoroughly prepared the orchestra in all of the works before the composer himself arrived.

Tuesday 22 March turned out to be a bright, pleasant day, and Cheltenham was full of visitors who had come 'from all corners of the county' for the event.[18] There were to be two performances of the complete programme: one in the afternoon, and another the same evening. At 3 p.m. the audience was in its place in the Town Hall as the official party arrived, including Holst, the Mayor, Town Clerk, Aldermen, and Councillors, together with members of the organizing committee. The first part of the concert included Holst himself conducting the *Somerset Rhapsody*, and during the interval the Mayor made a speech congratulating him on his achievement, and presented him with a pastel painting by Harold Cox, showing the planets in their positions in the sky as seen from Cheltenham on 25 May 1919, on which date the artist believed *The Planets* had been first performed. The precise positions of the planets had been especially calculated for the committee by the Astronomer Royal, those depicted being Saturn, Neptune, Jupiter, and Venus, 'subject to a slight artistic licence in making the very distant Neptune visible to the naked eye'.[19] No one quibbled that the suite had not in fact been performed on 25 May 1919, and the Mayor went on to suggest that as Holst had written a *Cotswolds Symphony* and a *Somerset Rhapsody*, perhaps he should now consider writing a *Cheltenham Idyll* (a suggestion which was not subsequently taken up). In his reply, Holst expressed his gratitude and made a plea for the cause of the British composer, particularly on behalf of living composers in preference to dead ones. He also thanked the organizing committee for providing a generous amount of rehearsal time, describing this as 'almost unique'.[20] The second half of the programme was entirely taken up by *The Planets* conducted by the composer, after which he received an enthusiastic ovation from the audience. The evening performance was even more successful, with a crowded audience which included many younger people who were unfamiliar with works such as *A Somerset Rhapsody*, which had not been performed for years and which had only recently been accepted for publication. Other members of the audience included colleagues and old friends of the Holst family from various parts of the Cotswolds, including some who remembered the composer's father and grandfather as eminent local musicians.

During the interval, congratulatory letters from various individual musicians and organizations were read out, including Elgar, Vaughan Williams, Henry Wood, Walford Davies, Landon Ronald, Hugh Allen, the British Music Society, and the Incorporated Society of Musicians.

When the Festival was over and the final accounts drawn up, the committee found itself in the happy position of having a surplus of funds, and decided to use this to commission a portrait of Holst after all, as had been originally intended. The oil painting, by Bernard Munns of Birmingham, was duly presented to Holst, and now hangs in the Holst Birthplace Museum, together with Harold Cox's painting of the planets.

At the end of the spring term a performance of the *Seven Choruses from the Alcestis of Euripides* was given at St Paul's Girls' School, after which Holst set off on a walking tour in Yorkshire, to obtain some solitude after so much socializing. He travelled to Beverley by train on 13 April, and before setting out visited the famous Minster, particularly enjoying the carvings of minstrels and musical instruments in various parts of the building. He sent a postcard advising Whittaker: 'When you go to Beverley Minster tell the verger that you are a musician and he'll show you the 14th century town band. When you come to the pipe and tabor ask him (the verger not the piper) for his story of Dancing Ducks. I am on a walking tour (I mean a "'Walking'" (?!!) one).'[21] From Beverley he walked to Driffield, Flamborough, and Scarborough, and after spending Easter there, continued his tour via Whitby and the North Yorkshire moors as far as Castleton, from where he took a train back to London, feeling thoroughly refreshed after so much time in the open air.

On his return he found a telegram awaiting him from the New York Symphony Orchestra offering a commission for an orchestral work, and he immediately recognized this as an opportunity to write a piece which had been in his mind for some time. Since his walk over the Wessex heathland the previous Easter, he had been considering the possibility of a composition based on Thomas Hardy's Wessex, and when Austin Lidbury had sent him a copy of *The Return of the Native* Holst read it avidly while the idea of the work formed in his mind. He began to make sketches in his notebook at the beginning of May 1927, and by the end of the summer term the score was half finished. At the beginning of August, he wrote to Hardy: 'I write to ask you whether I may dedicate my new orchestral composition to you as a little token of respect and gratitude. It is entitled "Egdon Heath" and is the result of reading the first chapter of "The Return of the Native" over and over again and also of walking over the country you describe so wonderfully.'[22] Above the music Holst inscribed a quotation from the novel, describing the heath as: 'A place perfectly accordant with man's nature—neither ghastly, hateful, nor ugly; neither commonplace, unmeaning, nor tame; but, like man, slighted and enduring; and withal singularly colossal and mysterious in its swarthy monotony!'[23] Holst captured this mood with a mysteriously evocative opening (recalling the atmosphere of the Prelude to the *First Choral Symphony*) in which the inexorable imitative counterpoint of slowly-moving motifs reflects the timelessness of the landscape. Into this scene flurries of activity are thrust in fragmentary musical gestures, followed by a ghostly pastoral folk-tune echoing an atavistic past, and the work ends as it began, in an atmosphere of awesome mystery.

During this work in progress, Holst carried on with his usual routine of teaching and conducting. On 24 May he attended the first public performance of *Assemble All Ye Maidens*, one of the *Seven Part-Songs* to words by Robert Bridges, which was performed in the Queen's Hall by the Bach Choir conducted by Vaughan Williams. The *Monthly Musical Record* described the part-song (which was sung twice during the concert) as 'a very beautiful and distinguished example of Holst's latter style',[24] and commended Dora Labette for her singing of the solo part, while the *Musical Times* described it as a 'most beautifully planned and executed piece', going on to say that 'the whole conjures up a vision of a group of Burne-Jones maidens . . . a picture without any softness, but imaginative and consistent in quite a rare way.'[25]

At the beginning of July, it was arranged that Holst should take some of his singers and players from St Paul's to visit Robert Bridges at his home near Oxford to perform for him the whole set of *Seven Part-Songs* for female voices and strings. This visit was a great success, both for the performers (with Imogen among the second sopranos) and for Bridges and his wife, together with several musical and literary friends whom they had invited to hear the songs. On 4 July Bridges wrote to Holst, thanking him for the performance and adding: 'You asked me once or twice about the music, whether I liked it: if I did not say much it was because I felt it impertinent of me to pretend to judge of your work, and I thought that the pleasure, which I could tell the professionals were feeling, was a better compliment than mine would be, because they are accustomed to modern writing, whereas I am old fashioned. I was relieved to find that they were somewhat in my predicament: which was that I did not understand any piece well on the first hearing, but liked it at second hearing and came in the end to full pleasure. I liked all the "songs" especially *When first we met* and *Sorrow and joy*. The only piece that I did not take to was "Assemble all ye maidens" and that could be accounted for by the great dislike that I have for the *poem*. Its history is queer. I will tell you of it some day. Our gratitude is enormous. We had a most delightful time: all our guests were enthusiastic. We hope you will do it again some day. Your way of treating the words is so novel, and so unlike anything I could have imagined, that I think I got on astonishingly well in appreciating your writing as far as I did. For I really liked them very much: and want to hear them again.'[26]

In his reply, Holst thanked Bridges for these comments, and added: 'We would love to come again another year. The chief obstacle to doing so is the fact that I am now setting some of your poems for *male* voices. This may be a mistake—it certainly is to some of last Saturday's singers' [St Paul's schoolgirls].[27] Holst was probably referring to two settings which he made of words by Bridges at this time, which are in fact for mixed voices, rather than male voices alone. *Eternal Father* is a short anthem for soprano solo, chorus and organ, with bells ad lib, to words from Bridges' *The Growth of Love* (with an Alleluia added by Holst), and *Man Born to Toil* is for similar forces (without a solo part) and was composed for the Bath and Wells Diocesan Choral Festival to be held the following year. When an extract from *Man Born to Toil* was published as a hymn, Holst named his tune 'Chilswell' after Bridges' home at Boar's Hill, where the poet had lived since 1907.

On 9 July Holst attended a concert organized by his ex-pupil Irene Bonnett at Spring Grove Polytechnic, Isleworth, and at the end of term there was a performance of *The Golden Goose* at St Paul's Girls' School Speech Day, in which 'every girl in the school took part, if only as one of the populace, singing in the big choruses', as one of them later recalled.[28] The Human Organ on this occasion was made up of pupils and masters from the Boys' School, wearing paper organ-pipes as head-dresses, 'who sang a marvellous Handelian fugue to "Oohs" and "Ahs" '.[29]

On 4 August, Holst travelled by train to Bristol and then set out to walk to Dorchester with the intention of paying a further visit to Thomas Hardy. He had written to Hardy to say that he was coming, that he was working on *Egdon Heath*, and that he intended to dedicate the work to him. He walked through the Mendips to Wells, and then on to Castle Cary and Sherborne, arriving in Dorchester on 8 August. The following day he had an 'unforgettable lunch' with the Hardys at Max Gate,[30] and they then went on a motor trip through the heathland, with the object of visiting Puddletown Parish Church, to see the wooden musicians' gallery in which Hardy's grandfather had often performed. During the trip Hardy pointed out features such as Melstock and Rainbarrow (which he recommended Holst to see by night) and remarked that the summer was the wrong time to see the heath—in November it would be at its best. Hardy accepted the dedication of *Egdon Heath* 'with pleasure' and said that he was sure that the work when completed would be 'very striking'.[31] In view of Hardy's professed ignorance of music, Holst was surprised to find that he was familiar with *The Planets*, and even more so when he learnt that Hardy had heard the work on gramophone records belonging to T. E. Lawrence (of Arabia) who had been stationed at a Royal Tank Corps depot nearby.

Holst took Hardy's advice and walked over Rainbarrow on the night of 11 August, arriving in Puddletown early the next day. From there he walked on to Wareham, but rain dampened the pleasure of his journey, and he decided to return to London by train. The whole visit had made an indelible impression on Holst ('It's been an unbelievable day,' he wrote to Imogen[32]), and some years later when lecturing on Haydn he compared the character of Thomas Hardy with what he considered to be Joseph Haydn at his best: 'There was a wealth of experience of town and country, deep and controlled emotion, wisdom and humour, all clothed in perfect courtesy and kindliness,' he declared.[33]

15

Commissions and Competition
(1927–1928)

At this time Vaughan Williams let it be known that he intended to give up the conductorship of the Bach Choir, and Stanford Robinson, then conductor of the BBC Wireless Chorus, wrote to Holst to ask him to recommend him for the post. This request must have been rather embarrassing for Holst, as he himself had already been offered the job and was undecided whether to take it. He did in fact eventually accept, and his appointment was duly announced in the press in January 1928, but when the time came to begin work with the choir his doctor advised him against it because the strain might prove too much for his heart, and he reluctantly had to resign from the post without ever having taken a rehearsal.

The Hymn of Jesus was performed again at the 1927 Three Choirs Festival in Hereford, and on 14 September Holst conducted *A Somerset Rhapsody, A Fugal Concerto,* and *Beni Mora* at a concert of British music at the Winter Gardens, Margate. He had meanwhile been working hard on *Egdon Heath,* and by mid-September it was finished. After playing it over to Vaughan Williams, Holst remarked: 'I don't think he likes it much but he gave me a good lesson on it. I've adopted three of his suggestions which means putting [in] patches . . .'[1] He sent a copy to Harold Brooke at Novello with a covering note: 'Although *Egdon Heath* looks unsatisfactory as a piano solo it might do for some sort of arrangement—piano and strings or string orchestra. I'll think it over.'[2] He also showed the score to the Oxford University Press, but Brooke accepted it for Novello who published it the following year.

At the beginning of October Holst received an invitation from George Bell, then Dean of Canterbury, to write some incidental music for a dramatic production to be performed in the cathedral. Bell was interested in the possibility of using drama to convey a religious message, and had asked John Masefield to write a suitable play, for which Holst would write the music, and which Charles Ricketts would produce. This was a radical proposal at that time, for although church dramas had been widely performed in the Middle Ages, the practice had fallen out of favour over the centuries, and although some parishes occasionally put on a play, such a thing had not been done in a British cathedral in modern times. Plans for the production, to be called *The Coming of Christ*, were submitted for the approval of Archbishop Davidson, who gave his consent on condition that the figure of Christ should not actually be portrayed before the audience.

Holst began to sketch the music, but immediately the project ran into some opposition from the cathedral organist and choirmaster, C. Charlton Palmer. Although Bell had previously discussed the plans with him, Palmer was not at all convinced that the performance was a good idea, and Bell therefore called a meeting between himself, Holst, and Palmer in Canterbury on 14 October to discuss the situation. He received a terse reply from Palmer: 'I will call at the Deanery about 10 on Friday morning and we can go into the matter of the music for the Masefield play . . . which I still think quite unpracticable.'[3] Palmer considered himself snubbed, and was annoyed that Bell had gone 'over his head' to invite Holst to compose the music. But the meeting appears to have mollified him, and Holst returned to London to continue sketching the music, meeting Masefield on 11 November for a discussion of practical details. On completion of the main choruses, Holst sent them to Bell, who in turn showed them to Palmer, which was sufficient to rekindle his animosity, and he declared that some of them were impossible to perform. Bell decided that another meeting was called for, and on 25 November wrote to Holst, asking him to come to Canterbury the following week. Bell also wrote to Palmer, with thinly-concealed irritation: 'I wrote last night to Holst and asked him to come down as soon as possible next week to talk over the situation. When talking last night you said there was one Chorus, I think the Chorus of the Host of Kings, which was "impossible". It would be a great help if you could tell me which Chorus or Choruses are so supremely difficult as to be at this stage "impossible". The first Chorus, you said, is not so bad, and others as you looked through them seemed difficult but not supremely so. You know that I am very loth to give up, and if you could tell me what is really the greatest obstacle in the music I should know better where things stood.'[4] Once again, the friction was smoothed over by a further meeting between the three men, and it was agreed that the performance would take place in the cathedral the following Whitsun, and that Holst would bring his performers from Morley College and St Paul's, so that the event would in effect be their Whitsun Festival for 1928.

Holst tried to get away from London to Essex as often as he could, as a substantial gift from Balfour Gardiner had enabled Isobel to have the barn at Brook End converted into a music room where he could work in peace, and it was there that he had completed *Egdon Heath*. Occasionally he would attend London concerts simply as a listener, and on 21 September after dining with Jane Joseph and some friends at a Soho restaurant, he went to a Queen's Hall Promenade concert devoted entirely to the works of J. S. Bach. The violin soloists were Adila Fachiri and her sister Jelly d'Aranyi, and their performance of Bach's *Double Concerto* made such an impression on Holst that he resolved to write a *Double Concerto* of his own, although it was to be two years before he could find the time to do so.

On 12 November 1927 Holst revisited Morley College to give a lecture on 'England and Her Music', and a week later gave the first of three weekly lectures on the music of Robert Lucas Pearsall and Samuel Wesley ('Old Sam' as he called him[5]) at the Royal Institute in Albemarle Street. The lectures were to be illustrated with examples sung by the Morley College choir, and Holst spent some time carefully selecting the music. Although he considered Pearsall to be a 'second-rate' composer,[6] he particularly admired the six-part *Take Heed ye Shepherd Swains*, and to this he added five other part-songs to illustrate the lecture. He was uncertain about the *Song of the Franc-Companies*, a part-song which exists in several versions, but when he was shown a copy of the original autograph manuscript, which differs considerably from the

. versions he had been looking at, he immediately exclaimed 'That's the thing!' and decided to include it.' This original version was published by the Year Book Press in time to be used for his lectures.

A more dramatic turn of events took place regarding one of the Wesley pieces. At the second lecture the choir was to have sung the six-part Christmas motet *O Magnum Mysterium* which Holst and Nora Day had transcribed from a volume of motets in Wesley's own hand in the British Museum library. The motet was duly published by Stainer & Bell and had been learnt by the choir, when two days before the lecture Holst received a letter from his ex-pupil Walter Gandy, pointing out that the music was not by Wesley at all but was note-for-note the same as William Byrd's setting in the *Gradualia* of 1605. Although this motet had long been regarded as being by Wesley and was included in catalogues of his works, it appeared that Wesley had merely copied out Byrd's setting for his own use. Holst was naturally very surprised, but sportingly told the whole story to his audience. Stainer & Bell were obliged to recall all their published copies, and the motet was later reissued with Byrd's name at the head of the music.

At the beginning of December Holst received a letter from the BBC asking whether he would be interested in writing a work for military band. The BBC at that time had its own band, and although a high level of technical proficiency had been attained, its musical scope was limited by the availability of suitable material. Accordingly, it was decided to commission 'one or two of the foremost British composers of today' to write especially for the band,[8] specifying that the work should be in one movement, last from twelve to fifteen minutes and be in the form of a concert overture, fantasy, or symphonic poem.

Holst accepted the offer, but suggested that he should not start work on the new composition until he had arranged one of Bach's organ fugues for band in order to reaccustom himself to the medium. He explained: 'I have had this at the back of my mind for many years,' and hoped that it would be possible for the BBC band to give the first performance of this arrangement. He also suggested that discussion of the details of the new work should be postponed until he had completed the arrangement, 'As I might wish to write something in more than one movement. Of course, if you have any particular reason for asking for a one-movement piece, I should be delighted to fall in with your wishes.'[9] The BBC however preferred a single movement, as the band repertoire already contained a considerable number of suites, in contrast to the dearth of single-movement works. Holst's fee was to be £50 for the complete broadcasting rights in the new work and £25 for similar rights in his Bach arrangement.

Holst was hoping to be able to spend a month in Vienna and Prague during the Christmas holidays, and decided to set off on the last day of term. On 19 December he directed the end-of-term singing at St Paul's Girls' School in the afternoon, and by 8.30 was on the boat train to Harwich, arriving in Karlsruhe the following afternoon. Two days later he went on to Munich, where he visited the picture gallery and saw a performance of *Salome*, and then set off for Vienna, arriving on Christmas Eve. On Christmas Day he heard a performance of a Bruckner Mass in the Burgkappelle and attended a performance of *Fidelio*, and then spent the next ten days exploring the city, visiting the Schuberthaus, the Haydn Museum and the art gallery, meeting various musicians including Egon Wellesz and Alfred Kalmus of Universal Edition, going to concerts, the opera, the cinema, and a dress rehearsal of Křenek's *Jonny Spielt auf*. Preferring to avoid large hotels where possible, Holst stayed in private accommodation and later reported that 'The hot bath there is a myth but the kindliness and comfort and sense of freedom were facts.'[10]

On 6 January he took a train to Prague, where he explored the city on foot, seeing the sights (including Mozart's house) and meeting eminent musicians such as Janáček and Hába, who introduced him to the mysteries of his quarter-tone piano. Holst's name was already known to musicians in the Czech capital, as his *Fugal Overture* had been performed there a few weeks before by the Czech Philharmonic Orchestra conducted by Václav Talich during a Festival of Contemporary English Music. He also attended choral and orchestral concerts and saw *The Tales of Hoffmann* and Smetana's *Two Widows*. As he was enjoying his holiday so much, Holst decided to extend it to include a visit to Leipzig, and therefore left Prague on Saturday

14 January, arriving in Leipzig early the next day. After attending a church service, he heard a concert of madrigals at the Conservatorium, and in the evening saw a performance of *Die Fledermaus*, afterwards strolling round the town to look at the Thomaskirche and Bach's statue. The next few days followed the same pattern; visits to museums and churches, attending concerts and recitals, and meeting musicians, and he also took the opportunity to call on the publisher's Breitkopf & Härtel and Peters Edition. On 19 January he left Leipzig by train for England, making his way to his country home at Brook End to rejoin his family.

A few days later a letter arrived from the BBC specifying the instrumentation of the Wireless Military Band, but Holst was prevented from starting work on his proposed Bach arrangement by the arrival of a more urgent commission. He was asked by the organisers of the National Brass Band Festival to compose a test-piece for their next annual championship, and as this had to be completed in time for publication so that the bands could practise it for the contest in September, he got to work straight away. As an ex-trombonist, Holst was on home ground with the brass band (which he preferred to the military band because of its more homogenous tonal blend), particularly enjoying the solution of technical problems and the challenge of making the music interesting for the players as well as effective for listeners. He called the resulting three-movement work *A Moorside Suite*, and after its performance at the 1928 championships it rapidly became known throughout the brass band world. The music has the imprint of Holst throughout, from the skipping 6/8 of the opening Scherzo to the vigorous melodic fourths of the concluding March; the intervening Nocturne bearing a family resemblance to the slow-moving procession of *Saturn*, but remaining within the feeling of traditional north-country brass band music.

On 12 February Walter Damrosch conducted the New York Symphony Orchestra in the first performance of *Egdon Heath* at the Mecca Auditorium, New York, and the following day the first European performance was given in Cheltenham Town Hall by the City of Birmingham Symphony Orchestra conducted by Holst himself. Thomas Hardy had died a few weeks previously, and Holst altered the dedication on his score, which now bore the inscription: 'Homage to Thomas Hardy'. Later in the same month the work was given its first London performance in a Royal Philharmonic Society concert conducted by Václav Talich. The reaction of the listeners to all three performances was much the same; according to the *Monthly Musical Record* the London audience 'only half took to it', partly because the conductor 'showed no sense of its form, but allowed it merely to drift in a sluggish way',[11] and partly because of the unfamiliarity of the idiom. The violist Bernard Shore later recalled that the players were disconcerted by the work: 'We felt that Holst had dropped us from his thoughts; the music seemed a bare skeleton which we, in our ignorance, knew not how to clothe with flesh and blood.'[12] Even Adrian Boult, a sympathetic interpreter of Holst's works, found difficulty in comprehending the score at first sight, but found that repeated hearings enabled him to come to terms with it: 'I remember particularly how enormously *Egdon Heath* grew on me when I heard him rehearsing it and playing it through three or four times in succession,' he later wrote.[13]

The audience were less favourably inclined: the quiet opening failed to rise above the level of conversation of the more inattentive listeners, and many simply did not comprehend the composer's intentions. Holst was particularly annoyed that the quotation from *The Return of the Native* had been omitted from the programme notes; this would have been a great help in understanding the music. (However, in a short story called 'The Third Partner' published a few years later, a character switches on the radio and hears a broadcast of Holst conducting *Egdon Heath* at the Queen's Hall. Without knowing anything of the quotation from the novel he finds that the mood of the music affects him deeply.[14]) Even Holst's wife was not won over; according to Thomas Armstrong, Isobel remarked to Hugh Allen: 'Oh dear, Sir Hugh, how I wish you could stop Gustav writing music like this, and get him back to his old style.'[15] In a review of Holst's work written a few years later, Francis Toye denounced the *First Choral Symphony* as still-born, going on to declare that '*Egdon Heath* can scarcely be said to have been born at all, so deficient was it in vitality. This aridity is very curious in a composer who started his career with such exuberance, who wrote not only uncommonly effective music for miltary bands, but a suite so eminently picturesque as *Beni Mora*.'[16]

As usual, Holst himself was unperturbed by the critical response, but felt that neither his own nor Talich's performance had done justice to the work. When Harold Brooke sent him the programme and press notices of the New York performance, he replied: 'I am, of course, disappointed at the reception of *Egdon Heath*. On the other hand I have my own very decided opinion of the work which prevents me from being as disappointed as I ought to be from the business point of view. I have written fully (and privately) to Henry Wood and trust that *Egdon Heath* will be heard in London this autumn exactly as I meant it to be heard.'[17] As was often the case when his latest works were performed, Holst considered it to be the best thing he had written, but instead of subsequently transferring his allegiance to other works, he continued to hold this view of *Egdon Heath* until his death. After a performance of the work in 1932, Holst remarked: 'It was not the result of that lunch with Hardy as the program stated but the result of years of knowing him, his books, and, above all, the heath. It was the first serious work I wrote after my accident ten years ago and it means much to me.'[18] Time has cast a different perspective on *Egdon Heath*, which can now be seen to embody all the characteristic features of Holst's mature style, from atmospheric orchestral effects to a 'sad procession' with ostinato bass, and the mysterious veiled folk-dance in 6/8 time, once regarded as out of keeping with the rest of the work, is now accepted as an essential element in the structure.

At Easter 1928 Holst was invited to lecture at an Easter School held by the English Folk Dance Society at Chester, and wrote to his ex-pupil Dorothy Callard: 'It is settled that I go to Chester for the week beginning April 9th. I should like to talk about R.V.W. and to try to get some singers to sing some of his choral folk-songs and his Christmas Fantasia. You might pass this on and let me know how many singing Morleyites will be there.'[19] He decided that this visit would be an ideal opportunity for some country walking, and after seeking advice on a suitable route from E. H. Fellowes, took a train to Kidderminster, intending to walk as far as he could. From Bucknell, he sent a set of photographic views of the district to Adeline Vaughan Williams, on the back of which he had written:

Dear Adeline,

I have not managed to get to Clun today partly because I spent so long in looking round Ludlow that I did not leave it until one and partly because when I did leave it I took a wrong turning and went some miles out of my way, and partly because I felt lazy and took life easily. Shropshire remains an ideal walking country and the weather has been better today for I have actually had two hours sun! Looking at the map of Shropshire has made me wonder where one could go if one chose to go to places because one was attracted by their names. For instance, one would avoid Llanfrihangelrlynthon especially if one had to ask the way. It would be far better to go to Everyjobb in spite of its extra 'b'. And although I had an excellent tea at Leintvardine today yet if one had the choice one would possibly be more attracted by Albright Hussey especially as Fidler's Arm, which I passed today, is not a pub but a gorge. And by that I mean a narrow valley between two hills & not the meal that I've just finished. Although it is strictly speaking off the point I think it worth mentioning that the rate collector at Ludlow is Mr Tantrums. Which—like most other details of life—is improbable. Last night's inn was a real hotel with a hot bath containing water that was hot as well as writing paper and electric bells & other luxuries. This place is a real country inn and as they don't seem to have any writing paper I am using the backs of these photographs. I shall post it in Clun if I ever get there, which, like everything else on a walk is uncertain. The great rule in walking tours is to plan to go somewhere and then drift somewhere else by mistake. Which I am doing.

Y. Gustav.[20]

He arrived in Shrewsbury on 6 April, and completed the rest of his journey by train. Although he had survived the walk very well, during the Easter School itself he caught a chill, and a week later wrote to Whittaker: 'I am only just getting over some sort of internal chill that spoilt my temper and other things last week in Chester. Previously I had had a glorious walk in Shropshire. I am now playing the professional invalid with great success and enjoying it thoroughly.'[21]

While convalescing, Holst started to make sketches for two

new works: an 'organ concerto' (later to become *A Choral Fantasia*), and a one-act opera, *The Tale of the Wandering Scholar*. Having read Helen Waddell's book *The Wandering Scholars* some time before, he asked Clifford Bax to write a libretto based on one of the incidents in the book, this being the first time that Holst had collaborated with a librettist rather than writing or adapting the words himself. Despite the reception given to his previous operatic ventures, he was clearly still interested in writing for the stage and although he had parodied operatic conventions in *The Perfect Fool*, the medium held such a fascination for him that he seemed unable to leave it alone. It is tempting to speculate whether this aspect of his musical interests might have matured in later life had he lived to a similar age as, say, Verdi. Holst had become 'immeasurably fond' of Helen Waddell's book, as Bax remarked, 'not without cause'. The meetings between the two men to discuss the project were described by Bax:

Every now and again he would summon me to sup with him at the George Hotel in Hammersmith Broadway, and here he had a corner-table which was regarded as his property and even a special waiter who became his portly Ganymede. Perhaps an epicure would not consider that Burgundy was a suitable accompaniment to a plate of fried onions, but these were usually our drink and our main fare ... He never wore a hat; his thin white hair accepted the rain and the wind; he always carried an ancient music-case: and he always peered doubtfully, through his magnifying glasses [spectacles], at the approaching guest. By the grace of fortune I had become acquainted with Miss Waddell and was therefore able to bring her to one of our reunions at the George. She talked so brilliantly that Gustav was in an enchanted state, nor shall I ever forget his complete happiness when she told us the long and romantic story of St Pelagia, who had once been a courtesan.[22]

According to Bax, 'Her easy eloquence amazed and intoxicated Gustav, who both as a talker and as a lecturer was somewhat naif and gauche.'[23] The plot of *The Wandering Scholar* is a short, bawdy incident with a strong medieval atmosphere, which was just what Holst needed for a fast-moving, entertaining one-act opera. It concerns a hungry young scholar who calls at a farmhouse, interrupting an assignation between the housewife and the lascivious parish priest. The woman refuses the scholar's request for food and drink and sends him on his way, but he soon returns in the company of her husband, and by clever subterfuge blackmails her into providing the much-desired victuals. The husband detects his wife's infidelity, and sends the priest packing.

This work is much more concentrated than Holst's previous operas, and shows that he had acquired a sense of timing and stagecraft as a result of his earlier experiences. Words are set to folk-like tunes with an ease that stems from *At the Boar's Head*, but this folksy aspect is not overdone, and the musical material is always appropriate to the dramatic situation. The accompaniment is simple, and the musical material economical but effective, being held together by the recurrence of a 'signature' motif which imparts its character to many of the vocal lines. There is no overture—only a few introductory bars, and the opera ends with an abruptness which took its first audiences by surprise. Edmund Rubbra pointed out that the phrase sung by the priest to the words 'Ascendit in secula seculorum' also appears in the *Hymn of Jesus*, and suggested that perhaps Holst was deliberately quoting from his own earlier work in this opera.[24]

After recovering from his chill, Holst immediately put all his energies into preparing for the performance of *The Coming of Christ*, to be given in Canterbury Cathedral at Whitsun 1928. When visiting Canterbury for the rehearsals, he took the opportunity of walking along the ancient Pilgrim's Way, the principal route through Kent long before the days of Christianity. Besides rehearsing the singers from Morley College and St Paul's Girls' School, he attended to various practical matters such as travel and accommodation, to ensure that everything would go smoothly. With characteristic generosity and attention to detail, he made discreet enquiries as to which pupils were unlikely to be able to afford the train fare, and arranged that their tickets should be already paid for when they arrived at the booking office. When buying the tickets he was asked by the clerk as to the name in which the seats should be reserved. Holst replied that they were called the 'Heavenly Host' (their part in the play), but on arrival at the station they found their compartments labelled 'A Poetical Play Party'.[25] At Canterbury they were met at the station by Bishop Bell and other organizers of the performance, to whom they sang on the platform before dispersing to their lodgings in various parts of the town. The previous friction with the choirmaster seems to have abated by this time, as Holst stayed in his house in the cathedral precincts for the duration of the festival.

There were to be five performances of the play, from 26 to 29 May, and Holst's singers also performed other music in the cathedral for Communion and a special Whitsun festival evening service, including Vaughan Williams's Mass in G minor (Holst wrote to Adeline Vaughan Williams: 'We are singing *His* (we mean *Our*) Mass from time to time and have discovered that He wrote it for this cathedral'[26]). The actors involved in the play included only one professional; the rest were made up of students whom John Masefield had brought from Oxford, clergy of the cathedral, masters from the King's School, and citizens of Canterbury; the part of Christ being taken by a soldier.

This first drama performance in an English cathedral since the Middle Ages drew protests from fundamentalists, several of whom sent stereotyped letters criticizing the church authorities ('If you allow this, God's judgement will speedily follow'[27]) but despite such dire prophesies the performances were very successful, attracting 6,000 people in all. The play was performed on the steps which lead down from the choir-screen to the nave, and Holst took advantage of the setting to position his singers on top of the choir-screen itself. Wearing white robes and standing high above the congregation, they had the appearance of a Heavenly Host, the musicians being located some distance below in the Warriors' chapel. The music was scored for mixed chorus, male voice chorus, piano, organ, and trumpets, and when at the dress rehearsal someone suggested that tubular bells might be added to the final chorus, Holst went back to his room and wrote out a special part which was played by a boy from the King's School.

On paper, Holst's music seemed rather sparse: unison chanting with simple chordal accompaniment, interspersed with unaccompanied choral passages, but in the resonant acoustics of the cathedral it was very effective—any complex counterpoint would have become confused in the reverberation of that vast building. Three of the actors sang solos as archangels, and the chorus of retainers of the Three Kings was accompanied on the piano rather than organ, providing an effective change of tone-colour. The final hymn *By Weary Stages* was sung by cast, chorus, and congregation (Holst gave this tune the name *Hill Crest*).

The production was an overwhelming experience for the performers, being the most elaborate Whitsun festival Holst's singers had ever attempted; and also for the listeners. The *Daily News* reported dramatically: 'Since the murder of Thomas à Beckett, Canterbury Cathedral has not been the scene of a more startling event than the performance of John Masefield's *The Coming of Christ.*'[28] The play had been presented as an act of worship to which admission was free, but the voluntary donations amounted to over £800, a considerable sum in those days, of which a substantial proportion was set aside to commission new plays in future years (the first was to be T. S. Eliot's *Murder in the Cathedral*). In gratitude for the hospitality provided by George Bell and his wife during the Whitsun singers' stay in Canterbury, Holst composed two rounds under the title *Canterbury Bells* to words especially written by Mabel Rodwell Jones, which the choir sang to their hosts in the Deanery garden on 29 May. The rounds were entitled *Within This Place All Beauty Dwells* and *To Bother Missis Bell*; the first being sung by female voices and the second by mixed voices.

When all was over and the last of the performers had been seen safely on to the London train, Holst set off on a two-day walk through Kent to clear his mind, for although he enjoyed the company of groups of friends, he also found it something of a strain. Leaving Canterbury on the morning of 30 May, he walked to Ashford via Chilham and Wye, and the next day went on to Rye via Ham Street and Appledore, finishing at Winchelsea the following day.

On 14 June the anthem *Man Born to Toil* was given its first performance in Wells Cathedral at the annual Festival Service of the Bath and Wells Diocesan Choral Association, and on the same day Stanford Robinson conducted the BBC Wireless Chorus in the first broadcast performance of the Third Group of *Choral Hymns from the Rig Veda*. Robinson was also planning an entire programme of Holst's choral music for a

Sunday broadcast, but was concerned about the innocuous part-song *Bring Us In Good Ale*, which the paternalistic BBC of those days considered too boisterous for Sunday-evening listening. He therefore wrote to Holst, outlining the proposed programme and asking whether he could suggest any of his other choral works. Holst replied: 'Could you *not* do "Autumn" which is 29 years old and "The Swallow leaves" which I don't like? . . . I am longing for a good London performance of my two motets "The Evening Watch" and "Sing me the men" . . .'[29] Consideration was given to these two works, but they were rejected for the proposed programme, and it was to be some years before the motets were eventually broadcast.

The BBC was nevertheless still keen for Holst to be associated with the Wireless Military Band, and invited him to conduct a performance of his two band Suites, broadcast from the London and Daventry stations on 22 July 1928. Holst's projected arrangement of a Bach fugue was well in hand; he had signed a contract with the BBC on 8 May, and had given the arrangement the title *Fugue à la Gigue*. He had chosen the fugue in G major, BWV 577, from Book 3 of Bach's organ works, explaining: 'When I was studying the organ some forty years or more ago it struck me that of all Bach's organ works, just one, this fugue, seemed ineffective on the instrument for which it was composed.'[30] When the arrangement was complete, Holst added the following note to the score: 'The title "Fugue à la Gigue" describes the work perfectly, but there is no reason to think that it was so named by Bach.'[31] Having completed the wind band version, Holst went on to make an orchestral transcription of his arrangement, so that it could be performed by a full symphony orchestra.

At the beginning of September Holst took a brief holiday in Paris, during which he visited the usual tourists spots, went on a motor trip to Fontainebleau, Sens, and Troyes, and met the music critic Henri Prunières. On his return he decided to set out on a one-day walking tour through London, having realized that in all his tramping through the English countryside he had neglected the city in which he spent most of his working life. His timetable was meticulously planned: 'Ealing 9.25, SPGS 10.35–10.50, Barkers (bus) 11.5, Marble Arch 11.30, Selfridges 11.35, leave Marble Arch 1, St Barts 2–2.15, Guildhall 2.40–3.0,

Whitechapel, Limehouse, Poplar, Canning Town 4.15.'[32] As this was a Tuesday, his progress must have been considerably impeded by the bustle of daily life in the city. On 20 September he conducted a performance of *Egdon Heath* at a Queen's Hall Promenade concert, and on 24 September his term of teaching began. But the mood of the holidays was hard to shake off, and after his first session he took a train to Haslemere for a two-day walk in Surrey and Sussex, arriving in Pulborough on 26 September.

He was back in London in time for the National Brass Band Festival on 29 September, for which the *Moorside Suite* was to be the test piece. Bands converged on the Crystal Palace at Sydenham from all parts of the country, and the performances took place in an atmosphere of tense excitement which was generated as much by anxiety as to the fate of wagers which had been placed on the outcome as from strictly artistic considerations. Holst listened to fifteen performances of the *Moorside Suite*, and was impressed by the technical skill and muscianship of the amateur performers. The judges awarded the prize to the Black Dyke Mills Band, which included the young Harry Mortimer in the cornet section, and the band was immediately engaged by the Edison Bell Company to record the work. A few days later Holst wrote to the Editor of *The British Bandsman*, which had organized the competition, complimenting the players on their performances. He remarked that it was some time since he had had contact with the brass band world, and although the players displayed the same technical prowess as had been achieved by their predecessors, he noticed that they were now much more musical in their approach: 'Last Saturday I listened to musicians conducted by musicians.' He was impressed by the flexibility of rhythm in the performances of the best bands, but was 'a little disappointed that certain cornet and euphonium soloists still indulge in *vibrato* when the music calls for a calm, smooth *cantabile*'. He also noticed a tendency for soloists to turn equal quavers into dotted notes in slow passages, but these were minor blemishes in performances which pleased him greatly. He ended his letter: 'And while congratulating the many players I heard that afternoon I also congratulate myself on having a new work produced with such enthusiasm, understanding and musicianship.'[33]

During the autumn term Holst fulfilled various engagements as a conductor and lecturer in addition to his teaching at St Paul's. On 14 October he conducted the Birmingham City Police Band at the West End Cinema, Birmingham, in a concert which included the two military band Suites, an arrangement of the *Nocturne* from the *Moorside Suite* and the *Fugue à la Gigue*. He also visited Oxford, Cambridge, and Bristol during the following weeks, and lectured on Pearsall in Newcastle on 1 December. On 4 December he returned to Canterbury, this time for the enthronement of Cosmo Gordon Lang as Archbishop: Holst was included in the specially invited group of guests representing artists and musicians; and on 8 December he again lectured on Pearsall at the Wigmore Hall in London to a meeting of the Incorporated Society of Musicians.

But he was not getting much composition done; partly because of his teaching, conducting, and lecturing commitments, but also because he had not been feeling very inspired in recent months. In particular, he had not been able to make a start on the one-movement work for military band which the BBC had commissioned the previous year, and was beginning to feel guilty about his failure to comply with the contract. He decided that he needed a holiday to refresh his mind, and wrote to Percy Pitt explaining that 'For some queer reason I've not been able to write a note since Easter . . . I'm not going to begin trying until next Easter and between now and then I'm going to have a long holiday abroad.' He added: 'I have no right to expect the BBC to wait indefinitely but if during 1929 I manage to write a piece of military band music I will send it to the BBC before anyone else on the understanding that they will be entitled to refuse it if they wish.'[34]

Another project which required Holst's attention was a repeat performance of *The Coming of Christ* to be given in Canterbury Cathedral the following Whitsun, for which extra music was needed to match some changes in the play, and he had also been asked to write the incidental music for a proposed Easter play. He felt unable to cope with either of these projects, and in mid-December George Bell wrote to John Masefield: 'I have just had a card from Holst asking whether anything is settled about next Whitsuntide, as he is having a term off from Thursday till Easter . . . You said that you were intending to make certain changes in the Play, especially shortening some of the dialogue and, still more, adding an opening chorus, which Holst was to set to music.'[35] In default of additional music from Holst, Masefield decided to use some of the existing music for the new chorus, and replied: 'I had better make the opening chorus go to the Hill Crest tune, for a host of little angels going *up* the steps of the transepts . . .'[36]

Having thus made his apologies to the BBC and settled the matter of the Canterbury play, the way was now clear for Holst to take leave of absence from his teaching commitments and get away from his worries and responsibilities for an extended holiday abroad. He decided that the sun and sights of Italy would be ideal for refreshing his imagination, and so on 20 December he said farewell to Isobel and embarked at Tilbury, *en route* for France and the distant Mediterranean.

16

'Life is Moderately Pleasing'
(1929–1930)

After travelling south by train via Chambéry and Genoa, Holst arrived in Rome on Christmas Eve in time to register at his hotel before attending midnight Mass. He met several friends there, including Louise Dyer, who had visited him in London a few months previously, and who enthusiastically outlined her plans for the establishment of an Australian library of Holst's published works under the auspices of the Victorian Branch of the British Music Society. Mrs Dyer and her husband James invited him to a Christmas Day dinner party at their hotel, and the following day Holst returned for further discussion of the proposed scheme. It was agreed to proceed with the plan, on condition that appropriate hire fees were paid to the publishers of music borrowed from the library for performance purposes.

During the next few days, Holst wandered round the city, walking in the Borghese Gardens and along the banks of the Tiber, and when it came on to rain he sheltered in the Pantheon, only to discover that the rain came in through the circular hole in the roof. Although he had glimpsed the city in 1918, Rome came as something of a disappointment to Holst, having seen the splendours of Athens during his YMCA service, and he later remarked: 'Rome's no good after Greece.'[1] On 29 December, after a walk on the Janiculum hill, he left by train for Naples, where he was again met by friends, and after registering at his hotel immediately set off to walk through the slum district of the city. He stayed in Naples for five days and had ample opportunity to visit all the sights, in weather ranging from clear sunshine to pouring rain. He visited the ruins of Pompeii ('not more than "interesting" ', he reported to Imogen[2]) and saw Vesuvius covered in snow, shimmering in the winter sunshine. On 5 January 1929 he left by ship for Sicily across a calm sea, arriving in Palermo early the next day. Once again, his first act was to set off to walk through the city, later making the customary excursion to Monreale to see the mosaics in the Norman cathedral. On 11 January he took a train to Agrigento (Girgenti) and was so impressed by the Greek temples that he stayed for over a week, viewing the ruins in all kinds of light and weather, in rain, sunshine, and most effectively of all, by moonlight. He walked so much that his ankle became weak, but the fascination of the place was such that any pain was pushed to the back of his mind. He considered the Valley of the Temples to be 'as good as Athens',[3] especially as the crowds of tourists to be found in the Greek capital were completely absent here, and he could wander alone among the temples and fallen columns which lay amid groves of fruit-laden orange and lemon trees. His favourite building was the Temple of Concord, which had survived the centuries substantially intact. He wrote home: 'I'm having a glorious sunny holiday. So far I like Girgenti the most and Naples the least!'[4] At last he managed to tear himself away, and took a train to Syracuse on 20 January. Once again he was astonished by the surviving Greek remains, especially the temple of Athena, amid whose columns stands the cathedral of Syracuse, and was fascinated by the ancient Greek theatre, to which he returned several times during his stay. He also visited the Roman amphitheatre and the ancient stone quarries, including the so-called Ear of Dionysus. On 25 January he started to walk the seven kilometres to the beauty spot of Fonte Ciane, but found the road to be 'too ugly'[5] and so turned back to spend some more time at the ancient sites before going on to Taormina by train. Here he found another open-air theatre, in a much more spectacular setting, and although he tried to explore as much of the town as possible on his first day, bad weather soon forced him to retreat into the tea-room and library. However, he was not to be daunted, and made a special point of watching the progress of the storm from the ruins of the theatre; a spectacular and dramatic setting, with the snow-clad mass of Mount Etna as a backdrop. He also set out in the midst of a gale to climb up the heights at the back of the town to the rock-cut church of the Madonna della Rocca, the Castello, and as far as the village of Mola, from which vantage-point he had a magnificent view of the town before his glasses were blown off by the wind.

One of his favourite pastimes in Taormina was to visit the marionette shows which took place in tiny theatres in side alleys off the main thoroughfare, and when Frances Ralph Gray and her sister arrived from England, he immediately took them to a show, where they saw dramatic re-enactments of scenes from Sicilian history in a dialect understandable only to the locals, who encouraged the puppets in their exploits, to the accompaniment of raucous music. Holst noted down one of the tunes and later made use of it in his *Brook Green Suite*. Miss Gray brought with her the worrying news that Jane Joseph had been taken seriously ill, but Holst was able to put his concern to the back of his mind, and wrote home: 'Sicily has been a brilliant success. Girgenti was my happiest place.'[6]

On 30 January he left Taormina on a leisurely journey back to England via various places in Italy, which was to take him the best part of two months. He had originally intended to go on to Hungary, but had to abandon this idea for financial reasons. The return journey took him via the Straits of Messina to Rome, where he once again met Louise Dyer. He explored parts of the city which he had missed on his previous visit, and the Dyers took him on motor-trips along the Appian Way and to Viterbo, where they narrowly avoided injury when their car skidded off the road into a snowbank. After attending a concert at the Mausoleum of Augustus and dining with the Dyers at the Excelsior, he left Rome for Orvieto, going on to Siena on 6 February. From there he wrote: 'I continue to have a very good time although I miss the warm sun of south Sicily.'[7] He visited all the major buildings, 'with walks between to keep warm',[8] and climbed to the top of the tall Torre di Mangia, from where he could view the contrapuntal arrangement of the city's rooftops. Then on to Florence, where the weather deteriorated, with frost and heavy snowfalls. To make matters worse, the central heating in his pensione expired, but he accepted several invitations from friends and also spent much time in visiting churches and museums, so that he did not have to linger long in his room. A thaw set in a few days later, enabling him to extend his explorations, and he found enough of interest to detain him for two weeks, during which he noticed that the city seemed to be full of White Russian refugees, and one evening he attended a concert given by what he described as 'The World's Worst Russian Choir'.[9]

He then went on a three-day excursion to Lucca and Pisa, returning to Florence on 24 February, and then set out southwards to Arezzo and Perugia, where he had to walk from the station to his hotel through snow and mud. After visiting Assissi he returned via Perugia to Florence, and then turned northwards to Bologna, arriving on 2 March. Here the weather was better; the sunshine made the exteriors of the buildings look 'splendid', but he found that the interiors were 'Baroque or dull or both'. The paintings in the museum he rated as 'NG'.[10]

His next main stop was at Ferrara, from where he diverted to Ravenna ('one of the very best places I've seen so far'[11]) for two days. Besides inspecting the famous mosaics, he also walked three miles out of town to the abandoned port of Classe to see the equally fine mosaics in the Church of St Apollinare, noting in his diary: 'Road clear of snow'. Returning to Ferrara, he then proceeded to Padua and thence to Venice, arriving on 9 March. Here he found several letters awaiting him, but one which was to cause him much anguish arrived a few days later, informing him of the death of Jane Joseph at the age of thirty-five. This brought him much grief, for he had considered her to be 'the best girl pupil I ever had',[12] and she had helped him enormously with the preparation of his scores and also with practical arrangements for concerts and the Whitsun festivals. This news cast a pall of gloom over his holiday, but he explored Venice none the less, finding it quite easy to follow his usual method of getting lost as the best way to explore an unfamiliar city. There was mist over the sea, combined with sunshine, but these Turneresque effects were spoilt by incidents such as hearing a 'loud loudspeaker' on a canal and a row in a café a night.[13]

While in Perugia he had received a cable from the USA inviting him to attend the twenty-first anniversary celebrations of the American Academy of Arts and Sciences as a representative of the arts in Britain. He now cabled his acceptance, and received a response from Yale University asking him to give the lecture which he had been too ill to deliver when awarded the Howland prize five years previously. He decided to accept this invitation, and applied to the American consul in Venice for the necessary visa.

On 16 March he left for Verona and found so much to see there that two days later he nearly missed his afternoon train through trying to cram in too much sightseeing. The next day in Milan he found most places closed as it was a public holiday, but he went to a performance of Rossini's *Barbiere di Siviglia*, saw a ballet at the Teatro Lirico, and walked around the city. In the evening he wrote home about his plans for the following day: 'I go first to have my hair cut, then to Ricordi the music publisher, then to the British consul then I shall have to find a fresh victim. A relation of Mussolini is lecturing here today and I might try him but I fear I could not get near enough to him as my shirt is not black enough. I stupidly put on a clean collar this morning.'[14] After more exploring, he found himself so tired that he had to go to bed in the afternoon and tried listening to the radio, which he found to be 'NG'.[15] In the evening he managed two acts of *Boris Godunov* at La Scala before being obliged to retire to his hotel. By 21 March he was en route for England, via Basle and Strasburg, sailing from Dunkirk on 22 March.

After spending a week at home with his family, Holst accompanied Imogen on a journey to Keswick where she was to attend an English Folk Dance Easter School. During this school Holst gave a lecture on 'The teaching of Art', judged a competition, and got in some hill walking 'in rain and snow'.[16]

From the Lake District he went direct to Liverpool, where he sailed for America on board the *Scythia* on 6 April. The Atlantic crossing was rough, and Holst soon became sick of the sea and the voyage, and so decided to get off at Halifax to complete the remainder of his journey by train. The ship had to wait outside the port for a whole day before the weather abated sufficiently to allow it to enter harbour, and Holst eventually arrived at New Haven, Connecticut, on 16 April, where he was accommodated in the Graduate's Club. Then followed a busy round of dinners, concerts, lectures, and visits packed into a few days, culminating in his Howland lecture on 'The Teaching of Art' on 19 April. After this, he was relieved to get away to New York to spend some time with his brother Emil, his niece Valerie, and his friend Austin Lidbury. On 23 April he duly attended the ceremony and dinner of the American

Academy, which was the real purpose of his visit, and spent the next few days in the company of Emil and Valerie, during which he heard a performance of Stravinsky's *Les Noces* and some of his own *Choral Hymns from the Rig Veda*. He took an overnight train to Boston on 25 April where he lectured at Harvard University, returning to New York the following night, and a day later, after breakfasting with Emil, Valerie, and Claude Bragdon, was on board the *Samaria, en route* for England. In contrast to his outward journey, the sea on his return trip was fairly calm and the weather 'fine and warm on the whole', although he found that 'Life on board ship is boring and demoralising'.[17] He arrived in Liverpool on 5 May, and after spending the night at Fred Wilkinson's house, took a train to London.

He felt that he had done enough travelling to last him a long while, and was looking forward to getting back to a regular routine of work. As he had written to Isobel: 'The truth is that I've had too much gadding about—four months on end. And when I get home I want to live a humdrum monotonous existence with lots of routine work, lots of new "things" that don't disappoint me too much, and occasional conducting jobs and three day walks—I want this for the next three or four years! It doesn't seem an unreasonable desire!'[18]

While Holst had been abroad in Italy and the USA, George Bell and John Masefield had been trying to cope with the problems of putting on a repeat performance of *The Coming of Christ* at Whitsun 1929. In February, Masefield had written to Bell: 'I have written a new chorus, to go to the final hymn tune... What would an invigorated, refreshed and rumbustious Holst think of setting the Three Kings to music, and letting them sing their parts? I could rewrite the three parts, if Gustav Holst would like this, and you liked it, and had the necessary singers, baritone, tenor and bass.'[19] Bell's reply must have been discouraging, for on 7 March Masefield wrote again: 'I hate the thought of giving up the play ... I do beg you let Holst (if he be willing for it) and myself to do two performances ... It would be quite another thing to do it after the lapse of another year.'[20]

But the problems of arranging the performance were too

great. Besides the difficulty of communication during Holst's travels (unbeknown to each other, Bell had arrived in Venice on holiday shortly after Holst had left), there were practical problems, and as a General Election was also imminent, Bell decided to abandon the play and to organize instead a festival of music and drama to be held in Canterbury Cathedral during August.

So for the first time in many years Holst found himself at a loss over the Whitsun weekend, but discovered that his holiday had refreshed his imagination and he once more felt the urge to compose. He had been reading some poems by Humbert Wolfe and began to set a selection of them for voice and piano, a combination for which he had not written since the early days of his career. He set thirteen of the poems altogether, but later discarded one of them, leaving the order of the remaining twelve to the performers. He did not intend the songs to be sung as a cycle—the performers were at liberty to use as many of them as they wished. The resulting *Twelve Songs* show a simplicity of texture and freedom of vocal line, coupled with unexpected turns of harmony and a lyric warmth which verges on sensuous romanticism. These settings reflect Holst's sympathetic response to Wolfe's poetry, especially the evocation in *The Dream City* of the atmosphere of certain parts of London (which Holst considered to be 'the most adorable city in the world'[21]) and of the strangeness and incomprehensibility of outer space in *Betelgeuse*, a theme which had already been touched on in *Neptune* many years before.

At about this time, Holst, Vaughan Williams and Rutland Boughton had a long meeting to discuss a proposed Welsh Festival which Boughton was hoping to organize. After Boughton had left, Holst and Vaughan Williams drew up a memorandum of suggestions regarding the organization of an opera tour in Wales, which they duly sent off to Boughton, but nothing ever came of this tour or of the projected Festival.

As with the previous year's performance of *The Coming of Christ*, arrangements for the proposed August festival of music and drama in Canterbury Cathedral were not going entirely smoothly. Holst had been asked to conduct the BBC Symphony

Orchestra in a performance of *The Planets* as part of the festival, and as it was to be held in the cathedral he suggested that the boys' voices of the cathedral choir could be used in *Neptune* instead of a female chorus. When the choirmaster C. Charlton Palmer heard about this proposal, he flew into a huff, claiming that arrangements were being made behind his back, and refused permission for his choir to have anything to do with the performance. George Bell (who had recently heard of his forthcoming appointment as Bishop of Chichester) tried to smooth things over and wrote an explanatory letter to Holst, in which he explained that Palmer had in fact been consulted at an early stage in the proceedings, and suggested that the women's voices of the Maidstone Choral Union could be used instead of the cathedral's choristers. On 23 May, Holst replied:

Dear Bell,

Thanks for your long letter of May 14 which has only just reached me ... I am deeply sorry about the matter but please don't worry about my chorus—women will do better than boys probably. I only suggested boys in case it would save trouble. All I knew about the matter was that I was engaged to conduct the 'Planets' in Canterbury on August 21 by the BBC. This will make it easier for me if I see Palmer. But once more, I am deeply sorry that your farewell to Canterbury should be clouded like this. I thought on my return to England on May 6 that you were already in Chichester. My best wishes to you there and cordial greetings to Mrs Bell.

Yours Ever,

Gustav Holst.[22]

At the beginning of July, Holst travelled to Warwick where open-air performances of *The Golden Goose* were to be given in the castle grounds on three successive days. He followed his usual practice of walking part of the way, taking the opportunity to stay overnight with Arthur Forty, a member of the family which had been close to the Holsts for many years. After seeing the final rehearsals and the first day's performance, Holst returned to London for yet another rehearsal of the work, this time by girls of St Paul's, who were to give three performances in one day in the grounds of Bute House on 6 July. Then at the end of the month Holst took his singers to Boar's Hill once again to sing the *Seven Part-Songs* to the poet laureate ('the old chap', as Holst described Bridges[23]) and the occasion seems to have been just as successful as their previous visit two years before.

Holst now began to sketch his long-postponed *Double Concerto* for two violins and orchestra. Since hearing Jelly d'Aranyi and Adila Fachiri perform Bach's Double Concerto two years previously at a promenade concert, he had had the intention of writing a concerto for them, but had been unable to make a start on it. 'And then luck changed,' he wrote,[24] and he began the concerto in August 1929, finishing the first sketch a month later. In this work Holst treated the soloists not as virtuoso exhibitionists, but as individual voices contributing to the overall design by contrasting their timbre with the sonority of the orchestra. For this reason the concerto has perhaps been regarded by soloists as being too reticent, and because of its brevity it is rather difficult to programme satisfactorily. Although Holst suddenly felt an urge to compose this work, his imagination did not provide all the material he needed, and he therefore incorporated some material from the second movement of his 1925 *Terzetto* into the work, including a country dance theme reminiscent of the *Lure* ballet music. The *Double Concerto* is in three short movements which are played without a break, and in it Holst made extensive use of bitonality, while still avoiding the dissonant clashes characteristic of many other composers' use of this technique.

On 16 August he was in London for the first rehearsal of *The Planets* with the BBC Symphony Orchestra for the Canterbury festival later in the month. Adrian Boult was to conduct the remainder of the programme, and to add to the friction already existing between George Bell and his choirmaster, Boult confided to Holst that he had 'had a row' with Elgar,[25] who would probably refuse to attend the festival if he knew who was conducting. In spite of these difficulties, the rehearsal went ahead, and afterwards Holst travelled by train to Rochester, setting out 'in a terrific storm' to walk to Maidstone, where a hotel provided him with 'lots of bed, bath and brandy' while he sat in the landlord's dressing gown waiting for his clothes to dry.[26] He finally arrived in Canterbury two days later in time to attend Evensong at the cathedral.

During rehearsals it was decided to position the choir in the cathedral's triforium, but as there were no doors which could be closed to obtain the fade-out effect in *Neptune*, the singers were instructed to walk away into the distance until they could no longer be heard. Boult considered this an ideal solution, and later remarked: 'I usually now adopt this practice in concert halls. It is more difficult for the singers, but much more effective.'

The performance was successful, and when the festival was over, Holst returned to London where he conducted three movements from *The Planets* at a British Composers' concert at the Queen's Hall, afterwards taking a motor coach to Oxford to spend a well-earned weekend with Balfour Gardiner. He wrote to Imogen, then on tour in Canada and the USA: 'Just now I am feeling that Life is Moderately Pleasing.'[27] He was getting plenty of fresh air during country walks, and the pressures of teaching were considerably reduced now that he had only one school to contend with, and was giving fewer lectures.

At the end of September Dorothy Silk called on him to collect the manuscript of the *Twelve Songs*, which she was to perform in Paris in November, and at the beginning of October the *Double Concerto* was tried through before being handed over to its dedicatees, Jelly d'Aranyi and Adila Fachiri. On 15 October, Holst and his daughter set off for Paris, to hear the first French performance of *Egdon Heath*. On arrival, they were taken in hand by the Dyers, who had moved on from Italy, and were invited to dinner and taken on motor trips to Sèvres and Versailles. The concert was given by l'Orchestre symphonique de Paris conducted by Pierre Monteux, and although the rehearsals went well, the performance itself was hissed by the audience, giving audible expression to feelings which English audiences had been too polite to articulate. Following this afternoon concert, Holst and Imogen had tea with the Dyers and then left for home on the evening train.

A week or so later, Holst spent a day with Vaughan Williams at Dorking, having a 'field day' devoted to their latest compositions, a way of passing the time which Holst greatly preferred to socializing in foreign cities. At that time Vaughan Williams was working on his 'masque for dancing' *Job*, and some years after Holst's death wrote: 'I should like to place on record all that he did for me when I wrote *Job*. I should be alarmed to say how many "Field Days" we spent over it. Then he came to all the orchestral rehearsals, including a special journey to Norwich, and finally, he insisted on the Camargo society performing it. Thus I owe the life of *Job* to Holst . . . I remember after the first orchestral rehearsal of *Job* his almost going on his knees to beg me to cut out some of the percussion with which my inferiority complex had led me to overload the score . . . Holst's orchestra could be naked and unashamed.'[28] (In the event, Vaughan Williams restored one of the deleted cymbal clashes after being implored to do so by a disappointed percussionist.) Arthur Bliss later recalled Holst at this rehearsal: 'I was sitting next to him at a first run-through of Vaughan Williams's *Job* in Norwich. The composer was taking the rehearsal. Suddenly Holst, and when he was listening to music he listened with a frightening intensity, said to himself "That doesn't come off. I must go and tell him". He stepped on to the platform, looked at the score with Vaughan Williams, discussed and suggested, and then came back to his place, while the composer spoke to the players. The section was then tried over again, but with what a difference of sound!—clarity instead of thick obscurity. Holst always probed like a fine surgeon to the root of the difficulty.'[29]

The first performance of the *Twelve Songs* was to take place at a private party given by Louise Dyer at her Paris apartment, and on 7 November Holst once again set out for France, together with Dorothy Silk, Nora Day, and Vally Lasker (who was to play the piano accompaniment). Their train arrived in Paris four hours late, and the staff at their hotel had to turn out at 3.30 a.m. to receive them. The following day Holst lunched with Mrs Dyer and supervised rehearsals of the songs, and on the day of the performance he walked alone in Paris in the morning, joining the others in the afternoon. The party lasted from 9.30 p.m. until 1 a.m., during which the songs were performed under the collective title *The Dream City*, with the omission of *Rhyme* and *Betelgeuse*; Louise Dyer had had a programme specially printed for the occasion, giving the words of the poems, together with a French translation. Dorothy Silk sang well, and the songs were favourably received by the large group of friends whom Mrs Dyer had invited for the performance. The next day Holst said farewell to Dorothy Silk at the station and then spent the next three days in the company of Nora Day, Vally Lasker, and the Dyers, during which he visited Chartres on a motor trip, and met Nadia Boulanger and her mother. On 13 November he left Paris for England.

By this time he had made a considerable amount of progress on *The Wandering Scholar*, and finished the first draft on 13 January 1930. Another composition which he completed at this time was a short piano piece written for Imogen in response to a request for some piano music without any folk-tunes in it. Untitled at first, Holst later named the piece *Nocturne*. This 'belated twenty-first birthday present' was the first of a projected pair,[30] but its intended companion piece was not completed until two years later.

At the beginning of 1930 George Bell, now Bishop of Chichester, wrote to Holst: 'The Dean of Chichester and I are very anxious to persuade you to bring yourself and the Heavenly Host to Chichester Cathedral and Palace for Whitsuntide, 1930.' Bell went on to explain that he hoped to include some folk dancing in the festival, and that he had asked John Reith of the BBC to provide 'a tiny orchestra of six or eight for an octet or a sextet for a sort of Chamber Music'.[31]

Holst replied on 6 January: 'Dear Bell, Thank you for a most delightful New Year's Greeting! Of course the HH will be longing to come. The drawbacks are 1) We have half promised to go to a church in Ealing. It has been suggested that we get the latter to invite us the previous Sunday. 2) Extra train fares will be a nuisance to some of the HH. 3) (This is rather important) I don't see what a scratch lot of amateurs, as we are, could do that Dr Conway's Singers could not do infinitely better. The virtues of my little lot are the virtues of first rate amateurs—enthusiasm and adaptability—they can sing, play, folk dance and do most other things when told to. But collecting them together often enough to learn one thing well instead of several things rather well is a problem sometimes. However I'd love to discuss possibilities so look forward to doing so with you, the Dean and Dr Conway . . .'[32]

Holst arranged this meeting for 15 February, and wrote to

Dorothy Callard: 'The Bishop of Chichester (late Dean of Canterbury) wants us to go to Chichester at Whitsun. There is a lot to be considered first and so I have suggested that you, Palmer, Miss Lasker and I go there next weekend to discuss everything. All expenses will be paid . . . Make a list of people you think ought to be invited but don't speak a word to anyone!'[33] (the Palmer referred to here was Holst's Morley College pupil Wilfred Palmer, not the Canterbury organist). Having arranged for his colleagues to go off to Chichester by train, Holst himself travelled by train only as far as Midhurst, and then walked over the Downs to Chichester, where he stayed in the Bishop's Palace with George and Mrs Bell. When the weekend was over and details of the proposed Whitsun festival had been settled, Holst left his friends to make his own way home, walking alone back over the Downs to Pulborough, from where he took a train to London.

A few days later he was again on the move: on 21 February a friend took him by car to Bourton-on-the-Water, where he spent a pleasant evening with the Wilkins family, reminiscing about the early days when he was organist and choirmaster there as a young man before entering the Royal College of Music. The next day he walked through the Cotswolds to Cheltenham, where he was to conduct the first concert performance of *The Golden Goose* on 24 February. Besides the choral ballet, the concert also included the first performance of his orchestral transciption of the *Fugue à la Gigue*. His performance of this with the City of Birmingham Symphony Orchestra drew demands for an encore from the audience, with which he was obliged to comply.

After staying overnight in the home of the Cheltenham musician Lewis Hann (whose pupils had performed movements of an early string suite by Holst in 1899), Holst set off to walk through the Cotswolds, through 'mist, East wind and snow', arriving in Bampton on 26 February ('sun in afternoon, starlight in evening'),[34] finishing in Oxford, where he stayed for a few days with Balfour Gardiner.

In recognition of his musical achievement, Vaughan Williams was awarded the gold medal of the Royal Philharmonic Society in March 1930, and the following month it was Holst's turn. At a Queen's Hall concert on 3 April, Adila Fachiri and Jelly d'Aranyi gave the première performance of the *Double Concerto* conducted by Oskar Fried, and during the interval Frederick Austin presented Holst with the Society's medal. By this honour, Holst and Vaughan Williams were acknowledged by the musical professional as being at the apogee of their careers, and in comparing the two composers, Austin described them as 'contemporaries, life-long friends, Arcadians both.'[35] Although they were indeed the closest of friends and each had acquired an international reputation, both composers maintained an objective attitude to the other's work, each taking it for granted that the other would speak his mind frankly if he perceived deficiencies in his friend's music. The day after Holst's première, Vaughan Williams wrote to him about the *Double Concerto*: 'The Lament & Ground are splendid—I'm not *quite* so sure about the scherzo—and even that boils down to not being quite so sure about the 6/8 tune.'[36] Although the two soloists coped with the work admirably, it seems that Oskar Fried's conducting was not up to standard; the musical press describing him as 'quite the least acceptable conductor heard at a London symphony orchestra concert for a long time . . . his performance of *Till Eulenspiegel* was a disgrace'.[37] However, despite the quality of conducting, some critics did not rate the *Double Concerto* very highly either, *The Sackbut* describing it as 'absolutely threadbare'.[38]

Holst decided to get away from it all by going on a walking tour in Holland during the Easter holidays. He took a boat from Gravesend, arriving in Rotterdam on 10 April, and after exploring the city, set out on foot for Delft. The next two weeks were spent in visiting museums and art galleries in The Hague, Leiden, Haarlem, and Amsterdam, where he also heard a performance of the *St Matthew Passion*. Wherever possible, Holst walked from town to town, despite being sometimes delayed by the weather or by getting lost and going round in circles, but soon began to suffer from a weak ankle, and although he sometimes took a train or bus to alleviate the strain (and accepted a lift on one occasion from the pianist José Iturbi), he decided to end his holiday at Middleburg, and returned to England.

On 28 April Holst was at Dorking for Vaughan Williams's Leith Hill music festival, and during May spent a considerable amount of time preparing for the forthcoming Whitsun festival to be held at Chichester. Despite these activities, he still managed to find time for composition, and during the first part of 1930 concentrated on *A Choral Fantasia* for soprano solo (or semi-chorus), mixed chorus, organ, strings, brass, and percussion. This was a setting of words from Robert Bridges *Ode for the Bicentenary Commemoration of Henry Purcell* (which had been set by Parry as a cantata for the 1895 Leeds Festival), and was composed for the Three Choirs Festival at the request of the Gloucester Cathedral organist Herbert Sumsion, who had asked for a work with a concertante organ part. Because of the difficulty of this organ part, Holst often referred to the work as his 'organ concerto'.[39] An important motif in the work bears an uncanny resemblance to the chorale 'Es Ist Genung', which was also used by Alban Berg in his violin concerto a few years later. While the composition was in progress, Holst heard of the death of Bridges on 21 April 1930 at the age of eighty-five, and inscribed his score with the dedication: 'In Homage, Robert Bridges'.[40]

Another smaller composition which he undertook at this time was some incidental music for a production of George Moore's play *The Passing of the Essenes*. Holst was asked to contribute only two chants for the Psalms in the play, but was by habit so thorough in his approach that he immediately went out and bought a copy of Moore's long novel *The Brook Kerith* on which the play is based, and read it from cover to cover before writing the tunes.

At the end of May, Holst was involved with rehearsals for the Chichester festival, and with helping Vaughan Williams put the finishing touches to his piano concerto which had been in progress since 1926. The concerto was tried out in a two-piano version in Holst's room at St Paul's on 29 May by Vally Lasker, Nora Day, and Astra Desmond. Helen Bidder was also to have taken part, but was taken ill, and Holst wrote to her: 'I rang up Uncle Ralph and have explained that when you are well and strong he shall hear his concerto properly played. Meanwhile he and his missus are coming tomorrow to hear a strictly improper mess up of it by Vally, Nora and Astra. They've refused to even look at the finale and the composer will only be admitted at owner's risk.'[41]

From 2 to 5 June Holst was in Chichester to conduct rehearsals for the Whitsun festival. As usual, the music included pieces by his favourite composers: Purcell, Bach, Byrd, Weelkes, Vittoria, and Pearsall, and there was also to be country dancing in the gardens of the Bishop's Palace. The Whit Sunday evening performance in the cathedral was given by more than 120 singers and players from St Paul's Girls' School and Morley College, together with a similar number of local performers, including students from Bishop Otter College. For this occasion, Holst grouped his performers in the three western bays of the nave, conducting them from the steps inside the west door. The performers were thus behind and out of sight of the congregation, which faced the correct way for the prayers conducted at the altar by Bishop Bell and the Dean, A. S. Duncan-Jones. The cathedral was filled to capacity, and a collection was taken in aid of urgent repairs to the fabric of the building. On Whit Monday, Holst's singers performed again for the morning service in the cathedral, and in the afternoon sang madrigals in the Palace Gardens, afterwards joining in country dancing with the West Sussex Folk Dancers. The festival closed with an evening service in the cathedral, including a procession round the building, pausing by the memorial tablet to Thomas Weelkes, who had been organist of the cathedral in the early seventeenth century, where his *Hosanna* was sung. In recognition of Holst's work in making the festival a success, a medallion was presented to him to commemorate the event (this is now on display in the Holst Birthplace Museum).

After the festival, Holst went by car to Cocking with his friend Austin Lidbury who was on a visit from America, and walked with him to Arundel; one of the rare occasions on which Holst shared his country rambles with another person. On 14 June he directed his singers in a 'Recital of Sacred Music' at All Saints' Church, Ealing Common, and on 23 June set off on yet another journey taking a train to Buckingham, walking to Blishworth, and going on by train to Northampton and thence by car to Overstone. After returning to London on 25 June, he was off once more the next day, this time to Oxford from where he walked to Cirencester, returning to London on 28 June to spend an evening with Austin Lidbury.

On 7 July, Imogen gave a piano recital at the Royal College of Music, including the first performance of the *Nocturne* (under the title *An Un-named Piece*), and works of her own were played at concerts on 12 and 15 July. After this second concert, which also included his *Fugal Concerto*, Holst travelled again to Sussex to visit Chichester for a choral festival, managing to get in some walking on the Downs before and after the event. On 19 July he left London once more, this time travelling by train direct to Cirencester, where he had been asked to conduct and speak at a hymn festival in the parish church the following day. The singing was led by the combined choirs of the Parish Church and Holy Trinity Church, and Holst addressed the congregation from the pulpit, making some introductory remarks, and then commenting on each hymn as it was sung (all selected from *The English Hymnal*). He declared that the most important thing in any piece of music was the first note, and insisted that the congregation should be standing and ready to sing as soon as the organist had played the introduction. He made his audience sing in unison and regulate their breath and diction so that the singing was well controlled and effective. The large congregation seemed to enjoy being put through their paces in this way, and by the end of the session were beginning to sing the hymns to Holst's satisfaction. In concluding his talk, he recalled that his mother and grandmother had attended services in the same church many years before.

After returning to London, he was off again a few days later for a week's walk from Southwell to Lincoln, where he attended a service in the cathedral and visited the cathedral library. From Lincoln he went to Alford and thence to Peterborough by train, returning to London on 7 August.

17

From Hammersmith to the USA
(1930–1932)

Holst now felt ready to begin work on the much-postponed work commissioned by the BBC for the Wireless Military Band. He had been turning over in his mind the notion of depicting in music that part of London with which he was most familiar: the slow and inevitable flow of the river at Hammersmith contrasted with the bustle of human life in the adjacent streets. Accordingly, in the summer of 1930 he began work on *Hammersmith*, working partly in his sound-proof room at St Paul's Girls' School, not far from the river itself, and partly in the cottage which he had recently rented to replace his previous one in the Thaxted area: Hill Cottage, at Great Easton, near Dunmow. *Hammersmith* was at first subtitled 'Prelude and Fugue', but Holst changed 'Fugue' to 'Scherzo' while he was writing the work. In the Prelude he used shifting bitonal lines to evoke the constant, dark flow of the river, breaking off for the bustling Scherzo, but returning at the end to the mood of the Prelude, as the river continues on its way regardless of the activities of man (a concept similar to that which he had previously expressed in *Egdon Heath*, and earlier still in *A Somerset Rhapsody*). There is no attempt to reconcile these two elements, and although motifs from the two sections are combined at the end, each retains its independence, remaining unchanged by the presence of the other.

Holst later wrote to Adrian Boult: 'As far as the work owes anything to outside influences it is the result of living in Hammersmith for thirty-nine years on and off and wanting to express my feelings for the place in music . . . Just as I was going to start on the work, I read A. P. Herbert's "Water Gypsies". There is no programme and no attempt to depict any person or incident. The only two things that I think were in my mind were 1) a district crowded with cockneys, which would be overcrowded if it were not for the everlasting good humour of the people concerned and 2) the background of the river, that was there before the crowd and will be there presumably long after, and which goes its way largely un-noticed and apparently quite unconcerned.'[1] These two factors are represented by a slowly-moving ground bass with flowing counterpoints above, and a querky triplet figure as might be whistled in a Cockney street market. There is also a 6/8 pastoral tune which might seem out of place in the brick-and-mortar landscape of Hammersmith, but which nevertheless fits nicely into Holst's musical design.

On 1 October *The Passing of the Essenes* opened for a short run at the Arts Theatre Club in Great Newport Street, and Holst attended the first night to hear how the actors were coping with his chants. On 14 October he visited Morley College to give a lecture on 'England and her Music' as part of a series of lectures by various distinguished guest speakers on the general theme of 'England Today and Tomorrow', and during October there were several rehearsals of Vaughan Williams's *Job* which Holst did his best to attend, travelling to Norwich on 20 October to hear the final rehearsal and first performance. Holst was so keen on *Job* that he set about persuading the newly-founded Camargo Society to stage a performance of the work. The aims of the Society were to promote dancing and the production of ballets, and besides its founder Edwin Evans its leading members included the economist Maynard Keynes and his wife the ballerina Lydia Lopokova. As a result of Holst's advocacy, the Society agreed to perform the work, and it was given in July of the following year at the Cambridge Theatre in London.

By the end of October Holst had completed *Hammersmith* in a version for two pianos, and wrote to Walton O'Donnell, conductor of the Wireless Military Band, asking him to come to St Paul's to hear it and to give him some advice on band scoring. He was also working on the *Choral Fantasia* and although it was now completely sketched out, he was still uncertain about some details and sought advice from conductors such as Henry Wood and Adrian Boult: 'The matter in point is my bewilderment as to how to bar my new thing now it is fully sketched.'[2] After jotting down some possibilities in his notebook, he added a reminder to himself: 'Don't be logical —decide each case by other parts.'[3]

On 4 November Nora Day and Helen Bidder played the two-piano score of *Hammersmith* to Walton O'Donnell, and a week later Vally Lasker and Helen Bidder played it to Vaughan Williams, who subsequently confessed to Holst that his evident lack of enthusiasm was probably due to hearing the work in piano reduction rather than on the intended instruments. At this time Vaughan Williams was working on his opera *Riders to the Sea*, and when he was approached by Adrian Boult to set some Welsh folk-songs for unaccompanied chorus he declined on the grounds that he was too busy. Boult then turned to Holst, explaining that he was making the request on behalf of the Misses Davies of Gregynog, Montgomeryshire (subsequently Powys), describing the two sisters as 'those delightful ladies that used to do so much entertaining in the happy days when we used to go to Aberystwyth . . .'.[4] Both Holst and Vaughan Williams had heard the songs sung at a London concert by Dora Herbert Jones (who worked at the Davies's printing works at Gregynog), and Holst invited Mrs Jones to sing at a meeting of the St Paul's Girls' School Music Society on 12 November so that he could hear the tunes again and discuss them with her. After obtaining copies of the melodies and their Welsh words, Holst asked Steuart Wilson to make English translations, and on receiving these began to set the tunes for mixed chorus, a task which was to occupy him into the first months of 1931.

Besides this project and his usual teaching, most of November and December were taken up with putting the finishing touches to *A Choral Fantasia*, *Hammersmith*, and *The Wandering Scholar*, all of which were all tried out at the piano in Holst's room at St Paul's on 12 December. Vaughan Williams was present, and subsequently told Holst that he thought the opera contained rather too much 6/8 time (these folksy tunes suggest that the experience of composing *At the Boar's Head* was still strong in Holst's mind).

A few weeks earlier Holst had written to Imogen: 'One evening last August I thought how wonderful it would be if I could pull off all the things I was trying to write, by the end of the year . . . But I've just realised that, given decent luck, I shall get everything done by Xmas! Which means that I must have a superb holiday to work it all out of the system and to start 1931 with a clear mind . . .' He was feeling rather tired, and explained: 'I find I can only be a Gay Young Thing for one night at a time—and even then only for a short time. At Mrs Courthould's supper party I fear I was less a G.Y.T. and more of a Boiled Owl.'[5] A few days before Christmas, Holst composed a short hymn entitled *God Be In My Head* in response to a request from Nora Day, and sent it to her with a note: 'I wrote it quite unexpectedly last night & find that I don't dislike it sufficiently to tear it up to-day.'[6] In the event the 'superb holiday' turned out to be only a few days of walking; from Ealing to Wealdstone in fog, and on to Elstree in sunshine, returning by train to London, and the next day by train to Broxbourne, walking in fog to Bishop's Stortford. By Christmas Eve the fog had cleared, and he walked on to Thaxted, arriving in time for midnight Mass. He stayed in the Vicarage over Christmas as the guest of Conrad Noel, who witnessed his signature on the commissioning contract for *Hammersmith* on Boxing Day, and on 27 December Holst walked back to Bishop's Stortford in the rain, taking a train to London. The following day (a Sunday) he tramped over Hampstead Heath and through the deserted streets of the city.

Early in the new year Holst received a letter from Boult concerning a forthcoming broadcast: 'We are doing *Savitri* soon, I believe, at a studio performance, and I was wondering whether you would like to have fuller Strings at any time or whether we shall stick to the double quartet?'[7] As one of the characteristic features of *Savitri* is the economy and subtlety of its instrumentation, Holst felt strongly that expansion of the string section would not be at all appropriate, although it may have to be necessary to produce an effective sound through the limited broadcasting equipment of those days. He replied: 'Will you decide about the strings in *Savitri*—I don't know what is best for broadcasting but I am all in favour of leaving the score as it is because I've usually found that solo instruments come through so well.' He went on: 'I've heard a rumour that the BBC tried to get Dorothy Silk to sing *Savitri* on Febr 13 but found that she was engaged. If it is not a) too late

b) too interfering would you consider altering the date? DS does it so beautifully.' The proposed broadcast also brought other ideas to Holst's mind: 'Your coming performance of *Savitri* has awakened my old dream of writing a real radio opera. But it remains a dream.'[8] It is tantalizing to speculate as to what such a work might have been like; Holst's recurrent problems with stagecraft in the theatre would be minimized in a radio production, allowing full rein to his creative imagination. (In the event, *Savitri* was dropped from the programme at the last minute, 'for technical reasons', according to the *Daily Mail*.[9])

In February Holst lectured on 'England and her Music' at Rugby, attended Boult's rehearsals and broadcast performances of *The Planets* and *Beni Mora* in London, visited Balfour Gardiner in Oxford, and attended a performance of *The Fairy Queen* in Cambridge. During the first months of 1931, he rescored *Hammersmith* for full orchestra, and also made some changes in the original band version, sending the score to Walton O'Donnell 'after having revised the score thoroughly. If the parts are already copied, I fear that this will give some trouble.' He added: 'The orchestral score is now complete. I am sending it to ACB [Adrian Boult] in a few days.'[10]

It was at this time that Holst was asked to write the music for a film; an unusual commission for a 'serious' composer in those days, as directors preferred to work with musicians who had served in cinema orchestras in the days of silent films. On 20 March Holst attended a meeting at the studios of Associated Sound Film Industries at Wembley, where he learnt that the film was to be called *The Bells*, being an adaptation by C. H. David of J. R. Ware's melodrama *The Polish Jew*. Having left consideration of the music to a very late stage in the proceedings, the directors wanted Holst to work quickly so that the recordings could be made the following month. Holst accepted this offer as he had no other major work in hand and had by now completed his settings of the Welsh folk-songs. But he had already decided to have an Easter holiday in Normandy, so after making preliminary sketches for the film score he set out on 27 March for what he described as 'a week's middle-aged walking'. He travelled by train from Victoria, via Dieppe to Rouen, from where his walks took him to Duclair, and thence along the Seine to Jumièges, returning on the main road in hot sunshine. He then went on to Caudebec, this time walking against a cold wind, and after walking to St Wandrille in the rain, decided to return to England as the weather was so bad. This holiday did him little good, as his health was no longer equal to such exercise, and he developed a throat infection as a consequence of his exposure to the elements in France. By 9 April he was sufficiently recovered to accompany Imogen to an English Folk Dance Society Easter School at Belstead House, then at Aldeburgh (which later became her permanent home), and to direct the folk-singing there.

On his return from Aldeburgh, Holst immediately immersed himself in work on music for *The Bells*. The press reported that the items Holst had agreed to compose would include 'a storm prelude, a wedding feast, and dance music, and several drinking songs',[11] and by 20 April he was able to note in his diary that sketches for the dances were complete. He had decided to use a small orchestra consisting of wind, brass, strings, percussion, harp, piano, and celesta, with a sousaphone to give extra weight to the bass line which often needed reinforcement on film sound-tracks. He spent several days at Wembley recording the music in the sound studios, and during one of the inevitable delays which arise during the making of a film, on hearing that more extras were needed for a crowd scene, volunteered his own services. He wrote excitedly to Adeline Vaughan Williams: 'I have appeared in a film! At least I think I have. Or, rather, I probably shall when its developed. Unless I am "killed in the cutting room".' Holst was particularly bemused by a scene in which a young couple go shopping on Old London Bridge (long demolished): 'I haven't asked why —it isn't done. I imagine that the reason is that a replica of old London Bridge was made for the Wembley exhibition and my film's studio is at Wembley.' He also told Adeline: 'I've had a first rate day and have written quite a lot of music that makes me purr and feel good all over. And on playing it through I find that it is all *Job*! It really isn't fair. Your old man ought to let me get in front sometimes.'[12]

In March Holst had received a letter from Dorothy Callard asking him to direct the music at the Whitsun festival which was to be held at Bosham in Sussex that year. Because of his various commitments he was unable to give a firm answer: 'I would certainly like to come to Bosham at Whitsun but it must be clearly understood that *I cannot promise anything* before June 1,' he wrote; 'Two months ago I was asked to write music for a film. They hoped to get everything finished by May 1 but it is quite certain that it cannot be ready before June 1 and until everything is in working order I cannot undertake any more work. Another point is that my old arm trouble has cropped up again and the less I conduct the better.'[13]

Despite this resurgent neuritis, he did his best to complete the recordings for *The Bells*, but his enthusiasm for film making began to fade when the directors suddenly asked him to make changes in the music to correspond with cuts they had made in the film. His disillusion was complete when he visited the studios for a private preview of the finished film—the sound which emerged from the loudspeakers was of such poor quality that it bore little resemblance to the music which he had conducted in the studio, and Imogen, who was with him in the viewing room, recalled that his 'white-faced look of dismay' increased as the showing of the film progressed.[14]

For some reason the company made little effort to distribute the film. Although its imminent release was announced in the press in 1931 and again in 1932, this produced few advance bookings and it was eventually sold off to an American company. It seems that the film was never shown in the USA either, and neither the American company nor the present whereabouts of the film can now be traced. Holst's score and orchestral parts have apparently disappeared just as completely, and the only person who could recall the music was an official of Associated Sound Films, who remembered a two-track sequence in which a brass band and a pipe band, playing their own tunes, marched from different directions and came together; an idea similar to that which had appeared many years before in the Finale of the *Beni Mora* suite. Although Holst was relieved that the distorted sound-track was not after all to be heard by the public, this was tinged with a little regret at the demise of his brief appearance as a film 'extra'.

On 23 April 1931 the original version of *Hammersmith* was rehearsed by the Wireless Military Band in the BBC studios under the arches of Waterloo Bridge, and again on 19 May. Holst wrote to Walton O'Donnell: 'If you are able to do it twice, may I conduct it one of the times?'[15] Although Holst had sent the score to O'Donnell the previous December in the hope that it might be included in an international military band festival, this performance had not materialized, and despite the work being rehearsed several times by the BBC band in 1931 it was not performed in Britain in its original version until several decades after Holst's death.

At the beginning of May, Holst took a train to Midhurst and then walked over the Downs to Chichester, staying overnight as the guest of George Bell in the Bishop's Palace ('Our palace', as Holst and his singers came to call it[16]) before going on to Bosham and returning to London the following day. On 9 May he visited the BBC studios for a rehearsal of the postponed performance of *Savitri*, and after the 19 May rehearsal of *Hammersmith* returned to Chichester for the Whitsun festival which was held in the ancient parish church at Bosham, by the water's edge on Chichester harbour.

The following month, Holst was engaged to lecture in Bournemouth ('doing a jaw', as he called it[17]) and once again took the opportunity of walking in the countryside, through the New Forest from Romsey to Ringwood. From there he made his way by bus and train to Bournemouth, where on 13 June he lectured at Holy Trinity Hall on 'England and her Music', afterwards going on by train to Christchurch. The next day he walked to Brockenhurst and Burley, returning to London in the evening.

On 11 July Holst travelled to Gregynog, where three of the *Twelve Welsh Folksongs* were to be performed by the Gregynog Choir. The settings are practical and effective despite their simplicity, and Holst added the following note to the score: 'There are no indications of tempo or of expression. These will arise out of the singing of the song, and are left to the judgement of the conductor and the singers.'[18] On this occasion he had no need for concern about the result, for the choir was under the direction of his reliable interpreter Adrian Boult. After the performance Boult took Holst back to London by car, but Holst was on the move again the following day, this time to Gloucester, where rehearsals of *A Choral Fantasia* were due to begin for its première at the Three Choirs Festival in September. He travelled via Oxford and walked through the Cotswolds, sometimes being forced to take a bus because of rain, arriving in Gloucester in time for rehearsals of the organ part in the evening. He stayed overnight with Herbert Sumsion, and the next day conducted a full choral rehearsal, after which he returned to London. On 21 July Holst left London again for Oxford, this time to hear some of the concerts of the ninth festival of the International Society for Contemporary Music, which included performances of Vaughan Williams's *Benedictie* and *Job* conducted by the composer.

At the end of July Holst travelled to Chichester to conduct his Whitsuntide singers in a performance in the cathedral. The programme included works by Byrd, Weelkes, Pearsall, and Jane Joseph, and a performance of Vaughan Williams's Mass in G minor, whose composer was in the audience, and described by Holst as 'happy'.[19] During the weekend, he stayed in the home of the organist Harvey Grace, and afterwards Holst and Dorothy Callard went by car to Malvern, where he was to teach singing at an English Folk Dance Society summer school. The demands of his very full schedule of conducting combined with his normal teaching duties were putting a considerable strain on his energies and had the effect of inhibiting his creative imagination—when the time came to relax and get down to composition, he found himself devoid of ideas, writing to Imogen at the end of August: 'I'm having an infernal time. After two good Augusts I can't write a note and my temper is even more unmentionable than the weather.'[20]

He returned to Gloucester on 5 September for a busy week of rehearsals and concerts, for besides *A Choral Fantasia* , his *Fugue à la Gigue* and *The Hymn of Jesus* were to be included in the Three Choirs programme. On 8 September he directed the first performance of the *Choral Fantasia*, with Dorothy Silk as soloist, and Herbert Sumsion playing the organ part. The instrumentation was well suited to the resonant acoustics of the cathedral, with the brass coming over particularly well, but this did not impress the critics, who were disturbed by Holst's latter-day style of composition. One went so far as to declare: 'When Holst starts his new *Choral Fantasia* with a six-four on D and a C sharp below that, with an air of take-it-or-leave-it one is inclined to leave it.'[21] But Holst was pleased that

Vaughan Williams had found the performance moving, and the feelings of his friend mattered more to him than the opinions of all the critics put together. The *Choral Fantasia* was not widely performed after this première, partly because of its difficulty, and partly because the acoustics of a large building are essential for its best effect. When the BBC came to consider the work for possible inclusion in their programmes, Stanford Robinson commented: 'I think it would be a hopeless proposition for broadcasting' (this was before the days of hi-fi); 'It would probably be very impressive in a cathedral with a large organ, but by wireless I think it would sound tedious. I do not recommend a performance.'[22]

After returning to London, Holst departed again on 12 September for a walking tour in Dorset, visiting Blandford Forum, Dorchester, Abbotsbury, and Chesil Beach. Despite driving rain, he clambered up the earthen ramparts of Maiden Castle, which he called by the Celtic name of John Ireland's tone-poem *Mai Dun*.

On 22 September he was at the BBC studios again to hear Helen Bidder and Vally Lasker play the two-piano arrangement of *Hammersmith* to officials of the BBC Music Department, and two days later he conducted *The Planets* at a BBC promenade concert broadcast from the Queen's Hall on the National wavelengths.

At the beginning of October, Holst was in Huddersfield to conduct some of his works at the Greenhead High School for Girls, and on 13 October he conducted the Huddersfield Glee and Madrigal Society in a concert at the Town Hall, described as a 'Special "Holst" Programme', including songs sung by Elsie Suddaby, part-songs by the choir, and piano pieces played by Imogen. Holst stayed with Mr and Mrs A. L. Woodhead during his visit, and was headlined in the local newspapers: 'A Great Composer to conduct Glee & Madrigal Concert'.[23]

He returned to London on 14 October in time for another BBC concert at the Queen's Hall, and a further one the following week. At the beginning of November he sent Adrian Boult the score and parts of the orchestral version of *Hammersmith* in readiness for the first performance later in the month, with a note on interpretation: 'With regard to pace, the Prelude should flow calmly and fairly slowly without being impressive, and the Scherzo should be as quick as possible, as long as it sounds easy and good-tempered and not brilliant, hard or efficient. In short, it must sound like London and not Paris.'[24] The première took place on 25 November in the Queen's Hall, in a programme which included the first London performance of William Walton's *Belshazzar's Feast*. Holst's new composition did not make a strong impression, perhaps being overshadowed by the larger choral work, but also because it did not quite succeed in this orchestral version. Although the audience had not had a chance to hear the original wind band version and were therefore unable to make a comparison, there is no doubt that the orchestral version is the less effective of the two, perhaps because of the technical demands which are made of the wind band players, tending to produce a more tense, concentrated performance, but also because much of the original wind writing does not readily transfer to the string idiom. As Vaughan Williams remarked to Holst: 'You are almost unique in that your stuff sounds better when it is played on the instrument it was originally written for.'[25]

Towards the end of the year, Holst received an invitation from Harvard University to accept the post of Horatio Lamb Lecturer in Composition for the second half of the academic session, from February to May 1932. He also received a request from the Boston Symphony Orchestra to conduct a concert of his own works in January, and therefore decided to accept both invitations, booking a passage to the USA for early in the New Year. In order to lessen the pressures which would come to bear on him as a visiting celebrity, he decided to employ an agent to deal with his business affairs in America, and asked Duncan McKenzie of the Oxford University Press in New York to undertake this task. McKenzie agreed to do so, and in early December Holst wrote to him:

Dear Mr McKenzie,
    I thank you for your most helpful letter and should be delighted if you would be my agent and accept 20% commission for every engagement you get me. I have never had an agent before and am quite ignorant as to the details but take it for granted that I may make final arrangements about two or three offers of conducting engagements, that have been offered me by friends, without consulting you . . .

After promising to send copies of articles about his work and to ensure that performing materials of his compositions would be available in the USA, Holst went on:

I hope to come over on the 'Bremen' which sails on Jan.8 and shall go direct to Harvard as I believe I am to conduct in Boston about the 22nd. I hope to have at least a week in New York before I begin work at Harvard on Feb.8 and shall probably stay at the University Club. As far as I know I am free to do anything (or nothing!) between Jan.2 and Feb.8. I understand that I shall be free at week-ends during my stay at Harvard but Mr Hill of the Division of Music there would tell you definitely about my duties. My lecture subjects are: 'England and her music' (either one or two on this subject), 'The Teaching of Art', Joseph Haydn. I will conduct any work of mine with the proviso that if 'The Planets' are wanted I must have all seven done or none. Although I am sincerely grateful to you for your offer yet I am a also little anxious. In fact I rather hope that you won't get me too many engagements! I am not as strong as I was and public engagements are best for me if they come singly. Normally I lead a very quiet life and have to forego much that would otherwise give me great pleasure. One great favour I would ask and that is to be quiet and alone before any public appearance.[26]

Before departing for the USA, Holst devoted his time to dealing with details of performances of his works and seeing old friends (he wrote to Dorothy Callard on 19 December: 'The time has flown and we have not met and I shall be in town only a few days before I go to America'[27]). He was hoping to be able to conduct a performance of the original band version of *Hammersmith* in Washington, and asked Walton O'Donnell to send the score to the publishers for a copy to be made as the original score and parts would be going with him to America.

On New Year's day 1932, Holst visited Adeline and Ralph Vaughan Williams at their home near Dorking. Vaughan Williams was at that time working on his Fourth Symphony, and he and Holst discussed the music together and had a further 'field day' on it at St Paul's on 6 January, when Vally Lasker and Helen Bidder played it through on two pianos.

Two days later Holst boarded the S.S. *Bremen* at Southampton for an uneventful voyage to the USA: 'Owing to the vibration the only things I can read with ease are my own scores which I have been trying to memorize while walking up and down the deck 3½ hours per day. In short, Life has been Dull,' he wrote.[28] He arrived in New York on the evening of 13 January, where he was met by a group of friends, including his new agent Duncan McKenzie. They saw him safely on to the 12.45 a.m. train to Boston, where he was met early the next day by Archibald and Mrs Davison, and taken to stay at their house at 22 Francis Avenue. During the next few days the Davisons showed him the local sights, including Plymouth Rock, and took him to concerts and recitals in the evenings. At these he was pleased to meet some old friends, including Steuart Wilson, who sang in a Bach cantata, and Jelly d'Aranyi, who played Bach partitas, and he also made the acquaintance of the composer Walter Piston. On 19 January Holst conducted the Boston Symphony Orchestra at the Albee Theatre, Boston, in an all-Holst programme consisting of the *St Paul's Suite, A Somerset Rhapsody*. the *Perfect Fool* ballet music, and the orchestral versions of the *Fugue à la Gigue* and *Hammersmith* (its first orchestral performance in the USA). The same programme was repeated on 22 and 23 January, and Holst wrote home: 'I, who previously had never conducted an entire symphony concert, had to conduct three in one week, also four rehearsals.'[29]

On 26 January Holst travelled by train to New York, where he was able to spend some time with his brother Emil and niece Valerie. He stayed at the University Club on West 54th Street and explored the city by day (including a walk in Central Park during a gale) and spent several evenings at the theatre, where he saw Valerie perform in *Hay Fever* at the Avon Theatre, and Emil in *The Devil Passes* at the Selwyn Theatre: 'They both had small parts and they both acted very well indeed,' he wrote to Vally Lasker; 'Altogether I feel proud of my family.'[30] He was astonished at the pace of life in New York, and complained: 'My time in New York seems to consist largely in telephoning . . . New York fascinates and sometimes terrifies me. One can compare Cambridge Massachussetts with Cambridge England but New York is like nothing else I know. Perhaps Nineveh and Constantinople were like it when they were young. But the telephone habit must be unique. New Yorkers rush to the telephone as a drunkard to whiskey, —or rather, as an inveterate smoker does to cigarettes. And I'm convinced that it does not help one to get things done a bit. It's an amazing place to visit but give me Emma [Hammersmith] for living in.'[31] He was glad to be able to escape from the city occasionally to visit his brother's home at Spuyton Duyvil, set amongst rural surroundings with a wide view over the Hudson river.

On the afternoon of 31 January 1932, Holst gave a talk to a meeting of the Beethoven Association, at which he was a guest of honour, and on 2 February he lectured on 'England and her Music' at a dinner given by the National Association of Organists at New York's Pythian Temple. Another, non-musical, event was an informal dinner given in his honour at the Players Club by a group of Gloucestershire friends and admirers resident in New York.

One of the musicians Holst met at this time was Nathaniel Shilkret, director of the popular Victor Orchestra, who gave frequent concerts and broadcasts of jazz-based material. The two men had a working breakfast at the University Club on 4 February, during which Shilkret commissioned a new piece from Holst, with the proviso that it should be based on an English or American folk-tune. After the meal they went along to the Columbia Radio Studios to hear the orchestra in action, and Holst immediately started to make plans for the new composition, writing excitedly to Vally Lasker: 'This morning I had breakfast with The Man Who Makes More Money In Music Than Anyone Else In The World!'[32]

Two days later Holst bade farewell to his New York friends and relations, and in the afternoon boarded a boat for Boston. As it crept slowly northwards, he watched the snow-covered New England coastline until the light faded, and on arrival in Boston early next morning was driven immediately to Harvard to settle into his rooms in Eliot House. He was soon busy making arrangements for his composition classes and for tutorials for individual pupils, and when a piano was moved into his rooms he was able to get down to serious composition. He wrote to Imogen: 'My appartment at Eliot House is the only place I've struck in the last 20 years barring my room in SPGS where I can spoil music paper easily. It looks as if I shall write steadily while I'm here.'[33] The previous year he had begun setting some poems from Helen Waddell's *Medieval Latin Lyrics* for male-voice chorus, strings, and organ, and during 1932 completed a set of six such choruses. Although he did not attempt to emulate the style of medieval music in these pieces, the resulting settings seem well-meaning but dull, as exemplified by the *Drinking Song*, which is quite lacking in any sense of inebriation.

He was also hard at work copying out extra parts for *Hammersmith* to match the instrumentation of American bands, and although it is surprising that the University did not provide a student copyist to undertake this chore, Holst probably did not make any such request, preferring to cause the minimum disturbance by doing the job himself. (He did in fact have help with some of his other scores, particularly from Elliott Carter, who studied composition with Holst at this time as a graduate student. Although Carter was more than willing to assist in this way, he did not hold unlimited admiration for Holst's music, and in a review some years later described a work as 'an unfortunate step in the direction of pompous works like Gustav Holst's *Hymn of Jesus*'.[34] However, Holst did manage to convince Carter that free counterpoint was more interesting than strict imitation, a notion which the pupil was later to take to extraordinary lengths in his mature compositions.)

Despite his teaching commitments, Holst was able to devote several mornings a week to composition, and could often write all day without interruption. As he reported to Whittaker: 'They have given me delightful rooms and I find that I can get a fair amount of writing done,'[35] and to Vally Lasker: 'I can spoil music paper here . . . I have five rooms all to myself. The front looks on to the river, on the other side of which is Boston. There is a large sitting room which I don't use much because my neighbour that side is addicted to jazz . . . But my neighbour this side is a real dear. A professor of comparative religion from Cambridge England, who quotes almost in one breath from Plato, St Augustine and P.G. Wodehouse, and who has decided views on and a delicate taste in alcohol.'[36] The students he found more difficult to fathom. As he wrote to Vaughan Williams: 'My idea of composition is to spoil as much MS paper as possible. But my pupils here would far rather write a thesis on Schoenberg's use of the bass clarinet compared with von Webern's: or, better still, talk vaguely about the best method of introducing the second subject in the recapitulation. And some of these boys have really studied hard—if not music, anyhow books on music. Is this University or is it America?'[37]

On 11 February he conducted the *Perfect Fool* ballet music with the Boston Symphony Orchestra in a concert at the Sanders Theatre, and two days later wrote to Vally Lasker: 'We've had hot sun, blue sky and snow on the ground . . . I have spent nearly the whole day trying to set another of Helen Waddell's Medieval Latin Lyrics. It isn't exactly a birthday ode [he was writing on her birthday] but it's a cheerful poem— "How mighty are the Sabbaths" from Peter Abelard. After breakfast tomorrow I shall have to decide whether today's work makes me feel sick—I'm not going to look at it tonight.' He added: 'I've not been able to finish the string arrangement of my brass band suite [*A Moorside Suite*] because other things are pressing. I am to conduct the military band version of *Emma* [*Hammersmith*] at Washington in April and have to add four extra parts p d q. Then I do want to dedicate two male voice choruses to Davison and he wants to do them at a concert they are giving in my honour in April (the second isn't written yet!) . . . I'm down to lecture on Haydn in Washington next month. Why oh why? Later on I'm to lecture about my work at Morley in Cleveland . . .'[38] By way of relaxation he visited local places of interest such as the Fogg Museum, was invited to dinner by acquaintances, and went to concerts, including one at a girls' school in Concord on 24 February, where his *Hecuba's Lament* was performed. At the end of February Emil visited Boston where he was appearing as the Colonel in Bernard Shaw's *Too True to be Good,* and lodged at Eliot House with Gustav, who remarked that it was the first time that the two brothers had stayed under the same roof for forty years.

Holst was by now making arrangements for the remainder of his stay, during which he planned to visit Canada for a lecture and concert tour, returning home at the beginning of June. He wrote to the Rural Music Schools Association: 'By the end of April I would like to have my Canadian tour planned and also my passage home from Montreal. I would like all tickets and, if possible, all hotel bills paid so that I have not to carry so much money about. If this cannot be done I can easily arrange for money to await me at certain places. I suppose I should be travelling by CPR the whole time. I have been told that their new boats are excellent and probably the sooner I book my passage the better. I ought to arrive in England any day between June 30 and July 5—the latter is the *very* latest—in fact it is a bit too late but nothing serious. An outside cabin is not important on these modern boats but I very much want a cabin to myself, being a bad sleeper. Would this be possible? Also if there is much night travelling in trains could I sometimes have a private sleeping saloon if there are such things and if they are not too dear?' In keeping with his concern for amateur music-making, he went on: 'If there were a genuinely musical group in some out of the way place in Canada who were as poor as they were musical ... I would consider it both an honour and a delight if I could help them by lecturing or conducting a rehearsal or anything of the sort without any sort of fee whatsoever. Outside actual composition these things mean more to me than anything else in the world ... *But it must be the real thing*—Music for music's sake.'[39]

He made a preliminary visit to Canada during March, having been invited to conduct and lecture in Montreal, where he arrived on 11 March 'at wrong station', eventually being located and taken to his hotel by Douglas Clarke, conductor of the Montreal Symphony Orchestra (who had been one of his pupils at University College, Reading). Holst was to conduct just one movement (*Jupiter*) from *The Planets*, and after rehearsing on the day after his arrival, conducted it at His Majesty's Theatre on the afternoon of 13 March, being obliged to repeat it as an encore. In the evening he lectured on 'England and her Music' at the People's Forum, and then left Montreal that night by train for New York. After spending a day with Emil, Valerie, and Duncan McKenzie, he attended an evening concert, including his *Two Psalms*, given by the New York Oratorio Society conducted by Albert Stoessel at Carnegie Hall, before catching the overnight train back to Boston.

18

Final Years
(1932–1934)

Two important events were now approaching: a visit to the Library of Congress at the end of March, where he was to give a lecture commemorating the bicentenary of Haydn's birth, and the first performance of the original band version of *Hammersmith*, which he was to conduct on 17 April at Constitution Hall, Washington, during the third annual convention of the American Bandmasters' Association. Although *Hammersmith* had been commissioned by the BBC, it had not yet been performed by their band because of Holst's suggestion that its première might be given in the context of a public concert, rather than being simply broadcast from the studio. As the Washington concert had by this time been arranged, Walton O'Donnell waived any objection to Holst giving the first performance, and Adrian Boult wrote to the composer at the beginning of March: 'O'Donnell tells me that he only held it up because he wanted to put it into an important military band programme when he gets a public concert, but this is not likely to be yet I am afraid, and you must go ahead with it in Washington if you wish.'[1] Holst replied: 'I think it is very generous of you and O'Donnell to let me have the first military band performance of *Hammersmith* in America and I thank you most heartily.'[2]

In between teaching and work on the *Six Choruses*, Holst drafted his Haydn lecture. On 18 March he went to a concert which included Liszt's 'Dante' Symphony, after which he had to walk home 'to get over it'.[3] By 21 March the lecture was ready, and the following day Holst read it over to Archibald Davison for his comments. On 23 March he made a few alterations to the text, and then began to sketch some themes for the piece commissioned by Nathaniel Shilkret, which eventually became known as the *Capriccio*. Two days later he took the morning train to New York, where he was met by Duncan McKenzie and taken across the city to New Jersey, where he boarded another train for Washington. On the afternoon of 26 March 1932 (Easter Saturday) he delivered his lecture in the Chamber Music Auditorium of the Library of Congress, and this was followed by a performance of Haydn's Quartet in D, Op. 76 no. 5, given by the Roth Quartet of Budapest (who played 'divinely', in Holst's estimation[4]); the whole event being presented under the auspices of the Elizabeth Sprague Coolidge Foundation.

After the lecture Holst felt rather faint, but nevertheless took a train back to Boston via New Jersey, arriving at Eliot House at 8 a.m. on the morning of Sunday 27 March. He seemed so ill that his colleagues called a doctor, who immediately ordered Holst to be taken to the Deaconess Hospital where haemorrhagic gastritis caused by a duodenal ulcer was diagnosed. All his forthcoming engagements were cancelled, including conducting the Washington première of *Hammersmith* (which was taken over by Captain Taylor Branson) and he remained in hospital until 11 April, when the Davisons took him back to their home to recuperate. He described his hospital experiences in a letter to Vaughan Williams: 'I learnt the real meaning of the phrase A Bloody Nuisance. They reckoned that I lost two quarts. They gave me a) blood transfusion which was invigorating at first but which gave me a high temperature the next day: b) morphia which is altogether delightful: c) five days of creamed milk every hour which was infernal.'[5] His niece Valerie visited him frequently in hospital, but on 14 April had to rejoin her theatre company, whereupon Holst developed 'a severe attack of home sickness'.[6] Despite this, and with the valuable contribution of the Davisons' kindness and care, he began to regain strength and energy, so much so that he began to think in terms of fulfilling an engagement to conduct at Ann Arbor in May and perhaps going ahead with his planned Canadian tour after all.

He began to pick up his various projects where they had been left off. On 17 April he finished his arrangement for strings of the *Moorside Suite*, which was intended for the junior orchestra at St Paul's, and sent the score to Vally Lasker with a covering note: 'At present I feel it just *won't do*! I only like the music in places. But apart from that I've not been able to make it easy enough. The obvious truth being that it is not real string music.' He added a postscript: 'When you have been through it I think you'll agree that it is my duty to write a Real string suite for the SP Jun Orch.'[7] (This was to emerge as the *Brook Green Suite*, composed the following year.)

On 18 April Holst moved back into his rooms in Eliot House, where he continued to work on the *Six Choruses* and resumed his teaching duties with renewed enthusiasm, even taking one of Davison's classes in choral composition on 25 April. On the 27th, after resting for most of the day (the weather was cold with snow showers) he attended a special concert given in his honour by the University at the Sanders Theatre. The programme included the *St Paul's Suite*, *A Dirge for Two Veterans*, *Hecuba's Lament*, the *Two Psalms*, two of the *Six Choral Folksongs*, and the first performance of *Before Sleep* from the *Six Choruses*, sung by its dedicatees, the Harvard Glee Club conducted by Archibald Davison. There was also a setting of the theme from *Jupiter* to words by Mark A. de Wolfe Howe, under the title *The Shores of Harvard*. Holst was pleased with the concert, which he described as 'The happiest night I've had in the USA . . . it was like Morley College on a large scale. Those youngsters sang some of my things by heart. One can't have a higher compliment than that! And the first trumpet of the Boston Symphony Orchestra *wanted to return his fee*!!'[8]

At the beginning of May, Holst took up his sketches for the Shilkret commission, finishing the first sketch three days later, and on 8 May completed the full score and started work on a two-piano version which he finished on the 11th. This was uncharacteristically speedy work for Holst, who remarked: 'Usually when I write things in a hurry I feel unwell when the result is played.'[9] Although Shilkret had requested a piece founded on folk-tunes, Holst had decided to use his own thematic material 'because I prefer my own',[10] and there was therefore a possibility that the completed work might not be acceptable. Despite this, Holst was hoping to be able to hear it played in New York by the Shilkret orchestra before he left the USA. He gave the piece the title *Mr Shilkret's Maggot*, following English country-dance precedents, but perhaps also prompted by Sylvia Townsend Warner's novel *Mr Fortune's Maggot* which was popular at that time. The novel is prefaced by a quotation from the *New English Dictionary*: 'MAGGOT. 2. A whimsical or perverse fancy; a crotchet.'[11] As Holst had feared, the piece was rejected by Shilkret, and in November Duncan McKenzie pursued the matter with the bandleader, receiving the following reply: 'I spoke to Holst about writing something for my composers' series on folk-music themes, for a short radio piece (not longer than 5 or 6 minutes). Instead, Mr Holst have me a short modernistic composition called "Shilkret's Maggot". I am very enthusiastic about this little number and hate to give it up, but I cannot play it because it is not based on a definite English or American folk theme. Will Mr Holst write me another composition (I think I mentioned "Three Blind Mice" to him) for the stipulated $200?'[12] Holst however did not feel inclined to compose another piece for the band, and there the matter rested.

Many years after his death, the work was rescored for small orchestra by Imogen Holst, who gave it the title *Capriccio*, and in this version it was first performed under her direction in London in 1968. Falling neither into the category of jazz nor of serious music, it aroused little enthusiasm among those who heard it, particularly the jazz enthusiasts, who were expecting something quite different. Steve Race found it to be 'merely Holstian music jazzed up and scored for a comic combination'[13] (surely the only time a jazz critic has complained about a work being 'jazzed up'!). Race deplored the 'bizarre element which seems to affect all orchestral composers when they think of jazz (and which is usually referred to as "humour")', and pronounced it to be a failure from the jazz point of view. The work seems to have suffered from the consequences of Holst's illness and the speed of its composition, as the score exhibits a debt to several of his previous works, particularly *Hammersmith*, the *Suite No. 2* for military band, and even the *Country Song* of twenty-six years before. But the main problem was his failure to comprehend the nature of the radio orchestra and the style of its repertoire. Although he introduced some lively material in contrast to the improvisatory folk-like opening, the music remains dull in concept and symphonic in sound throughout; perhaps it is merciful that this rather naïve attempt at entertainment music was never put to the test before a New York radio audience.

As Holst's health was improving so much, he now decided to go ahead with his engagement to conduct at Ann Arbor, although he had meanwhile given up any hope of proceeding with his Canadian tour. On 13 May he left Boston, arriving in Ann Arbor the following morning. Here he met many friends from his 1923 visit, and his step-brother Thorley came over from Chicago to see him. On 19 May Holst conducted a concert in the Hill Auditorium, including the *Fugue à la Gigue*, the *Perfect Fool* ballet music, and the first performance in the USA of *A Choral Fantasia*. The following day he returned to Boston via Detroit, and spent the remaining days of May in making preparations for his return to England. He would be travelling alone, but Emil was to follow soon afterwards for a short holiday, so that 'we are going to stroll over the Cotswolds together for the first time for over 40 years!'[14] On 23 May Holst conducted the *St Paul's Suite* at a Boston 'Pop' concert at Symphony Hall, in which Davison conducted *A Dirge for Two Veterans*, and after making his final farewells, Holst took a boat for New York on 26 May, enduring a violent storm which hit the ship before it reached the Cape Cod canal. On arrival early the next day, he walked through the Bowery to Cooper Square to see McKenzie, attended a rehearsal of Shilkret's band in the afternoon, and spent some time with Emil before boarding the *Europa* late in the evening.

After an uneventful voyage, he was back in London by 2 June, and Emil arrived two weeks later. On 21 June the two brothers set out by train for Oxford to begin their Cotswolds holiday, and were joined by Imogen, and unexpectedly by the Montreal conductor Douglas Clarke, who arrived in a large car and offered to drive them anywhere they wished. As Holst had still not fully recovered from his illness, this offer was gratefully accepted, and they visited Broadway, Cheltenham, and Cirencester before returning to London by train on 23 June. Although Emil had to leave a couple of days later, a further holiday was planned for August when Valerie was due to arrive from the USA.

Meanwhile Holst did some walking by himself, which he found he could manage provided he did not push the pace. As he wrote to Whittaker: 'I'm all right now except that my walking is even more middle-aged than before and I've got to keep off alcohol which I don't mind and fresh fruit which I do.'[15] He visited Worcester on 7 July, and on 27 July took a train to Arundel with Mabel Rodwell Jones, setting off alone to walk over the Downs to Chichester for the August festival which was to be directed by Vally Lasker. But his health was not up to the task, and he had to complete the journey by bus. The Bank Holiday music in the cathedral included Byrd's Mass for three voices, motets by Byrd and Vittoria, and *This Have I Done for My True Love*. When it was over Holst took a bus to the Downs, where he walked alone in the woods before accepting a lift from Irene Bonnett's family to Guildford, from where he returned to London.

On 12 August he travelled to Durham, where he stayed for three days, 'writing tunes in the Cathedral nearly all day and each day'.[16] He wrote to Vally Lasker: 'I wandered about the Cathedral and Castle all day and at intervals I found myself writing down tunes in the notebook you gave me. In the evening I found I had filled two pages. It seemed a nice change after the previous ten days so I spent all Sunday doing the same. Of course the services were much in the way (the music was quite bad on the whole) and they shut the cathedral too early: also there were too many people. But I found a chapel reserved for private meditation and when I wasn't there I was usually in the crypt. Result—another two pages. On Monday I settled down to it and by 3 PM evensong (at which I left the cathedral) I had filled five pages. I did a sixth by the river and then caught the 4 PM train to town. During the three days I didn't read what I had written but put the book away as soon as I'd put down something and then waited for the next . . . It was a quite intoxicating experience, wandering about that cathedral, waiting for the next!'[17]

Since his return from the USA he had written some canons for unaccompanied equal voices ('One of them is for two choirs and three keys,' he wrote, 'However the attack is nearly over and I don't think I shall repeat the offense'[18]), and also completed the remaining male voice choruses. When six of the canons were finished in June he invited Vally Lasker, Nora Day, and Helen Bidder to Kew Gardens, where they sang them through, and he later sent a published copy to Helen Bidder with a note conveying 'My best wishes for one of the happiest afternoons of 1932'.[19] He then added two further canons with piano accompaniment, the whole set of eight exhibiting his own personal brand of polytonality. He was also trying to complete the second piano piece which he had promised his daughter as a companion to the 'un-named' (the *Nocturne*). He had made a start before leaving for Durham, writing to Imogen: 'I've done nothing else these two days ... and my idea was to get something down on paper and then ask you to rewrite it and make it sound more or less like music. But I've just crawled through it twice (Molto Adagio instead of Vivace) and it really isn't fit to be seen even by you. So I'll put it aside until I come back ... It's a jig—probably. And I think the "un-named" is a nocturne. Do you?'[20]

On his return from Durham Holst reviewed the tunes jotted in his notebook. 'The first try through was most depressing,' he wrote, 'But after that I settled down to sort them out and I think quite a lot of the tunes will do.'[21] He then set off for two days in Oxford and the Cotswolds with Isobel, Imogen, and his niece Valerie, writing to Whittaker: 'I shall be in the Cotswolds with a New York actress with whom I fell in love. She will be accompanied by her aunt and cousin but they are old pals of mine and they won't get in the way seriously so I am looking forward to a good time.'[22] After this brief holiday he tried to get down to composition, but with little success: 'I've not had much luck. I'm feeling obstinate and I stick in my room by the hour but there is not much to show for it ... I wish I didn't feel such a damn dull fool and could spoil more music paper.'[23] On 23 August he conducted three movements from *The Planets* in a BBC promenade concert broadcast from the Queen's Hall, and during the following few days conducted rehearsals for the forthcoming Three Choirs Festival. Then on 31 August he left London by train for Oxford, on the first stage of his journey to Worcester for the Festival. After taking a bus as far as Burford, he set off on foot through the Cotswolds via

Wyck Rissington, visiting William Webb (his first harmonium pupil) and other old friends in celebration of 'the 40th anniversary of my Wyck organistship',[24] and also nearby Bourton-on-the-Water, where he stayed overnight with Cecil Wilkins at his family home in the centre of the village. The following day he walked to Winchcomb, accompanied for part of the way by nineteen-year-old David Wilkins, son of Edgar Wilkins. After another overnight stop at Malvern Link, Holst arrived in Worcester on 4 September, in time for the opening service of the Festival. On 7 September he conducted the ballet music from *The Perfect Fool*, and the following day *The Hymn of Jesus*, both of which were successful, and by 9 September was back in Malvern Link. After accepting a lift part of the way, he set out to walk over Bredon Hill to Overbury and thence to Broadway. Shipston on Stour, and Banbury, a total distance of some forty miles.

Once again term started at St Paul's, and although his friends had often urged him to reduce his teaching, he knew that it had become a part of his life which would be difficult to give up. His modest income from teaching was not so important at this time—as he wrote to Helen Bidder, offering her financial help after the death of her father: 'For the first time in my life I have more money than I need—just at a time when everyone else is hard up. It is partly owing to living in Harvard being cheaper than I had expected and partly to having been paid in dollars with the pound off gold standard.'[25]

He accepted several conducting engagements, and by way of relaxation took up the trombone again in preparation for a performance of Vaughan Williams's *Fantasia on Christmas Carols* to be given at St Paul's Girls' School at the end of term. But he was not yet in perfect health, and wrote to Whittaker on 17 October: 'I find it impossible to sit up at night. Although I am quite well the doctor tells me that I have got to go easy because my blood is not up to the mark either in quantity or quality as a result of my trouble in America. This should all come to an end, I hope, next Easter, but until then I must live as quietly as possible ... The worst of this business is that I cannot write. When I settle down to compose I usually fall asleep. However, it is only temporary.'[26]

On 29 October Holst was the guest of honour at the Annual General Meeting of the Music Teachers' Association, held at the Langham Hotel in London. The meeting was followed by a concert of his works, including pieces for string orchestra, part-songs for mixed and female voices, solo songs sung by Rose Morse accompanied by Vally Lasker, and piano pieces played by Imogen and Helen Bidder. Other performances during the term included the Second Group of *Choral Hymns from the Rig Veda* in Edinburgh on 6 November, the *Ode on a Grecian Urn* at the Queen's Hall on 10 December, the first performance of *Good Friday* (second of the *Six Choruses*) by the Westminster Abbey Choir on 13 December, and two Scottish premières: *The Cloud Messenger* on 16 December, and *Egdon Heath* the following day, both in Glasgow. Holst was content to leave the conducting of these performances to others, but insisted on playing the trombone in the St Paul's school orchestra when Vaughan Williams came to conduct his *Fantasia* just before Christmas.

Term ended on 20 December, and by way of celebration Holst set out on two one-day walks, the first through Southwark, Rotherhithe, Greenwich and Poplar to Barking, and the second from Barking to Theydon Bois, returning by train. Then on 23 December he travelled by train to Bishop's Stortford and walked via Takeley and Bambers Green to the cottage at Great Easton where he spent Christmas. On Boxing Day he wrote to Whittaker: 'We've had a week's sunshine in Essex and I had a lovely though distinctly middle-aged walk here. I hope to walk back another way into town and then come out again before term begins.'[27] But when the time came to do so he was unable to manage it: he lacked the stamina required for sustained country walking, and suffered a relapse from which it took him several months to recover.

However, the enforced physical idleness of illness prompted his brain into action, and he found with pleasure that he was able to compose once more, despite the distracting environment of the London nursing home in which he was confined. During his preceding 'blank' period he had been unable to fulfil commissions, such as a request to contribute a setting of words by James Joyce for inclusion in *The Joyce Book* (published in 1933), but he now started work on a piece for viola and

orchestra, the *Lyric Movement*, written for Lionel Tertis, and a
suite for the junior orchestra at St Paul's, subsequently given
the title *Brook Green Suite*.

In mid-January Holst replied to a letter from Dorothy Callard
about arrangements for a possible 1933 Whitsun festival at
Chichester: 'By all means have a Whitsun—and please tempt
me to come later on!'[28] Although he described himself at this
time as a 'gray haired old buffer',[29] he was still keen to be
actively involved in music-making, but was unsure as to what
state his health might be in by Whitsun. One invitation he
immediately accepted was a request to conduct a concert at
Her Majesty's Theatre in Carlisle on 12 February. This event
was in memory of his uncle Henry Ambrose Lediard, and
consisted of various works by Holst for military band, brass
band, chorus, and solo voice, including the first performance of
How Mighty are the Sabbaths from the *Six Choruses*. The
concert also included a military band work by Imogen, *The
Unfortunate Traveller*, which she conducted herself—perhaps
the first time a military band had ever been conducted by a
woman (she was later to conduct many performances and
recordings of her father's band music).

On 15 March Holst had a discussion with Lionel Tertis at St
Paul's Girls' School about the *Lyric Movement*, but the
following day had to take to his bed, and his engagements for
the next month were cancelled. He wrote to Whittaker: 'Just
now I'm in bed for three weeks on a milk diet in order to get rid
of the last vestige of that ulcer,'[30] but it was to be some time
before he could make an attempt at returning to his normal
activities. During April and May he led the restricted life of an
invalid and was unable to attend the Whitsun festival directed
by Vally Lasker in Chichester Cathedral at the beginning of
June. His diet was restricted to milk, eggs, fish, vegetable
purées, and brown bread, with a little chicken, lamb, and tea or
weak coffee, but he was forbidden beef, sausages, game, all
spiced foods, salads, new bread, and alcohol. By the end of June
he had regained sufficient strength to be able to go on a trip to
Gregynog to hear Dora Herbert Jones sing Welsh folk-songs
once again, and his doctors allowed him to teach for one day a
week at St Paul's.

At this juncture he received a request from a Hollywood author, Vadim Uraneff, to write some music for a pageant entitled *The Song of Solomon*. Uraneff had already obtained permission from Holst's publishers to include extracts from *The Planets* in the production, but needed some additional music. He therefore asked Holst to compose some music especially for the pageant, hoping that he would approve of the way in which the *Planets* extracts were to be used. Holst replied that he would be pleased to write the required music, but stipulated that no alterations should be made to the music of *The Planets*; if a particular section were too long, it should be simply faded out on a suitable chord. In the event it seems that the pageant was never produced, and apart from a few manuscript fragments now in the British Library, the music written by Holst cannot now be traced—perhaps it exists in some private collection in the USA. Another request he received was for some film music, which he also accepted despite his depressing experiences with *The Bells*, but like the pageant this project also came to nothing, and any music Holst may have written for it seems to have disappeared.

A small composition written under more auspicious circumstances was a canon composed for the marriage of Adrian and Ann Boult on 1 July 1933. After the ceremony, Holst handed the couple an envelope inscribed: 'To be opened in Italy and not before',[31] which in due course was found to contain a two-part setting of Marlowe's poem *Come live with me and be my love*, with the title *A Canon for A and A* 'from GH, for use in Italy, King's Langley, Gregynog and other nice places'.[32] At this time he also wrote a setting of James Elroy Flecker's *O Spiritual Pilgrim* for the Gregynog Choir, which was performed there in July 1933.

Holst also had more substantial works on his mind; on 30 July he started work on a *Scherzo*, finishing the first sketch on 18 August. This was intended as part of a full-scale symphony, his first purely orchestral work in this form since the *Cotswolds Symphony* of 1899–1900, but for reasons of health he was unable to compose the remainder of the work, although he did manage to orchestrate the *Scherzo* between bouts of illness. In many ways this movement is a summing up of

Holst's orchestral art. It begins with an angular syncopated
figure which is soon abandoned in favour of a more conventional 6/8 rhythm, with querky turns of phrase and sudden
changes of mood. Chromatic brass portamentos recall the
Prelude of *Hammersmith*, and a sudden cut-off leaving a soft
chord hanging in mid-air echoes the magic of *Uranus*. The
ending is rather abrupt, provoking speculation as to what kind
of music Holst might have had in mind to follow this
symphonic movement.

On 8 September he finished the first sketch of the *Brook
Green Suite*, and on the 16th completed a two-piano version of
the *Scherzo*, so that it could be tried through in his room at St
Paul's. The new term began on 20 September, and on the
following day, Holst's birthday, there was an informal celebratory concert at the school, during which his new *Canons*
were sung; probably their first complete performance. On 26
September (Nora Day's birthday) he finished making a copy of
the two-piano version of the *Scherzo*, inscribing it: 'Scherzo for
two pianos and The Birthday of Nora Day'.[33]

At the beginning of October there was a sudden spate of
correspondence in *The Times* concerning the hymn *O Valiant
Hearts*. The music critic of the paper had complained about a
new tune by the Revd. C. Harris which had been set to John
Arkwright's words, describing it as 'disastrous' and a 'bad copy
of the worst type of nineteenth-century hymn tune'.[34] After
faintly praising the original tune (*Ellers*) by E. J. Hopkins, the
critic went on to suggest that 'Farley Castle' by Henry Lawes
would be an ideal tune for the hymn, which had become
'generally accepted as a feature of services commemorative of
the men who fell in the war', a topical subject as the annual
Armistice remembrance ceremonies were soon to be held.
Charles Harris wrote to say that the words had originally been
written to go with *his* tune, and not for *Ellers* at all, while
several correspondents wrote in support of Holst's setting. The
last word was had by the Revd. L.T. Towers, who commented:
'To my mind Holst's magnificent setting in "Songs of Praise"
suffers from the drawback of so many modern tunes, in that it
is too difficult for average congregational singing and requires
the musical ability of a trained choir. The most essential

characteristic of any setting to "O Valiant Hearts" should surely be that it can be sung with heart and voice by the ordinary man, and this requirement "Ellers" eminently and nobly fulfils.' Holst did not allow himself to be drawn into this controversy, although there was certainly a case to be made in defence of his own setting, which was intended not for specially-trained choirs, but for ordinary congregational singing.

On 11 October Archibald Davison and his wife arrived on a visit to England, and Holst was determined to repay the hospitality which he had received from them during his stay at Harvard: 'They were most kind to me last year and I want them to have a first rate time now.'[35] But he was unable to put this into effect as he was taken ill again soon after their arrival, spending most of the following weeks in bed. It was however an opportunity to turn his thoughts to music, and on 18 October he began work on the music for the *Song of Solomon* while still in his bed.

By December 1933 his health had not improved, and three days before Christmas he was admitted to New Lodge Clinic, Windsor Forest, for treatment and a series of X-rays and other tests. While in the clinic he received a letter from Vaughan Williams saying that he had taken Holst's advice and expunged the 'nice' tunes from the Finale of his Fourth Symphony—a demonstration of the continued respect which Vaughan Williams had for Holst's opinion after nearly forty years of friendship. Holst also heard from Adrian Boult that the first performance of the *Lyric Movement* was to be given in a BBC broadcast the following March, and that there was also to be a broadcast of the *First Choral Symphony* in April, with a chorus of 200 voices and a semi-chorus of 'trained professional singers' numbering 40. Holst was hoping to be well enough to attend these performances, and perhaps also the 1934 Whitsun festival, writing to Dorothy Callard: 'I fear we must wait until I'm let loose before considering Whitsuntide. But I hope it won't mean waiting much longer!'[36]

At the beginning of the new year he wrote: 'I have been here during Xmas and hope to be let loose in a fortnight in the condition of 100% The Man instead of something on a fifty-fifty basis.'[37] But he was still in the clinic at the end of January when the first performance of *The Wandering Scholar* was given in the Davis Lewis Theatre, Liverpool, by the University of Liverpool Muisc Society conducted by J. E. Wallace. Holst sent his best wishes to the performers (who included Irene Eastwood, later known as Anne Ziegler, in her first role as Alison) and was pleased when the producer Frederick Wilkinson visited the clinic a few days later to tell him how the performance had gone.

In addition to worries about his health, Holst was concerned about his inability to carry out his teaching obligations at St Paul's Girls' School, and therefore decided to resign from his post as Director of Music. He wrote to the High Mistress, Miss Strudwick (who had succeeded Miss Gray in 1927), with the result that she appeared at the clinic the very next day and firmly put him in his place. He described the incident in a letter to Amy Kemp: 'After reckoning up the months I have been away from school during the last two years and adding the possible period the doctors had just told me I might have to be away in the near future, I wrote to Miss Strudwick and suggested that I really ought to resign. Her reply was a Perfect Crusher! She and Vally came yesterday and I grovelled before her.'[38]

Holst endured his treatment in the clinic with good spirits but by February it was clear that there had been little improvement in his health. On 11 February he wrote to Adrian Boult: 'If my ulcer has not healed by the 22nd the doctors suggest my leaving the nursing home and either having an operation or leading a "restricted life". I shall certainly do the latter in order to get further advice on the matter. But "restricted life" will mean no going out at night (amongst other disablements) so that I shall not be able to come to the concert on March 18 [first performance of the *Lyric Movement*]. So please invite me to all the rehearsals.'[39]

On 23 February 1934 Edward Elgar died at the age of seventy-six, and many people felt that an era had now come to an end in English music. A few days later Holst left the clinic to ponder over his own future, and soon received news that his friend Norman O'Neill had died on 3 March after a motor accident. On 5 March Holst wrote to Boult:

I left the clinic 10 days ago unhealed. The doctors there wanted me to be operated on at once as they said I was in such good condition. I did not feel so at all and felt and still feel much disappointed and quite cross. I have gone back to my regular doctor who is a sensible unpretentious G.P. But he feels that as medicine has failed I ought to try surgery. A year ago I wanted to (he was against it then) because I thought that surgery was a matter of kill or cure and I'm all for that. But now they tell me that at my age the only really useful operation would take me probably a year to get over!!! So I've warned my G.P. that I'm thinking of trying quacks and he has promised not to be huffy. But for the next week or so I want to try and lead a quiet normal life and to think things over and to lose my bad temper. I've no brains for spoiling music paper yet and am not allowed to wave a stick so Misses Day and Lasker do the latter for me when I teach and the nearest I get to the former is to correct extremely badly copied parts.[40]

He was however able to hear one of his recent compositions tried through at St Paul's: the *Brook Green Suite*, named after the green on which the school stands. He had written four movements: *Prelude, Gavotte, Air*, and *Jig*, but after listening to the rehearsal he decided that the *Gavotte* did not go with the other movements and withdrew it, changing the title of the last movement to *Dance* (the *Gavotte* was eventually arranged for recorders by Imogen Holst and published separately). The music is simple in concept, and more sparsely scored than the earlier *St Paul's Suite*, with a virtual absence of octave doublings. The *Prelude* is serene and folk-like in character, with modal touches in the melody; the *Air* has the quality of a courtly dance, with a hint of a Ravellian cadence; and in the Fnale he managed to incorporate a tune which he had heard in a marionette theatre in Sicily during his 1929 holiday without any sense of incongruity to the English country-dance atmosphere.

Dorothy Callard was at this first rehearsal; she had joined the Morley College orchestra after taking up the double-bass a few weeks previously, and had been practising the scale of C major. Holst asked her to come to the school for the try-through of the Suite, whereupon she found that her part had several descending C major scales, except for one passage which was full of accidentals. 'When I met this I stopped,' she recalled. 'He asked me, very innocently, why, and when I said I couldn't manage that, he said in a loud stage whisper, "Play the same old C major with lots of mistakes". So I obliged, and at the end he said "You know, that wasn't what I wrote but I rather think I like your version better than mine" and he took out his pencil and made some alterations in the score. When I hear the Suite broadcast, I often wonder which were the notes I composed.'[41]

Following this brief spell of activity, Holst again suffered a relapse, but by 12 March he was up and about again, writing to Boult: 'This is my first day out of bed. The attack was a very slight one but I've got to go easy and shall not be allowed to come to either the rehearsals [of the *Lyric Movement*] or concert next week-end. But I hope to listen in ... My present idea is to get the only two doctors in London who have done me any good so far—the Ealing one, Dr Hobbs and William Brown—to tackle me together.'[42]

Two days later he was feeling much better and planned to be at St Paul's the following week ('Also I've done a little scoring!' he wrote[43]). But in the event his strength was not up to it and he had to give up any idea of being present in the studio when the *Lyric Movement* was broadcast. He wrote to Boult: 'You and Tertis are to have an absolutely free hand over my new thing. Just do what you like with it. And accept my thanks in advance, also my blessing. And the same to LT and the other players.'[44] Holst listened to the broadcast on a radio which Boult had provided for his sick-room, and was very pleased with the performance, especially as Lionel Tertis had gone to the trouble of discussing the work in detail with him beforehand so as to be sure of complying exactly with the composer's wishes. As with his other works for solo performers, the *Lyric Movement* is not a vehicle for virtuosity, but thoughtful music in which the soloist contributes an essential part to the overall design, contrasting his single line against the sound of the orchestra. Although the improvisatory beginning is reminiscent of the opening of the 'Song' of the *First Choral Symphony*, Holst managed to avoid many of the mannerisms which had permeated his work in the previous ten years or so, and achieved a free, relaxed lyricism, harking back to earlier works such as the *Invocation* of 1911, contained in a rhapsodic but well-organized form. Despite this, the result seemed rather dull and not entirely idiomatic for the instrument, and these factors, together with the unfamilarity of the style prevented its qualities from being immediately appreciated by the performers. Writing many years later, the violist Bernard Shore recalled: 'It made on us the usual impression of the later Holst —bare, impersonal music, terribly aloof. Tertis himself was mystified at first ... but the *Lyric Movement* is now appreciated as a cherished gift to the viola player.'[45]

Another broadcast which Holst listened to took place on 11 April when the *First Choral Symphony* was performed by the BBC Symphony Orchestra and Chorus conducted by Adrian Boult. Holst had previously written to Boult suggesting Dorothy Silk as soloist: 'If you honour me by doing my Choral Symphony I want you to have a free hand. But the more I think of it the more I want D. Silk,'[46] but in the event the solo part was taken by Miriam Licette. Holst was to have been represented at the rehearsals by Vaughan Williams, but he too was ill at this time and was unable to attend any of them, having to be content, like Holst, with listening to the broadcast over the radio.

During his convalescence Holst had been turning over in his mind the alternative possibilities of leading a 'restricted life' or of undergoing a major operation, eventually deciding on the latter course. At the end of April he entered Beaufort House nursing home at Ealing, but the operation could not be carried out immediately because of his weak and anaemic condition. Clifford Bax visited him there and was shocked to discover that 'his lips were as white as his face'.[47] On 1 May, Holst wrote to Boult: 'Just heard definitely that my "op" (not a musical one) is postponed for 2½ or 3 weeks.'[48] He passed the time by working through some algebraic problems from Durrell's textbook, making suggestions on R. O. Morris's draft for his forthcoming book *The Structure of Music*, doing a little scoring ('although its very uncomfortable in bed'[49]), and writing letters to his friends. The annual Whitsun festival was to be held at Chichester, and on 18 May Holst sent a postcard to the vicar of Bosham, the Revd. George Street (with whom he had sometimes stayed) bearing a message of greeting to all the participants in the festival, ending with optimism: 'And I wish myself the joy of your Fellowship at Whitsuntide 1935.'[50] On 20 May he wrote to Adine O'Neill after hearing her give a broadcast recital: 'Dear Adine, The great treat is just over and so I write at once to thank you very much for it. But I hope I shall never have to go so long without hearing you—it must be nearly a year which is ridiculous. One thing that will help to bring us together soon is that my operation is fixed for next Wednesday. It is a great relief after all this waiting. Nora and Vally will keep you and the rest of St Paul's posted up with the latest news.'[51]

On 23 May he underwent a major operation at Beaufort House for removal of the duodenal ulcer. The surgery took three hours to carry out, and afterwards the hospital announced that although the operation had been successful, he would not be out of danger for three days and that convalescence was 'bound to be slow'. In fact the operation had been a severe shock to his entire system, and the struggle to recover proved to be too great, with the result that two days later, on 25 May, he died of heart failure. Isobel was constantly at his bedside, but he failed to recognize her on recovering from the anaesthetic, and eventually 'passed away quietly and peacefully like a little child'.[52]

Holst's family and friends were stunned—they had realized the risks involved but had not really prepared themselves for this worst possible outcome. His wider circle of musical associates were also deeply shocked, especially a group of singers who were to give a concert in the little Saxon church at Greensted in Essex the following day. Holst had supervised some of the rehearsals, and had made the singers promise that whatever should happen to him, they were to carry on with the concert under the direction of Albert Cox, one of the basses. Dorothy Callard recalled the scene on that day:

We went down by coach, and we cried all the way. When we got to Greensted Sir Adrian Boult came out to meet us. The lanes were lined with cars, and the church was overfull. We said we were sorry but we couldn't possibly go through with the music. Sir Adrian said: 'You know what you promised'. So we went into the church, red-eyed and red-nosed. We said we would start with 'Ave verum' as we could do that from memory. Sir Adrian gave us the chord, and we made a dreadfully wavering watery start, but as soon as we heard ourselves, something happened, and we went through the programme without any distress. Afterwards we agreed that it was Mr Holst who was conducting us, not Bert Cox.'[53]

The whole musical world was similarly shocked, and obituary notices appeared in all the major national newspapers and musical publications. At the beginning of June, Isobel wrote to Bishop Bell asking permission for Holst's ashes to be buried in Chichester Cathedral: 'I am really glad now that he has passed on,' she explained, 'because if he had lived he would have been an invalid and he would have been most unhappy. I was with him to the end and his going out was so peaceful and beautiful and he suffered no pain.'[54]

19

Epilogue
(1934–)

Soon afterwards, news came that Frederick Delius had died at Grez-sur-Loing on 10 June at the age of seventy-two, so that in that year three of the foremost British composers, Elgar, Holst, and Delius died within a few months of each other.

On 19 June a Holst memorial service was held by St Paul's Girls' School at St John's, Smith Square. Bishop Bell gave an address in which he paid tribute to Holst's life and work, the school choir sang music by some of his favourite composers, and Rose Morse and Dorothea Walenn performed two of the *Four Songs* for voice and violin.

The BBC organized a Holst Memorial Concert on 22 June, broadcast from Studio X at Waterloo Bridge, where Holst himself had conducted many performances, and which could accommodate up to 250 people. Besides the orchestra and chorus, there would be room for 20 members of the BBC staff, and a further 85 places for family, friends, Paulinas, Morleyites, and the press. Adrian Boult conducted the BBC orchestra and the Wireless Chorus (augmented by singers from Morley College) and the programme consisted of a representative selection from Holst's works: three movements from the *Suite de Ballet*, three of the *Choral Hymns from the Rig Veda* from Groups Two and Three (in which Sidonie Goossens played the harp part), the *Dirge for Two Veterans*, *Egdon Heath*, the *Ode to Death*, and *Turn Back, O Man*. Ralph Vaughan Williams gave an introductory talk before the music began.

On Sunday 24 June (midsummer day), Holst's ashes were buried in the north transept of Chichester Cathedral beneath a paving stone just below the wall memorial to Thomas Weelkes, a spot where his singers had stood to sing Weelkes's music during the Whitsun festivals. The service was conducted by Bishop Bell, and singers from St Paul's Girls' School and Morley College conducted by Vaughan Williams sang Weelkes's *Let Thy Merciful Ears*, the Kyrie from Vaughan Williams's *Mass in G minor*, and music by Holst, including *This Have I Done for My True Love* and *Turn Back, O Man*.

During the following months music by Holst was performed by various musicians and singers in their concert and recital programmes by way of tribute, including Astra Desmond, Rose Morse, the Newcastle Bach Choir and the Oriana Madrigal Society. On 20 October the Society of Woman Musicians presented a concert in memory of Delius, Holst, and Norman O'Neill, and on 3 November the Royal Choral Society presented a concert conducted by Malcolm Sargent in honour of Holst, Delius, and Elgar, which included *The Planets* and the *Ode to Death*.

Following Holst's death, there was the usual flurry of obituary appreciations and reminiscences, followed by the inevitable period of neglect. Some enthusiasts were determined to keep Holst's name alive, such as Havergal Brian, who declared: 'There should be a Holst Society in every shire of England and in every capital town of the Colonies,'[1] but it was left to Imogen Holst to shoulder the main burden of the task, and through her unstinting devotion to her father's music, his work was sustained through a period of indifference, to be appreciated anew in the changed world of the late twentieth century. Other musicians also contributed to keeping the name of Holst before the public, particularly Adrian Boult, whose performances of *The Planets* did much to make the work an enduring popular success.

As early as November 1934, Boult was making efforts to secure a hearing for some of Holst's lesser-known works. He wrote to Adine O'Neill and Nora Day at St Paul's about the possibility of arranging a broadcast performance of *The Vision of Dame Christian*, despite Holst's own stipulation that the music should never be performed outside the School. The High Mistress, staff, and governors were keen on the idea, but undecided whether to comply with Holst's wishes or go against them in the interests of bringing his music to the attention of a wider public. Leslie Woodgate attended a performance of the Masque a few months later and described it as 'One of the most impressive and beautiful things I have seen for years. The simplicity and charm with which it was performed has left an indelible impression on my mind. Gustav Holst's music, though written in his early manner, was so refreshing and fitted into the picture so perfectly, that it gave me the impression of being other-worldly.'[2]

At Ottershaw College near Woking, a scholarship was founded in memory of Holst, and record companies began to look at their catalogues with a view to increasing their coverage of his works; Decca recorded the *St Paul's Suite* in a performance by the Boyd Neel String Orchestra, which was issued the following February.

On 6 February 1935 Adrian Boult conducted the BBC Symphony Orchestra at the Queen's Hall in the première performance of the *Scherzo*, which Holst had completed just before his death, but had never heard. Because of its brevity and unfamiliarity Boult later suggested that it should be performed twice in one concert: 'It is fiendishly difficult to play, and I imagine not too easy to listen to, and so I think a case for immediate repetition might be made.'[3] The *Musical Times* later wrote of the *Scherzo*: 'As it stands, it sounds too inconclusive, but it is characteristically angular, rather chilly in temperature, and European rather than national in style . . . as if Hindemith had taken a hand in a scherzo by Vaughan Williams.'[4]

Holst memorial concerts continued to be given by performers with whom he had been associated, particularly by the Oriana Madrigal Society, and also at Morley College, where a scheme was afoot for a more lasting and practical tribute to his life and work. Although since Holst's time the College had moved from its original premises to a different location in the Waterloo Bridge Road, students and staff still found the accommodation too cramped for the various activities which took place there, and although plans had been drawn up for an extension to the building it had been impossible to find the necessary funds during the years of the depression. However, in 1935 the Board of Education and the London County Council at last gave their consent to the scheme which had been postponed for some years, and a group of Holst's friends and admirers immediately launched an appeal for funds so that part of the new extension could be provided with a recital room and practice rooms as a fitting memorial to Holst. The leading figure in this campaign was Vaughan Williams, who used his influence to persuade several friends and associates to form a steering committee, including such distinguished figures as Hugh Allen, Adrian Boult, Bishop Bell, Archibald Davison, Gerald Forty, Frances Ralph Gray, Eva Hubback, J. W. MacKail, John Masefield, and W. G. Whittaker. They set about the task of raising money with enthusiasm, issuing a declaration that 'We feel that such a memorial as this will be one of which Holst himself would have approved, and which will in some measure help to carry on his work.'[5] Joan Western was appointed Secretary of the Fund, and contributions large or small were invited from anyone who admired Holst and his work.

By November plans for the Holst room were well advanced; the architect Edward Maufe had designed a fan-shaped room, giving special attention to the acoustics. The total amount of contributions to the Memorial Fund now stood at just over £800, and a determined effort was made to reach a target of £1,000 by fund-raising concerts given at Morley and elsewhere. Work on the extension began, and by the beginning of 1937 the Fund had reached a total of £1,100, which permitted the provision of two smaller teaching rooms in addition to the Holst room.

The work was quickly completed, and on 6 March 1937 Queen Mary visited the College to perform the opening ceremony. Isobel and Vaughan Williams were among those presented to the Queen, and after declaring the extension open, the royal visitor was taken on a tour of the premises while a quintet drawn from the South London (Morley College) orchestra of unemployed professional musicians provided light background music. When the official proceedings were over, the appeal committee held its own celebrations in the Holst Room. Vaughan Williams and J. W. MacKail spoke of Holst's work and music-making at Morley College, Imogen conducted the choir in some of her father's part-songs, and Harriet Cohen tried out the new Steinway grand piano whih had been specially selected by Myra Hess. The guests admired the unusual design of the room and the subtle use of woods: Jarrah for the floor and pear for the resonator at the back of the platform and the remainder of the woodwork. Special attention had been given to commemorating Holst's music: the planets were painted on the ceiling against a blue background, and on the outside of the windows the keystones also represented the planets, in carvings by Edmund Burton. In spite of the destruction of much of the building by enemy bombs in 1940, the Holst Room survived intact, and has since been used by generations of appreciative students.

But these activities were all the result of the determination and enthusiasm of Holst's friends and associates; in the musical world at large, interest in his music had already begun to wane. Writing in June 1936, Gerald Abraham reported: 'Today, barely two years after his death, his works are as rarely heard as Parry's or Stanford's,'[6] while two years later R. W. Wood complained that many of Holst's works were languishing in 'total oblivion'.[7] It was to counteract this state of affairs that Imogen Holst wrote her biography of Holst, published in 1938, but it was not until after the Second World War that a revival of interest took place, and then only after a hard and persistent struggle on the part of Miss Holst and other dedicated enthusiasts.

In 1944 Chester published the virtually unknown *Terzetto*, and in the same year His Master's Voice issued a recording of *The Hymn of Jesus* by the Huddersfield Choral Society and the Liverpool Philharmonic Orchestra conducted by Malcolm Sargent. HMV also recorded *The Planets* the following year, with the BBC Symphony Orchestra and Chorus conducted by Adrian Boult, the recording being made in Bedford where the orchestra had been evacuated because of the war. This was followed by discs of some of Holst's other works, but it was not until the advent of the long-playing record (and subsequently the compact disc) that recordings were able to do full justice to the colour and dynamic range of his larger compositions.

In 1949–50 Curwen published Holst's original two-piano version of *The Planets* from the manuscript which had been in the possession of Vally Lasker since his death, and 1951 saw the publication of Imogen Holst's second book, *The Music of Gustav Holst*. In that year the English Opera Group presented *The Wandering Scholar* at the Cheltenham Festival in a version especially prepared by Benjamin Britten and Imogen Holst, and in 1954 Robert Cantrick conducted a performance of the original band version of *Hammersmith* in Pittsburgh, Pennsylvania, using parts which he had prepared from the long-neglected manuscript score. But by the mid-1950s interest in Holst's music in Britain had sunk to a low ebb, and the distractions of the continental avant-garde led many critics to dismiss both Holst and Vaughan Williams as antediluvian representatives of the native 'cow- pat' school of composition. But some were more perceptive; the magazine *Musical Opinion* compared Holst's position with that of Vaughan Williams: 'History . . . was against Holst. He was cosmopolitan at the wrong moment. What was required, and supplied by Vaughan Williams, was the selfconscious, militant national ideal. Holst, often, was an exotic, an alien, and thus historically unacceptable. Vaughan Williams, by one of those ironic twists of cultural fate, has cleared the path for an appreciation of Holst's art, which in so many ways stands closer to the music of our own day than does Vaughan Williams's own.'[8]

In 1956, at the age of eighty-four, Vaughan Williams founded the RVW Trust so that the income from his royalties could be used for the benefit of other musicians, and one of the first acts of the Trustees was to arrange a concert of Holst's lesser-known works in the Royal Festival Hall on 10 December 1956. The concert was conducted by Adrian Boult, and consisted of the *Ode to Death*, *Egdon Heath*, the *Fugal Overture*, *Assemble, All Ye Maidens* (from the *Seven Part-Songs*), *The Morning of the Year*, *A Choral Fantasia*, the *Perfect Fool* ballet music, and the *Fugal Concerto*. Such was the level of interest in Holst's music at that time that the hall was half empty, but those who did attend were enthusiastic about the music, much of which had not been heard for many years.

Throughout the 1950s and 1960s interest in Holst's music gradually increased and recordings began to proliferate, especially of *The Planets*, which became one of the best-known works in the recorded repertoire. This revival of interest was largely due to the tireless work of Imogen Holst, whose advocacy of her father's music through lectures, broadcasts, concerts, and recordings did much to change the views of the listening public. In the years since the composer's death, musical fashions had changed considerably, and audiences now found it easier to listen to his music objectively without being blinkered by the natural antipathy which follows any period of musical history. Besides her many and varied activities, Imogen Holst found time to attend to such practical matters as the placing of commemorative plaques on houses where Holst had lived. The approach of the centenary of Holst's birth assisted her in the task of persuading others of the justice of her cause, and besides an increasing number of performances, recordings and broadcasts of his music there were plans to commemorate his life and work by opening to the public the house in which he was born in Cheltenham. This was put into effect by the Cheltenham Borough Council, with the aid of a public appeal launched by Arthur Bliss, Master of the Queen's Music.

The centenary year of 1974 was a whirl of activity for Imogen Holst, who had the satisfaction of seeing the fruition of her dedicated labour throughout many difficult years, and in recognition of her work she was awarded a CBE in the subsequent New Year's honours list. Exhibitions on Holst's life and work were shown during the Aldeburgh Festival (of which Imogen Holst was an artistic director) and at the Royal Festival Hall, while at St Paul's Girls' School a number of events were organized, including the recording for the first time of the music for *The Vision of Dame Christian*. For this project, a chorus and chamber orchestra of Old Paulinas were assembled and conducted by Irene Swann, who as Irene Bonnett had been present at its first performance in 1909, had sung in the first performance of *The Planets* in 1918, and had played in the orchestra at the Thaxted festivals. A new wing at the school was named the Gustav Holst wing, a Holst Memorial Scholarship was founded, and the school orchestra was filmed playing the *St Paul's Suite* for a television programme about the composer.

Perhaps the most salutary effect of the centenary celebrations was to make Holst's music known to a wider public than ever before. Although the value of his work was recognized by musicians, and publications such as the Collected Facsimile Edition and the reissue of his own recording of *The Planets* would appeal to enthusiasts, it is only through mass media such as radio and television that the message can be communicated to the public at large. Holst himself said that although some people despise centenary celebrations, he thought that England needed 'at least one a week', declaring that: 'Only in England are the claims of her great composers almost ignored.'[9] He once made the dismal prediction: 'The epitaph that can be written on every British composer, with only one exception, is that 50 years after his death music in England was as if he had never lived.'[10] The exception which Holst had in mind was that of Henry Purcell, to whose illustrious achievements may now be added those of Holst himself.

20

The Legacy

Although Holst did not become the leader of a 'school' of composition, his influence is none the less widespread, albeit unacknowledged or even unrecognized. Imogen Holst remarked that listeners sometimes comment that *The Planets* is full of quotations; ample evidence that hard-pressed film and television composers have often turned to this work for inspiration, with the result that the public's familiarity with the original is often via such second-hand sources. Many of Holst's own compositions have been used as incidental and background music to radio and television programmes (*Mars* was used particularly successfully in a BBC radio serialization of H. G. Wells's *The War of the Worlds*) and have therefore entered the collective subconscious of the listening public; many people might recognize the music without having any idea as to the identity of the composer.

Nor have creative musicians escaped the influence of Holst: specific instances abound, particularly in the work of Vaughan Williams, who described Holst as 'the greatest influence on my music'.[1] Although Vaughan Williams's musical personality was more robust and forthright, using traditional materials in new ways rather than seeking fresh paths, he admired his friend's work so much that stylistic traits inevitably crept into his own music. This is perhaps most apparent in the *Pastoral Symphony* of 1922, the Fourth Symphony (written a year after Holst's death) which uses perfect fourths extensively and has a typically Holstian tritone relationship in the Scherzo, the Sixth Symphony of 1948, whose pianissimo Finale ends with an alternation of two chords in the manner of *Neptune*, the *Sinfonia Antarctica* of 1953, and the 1926 cantata *Flos Campi*, although Holst himself said that he 'couldn't get hold of' this last work and was disappointed by it.[2] Moreover, this influence was mutual; despite their differences of outlook and creative methods, Holst firmly believed in objective principles in art, and it was therefore unimportant to him that Vaughan Williams pursued a different path from his own; it was his musical opinion which mattered most.

Technical features such as the characteristic tritone key relationship appear in the music of several later composers, noticeably in the *War Requiem* of Benjamin Britten, who was an admirer and editor of Holst's work, and whose church parables such as *Curlew River* emulate the economy of *Savitri*, while fleeting reminiscences of melody and orchestral texture appear in the works of William Walton (First Symphony and *Belshazzar's Feast*) and Holst's pupil Edmund Rubbra. Holst's angular, asymmetrical scherzo style crops up in the Allegro section of Matyas Seiber's cantata *Ulysses*, and the introduction to the same work has something of the atmosphere of the beginning of *Hammersmith*, even including parallel triad chords for the trombones. Whether composers outside Britain have been much influenced by Holst's music is more difficult to ascertain, although during the 1920s *The Planets* was widely performed internationally and would have been well known to musicians in many countries. The rising fourths motif from *Jupiter* can be heard in Aaron Copland's *Appalachian Spring* (although here typically derived from the basic material), while its characteristic rhythm appears in Prokofiev's *Peter and the Wolf* of 1936. The unaccompanied opening of the Lament in Holst's *Double Concerto* has the lean, contrapuntal atmosphere of much of Shostakovich's later music, and there is a brief passage in Stravinsky's ballet *Agon* which bears a resemblance in orchestral texture to a similar passage in *Egdon Heath*. *The Hymn of Jesus* may be regarded as a precursor of Stravinsky's later religious works, such as the *Symphony of Psalms* and the hieratic serial cantatas, although it is doubtful whether Stravinsky was familiar with, or even aware of this work (if he were, such an influence would nicely return his own influence on Holst of many years before). Although direct connection in these cases is doubtful, or even improbable, they do show that Holst was forward-looking in his musical thinking, rather than fossilized in the English pastoral tradition, in which he is often categorized.

Perhaps the most significant artistic successor to Holst is

Michael Tippett, whose formative years as a music student in London coincided with the zenith of Holst's career; not simply because of superficial influences, such as the resemblance of the opening of the Ritual Dances in *The Midsummer Marriage* to *Mercury*, or because he continued the spirit of Holst's work as Director of Music at Morley College, but because he was one of the few British composers to develop Holst's notion of linear, contrapuntal music within a tonal framework, bringing this line of thought to a richer, more complex peak of achievement, based on a musical heritage stemming from Purcell, rather than being swayed by the lure of the Central European avant-garde. In the last movement of Holst's *Fugal Concerto* for example, passages of counterpoint between the upper lines and the bass foreshadow the taut, vigorous contrapuntal technique subsequently employed so successfully by Tippett in his works for string orchestra, while such moments as the sudden change of mood to woodwind and harp in Holst's late *Scherzo* and the instrumental passage in the coda to the Scherzo of the *First Choral Symphony* are pointers towards Tippett's first mature style. A striking feature of Tippett's second manner is his development of the juxtapositional possibilities of sectional structures, first explored by Holst in works such as *Egdon Heath*.

Later composers have reason to be grateful for Holst's work, even if they have not been specifically influenced by him or do not find themselves able to admire his music. As Wilfrid Mellers has written: 'Holst's importance as a representative figure lies in his honest pre-occupation with, rather than in his solution of, the problems which English composers are obliged to tackle. He was, indeed, one of the first to teach English composers of the twentieth century what these fundamental problems were,'[3] while Imogen Holst went further in declaring that 'The lessons he learnt so painfully are now taken for granted, and the mistakes he made will never have to be made again'[4] (although this contradicts Holst's own view that a composer learns most by making his own mistakes). She also remarked that her father made important achievements in bridging the gap between composer and listener, helping to 'put an end to the false distinction between music and contemporary music';[5] a malaise which has unfortunately reappeared in the latter part of the twentieth century.

Holst believed that the duty of a composer is to fulfil practical needs, and if music were needed for his school classes or for amateur musicians, he did not hesitate to supply it. He could thus quite easily write mundane arrangements of Christmas carols or hymn-tunes as well as major 'serious' works without any sense of incongruity. Whether a work was 'great' or not was of no concern to Holst, who devoted as much care to a song for voice and violin as he did to a full-scale choral symphony. As a result of this attitude, many people who may never have heard any of his major works, nor even of *The Planets*, have nevertheless derived great pleasure from hearing or singing such small masterpieces as the carol *In the Bleak Mid-winter*. Although Holst never sought popularity or success for its own sake, he would doubtless have been gratified to know that his music has given considerable pleasure to increasingly large numbers of people as the years go by.

Holst's lighter style still has a pervasive influence today, although doubtless quite unrecognized by the listeners it reaches. The 'signature tunes' used for popular radio and television programmes are heard by millions of people who perhaps would never consider listening to concert music, but such works as Arthur Wood's *Barwick Green* from his *Dale Dances* (used for the BBC radio programme *The Archers*) and Trevor Duncan's *Little Suite* (used for *Doctor Finlay's Casebook*) are direct descendants of Holst's *St Paul's Suite, Brook Green Suite*, and his suites for military band. In the words of Edmund Rubbra: 'His influence is lasting in the work of all of us who value directness and sincerity and who view music as not so much a secret preserve for the leisured few as a vital part of everyday life.'[6]

During his own lifetime Holst had few imitators: other British composers were content to acknowledge his achievements and go their own way, but the critics were markedly divided as to the worth of his music. It is remarkable how a group of professional writers could hold such diverse views of a composer who had achieved world-wide success, although it was perhaps this very success which turned some critics against him (one later referred to the 'suspicious popularity' of *The Planets*[7]). Robert H. Hull was moved to describe *Mars* as 'the least creditable' movement of *The Planets*, going on to declare: 'Here we see, at its weakest, Holst's devotion to rhythmic qualities. The rhythm is frankly barbaric and unimaginative. The harmonic usage is of a crudity which not even the title of the movement can be held to excuse. The claims of musical invention appear scarcely to have been considered,'[8] while Bernard van Dieren revealed his own prejudices by complaining that: 'His ever-recurring sequences of tritely articulated brief phrases and motives leave anything that even Tchaikovsky has perpetrated in this dreary field very literally panting behind.'[9]

In a 1934 obituary notice, Kaikhosru Sorabji assessed Holst as 'third-rate', and although crediting him with an unfashionable 'width of aim', went on to complain that 'Holst was lamentably lacking both in intellectual sweep, spaciousness of style, and any real magisterial authority of that unmistakable kind that marks the Master . . . The inadequacy of the man to grapple with the vast and mighty conceptions that, for want of a better word, one must say "inspired" him, was at times pitiful to the point of painfulness.' Sorabji was at pains to deny Holst even that quality which most others conceded to him; the personal identity of his works: 'Over all his work, as over so much of his contemporaries was a general nondescriptness, a lack of well-marked physiognomical characteristics, that made it, at least, for one among his audience, impossible to be able to say of any page or bar, that it was signed, definitely and unmistakeably, as any page of Elgar, Delius, or any other of the really outstanding figures of music.'[10]

Even his erstwhile friend and colleague Richard R. Terry was moved to write in 1927: 'Holst, who soared upwards to *The Planets*, has managed to weave his own winding sheet with "The Boar's Head", and to dig his own grave with his "Choral Symphony".'[11] When at a loss for specific examples of iniquity, certain critics simply resorted to insinuations about Holst's ancestry—as Dyneley Hussey wrote in 1928: 'His share of foreign blood may well account for something strange and alien in his works . . . There is something cold-blooded and repellent even in his best music.'[12]

Some critics suggested that Holst's technical gifts were not matched by a corresponding imaginative facility, and that his works were mere empty shells devoid of content or meaning.

W. J. Turner wrote in 1928: 'As a musician, Mr Holst may be compared with a highly trained political orator; he can speak eloquently and at length, but the value of what he has to say is nearly always completely negligible,'[13] and Dyneley Hussey remarked: 'Like the hero of his own comic opera *The Perfect Fool*, he is unable or unwilling to grasp his good fortune.'[14] These views contradict Holst's own admission that his technique was not always capable of dealing with the products of his imagination, and that for him composition usually meant a struggle to find the right notes. Moreover, it is clear that his works do stem from a creative imagination of considerable fertility, and do not dwell on technique for its own sake, but always use it for the expression of a higher creative purpose.

R. W. Wood wrote in 1938: 'Real originality—the originality that counts for something in the long run—is unselfconscious, involuntary, a matter of ingrained, automatic individuality of outlook, and not of artificial, technical explorativeness,'[15] and although Wood was here criticizing Holst, with hindsight it is easy to see that Holst did have such originality, and that any technical explorations he may have indulged in were simply a means to an end. This accounts for what Harvey Grace called the 'strange—even baffling—mixture of the hazardous and the calculated' in Holst's work,[16] and which led Hubert Foss to remark: 'Was there ever a musician who to such a degree combined dexterity of technique with angularity of outline and clumsiness of drawing?'[17] However, Edmund Rubbra justly pointed out that 'Art does not grow out of a deliberate choice of technique or method: art begins where selfconscious adaptation of other techniques and methods ends,'[18] and there is no doubt that Holst was able to surmount this barrier and to create music bearing the unmistakable imprint of his own artistic personality.

In 1919, when *The Planets* was about to make its mark on the musical world, Edwin Evans could foresee a glorious future for Holst, speculating: 'Will he join the ranks of the symphonists . . . or will he turn more and more to the composition of those massive choral works which have always been a characteristic feature of the English province? There is no reason why he should not fulfil both predictions.'[19] In the event, Holst combined both these prophesies in the *First Choral Symphony*, but the result was so removed from general expectation that it precipitated a decline in his public esteem, leading to the virtual isolation of his later years. For this he was himself partly to blame: instead of attempting to sustain his popularity, Holst chose to follow his own path regardless of public opinion, with the inevitable alienating result.

The process was summed up by Hubert Foss: 'What began as a real originality of outlook became almost a determination not to please with his music in the way other composers were trying to do. He was absorbed in the problem of being truthful. He was not blunt or outspoken in his compositions: he was deliberate in seeking precision of meaning to an almost irritating degree . . . His dislike of "padding" made him afraid of his own spontaneity. His native simplicity of outlook was cultivated by his own fears, and was complicated by a quite extraordinary intellectual power, a puzzle-solving power coupled with an introspective inquisitiveness. He was an explorer by type, an experimenter, for whom the writing of each new work was a process of discovery. We have the shyest of men producing music that can give us electric shocks: music that moreover is not very positive while it is assertive. Though it is not in the forefront of the attacking army of the English revival, this is music of reaction, not of action, music that will not charm, will not delight, will not be comfortable, lest it should be suspect.'[20] Eric Blom also drew attention to this lack of spontaneity in the works of Holst's later period: 'It would seem impossible to be so in earnest about one's intentions without appearing absolutely natural in the results; but to my mind that is exactly where Holst failed . . . Too much of what he wrote was over-deliberately contrived.' Blom considered Holst's music to be very original, but that it resulted from 'carefully-laid plans' rather than 'the direct outcome of inspiration'.[21]

In the years which have passed since these critical comments were written, the public have come to regard Holst's music in a different light. With the decline in organized religion, many listeners have come to seek in music some of the spiritual certainties which were previously realized only through faith. The enormity of the universe revealed by science cannot readily be grasped by the human brain, but the music of *The Planets* enables the mind to acquire some comprehension of the vastness of space where rational understanding fails. Holst sensed that through music the limitations of human thought could be transcended and concepts expressed which were not otherwise capable of formulation. As he wrote to Adrian Boult: 'Of course there is nothing in any of the planets (*my* planets I mean) that can be expressed in words.'[22] As Holst's concern with the planets was more astrological rather than astronomical, increased interest in 'alternative' disciplines such as astrology and Eastern religion and philosophy have provided additional points of contact with Holst's music for modern audiences. He himself once wrote: 'Great Art has the power of being obviously the product of its age and yet of equally obviously belonging to all ages,'[23] and he must have been particularly flattered to read Dan Godfrey's comment on *The Planets*: 'It is not music for a passing hour; it is an artistic creation to which we shall turn back in days to come with immense satisfaction and pride.'[24]

It is often said of composers that they were 'ahead of their time', but this is not applicable to Holst. He was of his time, in that he achieved considerable success during his lifetime, but he also created music which has relevance to all epochs—the same quality which can be discerned in the works of all great masters of musical composition. If he had not written *The Planets*, he would doubtless be regarded today as only a minor composer, but the popularity of that work had led many listeners to appreciate qualities in his other compositions which they might not otherwise have discovered.

In any other country but Britain, Holst would doubtless be revered as a national hero, but perhaps such adulation would be counter-productive, having the adverse effect of fossilizing his music in the past. Music cannot remain stagnant; it must constantly renew itself if it is to retain any of its vitality, so that besides admiring a past composer's work it is important to see how its qualities can relate to the music of our own time. A single lifetime is not long enough to achieve all, especially when cut short in Holst's case at a time of full maturity, and it is for later generations to take up the struggle and keep alive the principles in which he believed.

21

Holst's Musical Style

Holst made tantalizingly few statements about his methods of composition and the mental processes which led to the creation of his works. He believed that composers should get on with the business of creating music and leave analysis to critics, academics, and musicologists. When asked on one occasion about his work-in-progress, he retorted: 'Good gracious, I don't talk about what I'm doing until it's done.'[1] And when it was done, he was no less reticent. In response to a questionnaire circulated to several composers in 1928 he replied: 'I regret I cannot make any definite statement on the matter as I feel that the psychology of composition varies according to the composer much more than any writer has yet realised. It seems to me that in such matters as psychology and heredity a writer will start a theory and find plenty of examples, but will tend to ignore exceptions. Also I think that every composer has more than one way of writing. Finally, a composer is usually quite unconscious of what is going on and therefore easily deceived.'[2]

Although he declined to go into the reasoning behind his beliefs, they were none the less deeply held, and with a tenacity and conviction which could be disconcerting, even to his associates. Thomas Armstrong recalled his days as a student in Holst's composition class: 'His mind was full of plans for a choral symphony and the poetry of Keats: and he constantly quoted a letter of 1829 in which the poet was urging Shelley to be more disciplined in his writing "... you might curb your magnanimity, and be more of an artist, and load every rift of your subject with ore". And today, after 50 years I can see Holst as clearly as if it were yesterday, at an ink-stained table in the Royal College of Music, pencil in hand, emphasizing over and over again those last words of a sentence that greatly influenced his own work, leading him, at the end of his career, into efforts of concentration that made his music difficult even for those who most admired him.'[3]

Holst once wrote: 'I'm greatly averse to fixed principles in art and I like everything—form, melody, harmony, etc.—to grow out of the original inspiration which latter is one of the mysteries and therefore quite unfit for polite conversation!'[4] How these elements are to grow out of the initial idea we are not told: his reticence on such matters was clearly motivated by a belief that the music should speak for itself—if an explanation is required, then the music is not doing its job properly. Perhaps there was also an element of fear that once the inner workings of music are exposed, its mystery may be lost.

He had a strong distrust of theory for its own sake, and insisted that in art practice should come first and theory, if any, second. He compared the study of technique with studying the Parthenon from an engineering point of view: 'It is quite interesting and not dangerous as long as you do not imagine that it has any direct bearing on Art. You are learning facts about Art; but Art is a vision, complete in itself, and an intimate one.'[5]

Paradoxically, he also played down the importance of inspiration in his own music, declaring that: 'When I sit down to compose it is as though I were a mathematician attacking some absorbing problem.'[6] Evidence of this approach can be found in his work throughout his career; it is apparent that the music has been constructed by rational thought and the methods by which it has been done are often obvious, but the resulting effect generally transcends the means of construction, becoming something quite different with a unique character of its own. In Holst's own words: 'Above all, art is not the sum total of its details . . . Art is an emotion.'[7]

Despite this forthright declaration, his music is perhaps at its best when most restrained, operating within narrowly-confined stylistic and expressive limits. By this means, unrestricted self-indulgence can be avoided, to produce a kind of music which is capable of transcending the composer's self-imposed limitations. Holst believed that concentration on technique could produce the required transcendence, and went so far as to declare that 'The mastering of technical problems is the highest source of emotion';[8] that is, the most effective technique is that which enables the musical ideas to be communicated to the listener with the minimum technical impedance.

Holst's musical language developed gradually throughout his career, not only in the usual sense of continually building on technical expertise, but also by way of achieving a deeper self-knowledge, to create a kind of music which was most in keeping with his own musical nature. Having in his early years discovered the simplicity and economy of English folk-song, these factors stayed with him throughout his life, so that many of his later works seem sparse, even bare, in content and outline. But this exactly reflected his own insistence on paring down every idea to its essentials, refusing to admit any superfluous decoration or material which added nothing to the basic musical statement. Perhaps his lack of time and recurrent neuritis may have have influenced this attitude, as well as his interest in Eastern philosophy, all of which would have prompted a concentration on essentials, but it is clear that he considered functionalism to be valid in itself—if a musical motif or phrase served its purpose, there was no need to elaborate it.

This functionalism was rooted in clarity and directness of communication. Much of the deceptively simple music of his later years turns out to be much more subtle on closer inspection, and what may appear at first sight to be simple-minded is in reality carefully calculated to produce the maximum effect with the minimum of resources. He had a hatred of 'padding', which he felt got in the way of clear expression of the basic musical ideas, and would use complex techniques only when he felt they were essential for the musical result. As Vaughan Williams remarked: 'Holst had no use for half measures . . . what he wanted to say he said forcibly and directly. He . . . was not afraid of being obvious when the occasion demanded it—nor did he hesitate to be remote when remoteness expressed his purpose.'[9] Holst was thus willing to wear his heart on his sleeve, accepting the risk of being accused of naïvety, rather than disguising his basic musical thought behind a smokescreen of complications.

In many of Holst's works we find recurrence of particular motifs used in different ways or in slightly varied forms, as if he were constantly trying them out in new surroundings until he found their ideal setting. Thus, some motifs which originated in the *Phantastes* suite of 1911 were subsequently incorporated into the incidental music for the play *The Sneezing Charm*, eventually to find their true home in *The Perfect Fool* ballet music. Similarly, other motifs in *The Perfect Fool* were previously used in the *St Paul's Suite* of ten years before. Such methods made for slow technical progress (he was in fact in mid-career before he discovered that a 'fraction' line between the figures of a time-signature was unnecessary), and could be interpreted as a lack of creative invention. Holst once wondered whether such invention could be developed by writing several themes each day and then assessing them at the end of the week, and this eventually took the form of writing fragments in a notebook as and when he could, subsequently incorporating them in his works at a later date. He advocated slow dogged work, rather than facile speed, writing to Vaughan Williams in 1903: 'When you spoil good ideas is not that because you write too much—that is you go ahead too fast—instead of grinding away bar by bar which is the only true hard work?'[10]

Hand in hand with his insistence on clarity was a pragamatic attitude, resulting from constant contact with practical performance. His orchestral works contain many cued-in passages in case certain instruments are missing, and instructions on performance when the full complement of instruments is not available; he also made arrangements of several of his works for alternative ensembles, such as piano and strings. This attitude to instrumentation was often extended to the notes themselves; having himself been an orchestral musician, he understood the viewpoint of the players, always making their parts technically feasible though challenging, and would set great store by their opinion, often taking their remarks to heart to the extent of rewriting sections of his scores. As he wrote to Amy Kemp when sending her the manuscript of his recently completed *Toccata* for piano: 'If you find anything awkward to play *alter it!*'[11] In his early days he advocated rewriting all his compositions as a matter of course, writing to Vaughan Williams in 1903: 'Would it be good, do you think, for you to rewrite as a matter of course *everything* you write about six months after it is finished? (*Really* finished, not merely sketched). Whenever I have re-copied or re-scored anything, I have improved it very much. Anyhow I would never score at once—wait until your mud pie is hardened and until you can compare it in cold blood to others.'[12] In later life however, lack of time prevented realization of this youthfully idealistic proposal.

His pragmatism is perhaps at its most evident in his music for amateur performers. Music for amateurs must be technically feasible, but none the less interesting, not too difficult, but not too easy; rewarding, but with an element of challenge. Holst was well aware of these factors, and ensured that his own music for amateurs took account of them. He pointed out that the amateur music of the Elizabethan period was very well written for the voices or instruments (often by major composers of the day), and was in fact often easier to perform than much music of later times, despite its apparent complexity.

Although it is difficult to separate particular elements from the cohesive continuum which constitutes a piece of music, this is often the only way of identifying characteristics which contribute to the formation of an individual style, and the following sections therefore examine separate aspects of Holst's music, while recognizing that these elements are interdependent, each influencing the others to a considerable degree.

RHYTHM AND METRE

In considering characteristic features of musical style, rhythm can perhaps be discussed first as being the most basic of musical elements, without which all else would lack momentum. In Holst's case this is particularly relevant, as he considered rhythm to be of vital importance, both in performance as well as in composition. His works exhibit a variety of rhythmic devices, sometimes to the detriment of attention to other factors, and in much of the character of his rhythms there is a connection with physical movement, whether it be the dancing patterns of the *St Paul's Suite* and the *Perfect Fool* ballet music, or the 'sad procession' found in several of his works. This association may have been influenced by his contact with the Ballets Russes: Holst's compositions contain much more dancing music after he had heard the ballets of Stravinsky.

In his own lifetime, Holst's rhythmic structures were frequently denigrated as being too intellectual, arranged for the benefit of the eye rather than the ear, but such criticism may have been the result of unfamiliarity with the style; in a later age, when composers have taken rhythmical complexity to extraordinary lengths (and many are now in retreat from such extremism), Holst's techniques do not seem particularly complex and often have a naturalness about them, seemingly devoid of contrivance.

In much music it is often difficult to dissociate the element of rhythm from the musical context in which it is embedded, but in Holst's case rhythmic structure can often be isolated, particularly because of his use of ostinato. Although this device is closely associated with his music because of its most effective use in *Mars*, it occurs in many of his works, although surprisingly a true rhythmic ostinato consisting of nothing but reiteration of a basic pattern without change of pitch is fairly rare; it generally appears in combination with other elements, often as a pedal-point, above or below which harmonies or other motifs move. (Holst's use of ostinato may have sometimes have arisen from non-musical reasons; he facetiously referred to the repeat sign ⅍ as 'the joy of life',[13] as it saved his neuritic arm from the labour of writing out diverse patterns.)

As early as 1909, he used such an ostinato in the hymn *To Agni* in the Second Group of *Choral Hymns from the Rig Veda*, using a five-beat rhythm which later bore fruit in a more developed form in *Mars*, and in *The Hymn of Jesus* a similar ostinato pattern is used, but for quite different expressive purposes; instead of evoking the savagery of war, the figure here forms an accompaniment to the words 'Divine Grace is dancing' (Ex. 1). A related type of ostinato can be found in the

Ex. 1

(a) *To Agni*   (b) *Mars*   (c) *The Hymn of Jesus*

ballet music of *The Perfect Fool* (Ex. 4c) and the Bacchanal of the *First Choral Symphony*, although not used so hypnotically, being varied and interspersed with other material. Towards the end of his life, Holst used an ostinato pedal-point in the *Choral Fantasia* of 1930, showing that he did not consider that its possibilities were exhausted or overdone, and that it could still be used to good effect (Ex. 117c).

One of Holst's most extraordinary uses of rhythm for its own sake is not in fact an ostinato, but the reiteration by brass and percussion of the rhythmic pattern of the first theme of *Jupiter*, in a form completely stripped of its original melodic content (Ex. 2).

Ex. 2 *Jupiter*

In his early years, Holst naturally made use of the conventional rhythmical gestures of the late nineteenth century, set within metres in simple and compound time, and despite his explorations into other fields, continued to use such metres throughout his career. He was particularly fond of the folksy 6/8, sometimes verging on excess, which led Vaughan Williams to wonder about the extent of its use in the *Double Concerto* and even more about *The Wandering Scholar*: 'Do you think there's a *little* bit too much 6/8 in the opera?' he remarked.[14] In the 1929 song *Rhyme*, however, compound metres are effectively used to produce a lightweight, floating effect.

But although these commonplace metres served their purpose in an appropriate context, Holst also felt a need to develop an individual rhythmical language of his own, which he did more by extending the possibilities of metre, than by the invention of rhythms within the metre. Despite his fondness for 6/8, he found that remaining within it for an entire movement was too restrictive; the Jig of the *St Paul's Suite* contains groups of 9/8 bars inserted into the prevailing 6/8, and the Dance of Maidens in *The Morning of the Year* has single 9/8 bars similarly inserted. There are also implications of 9/8 phrasing in the Scherzo of *Hammersmith*, although notated within the prevailing 6/8. Such divergences from a regular metrical scheme arise from the needs of the musical material, as can be seen in *Beni Mora*, where the insertion of single 4/4 bars into a 3/4 context follows the requirement of the melody for an extra beat, and in the Dance of Youths from *The Morning of the Year* the insertion of 3/4 bars into a prevailing 2/2 allows the music to move on without waiting for a hiatus at the end of each phrase.

Once the notion that the metre can be changed at will within the course of a piece has been accepted, the way is open for freedom of application of bar-lengths according to the degree of flexibility required, as is evident in the carol *Of One That Is So Fair and Bright*, in which 4/4, 5/4, and 3/4 are mixed to produce a flowing rhythmic motion, and in the Scherzo of the *First Choral Symphony* where the combination of different metres produces an angular, dislocating effect.

From the free admixture of bars of different length to the consistent use of irregular, or asymmetric, metres is but a short step, as such metres often consist simply of systematic combination of shorter bars, but in Holst's case this did not happen as a chronological development, as he used both techniques extensively during his career. Although there are dangers in the use of asymmetrical metres, which can begin as liberating devices but quickly become irritating mannerisms, Holst wanted to extend the expressive possibilities of rhythm and metre, in particular believing that metres consisting of groups of five or seven beats are ideal for setting texts in the English language, since the words fall naturally into such patterns.

His interest in such ideas seems to have begun at an early

age, and continued throughout his career, showing a diversity of types and applications. In 1894 he was already using a 7/4 metre (divided into 3 + 4) in the Vivace movement of a student Trio for strings; a year later we find a 5/4 metre in the first of two Dances for piano duet, and in the part-song *Soft and Gently* of 1896 a 5/4 metre also appears.

The opera *Sita*, written between 1899 and 1906, contains such metres as 7/4, 9/4, 5/4, and 15/8, but it is in the *Vedic Hymns* that asymmetric metres are first used consistently and systematically, albeit within relatively restricted musical structures. In the up-tempo *Song of the Frogs* Holst uses a seven-beat metre divided into 4 + 3, within which an arpeggiated accompaniment figure gives support to a flowing vocal line which proceeds unhampered by the regular stress patterns which would have been imposed by the use of common time. The accompaniment is written in three groups of four quavers, with a crotchet rest at the end of each bar, as if it were a 3/2 with a hesitating pause at the end of each bar (Ex. 3). In the

Ex. 3   *Song of the Frogs*

seventh song, *Vac* (Speech), Holst gives the voice a declamatory line in 5/4 while the piano supplies chords mostly of a whole bar's duration, thus avoiding any implication of regular divisions of the bar, and allowing the voice greater freedom of rhythmical accent.

In the chamber opera *Savitri*, he uses the same device when setting the words 'I am with thee . . . When thou art weary I am watching' to a simple melody which is accompanied only by sustained thirds in the flutes, to obviate any suggestion of metrical division and to allow the voice the maximum amount of rhythmic flow, as in plainchant. When setting the words of both Satyavan and Death, however, Holst divides a 7/4 metre regularly into 4 + 3, in the first case to express Satyavan's physical vigour, and in the case of Death to convey a feeling of unease at his approach.

But it was in the four groups of *Choral Hymns from the Rig Veda* that Holst fully explored the use of asymmetric metres. In the first hymn of the First Group, *Battle Hymn*, the accompaniment lays down a persistent metrical rhythm in 5/4, accented on the second and fourth beats, above which the vocal rhythms are grouped into patterns of 3 + 2, while in the *Funeral Hymn* which ends the group, a 7/4 metre is divided sometimes into 4 + 3 and sometimes 3 + 4. In the second hymn of the Second Group, *To Agni*, this device of changing stress patterns is codified into a regular system, in which the relentless ostinato accompaniment rhythm in 5/4 is presented as 3 + 2 and 2 + 3 in alternate bars. The Third Group contains similar devices, the *Hymn to the Waters* employing a seven-beat metre divided into 4 + 3 which is given an added complexity by the voices singing in a triple rhythm (21/8) while the accompaniment has a duple figuration in demisemi-quavers, and in the final *Hymn of the Travellers* a five-beat melody divided into 3 + 2 with occasional 2 + 3 is set over an isorhythmic accompaniment. All four groups of *Choral Hymns from the Rig Veda* form a compendium of Holst's use of unusual metres, and are the foundation of his later use of such techniques.

Although a 7/4 metre (divded into 4 + 3) is used in the *Invocation* for cello and orchestra of 1911 and also the *Hymn to Dionysus* two years later, it is in *Mars* that Holst's most well-known and effective use of an asymmetrical metre appears. Here, the relentless rhythm in 5/4 is clearly derived from the simpler version in *To Agni*, but becomes an obssessive pedal-point which continues single-mindedly amid the prevailing violence. Surprisingly, in view of Holst's notoriety for the use of such metres, *The Planets* contains only one other example of an asymmetric metre; the subtly shifting 5/4 of *Neptune*, the antithesis of its strident use in *Mars*, demonstrating the wide possibilities of expression inherent in such metres.

In *The Hymn of Jesus* (1917), the five-beat rhythm found in *To Agni* and *Mars* is transformed by dotting the first beat, to produce a 2 + 3 dancing rhythm (Ex. 1c), while the *Ode to*

Death of 1919 is barred mainly in 7/4 (4 + 3) and 5/4 (usually 2 + 3) with only short sections in 4/4 and 3/4, producing a cool, flowing, ethereal effect.

The 'dancing' possibilities of a seven-beat metre were realized to the full in *The Perfect Fool* ballet music, where Holst changed his original notation from 7/4 to 7/8, giving a psychological lightness to the rhythm, which has the feeling of a 3/4 with the last beat extended by one quaver. This basic accompaniment supports a jocose melody, while repeated chords reminiscent of *To Agni* are here enhanced by the use of semiquavers, to produce a rhythmically pulsating pedal-point (Ex. 4).

Ex. 4   *The Perfect Fool*

(a)   (b)   (c)

The same kind of devices occur in the *First Choral Symphony*, which includes examples of a dancing 7/8 in the Bacchanal and a 5/4 with changing subdivisions of 3 + 2 and 2 + 3 in the Finale, while *The Morning of the Year* begins with a flowing 5/4 which allows considerable flexibility of melodic phrasing. The *Seven Part-Songs* of the same period include *Sorrow and Joy*, which is entirely in 7/4, and *Assemble, All Ye Maidens*, in which 5/4 alternates with other metres, while the orchestral *Egdon Heath* begins in 7/4, changing to a 5/4 within which the strings play triplets to produce a 15/8 metre.

Holst remained interested in the possibilities of asymmetrical metres until the end of his life; the Lament of the *Double Concerto* (1929) is entirely in 5/4; the *Choral Fantasia* of 1930 includes a flowing 7/4 section at 'Rejoice, ye dead' in which a regular divison of the bar is avoided, and in the chorus *How Mighty are the Sabbaths* the 7/4 melody seems to belong to a regular 4/4 in which the natural pause at the end of each line has been curtailed.

The use of asymmetrical metres in Holst's music is perhaps most effective in an instrumental context, in which rhythm can take precedence in the musical texture. In choral music he seemed so anxious to follow the natural stress of the text that he allowed such needs to override purely metrical considerations, with the result that changing durations and accentuation within a metre which is itself irregular can tend to produce a nebulous, diffuse effect which detracts from the effectiveness of that metre, although admittedly avoiding over-rigid adherence to the metrical pattern.

Sometimes Holst felt that his material necessitated a complete abandonment of regular metrical divisions: the *Four Songs* for voice and violin contain no time-signatures at all, and although bar-lines are used for co-ordination purposes, the length of each bar varies freely according to the melodic line. The same approach is used in the later Humbert Wolfe songs *Things Lovelier* and *The Thought*, and while this is perfectly practicable with only two performers, Holst also used the idea in a larger context when he began the Prelude to *The Hymn of Jesus* 'senza misura', without bar-lines, in emulation of the flexibility of plainsong, while later in the same Prelude the semi-chorus sings a plainsong theme in free time while the orchestra repeats an accompaniment bar until the singers have finished their music.

But he was also to discover that interesting effects can be obtained within the confines of a regular metre, without going to the lengths of inventing new metres or abolishing bars altogether. As early as the *Suite de Ballet* of 1899 a syncopated phrase appears, which was to re-emerge some years later as the striking rhythm of *Jupiter* (Ex. 5). In his setting of the folk-song *The Song of the Blacksmith* he uses a syncopated off-beat rhythm to portray the hammer-blows of the smithy; in *The Lure* occasional passages of syncopation appear, and rhythmic dislocation is also a feature of the Scherzo theme of *Hammersmith*; Holst's sketches show that he shifted his original metrical placing of the motif by one beat, so that the first note comes after an implied initial beat, producing that angular hiatus so characteristic of his scherzo themes (Ex. 6).

Although syncopation usually consists of displacement of a rhythmic accent from its normal place in the metre, Holst also developed a related technique of permutating the position of a

Ex. 5

(a) *Suite de Ballet*

(b) *Jupiter*

Ex. 6 *Hammersmith*

fixed motif in relation to the metre, thus producing dislocation of the implied accent. Such motifs usually consist of only a few notes, and Imogen Holst pointed out that the earliest example can be found in his student opera *The Revoke*. A similar rising motif of three notes with changing accents appears in the *Fugal Concerto* of 1923, here constrained within the confines of a 6/8 metre (in an identical rhythm to an arpeggiated phrase in *Mercury*), while in the *Double Concerto* the motif is reduced to only two notes which repeat with disconcerting pauses between them (Ex. 7). The same idea is used in the *Scherzo* of 1934, where the chromatic expansion of the motif emphasizes the disorientating effect of the rhythmic displacement (Ex. 8). In using such techniques, Holst was doubtless aiming at a breathless, angular syncopation, but the net effect is often to slow down the music, thus losing the momentum of the metre. The example from the *Double Concerto* for instance, can easily sound as if the pairs of quavers were grouped in threes with a rest between them, as if in a minim

Ex. 7

(a) *The Revoke*   (b) *A Fugal Concerto*

(c) *Double Concerto*

Ex. 8   *Scherzo*

metre at a slower tempo—probably the opposite effect of that intended (Ex. 7c).

A simple example of such rhythmic displacement can be found in the first movement of the *Fugal Concerto*, where the motif ♪♫♪ appears both on and off the beat, and a more complex version of the same thing occurs in *The Golden Goose* (Ex. 9). Imogen Holst recalled that as a girl she had found this particular phrase very difficult to dance to, and suggested that it should be rebarred in 5/8 and 6/8 (thus defeating Holst's original intention of laying the phrase across a constant metre).

Ex. 9   *The Golden Goose*

Allegretto

In the opera *At the Boar's Head* Holst used the same device to emphasize the agitation and indignation of Falstaff's insults, and in the Prelude of *Hammersmith* the rhythmic displacement of the counterpoint in relation to the regularity of the underlying bass helps to portray the shifting nature of the waters of the river Thames. An interesting combination of rhythmic displacement and syncopation appears in the March

Ex. 10 *A Moorside Suite*

of *A Moorside Suite* (Ex. 10), while in the Finale of the *Double Concerto* Holst reversed the process by repeating a twenty-four-beat theme in two different metres (2/2 and 3/4) thus completely altering the implications of its accents (Ex. 11).

Ex. 11 *Double Concerto*

In addition to such techniques as syncopation and rhythmic displacement, Holst also explored the possibilities of asymmetrical division of regular metres. In the *Fugal Overture* of 1922 he grouped the eight quavers of the 4/4 into a 3 + 3 + 2 pattern, producing a bar of three unequal beats, and in the song *Persephone* the same idea is used in crotchet patterns of 2 + 3 + 3, contrasted with the more usual 4 + 4 (Ex. 12). The

Ex. 12

(a) *A Fugal Overture*

(b) *Persephone*

Come back Per-se-pho-ne! As a moon-flake thin,

Choral Fantasia presented some problems of how to notate irregular subdivisions of an 8/4 metre, and after seeking advice Holst wrote a note to himself:

> Ch Fan 8/4 dotted lines
> Prefer 3/4 3/4 2/4 for voices
> Don't be logical
> Decide each case by other parts.[15]

In the event, the passage was published without dotted bar-lines indicating the subdivisions, as these may have impeded the natural flow of the music.

A more systematized method of subdividing regular metres is the procedure known as hemiola, whereby a 3/4 bar may be divided into two groups of three quavers (forming 6/8) rather than the usual three groups of two, the effect of which is to imply a new tempo with a new durational beat; the basis of what has later come to be known as metric modulation. This idea can be additive as well as divisive, as two 3/4 bars can be turned into one of 3/2 or three of 2/4 by grouping the crotchets in pairs, and vice versa (Ex. 13). Such techniques were well-known to Renaissance composers, but examples can be found in Holst's work long before he became acquainted with Fellowes's published editions of early music. In common with the early madrigalists, Holst used these devices in his vocal

Ex. 13
(a)   (b)

and choral works in response to the needs of the text; a fleeting hint of such rhythmic suppleness appears in the early *King Estmere* in an otherwise four-square rhythmical context, and a true hemiola appears in *Savitri* at the words 'my feet may never travel the path', in which the vocal stress combines two 3/2 bars into an implied 3/1 (Ex. 14). The technique is put to beautiful use in illustration of the text in *To Varuna* from the Second Group of *Choral Hymns from the Rig Veda*, where at the words 'Then in thy boat we embarked' a three-part sub-division of the chorus sings imitative flowing phrases in 6/4, while the remaining singers provide harmonizing chords in 3/2, the resulting cross-rhythm producing the effect of a boat gently rocking on water.

In instrumental music, too, Holst was intrigued by the possibilities of hemiola cross-rhythms; one of his favourite devices being to accompany a 3/4 melody with a 2/4 figure laid

Ex. 14

(a) *King Estmere*

(b) *Savitri*

across the metre. The Elegy of the *Cotswolds Symphony* begins with a two-beat horn pedal-note figure which is effectively in 2/4 within the 3/4 (Ex. 15a), while examples of a 2/4 hemiola accompaniment to material in 3/4 can be found in the *Country Song*, *The Cloud Messenger*, and *A Fugal Concerto*. In the Ostinato of the *St Paul's Suite* a turning 2/4 figure continues throughout the movement independently of the 3/4 melody (Ex. 15b), and the Finale of the same work contains what is probably Holst's most famous use of cross-rhythm, in which the 'Dargason' in 6/8 is combined with 'Greensleeves' in 3/4, the juxtaposition being all the more effective for the two-bar delay between the beginning of the two tunes (Ex. 16). A brilliant instrumental example of hemiola occurs in *Mercury*, in which the alternation in 6/8 of three crotchets with the usual 3 + 3 quaver grouping produces an exhilarating, free-wheeling feeling, which is further intensified when the crotchets are themselves divided into quavers (Ex. 17).

Holst also realized that the technique of hemiola could be applied to other metres besides the usual triple time. In *Mars*, for example, he boldly combined pairs of 5/4 bars to produce a

Ex. 15

(a) *Cotswolds Symphony*   (b) *St Paul's Suite*

Ex. 16   *St Paul's Suite*

Ex. 17   *Mercury*

(a)   (b)

5/2 effect (subsequently writing an actual 5/2), and in the
Perfect Fool ballet music he did the same thing with a 7/8
metre, to produce a 7/4 cross-rhythm which is quite practicable
for the players but can be hair-raising for the conductor (Ex. 18).

Ex. 18

(a) *Mars*   (b) *The Perfect Fool*

Most of the more common musical cross-rhythms occur
throughout Holst's work, such as two quavers against three in
6/8 time in the *St Paul's Suite* and the *Double Concerto* (which
includes not only hemiola, but also a section taken from the
Terzetto in which the soloists play simultaneously in 2/4 and
6/8), and in the Wind Quintet of 1903 four crotchets against
three can be found, a device which later emerges magnificently
in *Uranus* where the decrease in note duration serves to
accelerate the rythmical impetus (Ex. 19). *Mercury* contains
cross-metres such as 2/4 against 6/8 (both normal and hemiola)
and cross-rhythms of four semiquavers against three quavers

Ex. 19   *Uranus*

within the 6/8. Other examples occur in *The Lure* ballet music, and at the end of *At the Boar's Head,* where Doll Tearsheet's triadic motif appears in 3/4 and 6/8, in two different keys (Ex. 20). An excellent example of simultaneous metres appears in *Hammersmith,* when the augmented Scherzo theme in 2/4 crotchets is combined with the dancing 6/8 material.

Ex. 20   *At the Boar's Head*

Holst was clearly fascinated by the permutational possibilities of cross-rhythms; as they get out of phase with each other, the time taken for them to 'catch up' varies according to the difference in duration of the motifs. In the Second Dance of *Beni Mora* the opening timpani ostinato continues its 5/4 pattern against music in 3/4 in the rest of the orchestra; in *Saturn* he lays a 4/2 ostinato figure over an underlying 3/2; in the *Perfect Fool* ballet music a 2/4 figure in semiquavers is set against a 3/8 bass; in the *First Choral Symphony* an implied 9/8 appears across a 2/4 metre; the *Choral Fantasia* contains a five-beat ostinato pedal set within an 8/4 metre; and in the chorus *How Mighty are the Sabbaths* an eight-beat descending scale goes in and out of phase with its seven-beat metre. In the *Fugal Overture* the implied 5/8 and 2/4 metre of one of the principal themes contrasts effectively with the notated 4/4 (Ex. 21). Sometimes these cross-rhythms are quite involved, as in the *Perfect Fool* ballet music, in which an ostinato 3/8 bass is continued into a succeeding 7/8 section, the effect being made all the more complex by the combining of the 7/8 bars

Ex. 21   *A Fugal Overture*

into hemiola phrases, so that the percussion (jingles) is the only instrument playing in the true metre of the passage. Such techniques can produce intriguing results if handled musically, and Holst's interest in them remained strong throughout his life, as is evident in the *Jig* for solo piano of 1932. Here he used the technique of combining 3/4 with 6/8, but then grouped the crotchet beats in pairs to produce a separate augmented hemiola, with the overall effect of a 3/2 in the right hand against 12/8 in the left (Ex. 22). Two years later in the *Lyric Movement*, some of the viola phrases sound as if in metres of 6/8, 2/4, 9/8, and 5/8, although the notation remains steadfastly in 4/4 (Ex. 23).

Ex. 22   *Jig*

Ex. 23   *Lyric Movement*

Codified systems for dealing with combinations of rhythmic material were not always flexible enough to produce the required effect, and in *A Somerset Rhapsody* for example, Holst freely augmented and extended one of his folk-themes in order to make it fit with another, while in *Beni Mora* he combined several motifs in constantly changing relationships, similar to the interplay of jazz improvisation.

Most of the common techniques of rhythmic augmentation and diminution are to be found in Holst's work, usually employed with effortless musicality rather than contrived artificiality. In the Jig of the *St Paul's Suite*, the second theme appears unselfconsciously in single and double augmentation following the appearance of its original form, and in the *Fugal Overture* augmentation of the main theme is coupled with a change to minor mode, giving it added emphasis. *Hammersmith* contains some splendid and dramatic examples of rhythmic augmentation. Diminution can also be a dramatic device, and has the effect of hurrying the music forward. Examples can be found in *The Lure* ballet music, and most effectively in *The Mystic Trumpeter* and *Mars*, where the tightening of the brass calls produce an effect of increasing tension. An early example appears in the Wind Quintet of 1903, where 'tightening-up' phrases appear in the context of a rhythmic hemiola, and in the March of *A Moorside Suite* rhythmic diminution is used to bring a melodic phrase to an abrupt termination (Ex. 24).

Ex. 24   *A Moorside Suite*

Allegro

Closely associated with the concept of rhythm is that of tempo, but here Holst seems to have slipped from the standards with which he notated his rhythmic structures. He rarely provided metronome marks, apparently believing that performers would understand what was meant by such phrases as *poco vivace, poco adagio,* or *andante quasi allegretto.* His own recordings are not necessarily an authoritative guide to tempi because of the difficult studio conditions in those early days. Also, his conducting changed throughout his career, so that his performances altered quite noticeably as his technical competence developed.

This lack of precise information on tempo has led to wide divergences in subsequent performance, giving conductors scope for indulging in their own interpretative fancies. *Mars* is perhaps the most frequent victim of this: although Holst marked his score *Allegro,* many conductors take the movement at a *Moderato*, or even an *Andante*; recorded performances differing by as much as 25 per cent in duration. A metronome mark would have obviated the worst of such misunderstandings, so that any divergences could be blamed fairly and squarely on the conductor. Holst himself always insisted that *Mars* should be played quickly, and Imogen Holst recalled seeing him practising conducting the movement and thinking: 'If he does it any quicker, the crotchet will be too quick to *walk* to.'[16] Dulcie Nutting considered that 'If *Mars* is done as it ought to be done, it's almost unbearable. He told Jane Joseph nobody could play it as fast as he wanted it.'[17] But for most of Holst's other works, the relationship with actual physical movement is perhaps the best guide to tempo. Dancing and walking rhythms abound in his music, and the appropriate tempo is clearly the one which feels natural to move to. Imogen Holst recalled that as a girl she danced to the 'Dargason' on the vicarage lawn at Thaxted while thinking of its setting in the *St Paul's Suite*, and found that the tempo of the folk-dance fitted the Suite's music perfectly.[18]

MELODY AND COUNTERPOINT

Holst's youthful enthusiasm for the music of Sullivan, Grieg, and Mendelssohn, all noted for the directness and clarity of their melodic styles, is evident in schoolboy works such as the operetta *Lansdown Castle*, and even during his Wagnerian period some of his works, such as the cantata *King Estmere*, exhibit a simple lyricism. The influence of English folk-song brought him back to this melodic path, and although much of the thematic material of his mature work is motivic rather than fully phrased, lyricism is not far from the surface, as is apparent as late as 1929 in the *Twelve Songs* to words by Humbert Wolfe.

Besides his use of actual folk tunes, folk-like melodies can be found throughout Holst's work, particularly in the *Two Songs Without Words*, the *Four Old English Carols*, the *Suite No. 1* for wind band (here characteristically being derived from the original motif), *A Dream of Christmas*, *This Have I Done for My True Love*, the *Terzetto*, *A Moorside Suite*, the *Double Concerto*, and *The Wandering Scholar*. The influence of the

folk-music of other cultures can be found in works such as
Beni Mora and the *St Paul's Suite*, which contain echoes of his
1908 Algerian holiday.

The main melodic lesson which Holst learnt from English
folk-song was that a melody should be allowed to follow its
own natural course in terms of note duration, phrase length,
and intervallic construction, rather than being forced into a
strait-jacket of regularity, while remaining within the practicable singing range of the human voice. Although such an
approach can all too easily lead to aimless meandering, and
Holst is occasionally guilty of this, on the whole his music
uses the flexibility to good advantage. The works of his
Sanskrit period, which overlapped with his discovery of folk-
song, show considerable exploration on these lines, being
particularly successful in the *Vedic Hymns*, *Savitri*, and the
four groups of *Choral Hymns from the Rig Veda*.

Holst's melodic style exhibits certain features, which although
musically commonplace, give character to much of his thematic
material. Rising scale figures are frequently found, as at the
beginning of *Venus* and of *A Choral Fantasia* (Ex. 25), and their
descending converse appears in the chorus *Before Sleep* (Ex. 68)
and as a phrase ending in many other works, such as *The
Perfect Fool*, the *First Choral Symphony*, and the *Seven Part-
Songs* (Ex. 26).

Ex. 25   (*a*) *Venus*   (*b*) *A Choral Fantasia*

Although he often worked within the constraints of particular scales, it is evident that Holst also regarded intervals as
compositional elements in their own right, dissociated from
the implications of particular scale degrees. Such an interval is
the minor second which characterizes the *Battle Hymn* of the
First Group of *Choral Hymns from the Rig Veda* and also *Mars*
and *Saturn* (Ex. 27), while augmented seconds appear in
response to the needs of declamatory recitative, particularly in
Savitri (Ex. 34*a*).

Ex. 26
(a) *The Perfect Fool*   (b) *First Choral Symphony*

(c) *Say Who Is This?*

Ex. 27
(a) *Battle Hymn*   (b) *Mars*

(c) *Saturn*

Concentration on such intervals for their own sake led Holst to a type of thematic material in which melody in the usual sense hardly exists at all, being based on manipulation of motivic fragments built up from freely combined intervals of various kinds (although he would occasionally relax with a 'big tune', as in the Finale of the *First Choral Symphony*).

The interval which is perhaps most characteristic of Holst's music is the perfect fourth, which in conventional use usually appears in association with major and minor thirds, in triadic combinations. But Holst uses the interval as an independent element for its own sake, sometimes to the point of excess. Early examples of its use, in a diatonic context, can be found in *Lansdown Castle*, *The Magic Mirror*, and the *Cotswolds Symphony*, while in *Jupiter* it is used boldly as a characteristic feature, and permeates many subsequent works, including the *First Choral Symphony*, the *Terzetto*, *A Moorside Suite*, and

The Wandering Scholar. Even at the end of his life Holst was still interested in the possibilities of this interval, which features prominently in *Hammersmith*, the *Capriccio*, and the final *Scherzo*.

In these examples, two intervals of a perfect fourth are usually placed above each other, one of them substituting for the expected major or minor third of conventional diatonic syntax, implying an unresolved suspended third, but Holst also often uses two such intervals separated by a major or minor second. The opening of *The Golden Goose* uses two perfect fourths separated by a major second to produce a striking motto theme (Ex. 28a), while in several other works the articulating interval is contracted into a minor second, so that the two fourths 'side-slip', producing a chromatic motif which goes out of the base key. Characteristic examples of this appear in *Egdon Heath* and the *Double Concerto* (Ex. 28b,c), while in the opening of *The Wandering Scholar* a rising series of side-slipped fourths go in and out of the key of G major. In *The Morning of the Year* Holst pares this idea down to simply adding a chromatic semitone to the top and bottom of a perfect fourth to construct a characteristic musical motif (Ex. 29).

Ex. 28

(a) *The Golden Goose*   (b) *Egdon Heath*   (c) *Double Concerto*

Ex. 29   (a) *The Wandering Scholar*   (b) *The Morning of the Year*

The interval of the perfect fifth also fascinated Holst, and he seems to have used it with as much freedom as the fourth. Apart from an early appearance in *The Mystic Trumpeter*, obviously prompted by the subject-matter, it appears in a variety of works, particularly the carol *Terly Terlow* and the *Ode on a Grecian Urn* in the *First Choral Symphony*, in both of which perfect fifths are placed vertically above each other with harmonic rather than melodic implications (Ex. 30). In the part-song *Assemble, All Ye Maidens* the fifths appear in an ostinato bass figure, but here as an appoggiatura to the main key rather than being thought of in their own right (Ex. 31). But more often the fifths are 'side-slipped', either diatonically or chromatically: in the *Hymn to the Dawn* in the Third Group of *Choral Hymns from the Rig Veda* rising fifths are separated by a semitone, and by a whole tone in the *Nunc Dimittis* and *Terzetto*, while the *Lyric Movement* begins with three perfect fifths which are linked together by a semitone and a whole tone (Ex. 32).

Ex. 30   (*a*) *Terly Terlow*   (*b*) *First Choral Symphony*

Ex. 31   *Assemble, All Ye Maidens*

Ex. 32

(*a*) *Hymn to the Dawn*   (*b*) *Nunc Dimittis*

(*c*) *Terzetto*   (*d*) *Lyric Movement*

But rather than being confined to a single interval, a much more interesting effect can be produced by a mixture of fourths and fifths, which, because of the complementary nature of those intervals in forming an octave, together with the use of the side-slipping technique, can produce a wide variety of motifs and tonal implications. Examples occur in *Venus*, where it is used with great lyrical beauty, and *Hammersmith* and the *Scherzo*, where it produces an angular effect ideally suited to the lightweight mood of the music (Ex. 33).

Ex. 33

(a) *Venus* (b) *Hammersmith*

(c) *Scherzo*

Thematic material constructed by such methods can range widely in pitch according to the intervals used, but in his more declamatory, recitative-like passages, Holst often uses one particular note as a base, or pivot-note, from which melodic motifs can diverge and return. Although this relates to the function of the key-note in diatonic music, Holst did not confine himself to particular scales, simply regarding the pivot as a reference-point from which any interval can depart. Characteristic examples can be found in *Savitri* and *To the Unknown God* in the First Group of *Choral Hymns from the Rig Veda*, in both of which upward movement away from the pivot is counter-balanced by a corresponding downward turn of phrase (Ex. 34). Characteristic intervals used here are the minor second and augmented second, giving the material something of an oriental feeling, while in *The Perfect Fool* and

Ex. 34

(a) *Savitri*

(b) *To the Unknown God*

Be - got -ten in mys-ter-y,——— Lord —— of cre-a - ted things.

Ex. 35

(a) *The Perfect Fool*

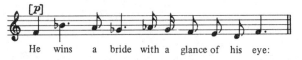

He wins a bride with a glance of his eye:

(b) *First Choral Symphony*

She can-not fade, ——— though thou hast not thy bliss,

the *First Choral Symphony* a similar technique is used, employing additional larger intervals such as the major third and perfect fourth (Ex. 35).

Holst's innate lyricism is also evident in his use of counterpoint, which is always musical despite the sometimes rather mechanical procedures evident in its construction. Commonplace imitative and sequential passages occur in many of his works, notably *King Estmere, Invocation, The Hymn of Jesus, Ode to Death, Terzetto,* and the motet *Sing Me the Men,* but he was also interested in the possibilities of more rigorous imitation. Examples of canon can be found in the Minuet of his 1903 Wind Quintet and in the later *Double Concerto,* and his use of the technique in choral music shows a wide range of application. The part-song *Tears, Idle Tears* from the 'Princess' set is a *tour de force* of four-part canonic writing in a tonal context of two subjects at the fourth and fifth; the *Funeral Chant* in the Second Group of *Choral Hymns from the Rig Veda* consists of canonic imitation of pentatonic motifs at the unison by three pairs of voices, each doubled in parallel sixths; while less complex, but none the less effective, is the two-part canon doubled in octaves in *A Choral Fantasia* at the words

'Then he hideth his face'. Towards the end of his life Holst used canon in the male-voice choruses *A Love Song* and *Before Sleep*, and demonstrated considerable skill in the *Eight Canons*, which exhibit a wide variety of imitative devices. Besides two-and three-part canons, some with piano accompaniment, the set includes the unaccompanied *Truth of All Truth* for two three-part choirs, and *O Strong of Heart* for three three-part choirs, all handled with consummate mastery.

A particular kind of canon which attracted Holst was the round, or perpetual canon, which he found useful in teaching counterpoint to schoolchildren and amateurs. He even went so far as to arrange for the publication of his student's work under the title *Morley Rounds*, and edited examples by various composers in the three sets of *Sacred Rounds and Canons*. A fine example in his own work is the round in praise of water in *The Perfect Fool*, and in the part-song *When First We Met* the round entries are distributed between the voices and the string accompaniment, including augmented durations.

Fugue, the logical development of canon into a more sophisticated structure, does not appear as such in Holst's work (apart from the facetious but well-made Laughing Fugue in his schoolboy operetta *Lansdown Castle*), but there are many passages of fugato style which catch its spirit, such as the fugal passage on a chromatic subject given to the chorus in *The Perfect Fool* to the words 'Where is the fire?' Despite their titles, the *Fugal Concerto* and *Fugal Overture* pay only lip-service to the form, and apart from the delicate three-part invention in the song *The Floral Bandit*, the nearest approaches Holst made to the fugue proper are the opening of the Prelude to the *First Choral Symphony* and the extended organ solo at the beginning of *A Choral Fantasia*.

Both canon and fugue involve the combination of a thematic motif with versions of itself or contrapuntally related subjects, but Holst was also interested in the juxtaposition of themes of diverse character. Mention has already been made of the conjunction of 'Greensleeves' and the 'Dargason' in the *St Paul's Suite* and *Suite No. 2*, and the same idea is used in *A Somerset Rhapsody*, where folk-songs are combined simultaneously. Whether such tunes can be made to fit together is largely a matter of good fortune, and a more practicable method is to compose a counter-melody to an existing tune. A simple but effective example is Holst's setting of Psalm 86, where the tenor soloist's phrases combine with the choir's presentation of the tune, and in *A Welcome Song* he adds free contrapuntal phrases to a repeated two-bar motif. In the Finale of *A Fugal Concerto*, the initial motif subsequently becomes a counterpoint to the country-dance tune 'If All the World Were Paper', giving rise to the suspicion that it was originally contrived with this purpose in mind. Such combination of motifs towards the end of a movement is a feature of many of Holst's formal structures, and can be found in the *Suite No. 1* for wind band, *A Fugal Overture*, and *Hammersmith*. The same device is useful in theatrical music to provide a degree of musical cohesion to an otherwise sequential narrative, as in *At The Boar's Head*, where Holst's own melody to the sonnet 'Devouring Time' later becomes a counterpoint to the folk-tune 'Chevy Chase', leading to a masterly passage in which a trio based on the sonnet tune is combined with 'Chevy Chase' in a lower part, the whole texture in due course being penetrated by the traditional march tune 'The Queen's Birthday'. In *Savitri*, Death's initial summons appears again beneath Savitri's opening words, and subsequently during the work as a kind of haunting leitmotif. Perhaps Holst's most effective combination of themes is the Finale of *Beni Mora*, in which various motifs are combined in a free and flexible counterpoint, liberated from the constraints of conventional imitation and regular patterning. Despite his skill in combining diverse thematic material, Holst's counterpoint is often most effective when it is simplest, as in his setting of Psalm 86, in which the chorus sings falling and rising Alleluia's in scale phrases doubled in parallel sixths and thirds, while the melody is played by the orchestra.

A persistent characteristic of much of Holst's music is the use of repetitive scales in the bass line as a counterpoint to the upper parts. Such a device might easily be dismissed as a failure of contrapuntal invention, and there is some truth in this as Holst often lapsed into such mannerisms in order to relieve the strain on his neuritic hand, but he may have acquired the idea from the Credo of Bach's Mass in B minor, where it is used most effectively and musically. The use of bass scales, particularly in steady crotchet beats, gives the music a kind of tramping inevitability, especially in the slow, 'sad procession' type of music, and examples can be found throughout Holst's career. Ascending bass scales appear in *To Agni*, Psalm 86, *Seven Choruses from the Alcestis of Euripides*, and *Intercession*, while the scales descend in *To Varuna*, *To the Unknown God*, *Turn Back, O Man*, *The Hymn of Jesus*, *Eternal Father*, *A Choral Fantasia*, and *How Mighty are the Sabbaths*. Rising and falling scales are mixed in the *Toccata*, *Egdon Heath*, and *A Moorside Suite*. The rhythmic motion of all these examples is in steady crotchet beats, but half-beat scales can be found in *A Somerset Rhapsody* and the *Brook Green Suite*, whose descending quaver passages evoke the effect of bell-chimes, while in the *Funeral Chant* in the Second Group of *Choral Hymns from the Rig Veda*, a descending bass scale appears augmented in very long note durations.

Such scales are contrapuntal in nature rather than harmonic, as they generally rise and fall within the prevailing harmonic scheme, but a related technique is to use a gapped scalar pattern (often descending) to outline the notes of a triad, as is done in *Saturn*, *Jupiter*, the carol *Masters in This Hall*, and in a rising form in *Hammersmith*, where it forms part of a bitonal ostinato (Ex. 36). Other ostinato bass figures in Holst's work include a motif in fourths in the *First Choral Symphony*, and smaller intervallic fragments in the same work ('Folly's Song') and the *Ode to Death* (Ex. 37). In the Chaconne of the *Suite*

Ex. 36

(a) *Saturn* (b) *Jupiter* (c) *Masters in This Hall* (d) *Hammersmith*

Ex. 37

First Choral Symphony

(a) (b) (c) *Ode to Death*

No. 1 for wind band he uses a true ground bass in the traditional sense, constructing upon it a series of interesting and effective variations.

TONALITY

The use of melodic pivot notes and scalar patterns implies some kind of concept of tonality; the one a 'tonic' or base note from which intervals can depart or return, and the other a set order of notes within the octave from which the composer can choose. These two approaches perhaps reflect the dichotomy between the pragmatic methods of folk-music and the theoretical academicism which has pervaded European art music for many centuries. His training at the Royal College of Music enabled Holst to acquire a good working knowledge of the latter approach, and his enthusiasm for Wagner and admiration for Strauss enabled him to realize the possibilities of extended chromaticism over the entire musical spectrum. However, Holst did not follow this line of development to its logical conclusion as did Schoenberg, but rather developed his own system of tonality, which fuses elements of traditional pitch relationships with a wide-ranging view of the availability of the entire chromatic spectrum. Evidence of this approach can be found in his attitude to key signatures: sometimes he uses them, sometimes not; even within a single work—in *Hammersmith* key signatures are given in the opening Prelude and on two occasions in the Scherzo, but do not appear in the final Poco Adagio, which is similar to the Prelude.

Unwilling to be bound by the constraints of textbook practices, or even by the extended use of Wagnerian chromaticism, Holst was always searching for ways of extending his own musical vocabulary. One way of doing this is to work within scales which diverge from the usual major/minor systems, such as the whole-tone scale, and the pentatonic scale, which can be regarded as a 'gapped' version of the common major scale. A rising whole-tone phrase appears in an otherwise diatonic context in the student opera *The Revoke*, while in *Savitri* there is a descending phrase of whole tones (Ex. 38); both examples demonstrating the capacity of this technique to give an indeterminate feeling to the tonality and

Ex. 38 *Savitri*

a world where all is name - less, un-known,

an inconclusive ending to the melodic phrase. The accompaniment to the song *Creation* in the *Vedic Hymns* introduces a whole-tone arpeggio at the word 'desire', while a more extended use of whole-tone scales can be found in the Second Group of *Choral Hymns from the Rig Veda*, where in *To Varuna* a whole-tone melodic phrase expresses the fluid nature of the subject (God of the Waters) while obscuring the minor tonality, which is nevertheless stated in the harmonization (Ex. 39)—later, a long rising whole-tone scalar melodic line is accompanied by an ostinato of descending whole-tone scales in the bass. In the *Funeral Chant* in the same Group, a whole-tone accompaniment figure is presented first in single notes, then in four-part chords, all drawn from the same scale (Ex. 40). *The Cloud Messenger* contains descending whole-tone bass scales, while in the *Invocation*, the *Perfect Fool* ballet music, and the *First Choral Symphony*, use is made of a fragmentary descending whole-tone motif which gives a characteristic turn to the melodic material (Exx. 41; 26a, b). Occasional pentatonic scales also appear in Holst's work, notably in the *Funeral Chant* from the Second Group of *Choral Hymns from the Rig Veda*, the brilliant opening of *Jupiter* (Ex. 42), and the motet *Sing Me the Men*.

Ex. 39

(a) *Creation*   (b) *To Varuna*

Ex. 40 *Funeral Chant*

Ex. 41

(a) *Invocation*   (b) *First Choral Symphony*

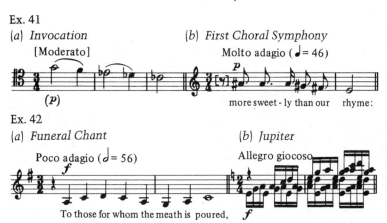

Ex. 42

(a) *Funeral Chant*   (b) *Jupiter*

Another path of divergence from the conventional patterns of diatonic tonality is through the use of modes, which Holst came to use more frequently after his contact with English folk-music, although he had previously come across them in the music of Grieg, and during his organ studies and work on *The English Hymnal*. His orchestral settings of folk-songs in *A Somerset Rhapsody* enabled him to savour the qualities of the Dorian and Aeolian modes, and this influence begins to be apparent in *Savitri*, for example in the sparsely-accompanied 'I am with thee', and in his incidental music for *The Pageant of London* (Ex. 43). Further settings of folk-songs permitted greater familiarity with these particular modes, as in the *Suite No. 2* for wind band, but their use in original composition can cease to be effective if over-used, and Holst soon dropped them except for special purposes such as the quasi-archaic Dorian at the beginning of the *Short Festival Te Deum* and at the mention of the word 'psalms' in *At the Boar's Head*, and the

Ex. 43

(a) *Savitri*

(b) *The Pageant of London*

beautifully fluid Dance of the Spirits of Water in the *Perfect Fool* ballet music (Ex. 44). Sometimes a touch of flattened-seventh modality adds richness of colour in a prevailing diatonic context, as at the end of the first movement of the *Suite No. 1* for wind band, or for expressive purposes, as in his setting of Psalm 86, in which the word 'sadness' is harmonized with a modal cadence venturing outside the main mode of the melody (Ex. 45).

Ex. 44

(a) *At the Boar's Head*   (b)   *The Perfect Fool*

Ex. 45   Psalm 86

Holst found greater possibilities in other modes: in the second of the *Two Eastern Pictures* he uses the Lydian mode (with major/minor ambiguity of the third degree), and the *Hymn to Manas* in the Fourth Group of *Choral Hymns from the Rig Veda* includes both the Lydian and Mixolydian (Ex. 46).

Ex. 46

(a) *Summer*   (b) *Hymn to Manas*

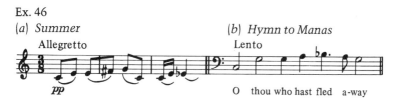

(c) *ibid.*

The Lydian mode crops up again in several works, notably the third movement of the *St Paul's Suite*, the *Perfect Fool* ballet music, and *A Fugal Overture* (Exs. 47;12*a*), while the Mixolydian can be found in *The Hymn of Jesus*, at the beginning of the part-song *Love on My Heart from Heaven Fell*, in *The Coming of Christ*, and the Humbert Wolfe song *Envoi* (Ex. 48). Holst sometimes uses the Mixolydian's implied combination of major scale and flattened seventh to give a touch of folksiness, as in the Wizard's aria 'Looking is loving' in *The Perfect Fool*, or of religiosity, as at the word 'grace' in *The Hymn of Jesus*, or otherwise at the beginning of a piece to give a feeling of tonal indeterminacy and expectancy.

Ex. 47

(*a*) *St Paul's Suite*   (*b*) *The Perfect Fool*

Ex. 48

(*a*) *The Hymn of Jesus*   (*b*) *Love on My Heart from Heaven Fell*

(*c*) *The Coming of Christ*

(*d*) *Envoi*

Having explored Dorian, Aeolian, Lydian, and Mixolydian, Holst turned his attention to the Phrygian mode, which occurs less frequently in English folk-music, but which offers considerable expressive possibilities because of its flattened second degree. An excellent example is the song which begins the first movement of the *First Choral Symphony*, the mode enabling a distinction to be made between the tonic and flattened supertonic, as if the higher note were 'leaning' on the lower, or were a semitonal departure from it, as in Holst's pivot-note technique (Ex. 49). Another example is the rising fragmentary phrase at the beginning of *A Choral Fantasia*, although the harmonization here includes notes which do not lie within the mode (Ex. 25*b*). The tritone formed between the second degree and fifth note also gives the mode its special character, as is evident in the Humbert Wolfe song *Persephone* (Ex. 12*b*).

Ex. 49 *First Choral Symphony*

Holst rarely remains long in any one particular mode, and sometimes alters notes to suit his purposes as he goes along, as in the use of two simultaneous versions of a mode in *The Morning of the Year* (Ex. 50), the sudden change from minor to major tonality in the first of the *Four Songs* for voice and violin, and the piquant use of both G and G sharp, and C and C sharp, in the song *Now in these Fairylands* (Ex. 82). He often abstracts the characteristic features of particular modes, rather than applying their note-patterns rigorously: in the song *The Thought* a Lydian dissonance between sharpened fourth and perfect fifth appears at the word 'tenderness', although with a

Ex. 50 *The Morning of the Year*

minor third (Ex. 51*a*), his chant *In the Lord Put I My Trust* for *The Passing of the Essenes* has the flattened second of the Phrygian, the sharpened fourth of the Lydian, and the flattened sixth of the Aeolian, and in *The Perfect Fool* he introduces a triad in Lydian relationship to a held-over note (Ex. 51*b*). The pivot-note construction of Death's opening aria at the beginning of *Savitri* implies at first some of the characteristics of the harmonic minor scale on A, then of the Lydian mode on A, then of the Phrygian mode on G sharp, while the Mother's phrase in *The Perfect Fool* has something of the character of the harmonic minor scale coupled with the Lydian mode (Exx. 34*a*; 35*a*). The opera *At the Boar's Head* contains a brief passage in which major-third melodic fragments imitated at the interval of a major third produce a whole-tone effect despite the inclusion of a semitone within the scale (Ex. 52).

Ex. 51

(*a*) *The Thought*   (*b*) *The Perfect Fool*

Ex. 52   *At the Boar's Head*

From such alteration of modes and extraction of particular features from within them it is a short step to the construction of entirely new scales which fall neither within the usual major/minor system nor conform to fully modal patterns. Besides the self-consciously 'oriental' scales (emphasizing the augmented second between the sixth and seventh degrees of the harmonic minor scale) which are used in *Beni Mora* and the *St Paul's Suite*, in the early *Mystic Trumpeter* there is an example of a phrase based on a major scale with a flattened sixth as pedal below (Ex. 53), and composite scales first begin to appear systematically in the *Choral Hymns from the Rig Veda*. *To Agni* in the Second Group contains passages of alternating chords which imply an overall scale having features of diatonic major and minor and the Phrygian mode (Ex. 54), and in *To the Unknown God* in the First Group, a descending bass scale embodies elements of the melodic minor scale and Lydian and Phrygian modes to produce a completely new scale, which is also the basis of the *Hymn of the Travellers* in the Third Group (Ex. 55). This same scale appears in the male-voice chorus *Good Friday* as a result of harmonic apoggiaturas, but with the insertion of an extra note, thus producing an eight-note scale within the octave rather than the customary seven (Ex. 56). Another eight-note scale appears in the sketches for *The Song of Solomon* (Ex. 57), while in the part-song *Assemble, All Ye Maidens* the effect of a declamatory melodic line against a sustained perfect fifth accompaniment is to produce an eight-note scale which combines features of the diatonic major and Lydian and Phrygian modes (Ex. 58). A different kind of eight-note scale appears both in *Mercury* and the ballet music from *The Perfect Fool*, here consisting of two

Ex. 53   *The Mystic Trumpeter*

[Moderato]

ppp

Ex. 54   *To Agni*

Allegro (♩ =200)

f >

Flame   for   us   O   Ag - ni!

Ex. 55   (a) *To the Unknown God*   (b) *Hymn of the Travellers*

Adagio

Basic scale:

pp staccato

disjunct tetrachords a tritone apart (Ex. 59), while the opening of *Egdon Heath* makes do with a scale of only six notes within the octave (Ex. 106). Holst seemed particularly fond of an ambiguous scale constructed from the upper notes of a descending melodic minor and the lower part of the major scale, which can be found in *The Hymn of Jesus*, the Scherzo of the *First Choral Symphony* (where it shoots upwards, to return on a descending Aeolian scale a semitone higher), and the male-voice chorus *Drinking Song* (Ex. 60).

Ex. 56   *Good Friday*

Ex. 57   *The Song of Solomon*

Ex. 58   *Assemble, All Ye Maidens*

Ex. 59

(a) *Mercury*   (b) *The Perfect Fool*

Ex. 60

(a) *The Hymn of Jesus*   (b) *First Choral Symphony*

(c) *Drinking Song*

To you, con-sum-mate drink-ers Though lit - tle be your drought,

An alternative view of this last-mentioned scale is as a combination of two major tonalities a major third apart, a pitch relationship which often appears in Holst's work, supplanting the traditional tonic/dominant polarity of conventional diatonicism. Characteristic examples can be found in the song *The Heart Worships* (D/Gb/Bb), the *Hymn of the Travellers* from the Third Group of *Choral Hymns from the Rig Veda* (Dm/F♯m), *Neptune* (Em/G♯m), *The Hymn of Jesus* (C/E, G/B, A/Cm, D/F♯), and the *First Choral Symphony* (Bm/D♯m, Dbm/Fm). Sometimes this is achieved by enharmonic means, as in the *Dirge for Two Veterans*, where the change from F sharp to B flat minor is carried out by the equivalences of A♯/Bb and C♯/Db. In his harmonization, Holst sometimes used the characteristics of the augmented triad, which itself contains implications of this major-third relationship, as in the song *The Thought* and the male-voice chorus *A Love Song* (Ex. 61). The pivotal construction of Death's aria in *Savitri* results in a similar implied major third relationship, between A minor and F minor (Ex. 34a). These examples are all on the small scale, often consisting of simple alternation of chords, but the same pitch relationship can be found in larger dimensions, as in the *Hymn to Dionysus* where the tonality moves to A major after an opening section in F, and in Psalm 148 where the central section is in E major, flanked by opening and closing material in C. Other pitch relationships favoured by Holst include the semitone and the tritone, the first of which can be found

Ex. 61

(a) *The Thought* (b) *A Love Song*

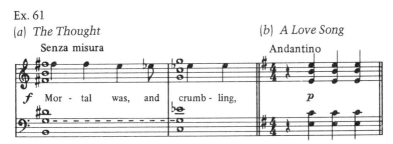

throughout his work. As early as the schoolboy operetta *Lansdown Castle,* he received critical approbation for a 'cleverly handled' modulation from G major into 'the very extraneous key of F Sharp minor';[19] the opera *Sita* and the cantata *King Estmere* contain examples of key change by rising or falling a semitone; the *Ode to Death* and the *First Choral Symphony* both contain passages based on tonalities a semitone apart; and the late canon *If You Love Songs* has a key scheme which remains closely adjacent to its key-note: Am, A, Gm, A♭, A. The tritone relationship appears in the mysterious alternating chords at the beginning of *The Mystic Trumpeter* (Ex. 62), and is a characteristic feature of *Mercury* (Ex. 97e) and the *Perfect Fool* ballet music, whose scales built on tetrachords a tritone apart have already been mentioned.

Ex. 62   *The Mystic Trumpeter*

While still at work on *The Planets,* Holst advised W. G. Whittaker in the matter of tonality: 'Avoid jumping about from one key to another. The modern tendency is to enlarge the scope of a key—a very different thing.'[20] Scant evidence of this principle can be found in Holst's own work however; even in his recently completed *Jupiter* there is an example of a sudden leap from G Mixolydian on to the totally unrelated chord of F♯ major, and in much of his later music it is clear that he regarded the entire chromatic spectrum as available for instantaneous transition without preparation, as is particularly evident in the opera *At the Boar's Head* and the piano *Toccata.* Such an attitude can sometimes have unexpected results, as in the second movement of *A Moorside Suite,* where the seemingly conventional move from F minor/Aeolian to C major has little of the feeling of a tonic-dominant relationship, sounding more like a shift to a new and fresh key, because of the absence of modulatory procedures.

Such an unconstrained approach naturally led him towards bitonality and polytonality, perhaps encouraged by hearing early examples such as Stravinsky's *Petrushka*, although the roots of the technique lie much further back in Holst's own work. The horn and trumpet calls at the beginning of *The Mystic Trumpeter* give an impression of a bitonal combination of the keys of D and B flat (another major-third relationship), and the coda of the second movement of the *Suite No. 1* for wind band combines a Dorian melody on D with a quasi D major melody, over a fifths pedal on C and G. In the second movement of the *St Paul's Suite* the turning ostinato figure continues at the same pitch despite excursions of tonality into the dominant and subdominant keys, as its three notes form part of those scales as well as that of the tonic. The Finale of *Beni Mora* is a *tour de force* of combination of different motifs, each having its own tonal implications, but it was not until Holst became acquainted with the ballets of Stravinsky that he was able to acquire sufficient self-confidence to be able to write polytonal combinations which would predictably come off in performance. The shifting juxtaposition of E minor and G♯ minor in *Neptune* is an excellent example of such confidence; on paper it seems likely to be rather muddled, but the resulting sound is a wonderfully evocative and nebulous expression of far-distant space, without a hint of untoward dissonance.

Sometimes Holst prepares his bitonality in a manner similar to the traditional method of dealing with dissonance in conventional harmony; in *The Hymn of Jesus* he writes an E major triad above a composite scale which contains elements of E major and therefore does not clash too much with the upper parts, but then changes the bass to the Phrygian mode while retaining an E major feeling above, producing an ambiguity between the G natural below and G sharp above, although the music is carefully arranged so that the notes do not clash simultaneously (Ex. 63). A similar method is used in the motet *The Evening Watch*, where he sustains a residual perfect fourth G–C from a C minor chord, and adds to this a solo line in A flat minor, thus producing a composite scale which includes elements of both tonalities (Ex. 64a).

Ex. 63 *The Hymn of Jesus*

Ex. 64

(a) *The Evening Watch* (b) *First Choral Symphony*

In his bitonal combinations, Holst favoured the same pitch relationships as he used for alternating tonalities: the semitone, major third, and augmented fourth. Examples of the semitone relationship can be found in the coda to the Scherzo in the *First Choral Symphony* in which the chords of C and Db minor share an enharmonic E (Ex. 64b), and at the end of *At the Boar's Head* (Ex. 20), both of which are formed from superimposed triads in a harmonic bitonality, while a more linear approach can be found in the Prelude to *Hammersmith*, where a quietly moving melodic line in E major is underlaid by an F minor ostinato. In the *Lyric Movement* the soloist plays a line based on E major, over a sustained perfect fifth on F in the orchestra (Ex. 65). The bitonal interval of a major third can be found in the first movement of the *Double Concerto*, where the soloists play in A Mixolydian and F major simultaneously (Ex. 66), and also in the following Lament, where the keys are G sharp minor (Aeolian) and E minor (Aeolian), although the effect here is much less nebulous than in *Neptune* because of the avoidance of vertical abrasion, and the result sounds more like a modified version of B major or its relative minor (Ex. 67).

Ex. 65 *Lyric Movement*

Andante quasi allegretto

Ex. 66 *Double Concerto*

Allegretto

Ex. 67 *Double Concerto*

Andante

Other examples of major third bitonality occur in the male-voice chorus *Before Sleep*, where A minor (Aeolian) and F minor (Aeolian) are underpinned by a sustained pedal E which is extraneous to both scales (Ex. 68), and the canon *Evening on the Moselle* (Em/Cm Aeolian), whose piano accompaniment figure alternates between the two keys. The tritone relationship appears in later works, such as the *Choral Fantasia*, in which brass calls based on A flat and D recall the opening of *The Mystic Trumpeter*, the canon *If 'Twere the Time of Lilies*, and in *Egdon Heath*, where an ostinato figure is imitated at the interval of an augmented fourth, although once again Holst avoids dissonance by keeping the melodic intervals small so that each figure takes up only a small part of an octave, to produce an almost complete diminished scale (Ex. 69).

Ex. 68   *Before Sleep*

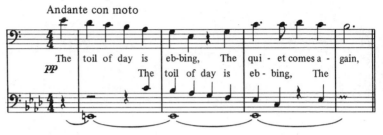

Ex. 69

(a) *A Choral Fantasia*

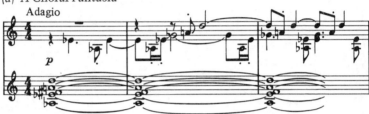

(b) *If 'Twere the Time of Lilies*

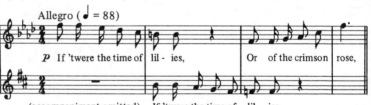

(c) *Egdon Heath*

Other intervallic relationships rarely appear in Holst's bitonal passages, although in the Prelude to the *First Choral Symphony* he writes five entries of a chromatic fugal subject at intervals of a perfect fifth, gradually getting further away from the main key, over a sustained pedal note held throughout by the choir and orchestra. At the beginning of the male-voice chorus *How Mighty are the Sabbaths*, the upper parts carry out a modulatory sequence of chords, while the bass keeps to a descending ostinato scale pattern, although these are largely pedal effects rather than of polytonality.

In the *Terzetto* and some of the *Eight Canons*, more extended examples of polytonality can be found in which the parts are written with their own key-signatures, but once again Holst avoids dissonance as much as possible in vertical combinations, the result sounding more like a composite tonality than simultaneous key-centres. He assumes enharmonic equivalence of all chromatic notes, so that in the *Terzetto* some homophonic passages actually boil down to nothing more than a simple sequence of major and minor triads (Ex. 70). Because of this approach, Holst's bitonality lacks the abrasiveness of that of Milhaud or Stravinsky, and of the *Eight Canons* Holst himself wrote: 'I do like both the singers and listeners to feel the two keys quite distinctly and I think that making the former do so helps the effect to the latter ... It is something quite apart from the hits and squashes of conventional modern harmony. And I felt secretly flattered when an excellent musician complained that my two-key writing won't do because it has no "wrong notes" in it.'[21]

Ex. 70 *Terzetto*

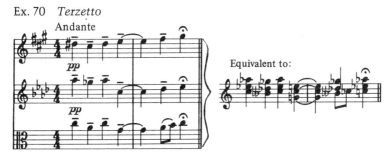

HARMONY

Holst's avoidance of dissonance in his polytonal writing does not imply that he was averse to it or insensitive to the nuances of more complex harmony, as his work shows ample evidence of his awareness of the evocative power of particular chords and of his willingness to try out various harmonic possibilities. But such an exploratory attitude went hand in hand with use of harmony in more traditional guises, and it is this mixture of the unusual and the conventional which has often disconcerted even sympathetic listeners.

Many examples can be found of Holst's use of simple triadic

harmony, although as his career progressed he came to disregard conventional usage and often used triads simply to double melodic lines, as in the first inversions used in *A Choral Fantasia*, taking enharmonic equivalence for granted and regarding the entire chromatic scale as his province (Ex. 71). In *Mars*, a winding melodic line is doubled in parallel triads whose chromaticism ventures outside the ostensible key of the movement (Ex. 18*a*), thus reinforcing the inherent acoustical properties of the melodic notes (as Ravel was later to do in his *Bolero*). A similar device appears in *The Perfect Fool* in much faster figuration, impossible to play single-handedly on the piano but very effective in an orchestral context (Ex. 72), and in *The Lure* imitative whole-tone melodic fragments are doubled in triads, producing a chromatic effect (Ex. 73).

Ex. 71   *A Choral Fantasia*

Ex. 72   *The Perfect Fool*

Ex. 73   *The Lure*

Another characteristic way of dealing with triads which leads to chromatic results is Holst's habit of moving the outer notes of a triad by a semitone (or whole tone) often in contrary motion, while the central note either remains static as a pivot, or itself moves by a semitone. This generally works best with minor triads, and examples can be found in *Savitri*, *To Varuna*

in the Second Group of *Choral Hymns from the Rig Veda*, the *Seven Choruses from the Alcestis of Euripides*, and as late as the cadence at the end of the canon *Lovely Venus* (Ex. 74). This technique assumes total enharmonic equivalence of chromatic notes, which Holst takes for granted throughout his work, in both instrumental and vocal music, often using the pivot-note technique to link harmonies together, as in the song *The Thought* (Ex. 61).

Ex. 74

(*a*) *Savitri*   (*b*) *To Varuna*   (*c*) *Seven Choruses*   (*d*) *Lovely Venus*

Such a free-ranging attitude to chromaticism doubtless originated during his Wagnerian period, when in works such as *A Winter Idyll*, the overture *Walt Whitman*, *Sita*, and *The Mystic Trumpeter*, Holst demonstrated a competence in handling nineteenth-century harmonic techniques, even though the result was often rather dull and lacking in originality. In *A Somerset Rhapsody*, he combined chromatic harmonization with modal melodic material in a most expressive way, but from this point onwards harmonic chromaticism began to decline in his work, and *The Cloud Messenger*, the *Hymn to Dionysus*, and the *Ode to Death* are virtually the last examples of it, although in the Wagnerian parody in *The Perfect Fool*, he showed that he was still capable of emulating the style of his former hero.

Coupled with this changing attitude towards conventional chromaticism was his development of the notion of the use of harmony for its own expressive and evocative properties rather than for its ability to hold together melodic phrases or for modulatory purposes: he was discovering non-functional harmony. An interesting example of this change in attitude can be seen by comparing a phrase in *King Estmere* with its later reuse in *Mars*. In the earlier cantata Holst finds it necessary to resolve his seventh chords conventionally on to a triad, but in *Mars* he simply uses them for their own sake, sometimes moving to plain triads, sometimes to further dissonance, according to the needs of the music, always avoiding a feeling of harmonic or tonal repose (Ex. 75).

Ex. 75

(a) *King Estmere* (b) *Mars*

Holst was clearly sensitive to the expressive feeling of particular chords, as in Savitri's cry of 'Satyavan' on the major seventh of an F minor harmony, his use of a similar chord in diminished form to evoke mystery and suspense at the beginning of *Beni Mora*, and the plaintive diminished seventh in Psalm 86 (Ex. 76). Other examples of chords used for their own sake include the augmented ninth at the phrase 'with one word' in *The Perfect Fool*, and the famous 'magic' ninth chord in *Uranus*. At the word 'pierce' in *The Hymn of Jesus* Holst uses a seventh-chord with false-relation thirds, and at the word 'soar' in the Scherzo of the *First Choral Symphony* there is an augmented chord with major seventh, a chord which contains implications of Holst's two-key major third polarity (Ex. 77). In the carol *Terly Terlow* the use of a thirteenth-chord on G

Ex. 76

(a) *Savitri* (b) *Beni Mora* (c) Psalm 86

Ex. 77

(a) *The Perfect Fool* (c) *The Hymn of Jesus*

(b) *Uranus* (d) *First Choral Symphony*

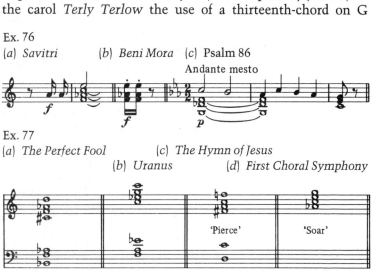

following E major expresses the words ('Light-stream') beautifully, as does the third-inversion seventh-chord at 'Slumbering
men' in *The Coming of Christ*, while in *Beni Mora* there is
even a Stravinskian neo-classical harmony containing elements
of more than one chord, an effect which recurs in a rich
cadence near the end of the *Lyric Movement* (Ex. 78). Plain
triads could also function expressively in Holst's vocabulary,
as in the first inversion E flat chord (following a phrase in D
major) in *King Estmere* at the words 'Fight or go home' (Ex. 79),
and the extraordinary reiteration of the opening rhythm of
Jupiter, again on a first inversion, of F sharp (Ex. 2).

Ex. 78 (*a*) *Terly Terlow* (*b*) *The Coming of Christ* (*c*) *Beni Mora*
(*d*) *Lyric Movement*

Ex. 79 *King Estmere*

Other elements of traditional harmonic usage appear throughout Holst's work, which he seems to use side by side with
more radical procedures without any sense of incongruity.
Venus ends on a restful root-position sixth-chord, as does the
Prelude of the *Japanese Suite* (second inversion), while the
motet *The Evening Watch* also ends on a second inversion
sixth chord, for all its preceding austere fourth-chord progressions. Even the appoggiatura makes an appearance in the
sequence of chords towards the end of the Finale of the *St*

Paul's Suite (Ex. 80), and in a passage in *Beni Mora* which also
reappears in a very effective form in *Mars* (Ex. 81). By the time
of the *Twelve Songs* of 1929, Holst felt free to use any
conventional harmonic combination if it suited his purpose,
without any self-conscious feelings of being old-fashioned,
reactionary, or academic. So in *Now in these Fairylands* we
find suspended fourths, in *The Thought* some beautifully
expressive appoggiaturas, in *Journey's End* various major and
minor seventh-chords (ending with a doom-laden second-
inversion A minor seventh), in *Envoi* minor chords with major
sevenths and unresolved augmented fourth degrees, and in
Rhyme a harmonic scheme based mainly on first-inversion
triads (Ex. 82).

Ex. 80   *St Paul's Suite*

Ex. 81

(a) *Beni Mora*

(b) *Mars*

Ex. 82
(a) *Now in these Fairylands*

Lento

Now in these fair - y-lands ga - ther your wear - y hands

(b) *The Thought*

Senza misura

What words can do - stir the air,

(c) *Journey's End*

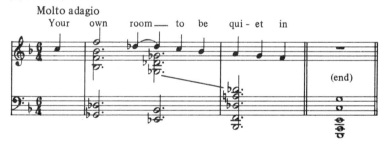

Molto adagio

Your own room — to be qui - et in

(end)

(d) *Envoi*

Moderato

spell of dust lies on all that was well be - thought

(e) *Rhyme*

Poco vivace

p We hear ring- ing, far- off and clear,

Apart from using conventional resources in his own way, Holst also turned towards making new harmonic combinations, the simplest method of which is to add extra notes to triads by way of extending their possibilities. But although the traditional method of doing this is to extend them upwards, reinforcing their overtones by adding further notes of the harmonic series such as sevenths, ninths, and thirteenths, Holst's method was frequently to add notes below them, often in the form of pedal-points, so that the notes of the original triad now become overtones of the new bass note.

There are many examples in his work of a dissonant note being placed beneath a triad, from the *Invocation* of 1911 to the *Lyric Movement* of 1933, including *The Perfect Fool*, the *First Choral Symphony*, *The Wandering Scholar*, and *A Choral Fantasia*, in all of which there are instances of a major triad with a sharpened fourth degree placed below (Ex. 83). Holst was particularly attracted by the sound of this Lydian relationship, and in *Egdon Heath* it is made a prominent feature of the thematic material. The expressive semitonal clash is also evident in the second movement of the *Fugal Concerto*, but here as an abrasion between major and minor thirds of an implied triadic harmony. The other dissonant note which often appears in his work is the major seventh: in *The Hymn of Jesus* it resolves on to a two-note chord which itself contains a Lydian dissonance, while in other works it is simply added to the triad for extra spice (sometimes in addition to a sharpened fourth) without preparation or resolution, generally in the lowest part, but sometimes in other voices (Ex. 84).

Holst's use of pedal notes can be traced back to his early organ studies and schoolboy enthusiasm for the music of Grieg, an influence which can be found in such works as the

Ex. 83
(a) *Invocation*   (b) *The Perfect Fool*   (c) *First Choral Symphony*
(d) *The Wandering Scholar* (e) *A Choral Fantasia* (f) *Lyric Movement*

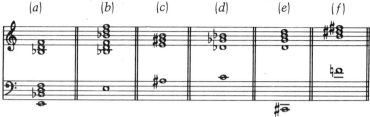

Ex. 84
(a) *Egdon Heath*   (b) *A Fugal Concerto*   (c) *The Hymn of Jesus*

(d) *The Mystic Trumpeter*

early *Two Dances* for piano duet and the *Suite de Ballet*, in both of which there are drone pedal-points in perfect fifths, a device which reappears in as late a work as the *First Choral Symphony* (Ex. 85). *Savitri* contains examples of sustained pedal notes, but always in these examples the pedal has been conceived as part of the prevailing harmony. However Holst soon began to explore other possibilities, and in the *Hymn to Vena* in the Third Group of *Choral Hymns from the Rig Veda* the singers sustain an internal pedal point while the harmonies of the accompaniment gradually change, an effective and atmospheric device which he was to use on a more extended

scale in the Prelude to the *First Choral Symphony*. In his
setting of Psalm 86, besides a long dominant pedal beneath a
modal melody, there is a strident and emotive clash of a chord
on the flattened second degree of the scale against a tonic
pedal, and this notion of chromatic upper parts conflicting
with a stable pedal bass was to become the basis of much of his
harmonic thinking in *Mars*, composed two years later (Ex. 86).
The same idea is used in the ballet music from *The Perfect
Fool*, particularly the dance of the Spirits of Fire, in which a
stable G pedal note is held against changing tonalities in the
upper parts, and in the slow movement of the *First Choral Symphony* where a basic C pedal underlies various upper harmonies.

Ex. 85

(*a*) *Two Dances*   (*b*) *Suite de Ballet*

(*c*) *First Choral Symphony*

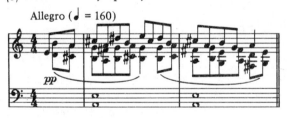

Ex. 86   Psalm 86

A further stage in harmonic exploration is to abandon altogether the idea of the triad as the fundamental unit of harmony
and to seek intervallic combinations based on intervals other
than the major and minor third. Holst turned to fourths and
fifths as offering possibilities for harmonic exploration, perhaps
initially because they can be simply regarded as parts of triads
from which the third has been omitted, thus offering an
ambiguity of major/minor implications, but also because of
their qualities of primitive evocation, as in the Vedic Hymn
Varuna I and his early operetta *Lansdown Castle*, in which
Holst harmonized a plainchant phrase in parallel fourths as a
magic incantation. This evocative power of unadorned fourths
and fifths is used by Holst to produce an archaic effect in the
Hymn of the Travellers in the Third Group of *Choral Hymns
from the Rig Veda* and a soothing atmosphere at the beginning
of the *Ode to Death*, while in *Mercury* an ostinato in parallel
fifths accompanies the fleeting violin melody, in all cases
involving the harp, an instrument with archaic connotations
(Ex. 87). In the *Perfect Fool* ballet music, the melody of the
Spirits of Water is enhanced by doubling in parallel fifths and
octaves within the mode (Ex. 44*b*), while the Dance of the
Spirits of Earth contains melodic lines doubled mainly in

Ex. 87

(*a*) *Hymn of the Travellers*   (*b*) *Ode to Death*

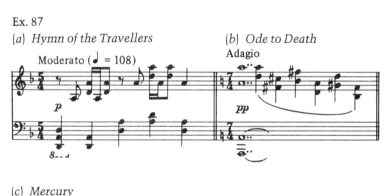

(*c*) *Mercury*

perfect fourths, necessitating the use of chromatic notes outside the tonality. Such doubling in fourths can be found in *Egdon Heath*, which also includes an example of the use of stark open fifths emphasizing the nature of the subject-matter (Ex. 88). Doubling of the melodic line in parallel fourths within the mode can be found in the *Fugal Overture* and the part-song *Angel Spirits of Sleep*, in which the accompaniment consists of two lines in contrary motion, the upper a pentatonic line doubled in perfect fourths and the lower in parallel sixths (Ex. 89). A version of the main theme of *A Fugal Overture* is given out in strident perfect fifths at one point, and other examples of harmonic doubling in parallel fifths can be found in the *Double Concerto* and *Hammersmith*.

Ex. 88

(a) *The Perfect Fool*   (b) *Egdon Heath*

Ex. 89

(a) *A Fugal Overture*   (b) *Angel Spirits of Sleep*

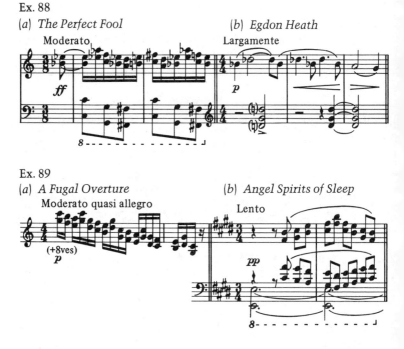

From such doubling of melodic lines, it is clear that Holst did not consider an interval such as the perfect fourth as a dissonance requiring eventual resolution, but regarded both fourths and fifths as entities in their own right, each having its own characteristic quality. This opens the way for the use of such intervals as elements in new chords, the actual building process being exposed in such passages as the opening of the *Ode on a Grecian Urn*, in which successive perfect fifths are sustained vertically above each other (Ex. 30*b*). The inverse process can be observed at the beginning of *The Lure*, where fourth- chords are built downwards with magical effect, but having established that chords can be made up from fourths as well as thirds, Holst generally did not bother to exhibit the constructional process, and simply used them in the same way as ordinary triads. The *First Choral Symphony* contains many examples of fourth-chords, often consisting of an upper and lower group, sometimes in contrary motion, revealing the keyboard origins of this and much else of Holst's harmony. Perhaps his most characteristic use of fourth-chords is in the motet *The Evening Watch*, in which the intervals are piled up almost beyond the reach of fingers on a keyboard, and involving considerable pitching problems for the singers, but the resulting sound is very atmospheric (Ex. 90*c*).

Ex. 90

(*a*) *The Lure*   (*b*) *First Choral Symphony*   (*c*) *The Evening Watch*

In the song *Betelgeuse* Holst used the sustaining properties of the piano to build up skeletal chords which can be regarded either as the semitonal juxtaposition of two perfect fifths (F/C and B/E) with octave doublings, or as a mixture of fourths, fifths, and sevenths (Ex. 91). In fact he had soon realized that that the persistent use of chords built solely from one interval such as the perfect fourth soon leads to tedium, and that variety of intervallic construction is the path towards production of the most effective results. One such combination of which he was particularly fond is the superposition of an augmented fourth above a perfect fourth, which is used to strident effect in *Mars,* and of which there are frequent examples in his later work, such as the motet *Sing Me the Men,* the choral ballet *The Golden Goose, Egdon Heath, Hammer-smith,* and the *Lyric Movement,* often appearing at moments of climax or of static suspense in preparation for subsequent forward movement. Because of the augmented interval, such a chord contains suggestions of bitonality; in the *Capriccio* there is an example in which Holst gives the upper note to the strings in four octaves, while the remaining notes appear in the brass, giving this instrumental colour its own region of tonality, linked to the string sound via the tuba which doubles the cellos (Ex. 92).

Ex. 91   *Betelgeuse*

Ex. 92

(a) *Mars* (b) *Sing Me the Men* (c) *The Golden Goose* (d) *Egdon Heath*
    (e) *Hammersmith*   (f) *Lyric Movement*   (g) *Capriccio*

(a)   (b)   (c)   (d)   (e)   (f)   (g)

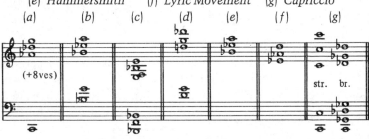

Some of Holst's dissonant effects arise through the movement of parts, rather than being conceived as static combinations. In several instances such dissonance is associated with words which refer to mirrors, light, or space, suggesting a strong connection in Holst's mind between harmonic abrasion and the mysterious behaviour of light. For example, in *Savitri*, at the words 'The forest is to me a mirror', the bass of the accompaniment reflects the notes of the melody beneath an augmented triad to produce an effect of strange mystery; the *Hymn to Manas* in the fourth Group of *Choral Hymns from the Rig Veda* contains a passage of contrary motion of chordal lines whose dissonances express the words 'Radiant light, whose flashing beams flow on through space'; the part-song *Angel Spirits of Sleep* has contrary dissonant motion in the accompaniment at the words 'With your moonlit play'; and in *A Choral Fantasia* a passage of contrary chordal motion with passing dissonances appears at the words 'He calleth the stars by name' (Ex. 93).

Ex. 93

(a) *Savitri*

(b) *Hymn to Manas*

(c) *Angel Spirits of Sleep* (d) *A Choral Fantasia*

Other examples of dissonance arising from movement of parts or chordal lines abound: in the *Japanese Suite* movement of a bass part produces a dissonance aginst the melody note above; in the *First Choral Symphony* triads move in contrary motion within the Lydian mode to represent 'Forest branches', and in the same work triads converge on to a dissonant bitonal chord at the word 'warm' (Ex. 94). In the motet *Sing Me the Men* imitative entries at the interval of a third result in a chord with bitonal implications; in *Egdon Heath* converging wood-wind lines in fourths and thirds arrive at a seventh chord with flattened fifth, while in *A Choral Fantasia* parts moving in

Ex. 94

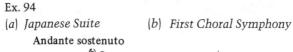

(a) *Japanese Suite* (b) *First Choral Symphony*

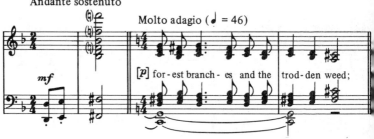

(c) *First Choral Symphony*

contrary motion again produce a bitonal chord (Ex. 95). The wonderfully atmospheric opening of the Finale of *Beni Mora* is achieved by contrary motion of string parts, producing only mild dissonance but in a much lower register than is usual, and the unaccompanied choral ending of *Neptune* also consists of chords in contrary motion (Ex. 96).

Ex. 95

(a) *Sing Me the Men*

(b) *Egdon Heath*

(c) *A Choral Fantasia*

Ex. 96

(a) *Beni Mora*

(b) *Neptune*

Instead of extended progressions, much of Holst's harmonization consists simply of alternation of chords, which hostile critics disparaged as 'merely irritating',[22] and even such a close friend as Balfour Gardiner declared to be 'a most terrible habit ... it ruins all his music'.[23] Such alternating chords can be found in *The Mystic Trumpeter*, *The Cloud Messenger*, the *Hymn of the Travellers* in the third Group of *Choral Hymns*

from the Rig Veda, Venus, Mercury, Saturn, and *Neptune* in
The Planets, and *The Hymn of Jesus,* in all cases the effect
being to produce a feeling of motion without modulation or
changing the essential atmosphere of the harmony (Exx. 97;
96b). Sometimes the chords are related and within the same
key or mode, while others are quite unrelated, as in *Mercury,*
where the alternating triads are a tritone apart. The effect of
exactly parallel chords which include notes outside the key, as
in *Saturn* (Ex. 97f), the effect is to obscure the key centre,
leaving a vague tonal indeterminacy.

Ex. 97

(a) *The Mystic Trumpeter*   (c) *Hymn of the Travellers*

(b) *The Cloud Messenger*

(d) *Venus*   (e) *Mercury*

(f) *Saturn*   (g) *The Hymn of Jesus*

From alternation of unrelated chords to simultaneous sounding of them is a step which may have been prompted by the sustaining effects of the piano, at which Holst composed, or by logical reasoning as was done by Darius Milhaud who evolved his own system of bitonality and polytonality at about the same time that Holst was making his own ventures into this field. In *Neptune* the former process can be seen at work; the two tonalities of E minor and G sharp minor first appear alternately, and are then combined to produce a scintillating bitonal atmosphere (Ex. 98a). This experience gave Holst the confidence to write simultaneous passing triads a semitone apart in *The Hymn of Jesus* at the words 'To you who gaze a lamp am I' (Ex. 98b), while in the *First Choral Symphony* he used bitonal chords extensively as a regular part of his harmonic vocabulary, particularly in the slow movement to express evocative words such as 'ecstasy' (Eb/D7), 'beauty' (Bm/C), 'young' (Dm/E+), 'panting' (Bb/A7), and 'escape' (Am/B+) (Ex. 99). In the Scherzo of that work, the chords of D flat minor and C major are combined into a sort of composite tonality which has much of the character of both keys and adds to the fleetness of the music (Ex. 64b). Even in *At the Boar's Head*

Ex. 98

(a) *Neptune*   (b) *The Hymn of Jesus*

Ex. 99   *First Choral Symphony*

(a)   (b)

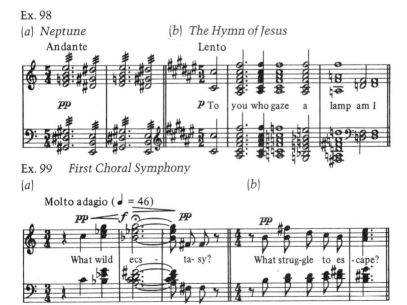

which is based almost entirely on traditional tunes, Holst made extensive used of bitonal chords, resulting mainly from keyboard patterns, but adding interest to what could otherwise have become merely conventionally routine harmonization.

FORM

Despite Holst's explorations in the fields of melody, tonality, and harmony, he still had to cope with the problem of form, a factor faced by all composers, both conservative and radical. Simply to have good ideas is not enough; they must also be expressed in a coherent and satisfactory way. Curiously, Holst's interest in Eastern literature and philosophy did not lead him to the conclusion reached by some later twentieth-century avant-garde composers influenced by Zen Buddhism: that independent objective beauty of form does not exist, and that the most important factor is the attitude of the perceiver towards a work of art. On the contrary, he believed strongly in the existence of certain abstract principles: 'Clearness of outline, fineness of texture, beauty of form in relation to content',[24] and that these factors were independent of style or epoch. 'We all should know that the essentials in Art are eternal,' he declared, 'and beneath the surface one feels the essentials in a beautiful piece of music of the 16th century just as much as in one of the 20th century . . . All Art is one below the surface.'[25]

But by this he did not mean that form was simply a matter of filling in pre-existing structures with fresh ideas. 'Significant Form is not and cannot be imitation,' he declared; 'Art like Nature is always creating and never repeating. . . So one of the safe uses of your knowledge of Mozart's Form is to remember that, as you are not Mozart and are not living in his age or circumstances, if you produce music which has Significant Form, its external details will probably be different from his.'[26]

He also wrote: 'If Mozart's sonata form be beautiful in this sense, then certain critics were right in blaming Beethoven and others for not keeping to it. But ideally beautiful form is that which—among other ·qualities—is at one with that which it enfolds.'[27] He believed that each piece of music should have its own form which is the ideal expression of its content: 'Each Significant form in Art occurs once and is unique'; nor can form be calculated or codified with any scientific exactitude: 'Artistic Form to me has a wonderful live quality . . . it seems to transcend all ordinary laws instead of ignoring or flouting them.'[28]

Although Holst understood that form is what distinguishes art from mere self-expression, he was wary of the dangers of concentrating on form for its own sake: ' "Beauty of form" is good, but it has misled people to think that any form can be beautiful apart from its relation to its contents.'[29] . . . 'No composer has given us true form without true inspiration; he has only given us "cold storage".'[30]

Such idealistic remarks are easy to make, but much more difficult to put into practice. However, as usual Holst was undeterred by the enormity of the task, and set himself to finding solutions to these problems. His approach was partly negative rather than constructive, in the sense that he tended to avoid those types of form with which he was not in sympathy. So we find little in the way of sonata form in Holst's music, as neither of its two essential characteristics—tension between tonal centres and development of thematic material —were intrinsic to his style. Because of Holst's radical attitude to unrelated keys, in which he regarded the entire chromatic spectrum as available for instant use, the construction of forms on the basis of departure from a tonic key and eventual return to it did not appeal to him. The reasons for his aversion from development are harder to ascertain, perhaps connected with his dislike of 'padding', which he regarded as simply a long-winded way of saying something when a concise statement would serve just as well, but perhaps also influenced by his experiences in folk-song setting in which the character of the original tune must remain sacrosanct. Development techniques involve mutation of the original material, thus destroying some of its original character, and breaking the atmospheric unity of a piece. Holst evaded this problem to a certain extent by his techniques of patterning, whereby repetition of phrases and slightly changing patterns provide variation and push the music forward, while retaining the essence of an idea. Although he claimed that *A Fugal Overture* was in strict sonata form, despite the outlines of the shape being present, the interplay between functionally related keys and the development and transformation of material are not.

Few other conventional forms appear in Holst's music. As a student he was required to write pieces in the form of Air and Variations, and this experience led to his use of variation technique in the Wind Quintet of 1903, and perhaps later to his treatment of the 'Dargason' in the Finale of the *St Paul's Suite* and *Suite No. 2* for wind band. From Purcell he acquired an appreciation of the ground bass, resulting in the elegantly constructed Chaconne in the *Suite No. 1* for wind band and the Variations on a Ground of the *Double Concerto*. His early works contain examples of genre forms, such as March, Valse, Ländler, Minuet, and Scherzo, most of which were soon abandoned, with the exception of the Scherzo, which crops up throughout his career as a manner rather than a formal structure, as is evident in *The Planets*, the *First Choral Symphony*, *A Moorside Suite*, the *Double Concerto*, *Hammersmith*, and the final *Scherzo*.

Rather than accepting the formal structures of musical consensus, Holst was much more at home inventing his own, an achievement for which he has been given little credit. Each one of his works has its own form, based on his own principles of Clarity, Balance, and Unity,[31] producing coherent structures in which nothing is out of place and whose proportions are satisfying to the listening ear. Even such works as *A Somerset Rhapsody*, *Beni Mora*, *Egdon Heath*, and *Hammersmith*, whose inspiration derives from programmatic, literary, or visual connotations, are in fact constructed according to well-organized musical schemes.

The way in which Holst carried this out was by creating sectional patterns of contrasting material which are held together by cross-references and thematic relationships, a technique in which organic growth plays little part, and which has more in common with the structures of later twentieth-century music than those of his contemporaries. Such a method works well with the smaller durations within which Holst often worked, but also with the individual movements of a full-scale symphonic work such as *The Planets*. So successful was he that one critic found the violently emotional expression of *Mars* to be 'severely, classically "tidy", without one futile note',[32] another declared the mosaic patterning of *Egdon Heath* to be nothing less than a 'one-movement symphony',[33] while Edmund Rubbra considered every piece Holst wrote to be 'a miracle of condensation',[34] later pointing out that Holst 'was fundamentally more interested in letting the light of the intellect play upon the *sensuous* nature of pure sound than in architectural design. As a formalist, Holst does not use the conventions of development, but substitutes a highly idiomatic use of pattern, upon which changes are rung and yet which do not move away from their particular position in musical space.'[35] This curiously static quality of Holst's structural technique can be observed in the second section of *Venus*, in which the music has feelings of movement and expansion, but only succeeds in ending up where it began.

By way of illustration of Holst's sectional forms, it is useful to look at some examples in terms of elapsed time, reducing the various changes of metre and tempo to one durational continuum which can be regarded as a chart of the time-span of the piece.

An early example is the *Somerset Rhapsody*, which although deriving from programmatic considerations, is in fact much more rigorously constructed than may be apparent at first hearing. The work is built out of four folk-tunes: the 'Sheep-Shearing Song', 'High Germany', 'The True Lover's Farewell', and 'The Cuckoo', which are presented sequentially in sections which form an interrelated pattern. It begins with a statement of the 'Sheep-Shearing Song', which is repeated in a different setting and tonality. Then follows a transitional section in which fragments of this tune are mingled with fragments of 'High Germany', which has a further fragmentary section to itself before being presented in full, followed by a repeated version. The next tune, 'The True Lover's Farewell', begins without any link to the preceding material (except for being in the same key), but its expected repeat turns out to be the second half only, the remainder of the section being taken up by a fragmentary version of 'High Germany'. These two tunes are then combined, before 'High Germany' emerges triumphant, first in fragmentary form, and then in full presentation. 'The Cuckoo' then appears, without any linking material, followed by a reappearance of 'The True Lover's Farewell' in a luscious chromatically-harmonized version. This tune is repeated, and fragments of the original 'Sheep-Shearing Song' begin to appear, eventually leading to a recapitulation of this tune, to which is added 'The Cuckoo' in a faster tempo, before the mood reverts to that of the beginning. Such a verbal description belies the essential simplicity of the form, in which the sections containing the various tunes are arranged in linked pairs within the structure. It is interesting to note that the points at which new tunes are introduced without first being presented in fragmentary form coincide exactly with the Golden Section proportions of durational time, although whether Holst consciously calculated this is open to speculation (Fig. 1).

Fig. 1   *A Somerset Rhapsody*: approximate durational proportions of the sections.

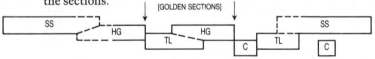

[SS=Sheep Shearing song, HG=High Germany, TL=The True Lover's Farewell, C=The Cuckoo]

The success of *A Somerset Rhapsody* as a musical structure confirmed Holst's intuitive belief that effective musical forms could be built without resorting to traditional techniques of development or variation, and he applied the same method to most of his subsequent works. All the movements of *The Planets*, for example, are built on a sectional basis, contrasting various types of material. Some, such as *Venus* and *Saturn*, have only two basic types of material; *Mars* has three; *Mercury, Jupiter,* and *Uranus* four. These structures all involve cross-relationships between the sections, although literal repetitions are generally avoided, but perhaps the most remarkable of all is *Neptune*, in which there is no such reference back—the sections succeed each other without recapitulation to produce an ideal representation of a journey into the outer reaches of the universe, from which there can be no return (Fig. 2).

All these movements seem to 'work' in the sense that the proportions seem right, nothing is out of place, and they are neither too short nor outstay their welcome. As in the *Somerset Rhapsody*, this is achieved by division of the durational time into harmonious proportions commensurate with the musical content of the sections, generally with a 'centre of gravity' at or near the Golden Section division. Within such a method, Holst achieves a variety of forms in his works, the linking of related sections in pairs tending to produce an 'arch' form, which is particularly noticeable in *Hammersmith* because of the contrast between the slow music of the Prelude at the beginning, middle, and end, and the fast Scherzo material between. His most extraordinary formal achievement must surely be the one-movement *Egdon Heath*, which holds together despite being made up of a large number of short sections based on no less than six distinct, yet related, undeveloping motifs (Fig. 3).

Such fragmentary structures might easily degenerate into incoherence unless they are held together by thematic relationships in addition to recapitulation of recognizable material, and there is ample evidence that Holst gave considerable thought to this problem. One of his early devices was the combination towards the end of a movement of themes which have previously been heard separately, as if revealing that they had been meant for each other all along. This happens at the end of both the *Country Song* in the *Two Songs Without Words*, and the Intermezzo in the *Suite No. 1* for wind band, and reappears as late as the final section of *Hammersmith*. But more pervasive is his method of providing cross-references between the thematic material of the various sections of a single movement. Although Vaughan Williams wrote of the central theme of *Jupiter*: 'It is a pity that this theme is hidden in the middle of "Jupiter" which it does not seem altogether to fit,'[36] it is clear that the various sections of that movement do in fact have close motivic relationships, and the ternary form holds together despite Vaughan Williams's contention that the

Fig. 2 *The Planets*: approximate durational proportions

(*a*) *Mars*

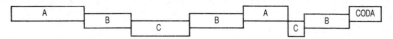

(*b*) *Venus*

(*c*) *Mercury*

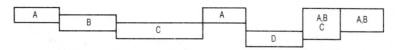

(*d*) *Jupiter*

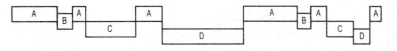

(*e*) *Saturn*

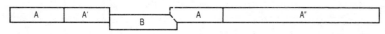

(*f*) *Uranus*

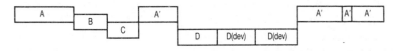

(*g*) *Neptune*

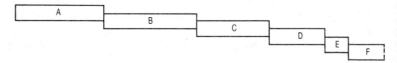

Fig. 3   Approximate durational proportions of sections:
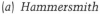
(a) *Hammersmith*

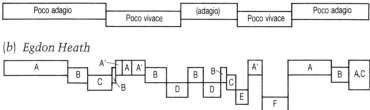

(b) *Egdon Heath*

tune 'ought to be the climax of some great movement which
would take the place in the public affections of the sentiment-
alities of *Finlandia*'.[37] In this movement, Holst used the very
first opening notes of minor third plus major second to derive
the diverse thematic material of the various sections, sometimes obviously, and sometimes subliminally, as in the
permutated version in 3/4 (Ex. 100). In *Mars* the twining
semitonal melody of the second section (Ex. 18) is clearly
derived from the dramatic semitone of its opening, in the same
way that the 'four-flute' tune in *Saturn* is derived from the
semitone in its own opening phrase. In *Egdon Heath* much use
is made of a melodic major second as a unifying device, while
in *Hammersmith* motivic relationships can be traced between

Ex. 100   *Jupiter*

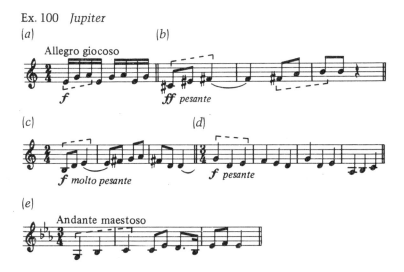

the music of the Prelude and the ensuing Scherzo, and also within the Scherzo itself.

These cross-references are not confined to sections within a single movement, as Holst's multi-movement works abound with links between the movements. The most celebrated example is his derivation of the thematic material for all three movements of the wind band *Suite No. 1* from the bass of the opening Chaconne (Ex. 101), and in the suite *Beni Mora* the semiquaver duplet of the first movement provides the basis for the timpani ostinato of the second (Exs. 76*b*;117). The seven large movements of *The Planets* exhibit links as well as contrasts, providing the Unity and Balance of Holst's own philosophy. The menacing opening motif of *Mars*, consisting of a rising fifth with adjacent falling semitone, reappears at the beginning of *Saturn* in a slightly altered version with the semitone rising to the fifth, to be transformed into the theme

Ex. 101   *Suite No. 1*

(*a*)

(*b*)

(*c*)   (*d*)

(*e*)

of a 'sad procession' as a perfect fourth with major second, which re-emerges at the end of the movement in a mood of peaceful resignation. The same three notes from the beginning of *Saturn* also form the basis of the accompaniment material of *Uranus* (Exx. 27*b,c*; 19), whose end is linked to the beginning of the following movement *Neptune* by the mutation of the prominent thematic falling major third into a minor version. The ostinato chords of *Saturn* can be regarded as a rhythmic augmentation of the alternating chords in *Venus* (Ex. 97); *Saturn* and *Uranus* are linked by the use of a major second in their thematic material (Ex. 102); similar woodwind figurations appear in both *Jupiter* and *Saturn*; and *Neptune* contains a reminiscence of the rising scale figure first heard in *Venus*. These selected examples show that the sequence of seven apparently diverse movements actually contains a complex web of interrelationships acting as cohesive links within what is in fact a kind of double four-movement symphonic structure: Allegro, Adagio, Scherzo, Allegro; this last acting as the pivotal beginning of a new sequence of four: Allegro, Adagio, Scherzo, with a final Adagio instead of the expected Allegro.

Ex. 102

(*a*) *Saturn*   (*b*) *Uranus*

Similar examples of linkage can be found in many of Holst's other works: several themes in *The Perfect Fool* are related by anapaestic rhythm and melodic shape (Ex. 44*b*;47*b*;111); in the *Fugal Concerto* an anapaestic fragment in the first movement is echoed by a minor triplet version in the Finale; and in the *Double Concerto* the opening minor second motif is a precursor of later themes, the second movement develops material from the first, while the Finale contains quotations from both preceding movements.

In the field of choral and vocal music, the possibilities for purely musical construction are obviously much more limited because of the constraints of the text. Although bearing an ostensible resemblance to a multi-movement orchestral symphony, the *First Choral Symphony* shows little of the internal structure of a purely instrumental work, as Holst was obliged to follow the sequence of poetic lines. But he did attempt to provide points of reference by repetition of material and by means of overall stylistic character. There are also indications in his other choral works that he attempted to provide formal coherence, apart from the obvious use of simple strophic forms in which the music is the same for each verse of a song or part-song, as in the *Hymn to the Dawn* in the Third Group of *Choral Hymns from the Rig Veda*. In *The Hymn of Jesus* Holst used the triadic 'Amens' of the semi-chorus to separate the phrases of the Hymn itself, and the opening plainsong melodies are brought into the choral texture towards the end to provide a reflection of the beginning of the work, which ends not as it began but on one of the previously intermediary 'Amens'. Repetition of the opening material also occurs in the *Choral Fantasia*, but as ever, avoiding literal recapitulation: the opening soprano solo reappears sung by male voices, while the organ 'fugue' becomes an imitative choral passage. On a smaller scale, such structural organization did not seem to apply: after completing the *Twelve Songs*, Holst stated that they could be performed in any order, and most of them are through-composed, with little in the way of literal recapitulation.

In opera, the use of thematic references raises the spectre of the Wagnerian leitmotif, which Holst generally rejected as a method of characterization, although he was obliged to fall back on it at times in *At the Boar's Head*, simply because the traditional tunes which he used as thematic material were not open to modification in the same way as in an originally-composed work. Doll Tearsheet's motif permeates the scenes in which she appears and dominates the texture of the final pages of the work. Although Holst otherwise spurned the leitmotif, he did make use of thematic fragments to provide coherence in his other operas, as in *Savitri*, in which Death's opening phrase reccurs at various points, and *The Wandering Scholar*, whose opening motif reappears in diverse contexts, not associated with any particular individual, but ensuring that much of the material has a similar character. In *The Perfect Fool*, a structural link is provided by the fact that events prophesied in the earlier part of the work later become true, thus providing opportunities for recapitulation of material.

Most of the thematic material of this opera is contained in its opening ballet music, and reappears during the work in various parts without development or modification; as Edwin Evans pointed out at the time of its first performance, this method 'Gains in clarity, but loses in symphonic opportunity'.[38]

ORCHESTRATION AND INSTRUMENTAL WRITING

Holst learnt his orchestral technique in the hard schools of theatre pits and among the players of symphony orchestras, rather than from textbooks. This had the effect of fixing the sound of the orchestra in his mind, so that his musical ideas were not simply abstract black-and-white notes waiting to be clothed in instrumental sound, but were already conceived in terms of their own tone-colours. Such an approach may even have had its origins as far back as his boyhood acquaintance with the organ at Cheltenham's All Saints' Church, from which a wide variety of sounds could be extracted, a totally different experience from the rather monochrome effect of the piano keyboard.

When once asked for his views on orchestration, Holst replied: 'Orchestration! What do you mean? That's a question I can't possibly answer. You see, I can't dissociate orchestration from the material which is being orchestrated . . . Once I tried to teach orchestration at the College, but I found it was impossible. The whole thing goes together, the material indicating the orchestration. If a drawing's bad, you can't show a student how to colour it.'[39] His success in applying this philosophy led one critic to declare of *The Planets* that it was doubtful whether Holst had a living rival as an orchestrator,[40] and at a time when composers such as Stravinsky and Ravel were at the height of their achievement, this was praise indeed, if a trifle too partisan.

His early practical experience of orchestral playing also ensured that his own music always took into account the attitudes and expectations of the players in addition to the needs of the composer and his audience. Having been an orchestral musician himself, he was able to obtain the sympathy and co-operation of the players, a factor vital to the success of any orchestral work, however good the composer or conductor. Holst understood what kind of writing was most appropriate to each type of instrument, what was possible within the general consensus of technique, and what the players would find interesting and challenging. Sometimes this relationship took the form of friendly banter between composer and players: Bernard Shore recalled that the orchestral musicians were convinced that Holst had deliberately tried to catch them out in his string writing in *Mercury*,[41] although this is not borne out by a letter in which Holst explained to Adrian Boult that he wanted to alter one of the passages: 'I have arranged it very clumsily between the instruments. It sounds quite well later on the wind . . . But I am now wishing that I could re arrange the string parts better.'[42] This practical experience also gave him confidence in writing for combinations of instruments—he knew exactly what would 'come off' and what would not, and arranged his musical material accordingly.

Holst was always willing to alter his music as a result of performance experience or comments from players, and to add parts for available instruments even if they were not specified in the original instrumentation. In his early days as conductor of the choral society at Wyck Rissington and Bourton-on-the-Water he heard of a lady harpist living nearby, and persuaded her to join in the performance. Despite his sketchy knowledge of the harp at that time, he showed her what was needed at the piano, and she in turn showed him how it would sound best on the harp, with the result that in mid-career Holst declared it to be 'the best harp part he has ever written'.[43] Even as late as the 1928 performance of *The Coming of Christ* he was quite prepared to provide an extra part for tubular bells at the last minute at someone's suggestion, after the music had been printed and just before the final rehearsal.

He was always pragmatic, particularly when arranging other composers' music, and would think nothing of altering or transposing notes in Bach's cantatas if he thought that practicalities demanded it, believing that Bach himself would probably have approved of such an approach. He applied the same attitude to his own music, and many of his scores contain detailed instructions on performance possibilities with smaller ensembles, the optional instruments being carefully cued in to the other parts, a skill which he developed from his early experience of helping his father prepare the material for his chamber orchestra concerts in Cheltenham. Sometimes this led to musical improvements: his incidental music for *The Sneezing Charm* includes a phrase for alto flute, cued in for cor anglais or horn, but Holst later decided that the viola would be more appropriate as a cue, and the phrase was in fact transferred to this instrument when the music was reused for *The Perfect Fool*. He also arranged many of his larger works for strings and piano or for two pianos, to encourage performance by smaller forces, and in the case of the *Two Psalms* arranged the organ part for brass band to facilitate an open-air perform-ance. His attention to practicalities would extend to the smallest details, always informed by his own experience. In a letter to Harold Brooke concerning one of his works, Holst explained: 'Trombones like plenty of time to put on mutes—I have added *con sordino* early in the parts,'[44] while for the unaccompanied plainsong melody given to the trombones at the beginning of *The Hymn of Jesus*, besides advising the players to study authentic vocal plainsong performance practice, he even went to the unheard-of length of specifying the slide positions, to 'avoid the unpleasant smearing of one note into another',[45] with the notes cued into the horn part in case the trombones are unable to manage the passage correctly. He had no time for theoretical niceties, preferring to concentrate on producing the required result, so that sometimes grossly exaggerated dynamic indications such as *ffff* or *pppp* appear, as he knew that this was the only way to make players take notice and produce a level of sound approximating to what he had in mind.

Apart from *The Planets*, whose gigantic orchestra seems to have emanated solely from artistic considerations dissociated from any immediate possibility of performance, Holst's or-chestral works normally call for instrumental combinations which are well within the provision of the normal symphony orchestra. Several of them are scored only for double woodwind, with doubling of piccolo and cor anglais, quite appropriate to small-scale works such as the *Two Songs Without Words*, and vital to a chamber opera such as *The Wandering Scholar* and a work of such delicacy as the *Double Concerto*, in which the composer must take care not to overwhelm the vocal or instrumental soloists. In the carols *A Welcome Song* and *Terly Terlow* he wrote effective accompaniments for the choir using only an oboe and cello, but perhaps his most remarkable scoring is the minimal group of instruments specified for *Savitri*, consisting of two flutes, cor anglais, two string quartets and double-bass; a chamber ensemble which is nevertheless capable of producing an almost orchestral quality of sound. In his large-scale works he specified triple woodwind (always with the possibility of performance by smaller forces), but occasionally a mixture of double and triple, as in *Egdon Heath* in which he abandoned his original idea of triple wind and added only the cor anglais and contra-basson to the usual pairs to provide the darker tone-colours needed for the work. Brass is generally in proportion to the winds, and in the larger works soon settled down to the usual complement of four horns, three trumpets, three trombones and tuba (after an early experiment with two cornets in the *Suite de Ballet*) to which was added percussion, strings, and keyboard instruments according to the nature of the work.

Holst's scoring techniques are fairly conventional, making use of the usual octave doublings, harmonic thickening, figurations, and filler parts, but after emerging from his Wagnerian period he began to use the orchestra more as a source of colour than of volume, as is evident in *Beni Mora*, whose large orchestra is drawn upon as a kind of instrumental palette, and which plays tutti for only a small proportion of the work's total duration. In this work he at last found his feet as a skilled and sensitive orchestrator, and apart from the aberration of the ill-considered *Phantastes Suite* in which he overdid certain grossly exaggerated orchestral effects, his technique remained basically unchanged for the remainder of his career.

All of his instrumental writing is eminently practical, and never makes undue demands on the players, although he was conversant with all the usual techniques of the various instruments. His string writing, for instance, requires a relatively modest technique compared with the demands of a Strauss, but Holst knew exactly what effects could be produced by the minimal means without recourse to showy virtuosity for its own sake. Although a brass player himself, he had studied the violin in his youth, and was therefore familiar not only with the techniques of string writing, but also with the feel of the instruments, both for the player and as part of an ensemble sound. From an early date his string writing shows a professional competence, with careful attention to details of articulation and bowing, an aspect which composers sometimes evade by assuming that such matters will be sorted out by the players. The *St Paul's Suite* is an exemplary work in which various groupings of instruments, together with techniques such as double, triple, and quadruple stops and octave doublings are freely used to produce a rich string sound, yet which is within the technical abilities of a school orchestra, while the later *Brook Green Suite* dispenses with such trappings, to produce a work which is elegant in its simplicity yet none the less effective in its musical expression.

Holst was always careful to ensure that everyone in the orchestra has something interesting to play, whether they be amateurs whose commitment must be encouraged, or professionals who are apt to become jaded if not provided with an element of challenge. In the string section this applies particularly to the double-basses, to whom Holst sometimes gives notes other than the usual role of doubling the cellos, occasionally using them as soloists, as in *The Perfect Fool* ballet music and at the beginning of *Egdon Heath*, where they play entirely alone in a high position to produce a mysterious and unique sound unobtainable from any other instrument (Ex. 103). At the beginning of the *First Choral Symphony*, double-basses divided into three parts provide a double-octave pedal-point for a large part of the Prelude. Holst gave similar attention to that other Cinderella of the strings, the viola, with

Ex. 103

(a) *The Perfect Fool*   (b) *Egdon Heath*

occasional solo passages providing a welcome change of tone-colour, and even indulging in the luxury of violas divided into three parts in the second movement of *Beni Mora*.

Most of his string writing uses normal methods of playing, which makes the use of different techniques all the more striking when they do occur. He used *col legno* to good effect in *Beni Mora* and *The Perfect Fool*, but most successfully of all at the beginning of *Mars*, where the mood is one of hushed menace rather than of blatant aggression. Sometimes the texture is enlivened by the use of pizzicato, particularly effective when used with simplicity as at the end of the Prelude of the *Brook Green Suite*, or in an unusual way, as in the rapidly articulated repeated semiquavers in *Jupiter* (Ex. 104). But on the whole, Holst preferred his strings to be played in the normal bowed manner, within which he was able to obtain a considerable variety of instrumental sound by grouping the sections in different ways, including unison doubling in double and triple octaves, contrast of solo against ripieni (as in *Mercury*), the vigorous pentatonic texture of the opening of *Jupiter*, and the true unison of violins, violas, and cellos, an effect of which he was particularly fond and used in several movements of *The Planets*, especially for *maestoso* effects. In *Beni Mora* an effective crescendo is achieved by bringing in divided first and second violins in delayed entries on the same sustained note, and to achieve the required *ppp* at the end of the same work the string parts are specified for single desks only. His most stunning invention for strings is probably the passage of pianissimo staccato parallel third-inversion seventh-chords in *Mercury*; a basically simple idea which is nevertheless virtually unplayable at this register and dynamic by any other group of instruments, and which produces an extraordinary effect of the slip-stream as the Winged Messenger rushes on his way (Ex. 105).

Ex. 104   *Jupiter*

Ex. 105   *Mercury*

Although he had never played a woodwind instrument, Holst had an intuitive feeling for their playing technique and the qualities of their sound, both as soloists and in ensemble. His use of wind instruments for colouristic effects began soon after his 1908 holiday in Algeria, and it was probably this experience which led him to realize the full expressive possibilities of woodwind tone-colour, although he had previously occasionally used it for atmospheric purposes, as in the brief passage for two flutes and piccolo in *The Mystic Trumpeter*, evoking the words 'now in the distance lost' (Ex. 106). In *Savitri* the dark timbre of the cor anglais provides the ideal instrumental counterpart to the threat and mystery of Death, while in *Beni Mora* the Arab allusions are overt, with oboes and cor anglais used for their nasal qualities, and the evocative and velvety low-register flute providing the mysterious and insistent ostinato in the Finale. Holst was attracted to the sound of the flutes in their lowest octave, and wrote chords for them in this register in *Savitri, Invocation*, and at the beginning of *Saturn*, where they are doubled by harp harmonics (Ex. 107; 97*f*). The 'four-flute' tune in *Saturn* also begins in this lowest register before moving upwards, with an alto flute playing the lowest notes of the chords (Holst always erroneously referred to the alto flute in G as a 'bass flute'). In the absence of an alto flute the composer suggested that a bassoon could be substituted, but when Adrian Boult heard this played by 'the finest bassoon

Ex. 106   *The Mystic Trumpeter*

player in London', he concluded that 'there is no doubt it lost from the alteration, thus showing it to be a justifiable extravagance to have the bass flute.'[46] The same remark could have been made of Holst's use of the bass oboe in *Neptune*, where its dark, hollow sound is quite different from that produced by the cued-in bassoon in the same register.

Ex. 107

(a) *Savitri*   (b) *Invocation*

Triadic figuration for flutes in a higher register appears in *The Mystic Trumpeter*, *The Hymn of Jesus*, and the *First Choral Symphony*, where it is used to evoke the static scenes depicted on the Grecian Urn (Ex. 108), and in *Venus* chords for flutes and oboes in contrary motion produce a cool, restful sound, which is reflected in the harmonic figuration later in the movement, in which woodwind pulsations form a background to string melody. The contrary motion idea appears again at the beginning of *Egdon Heath*, this time between flutes and bassoons, which also join forces later in the work to play the strange ritualized folk-dance in parallel fourths (Ex. 109).

Ex. 108

(a) *The Mystic Trumpeter*   (c) *First Choral Symphony*
(b) *The Hymn of Jesus*

Ex. 109

(a) *Venus*   (b) *Egdon Heath*

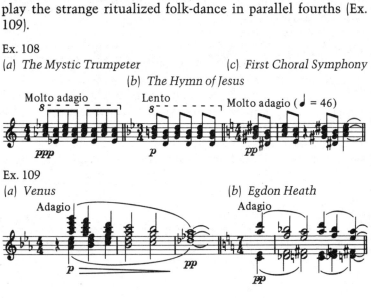

(c) *Egdon Heath*

Andante

p

Once again, Holst tried to ensure that every instrument has something worthwhile to play; in the *Fugal Overture* there is a duet between piccolo and bassoon, and the *Japanese Suite* begins with a bassoon solo, in the manner of *The Rite of Spring*. Only the clarinet seemed to find little favour with Holst's musical ear, but this instrument is given its chance to shine in the military band works, in which it provides the mainstay of the thematic material.

With the brass, Holst was on home ground and knew precisely the capabilities of each instrument, although surprisingly he did not use this specialized knowledge to extend and develop their possibilities, always keeping well within the normal playing range and technique. In both his horn and trumpet parts for example, he rarely ventures into ledger lines above the stave, although his habit of writing for trumpets in C means that the notes are produced in a slightly higher register when played on the modern B flat instrument. Even in *A Moorside Suite*, specially commissioned as a brass band test-piece, he resisted the temptation to indulge in dazzling technique for its own sake, and eschewed such tricks as double-tonguing, opting instead for solid musicality, for which control of sustained legato is necessary. Nevertheless, his brass parts are interesting, often melodic, and always practical, allowing plenty of time for breathing.

As a trombonist, Holst was naturally partial towards his own instrument, and gave important thematic material to the trombones in the 'slow processions' of *Saturn* and *Egdon Heath*, and the opening gesture of *The Perfect Fool* (Ex. 110). He demonstrated the instrument's agility in scale passages in *The Perfect Fool* ballet music and a counter-melody in *Jupiter* which sounds against the entire orchestra (Ex. 111), and also its nuances, as in the subtle semitone glissando in the Prelude to *Hammersmith* and the nebulous interchange with the trumpets of pianissimo bitonal chords in *Neptune* (Ex. 98a). Apart

Ex. 110

(a) *Saturn*   (b) *Egdon Heath*   (c) *The Perfect Fool*

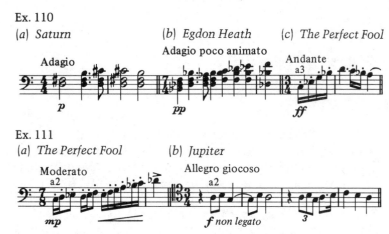

from the martial calls in *The Mystic Trumpeter*, the *Pageant of London*, *Mars*, and *The Perfect Fool*, the trumpets also get their due share of thematic material, sometimes in a solo role, as in the desolate phrase at the end of *Egdon Heath*, and sometimes in combination with the trombones, producing the commanding invocation at the beginning of *Uranus* (Ex. 112). Both trumpets and trombones occasionally appear with mutes, but apparently with the intention of simply quietening the sound, rather than by way of change of tone-colour.

Ex. 112

(a) *Egdon Heath*   (b) *Uranus*

Holst's use of the horns often fulfils the common function of providing harmonic background, but he also frequently gives them thematic material, allowing them to join in the string unisons in *Jupiter* to happy effect, and beginning *Venus* with a solitary horn motif. In the *Phantastes Suite* he went rather too far in giving them bizarre lip glissandi on the upper notes of the natural series, but in *The Perfect Fool* the horns make a magnificent sound in *fff* staccato block harmonies in the Dance of the Spirits of Fire (Ex. 113). The tuba is not forgotten,

Ex. 113

(a) *Phantastes Suite*   (b) *The Perfect Fool*

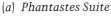

and has its own solo passages in the *Phantastes Suite, A Fugal Overture,* and the *Scherzo* (Ex. 114), while in *The Planets* Holst included a tenor tuba (euphonium) in his already large brass section, adding an urgent tone to the tightening motifs in *Mars,* and allowing it to join in a rollicking trombone theme in *Uranus* (Ex. 115).

Ex. 114

(a) *Phantastes Suite*

(b) *A Fugal Overture*

(c) *Scherzo*

Ex. 115

(a) *Mars*

(b) *Uranus*

Despite specifying sometimes quite large instrumental forces, Holst occasionally found himself in need of still greater reserves of power, for which he turned to the organ, although usually making its use optional in case such a requirement should restrict performance possibilities. In *Mars* the organ is thrown in at a moment of climactic violence, when all the resources of the vast orchestra have already been fully committed, while elsewhere in the movement it is used to add emphasis to brass chords. He resisted the temptation to use the organ for an effect of smug self-satisfaction in the *maestoso* section of *Jupiter*, but in *Uranus* came up with the astonishing idea of an organ glissando, although Adrian Boult found that the original notation had to be curtailed in performance because the lowest notes 'had hardly time to speak'.[47] The organ is sometimes used to give extra weight to the bass line by means of pedal notes, the exact stops required being specified in *Mars*, *Saturn*, and *Neptune* (where it is used *ppp*), and appears in the same role in *The Hymn of Jesus* and the *First Choral Symphony*, where in the Finale the pedal swells and builds up to another great climactic chord.

For more subtle effects Holst turned to the harp and celesta, without which he would have been unable to produce the limpid music of the Spirits of Water in *The Perfect Fool*. Sometimes he specified two harps, to no particular purpose in *Beni Mora*, as the music could just as well have been given to one, but in *The Planets* to add volume and intricacy to the textures and to cope with rapid changes of tonality which are foreign to the nature of a single instrument. Harp harmonics add their own unique quality to the alternating chords at the beginning and end of *Saturn*, and are used to give a veiled glimpse of the motif of *Uranus* before he finally vanishes into thin air, but the instrument is mainly used to provide harmonic texture and to assist articulation of phrases in other instruments. The celesta generally outlines or enhances material appearing in other parts, but sometimes stands alone, as in a lengthy chordal passage in the *Phantastes Suite* subsequently elaborated in *Mercury* (Ex. 116), and a single-note strand towards the end of the Scherzo of the *First Choral Symphony*. Very occasionally Holst added a piano to his orchestra; in *The Hymn of Jesus* it plays chords, rhythmic figures, and helps to

Ex. 116

(a) *Phantastes Suite*

(b) *Mercury*

double the bass line, but is very much an 'extra', playing as little part in his orchestral thinking as it did as a solo instrument.

Holst also regarded the percussion as something of an extra, sometimes designating it as optional in his instrumentation, and advised his composition students to make their scores effective without the use of such instruments. Nevertheless the percussion does play a vital role in several of his works, and he paid careful attention to the effects which could be drawn from it.

As early as *Beni Mora* there is a cross-metre ostinato played by one player on two timpani simultaneously, a device which is also used in the *Japanese Suite* and later in *A Choral Fantasia*, where they are tuned in fifths and octaves (Ex. 117). The idea of the timpani being given important thematic material instead of merely rhythmic or harmonic figures also appears in *The Planets*, which calls for two performers playing

Ex. 117

(a) *Beni Mora*   (b) *Japanese Suite*   (c) *A Choral Fantasia*

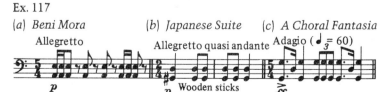

six drums, thus enabling the principal theme of *Jupiter* to be split between them, while in the Finale of the *Double Concerto* the theme of the Ground is played on three drums by one player (Ex. 118). Not content with the sound of the normal felt sticks, Holst sometimes directed that the timpani should be played with wooden sticks, producing a clearer, less rounded sound which is ideal for intricately articulated figures such as the ostinato at the opening of *Mars* and the rhythmic figuration of the *Japanese Suite* and the Bacchanale of the *First Choral Symphony*. Holst also specified wooden sticks for the long timpani rolls in *Neptune*, producing a hollow, other-worldly effect, in preference to the more conventional rather muffled tone. Sometimes the bass drum is also played with wooden sticks, as in the Finale of *Beni Mora* and the Dance of the Spirits of Earth in the *The Perfect Fool*, whose ballet music contains passages in which timpani and bass drum play alternate notes with felt and wooden sticks, a device which reappears in the ballet *The Lure* (Ex. 119).

Ex. 118
(a) *Jupiter*

(b) *Double Concerto*

Ex. 119
(a) *The Perfect Fool*

(b) *The Lure*

Of the other more common percussion instruments, the side drum is specified in only a few works, being used without snares in *The Hymn of Jesus*, but most effectively of all in the central section of *Mars*, in which by using only a few quiet notes in each bar, Holst succeeded in conveying an atmosphere of apprehension and menace (Ex. 120). Cymbals are often used, sometimes being suspended and played with a soft felt timpani stick, as in the early *Suite de Ballet*, *Neptune*, and *The Perfect Fool* ballet music, and the triangle occasionally occurs, together with tambourine, and 'jingles' (sleigh bells) which are called for in the *Japanese Suite*, *The Perfect Fool*, and *A Fugal Overture*. Holst seemed to be particularly attracted to the sound of the tam-tam (or gong, as he called it), using its frightening crescendo roll at the beginning of *The Perfect Fool* and *Mars*, and also in the *First Choral Symphony*, but realizing that its effect can be overdone, as is evident from a letter to Walton O'Donnell concerning the score of *Hammersmith*: 'Before sending it will you take out the *fff* gong note the bar before the final 4/2 and add it (the gong) *ppp* a bar later—at the 4/2 double bar.'[48] He occasionally used the glockenspiel to add sparkle to his musical material, as in the *Japanese Suite* and *Mercury*, in which it is used to provide an upper pedal note for the entire orchestra (Ex. 121), and the xylophone provides just the right kind of bizarre tone-colour for the galumphing dance of *Uranus*. *Saturn* could not exist without the off-beat alternation of tubular bell notes, which first appear in panic, played with a metal striker, and later in peaceful mood with a soft felt striker (Ex. 122).

Ex. 120   *Mars*

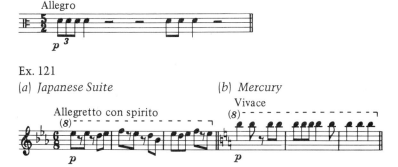

Ex. 121

(a) *Japanese Suite*   (b) *Mercury*

Ex. 122

(a) *Uranus*   (b) *Saturn*

Despite this imaginative invention and Holst's evident feeling for the tone-colours which could be produced from percussion instruments, his basic attitude is revealed in his firm conviction that *Egdon Heath* was his best composition, the evocative score of which is entirely devoid of percussion instruments.

There is one further instrument which Holst incorporated into his orchestra only once, but with astonishing musical effect: the human voice, in the form of the female chorus used at the end of *Neptune*. The treble voices first enter on a high sustained pianissimo G (originally optimistically marked *pppp*), a note which although present in the lower orchestral parts is dissonant to some of the upper notes of the harmony, producing a strange effect. Archibald Davison has written: 'It emerges from the orchestral texture as something disembodied increasing in intensity until it suggests, with an effect that is almost physical, a persistent and a chilling wind.'[49] The ending of this movement, and of the work, on a repeated fading alternation of two chords by the double female chorus is a master-stroke of musical imagination, as if Holst were acknowledging that the limit of musical expression by orchestral instruments had been reached, and that only voices, and subsequently silence, could carry the music any further.

CHORAL AND VOCAL WRITING

Although Holst was not a singer himself, he had an intuitive understanding of the human voice, the needs of singers, and what was needed for successful vocal writing. He never wrote choral and vocal music in the abstract, but always with the practicabilities and problems of performance in mind, and wrote in such a way that the result was singable and grateful to the voice without straining the vocal chords in the interests of musical expression. In support of this approach, he pointed out that Beethoven's writing for the chorus in the Ninth Symphony was bad, whereas singing the music of Byrd improved the voice.[50] So great was his understanding of the principles involved that Harvey Grace wrote that: 'Holst has a way of writing not for performers' abilities, but for their potentialities.'[51]

He was careful not to overstrain the vocal chords, and often included rests before demanding passages: as one reviewer wrote of *The Hymn of Jesus*: 'To borrow an analogy from pugilism—however gruelling the three-minute rounds may be, each is relieved by a one-minute rest.'[52] When approaching a complex chord, he would ensure that dissonant intervals are approached by step rather than by leap, and often used the octave or unison as a stepping-off point, to give the singers confidence before tackling their intervals, sometimes thickening the line in between to make a smooth transition. Typical examples can be found in *To Varuna* in the Second Group of *Choral Hymns from the Rig Veda*, *The Hymn of Jesus*, the *Ode to Death*, the *First Choral Symphony*, and *The Evening Watch* (Exx. 123; 99). Much of the choral writing in *The Hymn of Jesus* and the *First Choral Symphony* seems rather daunting on paper, but is in fact quite practicable because of this attention to part-writing, and works well provided the singers concentrate on their own lines and do not allow themselves to be diverted by what is going on elsewhere. As Norman Demuth pointed out, Holst's imaginative choral writing is effective when sung, but often sounds 'hideous' on the piano, thus proving the fallibility of Stanford's 'black and white test'.[53]

Holst excelled at writing for unaccompanied female voices, of which he had so much practical experience, and in his writing for amateurs and schoolchildren he was always careful to ensure that the individual lines are well within the capabilities of average singers and do not venture too high for voices which have not been professionally trained. Within these constraints the lines have their own logic and continuity and are always interesting, especially in the inner and lower parts, which are sometimes neglected by composers. In his unaccompanied female-voice writing for example, Holst's alto parts often range over their entire compass, instead of being restricted to their lower notes by the necessity of providing a bass. But when musical considerations required it, he did not hesitate to write demanding music for the voice, even if this meant that its

Ex. 123

(a) *To Varuna*   (b) *The Hymn of Jesus*

(c) *Ode to Death*

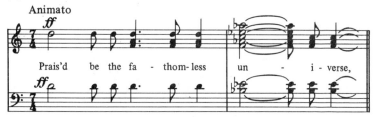

(d) *The Evening Watch*

performance would be restricted to the more accomplished choirs. The parallel fourth-chords of the unaccompanied *Evening Watch* present problems of pitching, both for the inner voices, despite their generally step-wise movement, and also for the basses, who have to cope with some low-range writing while providing a firm foundation for the upper parts (Ex. 124).

Ex. 124   *The Evening Watch*

Its companion motet *Sing Me the Men* contains a phrase in which the second bass part descends to an ad lib low B flat, although doubling the first bass at the octave in a consonant chord, while in the male-voice version of the folk-song arrangement *I Love My Love* the second basses have several optional low Ds and what one reviewer described as 'a long CC that is hardly likely to be more than a draught'.[54] At the other end of the register, the published version of *A Dirge for Two Veterans* contains some high writing for tenors and basses, having been transposed up a whole tone from the original manuscript version for some reason, perhaps from the publisher's desire to avoid the use of complicated key signatures.

From an early stage Holst showed great competence in handling techniques of choral writing, his scores containing a variety of ways of presenting musical material, including homophony, counterpoint (imitative and otherwise) of lines and chordal passages, unison and octave writing, contrary motion, pairing of voices, divided parts, contrast between male and female voices and between solo and tutti sections. His mastery of traditional techniques is evident in such works as the *Ave Maria* for unaccompanied female chorus, and the *Nunc Dimittis* for mixed voices, but he was also interested in extending the possibilities of any medium within which he worked, and he developed choral writing to a level at which it might be regarded almost as a form of vocal orchestration.

He did this partly through his experiments in rhythm, tonality, and harmony, as are evident in the *Choral Hymns from the Rig Veda*, but also by the deployment of voices in various combinations, introducing a spatial facet reminiscent of Renaissance techniques. His incomplete schoolboy anthem *The Listening Angels* specifies a hidden choir, probably suggested by the text ('Solemnly from distant voices rose a vesper hymn'), and this idea was developed in the female-voice *Songs from 'The Princess'* where in *Sweet and Low* and *The Splendour Falls* the main choir is supplemented by an echo choir placed in an adjoining room. In the *Funeral Chant* in the female-voice Second Group of *Choral Hymns from the Rig Veda*, the echo idea was taken even further by dividing the choir into three groups whose deployment is carefully specified: 'The first group is to consist of the front half of the choir:

the rest will be divided equally into the second group (behind the first) and the third at the back of all, so that these two latter groups will sound as echoes of the first group. Thus, if there are eight rows in the choir, the first four will form the first group, rows 5 and 6 the second group and rows 7 and 8 the third.'[55] The hymn *To Varuna* in the same Group includes independent parts for the first row of the whole choir, consisting of first trebles, second trebles, and altos, with separate parts for the remainder.

By means of such devices Holst was able to transcend the inherent limitations of the female-voice medium, but he also applied them to mixed-voice works with good effect. Apart from the dramatic placing of the Heavenly Host chorus on the choir-screen of Canterbury Cathedral in *The Coming of Christ*, the concert-piece *The Hymn of Jesus* is scored for two mixed-voice choruses and a female-voice semi-chorus, whose deployment is once again specified in detail: 'The two choruses should be of fairly equal strength, and, if possible, should be well separated. The semi-chorus should be placed above them and well apart.'[56] It is evident from this that spatial considerations form an important factor in the musical concept, and if ignored can reduce the effect to blandness, as is the case in monophonic recordings and broadcasts. In his other works for double choir, such as the *Ave Maria* and *Nunc Dimittis*, in which separation is not specifically called for, it is clear that a certain amount of separation can enhance the intentions of the music. Physical movement was also sometimes used; in *The Planets* and the *Songs from 'The Princess'* to achieve a fade-out as an alternative to closing doors to an adjoining room, but also for dramatic effect, as when Holst arranged for William Vowles to lead a small choir singing 'Sumer is Icumen in' while walking towards the main choir at the beginning of his 1919 Constantinople concert, and away again at the end.

In *Savitri* the hidden female chorus sings without words, to the vowel 'u', as in 'sun', to produce a magical intertwining texture, an effect which reappears in the later motet *Sing Me the Men* in which the sopranos are divided into four parts to sing a repeated five-beat pentatonic phrase in canon at the unison at one bar's distance, with a similar alto part, all to the vowel 'ah', as an accompaniment to tenors and basses below.

The idea of wordless music is reversed in *The Hymn of Jesus* where the double chorus is suddenly given musicless words in an unpitched spoken section in quasi-canonic entries, a device which was virtually unprecedented at the time, but much used later in the twentieth century. He also mixed singing and spoken dialogue in the opera *The Perfect Fool*, but in this case more as an aid to understanding the words. A choral effect of which Holst was particularly fond is the pianissimo chanting on a unison note found in *To the Unknown God* in the First Group of *Choral Hymns from the Rig Veda*, and the mysterious Prelude of the *First Choral Symphony*, while in *The Hymn of Jesus* he achieved a soft humming effect by instructing the chorus to close their lips on the final sustained syllable of the word 'wisdom', *ppp*. In his early operetta *Lansdown Castle*, Holst used the same effect to bizarre purpose when he wrote a fragment of liturgical chant to be sung through closed lips as a magical incantation.

Holst also made use of the possibilities of dynamic contrast between small and larger groups and between soloist and full choir. In the *Ode on a Grecian Urn* in the *First Choral Symphony* full chorus and half chorus alternate on successive phrases, and several of his choral works include solos for a singer drawn from the choir, sometimes for effects of timbre as well as dynamics, as in the alternating phrases for tenor solo and female voices in his setting of Psalm 86. The introduction of a solo voice did not always produce the intended effect however, as W. G. Whittaker reported after a performance of the Third Group of *Choral Hymns from the Rig Veda*: 'I took one liberty, of making the semichorus sing the closing three solo phrases in the "Travellers", because I found that when a solitary voice came in, it sounded almost like a mistake.'[57]

In the *First Choral Symphony* and *A Choral Fantasia* Holst added a soprano soloist, thus combining the sonority of his solely choral works with the possibilities of voice and orchestra which he had explored in the early scenas *Örnulf's Drapa* (baritone) and *The Mystic Trumpeter* (soprano). But on the whole he was not attracted to the solo voice, much preferring the anonymity of the chorus, even though in his early years he did write a number of songs for voice and piano, culminating in the *Vedic Hymns*, after which he wrote nothing more for this combination until the *Twelve songs* of 1929. In the intervening period his interest in the solo voice was confined to opera, in which he displayed an musicianly understanding of vocal technique; all his operatic writing is eminently singable, but with the unfortunate corollary that it does not place any undue demands or strain on the performers or offer them opportunities for vocal display, and therefore lacks the challenge which soloists might expect from an effective operatic part. It is really concert music which happens to take place on stage, rather than theatrical music as such, best exemplified by the vocal lines of *Savitri*, which are more like a heightened version of everyday speech than high-flown operatic lyricism.

In his earlier works Holst sometimes misjudged the weight of his orchestral accompaniments to the detriment of the singers, so that in the original version of *The Mystic Trumpeter* the soloist had to battle against the power of the orchestra, an effect which he later parodied in *The Perfect Fool*. In avoiding this pitfall, he sometimes went to the other extreme by providing only the minimal amount of support for the singers. The *Funeral Chant* in the Second Group of *Choral Hymns from the Rig Veda* is accompanied by nothing more than a very slow descending scale in the bass, which in the Wizard's wooing song in *The Perfect Fool* becomes fossilized into a static sustained pedal note, a device which also appears in his setting of Psalm 86, the *Seven Part-Songs*, and *The Coming of Christ*, although here probably for acoustical, rather than musical reasons. The scores of *The Perfect Fool*, *At the Boar's Head*, and *The Wandering Scholar* are all examples of economy in vocal support, while retaining interest in the accompaniment, an art which he brought to a high state of development in the *Twelve Songs* to words by Humbert Wolfe. This set of songs is a masterpiece of achievement for someone who was neither a pianist nor had touched the song medium for many years; the vocal lines express the words perfectly, while the accompaniments show an understanding of piano technique despite the composer's known aversion from the instrument. In general, the accompaniments do not mimic the words of the songs, but he was unable to resist the phrase 'old thin clavichord' in *The Floral Bandit*, and produced a delightful page of three-part invention involving the voice as well as accompaniment in the contrapuntal texture.

In most of his vocal writing Holst avoided melisma, being content with one note per syllable as the clearest means of allowing the words to be understood by the listener. He was also particularly careful about rhythmic matters in word setting, and came to believe that asymmetrical metres allowed a wider variety of word-stress than the more common times. At the end of his Sanskrit period a report declared that: 'He has long believed that few understand the peculiar genius of our language, and that until the proper rhythmic value of our phrases is understood, no thoroughly successful wedding of words and music can result. He believes that this is the chief stumbling-block in the formation of a national school of English opera.'[58] He was well aware of the disparity between the intrinsic stress-patterns of the text and the needs of the music, which he elided by not attempting to force the words into a strait-jacket of melodic lyricism, but to let them go their own way, guided by motivic consistency and a sense of linear continuity, an approach which was particularly successful in the *Four Songs* for voice and violin and the twelve Humbert Wolfe songs.

Such problems inevitably arise when setting pre-existing texts, even if they have been written by the composer himself, and one way round this is to evolve the text and the music simultaneously, thus ensuring their compatibility. Holst wrote of his own attempts to do this: 'I didn't get very far in Sita . . . But in all the Vedas matters improved and in the CM [*Cloud Messenger*] and Savitri, especially the latter, the words and music really grew together.'[59] He had been forced to write his own words after fruitless searching for suitable texts for songs and choral music, which resulted in his translations from the Sanskrit, which not only provided the words he needed but also reflected his own philosophy of life. His boyhood attempts at song-writing were based on poems which formed part of his school work or which he happened to come across on his father's bookshelves: Tennyson, Charles Kingsley, Thomas Hood, and songs in the novels of Walter Scott. For the libretto of his operetta *Lansdown Castle* he obtained the collaboration of a local resident, Major Cunningham, whose modest talents were those of a well-meaning amateur, and it was not until his student friendship with Fritz Hart that Holst came into contact with competent literary ability. This resulted in settings of several of Hart's poems as songs or part-songs, including Holst's first published work, the part-song *Light Leaves Whisper*, and some operatic collaborations, such as *The Revoke*, *The Magic Mirror*, and the children's operettas *Ianthe* and *The Idea*. Holst also tried his own hand at writing farcical plays under Hart's tutelage, but it was to be some time before he would turn this experience to use in writing words for his own musical works. Meanwhile he continued to set poems by other authors as his literary horizons expanded; besides Kingsley and Hood he added settings of Meredith, Francis Thompson, Bridges, Blake, Hardy, MacDonald, Alfred Hyatt, and William Morris, to whose influence he briefly succumbed as a member of the Hammersmith Socialist Society. Occasionally he would select verses from a historical anthology, in innocent ignorance of preceding and more famous musical settings, including poems by Jonson, Sidney, Heywood, Herrick, and Shakespeare. For his larger-scale works he turned to Ibsen (*Örnulf's Drapa*), Percy's *Reliques of Ancient Poetry* (*King Estmere*), and Walt Whitman (*The Mystic Trumpeter*), a poet whose words he was later to set in the *Dirge for Two Veterans* and the *Ode to Death*, and who also provided the inspiration for an orchestral overture.

It was at this point that Holst began to write his own words, both for opera libretti and for the texts of songs and part-songs. His first attempt, *The Youth's Choice*, was not successful, and he was advised by Vaughan Williams to improve his style, 'otherwise it will read like Corder's translation of Wagner'.[60] He was at this time discovering Sanskrit literature, and soon found that he could make his own versions of the ancient texts by using published translations as a model, and by this method wrote the libretti of *Sita* and *Savitri*, and also the words of the *Vedic Hymns*, the four groups of *Choral Hymns from the Rig Veda*, the *Two Eastern Pictures*, and *The Cloud Messenger*. Unfortunately, he was still much under the influence of Wagnerian verbiage, and his texts smack of the pseudo-archaic language of *King Estmere*, with pervasive use of the '-eth' suffix for the present tense ('breaketh'; 'leadeth'; 'awakeneth');

obsolete words ('hie'; 'yea'; 'tarry',); clichéd phrases ('mine eyes are open'; 'thou art pale and trembling'; 'what ails thee'); tongue-twisting alliteration ('fearfullest of foes'; 'we would fain welcome you fitly'); and needless inversions ('law eternal'; 'the warrior hither comes'). Doubtless this was intended to give the words a sense of ancient timelessness, but although perhaps acceptable in poetic usage, even at that period it must have sounded dated. The use of 'thee', 'thou', and 'thy' may be excusable in the Rig Veda hymns in evoking an atmosphere of religiosity, and in fact works quite well in *The Hymn of Jesus*, which Holst translated from the Greek. For the libretto of *The Perfect Fool* he adopted a more vernacular language, reserving such words as 'hither' and 'yonder' for archaic effect, but this was to be his last attempt at writing his own texts, as he had found a collaborator in Clifford Bax, who wrote the libretto for *The Wandering Scholar* as well as adapting and translating words for various other works.

During the First World War, Holst had come across Mary Segar's *A Medieval Anthology*, which revived his student interest in medieval poetry, resulting in several carol settings and the *Four Songs* for voice and violin. This interest was to re-emerge towards the end of his life through his acquaintance with Helen Waddell, when he set her translations of medieval Latin lyrics in the *Six Choruses* and *Eight Canons*, besides asking Clifford Bax to adapt a story from her book *The Wandering Scholars*. Bax was impressed by Holst's range of literary taste: 'Gustav read widely. He was more familiar than I with the works of Shaw, Wells, and Bennett. Indeed, he once pleased Arnold Bennett by praising a book called "A Great Man" which the world, it seemed, had already forgotten . . . He consulted me very often about the literary works which he desired to adorn with music.'[61] Among the other authors whose words Holst 'adorned with music' were Christopher Marlowe, Thomas Heywood, Robert Herrick, Henry Vaughan, Thomas Lovell Beddoes, Christina Rossetti, John Greenleaf Whittier, Alice M. Buckton, Digby Mackworth Dolben, George Moore, Gilbert Murray's translations of Euripides, and John Masefield's play *The Coming of Christ*. In his latter years, Holst resumed his interest in Robert Bridges' poetry, largely in consequence of personal acquaintance, and set his words as anthems, part-songs, and in *A Choral Fantasia*, and for the same reasons he also renewed his interest in Thomas Hardy, not by means of vocal settings, but through the orchestral *Egdon Heath*. Holst's lack of Christian orthodoxy did not prevent him from setting liturgical texts, which he did with success in the *Ave Maria*, the *Nunc Dimittis*, and the *Short Festival Te Deum*, in addition to his carols and hymn-tune settings.

Many of the words which he set were not of first-rate quality, but as with many other composers, he managed to produce excellent compositions from such material, as in the *Twelve Songs* to words by Humbert Wolfe. Holst doubtless recognized that the very best poetry has its own musicality, often destroyed by the act of setting it to music, but this did not deter him from using Shakespeare's words with impunity in *At the Boar's Head*, and even more so Keats's poetry in the *First Choral Symphony* in a manner which outraged literary purists of the time. But Holst's choice of words was simply a matter of providing the impetus necessary for the creation of his music; he was not concerned with pedantry, but with those twin artistic criteria so vividly expressed in Keats's *Ode on a Grecian Urn*:

> 'Beauty is truth, truth beauty,'—that is all
> Ye know on earth, and all ye need to know.

Holst's Character: A Phrenological Analysis

This analysis of the eighteen-year-old Gustav Holst is reproduced by courtesy of the Holst Birthplace Museum, Cheltenham.

You possess decidedly a large brain, but unfortunately the vitality is not equal to the brain power, and the natural consequence would be that, if you work your brain at high pressure, you will suffer a great deal from physical and nervous exhaustion. You will have to be very watchful of your health generally, and must guard against anything that will upset the health in any manner whatever. You are by nature active, but then, although you have an active temperament, a want of real vitality will check you considerably. In order to restore the balance between your mind and body, you must endeavour to get as much sleep as you possibly can in the early part of the night. Your brain, take it upon the whole, is indicative of a considerable amount of thinking power and ability. Causality is very large, and this will enable you to reason and argue well upon most subjects, but you must cultivate the organ of comparison in order to become more critical and analytical in your style. You will not be very fluent as a speaker, but will be very copious as a writer. The faculty of tune is very large. If you will honestly give your attention to music, you will decidedly excel and make great headway with it. With your very large development of constructiveness and ideality, you will be able to compose. You are naturally very imaginative and are able to look at life from a poetical point of view. You are imitative, and brim full of fun and wit; if you had studied drawing, you would be able to caricature remarkably well. Benevolence is very large and this organ will make you keenly sympathetic, and you will be most kind in your manner towards other people. You are so emotional that your feelings are very quickly aroused. Upon religious matters, you will be decidedly sceptical. You have very little faith and not much reverence, and you will never be overawed by greatness, neither will you bend too much to creed or ceremony. Although you have a mirthful disposition, the faculty of hope is small and, if disaster attend your efforts, you will become too despondent and will dwell too much upon life's difficulties. You must counteract this by endeavouring to cultivate the faculty of hope by always striving forward into the future. You have a keen sense of honour, and you will reason clearly upon moral subjects generally. You are weak in will power. Firmness is a faculty that you must endeavour to cultivate by being more decided and working out the ideas that your intellect may originate. Cultivate more confidence in your own judgement and capability; you undervalue your powers considerably, and you think too little of yourself generally. Approbativeness is only fully developed; you will not be inflated by a compliment, and you will never be unduly ambitious, still there is enough of this organ to spur you on to action. The commercial faculties are in a full state of development and therefore you will manifest a considerable amount of commercial tact and shrewdness. Destructiveness and combativeness are both well developed, and these two organs will give you courage and much defiance if the temper is aroused; you may argue well then. Continuity is small. Cultivate this faculty by finishing all things that you may once commence. Also cultivate the faculty of order, as you are rather weak in this respect and you are not quite so methodical as you should be. You will not mind much where you live; you can readily make yourself quite at home in new places and in new districts. You are guarded in making friends; you have somewhat a reserved disposition, and you will generally keep to yourself. You will never like making the first advance to strangers. You can appreciate the society of the fair sex, but you will not lose your heart over them as a rule. The faculty of amativeness is only fully developed. The summary of your character will be, if you give your attention to music, to any works connected with construction or designing, you will be successful, and if trained for business would succeed very well in a bank or in any commercial pursuit of that nature.

November 16th 1892.　　*W. Cross.*

References

References in the form 'GH to VL, 3 Jan. 1924' indicate letters; where no location or published source is given, ownership by the recipient or successor is implied. Those in the form 'ImH 1974*a*' or 'Rubbra 1947' refer to publications listed in the Bibliography (Harvard system). Thus 'GH to WGW, 13 Mar. 1917 (GH 1974)' indicates a letter from Holst to W. G. Whittaker, published in the 1974 edition under Holst's name in the Bibliography. Annotations in the form 'via ImH' indicate information acquired from secondary sources, while the form 'From ND' indicates information obtained by the author in the course of verbal conversation.

The following abbreviations have been used in addition to those listed before the Bibliography:

ACB	Adrian (Cedric) Boult		HF	Holst Foundation
AVW	Adeline Vaughan Williams		IB	Irene Bonnett
			ImH	Imogen Holst
BBC	British Broadcasting Corporation		IsH	Isobel Holst
			JM	John Masefield
BBC/WA	BBC Written Archives		LPL	Lambeth Palace Library
BL	British Library			
BM	British Museum		MC	Morley College
BPL	Britten-Pears Library, Aldeburgh		MK	Maja Köhler
			MS	Michael Short
DC	Dorothy Callard		ND	Nora Day
DCM	Dorset County Museum		RAM	Royal Academy of Music
EE	Edwin Evans		RB	Robert Bridges
ER	Edmund Rubbra		RCM	Royal College of Music
FRG	Frances Ralph Gray		RMSA	Rural Music Schools Association
GB	George Bell			
GH	Gustav Holst		RVW	Ralph Vaughan Williams
GTH	Gustav Holst		SPGS	St Paul's Girls' School
GvH	Gustav Holst		TH	Thomas Hardy
H	Gustav Holst		UVW	Ursula Vaughan Williams
HBd	Helen Bidder		VL	Vally Lasker
HBk	Harold Brooke		WGW	William G. Whittaker
HBM	Holst Birthplace Museum, Cheltenham		WO'D	Walton O'Donnell

PREFACE

1. From ImH, Apr. 1980.
2. ImH to MS, 14 Feb. 1980.
3. GH to VL, 13 Jan. 1919 (HF).
4. GH 1921a.

INTRODUCTION

1. RVW 1938.
2. Scott 1944.
3. GH 1921*b*.
4. Capell 1927*e*.
5. Bax 1939.
6. *CSMon* 1921.
7. Bax 1939.
8. Ibid.
9. Bax 1925*a*.
10. GH to Joan Spink, 10 June 1920.
11. Brian 1934.
12. From *VL*, 1974.
13. Bax 1925*b*.
14. GH to EE, 29 Jan. 1911.
15. Blackpool lecture, Feb. 1923 (via ImH).
16. ImH 1938.
17. Porte 1923.
18. RVW 1938.
19. GH to WGW, 1 Aug. 1917 (GH 1974).

1. EARLY YEARS (1874–1893)

1. Hannam-Clark 1949.
2. From ND, 27 Nov. 1979.
3. GH lecture, 3 Nov. 1907 (*MCMag*, Feb. 1908).
4. Autograph score (HBM).
5. *CheltLO*, 26 Dec. 1891.
6. GH to WGW, 8 Dec. 1924 (GH 1974).
7. Programme (HBM).
8. *MTimes*, Aug. 1892.
9. *GlosChr*, 11 Feb. 1893.
10. Programme (HBM).
11. As 9.
12. *GlosCit*, 9 Feb. 1893.
13. As 9.
14. *GlosEch*, 9 Feb. 1893.

2. THE STUDENT (1893–1898)

1. GH to HBk, 22 June 1922.
2. ImH 1938.
3. GH 1918.
4. ImH 1938.
5. Autograph score (HBM).
6. Hart 1943.
7. GH 1926*b*.
8. Autograph score (HF/BPL).
9. *Middleton Parish Magazine*, Sept. 1894.
10. 'A Musical Autobiography' (RVW 1953).
11. *MTimes*, Dec. 1895.
12. 'England and Her Music' (GH 1959).
13. GH to RVW, 1903 (GH 1959).
14. Grew 1922.
15. GH 1959.
16. Hart 1943.
17. *Times*, 26 May 1897.
18. UVW: *RVW* (OUP, 1964).
19. GH 1959.
20. Ibid.
21. RVW 1920.
22. RB to GH, 26 May 1925.
23. RB to GH, 9 June 1925.
24. *MTimes*, Jan. 1898.
25. Fac. in ImH 1978.

3. THE ORCHESTRAL MUSICIAN (1898–1903)

1. *London Music in 1888–89* (Constable, 1937).
2. GH 1959.
3. Eaton 1932.
4. GH 1959.
5. Prout to GH, 4 Mar. 1901.

6. *Minim*, Apr. 1901.
7. *English Music in the Nineteenth Century* (Richards, 1902).
8. WGW 1914.
9. Tippett 1958.
10. GH 1916.
11. GH to RVW, 15 Apr. 1932 (GH 1959).
12. GH 1959.
13. *Minim*, Oct. 1901.
14. Press-cutting, HBM.
15. GH to WGW, 23 May 1917 (GH 1974).
16. *Herald*, 26 Apr. 1902.
17. 26 Apr. 1902.
18. *Times*, 6 May 1902.
19. BL Add. 61951
20. Ibid.
21. Ibid.
22. GH 1959.
23. Ibid.
24. *MTimes*, Apr. 1904.

4. THE TEACHER (1903–1908)

1. DC to MS, 14 Oct. 1978.
2. GH to WGW, 30 Mar. 1916 (GH 1974).
3. Hogarth 1925.
4. *BMusn*, Aug. 1934.
5. William Wallace; *Times*, 30 May 1904.
6. *Times*, 21 May 1904.
7. *MTimes*, Jan. 1905.
8. *DTel*, 3 Dec. 1904.
9. Pamela J. Willetts: *RVW* (BM exhibition catalogue, 1972).
10. ImH 1974*f*.
11. *MMR*, Aug. 1905.
12. Swann 1974.
13. GH to DC, 28 Jan. 1918.
14. ImH 1938.
15. GH 1921*a*.
16. Swann 1974.
17. Strode 1974.
18. *Paulina* 159 (1978–9).
19. *CSMon* 1921.
20. Ibid.
21. Strode 1974.
22. Scholes 1921.
23. Bax 1936.
24. GH to EE, 9 Oct. 1924.
25. GH 1921*a*.
26. Reynolds 1974.
27. Lecture, 4 Feb. 1922 (Lumby 1974).
28. GH to EE, 29 Jan. 1911.
29. *RCMMag*, Easter term 1906.
30. GH to WGW, 9 July 1917 (GH 1974).
31. GH to EE, n.d.
32. *Bath Chronicle*, 8 Feb. 1906.
33. As 28.
34. *DNews*, 1 June 1906.
35. *MStnd*, 9 June 1906.
36. Ibid.
37. *Clarion*, 15 June 1906.
38. BL Loan 48.13/16(241).
39. WGW 1917.
40. MC Executive Committee minutes.
41. GH to MK [Apr.] 1907.
42. *MCMag*, May 1907.
43. ImH 1938.
44. GH 1921*b*.
45. *Hinrichsen's Musical Year Book*,1944.
46. C. 1934.
47. *DTel* 18 Nov. 1907.
48. Hart 1943.
49. *Times*, 28 Jan. 1909.
50. GH 1959.
51. Ibid.
52. GH to Muriel Davenport, 11 Mar. 1908.
53. *MCMag*, Apr. 1908.
54. BPL.

5. FROM SANSKRIT TO FOLK-MUSIC (1908–1911)

1. GH to WGW, 23 May 1917 (GH 1974).
2. IsH to MK, Jan. 1907.
3. Capell 1935.

4. *MTimes*, Apr. 1923.
5. WGW 1917.
6. EE 1919.
7. WGW to GH, 19 Dec. 1912 (GH 1974).
8. GH to EE, 15 Apr. 1925.
9. *DNews*, n.d. (press-cutting, HBM).
10. GH to IB, 5 Nov. 1916.
11. *MCMag*, Jan. 1909.
12. GH to MK [1909].
13. GH to EE, 29 Jan. 1911.
14. *MCMag*, Jan. 1909.
15. MC Executive Committee minutes.
16. *Paulina*, 1975.
17. FRG 1931.
18. GH to Mary Lediard, n.d. (HF).
19. Programme (HBM).

20. GH to BBC, 30 July 1928 (BBC/WA).
21. *Standard*, 7 Apr. 1910.
22. *DTel*, 7 Apr. 1910.
23. Capell 1926c.
24. *BirmDP*, 6 May 1910.
25. GH to WGW, 6 Mar. [1916] (GH 1974).
26. *Bath Chronicle*, 24 Nov. 1910.
27. *MCMag*, Mar. 1911.
28. GH to WGW, 4 June 1918 (GH 1974).
29. EE 1911.
30. Autograph score (BL Add 47826).
31. Joseph 1923.
32. Richards 1958.
33. GH 1920c.

6. FROM SCHOOL TO QUEEN'S HALL (1911–1913)

1. Dorothy Pybus to Wycombe Abbey School, 1978.
2. *Paulina*, 1912.
3. Sharp 1974.
4. *MTimes*, June 1912.
5. ImH 1938.
6. WGW 1914.
7. R. W. Wood 1938.
8. *MCMag*, Nov. 1912.
9. *Morning Post*, 24 July 1912.
10. *Yorkshire Post*, 24 July 1912.
11. *MTimes*, Aug. 1912.
12. *Manchester Guardian*, 25 July 1912.
13. *DMail*, 24 July 1912.
14. *BirmP*, 24 July 1912.
15. Francis Toye: *Bystander*, 7 Aug. 1912.
16. *The Mirror of Music* (Novello/OUP, 1947).
17. *MTimes*, Oct. 1912.
18. As 16.
19. From ImH.

20. WGW to GH, 19 Dec. 1912 (GH 1974).
21. FRG 1931.
22. Harvard lecture, 1932 (GH 1959).
23. GH to ACB, 20 Sept. 1925.
24. Strode 1974.
25. *MTimes*, Feb. 1913.
26. *MTimes*, Apr. 1913.
27. Stephen Lloyd: *H. Balfour Gardiner* (CUP, 1984).
28. RVW to GH, n.d. (GH 1959).
29. WGW 1914.
30. Brian 1940.
31. ER 1947a.
32. ImH 1938.
33. F. H. Wood 1913.
34. Bax 1925a.
35. Ibid.
36. Bax 1939.
37. *Paulina*, July 1913.
38. FRG 1931.

7. ASTROLOGY AND THE WAR (1913–1916)

1. GH 1922b.
2. GH 1926b
3. Grew 1934.

4. Nesta MacDonald: *Diaghilev Observed* (Dance Horizons, 1975).

5. *MTimes*, Aug. 1913.
6. *MCMag*, Nov. 1913.
7. Henry J. Wood: *My Life of Music* (Gollancz, 1938).
8. *MTimes*, Feb. 1914.
9. *The Mirror of Music* (Novello/OUP, 1947).
10. *MCMag*, Apr. 1914.
11. Maine 1934.
12. From ImH.
13. Bax 1936.
14. GH 1926*i*.
15. ImH 1938.
16. Fowler 1913.
17. Cf. H's 1926 recording (HMV HLM 7014).
18. Capell 1927*e*.
19. Charles Reid: *Thomas Beecham* (Gollancz, 1962).
20. ImH 1974*d*.
21. Bax 1936.
22. Ibid.
23. 'England and Her Music' (GH 1959).
24. DC to MS, 14 Oct. 1978.
25. Strode 1974.
26. Boult 1970.
27. Morris 1920.
28. GH to VL, 22 Aug. 1915 (HF).
29. *MTimes*, Dec. 1920.
30. GH 1915.
31. GH to WGW, 13 Dec. 1915 (GH 1974).
32. GH to WGW, 6 Jan. 1916 (GH 1974).
33. Morris 1920.

8. MUSIC AT THAXTED (1916–1917)

1. GH to EE, 6 Nov. [1919]
2. Michael Kennedy: *The Works of RVW* (OUP, 1964).
3. GH 1974.
4. GH to WGW, 18 May 1916 (GH 1974).
5. GH to WGW, 1 Feb. 1920 (GH 1974).
6. Bax 1939.
7. WGW to GH, 28 Mar. 1916 (GH 1974).
8. *Northerner*, May 1916.
9. *MCMag*, Sep–Oct. 1916.
10. GH to WGW, 18 June 1916 (GH 1974).
11. EE 1914*a*.
12. GH to WGW, 23 May 1917 (GH 1974).
13. From ImH.
14. Bax 1939.
15. GH to WGW, 23 Oct. 1916 (GH 1974).
16. ImH 1938.
17. GH to VL, Sept. 1925 (HF).
18. ND to MS, 2 Dec. 1975.
19. GH to VL, 22 Aug. 1915 (HF).
20. ND to MS, 2 Dec. 1975.
21. RCM MS 4556.
22. GH to WGW, 17 May 1917 (GH 1974).
23. ND: *Paulina* 159 (1978–9).

9. WARTIME IN LONDON (1917–1918)

1. Dent 1920
2. GH to WGW, 4 Feb. 1917 (GH 1974).
3. GH to WGW, 13 Mar. 1917 (GH 1974).
4. GH to IB, 17 Feb. 1917.
5. GH to IB, 15 May 1917.
6. GH to WGW, 4 June 1917 (GH 1974).
7. Ibid.
8. *MTimes*, Mar. 1921.
9. *MCMag*, Sept.–Oct. 1917.
10. GH to WGW, 4 June 1917 (GH 1974).
11. *MCMag*, Dec. 1917.
12. GH to WGW, 1 Aug. 1917 (GH 1974).
13. Trans. Mary C. Clarke (Novello, 2nd edn. 1858).
14. Capell 1927*a*.

15. GH to WGW, 18 Dec. 1917 (GH 1974).
16. GH to WGW, Feb. 1918 (GH 1974).
17. GH to EE, 15 Apr. 1925.
18. GH to ACB, 5 Feb. 1918 (Moore 1979).
19. *MCMag*, Feb. 1918.
20. Ibid.
21. GH to WGW, *c*.12 Mar. 1918 (GH 1974).
22. Green 1918.
23. As 21.
24. *MCMAG* 1918.
25. As 22.
26. GH to IB, 12 Apr. 1918.

27. GH to VL, 25 Dec. 1918 (HF).
28. GH to WGW, 8 July 1918 (GH 1974).
29. *MStnd*, 26 Oct. 1918.
30. *Paulina* 159 (1978–9).
31. GH to WGW, Sept. 1918 (GH 1974).
32. GH to FRG, 15 Sept. 1918.
33. Boult 1934.
34. Ibid.
35. GH to ACB, 30 Sept. 1918 (Moore 1979).
36. GH to ACB, 14 Nov. 1918 (Moore 1979).
37. Bax 1939.

10. BARRACK-ROOM AND UNIVERSITY (1918–1920)

1. GH to IsH, 10 Nov. 1918 (HF).
2. GH to IsH, 11 Nov. 1918 (HF).
3. GH to ACB, 14 Nov. 1918.
4. GH to ACB, 21 Nov. 1918.
5. GH to VL, 5 Dec. 1918 (HF).
6. GH to IsH, 10 Feb. 1919 (HF).
7. UVW: *RVW* (OUP, 1964).
8. GH to VL, 5 Dec. 1918 (HF).
9. Vowles 1934.
10. Eggar 1921.
11. GH to IsH, 25 Dec. 1918 (HF).
12. Vowles 1934.
13. GH to VL, 13 Jan. 1919 (HF).
14. GH to IsH, 15 Jan. 1919 (HF).
15. GH to WGW [Aug.1919] (GH 1974).
16. GH 1919*a*.
17. GH to WGW, 4 Feb. 1919 (GH 1974).
18. GH to RVW, 12 Apr. 1919 (GH 1959).
19. *MStnd* 1919.
20. GH to IsH, 25 Feb. 1919 (HF).
21. ACB to VL, 17 Nov. 1918 (Moore 1979).
22. GH to ACB, 14 Nov. 1918 (Moore 1979).
23. GH to IsH, 18 Apr. 1919 (HF).
24. GH to RVW, Mar. 1919 (ImH 1938).
25. GH to IsH, Mar. 1919 (HF).
26. GH to ImH, Mar. 1919 (HF).
27. GH to RVW, 1903 (GH 1959).

28. GH to WGW, 5 May 1919 (GH 1974).
29. GH to FRG, May 1919.
30. GH to VL, 13 Jan. 1919 (HF).
31. Ibid.
32. Carnegie UK Trust: 6th Annual Report.
33. As 23.
34. Vocal score (Stainer & Bell, 1919).
35. *MTimes*, Sept. and Nov. 1922.
36. GH to IsH, June 1919 (HF).
37. GH diary (HF).
38. Ibid.
39. GH to WGW, 12 July 1919 (GH 1974).
40. GH to Mrs Boult [Aug. 1919].
41. GH to IsH, n.d. ; YMCA notepaper (HF).
42. ImH 1938.
43. Bax 1936.
44. *MTimes*, Jan. 1920.
45. GH 1921*b*.
46. GH 1920*a*.
47. Probert-Jones 1935.
48. GH 1921*b*.
49. GH 1920*a*.
50. GH 1959.
51. C. 1934.
52. Joseph 1923.
53. ImH 1974*g*.
54. Bliss: *As I Remember* (Faber, 1970).

55. ER 1974*d*.
56. R. Bennett 1922.
57. GH to WGW, 13 Dec. 1915 (GH 1974).
58. GH to WGW, 23 May 1917 (GH 1974).
59. GH to IB, 25 Feb. 1917.
60. ER 1949.
61. ER 1934*b*.

11. GROWING FAME (1920–1922)

1. RVW to GH, n.d. [1925] (GH 1959).
2. Goddard 1936.
3. Servin 1963.
4. *MTimes*, Apr. 1921.
5. ER 1947*a*.
6. GH to WGW, 8 Apr. 1920 (GH 1974).
7. *MCMag*, June 1920.
8. DC to MS, 14 Oct. 1978.
9. GH to WGW, 12 Aug. 1920 (GH 1974).
10. GH to VL, 20 Aug. 1920 (HF).
11. GH to WGW, 17 Oct. 1920 (GH 1974).
12. GH to VL, 20 Aug. 1920 (HF).
13. GH to WGW, 5 Oct. 1920 (GH 1974).
14. *MTimes*, Dec. 1920.
15. GH 1920*c*.
16. Strode 1974.
17. Bliss: *As I Remember* (Faber, 1970).
18. GH to IB, 12 Dec. 1920.
19. Eggar 1921.
20. As 17.
21. *MTimes*, Aug. 1921.
22. *MTimes*, Oct. 1921.
23. C. L. Williams etc. : *Annals of the Three Choirs* (Minchin & Gibbs, 1931).
24. Grace 1934.
25. Nutting 1976.
26. *DGraph*, 28 Sept. 1921.
27. GH to WGW, 2 Oct. 1921 (GH 1974).
28. GH 1920*c*.
29. GH to WGW, 6 Oct. 1921 (GH 1974).
30. C. 1922.
31. GH 1922*a*.
32. Dan Godfrey: *Memories of Music* (Hutchinson, 1924).
33. Nutting 1976.
34. Letter in ImH 1963*b*.
35. *MCMag*, Sept.–Oct. 1922.
36. GH to RVW [1922] (GH 1959).
37. GH 1922*b*.
38. UC Reading to GH, 3 Aug. 1922.
39. ImH 1974*f*.
40. *MTimes*, Sept. 1922.
41. GH to WGW, 5 Oct. 1922 (GH 1974).

12. INTERNATIONAL ACCLAIM (1922–1924)

1. GH to WGW, 17 Nov. 1922 (GH 1974).
2. GH to WGW, 26 Mar. 1923 (GH 1974).
3. *MTimes*, Apr. 1923.
4. GH to VL, Apr. 1923 (HF).
5. GH to ImH, 2 July 1928 (HF).
6. Grace 1939*b*.
7. GH to WGW, 19 June 1923 (GH 1974).
8. Ibid.
9. GH to C. A. Sink, 11 Jan. 1923 (Univ. Michigan, Ann Arbor).
10. As 7.
11. As 7.
12. Antcliffe 1923.
13. Vocal score (Novello, 1923).
14. ImH 1951*a*.
15. Kalisch 1923.
16. Toye 1931.
17. Einstein 1923.
18. *MN & H*, 23 June 1923.
19. Turner 1923.
20. A. Bennett 1923.
21. Turner 1924.
22. Antcliffe 1923

23. EE 1923*a*.
24. *MTimes*, July 1923.
25. As 23.
26. Antcliffe 1923.
27. Williams 1934.
28. Mendl 1936.
29. Hussey 1928.
30. Bax 1936.
31. Capell 1923*b*.
32. GH to P. Pitt, 9 July 1923 (BL Egerton 3304/243).
33. BL Add. 57953.
34. *MTimes*, Nov. 1923.
35. GH to RVW [Dec.1923] (GH 1959).
36. RVW to GH, 31 Dec. 1923 (GH 1959).
37. GH to WGW, 23 Dec. 1923 (GH 1974).
38. Bax 1939.
39. GH to WGW, 28 Jan. 1924 (GH 1974).
40. Ibid.
41. Ibid.
42. GH to MK, 28 Jan. 1924.
43. ImH 1938.
44. Ibid.
45. Ibid.
46. Ibid.
47. GH to WGW [Feb. 1924] (GH 1974).
48. Ibid.
49. GH to VL, Apr. 1924 (HF).

13. 'REAL COMPOSER AND TAME CAT' (1924–1925)

1. GH to VL, 7 Apr. 1924 (HF).
2. Jacob 1934.
3. RVW 1934*b*.
4. GH 1920*a*.
5. *Morning Post*, 15 Oct. 1921.
6. *First Choral Symphony* sketch (RCM MS 4568/1).
7. GH to WGW, 7 Sept. 1924 (GH 1974).
8. Ibid.
9. GH to Adine O'Neill, 21 July 1924.
10. As 7.
11. GH to Amy Kemp [Sept. 1924].
12. Hogarth 1931.
13. EE 1919.
14. Derek Hudson: *Norman O'Neill* (Quality Press, 1945).
15. GH to WGW, 6 July 1924 (GH 1974).
16. As 7.
17. ImH 1973.
18. *Times* 1925*b*.
19. GH to Robinson, 6 Feb. 1931 (BBC/WA).
20. ImH 1974*f*.
21. As 7.
22. ImH 1938.
23. Bax 1939.
24. Yale to GH, 24 Oct. 1924 (HBM).
25. GH to HBk, 20 Oct. [1924] (BL Add 57953).
26. GH to VL, 26 Oct. 1924 (HF).
27. Ibid.
28. GH to WGW, 31 Oct. 1924 (GH 1974).
29. GH to WGW, 20 Nov. 1924 (GH 1974).
30. GH to WGW, 8 Dec. 1924 (GH 1974).
31. GH to WGW, 27 Mar. 1925 (GH 1974).
32. Grace 1925*b*.
33. 'Da Capo' 1925.
34. Hussey 1928.
35. Phyllis Hartnoll (ed.): *Shakespeare in Music* (Macmillan, 1964).
36. Bax 1936.
37. Bax 1925*b*.
38. Wilkinson 1974.
39. GH to VL, 5 Oct. 1925 (HF).
40. GH to EE, 15 Apr. 1925.
41. RVW to GH, *c*.1932–3 (GH 1959).
42. Pamela J. Willetts: *RVW* (BM exhibition catalogue, 1972).
43. RB to GH, 26 May 1925.
44. RB to GH, 9 June 1925.
45. ImH 1938.
46. GH to IsH, Aug. 1925 (HF).

47. GH to IsH, Aug. 1925 (HF).
48. *MOpin*, Oct. 1925.
49. As 39.
50. As 39.
51. *Times* 1925*a*.
52. C. Gray 1925.
53. Ibid.
54. Turner 1928.
55. Newman 1934.
56. EE 1934.
57. As 52.
58. RVW to GH [1925] (GH 1959).
59. As 52.
60. As 54.

61. *MN & H*, 31 Oct. 1925.
62. Ibid.
63. Grace 1925*c*.
64. EE 1954.
65. A.J.S. 1925.
66. As 64.
67. RVW to GH [1925] (GH 1959).
68. RVW to GH, 13 Apr. 1934
    (GH 1959).
69. Hussey 1928.
70. GH to WGW, 19 Mar. 1926
    (GH 1974).
71. C. Gray 1924.

14. LECTURES AND FESTIVITIES (1925–1927)

1. GH to VL, 13 Oct. 1925 (HF).
2. GH 1925*b*.
3. ImH 1938.
4. BL Add 57953.
5. GH to WGW, 18 Apr. 1928
   (GH 1974).
6. GH to WGW, 19 Apr. 1926
   (GH 1974).
7. Programme note; Cheltenham
   concert, 13 Feb. 1928.
8. ImH 1974*i*.
9. ImH 1974*h* and 1975.
10. GH to RB, 3 Sept. 1926.
11. GH to RB, 10 Sept. 1926.
12. GH to HBk, 22 Nov. 1926
    (BL Add. 57953).
13. GH to RB, 29 Dec. 1926.
14. GH to RB, 17 Jan. 1927.
15. BBC memo, 31 Aug. 1928
    (BBC/WA).

16. GH to PP, 24 Feb. 1927
    (BBC/WA).
17. Hannam-Clark 1949.
18. Nicholls 1927.
19. *GlosEch* 22 Mar. 1927.
20. Ibid.
21. GH to WGW, 15 Apr. 1927
    (GH 1974).
22. GH to TH, 4 Aug. 1927 (DCM).
23. Full score (Novello, 1928).
24. *MMR*, July 1927.
25. *MTimes*, July 1927.
26. RB to GH, 4 July 1927.
27. GH to RB, 6 July 1927.
28. Harris 1964.
29. Ibid.
30. GH to Austin Lidbury,
    11 Aug. 1927 (ImH 1938).
31. TH to GH, 6 Aug. 1927 (HF).
32. GH to ImH, 9 Aug. 1927 (HF).
33. Washington lecture,
    26 Mar. 1932 (GH 1959).

15. COMMISSIONS AND COMPETITION (1927–1928)

1. GH to VL, 6 Sept. 1927 (HF).
2. GH to HBk, 16 Sept. 1927
   (BL Add 57953).
3. Palmer to GB, 11 Oct. 1927
   (LPL).
4. GB to Palmer, 26 Nov. 1927
   (LPL).
5. GH to E. H. Fellows,
   29 Feb. 1928.

6. Newcastle lecture, 1 Dec. 1928
   (*NewcDJ*, 3 Dec. 1928).
7. Edgar Hunt: *Robert Lucas
   Pearsall* (Edgar Hunt 1977).
8. BBC to GH, 3 Dec. 1927
   (BBC/WA).
9. GH to BBC, 5 Dec. 1927
   (BBC/WA).

10. GH to WGW, 26 Jan. 1928 (GH 1974).
11. *MMR*, Apr. 1928.
12. Shore 1949.
13. BBC memo, 19 Nov. 1943 (BBC/WA).
14. *Pearson's Mag*, Aug. 1930.
15. Armstrong 1974.
16. Toye 1931.
17. GH to HBk, 20 Apr. 1928 (BL Add 57953).
18. GH to WGW, 26 Dec. 1932 (GH 1974).
19. GH to DC, 21 Feb. 1928.
20. GH to AVW, 4 Apr. 1928 (BL Add 57953).
21. GH to WGW, 18 Apr. 1928 (GH 1974).
22. Bax 1939.
23. Bax 1936.
24. Rubbra 1948.
25. DC to MS, 14 Oct. 1978.
26. BL Add. 57953.
27. LPL.
28. R. C. D. Jasper: *George Bell* (OUP, 1967).
29. GH to Robinson, 13 July 1928 (BBC/WA).
30. Darrell 1932.
31. BL Add. 57909.
32. GH diary (HF).
33. *British Bandsman*, Autumn 1928 (via ImH).
34. GH to PP, 6 Dec. 1928 (BBC/WA).
35. GB to JM, 18 Dec. 1928 (LPL).
36. JM to GB, *c.* 21 Dec. 1928 (LPL).

16. 'LIFE IS MODERATELY PLEASING' (1929–1930)

1. Bax 1936.
2. GH to ImH, 4 Jan. 1929 (HF).
3. ImH 1938.
4. GH to OUP, 21 Jan. 1929 (via ImH).
5. GH diary (HF).
6. GH to ImH, 29 Jan. 1929 (HF).
7. GH to OUP, 6 Feb. 1929 (via ImH).
8. As 5.
9. GH to ImH, 19 Feb. 1929 (HF).
10. As 5.
11. GH to ImH, 5 Mar. 1929 (HF).
12. GH 1929.
13. As 5.
14. GH to ImH, 19 Mar. 1929 (HF).
15. As 5.
16. As 5.
17. GH to VL, 13 Apr. 1929 (HF).
18. GH to IsH, 12 Apr. 1929 (HF).
19. JM to GB, Feb. 1929 (LPL).
20. LPL.
21. Haskell 1930.
22. GH to GB, 23 May 1929 (LPL).
23. GH to IB, 13 July 1929.
24. GH to ImH, 9 Sept. 1929 (HF).
25. LPL.
26. GH to VL, 23 Aug. 1929 (HF).
27. As 23.
28. 'A Musical Autobiography' (RVW 1953).
29. A. Bliss: *As I Remember* (Faber, 1970).
30. ImH 1974f.
31. GB to GH, 1 Jan. 1930 (LPL).
32. GH to GB, 6 Jan. 1930 (LPL).
33. GH to DC, *c.* 7 Feb. 1930.
34. GH diary (HF).
35. *MMR* 1930b.
36. RVW to GH, 4 Apr. 1930 (GH 1959).
37. As 34.
38. *Sackbut*, July 1931.
39. GH notebook (HF).
40. BL Add. 57903.
41. GH to HBd, 28 May 1930.

17. FROM HAMMERSMITH TO THE USA (1930–1932)

1. GH to ACB, 19 Oct. 1931.
2. GH to ACB, 3 Oct. 1930 (BBC/WA).
3. GH notebook (HF).
4. ACB to GH, 16 June 1930 (BBC/WA).

5. GH to ImH, 13 Nov.1930 (HF).
6. GH to ND, 21 Dec.1930 (BL Add. 60391 BB).
7. ACB to GH, 13 Jan.1931 (BBC/WA; Moore 1979).
8. GH to ACB, 18 Jan.1931 (BBC/WA; Moore 1979).
9. *DMail*, 14 Feb.1931
10. GH to WO'D, 16 Mar.1931 (BBC/WA).
11. *Times*, 15 Apr. 1931.
12. BL Add. 57953.
13. GH to DC, 30 Apr. 1931.
14. ImH 1974*f*.
15. GH to WO'D, 4 May 1931 (BBC/WA).
16. GH to VL, 29 Jan. 1932 (HF).
17. GH to Clare Mackail, 23 Aug. 1931 (via ImH).
18. BL Add. 57906.
19. ImH 1938.
20. GH to ImH, 25 Aug. 1931 (HF).
21. ImH 1938.
22. BBC memo, 16 June 1931 (BBC/WA).
23. *Huddersfield Examiner*, 10 Oct. 1931.
24. GH to ACB, 2 Nov. 1931 (BBC/WA).
25. RVW to GH, Dec. 1930 (GH 1959).
26. GH to McKenzie, 4 Dec. 1931 (via ImH).
27. GH to DC, 19 Dec. 1931.
28. GH to ImH, 13 Jan. 1932 (HF).
29. GH to ImH, 26 Jan. 1932 (HF).
30. GH to VL, 29 Jan. 1932 (HF).
31. Ibid.
32. GH to VL, 4 Feb. 1932 (HF).
33. GH to ImH, 19 Feb. 1932 (HF).
34. *Modern Music*, May-June 1939.
35. GH to WGW, 14 Feb. 1932 (GH 1974).
36. GH to VL, 13 Feb. 1932 (HF).
37. GH to RVW, 15 Apr. 1932 (GH 1959).
38. GH to VL, 13 Feb. 1932 (HF).
39. GH to RMSA, Mar. 1932.

18. FINAL YEARS (1932-1934)

1. ACB to GH, 3 Mar. 1932 (BBC/WA).
2. GH to ACB, 17 Mar. 1932.
3. GH diary (HF).
4. GH to WGW, 12 May 1932 (GH 1974).
5. GH to RVW, 15 Apr. 1932 (GH 1959).
6. GH to WGW, 19 July 1932 (GH 1974).
7. GH to VL, 17 Apr. 1932 (HF).
8. ImH 1938.
9. GH to ImH, 13 May 1932 (HF).
10. Ibid.
11. Chatto & Windus, 1927.
12. Shilkret to McKenzie, 29 Nov. 1932 (ImH 1974 f.).
13. Race 1955.
14. As 4.
15. As 6.
16. GH diary (HF).
17. GH to VL, 17 Aug. 1932 (HF).
18. As 6.
19. GH to HBd, 8 Jan. 1933.
20. GH to ImH [Aug. 1932] (HF).
21. As 17.
22. As 6.
23. GH to VL, 25 Aug. 1932 (HF).
24. GH to ImH, 4 Sept. 1932 (HF).
25. GH to HBd, 9 Aug. 1932.
26. GH to WGW, 17 Oct. 1932 (GH 1974).
27. GH to WGW, 26 Dec. 1932 (GH 1974).
28. GH to DC, 15 Jan. 1933.
29. GH to VL, 11 Feb. 1933 (HF).
30. GH to WGW, 16 Mar. 1933 (GH 1974).
31. Moore 1979.
32. Ibid.
33. RCM MS 4550.
34. *Times*, 7 Oct. 1933.
35. GH to WGW, 25 Oct. 1933 (GH 1974).
36. GH to DC, 30 Jan. 1934.
37. GH to Walter Gandy, Jan. 1934 (HF)
38. GH to Amy Kemp, 11 Feb. 1934 (HF).
39. BL Add 58079.

40. GH to ACB, 5 Mar. 1934 (BBC/WA).
41. DC to MS, 14 Oct. 1978.
42. GH to ACB, 12 Mar. 1934.
43. GH to ACB, 14 Mar. 1934 (BBC/WA).
44. GH to ACB, 17 Mar. 1934 (Moore 1979).
45. Shore 1949.
46. GH to ACB, 31 July 1933 (BBC/WA).
47. Bax 1936.
48. GH to ACB, 1 May 1933.
49. GH to ImH, 22 Apr. 1934 (HF).
50. *MTimes*, Aug. 1934.
51. D. Hudson: *Norman O'Neill* (Quality Press, 1945).
52. IsH to Thorley vH, 12 Aug. 1934 (HF).
53. DC to MS, 14 Oct. 1978.
54. IsH to GB, 1 June 1934 (LPL).

19. EPILOGUE (1934–)

1. Brian 1934.
2. BBC memo, 2 Apr. 1935 (BBC/WA).
3. BBC memo, 15 Oct. 1940 (BBC/WA).
4. *MTimes*, Jan. 1956.
5. RVW 1935*a*.
6. Abraham 1936.
7. R. W. Wood 1938.
8. *MOpin*, Apr./May 1955.
9. GH 1922*b*.
10. GH 1925*b*.

20. THE LEGACY

1. Armstrong 1974.
2. GH to RVW, 11 Nov. 1925 (GH 1959).
3. Mellers 1941.
4. ImH 1951*a*.
5. Ibid.
6. Rubbra 1949.
7. Raynor 1954.
8. R. H. Hull 1930.
9. Dieren 1928.
10. Sorabji 1934.
11. *On Music's Borders* (Fisher Unwin, 1927).
12. Hussey 1928.
13. Turner 1928.
14. As 12.
15. R. W. Wood 1938.
16. Grace 1925*c*.
17. Foss 1942.
18. 'The Greatness of GH' (ER 1974*a*).
19. EE 1919.
20. As 17.
21. Blom 1934*b*.
22. GH to ACB, 14 Nov. 1918 (Moore 1979).
23. GH 1921*b*.
24. *Memories and Music* (Hutchinson, 1924).

21. HOLST'S MUSICAL STYLE

1. Grew 1922.
2. GH 1928*a*.
3. Armstrong 1974.
4. GH to WGW, 23 May 1917 (GH 1974).
5. GH 1920*a*.
6. From ImH.
7. GH 1920*a*.
8. GH to ACB, 22 Dec. 1928.
9. RVW 1938.
10. GH 1959.
11. GH to Amy Kemp, 1924 (HF).
12. As 10.
13. As 11.
14. RVW to GH [Dec. 1930] (GH 1959).
15. GH notebook (HF).
16. ImH to ACB, 1 Feb. 1973 (Moore 1979).
17. Nutting 1976.

18. ImH to ACB, 18 Aug. 1965
(Moore 1979).
19. *GlosChr*, 11 Feb.1893.
20. GH to WGW, 13 Dec. 1915
(GH 1974).
21. GH to WGW, 25 Sept. 1932
(GH 1974).
22. Hussey 1928.
23. Stephen Lloyd: *H. Balfour
Gardiner* (CUP, 1984).
24. GH 1920*b*.
25. GH 1920*a*.
26. Ibid.
27. GH 1921*b*.
28. As 25.
29. As 27.
30. As 25.
31. As 27.
32. Capell 1927*e*.
33. Whittall 1974.
34. ER 1932*a*.
35. ER 1947*a*.
36. RVW 1920.
37. Ibid.
38. EE 1923.
39. Bax 1936.
40. Morris 1920.
41. Shore 1949.
42. GH to ACB, 14 Nov. 1918
(Moore 1979).

43. Joseph 1924.
44. ImH 1973.
45. Full score (Stainer & Bell, 1919).
46. 'The orchestral problem of the
future' (*ProcMA*, 1922–3).
47. ACB to GH, 20 Apr. 1919
(Moore 1979).
48. GH to WO'D, 14 Dec. 1931
(BBC/WA).
49. *The Technique of Choral
Composition*
(Harvard UP, 1945).
50. GH 1927*b*.
51. Grace 1925.
52. C.H. 1922.
53. Demuth 1952.
54. *MTimes*, Nov. 1925.
55. Vocal score
(Stainer & Bell, 1912).
56. Vocal score
(Stainer & Bell, 1919).
57. WGW to GH, 28 Mar. 1916
(GH 1974).
58. *Music Student* 1914.
59. GH to WGW, 23 May 1917
(GH 1974).
60. RVW to GH, *c*.1901
(GH 1959).
61. Bax 1939.

Personalia

Brief biographical notes on people connected with Holst's career.

ALLEN, HUGH PERCY: b. Reading 23 Dec. 1869. Organist & choir-master. Studied at Reading and Oxford; conductor of London Bach Choir 1907–20; Professor of Music, Oxford Univ. 1918– ; Director of RCM 1919–37; knighted 1920. d. Oxford 20 Feb. 1946.

AMBROSE (AMBROSSE), CAROLINE: great-grandmother of GH; mother of Mary Croft Lediard.

BARNS, ETHEL: b. London 1880. Violinist and composer; wife of baritone Charles Phillips. Studied at RAM; début at Crystal Palace 1899; professor at RAM; toured England and America. d. Maidenhead 1948.

BARTER, (WILLIAM) ARNOLD: b. 1876. Amateur musician: conductor and organist. Founded Bristol Philharmonic Society Choir 1901; organist and choirmaster Portland Chapel, Kingsdown, Bristol; Hon MA Bristol Univ. 1951; OBE; retired 1963. d. Bristol c.24 Apr. 1966.

BAX, ARNOLD (EDWARD TREVOR): b. Streatham, London 8 Nov. 1883. Composer and writer. Studied at RAM; knighted 1937; Master of the King's Music 1942– . d. Cork 3 Oct. 1953.

BAX, CLIFFORD LEA: b. London 13 July 1886. Critic, playwright, author and editor. Founded Phoenix Society for revival of plays. d. 18 Nov. 1962.

BEHR, EDWARD: b. 26 Mar. 1879. Conductor. Studied at RCM; bandmaster to Governor of Bombay 1907–12; conductor of Bombay SO 1921–c.1931. d. London 9 Dec. 1958.

BELL, GEORGE KENNEDY ALLEN: b. Hayling Island 4 Feb. 1883. Clergyman. Educated Westminster School and Christ Church College Oxford; Chaplain to Archbishop Davidson; Dean of Canterbury 1924–9; Bishop of Chichester 1929–58. d. Canterbury 3 Oct. 1958.

BELL, WILLIAM HENRY: b. St Albans 20 Aug. 1873. Composer, teacher and conductor. Studied at RAM; professor of harmony at RAM 1903–12; Musical Director of 1911 Festival of Empire at Crystal Palace; Principal of Cape Town Conservatoire of Music 1912– ; FRCM 1924. d. Cape Town 13 Apr. 1946.

BENSON, LIONEL SEYMOUR (SOLOMON): b. Whinfold, Hascombe 1849. Amateur musician: conductor. Founded Magpie Madrigal Soc. 1886 to give charity concerts; in 1911 it was renamed the Elizabethan Madrigal Soc. d. 1929.

BIDDER, HELEN: b. 1891. Pianist, teacher, and composer. Studied at RAM; taught piano at SPGS.

BLISS, ARTHUR (EDWARD DRUMMOND): b. Barnes, London 2 Aug. 1891. Composer. Educated at Rugby, Pembroke College Cambridge, and RCM; war service 1914–19; professor at RCM 1921–2; USA 1923–5; m. Gertrude Hoffmann 1925; Director of Music BBC 1942–4; Chairman Music Committee of British Council 1946–50; knighted 1950; Master of Queen's Music 1953– ; KCVO 1969; CH 1971. d. London 27 Mar. 1975.

BONNETT, IRENE *see* SWANN, IRENE

BOULT, ADRIAN CEDRIC: b. Chester 8 Apr. 1889. Conductor. Educated at Westminster School, Christ Church Oxford and Leipzig Conservatorium; professor at RCM 1919– ; Director of CBSO 1924–30; Conductor of BBC SO 1930–50; knighted 1937; Principal conductor of LPO 1950– . d. 23 Feb. 1983.

BRIDGES, ROBERT: b. Walmer 23 Oct. 1844. Poet. Educated at Eton and Corpus Christi College, Oxford; held medical posts until 1882; Poet Laureate 1913– . d. Boar's Hill, Oxford 21 Apr. 1930.

BULLOCK, ERNEST: b. Wigan 15 Sept. 1890. Conductor, organist, and composer. Organist of Exeter Cathedral 1919– ; Master of Choristers at Westminster Abbey 1928– ; professor of Music at Glasgow University 1941– ; knighted 1952; Director of RCM 1952– . d. Aylesbury 24 May 1979.

BURKE, CHARLES: b. 1849. Pupil of H at MC; composer of *St Patrick's Prayer*. d. 27 Feb. 1917.

BUTTERWORTH, GEORGE SAINTON KAYE: b. London 12 July 1885. English composer and folk-song collector. Educated at Eton and Oxford; friend of RVW; dedicatee of VW's *London Symphony*, the score of which he helped prepare. Killed at Pozières in the battle of the Somme 5 Aug. 1916.

CAPELL, RICHARD: b. Northampton 23 Mar. 1885. Writer and music critic, of *DMail* 1911– and *DTel* 1933– ; editor of *MMR* 1928–33 and *M&L* 1950–4. d. London 21 June 1954.

CLEGG, EDITH KATE: b. London. Operatic contralto. Studied at Guildhall School of Music, also under Jacques Bouhy in Paris; stage début in Lehmann's *Vicar of Wakefield*; sang at LSO concerts, with the London Philharmonic Soc. and at Covent Garden; taught singing at SPGS and RADA.

COLES, CECIL FREDERICK GOTTLIEB: b. Galloway 7 Oct. 1888. Composer and conductor. Studied at Edinburgh Univ. and Stuttgart Conservatoire 1908–11; assistant conductor at Stuttgart Royal Opera House 1911–13; married and moved to London 1913; teacher of singing and harmony at MC 1913–14; volunteered for war service 1914. Died of wounds in France, 28 Apr. 1918.

COSSART, ERNEST *see* HOLST, EMIL GOTTFRIED ADOLF VON

COWEN, FREDERICK HYMEN: b. Kingston, Jamaica 29 Jan. 1852. Pianist, conductor, and composer. Studied under Benedict and Goss, and in Leipzig and Berlin under Hauptmann, Moscheles, and Reinecke; works include operas, symphonies, and songs; conductor of various choral socs. and orchs.; conductor of Scottish Orch. 1900– ; knighted 1911. d. London 6 Oct. 1935.

DAMROSCH, WALTER JOHANNES: b. Breslau 30 Jan. 1862. Conductor and composer. Studied in New York, Dresden and Frankfurt; conductor of NYSO 1885–1928; musical adviser to NBC 1927– ; works include operas and incidental music. d. New York 22 Dec. 1950.

D'ARÁNYI, JELLY: b. Budapest 30 May 1895. Violinist; sister of Adila Fachiri. Studied with Hubay in Budapest; settled in London 1923; NY début 1927. d. Florence 30 Mar. 1966.

DAVIES, JESSIE ELIZABETH *see* HARRISON, JESSIE ELIZABETH

DAVISON, ARCHIBALD T.: b. Boston, Mass 11 Oct. 1883. Choral conductor. Studied at Boston, Harvard Univ. and Paris; organist and choirmaster Harvard Univ. 1911– ; Professor of Choral Music at Harvard Univ. and conductor of Harvard Glee Club 1912–34. d. Brant Rock, Mass. 6 Feb. 1961.

DAY, NORA: b. 26 Sept. 1891. Music teacher. Educated at SPGS 1907–10 and RAM; studied piano with Adine O'Neill; helped H prepare many of his scores; gave two piano performances with Vally Lasker. d. 1983.

DEARMER, PERCY: b. 1867. Clergyman. Professor of Ecclesiastical Art at King's College, London 1919– ; Vicar of Chelsea Church 1924– ; Canon of Westminster 1933– ; writer and Editor of *English Hymnal* and *Songs of Praise*. d. 29 May 1936.

DESMOND, ASTRA: b. Torquay 10 Apr. 1893. Contralto. Studied at Westfield College, London; career closely connected with Elgar and RVW; wrote articles on songs of various composers; m. Thomas Neame; CBE 1949. d. Faversham 16 Aug. 1973.

DUCKWORTH, FRANK: b. 1866. Organist and choirmaster. Conductor of Blackburn Ladies' Choir 1906–24; organist of St Mark's Church, Blackburn 1902–36. d. Blackburn 25 Nov. 1946.

DYER, LOUISE HANSON: Wife of James Dyer. Promoted performances of British music in Australia; founded Editions de l'Oiseau Lyre 1932. d. Monaco Nov. 1962.

EVANS, EDWIN: b. London 1 Sept. 1874. Writer and critic. Studied in Lille and Luxemburg; music critic of *Pall Mall Gazette* 1912–23 and *DMail* 1933– ; one of the founders of ISCM (President 1938–). d. Balham, London 3 Mar. 1945.

FACHIRI, ADILA (née ARÁNYI DE HUNYADVÁR): b. Budapest 26 Feb. 1889. Violinist; sister of Jelly d'Arányi. Studied with Hubay in

Budapest and with her great-uncle Joachim in Berlin; settled in London 1909; m. Alexander Fachiri 1915; gave many performances in Britain with her sister, often accompanied by Donald Tovey. d. Florence 15 Dec. 1962.

FORTY, FRANK: b. Cheltenham 1846. Amateur pianist, organist, singer, and composer. Co-founder with Henry Dale of the music firm Dale, Forty & Co. of Cheltenham. d. Cheltenham 1916.

FORTY, MABEL: b. 1875. Pianist and teacher; daughter of Frank Forty. Studied at Manchester College of Music under Olga Neruda, sister-in-law of Charles Hallé; taught piano in Manchester. d. early 1940s.

GARDINER, GEORGE BARNET: Scottish linguist and classics teacher at Edinburgh Univ.; spent the last five years of his life collecting English folk-songs. d.1910.

GARDINER, HENRY BALFOUR: b. London 7 Nov. 1877. Composer and patron of music; brother of Egyptologist Alan Gardiner. Studied at Frankfurt Conservatorium 1894–6 and New College, Oxford 1896–1900; in 1912–13 organized a series of concerts at QH to promote music by younger British composers. d. Salisbury 28 June 1950.

GEEHL, HENRY ERNEST: b. London 28 Sept. 1881. Composer and conductor. Studied in London and Vienna; professor at Trinity College of Music 1918– ; arranged music by various composers for school orch. and brass band. d. Beaconsfield 14 Jan. 1961.

GLEESON-WHITE, CICELY R: b. Christchurch, Hants 1877. Operatic soprano. Studied at RCM; sang at ROH and various provincial festivals and concerts; m. George Miller.

GODFREY, DAN II: b. London 20 June 1868. Conductor; son of Dan Godfrey I (1831–1903). Educated King's College School and RCM; founded Winter Gardens orchestra in Bournemouth (later the Bournemouth Municipal Orchestra) 1893; knighted 1922. d. Bournemouth 20 July 1939.

GOODRICH, HONORIA *see* HOLST, HONORIA VON

GOTCH, NANCY: b. Oxford 12 Apr. 1899. Daughter of Francis Gotch, Waynflete Professor of Physiology, Oxford Univ. Pupil of GH; educated privately in Oxford, and at SPGS 1913–17; m. Maurice Strode 1920. d. Aldeburgh 11 Jan. 1978.

GRAY, FRANCES RALPH: Teacher. Educated at Plymouth and Newnham College, Cambridge; Headmistress St Katharine's School, St Andrews 1894–1903; High Mistress SPGS 1903–27; OBE 1926. d. 10 Nov. 1935.

HALL, MARIE: b. Newcastle-upon-Tyne 8 Apr. 1884. Violinist. Studied in Prague and Vienna; London début 1903; married Edward Baring, concert agent, of Cheltenham 1911; dedicatee of GH's *Valse Etude* and VW's *Lark Ascending*. d. Cheltenham 11 Nov. 1956.

HAMMOND-DAVIES, AMY *see* KEMP, AMY

HARDY, THOMAS: b. Higher Bockhampton, Dorset 2 June 1840. Writer. Attended school at Dorchester; studied architecture in London; practised as an architect in Dorchester before becoming a full-time writer; m. Emma Lavinia Gifford 1874 (d. 1912), Florence Emily Dugdale 1914. d. Dorchester 11 Jan. 1928.

HARRISON, EMILY ISOBEL *see* HOLST, (EMILY) ISOBEL VON

HARRISON, GEORGE AUGUSTUS: Father of Ralph Augustus Harrison. Water-colour artist.

HARRISON, JESSIE ELIZABETH (née DAVIES): wife of Ralph Augustus Harrison; mother of Emily Isobel Harrison (Isobel Holst).

HARRISON, RALPH AUGUSTUS: b. Chartreux 4 July 1843. Father of Emily Isobel Harrison (Isobel Holst).

HART, FRITZ BENNICKE: b. Brockley, Kent 11 Feb. 1874. Composer, teacher, and writer. Chorister at Westminster Abbey; studied at RCM; became Director of Melbourne Conservatory of Music and of Honolulu SO; FRCM 1924. d. Honolulu 2 July 1949.

HAST, (HARRY) GREGORY: b. London 21 Nov. 1862. Tenor. Founded Meister Glee-Singers 1890; professor of singing at Guildhall School of Music; sang at various concerts and festivals in London and the provinces.

HOLST. N.B. The surname prefix 'von' was used by the German branch of the family, but not by the Russian ancestry of the English branch. It was first adopted in England by Gustavus Valentine (see below), but was abandoned by GH in 1918.

HOLST, ADOLPH (ADOLF/ADOLPHUS) VON: b. London 5 Feb. 1846. Father of GH; youngest son of Gustavus Valentine (v)H. Pianist, organist, teacher, and composer. Studied in Hamburg; taught music in Cheltenham, giving recitals at Assembly Rooms and Montpellier Rotunda; organist of All Saints' Church 1868–95; local examiner for RCM. m. Clara Cox Lediard 11 July 1871; Mary Thorley Stone 20 Aug. 1885. d. Cheltenham 17 Aug. 1901.

HOLST, BENIGNA ('NINA') HONORIA VON: b. Marylebone, London 1849. Aunt of GH; daughter of Gustavus Valentine (v)H; sister of Adolph vH. Pianist. d. 1920s.

HOLST, CAROLINE HELLENA MARIA VON: b. Danzig 1802. Aunt of Adolph vH. Harpist at the Prussian court in Hamburg; m. Joachim H. C. Friedrichs 1834.

HOLST, CATHERINE MARIA VON: b. 14 Nov. 1839. Aunt of GH; daughter of Gustavus Valentine (v)H; sister of Adolph vH. d. Glasgow 21 Jan. 1874.

HOLST, CLARA COX VON (née LEDIARD): b. Cirencester 13 Apr. 1841. Mother of GH; first wife of Adolph vH; fifth child of Samuel Lediard. Pianist; pupil of Adolph vH. d. Cheltenham 12 Feb. 1882.

HOLST, EMIL GOTTFRIED ADOLF VON (stage name: ERNEST COSSART): b. Cheltenham 24 Sept. 1876. Brother of GH. Actor. Left home to join touring theatre company; London début 1896; went to USA c1902; served in Canadian army in First World War and was severely wounded; after war appeared in musical comedy in London; returned to USA 1919, appearing on Broadway and as film actor in Hollywood. d. New York 21 Jan. 1951.

HOLST, EVELYN THORLEY VON: b. Cheltenham 25 June 1889. Stepbrother of GH; son of Adolph vH and his second wife Mary Thorley Stone. Lawyer. Taken to USA as a child; subsequently practised law in Chicago. d. 1969.

HOLST, GUSTAVUS MATTHIAS VON: b. London 1833. Uncle of GH; eldest son of Gustavus Valentine (v)H; brother of Adolph vH. Pianist and composer; organist of St John's Episcopal Church, Glasgow 1867–8. d. Keith 17 Jan. 1874.

HOLST, GUSTAVUS VALENTIN(E) JOHANN (VON): b. Riga 19 Sept. 1799. Grandfather of GH; eldest son of Matthias H; brother of Theodore H. Composer, harpist, and pianist. Brought to England by his family c.1803–4; settled in Cheltenham c.1832; taught harp and piano. Married Honoria Goodrich. d. Cheltenham 8 June 1870.

HOLST, HONORIA VON (née GOODRICH): Paternal grandmother of GH; wife of Gustavus Valentine (v)H. Native of Norwich; first English member of the H family. d. Glasgow 15 Feb. 1873.

HOLST, IMOGEN CLARE: b. Richmond, London 12 Apr. 1907. Daughter of GH. Writer, conductor, composer, and teacher. Educated at Eothen School 1917– , and SPGS 1921–5; studied at RCM; music organizer for CEMA 1941–4; Director of Music at Dartington Hall 1943–51; amanuensis to Benjamin Britten 1952–64; artistic director of Aldeburgh Festival 1956– ; Conductor of Purcell Singers 1953–67; CBE 1975. d. Aldeburgh 9 Mar. 1984.

HOLST, (EMILY) ISOBEL (VON) (née Harrison); b. 26 Mar. 1877. Wife of GH; daughter of Ralph Augustus Harrison and Jessie Elizabeth Davies. d. Stowmarket 16 Apr. 1969.

HOLST, LORENZ HENRY VON: b. 28 Oct. 1842. Uncle of GH; son of Gustavus Valentine (v)H; brother of Adolph vH. Emigrated to Australia. d. Victoria 28 Feb. 1913.

HOLST, MARY THORLEY VON (née STONE): Stepmother of GH; second wife of Adolph vH; daughter of Revd Edward Stone. Pianist, theosophist; emigrated to California c.1900.

HOLST, MATTHIAS: b. Riga 1769. Great-grandfather of GH. Pianist, harpist, and composer. Harp teacher to the Imperial family at St Petersburg; married Katharina Rogge (d. England 1838); settled in London, working as a teacher and composer. d. Hampstead, London 1854.

HOLST, MATTHIAS JOHANN VON: b. 4 Oct. 1839. Distant cousin of Adolph vH. Architect; studied in Hanover and Zurich 1867– ; m. Rosa Cayard (b. Nottingham, 1 Jan. 1836). d. Berlin, 21 Apr. 1905.

HOLST, MATTHIAS ('MAX') RALPH BROMLEY VON: b. 28 Nov. 1886. Stepbrother of GH; son of Adolph vH and his second wife Mary Thorley Stone. Became a professional cellist in London; m. Dorothy Louise Arden; ch. Theodore Lorenz. d. 1956.

HOLST, NINA VON *see* HOLST, BENIGNA HONORIA VON:

HOLST, ROSA VON: b. Riga 29 Dec. 1868. Distant cousin of GH; daughter of Matthias Johann vH. m. Harry Nyce, USA 1892.

HOLST, THEODORE: b. London 3 Sept. 1810. Great-uncle of GH; son of Matthias H; brother of Gustavus Valentine (v)H. Painter; pupil of Fuseli. d. London 12 Feb. 1844.

HOLST, VALERIE *see* LIVINGSTONE, (DOROTHY) VALERIE

JACOBI, GEORG: b. Berlin 13 Feb. 1840. Violinist, conductor, and composer. Conductor at the Bouffes-Parisiens; Director of music at the Alhambra Theatre; professor of composition at RCM 1896– . d. London 13 Sept. 1906.

JOSEPH, JANE MARIAN: b. London 31 May 1894. Composer, writer, and percussionist; pupil of GH. Educated at SPGS 1909–13 and Girton College Cambridge; wrote orchestral, vocal, and choral music; in 1921 organized performances of Purcell's *Dioclesian* at Bute House, Hyde Park, and the Old Vic; sometimes deputized for H as singing teacher at SPGS and helped him with the preparation of his scores. d. London 9 Mar. 1929.

KEMP, AMY (HAMMOND-DAVIES): b. Cairo 1897. Pianist. Educated SPGS 1911–16; taught at SPGS 1917–37; m. 1937. d. Newbury July 1986.

LASKER, VALLY: b. 13 Feb. 1885. Pianist and music teacher, at SPGS, MC, and Borough Polytechnic. Helped H prepare many of his scores; made piano arrangements and gave two-piano performances with Nora Day. d. London 29 Mar. 1978.

LEDIARD, ANNA *see* NEWMAN, ANNA

LEDIARD, CLARA COX *see* HOLST, CLARA COX VON

LEDIARD, MARY CROFT (NÉE Whatley): b. 2 Jan. 1806. Maternal grandmother of GH; wife of Samuel Lediard. d. 24 Jan. 1895.

LEDIARD, SAMUEL: b. *c*.1805. Maternal grandfather of GH. Solicitor, of Cirencester. d. 1 Nov. 1852.

LIVINGSTONE, (DOROTHY) VALERIE (née VON HOLST): b. 27 June 1907. Niece of GH; daughter of Emil Gottfried Adolf vH.

LONGMAN, DOROTHY (née FLETCHER): violinist and singer; member of London Bach Choir; married R. G. Longman 1915.

LONGMAN, R. G. ('BOBBY'): singer. Neighbour of RVW at Dorking; brother of pianist Margaret Longman: both were members of the Coldharbour Choir.

LOPOKOVA, LYDIA (LADY KEYNES): b. St Petersburg 1892. Dancer. Studied at Mariinsky Theatre; member of Diaghilev's Ballets Russes 1910– ; married economist J. M. Keynes 1925; founded with him the Arts Theatre, Cambridge 1936.

MACFARREN, WALTER CECIL: b. London 28 Aug. 1826. Composer, pianist, editor, and critic. Studied at RAM; professor of piano at RAM 1846–1903; treasurer of Philharmonic Soc. 1877–80. d. London 2 Sept. 1905.

MCINNES, JAMES CAMPBELL: b. Bury, Lancs 23 Jan. 1874. Baritone. Studied at RCM 1895– ; pupil of Santley; London début St James's Hall 1899; became well-known oratorio soloist. d. Toronto 8 Feb. 1945.

MACKAIL, CLARE: musician and artist. Granddaughter of Edward Burne-Jones; daughter of Professor J. W. Mackail; sister of Dennis Mackail and Angela Thirkell. Pupil at SPGS 1908–11; war service as VAD 1916– . d. 6 Jan. 1975.

MAITLAND, JOHN ALEXANDER FULLER: b. London 7 Apr. 1856. Pianist and music critic for various newspapers, including *Guardian* and *Times*. Folk-song enthusiast; helped to found EFDSS; edited much early music and 2nd edn. of *Grove's Dictionary*. d. Carnforth, Lancs. 30 Mar. 1936.

MASEFIELD, JOHN: b. Ledbury 1 June 1878. Writer. Educated at King's School, Warwick; trained as a seaman, then turned to literature; m. Constance de la Cherois-Crommelin (d. 1960) 1903; Poet Laureate 1930– ; OM 1935. d. Abingdon 12 May 1967.

MASON, EDWARD: b. Coventry 24 June 1878. Cellist, conductor, and teacher. Studied at RCM; London début Bechstein Hall 1900; conducted New SO at its first concert, QH 1906 and became its principal cellist; founded Edward Mason Choir; assistant music master at Eton for 15 years. Killed in action in France, 9 May 1915.

MORRIS, WILLIAM: b. Walthamstow 24 Mar. 1834. Poet, designer, printer, medievalist, and socialist. Educated at Marlborough and Exeter College, Oxford; founded the firm of Morris & Co., producing wallpapers, fabrics, and household furniture; in 1878 moved to Hammersmith, founding the Hammersmith Socialist Society. d. Kelmscott, Oxon. 3 Oct. 1896.

MUKLE, MAY HENRIETTA: b. London 14 May 1880. Cellist. Studied at RAM; London début 1907; toured extensively as soloist in orchestral and chamber concerts. d. 1963.

NAYLOR, EDWARD WOODALL: b. Scarborough 9 Feb. 1867. Organist, composer, and scholar. Studied at RCM; lecturer at Cambridge Univ. 1902– ; organist of Emmanuel College, Cambridge; author of *Shakespeare and Music* (1897). d. Cambridge 7 May 1934.

NEWMAN, ANN(A) EMILY (née LEDIARD): b. 1846. Aunt of GH; sister of Clara Cox Lediard. Married Richard Newman, a riding master, and moved to Barnes, where she ran St Mary's School with her daughter. d. 1908.

NOEL, CONRAD LE DESPENSER RODEN: b. 12 July 1869. Clergyman, writer, lecturer, and socialist. Vicar of Thaxted 1910– ; restored buildings there and encouraged the revival of folk-dancing and music in church ceremonies; organized Whitsun festivals with GH. d. Thaxted 22 July 1942.

O'NEILL, ADINE (née RÜCKERT): b. 1875. Pianist. Studied at Paris Conservatoire and with Clara Schumann in Frankfurt; m. Norman O'Neill 1899; taught piano at SPGS; played at the Proms 1904–17; London critic of *Le Monde Musicale*; President of Society of Women Musicians 1921–3. d. 17 Feb. 1947.

O'NEILL, NORMAN HOUSTOUN: b. Kensington, London 14 Mar. 1875. Composer. Studied at Frankfurt Conservatorium 1893–7; m. Adine Rückert 1899; musical director Haymarket Theatre, London 1908– ; examiner for Associated Board of RSM and Treasurer of Royal Philharmonic Soc.; professor of harmony and composition at RAM 1924– . d. 3 Mar. 1934.

O'NEILL, YVONNE PATRICIA: b. 26 Jan. 1916. Daughter of Adine and Norman O'Neill; married Derek Hudson.

PARRY, (CHARLES) HUBERT HASTINGS: b. Bournemouth 27 Feb. 1848. Composer, teacher, and administrator. Studied at Eton and Exeter College, Oxford; professor at RCM 1883– , Director 1894– ; Professor of Music, Oxford Univ. 1900–8; knighted 1898. d. Rustington, Sussex 7 Oct. 1918.

PHILLIPS, CHARLES: b. Ayr. Baritone and teacher of singing; husband of Ethel Barns. Studied at RAM and Milan; début at St James's Hall, London 1892; professor at RAM; founded Barns-Phillips Chamber Concerts 1897.

PITT, PERCY: b. London 4 Jan. 1870. Conductor, composer, organist, and pianist. Studied in Paris, Leipzig, and Munich; organist at QH 1896; Director of Opera at Covent Garden 1907–24; Director of BNOC 1922–4; Musical Director of BBC 1922–30. d. London 23 Nov. 1932.

RONALD, LANDON: b. London 7 June 1873. Conductor, composer, and writer. Performed widely as an operatic conductor and pianist; conductor of Scottish Orch. 1916–20, and of New SO 1910–14; gave concerts at RAH and QH; Principal of Guildhall School of Music 1910– ; knighted 1922; FRCM 1924. d. London 14 Aug. 1938.

SCHWILLER, ISIDORE: b. 1878. Violinist. Leader and deputy conductor of the Carl Rosa Opera Company orchestra; leader of Schwiller

Quartet; leader of Leith Hill Music Festival orchestra for nearly 50 years. d. 28 May 1956.

SCOTT, CHARLES KENNEDY: b. Romsey, Hants 16 Nov. 1876. Choral conductor. Studied at Brussels Conservatoire; founded Oriana Madrigal Soc. 1904; founded Philharmonic Choir 1919, Bach Cantata Club 1926; edited much early music. d. London 2 July 1965.

SHILKRET, NATHANIEL: b. New York 1 Jan. 1895. Conductor, arranger, and composer. Studied engineering, then music in Kansas; clarinettist in various orchestras; Music Director of Victor Records 1916–35; Hollywood film arranger 1935– .

SILK, DOROTHY: b. King's Norton, Worcs. 4 May 1883. Soprano. Studied in Vienna; London début at QH; sang at RAH, Aeolian Hall and provincial centres; professor of singing at RCM. d. Alvechurch, Worcs. 30 July 1942.

SOLLY, HARRIET L.: b. 1873. Violinist and composer. Leader of MC orchestra and Solly String Quartet.

STANFORD, CHARLES VILLIERS: b. Dublin 30 Sept. 1852. Composer, conductor and teacher. Studied at Queen's College, Cambridge, Leipzig, and Berlin; professor of composition at RCM 1883– ; conductor of London Bach Choir 1885–1902; Professor of Music, Cambridge Univ. 1887– ; knighted 1902. d. London 29 Mar. 1924.

STONE, MARY THORLEY *see* HOLST, MARY THORLEY VON

STRODE, NANCY *see* GOTCH, NANCY

SWANN, IRENE (née BONNETT): b. 4 Jan. 1897. Pupil at SPGS 1909–16; studied organ and composition with H; organ scholar at Girton College; studied violin and conducting at RCM; helped H with Whitsun festivals.

TERRY, RICHARD RUNCIMAN: b. Ellington, Northumberland 3 Jan. 1865. Organist and choirmaster. Educated at Oxford and Cambridge; organist and choirmaster Downside Abbey 1896–1901, Westminster Cathedral 1901–24; knighted 1922. d. London, 18 Apr. 1938.

VAUGHAN WILLIAMS, ADELINE (née FISHER): b. 16 July 1870. Pianist and cellist; daughter of Herbert W. Fisher and Mary Jackson; married RVW 9 Oct. 1897. d. Dorking 10 May 1951.

VAUGHAN WILLIAMS, RALPH: b. Down Ampney, Glos. 12 Oct. 1872. Composer. Studied at RCM and Trinity College, Cambridge, also with Max Bruch and Ravel; m. Adeline Fisher 9 Oct. 1897, Ursula Wood (née Lock) 7 Feb. 1953; music editor of *English Hymnal* 1906; collected English folk-songs; professor at RAM; conductor of London Bach Choir 1919– ; organized and conducted Leith Hill Music Festival 1905–53. d. London 26 Aug. 1958.

WHITTAKER, WILLIAM GILLIES: b. Newcastle-upon-Tyne 23 July 1876.

Choral conductor, composer, and writer. Taught at Armstrong College, Newcastle; conducted Newcastle and Gateshead Choral Union and Newcastle Bach Choir; first Gardiner Professor of Music at Glasgow Univ. and Principal of Scottish National Academy of Music 1930– . d. Orkney 5 July 1944.

WILSON, (JAMES) STEUART: b. Clifton, Bristol 21 July 1889. Tenor and administrator. Educated Winchester and King's College Cambridge; one of the original members of the English Singers; professor of singing at RCM; Music Director of Arts Council 1945–8; knighted 1945; Principal of Birmingham School of Music 1957–60; translated many songs into English. d. Petersfield 18 Dec. 1966.

WINDRAM, JAMES CAUSLEY: b. 1886. Conductor and composer. Studied at RMSM; Director of Music of Coldstream Guards; Bandmaster of 1st Battalion of Royal Northumberland Fusiliers 1914–30.

WOLFE, HUMBERT: b. 1885. Civil servant and poet. Principal Assistant Secretary in Ministry of Labour 1918–38, Deputy Secretary 1938– ; published several volumes of poems. d. 1940.

WOODWORTH, (GEORGE) WALLACE: b. Boston, Mass 6 Nov.1902. Conductor, organist, and teacher. Studied at Harvard and RCM; conductor of Radcliffe Choral Soc. 1924– and Harvard Glee Club 1933– ; Professor of Music, Harvard Univ. 1954– . d. Cambridge, Mass. 18 July 1969.

Holst's Compositions: A Classified List

All Holst's known compositions are listed here, including juvenile attempts and student exercises as well as mature works, together with his own arrangements, orchestrations, and transcriptions of works by himself and others. Full details of manuscripts, first performances, publication, and recordings can be found in Short 1974*a* and IH 1974*f*, whose system of H. numbers is used here to identify each work.

ORCHESTRA

Intermezzo (1891) H. App. I, 12
Scherzo (1891) H. App. I, 13
Funeral March (c. 1891–2) H. App. II, 3
Wedding March (c.1891–2) H. App. II, 2 (*incomplete*)
Symphony in C minor (1892) H. App. I, 14
Bolero (1893) H. App. I, 24
Children's Suite (1895) H. App. II, 8 (*incomplete*)
Two Pieces (1896–7) H. App. II, 10 (*incomplete*)
A Winter Idyll (1897) H. 31
Walt Whitman: overture, Op. 7 (1899) H. 42
Suite de Ballet, Op. 10 (1899) H. 43
Cotswolds Symphony, Op. 8 (1900) H. 47
Greeting: No. 3 of *Six Solos* for violin and piano (c.1901–2) H. 53, orch. GH
Indra: symphonic poem, Op. 13 (1903) H. 66
Dreaming by Berthold Tours, orch. GH (c.1906) H. App. III, 4
Minuet d'Amour by Frederick H. Cowen, orch. GH (c.1906) H. App. III, 5
Songs of the West, Op. 21*a* (1906–7) H. 86
A Somerset Rhapsody, Op. 21*b* (1906–7) H. 87
Two Songs Without Words, Op. 22 (1906) H. 88:
    1. *Country Song*   2. *Marching Song*
Beni Mora: oriental suite, Op. 29/1 (1909–10) H. 107
Morris Dance Tunes harm. Cecil Sharp, orch. GH (1910) H. App. III, 12
Phantastes Suite, Op. 29/2 (1911) H. 108 (*withdrawn*)
The Planets: suite, Op. 32 (1914–16) H. 125
Japanese Suite, Op. 33 (1915) H. 126
The Gordian Knot Untied by Henry Purcell, arr. GH (c.1916–18) H. App. III, 18

A list of compositions prepared by Holst himself c. 1918

The Married Beau by Henry Purcell, arr. GH (*c*.1916–18) H. App. III, 20
The Old Bachelor by Henry Purcell, arr. GH (*c*.1916–18) (*incomplete*)
The Virtuous Wife by Henry Purcell, arr. GH (*c*.1916–18) H. App. III, 19
A Magic Hour: ballet (*c*.1920)
The Lure: ballet (1921) H. 149
Ballet music from *The Perfect Fool*, Op. 39 (1918–22) H. 150
A Fugal Overture, Op. 40/1 (1922) H. 151
Egdon Heath, Op. 47 (1927) H. 172
Fugue à la Gigue by J. S. Bach (BWV 577), orch. GH from the wind
    band version (1928) H. App. III, 25
Hammersmith, Op. 52 (1931) H. 178, orch. GH from the original wind
    band version
Capriccio (1932) H. 185 (originally *Mr Shilkret's Maggot* for radio jazz
    orchestra)
Scherzo (1933–4) H. 192

STRING ORCHESTRA

Suite in G minor (1898) H. 41
St Paul's Suite, Op. 29/2 (1913) H. 118
Nocturne from *A Moorside Suite* (1928) H 173, arr. GH
Brook Green Suite (1933) H. 190

WIND BAND

Marching Song from *Two Songs Without Words*, Op. 22 (1906) H. 88,
    arr. GH
Suite No. 1, Op. 28/1 (1909) H. 105
Suite No. 2, Op. 28/2 (1911) H. 106
Morris Dance Tunes harm. Cecil Sharp, arr. GH (1911) H. App. III, 12
Three Folk Tunes (*c*.1911) H. 106*a*
Fugue à la Gigue by J. S. Bach (BWV 577), arr. GH (1928) H. App. III, 25
Hammersmith, Op. 52 (1930) H. 178

BRASS BAND

A Moorside Suite (1928) H. 173

SOLO INSTRUMENTS AND ORCHESTRA

A Song of the Night for violin and orch., Op. 19/1 (1905) H. 74
Invocation for cello and orch., Op. 19/2 (1911) H. 75
A Fugal Concerto for flute, oboe, and strings, Op. 40/2 (1923) H. 152

Double Concerto for 2 violins and orch., Op. 49 (1929) H. 175
Lyric Movement for viola and orch. (1933) H. 191

OPERA

Lansdown Castle, or The Sorcerer of Tewkesbury: operetta in 2 acts
   (1892) H. App. I, 21
Ianthe: romantic operetta for children (c.1894) H. App. I, 42
The Revoke: opera in one act, Op. 1 (1895) H. 7
The Magic Mirror: opera in one act (1896) H. App. II, 12 (*incomplete*)
The Idea: children's operetta in two acts (c.1896) H. 21
Cinderella: fairy pantomime for children (c.1901–2)
The Youth's Choice: a musical idyll in one act, Op. 11 (1902) H. 60
Sita: opera in three acts, Op. 23 (c.1900–06) H. 89
Savitri: an episode from the Mahabharata, Op. 25 (1908–9) H. 96
Opera as She is Wrote: parody (1917–18) H. App. II, 15
The Perfect Fool: opera in one act, Op. 39 (1918–22) H. 150
At the Boar's Head: a musical interlude in one act, Op. 42 (1924) H. 156
The Wandering Scholar: chamber opera in one act, Op. 50 (1929–30)
   H. 176

INCIDENTAL MUSIC

Stratford Revels (1905) H. App. III, 1
Nabou, or Kings in Babylon (c.1905) H. 94
The Vision of Dame Christian, Op. 27a (1909) H. 101
Stepney Children's Pageant, Op. 27b (1909) H. 102–3
The Pageant of London (1910) H. 114 (wind band)
The Sneezing Charm (c.1920) H. 143
Seven Choruses from the Alcestis of Euripides (1920) H. 146 (unison
   voices, harp and 3 flutes)
St Martin's Pageant (1921) H. App. III, 22
The Coming of Christ (1927) H. 170
The Passing of the Essenes (1930) H. 180 (male voices in unison)
The Song of Solomon (1933–4) H. App. II, 17

FILM MUSIC

The Bells (1931) H. 184

CHORAL BALLETS

The Golden Goose, Op. 45/1 (1926) H. 163
The Morning of the Year, Op. 45/2 (1926–7) H. 164

CHORUS AND ORCHESTRA

MIXED VOICES

Horatius (c.1887) H. App. II, 1 (*incomplete*)

Clear and Cool, Op. 5 (1897) H. 30

King Estmere, Op. 17 (1903) H. 70

Choral Hymns from the Rig Veda: 1st Group, Op. 26/1 (1908–10) H. 97:
   1. *Battle Hymn*
   2. *To the Unknown God*
   3. *Funeral Hymn*

Christmas Day (1910) H. 109

The Cloud Messenger, Op. 30 (1910–12) H. 111

News From Whydah by Henry Balfour Gardiner, orch. GH (c.1912) H. App. III, 14

Two Psalms (1912) H. 117 (strings and organ or brass):
   1. *To My Humble Supplication* (Psalm 86)
   2. *Lord, Who Hast Made Us for Thine Own* (Psalm 148)

Three Festival Choruses, Op. 36a (1916) H. 134:
   1. *Let All Mortal Flesh Keep Silence*
   2. *Turn Back, O Man*
   3. *A Festival Chime*

The Hymn of Jesus, Op. 37 (1917) H. 140

All People That On Earth Do Dwell arr. GH (c.1916–19) H. App. III, 17

Ode to Death, Op. 38 (1919) H. 144

Short Festival Te Deum (1919) H. 145

First Choral Symphony, Op. 41 (1923–4) H. 155 (soprano solo)

A Choral Fantasia, Op. 51 (1930) H. 177 (soprano solo)

MALE VOICES

Sailors' Chorus (c.1891–2) H. App. II, 4

Ode to the North East Wind (1892) H. App. I, 20

Choral Hymns from the Rig Veda: 4th Group, Op. 26/4 (1912) H. 100 (strings or piano, with brass ad lib):
   1. *Hymn to Agni* (the sacrificial fire)
   2. *Hymn to Soma*
   3. *Hymn to Manas*
   4. *Hymn to Indra*

Six Choruses, Op. 53 (1931–2) H. 186 (strings or organ/piano):
   1. *Intercession*
   2. *Good Friday*
   3. *Drinking Song*
   4. *A Love Song*
   5. *How Mighty are the Sabbaths* (full orchestra; also a simplified version for unison voices, strings and organ)

6. *Before Sleep*

[7. *When the Dawn at Early Morning*—discarded, *incomplete*]

FEMALE VOICES

Choral Hymns from the Rig Veda: 2nd Group, Op. 26/2 (1909) H.98 (or piano and violins ad lib):

    1. *To Varuna* (God Of The Waters)

    2. *To Agni* (God Of Fire)

    3. *Funeral Chant*

Hecuba's Lament, Op. 31/1 (1911) H. 115

Lord, Who Hast Made Us For Thine Own:No. 2 of *Two Psalms* arr. from the original mixed-voice version (1912) H. 117 (strings and organ or piano)

Hymn to Dionysus, Op. 31/2 (1913) H. 116

A Dream of Christmas (1917) H. 159 (strings or piano)

Seven Part-Songs, Op. 44 (1925–6) H. 162 (strings):

    1. *Say Who Is This?*

    2. *O Love, I Complain*

    3. *Angel Spirits of Sleep*

    4. *When First We Met*

    5. *Sorrow And Joy*

    6. *Love on My Heart from Heaven Fell*

    7. *Assemble, All Ye Maidens*

Christ Hath A Garden (c.1928) H. 167

UNISON VOICES

Three Carols (1916–17) H. 133 (or piano):

    1. *Christmas Song: On this Day*

    2. *I Saw Three Ships*

    3. *Masters in This Hall*

Seven Folksongs (c.1904–19) H. 85:

    1. *On the Banks of the Nile*

    2. *The Willow Tree*

    3. *Our Ship She Lies in Harbour*

    4. *I'll Love My Love*

    5. *Claudy Banks*

    6. *John Barleycorn*

    7. *Spanish Ladies*

I Vow To Thee, my Country arr. GH (c.1918) from *Jupiter* theme in *The Planets* (1914–16) H. 148 (or piano)

CHORUS AND OTHER ACCOMPANIMENT

MIXED VOICES

A Christmas Carol (c.1890) H. App. I, 7 (piano)

The Listening Angels (1891) H. App. I, 5 (piano) (*incomplete*)
New Year Chorus (1892) H. App. I, 16 (piano)
Winter and the Birds (c.1893–4) H. App. I, 40:2 (piano)
Not Unto Us, O Lord (c.1893–6) H. 22 (organ)
Four Old English Carols, Op. 20b (1907) H. 82 (piano):

    1. *A Babe Is Born*

    2. *Now Let Us Sing*

    3. *Jesu, Thou the Virgin-Born*

    4. *The Saviour of the World*

A Welcome Song (c.1907–8) H. 91: 1 (oboe and cello)
Terly Terlow (1916) H. 91: 2 (oboe and cello)
Man Born to Toil (1927) H. 168 (organ)
Eternal Father (1927) H. 169 (organ)

MALE VOICES

A Dirge for Two Veterans (1914) H. 121 (brass and percussion)

FEMALE VOICES

Four Old English Carols (1907) H. 82, arr. GH from the mixed-voice
    originals (piano)
Choral Hymns from the Rig Veda: 3rd Group, Op. 26/3 (1910) H. 99
    (harp):

    1. *Hymn to the Dawn*

    2. *Hymn to the Waters*

    3. *Hymn to Vena*

    4. *Hymn of the Travellers*

Two Eastern Pictures (1911) H. 112 (harp or piano):

    1. *Spring*   2. *Summer*

Dirge and Hymeneal (1915) H. 124 (piano)

EQUAL VOICES

Eight Canons Nos. 7–8 (1932) H. 187 (piano; also arr. IH for
    strings):

    7. *Evening on the Moselle*

    8. *If 'Twere the Time of Lilies*

CHILDREN'S VOICES

Clouds o'er the Summer Sky (c.1902) H. 40 (piano)
Four Part-Songs (1910) H. 110 (piano):

    1. *Song of the Ship-builders*

    2. *Song of the Shoemakers*

    3. *Song of the Fishermen*

    4. *Song of the Drovers*

Two Part-Songs (1917) H. 138 (piano):

    1. *The Corn Song*

    2. *Song of the Lumbermen*

UNISON VOICES

The Strain Upraise: anthem with treble solo (c.1891–2) H .App. I, 4 (organ)

Advent Litany (c.1891–2) H. App. I, 6 (organ)

Sanctus (1892) H. App. I, 15 (organ)

Our Ship She Lies In Harbour:No. 16 of *Folksongs From Hampshire* (c.1908) H. 83, arr. from the original song version (piano)

Song of the Shoemakers:No. 2 of *Four Part-Songs* for children (1910) H. 110, arr. from the original 3-part version (piano)

In Loyal Bonds United (*Coronation Song/An Empire Day Song*) (1911) H. 113 (piano)

Playground Song (1911) H. 118a (piano)

Roadways (c.1931) H. 181 (piano)

UNACCOMPANIED CHORUS

MIXED VOICES

Ah Tyrant Love (189–) H. 18

It Was A Lover And His Lass (189–) H. 59

The Stars Are With The Voyager: 2 settings (189– and 1895) H. 2

Love Wakes and Weeps (1894) H. App. I, 41

The Autumn Is Old (1895) H. 1

O Lady, Leave That Silken Thread (1895) H. 4: 1

Spring It Is Cheery (1895) H. 3

The Kiss (1896) H. 16

Light Leaves Whisper (c.1896) H. 20

There's a Voice in the Wind (1896) H. 15

Five Part-Songs, Op. 9a (1897–1900) H. 48:

    1. *Love is Enough*

    2. *To Sylvia*

    3. *Autumn (Song)*

    4. *Come Away, Death*

    5. *A Love Song*

Thou Didst Delight My Eyes (c.1903) H. 58

Five Part-Songs, Op. 12 (1902–3) H. 61:

    1. *Dream Tryst*

    2. *Ye Little Birds*

    3. *Her Eyes The Glow-Worm Lend Thee*

    4. *Now is the Month of Maying*

    5. *Come To Me*

Two Part-Songs (pre–1908) H. 76, 78:

    1. *In Youth Is Pleasure*

    2. *Now Rest Thee From All Care*

I Love Thee (c.1912) H. 57
Nunc Dimittis (1915) H. 127
This Have I Done for My True Love (1916) H. 128
Lullay My Liking, Op. 34/2 (1916) H. 129
Of One That Is So Fair and Bright, Op. 34/3 (c.1916) H. 130
Bring Us In Good Ale, Op. 34/4 (1916) H. 131
Six Choral Folksongs, Op. 36b (1916) H. 136:
    1. *I Sowed the Seeds of Love*
    2. *There Was a Tree*
    3. *Matthew, Mark, Luke and John*
    4. *The Song of the Blacksmith*
    5. *I Love My Love*
    6. *Swansea Town*
Diverus and Lazarus (c.1916) H. 137
Two Motets, Op. 43 (1924–5) H. 159–60:
    1. *The Evening-Watch*
    2. *Sing Me the Men*
Ode to C.K.S. and the Oriana (1925) H. 157
O Magnum Mysterium by William Byrd, ed. GH (1927) H. App. III, 24
Wassail Song (1931) H. 182
Twelve Welsh Folksongs (1930–1) H. 183:
    1. *Lisa Lan*
    2. *Green Grass*
    3. *The Dove*
    4. *Awake, Awake*
    5. *The Nightingale and Linnet*
    6. *The Mother-In-Law*
    7. *The First Love*
    8. *O 'twas on a Monday morning*
    9. *My Sweetheart's Like Venus*
    10. *White Summer Rose*
    11. *The Lively Pair*
    12. *The Lover's Complaint*
O Spiritual Pilgrim (1933) H. 188

MALE VOICES

The Homecoming (1913) H. 120
Six Choral Folksongs Nos. 1, 3–6 (1916) H. 136, arr. GH (1924) from
   the mixed-voice originals

FEMALE VOICES

Ave Maria, Maiden Mild (1894) H. App. I, 35
Fathoms Deep Beneath the Wave (1894) H. App. I, 36
Now Winter's Winds are Banished (c.1894) H. App. I, 37

Summer's Welcome (1894) H. App. I, 39

There Is Dew For The Flow'ret (1894) H. App. I, 38: 2

Winter and the Birds (1894) H. App. I, 40: 1

All Night I Waited By The Spring (1890s) H. 12

Three Short Part-songs (1896) H. 13:

    1. *In The Forest Moonbeam-brightened*

    2. *All The Nests With Song Are Ringing*

    3. *Soft and Gently*

O Spring's Little Children (1897) H. 24

Autumn Song (1899) H. 48: 3a

Ave Maria, Op. 9b (1900) H. 49

Songs from 'The Princess', Op. 20a (1905) H. 80:

    1. *Sweet And Low*

    2. *The Splendour Falls*

    3. *Tears, Idle Tears*

    4. *O Swallow, Swallow*

    (4a. *Home They Brought Her Warrior Dead*—unpublished)

    5. *Now Sleeps The Crimson Petal*

Adoramus Te Christe by Orlando di Lasso, arr. GH (c.1908) H. App. III, 10

Benedictus by William Byrd, arr. GH (c.1908) H. App. III, 8

Help Me, O Lord by Thomas Augustine Arne, arr. GH (c.1908) H. App. III, 9

How Merrily We Live by Michael Este (East), arr. GH (c.1908) H. App. III, 7

A Song of Fairies (c.1909) H. 104

Pastoral (c.1909) H. 92

The Swallow Leaves Her Nest (c.1913) H. 119

Old Airs and Glees by various composers, arr. GH (c.1913–16) H. App. III, 16

Here Is Joy For Every Age (c.1916–17) H. 142

EQUAL VOICES

Sacred Rounds and Canons by various composers, arr. GH (c.1910) H. App. III, 13

Short Communion Service by William Byrd, arr. GH (1916) H. App. III, 21

Morley Rounds by his pupils, ed. GH (c.1924) H. App. III, 23

Canterbury Bells: 2 rounds (1928) H. 171:

    1. *Within This Place All Beauty Dwells*

    2. *To Bother Missis Bell*

Eight Canons Nos. 1–6 (1932) H. 187: .

    1. *If You Love Songs*

    2. *Lovely Venus*

3. *The Fields of Sorrow*
4. *David's lament for Jonathan*
5. *O Strong of Heart*
6. *Truth of All Truth*
Come Live With Me (1933) H. 189

HYMNS, FOR UNISON OR HARMONIZED SINGING

From Glory to Glory Advancing (tune: *Sheen*) (c.1905) H. 73: 2
Holy Ghost, Come Down Upon Thy Children (tune: *Bossiney*) (c.1905) H. 73: 3
In the Bleak Mid-winter (tune: *Cranham*) (c.1905) H. 73: 1
God Is Love, His The Care (tune: *Theodoric*) arr. GH (c.1925) from No. 1 of *Three Carols* (c.1916–17) H. 133
I Vow to Thee, My Country (tune: *Thaxted*) arr. GH (c.1918) from *Jupiter* theme in *The Planets* (1914–16) H. 148
I Sought Thee Round About, O Thou My God (tune: *Monk Street*) (c.1925) H. 161: 4
In This World, the Isle Of Dreams (tune: *Brookend*) (c.1925) H. 161: 2
O Valiant Hearts (tune: *Valiant Hearts*) (c.1925) H. 161: 1
Onward, Christian Soldiers! (tune: *Prince Rupert*) (c.1925) H. 161: 3
By Weary Stages (tune: *Hill Crest*) arr. GH from *The Song of the Coming of Christ* in *The Coming of Christ* incidental music (1927) H. 170
Gird On Thy Sword/Lift Up Your Hearts (tune: *Chilswell*) arr. GH from *Man Born to Toil* (1927) H. 168

SOLO VOICE AND ORCHESTRA

Örnulf's Drapa, Op. 6 (1898) H. 34 (baritone)
The Mystic Trumpeter, Op. 18 (1904) H. 71 (soprano)
Vedic Hymns, Op. 24 (1907–8) H. 90; nos. 4, 5, 8, orch. GH:
    4. *Indra* (God Of Storm and Battle)
    5. *Varuna II* (The Waters)
    8. *Creation*

TWO SOLO VOICES AND ORCHESTRA

Duet: Herald and Tom (c.1891–2) H. App. II, 5 (tenor/treble and bass) (*incomplete*)
Shepherd, Shepherd, Leave Your Labours by Henry Purcell, arr. GH (c.1909) H. App. III, 11: 1 (2 sopranos)

The Stream Daughters by Henry Purcell, arr. GH (c.1909) H. App. III, 11: 2 (2 sopranos)

THREE SOLO VOICES AND ORCHESTRA

Song of the Valkyrs (1893) H. App. I, 22 (2 sopranos and alto) (*incomplete*)

SOLO VOICE AND PIANO

The Harper (1891) H. App. I, 1
Die Spröde/The Coquette (c.1891) H. App. I, 3
I Come from Haunts of Coot and Hern (1892) H. App. I, 18
Sing Heigho: 1st setting (1892) H. App. I, 19
Anna-Marie (1893) H. App. I, 27
A Lake and a Fairy Boat: 1st setting (1893) H. App. I, 25
There Sits a Bird on Yonder Tree (1893) H. App. I, 26
The White Lady's Farewell (1893) H. App. I, 28
Now Sleep and Take Thy Rest (189–) H. 77
There Is Dew For The Flow'ret (c.1891–2) H. App. I, 38: 1
Ah, Come, Fair Mistress (189–) H. 45
The Exile of Erin (189–) H. App. I, 2
Four Songs, Op. 4 (1896–8) H. 14:
    1. *Margrete's Cradle–Song*
    2. *Slumber–Song/Sluimer lied* (Soft, soft wind)
    3. *Softly and Gently*
    4. *Awake, my Heart*
I Scanned Her Picture (late 1890s) H. 38
Airly Beacon (1897) H. 27
A Lake and a Fairy Boat: 2nd setting (1897) H. 25
Not a Sound But Echoing In Me (1897) H. 32
O Lady, Leave That Silken Thread (1897) H. 4: 2
Sing Heigh-ho: 2nd setting (1897) H. 26
Song to the Sleeping Lady (1897) H. 17
Twin Stars Aloft (189–) H. 28
Autumn Song (189–) H. 35
The Day of the Lord (189–) H. 29
Two Brown Eyes (189–) H. 39
My Joy (1898) H. 36
Whether We Die Or We Live (1898) H. 33
Bhanavar's Lament (1898–9) H. 44
Draw Not Away Thy Hands (189–) H. 37
She Who is Dear to Me (c.1900) H. 46
The Ballade Of Prince Eric (c.1901–2) H. 19

Six Songs (baritone), Op. 15 (1902–3) H. 68:
    1. *Invocation to the Dawn*
    2. *Fain Would I Change That Note*
    3. *The Sergeant's Song*
    4. *In a Wood*
    5. *Between Us Now*
    6. *I Will Not Let Thee Go*
To A Wild Rose c.1902–3) H. 65
A Prayer For Light (c.1903) H. 62
Song of the Woods (c.1903) H. 64
To Hope (1900s) H. 79
Six Songs (soprano), Op. 16 (1903–4) H. 69:
    1. *Calm is the Morn*
    2. *My True Love Hath My Heart*
    3. *Weep You No More, Sad Fountains*
    4. *Lovely Kind and Kindly Loving*
    5. *Cradle Song*
    6. *Peace*
Dewy Roses (c.1904) H. 63
Darest Thou Now, O Soul (c.1904–5) H. 72
Stu Mo Run arr. GH (c.1906–7) H. 84a
Four Folksongs arr. GH (c.1906–8) H. App. II, 13 (*incomplete*):
    1. *On Monday Morning*
    2. *Pretty Nancy*
    3. *Jocky and Jenny*
    4. *Swansea* [Town]
Nine Folksongs arr. GH (c.1906–14) H. 84:
    1. *Sovay*
    2. *The Seeds of Love*
    3. *The Female Farmer*
    4. *Thorneyfield Woods*
    5. *Moorfields*
    6. *I'll Love My Love*
    7. *Claudy Banks*
    8. *On the Banks of the Nile*
    9. *Here's Adieu*
The Heart Worships (1907) H. 95
Vedic Hymns, Op. 24 (1907–8) H. 90:
    1. *Ushas* (Dawn)
    2. *Varuna I* (Sky)
    3. *Maruts* (Stormclouds)
  [3a.*Ratri* (Night): discarded]
    4. *Indra* (God Of Storm & Battle)
    5. *Varuna II* (The Waters)

    6. *Song of the Frogs*

    7. *Vac* (Speech)

    8. *Creation*

    9. *Faith (Sraddha)*

      [*Battle Song (Indra and Maruts)*]

      [*Manas*]

      [*Funeral Hymn*]

      [the last three are in GH's own list of works, but cannot now be traced]

Folk Songs From Hampshire arr. GH (*c.*1908) H. 83:

    1. *Abroad As I Was Walking*

    2. *Lord Dunwaters*

    3. *The Irish Girl*

    4. *Young Reilly*

    5. *The New-mown Hay*

    6. *The Willow Tree*

    7. *Beautiful Nancy*

    8. *Sing Ivy*

    9. *John Barleycorn*

   10. *Bedlam City*

   11. *The Scolding Wife*

   12. *The Squire and the Thresher*

   13. *The Happy Stranger*

   14. *Young Edwin in the Lowlands low*

   15. *Yonder Sits A Fair Young Damsel*

   16. *Our Ship She Lies In Harbour*

Glory of the West arr. GH (*c.*1911) H. App. II, 14

A Vigil of Pentecost (191–) H. 123

The Ballad of Hunting Knowe (192–) H. 147

He-Back She-Back arr. GH (*c.*1920s)

Twelve Songs, Op. 48 (1929) H. 174:

    1. *The Floral Bandit*

    2. *Journey's End*

    3. *Now in these Fairylands*

    4. *A Little Music*

    5. *The Thought*

    6. *Things Lovelier*

    7. *In The Street Of Lost Time*

    8. *Envoi*

    9. *The Dream-City*

   10. *Rhyme*

   11. *Betelgeuse*

   12. *Persephone*

   [13. *Epilogue*: discarded]

God Be In My Head (1930)

VOICE AND VIOLIN

Four Songs, Op. 35 (1916–17) H. 132:
  1. *Jesu Sweet, Now will I Sing*
  2. *My Soul Has Nought But Fire and Ice*
  3. *I Sing Of A Maiden*
  4. *My Leman Is So True*

VOICE AND TWO VIOLINS

May Day Carol (c.1918) H. 141

CHAMBER MUSIC

First Quartet for strings (1893) H. App. I, 30 *(incomplete)*
Theme and Variations for string quartet (1893) H. App. I, 29
Allegro for string quartet (c.1893–6) H. App. II, 6 *(incomplete)*
Scherzando for string quartet (c.1893–6) H. App. II, 7 *(incomplete)*
Air and Variations for piano and string quartet (1894) H. App. I, 32
Short Trio for violin, cello and piano (1894) H. App. I, 33
Trio for strings (1894) H. App. I, 34
Allegro for wind septet (1896) H. App. II, 9 *(incomplete)*
Fantasiestücke for oboe and string quartet (1896) H. 8
Quintet for piano and wind instruments (1896) H. 11
Sextet for oboe, clarinet, bassoon, violin, viola, and cello (c.1896) H. 10
Variations for oboe, clarinet, bassoon, violin, viola, and cello (1896) H. 9
Scherzo for string sextet (1897) H. 23
Quintet for wind instruments, Op. 14 (1903) H. 67
Bourrée by W. C. MacFarren, arr. GH for piano and strings (c.1906) H. App. III, 2
March by Berthold Tours, arr. GH for piano and strings (c.1906) H. App. III, 3
Minuet d'Amour by Frederick Cowen, arr. GH for piano and strings (c.1906) H. App. III, 5
Seven Scottish Airs arr. GH for piano and strings (1907) H. 93
Andantino by Edwin H. Lemare, arr. GH for piano and strings (c.1908) H. App. III, 6
Phantasy on British Folksongs for string quartet, Op. 36 (1916) H. 135 (*withdrawn*; arr. IH for string orch. as *Fantasia on Hampshire Folksongs*)
Terzetto for flute, oboe, and viola (1925) H. 158
Gavotte discarded from *Brook Green Suite* (1933) H. 190, arr. IH for recorder quartet

INSTRUMENTAL

PIANO SOLO

Arpeggio Study (c.1892) H. App. I, 17

Two Pieces (*Deux Pièces*) (c.1901) H.50

Country Song from *Two Songs Without Words* (1906) H. 88, arr. GH from the orchestral original

Beni Mora: oriental suite, Op. 29/1 (1909–10), arr. from the orchestral original

Tender Bars (1920s) (*fragment*)

A Piece for Yvonne (1924) H. 154

Toccata (1924) H. 153

Chrissemas Day in the Morning, Op. 46/1 (1926) H. 165

Two Northumbrian Folk Tunes, Op. 46/2 (1927) H. 166

Nocturne (1930) H. 179: 1

Jig (1932) H. 179: 2

PIANO DUET

Introduction and Bolero (1893) H. App. I, 23

Dances (1895) H. 5

TWO PIANOS

Duet (c.1899) H. 6

The Planets: suite, Op. 32 (1914–16) H. 125, arr. GH from the orchestral version

VIOLIN AND PIANO

Six Solos: Nos.1–5 (c.1901–2) H. 51–5

    1. *Song Without Words* (*Chant sans Paroles/Lied ohne Wörte*) H. 51

    2. *A Spring Song* H. 52

    3. *Greeting* H. 54

    4. *Maya*: romance H. 55

    5. *Valse Etude* H. 56

TWO VIOLINS AND PIANO

Ländler (c.1903) H. 53: No. 6 of *Six Solos*

ORGAN SOLO

Four Voluntaries (1891) H. App. I, 8–11

Neptune: No. 7 of *The Planets* suite, Op. 32 (1914–16) H. 125, arr. GH from the original orchestral/choral version

A Duet For Three Hands And No Feet: extract from the *Terzetto* (1925) H. 158, arr. GH from the original version

TROMBONE & ORGAN

Duet (1894) H. App. I, 31

Bibliography

This is a comprehensive listing of writings about Holst which have appeared in printed form. All items are in English and published in Britain unless otherwise stated. Some very brief items have been included, as these sometimes provide useful details on Holst's career, or throw interesting light on critical attitudes of the period. Certain categories of ephemeral publication, such as concert programmes and record sleeve notes, have been excluded.

In general, entries are listed under the name of the author. In the case of anonymous authorship, lecture reports are listed under the name of the lecturer, and interviews under the name of the interviewee; otherwise entry is made under the name of the journal in which the article appears.

The following abbreviations have been used:

ARRev	*Audio Record Review*
BMBull	*British Music Bulletin*
BMusn	*British Musician*
BirmDM	*Birmingham Daily Mail*
BirmDP	*Birmingham Daily Post*
BirmP	*Birmingham Post*
BIRS	British Institute of Recorded Sound
BlacknT	*Blackburn Times*
BlacknWT	*Blackburn Weekly Telegraph*
BMBull	*British Music Bulletin*
BMSJ	*British Music Society Journal*
BMusn	*British Musician*
BrisTM	*Bristol Times & Mirror*
BurnEx	*Burnley Express*
C&Rec	*Concerts & Recitals*
CBDNAJnl	*College Band Directors National Assocation Journal (USA)*
CheltCh	*Cheltenham Chronicle*
CheltLO	*Cheltenham Looker-On*
ClifCh	*Clifton Chronicle*
CSMon	*Christian Science Monitor*
DGraph	*Daily Graphic*
DMail	*Daily Mail*
DNews	*Daily News*

DTel	*Daily Telegraph*
ENews	*Evening News*
EngRev	*English Review*
FMJ	*Folk Music Journal*
G&IH	G & I Holst Ltd
GlasHd	*Glasgow Herald*
GlosChr	*Gloucestershire Chronicle*
GlosCit	*Gloucester Citizen*
GlosEch	*Gloucestershire Echo*
GlosStd	*Gloucestershire Standard*
GramRec	*Gramophone Record*
IAML	International Association of Music Libraries
Inst	*Instrumentalist*
JAGSMag	*James Allen's Girls' School Magazine*
JBASBWE	*Journal of the British Association of Symphonic Bands and Wind Ensembles*
JBR	*Journal of Band Research*
LivPM	*Liverpool Post & Mercury*
MAmer	*Musical America*
M&L	*Music & Letters*
M&M	*Music & Musicians*
M&Y	*Music & Youth*
MBull	*Music Bulletin*
MCMag	*Morley College Magazine*
MCour	*Musical Courier (New York)*
MHer	*Musical Herald*
MidMusn	*Midland Musician*
MinEd	*Music in Education*
MMir	*Musical Mirror*
MMR	*Monthly Musical Record*
MN&H	*Musical News & Herald*
ModMus	*Modern Music*
MOpin	*Musical Opinion*
MPM	*Musical Progress & Mail*
MQuart	*Musical Quarterly*
MRev	*Music Review*
MStnd	*Musical Standard*
MStud	*Music Student*
MTchr	*Music Teacher*
MTimes	*Musical Times*
MTRev	*Music Trades Review*
N&Ath	*Nation & Athenaeum*
NewcDJ	*Newcastle Daily Journal*
PhonMR	*Phonograph Monthly Review (Boston, Mass)*

Proc(R)MA	*Proceedings of the (Royal) Musical Association*
R&R	*Records & Recording*
RCMMag	*Royal College of Music Magazine*
RevMus	*Revue Musicale (Paris)*
RevRev	*Review of Reviews*
RSound	*Recorded Sound*
RTimes	*Radio Times*
STel	*Sunday Telegraph*
STimes	*Sunday Times*
WestDP	*Western Daily Press*
WiltGS	*Wiltshire & Gloucester Standard*

A., T. (1927). 'Some new part-songs by H'. *MTimes* 68/1007 (Jan.) 45–7. Review of *Seven Part-songs* with examples of H's choral technique.

ABRAHAM, GERALD E. H. (1924). 'The art of GH'. *MTchr* 3/7 (July) 387–8. Assessment of H's musical style.

—— (1934). 'On H and Scriabin'. *C&Rec* NS 11 (27 Oct.–3 Nov. 1934) 6, 8. Discusses the opposing polarities of the two composers, as exemplified by *Prometheus* and *The Planets*.

—— (1936). 'H in perspective'. *Listener* 15/388 (17 June) 1179–80. An assessment of H's standing at this date.

—— (1946). 'GH'. In *British Music of Our Time* ed. Alfred L. Bacharach. Pelican, 256pp. Review of his work, with a select discography.

ANDERSON, W. R. (1947). 'Some modern masters: 11. GH'. *MTchr* 26/10 (Oct.) 383–4, 389. Assessment of H's style, using ImH 1938 as a starting point.

ANDREWS, HILDA (1928). 'Outline class lesson: GH'. *MTchr* 7/7 (July), 403–4. General review of his life and main works.

ANTCLIFFE, HERBERT (1923). '*The Perfect Fool*'. *MN&H* 65/1625 (19 May) 494. Brief review of the first performance.

ARMSTRONG, THOMAS (1974). 'Mr H'. *MinEd* 38/368 (July/Aug.), 163–5. Consideration of H's achievement, by one of his pupils.

AUDIO RECORD REVIEW (1968). 'Music on record: GH'. *ARRev* 8/10 (June) 426–7, and 8/11 (July), 499. Comprehensive discography of recordings of H's works.

B., R. (1926). 'Artists of the day: GH'. *MN&H* 70/1771 (6 Mar.), 224. Brief summary of his life and work.

BAINTON, EDGAR L. (1911a) 'GH'. *MOpin* 34/402 (Mar.), 397–8. Calls attention to his neglect as a composer of major stature (RP in 1911b).

—— (1911b). 'A Cheltenham composer: Mr GH'. *CheltLO* 3910 (18 Mar.), 13. RP of 1911a.

BASHFORD, RODNEY (1987). 'H, horns and unharmonious blacksmiths'. *Winds* 2/2 (Spring), 26–7. Comments on horn writing in the military band suites.

BAX, CLIFFORD (1925a). *Inland Far: A Book of Thoughts and Impressions*. Heinemann (RP Dickson 1933), 332pp. Includes a description of H's holiday journey to Majorca in 1913.

—— (1925b). 'GH: the man'. *ENews* 13532 (20 Apr.), 6. Some conversational anecdotes, by one of H's collaborators.

—— (1936). *Ideas and People*. Dickson, 296pp. Includes a chapter on H, consisting of personal reminiscences and anecdotes about the composition of several of his works.

—— (1939). 'Recollections of GH'. *M&L* 20/1 (Jan.) 1–6. Anecdotes of H and Bax's collaboration with him as librettist.

BELL, GEORGE (1934). Address given at the memorial service for GH at St John's Church, Westminster on Tuesday 19 June (privately printed). Describes the effect H had on those with whom he came into contact during his career.

BENNETT, ARNOLD (1923). 'GH's *The Perfect Fool*'. *Adelphi* 1/1 (June 1923) 58–60. Review of the first performance.

BENNETT, RODNEY (1922). 'GH'. *Bookman* 63/374 (Nov.) 117–20. An interview with H, discussing his career as composer and teacher.

BLÄTTER DER STAATSOPER (1931). 'Planeten: Eine choreographische Fantasie nach der gleichnamigen Symphonie von GH'. *Blätter der Staatsoper* (Berlin) (May), 4. Description of a ballet based on *The Planets* (in German).

BLISS, ARTHUR (1934), 'GH: a lonely figure in music'. *RTimes* 43/559 (15 June), 819. Obituary appreciation and reminiscences (with Boult 1934).

BLOM, ERIC (1931). 'The listener's repertoire: H—*The Planets*'. *MTchr* 10/2 (Feb.), 91–2. Analytical notes on each movement.

—— (1934a). 'Mr GH: career as teacher and composer'. *BirmP* 23678 (26 May), 18. Obituary notice describing his career and main works.

—— (1934b). 'The world of music: the art of GH'. *BirmP* 23679 (28 May), 8. An evaluation of H's musical style (RP in Blom 1941).

—— (1941). *A Musical Postbag*. Dent, 307pp. Includes RP of 1934b.

BONAVIA, FERRUCCIO (1925). 'At the Boar's Head'. *M&L* 6/3 (July), 269–75. Assessment of the work, with discussion of the relative merits of words and music in opera.

—— (1933). '*Savitri*' and '*The Perfect Fool*' in *The Complete Opera Book* by Gustav Kobbe. Synopses of the two works.

BONNETT, IRENE (1934). 'Mr H in school'. *RCMMag* 30/3, 86–8. Reminiscences of his classes at SPGS, by one of his pupils.

BOULESTIN, X. MARCEL (1914). 'Les Post-Elgariens, ou la jeune école anglaise'. *RevMus* (Jan.), 19–30. Includes brief section on H (pp. 24–5) mentioning his main works to date (in French).

BOULT, ADRIAN C. (1917). 'Music students' social: a performance of Mr v H's part-songs from the Rig Veda'. *MCMag* 26/6 (May), 89–90. Report of a talk on Sanskrit by Mabel Bode and a performance of the 2nd Group of *Choral Hymns from the Rig Veda*.

—— (1925). 'St Paul's Suite (GH): analysis'. *MN&H* 69/1754 (7 Nov.), 416, 428. Practical notes on the performance of each movement.

—— (1934). 'GH: the man and his work'. *RTimes* 43/559 (15 June), 819. Obituary appreciation and reminiscences (with Bliss 1934).

—— (1970). 'Interpreting *The Planets*'. *MTimes* 111/3 (Mar.), 263–4. Discusses points arising from publication of a new edition of the score, and includes a letter from H commenting on Boult's first performance of the work in 1918.

—— (1974). 'GH'. *RCMMag* 52/2 (Summer), 52–4. Some personal reminiscences.

BOYER, D. ROYCE (1968). 'GH's *The Hymn of Jesus*'. Univ. of Texas at Austin doctoral thesis, 135pp. Detailed assessment and analysis of the work, with discussion of performance problems.

—— (1975). 'H's *The Hymn of Jesus*: an investigation into mysticism in music'. *MRev* 36 (Nov.), 272–83. Traces the influence of mysticism in this work.

BRAITHWAITE, WARWICK (1923a). '*The Perfect Fool*: an analytical survey'. *Opera* 1/6 (June), 26–8. Discusses the musical and dramatic techniques used in the work.

—— (1923b). '*Savitri*: an interpretation of GH's one-act music-drama produced recently at Covent Garden'. *Opera* 1/7 (July), 17–18. Describes the work and the original story on which it is based.

—— (1924). 'Musical analysis of *The Perfect Fool*'. *ClifCh* 3802 (10 Apr.), 11. Not in fact an analysis, but draws attention to some interesting points (based on 1923a.)

BRIAN, HAVERGAL ['La Main Gauche'] (1934). 'On the other hand' and 'The loss to English music: GH'. *MOpin* 57/682 (July), 860–1, 865. Obituary assessment of H's achievement, in comparison with that of Delius.

—— (1940). 'GH: an English composer'. *MOpin* 63/748 (Jan.), 154–5. A review of his life and main works.

BRITISH MUSIC SOCIETY (1928). *List of compositions: GH*. BMS Victorian Centre (Melbourne, Australia), 8 pp. Classified list of published works up to 1927 (see also Dyer 1931).

C. (1922). 'GH on Purcell'. *MTimes* 63/951 (May), 354–5. Report of a lecture given by H at University College, London.

C. [a Morley College student] (1934). 'An appreciation of GH'. *MCMag* 20/2 (Nov.), 27–8. Recalls the enthusiasm and integrity which H conveyed to his students.

CALLARD, DOROTHY (1934). 'GH'. *JAGSMag* (1934), 61–3. Reminiscences of his work at JAGS, by one of his pupils.

CALVOCORESSI, M-D. (1923). '*Le Parfait Sot* de GH à Covent Garden'. *RevMus* 9 (July), 262–4. Description and assessment of *The Perfect Fool* (in French).

CANTRICK, ROBERT (1956). '*Hammersmith* and the two worlds of GH'. *M&L* 37/3 (July), 211–20. Origins and analysis of the work, with an account of the 1954 performance.

CAPELL, RICHARD (1923a). '*The Perfect Fool* at Covent Garden'. *MMR* 53/630 (June), 161–2. Review of the first performance.

—— (1923b). '*Savitri*'. *MMR* 53/632 (Aug.), 236. Review of a performance at Covent Garden.

—— (1926a). 'The time and the place: introduction to a sketch of H'. *M&L* 7/2 (Apr.), 150–6. Discusses the circumstances which give rise to the emergence of composers of varying styles within the European musical tradition.

—— (1926b). 'Extract from an introduction to a sketch of GH: Gloucester to Paddington'. *M&L* 7/4 (Oct.), 310–21. Discusses the influence of English folk-song on H's work and his place in the development of contemporary English music.

—— (1926c). 'GH: notes for a biography'. *MTimes* 67/1006 (Dec.), 1073–5, 68/1007 (Jan. 1927), 17–19. Describes H's life and main works to date, including information on his early years in London.

—— (1927a). 'Introduction to The *Hymn of Jesus*'. *MMR* 57/674 (Feb.), 38–9. Further extract from Capell's unpublished study of H, discussing the nature of his art.

—— (1927b). *Programme of concerts given in honour of GH*. [Cheltenham Borough Council] 16 pp. Biographical note, with outline analyses of several works.

—— (1927c). 'Introduction to *The Planets* (extract)'. *MMR* 57/676 (Apr.), 99–101. Description of each movement, except 'Mars'.

—— (1927d). 'H festival at Cheltenham'. *MMR* 57/667 (May), 138. Review of two concerts given in honour of H.

—— (1927e). 'GH: 3'. *M&L* 8/4 (Oct.), 73–82. A study of H's artistic attitudes, based on a consideration of *The Planets*, movement by movement.

—— (1928a). '*The Coming of Christ* at Canterbury'. *MMR* 58/691 (July), 204. Brief review of H's music for the Mystery play.

—— (1928b). 'Stereoscopic views: 3. GH'. *Dominant* 1/12 (Dec.), 13–20. An enthusiastic appreciation, contrasted with the views of Bernard van Dieren.

—— (1931). 'The music of the spheres'. *RTimes* 30/384 (6 Feb.), 295, 328. Biographical notes, with a description of *The Planets*.

—— (1934). 'GH, 1874–1934: ave atque vale'. *DTel* 24651 (26 May), 15. Obituary notice assessing his life and work.

—— (1935). 'Death comes to Satyavan'. *RTimes* 49/629 (18 Oct.), 15. Discussion of the philosophy and musical style of *Savitiri*.

CHELTENHAM CHRONICLE (1927). 'GH festival: Cheltenham's famous son'. *CheltCh* (26 Mar.), 5. RP of *GlosEch* 1927.

CHELTENHAM LOOKER-ON (1910). 'GvH'. *CheltLO* 3863 (16 Apr.), 18. Quotations from reviews of *A Somerset Rhapsody*, with brief biographical notes.

CHRISTIAN SCIENCE MONITOR (1921). 'GH'. *CSMon* 13/87 (5 Mar.), 12. Review of his work and musical style.

COATES, ALBERT (1929). 'GH: tone-poet, musician, composer'. *Millgate* 24/2 (Sept.), 707–9. Review of his life and work to date, by a sympathetic interpreter of his music.

COLE HUGO (1974). 'Centenaries'. *Listener* 92/2375 (3 Oct.), 445. Evaluation of some of H's lesser-known works performed during the centenary.

CONFALONIERI, GIULIO (1923). 'GH'. *Critica Musicale* (1923), 2–3. Review of H's style, achievements and attitudes (in Italian).

COOLEY, NANCY (1974). 'Reflections on H'. *Paulina* 153 (1973–4), 17–18. Discussion of features of H's style.

COOP, NORA (1974). 'GH 1974: the Masque record', by Nora Coop, F.L. Partridge, and Irene Swann. *Paulina* 153 (1973–4), 14–16. Articles on the recording of *The Vision of Dame Christian* at SPGS in 1974, including a list of performers.

CORBETT-SMITH, ARTHUR (1923). *The Perfect Fool (H)*. Richards (National Opera Handbooks 11) 46 pp. A whimsical synopsis of the opera and H's musical attitudes, with biographical note and list of works.

'DA CAPO' (1925). 'H's new opera'. *MN&H* 68/1724 (11 Apr.), 346, 348. Review of the first performance of *At the Boar's Head*.

DAILY MAIL (1925). 'GH: a trombone player'. *DMail* (Brisbane, Australia) (press cutting in HBM). Includes information on his early career and aspects of his character.

DARRELL, R. D. (1932). 'H in America: an interview with one of the first contemporary composers to conduct his own works for recording'. *PhonMR* 6/5 (Feb.), 83–4. Anecdotes of H conducting the Boston SO.

DEMARQUEZ, SUZANNE (1929). 'Notes sur l'école anglaise contemp-oraine'. *Musique* (Paris) (15 Dec.), 114–19. Includes a brief section describing H's main works (in French).

—— (1931a). 'GH'. *RevMus* 115 (May), 385–401. Detailed account of his life and work (in French).

—— (1931b). 'GH: a French view'. *MMR* 61/726 (June), 167. A brief English synopsis of Demarquez 1931a.

—— (1934). 'Alfred Bruneau, GH, Frederick Delius'. *RevMus* 148 (July), 158–60. Brief obituary appreciation (in French).

DEMUTH, NORMAN (1952). *Musical Trends in the Twentieth Century*. Rockliff, 359 pp. Contains a chapter on H, giving a general assessment of his work.

DENT, EDWARD J. (1920). 'The Hymn of Jesus'. *Athenaeum* 4692 (2 Apr.), 455. Origin and significance of the text and H's compositional technique in the work.

DICKINSON, A. E. F. (1939). 'Music that is absolutely true: H's *Hymn of Jesus*'. *RTimes* 62/801 (3 Feb.), 10. Brief assessment of the work.

—— (1972). 'The neo-modal style'. *MRev* 33/2 (May), 108–21. Discusses the use of modes in *The Hymn of Jesus*.

—— (1974a). 'The art of GH'. *MOpin* 1157 (Feb.), 228–9. Centenary assessment of his life and work.

—— (1974b). 'The revival of H'. *Tempo* 111 (Dec.), 2–6. Assessment of H's technical resources.

DIEREN, BERNARD VAN (1928). 'Stereoscopic views: 3. GH'. *Dominant* 1/12 (Dec.), 13–20. Claims that H's status had been inflated by British chauvinism; contrasted with the views of Richard Capell.

DYER, LOUISE B.M. (1931) *Music by British Composers: a series of complete catalogues: 1. GH.* OUP, 12 pp. Classified list of works up to March 1931 (based on British Music Society 1928).

EAST, LESLIE (1974). 'Double anniversary'. *M&M* 22/261 (May), 30–2. Centenary assessment of his life and work.

EATON, QUAINTANCE (1932). 'GH, on America visit approves our ways'. *MAmer* 52/3 (10 Feb.), 6. Interview with H, attempting to elucidate his musical opinions.

EGGAR, KATHERINE E. (1921). 'How they make music at Morley College: a chat with Mr H and a sight of his work there'. *MStud* 13/6 (Mar.), 359–61. Whimsical report of an interview with H and an evening spent at the college.

EINSTEIN, ALFRED (1923). 'H's *The Perfect Fool*: some thoughts of a German musician'. *MMR* 53/631 (July), 198–9. Discusses German antecedents of the 'musical fairy-tale' and describes H's techniques of parody.

EVANS, EDWIN (1911). 'Music and Sanskrit literature: GH's compositions'. *BlacknT* 2878 (11 Mar.), 9. Describes H's method of making his own translations.

—— (1914a). 'GvH'. *Outlook* 33/842 (21 Mar.), 388. Review and assessment of H's work to date (RP in 1914b).

—— (1914b). 'GvH'. *MCMag* 23/7 (Apr.), 109–11. RP of 1914a.

—— (1919). 'Modern British composers: 6. GH'. *MTimes* 60/920 (Oct.), 524–8; 921 (Nov.), 588–92; 922 (Dec.), 657–661. Detailed assessment of H's career to date, with list of works based on information provided by H himself.

—— (1920). 'The new dispensation'. *Outlook* 46/1191 (27 Nov.), 539. Assessment of H's position as a musician of international importance.

—— (1923a). 'The Perfect Fool'. *MTimes* 64/964 (June), 389–93. Describes the action of the opera, giving examples of the main musical themes.

—— (1923*b*). 'The Perfect Fool at Covent Garden'. *MTimes* 64/964 (June), 423. Review of the first performance.

—— (1927). 'H'. In *Grove's Dictionary of Music and Musicians* 3rd edn, ed. H. C. Colles. Macmillan, 5 vols. Outline of H's life and work, with a list of works up to 1924 (see also Evans 1940 and 1954).

—— (1928). 'GH'. *Dominant* 1/6 (Apr.), 24–5. Impressions of H the man over a long period of friendship.

—— (1929). 'H'. In *Cobbett's Cyclopedic Survey of Chamber Music*, ed. Walter W. Cobbett; OUP, 2 vols. Brief description of the *Terzetto*.

—— (1934). 'GH'. *MTimes* 75/1097 (July), 593–7. Obituary notice summarizing his achievement, by one of his close friends.

—— (1940). 'H'. In *Grove's Dictionary of Music and Musicians* 4th edn., ed. H. C. Colles. Macmillan, 5 vols. A revision of Evans 1927, with a chronological list of works (see also Evans 1954).

—— (1954). 'H'. In *Grove's Dictionary of Music and Musicians* 5th edn., ed. Eric Blom. Macmillan, 9 vols. A revision of Evans 1940, with a classified list of works.

EWEN, DAVID (ed.) (1969). *Composers Since 1900: a biographical and critical guide*. Wilson (NY). Includes a section on H, giving a biographical summary, assessment of his work and list of main compositions.

FENNELL, FREDERICK (1975). 'The H *Suite* in E♭'. *Inst* 29 (Apr.), 27–33. Detailed description of the work and advice on performance (RP in Fennell 1980).

—— (1977*a*). 'GH's *Hammersmith*'. *Inst* 31 (May), 52–9. Detailed discussion of performance problems (RP in Fennell 1980).

—— (1977*b*). 'GH's second suite in F for military band'. *Inst* 32 (Nov.), 42–52. Detailed discussion of performance problems (RP in Fennell 1980).

—— (1980)*Basic Band Repertory: British band classics from the conductor's point of view*. Instrumentalist, 48pp. Includes reprints of Fennell 1975, 1977*a* and 1977*b*, and a postscript on *Hammersmith*.

FOSS, HUBERT J. (1923). 'GH: will he be permanent in music?' *Cassell's Weekly* 2/28 (26 Sept.), 35–6. Assessment of H's achievement and musical style.

—— (1942). 'H: the bringer of paradox'. *Listener* 28/714 (17 Sept.) 381. An assessment of H's standing at this date, drawing attention to some contradictions in his artistic attitudes.

FOSTER, ARNOLD (1934*a*). 'H and the amateur'. *RCMMag* 30/3, 88–90. Summarizes his attitude to teaching amateurs and his work in evening institutes.

—— (1934*b*). 'GH: an appreciation'. *MMR* 64/758 (July/Aug.), 126. Obituary notice describing H's teaching work and the Whitsun festivals.

Fox-Srangeways, A.H. (1925). 'H's choral symphony'. *Observer* 7012 (18 Oct.), 10. Description of the *First Choral Symphony*, giving the main musical themes.

Gallagher, Charles (1965). 'Thematic derivations in the H First Suite in E flat'. *JBR* 1/2, 6–10. Analysis of the motivic construction of the *Suite No.1* for military band.

Gibbin, L. D. (1950). 'The MTR guide to the music of GH'. *MTRev* 73/909 (July), 492, 494. Classified list of published works.

Gloucestershire Echo (1927). 'GH festival: Cheltenham's famous son'. *GlosEch* (22 Mar.), 6. Report of the H festival at Cheltenham, with biographical notes and summaries of the mayor's and H's speeches (RP in *CheltCh* 1927).

Goddard, Scott (1936). 'An original genius'. *RTimes* 51/654 (10 Apr.), 11. Describes *The Hymn of Jesus* and assesses its importance.

——(1962). 'H's *The Hymn of Jesus*'. *Listener* 67/1719 (8 Mar.), 449. Describes the work and its significance in H's output.

Grace, Harvey ['Feste'] (1921). 'Matters musical'. *BurnEx* 5372 (3 Sept.), 14. Discussion of the *Four Songs* for voice and violin, and problems of setting English poetry.

——(1925a). 'At the Boar's Head: H's new work'. *MTimes* 66/986 (Apr.), 305–10. Describes the plot of the opera, giving examples of the main musical themes.

——(1925b). 'Ad libitum'. *MTimes* 66/988 (June), 507–8. Discusses the extent to which the lack of success of *At the Boar's Head* could be attributed to the production rather than the composer.

——(1925c). 'H's choral symphony'. *MTimes* 66/992 (Oct.), 892–6. Description of each movement and main themes of the *First Choral Symphony*.

——(1925d). 'Ad libitum'. *MTimes* 66/994 (Dec.), 1086–8. Discussion of the relative merits of the Leeds and London performances of the *First Choral Symphony*.

——(1934). 'GH: teacher'. *MTimes* 75/1098 (Aug.), 689–96. An account of H's work at various schools and colleges.

——(1937). 'Music for worship'. *Listener* (9 June), 1165. Discusses H's use of fourths in choral harmonization.

——(1939a). 'H: a third period?' *MTimes* 80/1151 (Jan.), 30–2, 37. Considers the major works of H's later years and the reasons for their lack of success.

——(1939b). 'Ad libitum'. *MTimes* 80/1153 (Mar.), 182. Includes an anecdote about H in the USA, submitted by Duncan McKenzie.

Gray, Cecil (1924). *A Survey of Contemporary Music*. OUP, 261 pp. Includes a brief, strongly critical, paragraph on H.

——(1925). 'Vaughan Williams and H'. *N&Ath* 38/8 (21 Nov.), 290. Compares the *First Choral Symphony* with VW's *Flos Campi*.

GRAY, FRANCES RALPH (1931). *And Gladly Wolde He Lerne and Gladly Teche*. Low, 284 pp. Contains a chapter describing H's work at SPGS.

—— (1934*a*). 'Mr H: musician and friend'. *Times* 46768 (31 May). 19. Reminiscences of H by F. R. Gray and George Bell.

—— (1934*b*). 'GH'. *Paulina* 89 (July), 4. Brief obituary appreciation.

GREEN, L. DUNTON (1918). '*Opera as She is Wrote*'. *MCMag* 27/7 (Apr.), 90–1. A whimsical critique of H's operatic parody.

—— (1920). 'GH'. *Chesterian* NS 8 (June), 225–8. General assessment of H's development to date and his approach to composition.

GREGORY, ROBIN (1950). 'The uncompleted'. *MMR* 80/921 (Nov.), 233–7. Discusses works which were planned by various composers but never completed, using H's projected *Second Choral Symphony* as a starting-point.

GREW, SYDNEY (1914). 'GvH'. *MOpin* 37/437 (Feb.) 359–60. Review of H's work to date, particularly the Sanskrit works.

—— (1922). *Our Favourite Musicians: from Stanford to Holbrooke*. Foulis, 257 pp. Includes an anecdotal chapter on H as a person and composer, with an assessment of his work.

—— (1934). 'Problems concerning H'. *BMusn* 103, 10/7 (July), 155–6, 104, 10/8 (Aug.), 179–80. Considers the disparity between H's roles as 'mystical composer' and 'beloved instructor'.

H., C. (1922). '*The Hymn of Jesus* by Mr GH'. *Spectator* 128/4889 (11 Mar.), 303. Review of a performance at the Royal Albert Hall, London.

HANNAM-CLARK, GEORGE (1949). *GTH: his associations with Cheltenham and the Cotswolds*. Cheltenham Festival of British Contemporary Music, 3 pp. A rather inaccurate leaflet, which includes useful biographical notes on the H family.

HARRIS, JOANNA (1964). 'Some memories of H at St Paul's'. *Making Music* 55 (Summer), 7–8. Anecdotes of performances under H's direction, by one of his pupils (RP in *Composer* 52 (Summer 1974), 17–18).

HART, FRITZ B. (1943). 'Early memories of GH'. *RCMMag* 39/2, 3; 43–52, 84–9. Reminiscences by a fellow student, including information on the composition and performance of some early works.

HASKELL, ARNOLD (1930). *Penelope Spencer, and other studies*. British-Continental (Artists of the Dance 5). Contains a foreword by H, in the form of a brief letter to Penelope Spencer.

HEAD, RAYMOND (1986). 'H and India (I): *Maya* to *Sita*'. *Tempo* 158 (Sept.), 2–7. A re-examination of H's involvement with Sanskrit language and literature.

—— (1987). 'H and India (II)'. *Tempo* 160 (Mar.), 27–37. Further consideration of the Sanskrit works.

HEAD, RAYMOND (1988). 'H and India (III)'. *Tempo* 166 (Sept.), 35–40. Discussion of *Savitri* and *The Cloud Messenger*.

HEWARD, LESLIE (1923). 'GH and a method, or; composition without tears'. *Opera* 1/12 (Dec.), 12–14. Discusses the roots of H's melodic style in bi-chordal harmony, pedal-points and asymmetrical metres.

—— (1927). 'GH'. *Voorslag* (Durban, SA) 1/8 (Jan.), 31–4. An idiosyncratic review of H's career, containing many factual inaccuracies.

HIBBS, LEONARD (1934). 'GH 1874–1934'. *GramRec* (June), 8. Brief note on his work and character, with list of recordings currently available.

HILL, RALPH (1944). 'GH: 1874–1934'. *RTimes* 83/1077 (19 May), 5. Discussion of H's style, as exemplified by *Egdon Heath* and *The Planets*.

HOGARTH, BASIL (1925). 'The great English modernists: 5. GH'. *MMir* 5/8 (Aug.), 149. Review of his life and work.

—— (1931). 'Our modern music makers: 6. GH'. *MPM* 2/1 (Oct.), 26–7. Mainly about his early years as an orchestral musician.

HOLBROOKE, JOSEPH (1925). *Contemporary British Composers*. Palmer, 324 pp. Contains a chapter on H: an idiosyncratic but sympathetic view of his work.

HOLST, GUSTAV (1915). 'A British school of composers'. *MHer* 810 (Sept.), 401. Includes a letter from H, giving his views on British music.

—— (1916). 'The school orchestra'. *MStud* 8/6 (Feb.), 166. Report of a lecture given by H at a conference on musical education.

—— (1918). 'A memory of Parry as a lecturer'. *MStud* 11/3 (Nov.), 86. Very brief reminiscence of Parry at the RCM.

—— (1919*a*). 'Letter from the East: to the Morley students'. *MCMag* 28/6 (Mar.). Describes his experiences organizing music for the troops in Salonica.

—— (1919*b*). 'Music in the British Salonica force'. *MOpin* 43/505 (Oct.), 37. Some anecdotes of his activities as a YMCA organizer.

—— (1920*a*). 'The mystic, the philistine and the artist'. *Quest* 11/3 (Apr.), 366–79. Outlines his views on the function of the artist in society (RP in ImH 1938 and ImH 1969).

—— (1920*b*). 'Society of Women Musicians: reception and composers' conference'. *MStud* 12/12 (Sept.), 715. Report of a paper on the education of composers read by H at a conference in London.

—— (1920*c*). 'The composer of *The Planets*: Mr H and his work'. *Observer* 6757 (21 Nov.), 7. An interview with H and account of his work at MC and SPGS.

—— (1921*a*). 'On appreciation'. *BMBull* 3/2 (Feb.) 30–1. A statement of his views on the relationship between music and the listener.

—— (1921*b*). 'The education of a composer'. *Beacon* 1/1 (Oct.), 30–6. An exposition of his views on the relationship between musical tradition and the twentieth-century composer (RP in *Composer* 52, Summer 1974).

—— (1922*a*). 'Mr H on Purcell: *Diocelsian* performed'. *Times* 43002 (10 Apr.), 12. Report of a performance and lecture given by H at University College, London.

—— (1922*b*). 'The tercentenary of Byrd and Weelkes'. *ProcMA* 49 (1922–3), 29–37. H's lecture to the Association, with ensuing discussion (RP as a pamphlet; see also GH 1923*a* and 1923*b*).

—— (1923*a*. 'Mr H on English music: new factor in technique'. *Times* 43235 (10 Jan.), 8. Brief report of lecture (cf GH 1922*b*).

—— (1923*b*). 'Byrd and Weelkes'. *MTimes* 64/961 (Mar.), 199. Report of H's lecture to the Musical Association (cf GH 1922*b*).

—— (1925*a*). 'The education of a composer'. *MOpin* 48/572 (May), 831–2. Report of the inaugural Alsop lecture, given by H at Liverpool University.

—— (1925*b*). 'The British composer's epitaph'. *LivPM* 21947 (17 Oct.), 4. Report of the first of a series of lectures on 'England and her music' given by H at Liverpool Univ.

—— (1925*c*). 'In the blood: England's choral tradition'. *LivPM* 21953 (24 Oct.), 4. Report of second lecture given by H at Liverpool Univ.

—— (1925*d*). 'Sing we and chant it'. *LivPM* 21958 (31 Oct.). Report of H's third lecture at Liverpool Univ.

—— (1925*e*). 'English mode in music'. *LivPM* 21965 (7 Nov.), 4. Report of H's fourth lecture, on the age of Purcell.

—— (1925*f*). 'Mr H on his early days: playing the trombone in "foreign" bands'. *LivPM* 21971 (14 Nov.), 5. Report of H's fifth lecture at Liverpool Univ.

—— (1925*g*). 'Better dead: Mr H on his pet aversion'. *LivPM* 21977 (21 Nov.), 4. Report of H's sixth lecture at Liverpool Univ., and of another by him on the music of RVW.

—— (1925*h*). 'Mr GH lectures in Bristol on British music: the new Pastoral Symphony'. *BrisTM* 18995 (1 Dec.), 8. Report of a lecture on VW's Symphony, given by H at Bristol Univ.

—— (1925*i*). 'Mr GH lectures in Bristol: comments on VW's Pastoral Symphony'. *WestDP* 135/23044 (1 Dec.), 5. Report of H's lecture at Bristol Univ.

—— (1926*a*). 'My favourite Tudor composer'. *MidMusn* 1/1 (Jan.), 4–5. An appreciation of the work of Thomas Weelkes (RP in GH 1959).

—— (1926*b*). 'The orchestra: Mr GH and its history'. *GlasHd* 144yr/14 (16 Jan.), 11. Report of H's inaugural Cramb lecture at Glasgow Univ.

—— (1926*c*). 'Sunshine in art: Mr GH and Brahms' works'. *GlasHd* 144yr/15 (18 Jan.), 11. Report of H's second Cramb lecture at Glasgow Univ, discussing Brahms' orchestral technique.

—— (1926*d*). 'Air on G string: Mr H and a Bach fallacy'. *GlasHd*

144yr/20 (23 Jan.), 10. Report of H's third Cramb lecture at Glasgow Univ.

—— (1926*e*). 'Beethoven's no. 7: "a world masterpiece" '. *GlasHd* 144yr/21 (25 Jan.), 11. Report of H's fourth Cramb lecture at Glasgow Univ.

—— (1926*f*). 'Mr H's experiment in wood-wind'. *GlasHd* 144yr/26 (30 Jan.). Report of H's fifth Cramb lecture at Glasgow Univ.

—— (1926*g*). 'Wagner's genius: "inevitable scoring" of operas'. *GlasHd* 144yr/27 (1 Feb.), 11. Report of H's sixth lecture at Glasgow Univ.

—— (1926*h*). 'Mozart themes: beauties of the "E flat symphony" '. *GlasHd* 144yr/32 (6 Feb.), 11. Report of H's seventh lecture at Glasgow Univ., discussing the orchestration of Mozart's works.

—— (1926*i*). 'Mood pictures: Mr H's analysis of *The Planets*'. *GlasHd* 144yr/33 (8 Feb.), 13. Report of H's eighth lecture at Glasgow Univ.

—— (1926*j*). 'Music contrasts: a neglected Beethoven symphony'. *GlasHd* 144yr/38 (13 Feb.), 11. Report of H's ninth lecture at Glasgow Univ., discussing Beethoven's Second Symphony and Mendelssohn's *Midsummer Night's Dream* music.

—— (1926*k*). 'America's music: "frightful" British extravagance'. *GlasHd* 144yr/39 (15 Feb.), 13. Report of H's concluding lecture at Glasgow University, examining the current state of British orchestral music.

—— (1927*a*). 'Henry Purcell: the dramatic composer of England (1658–1695)'. In *The Heritage of Music* 1, ed. Hubert J. Foss, 44–50. OUP, 265 pp. A review and assessment of Purcell's work.

—— (1927*b*). 'English music: Mr GH on past triumphs'. *Times* 44738 (14 Nov.), 12. Report of a lecture on 'England and her music' given by H at Morley College.

—— (1928*a*). 'On inspiration', ed. L. Dunton Green. *Chesterian* 9/68 (Jan./Feb.), 114. Includes a letter from H in reply to a questionnaire, and facsimile scores of three of the *Four Songs* for voice and violin.

—— (1928*b*). 'The ocean of story': review of C. H. Tawney's translation of Bhatta Somadeva's *Katha Sarit Sagara*. Book review from an unidentified newspaper (press-cutting, HBM).

—— (1929). 'Jane Joseph'. *MCMag* 34/9 (June), 104–5. An appreciation of 'the best girl pupil I ever had' (see also GH 1931).

—— (1931). 'The younger English composers: 18. Jane M. Joseph, 1894–1929'. *MMR* 61/724 (Apr.), 97–8. An expanded version of GH 1929, with a list of her works.

—— (1959) *Heirs and Rebels: letters written to each other and occasional writings on music* by GH and RVW, ed. UVW and ImH. OUP, 111pp. (RP Cooper Square, NY, 1974). Also includes H's lectures on 'Haydn' and 'The teaching of art' (RP in ImH 1968) and his notes for lectures on 'England and her music', 'My favourite Tudor composer' (RP from GH 1926a), 'Samuel Wesley' and 'Musical education'. Four letters RP in ImH 1969.

—— (1965). *The Musician's World: great composers in their letters*, ed. Hans Gal. Thames and Hudson, 464pp. Contains shortened versions of several of H's letters.

—— (1974) *Letters to W. G. Whittaker*, ed. MS. Glasgow UP, 138 pp. A collection of letters 1913–34 in Glasgow Univ. Library.

HOLST, IMOGEN (1938). *GH: a biography*. OUP, 200 pp. A detailed study of H's life, with a note by RVW, a reprint of GH 1920a, and classified list of works (see also ImH 1969).

—— (1948). 'H's later orchestral works'. *Listener* 40/1017 (22 July), 141. Discussion of his style in the *Double Concerto* and other works.

—— (1951a)*The Music of GH*. OUP, 164pp. A comprehensive study of H's music, with a chronological list of works (see also ImH 1968 and 1986).

—— (1951b). 'H: the man and musician'. *RTimes* 110/1424 (23 Feb.), 13. Describes some works to be broadcast and his interest in Sanskrit and astrology.

—— (1952). 'H, the bringer of music'. *MCMag* 33/1, 9–11. An account of his work at Morley College.

—— (1963a). 'GH'. *Canon* (Sydney, Australia) 16/7 (Feb.) 13–15. An account of his work, mentioning his main compositions.

—— (1963b). 'A new look at H'. *MTimes* 104/1442 (Apr.) 262–3. Letters from ImH, Madeleine Smith, and Peter Jackson, commenting on Warrack 1963.

—— (1965). 'Unfamiliar H'. *Listener* 74/1905 (30 Sept.) 509. Describes some of his rarely-performed part-songs.

—— (1967). 'GH's manuscripts'. *Brio* 4/2 (Autumn), 2–4. Discussion of problems in H research (RP in *Composer* 27, Spring 1968, 11–14).

—— (1968). *The Music of GH* (2nd edn.). OUP, 169 pp. Revised RP of ImH 1951a, together with H's lecture on 'The teaching of art' RP from GH 1959 (see also ImH 1986).

—— (1969). *GH: a biography* (2nd edn.). OUP, 210 pp. RP of ImH 1938, with four letters from H to RVW RP from GH 1959.

—— (1972). *H*. Novello, 22 pp. (Short Biographies series). A condensed biography, with brief list of works.

—— (1973). *H*. Novello, 4 pp. List of works published by Novello, with an introduction.

—— (1974a). 'GH's debt to Cecil Sharp'. *FMJ*, 400–3. Discusses the influence of English folk-song on H's style.

—— (1974b). *GH, 1874–1934: centenary list of published works*. G&IH, 7 pp. List of works in print or available on hire.

HOLST, IMOGEN (1974c). *GH, 1874–1934: a guide to his centenary.* Cambridge Music Shop/G&IH, 22 pp. Details of performances, exhibitions, recordings, and publications, with extracts from several of his letters.

—— (1974d). 'GH and Thaxted'. RP from *Thaxted Bulletin*, 2 pp. Reminiscences of H's activities there, with a facsimile of *I Sing of a Maiden*.

—— (1974e). *H.* Faber, 96 pp. (Great Composers series). A biography for young people (2nd edn. 1981).

—— (1974f). *A Thematic Catalogue of GH's Music.* Faber, 285 pp. A comprehensive listing, with incipits of all works for which material exists.

—— (1974g). 'H and the RCM'. *RCMMag* 52/2 (Summer), 49–51. H's connections with the College.

—— (1974h). 'ImH talks to Alan Blyth'. *Gramophone* 52/616 (Sept.), 479–80. Discussion of H recordings, particularly his own performances.

—— (1974i). 'H's music: some questions of style and performance at the centenary of his birth'. *ProcRMA* 100 (1973–4), 201–7. Text of a lecture given on 9 Nov., discussing phrasing and rhythm in various works.

—— (1974j). *GH: centenary exhibition.* Cheltenham Art Gallery and Museum, 6 pp. List of exhibits, with an introduction.

—— (1975). 'Recordings of H's music'. *RSound* 59 (July) 440. An account of 50 years of H recordings.

—— (1978). *A Scrap-Book for the Holst Birthplace Museum.* Radford/G&IH, 48 pp. A pictorial account of H's career.

—— (1980a). 'The composer and the planets: ImH talks to Christopher Headington. *R&R* (Jan.). Discussion of the composition of *The Planets*.

—— (1980b). 'H'. In *The New Grove Dictionary of Music and Musicians* 8, 659–66. Macmillan. Survey of his career, with classified list of works.

—— (1982). 'H's *At the Boar's Head*'. *MTimes* 123/1671 (May), 321–2. Description of the work.

—— (1984). 'H in the 1980s'. *MTimes* 125/1695 (May), 266–9. A reassessment of the value of H's music.

—— (1986). *The Music of GH* (3rd rev. edn.) and *H's Music Reconsidered.* OUP, 178 pp. Shortened RP of ImH 1968, with comments on aspects of H's music.

HOLST, MATTHIAS R. VON (1951). Letter to the editor. *M&L* 32/3 (July), 302. Recollections of H's religious ideas and the causes of his giving up the piano.

HOWES, FRANK (1948). '*The Planets*'. *Hallé* 8 (Jan.), 7–10. Examines the work's position in H's output, giving examples of some of the main themes.

—— (1964). 'Choral ode'. *M&M* 12/5 (Jan.), 22. Discusses H's setting of Keats's verse in the *First Choral Symphony*.

HUGHES, ERIC (1975). 'The music of GH: a discography'. *RSound* 59 (July), 441–6. A listing of all known commercial recordings, plus BBC tapes and transcription recordings held in the BIRS.

HULL, ROBERT H. (1930). 'GH'. *EngRev* 50 (Mar.), 369–74. Assessment of his work to date.

—— (1931). 'Fixing the status of GH: a career of hard work'. *BirmDM* 20323 (1 Apr.), 5. Assessment of his life and work.

—— (1935). 'Notable music of the week: H's last Scherzo'. *RTimes* 46/592 (1 Feb.), 12. Compares the work with movements of *The Planets*.

HULL, ROBIN (1959). 'Three British composers: Elgar, Delius and H'. *MTimes* 100/1397 (July), 380–2. Brief assessment of H's standing, on the 25th anniversary of his death.

HURD, MICHAEL (1974). 'H's operas'. *MinEd* 38/368 (July/Aug.), 168–70. Suitability of the published operas for performance by amateurs.

HUSSEY, DYNELEY (1928). 'English musicians: 8. GTH'. *Landmark* 10/2 (Feb.), 119–22. Review of his life and work to date.

HUTCHINGS, ARTHUR (1959). 'The meditative English mind'. *Listener* 61/1569 (23 Apr.), 736. Compares H's musical style with those of Elgar and Delius.

HYDE, DEREK E. (1970). 'H's songs for female voices'. *MinEd* 34/345 (Sept./Oct.), 259–60; 35/347 (Jan./Feb. 1971), 370–3. Examines H's technique in the medium and lists songs suitable for school use.

—— (1974). 'H's *Seven Part-Songs*, Op. 44'. *MinEd* 38/368 (July/Aug.), 166–7. Description and assessment of the work.

JACKSON, PETER (1959). 'Do we pay only lip service to H?' *M&M* 7/9 (May), 17. Assessment of H's standing 25 years after his death.

JACOB, GORDON (1934). 'H the composer'. *RCMMag* 30/3 (Dec.), 81–3. Surveys the main works of his career (RP in *RCMMag* 80/2, Summer 1984).

JEAN-AUBRY, G. (1924). *GH*. Chester, 12 pp. (Miniature Essays series). Brief account of his career to date (parallel English and French texts).

JOSEPH, JANE M. (1923). 'Introductions: 4. GH'. *MBull* 5/4 (Apr.), 112–15. H's work as teacher and conductor, by one of his pupils (RP in Joseph 1924).

—— (1924). *Compositions of GH, with a short biographical sketch*. Gray (NY), 10 pp. RP of Joseph 1923, with classified list of works.

KALISCH, ALFRED (1923). '*The Perfect Fool*'. *EngRev* 36 (June), 593–6. Assessment of the work, following its first performance.

KENNEDY, MICHAEL (1959). 'Elgar, Delius and H'. *Hallé* 113 (Apr.), 8–12. Short account of H's life and work, on the 25th anniversary of his death.

—— (1982). 'The English musical renaissance 1880–1920'. *Gramophone* 60/711 (Aug.), 211–12, 217–18, 221–2. Useful background information.

—— (1984). *Elgar, Delius and H*. Finzi Trust, 8 pp. Compares the careers of the three composers.

KIDSON, ERICA (1954). 'GH'. *Canon* (Sydney, Australia) 8/4 (Nov.), 185–7. Assessment of his musical style and methods of expressing his ideas.

LIMBERT, K. E. (1946). 'Delius, 1862–1934; H, 1874–1934'. *Parent's Rev.* (May), 113–17. General review of H's work, with regard to its suitability for performance by children.

LUMBY, SHEILA (and HOUNSFIELD, VERA) (1974). *Catalogue of H's Concert Programme and Press Cuttings in the Central Library, Cheltenham*. G&IH, 141 pp. A valuable guide for H scholars.

LYLE, WATSON (1927). 'GH and his music: a personal study of the composer of *The Planets*'. *Windsor Mag* 65 (Jan.), 125–30. A sympathetic review of his life and work.

MAINE, BASIL (1934). 'GH and his music'. *Listener* 11/284 (20 June), 1046. Discusses the phases of H's development as a composer (RP in Maine 1945).

—— (1937). 'Four English composers'. *Choir* 17 (May), 70. Includes a general review of H's life and work.

—— (1945). *Basil Maine on Music*. Westhouse, 129 pp. Contains RP of Maine 1934.

MANNING, ROSEMARY (1949). *From H to Britten: a study of modern choral music*. Workers' Music Assoc., 80 pp. Includes a section on H, giving a Marxist view of his work as a choral composer.

MARK, JEFFERY (1925). 'VW and H'. *ModMus* 2/1 (Jan.), 24–6. Compares the artistic attitudes of the two composers.

MARTIN, T. L. (1931). 'H's *Choral Fantasia*'. *MMR* 61/729 (Sept.), 265. Brief description of the work.

MASON, ERIC (1962). 'H and Honneger'. *Choir* 53/2 (Feb.), 29. Brief review of a performance of *The Hymn of Jesus*.

MATTHEWS, COLIN (1984). 'Some unknown H'. *MTimes* 125/1695 (May), 269–72. Notes on rarely-performed and unpublished works.

MELLERS, WILFRID H. (1941). 'H and the English language'. *MRev* 2 (Aug.), 228–34. Examines H's techniques of word-setting and the influence of the English language on his musical style (RP in Mellers 1947).

—— (1944). 'Two generations of English music'. *Scrutiny* 12/4 (Autumn), 261–70. Outlines H's contribution to the 'English musical renaissance'.

—— (1947). *Studies in Contemporary Music.* Dobson, 216 pp. Includes RP of Mellers 1941.

—— (1952). 'Recent trends in British music'. *MQuart* 38/2 (Apr.) 185–201. Includes a short section on H and his use of principles derived from earlier English music.

MENDL, R. W. S. (1925). 'The recognition of genius'. *MTchr* 4/12 (Dec.), 741–3. Discusses the problem of assessing the real value of contemporary composers, taking H as an example.

—— (1936). 'Three English masters: 4. GH'. *MOpin* 59/700 (Jan.) 308–9. Brief description of H's main works and the essence of his style.

MITCHELL, JON C. (1983). 'GH: the band works in retrospect'. *JBASBWE* 2 (Spring), 10–18. Reviews H's works for band and smaller wind ensembles.

—— (1984). 'The premieres of *Hammersmith*'. *CBDNAJnl* 1/1 (Spring), 18–25. Circumstances surrounding the first performance of the work.

—— (1985*a*). *From Kneller Hall to Hammersmith: the band works of GH.* Ars Ventorum (Hanover, Indiana), 231 pp. A very detailed chronological discussion of H's works in the wind band medium (based on University of Illinois doctoral thesis 1980).

—— (1985*b*). 'Thematic "borrowings" in the H band works'. *JBASBWE* 4/1 (Spring), 28–9. Investigates the origins of thematic material in these works.

—— (1986). 'GH: the *Hammersmith* sketches'. *CBDNAJnl* 2/2 (Winter), 8–17. Detailed consideration of the compositional process.

MONTHLY MUSICAL RECORD (1928). 'In the concert room: H's *Egdon Heath*'. *MMR* 58/688 (Apr.), 109. Review of a performance at QH.

—— (1930*a*). 'GH's new songs'. *MMR* 60/711 (Mar.), 68. Review of the first English performance of the *Twelve Songs*.

—— (1930*b*). 'In the concert room'. *MMR* 60/713 (May), 140. Brief review of the first performance of the *Double Concerto*.

—— (1932). 'Opera at the Royal College'. *MMR* 62/733 (Jan.), 13. Very brief review of a performance of *Savitri*.

—— (1934*a*). 'Notes of the day' [editorial]. *MMR* 64/757 (June), 101. Brief obituary notice.

—— (1934*b*) 'Allotria' [editorial]. *MMR* 64/759 (Sept), 162. Includes very brief paragraph recording the foundation of a H memorial scholarship at Ottershaw College, near Woking.

MOORE, JERROLD NORTHROP (ed.) (1979). *Music and Friends: seven decades of letters to Adrian Boult.* Hamilton, 207 pp. Includes several letters from H to Boult.

MORLEY COLLEGE MAGAZINE (1916). 'The Whitsun festival at Thaxted'. *MCMag* 26/1 (Sept./Oct.), 9–11. An account of the festival.

MORLEY COLLEGE MAGAZINE (1918). 'English opera as she is wrote'. *MCMag* 27/6 (Mar.), 77–9. A preview of the forthcoming performance of *Opera as She is Wrote*.

MORRIS, REGINALD O. (1920). 'The Planets'. *Athenaeum* 4727 (3 Dec.), 768–9. Non-technical description of the character of each movement.

MUSIC STUDENT (1914). 'GvH'. *MStud* 3/NS72 (16 May), 461–2. Assessment of H and his work to date.

MUSICAL NEWS & HERALD (1926). 'Musical genealogies: 3. GH—Klingenberg'. *MN&H* 71/1800 (9 Oct.), 304. Short article tracing a pupil–master connection from H back to Gottlieb Klingenberg ('a rather obscure German musician of the 17th century').

MUSICAL STANDARD (1919). 'British music in Salonica'. *MStnd* 13/NS304 (10 May), 157. Report of concerts and lectures for the troops, given by H and other musicians (RP in *MTimes* June 1919, 311–12).

MUSICAL TIMES (1922). 'A new choral work by H'. *MTimes* 63/956 (Oct.), 689–90. Some of H's characteristic technical procedures, exemplified by the *Ode to Death*.

—— (1925). 'First "Choral" symphony by GH'. *MTimes* 66/993 (Nov.), 1007–8. Review of the first performance.

NEVE, WILLIAM (1974). 'H never mastered maths'. *Cotswold Life* (Aug.), 28. H's schoolboy years at Cheltenham Grammar School.

NEWMAN, ERNEST (1925a). 'At the Boar's Head'. *MTimes* 66/987 (May), 413–14. Discusses H's success in combining Shakespeare's words with folk-tunes.

—— (1925b). 'H's choral symphony'. *STimes* 5348 (11 Oct.), 9; 5349 (18 Oct.), 7. Description of the *First Choral Symphony*, discussing H's techniques of word-setting (RP in Newman 1956).

—— (1934). 'Words and music: some problems of the future'. *STimes* 5793 (22 Apr.), 7. H's techniques of word-setting, exemplified by the *First Choral Symphony* (RP in Newman 1958).

—— (1956) *From the World of Music*. Calder, 190 pp. Contains RP of Newman 1925).

—— (1958). *More Essays From the World of Music*. Calder. Includes RP of Newman 1934.

NEWMARCH, ROSA (1938). *The Concert-Goer's Library of Descriptive Notes* 5. OUP. Includes analytical notes on *The Planets* and *St Paul's Suite*.

NEWSON, ARTHUR (1921). 'A musical experiment: H's mediaeval songs for voice and violin'. *Musician* 18 (Feb.), 120. Description of the *Four Songs*.

NICHOLLS, HELLER (1927). 'H festival at Cheltenham'. *RevRev* 74/447 (Apr./May), 364, 366. Account of the festival, including a summary of H's speech.

NUTTING, DULCIE (1976). 'Dulcie Nutting talks to Roger Lucas about GH'. *More* (MC Mag) 3 (Summer), 4–7. Reminiscences by one of H's associates.

OTTAWAY, D. HUGH (1952). 'A lesson in style: ImH on the music of her father'. *MOpin* 893 (Feb.), 273, 275. A review of ImH 1951.

—— (1974). 'H as an opera composer'. *MTimes* 115/1576 (June), 473–4. The theatrical effectiveness of H's main operas.

PARKER, D. C. (1922). 'GH: a musical stalwart of Young England'. *MAmer* 36/13 (July), 5–6. Review of his life and work, with assessment of his character and musical attitudes.

PARROTT, IAN (1967). 'H's *Savitri* and bitonality'. *MRev* 28/4 (Nov.), 323–8. H's instrumental, rhythmic, and melodic techniques, and tonality in this work.

PATTERSON, ANNIE (1925). 'Great minds in music: GH'. *Great Thoughts* 9/9s/2170 (July), 146–8. Review of his life and work.

PAYNE, ANTHONY (1967). 'Inconsequential *Hammersmith*'. *M&M* 16/4 (Dec.), 47. Very brief review of a performance of the orchestral version.

PEARSON, DOROTHY K. (1971). 'GH: one of Gloucestershire's illustrious sons'. *Cotswold Life* 3/8 (May), 16–21, 33. Account of his life and work.

PIRIE, PETER J. (1957). 'In defence of GH'. *MOpin* 960 (Sept.), 723, 725. Argues against the neglect of H's work.

PORTE, JOHN F. (1923). 'GH'. *MCour* 87/15 (11 Oct.), 42–3. Review of his life and work.

PROBERT-JONES, W. (1935). 'GH'. *Tamesis* 33/2 (Lent), 57–60. Brief biography, with description of his main works and an account of his teaching at University College, Reading.

PRUNIERES, HENRY (1930). '*Egdon Heath* de GH, à l'O.S.P.'. *RevMus* 100 (Jan.), 66–7. Review of the first French performance (in French).

PUTTERILL, JACK (1974). 'GH'. *Making Music* 86/2 (Autumn), 12. Personal reminiscences by one of H's pupils and associates.

RACE, STEVE (1955). 'Jazz at the Museum'. *Melody Maker* (5 Feb.), 2. Assessment of the *Capriccio* from a jazz musician's point of view.

RAWLINSON, HAROLD (1946). 'Some famous works for string orchestra: 3. *St Paul's Suite*, Op. 29/2 by GH'. *Strad* 57/674 (June), 41–2. Some anecdotes of H, with practical points on performance of the work.

RAYNOR, HENRY (1954). 'The case of H: an interim report'. *MMR* 84/954 (Feb.), 31–4; 955 (Mar./Apr.), 70–3. Discusses H as the creator of an original technique in search of a content to which he could give expression.

REED, E. M. G. (1922). 'Music at St Paul's Girls' School'. *MTchr* 14/6 (Mar.) 318–20. Describes H's musical activities at the school.

REULING KARL F. (1970). 'Heirs and rebels: the spirit of two English composers lives on in their womenfolk'. *Opera News* (NY) (24 Jan.), 12–15. Discusses the operatic works of H and VW.

REYNISH, TIMOTHY (1984). 'A new wind work from H'. *MTimes* 125/1697 (July), 375–7. Discusses H's works for wind ensemble and military band, including the *Three Folk Tunes*.

REYNOLDS, GORDON (1974). 'Service and freedom'. *MinEd* 38/368 (July/Aug.), 161–2. H's work as a teacher.

RICHARDS, DENIS (1958). *Offspring of the Vic: a history of Morley College*. Routledge, 316 pp. Includes references to H's work at the College from 1907 to 1924.

ROTHENSTEIN, WILLIAM (1923). *Twenty-Four Portraits*, 2nd series. Chatto & Windus. Includes a reproduction of a pencil drawing of H and brief assessment of his musical character.

RUBBRA, EDMUND (1930). 'GH as teacher'. *MMR* 60/715 (July), 199–200. Some anecdotes of H's methods, by one of his most distinguished pupils.

—— (1932a). 'H: some technical characteristics'. *MMR* 62/740 (Oct.), 170–3. H's rhythmic, melodic and harmonic procedures, with examples mainly from vocal and choral works (RP in Rubbra 1974 a; see also 1947a).

—— (1932b). 'A H concert'. *MMR* 62/742 (Dec.), 230. Brief review of a concert given in H's honour by the Music Teachers' Association.

—— (1934a). 'GH (1874–1934)'. *Chesterian* 15/116 (July/Aug.), 153–7. Obituary notice assessing his achievement (RP in Rubbra 1974 a).

—— (1934b). 'H the teacher'. *RCMMag* 30/3, 83–6. Recollections of his work at the RCM, by one of his pupils (RP in Rubbra 1974 a).

—— (1935). 'The early manuscripts of GH'. *MMR* 65/768 (July/Aug.), 123–4. Examines the origins of H's mature style, to be found in his earlier, lesser-known works (RP in Rubbra 1974 a; see also 1947a).

—— (1938). 'A life of H'. *MMR* 68/801 (Nov.), 267–9. A review of ImH 1938.

—— (1947a). *GH*. Lyrebird (Monaco), 49 pp. Detailed study of H's work, with classified list of works and recordings available at the time of writing (incorporates material previously published in Rubbra 1932a and 1935).

—— (1947b). 'H and his Choral Symphony'. *Listener* 37/954 (8 May), 738. Discusses H's position in the development of English music, with a brief description of the work (RP in Rubbra 1974 a).

—— (1948). 'H's last opera'. *Listener* 40/1040 (30 Dec,), 1025. Discusses H's technique in *The Wandering Scholar* (RP in Rubbra 1974 a).

—— (1949). 'GH'. *Cresendo* 19 (Feb.), 15–17. An account of H's attitudes to the teaching of composition, by one of his pupils (RP in Rubbra 1974a).

—— (1974a). *GH: collected essays*. Triad, 54 pp. RP of Rubbra 1932a, 1934a, 1934b, 1935, 1947b, 1948, and 1949, with 'The Greatness of GH' RP from an unspecified issue of *The Listener*.

—— (1974*b*). 'Last week's broadcast music'. *Listener* 91/2345 (7 Mar.), 313. Brief description of *The Hymn of Jesus*.

—— (1974*c*). 'The musical vision of GH'. *Listener* 92/2373 (19 Sept.), 376–7. Centenary assessment of H's achievement.

—— (1974*d*). 'The Englishness of H'. *STel* 708 (22 Sept.), 17. H's character and methods of teaching composition.

S., A. J. (1925). 'H and Keats'. *BirmP* 21013 (19 Oct.), 6; 21019 (26 Oct.), 6. Discusses problems of choral composition, with particular reference to the *First Choral Symphony*.

SALAZAR, ADOLFO (1929). 'Dos ingleses: VW y GvH'. In *Sinfonía y ballet* (Editorial Mundo Latino, Madrid), 158 (in Spanish).

SANDERS, ALAN (1976). 'GH records *The Planets*'. *Gramophone* 54/640 (Sept.), 404. Discusses H's own recordings of the work.

SCHOLES, PERCY A. (1920). 'Music of the week: *The Planets*'. *Observer* 6757 (21 Nov.), 10. Review of the first complete public performance, briefly describing the work.

—— (1921). 'Personally speaking'. *MStud* 13/5 (Feb.), 297. Includes some remarks by H on composition.

SCOTT, MARION M. (1944). 'H: Cotswold man and mystic'. *Listener* 31/801 (18 May), 561. Describes some works to be broadcast on the tenth anniversary of his death.

SELDENSLAGH, C. (1923). 'GH'. *Belgique Musicale* (Apr.), 152–4. Assessment of his work to date (in French).

SERVIN, MAX (1963). 'Reflections on GH's *The Hymn of Jesus*'. *American Record Guide* 29 (Mar.), 512–14. Detailed information on the origin of the text.

'SFORZANDO' (1925). 'The first performance of H's new opera'. *MMR* 55/653 (May), 131. Very brief critical review of *At the Boar's Head*.

SHARP, G. B. (1974). 'GH'. *Church Music* 3: 27 (June), 14–17. Technical aspects of H's work and discussion of influences.

SHELDON, A. J. (1923). 'GH's *The Planets*'. *MOpin* 46/546 (Mar.), 551–3. Description of the work, with main themes of each movement.

SHORE, BERNARD (1949). *Sixteen Symphonies*. Longmans, 387 pp. Includes a biographical chapter on H, with an assessment of his work and an analysis of *The Planets*.

SHORT, MICHAEL (1974*a*). *GH: a centenary documentation*. White Lion, 285 pp. Complete catalogue of works, with discography and classified lists.

—— (1974*b*). *GH: centenary exhibition*. Royal Festival Hall/IAML, 19 pp. Annotated catalogue of exhibits, with biographical note.

—— (1974*c*). 'GH: what we can learn from him'. *Composer* 52 (Summer), 13–16. Relevance of H's work to present-day composition.

SHORT, MICHAEL (1980). 'The making of *The Planets'. BMSJ* 2, 22–7. Factors influencing the composition of the work.

—— (1982). 'H, un apasionado de la filosofia hindu'. In *Los Grandes Compositores* (Salvat, Barcelona) 5/86. Review of his life and work (in Spanish).

SLONIMSKY, NICHOLAS (1949). *Music Since 1900* (3rd edn.). Coleman-Ross (NY), 759 pp. Chronological list of important musical events, including several notable performances of works by H.

SORABJI, KAIKHOSRU (1934). 'Music'. *New English Weekly* 5/9 (14 June), 208–9. A brief, severely critical obituary notice.

SOUPER, F. O. (1933). 'Famous amateur orchestras: the Morley College orchestra'. *Strad* 44/522 (Oct,). 219–20, 222. Describes H's work with the orchestra and some notable performances.

SPEARING, ROBERT (1974). 'H the mystic'. *RCMMag* 52/2 (Summer), 58–9. H's interest in Sanskrit literature, religion and astrology.

STRODE, NANCY (1974). 'Across the years: a personal recollection of GH'. *Conductors' Guild Bulletin* (Summer). Reminiscences by one of his pupils at SPGS (RP in *Paulina*, 1975).

STUART, CHARLES (1951). 'Morley College music'. *MTimes* 92/1303 (Sept.), 393–8. Includes some details of H's work at the College.

SWANN, IRENE (1974). 'Dear Gussie'. *Paulina* 153 (1973–4), 13. Reminiscences of H's classes at SPGS, by one of his pupils.

TAYLOR, STAINTON (1934). 'GH (1874–1934)'. *Choir* 25/297. 195–6. Obituary notice assessing H's achievement and place in English music.

THOMPSON, KENNETH (1973). *A Dictionary of 20th-Century Composers.* Faber, 666 pp. Includes a detailed entry on H.

THOMPSON, OSCAR (ed.) (1939). *The International Cyclopedia of Music and Musicians.* Dodd, Mead (NY), 2287 pp. (RP 1975). Includes brief entry on H, with a classified list of works.

TIMES (1925a). 'Symphonies and poets: the new eclecticism'. *Times* 44083 (3 Oct.), 8. Assessment of the *First Choral Symphony* prior to its first performance.

—— (1925b) 'Two choral composers: H and VW'. *Times* 44095 (17 Oct.), 10. Compares the *First Choral Symphony* with VW's *Flos Campi*.

—— (1934). 'Mr GH: composer and teacher'. *Times* 46764 (26 May), 7. Obituary notice describing his life and work.

—— (1951). 'A hermit of music: H's artistic faith'. *Times* 51915 (2 Feb.), 3. A review of ImH 1951a.

—— (1952a). 'H manuscript discovered: unpublished wind quintet'. *Times* 52485 (3 Dec.), 8. Brief report of the discovery of the manuscript of the 1903 Quintet.

—— (1952b). 'H's unpublished music: discarded and revised compositions'. *Times* 52490 (9 Dec.), 11. Brief report of the volumes available to readers at the British Museum Library.

TIPPETT, MICHAEL (1958). 'H: figure of our time'. *Listener* 60/1546 (13 Nov.), 800. Discusses H's character and musical development.

TOVEY, DONALD F. (1923). '*The Perfect Fool*, or the perfect opera'. *N&Ath* 33/8 (26 May), 282, 284. Discusses the theatrical effectiveness of the work (RP in *MTimes* 64/965 (July 1923), 464–5).

—— (1935). *Essays in Musical Analysis: 2. Symphonies (2), variations and orchestral polyphony.* OUP, 212 pp. A collection of Tovey's programme notes, including short analyses of *A Fugal Concerto* and *A Fugal Overture.*

—— (1936). *Essays in Musical Analysis: 4. Illustative music.* OUP, 176 pp. Contains Tovey's brief programme note on *The Perfect Fool* ballet music.

—— (1937). *Essays in Musical Analysis: 5. Vocal music.* OUP, 256 pp. Includes Tovey's programme note analysing *The Hymn of Jesus.*

TOYE, FRANCIS (1931). 'Studies in English music: 7, Arnold Bax and GH'. *Listener* 6/133 (29 July), 184. Includes a brief section on H, suggesting that his invention had declined in recent years.

TREND, J. B. (1921). '*Savitri*: an opera from the Sanskrit'. *M&L* 2/4 (Oct.), 345–50. Description of the work, with information on the work of Richard John Samuel Stevens, the first English composer to write theatrical music on Indian themes.

TREND, MICHAEL (1985). *The Music Makers: heirs and rebels of the English musical renaissance: Edward Elgar to Benjamin Britten.* Weidenfeld & Nicolson, 269 pp. Contains a short section on Holst's life and work.

TURNER, WALTER J. (1923). '*The Perfect Fool*'. *New Statesman* 21/527 (19 May), 170. Assessment of the work, based on the first performance.

—— (1924). *Variations on the Theme of Music.* Heinemann, 316 pp. Contains a chapter on *The Perfect Fool*, describing its plot in a disparaging manner.

—— (1928). *Musical Meanderings.* Methuen, 206 pp. Contains a chapter on the *First Choral Symphony*. criticizing H's setting of the words.

UPTON, GEORGE P. (1930). *The Standard Concert Guide* (rev. edn.), by George P. Upton and Felix Borowski. McClurg (Chicago), 551 pp. Includes brief descriptive notes on *The Planets* and *Beni Mora* (RP in Upton 1947).

—— (1947). *The Standard Concert Guide* (new rev. edn.), by George P. Upton and Felix Borowski. Halsyon (NY), 486 pp. RP of Upton 1930, with a brief note on the *St Paul's Suite.*

VAUGHAN WILLIAMS, RALPH (1920). 'GH'. *M&L* 1/3 (July), 181–90, 1/4 (Oct.), 305–17. An appreciation of H the man and his music (RP in RVW 1953 and 1963).

—— (1934*a*). 'GH'. *MCMag* 20/2 (Nov.), 26–7. Reminiscences of H and his work at MC (see also RVW 1934*b*).

—— (1934*b*). 'GH: man and musician'. *RCMMag* 30/3, 78–80. Reminiscences by his closest musical associate (mainly taken from RVW 1934*a*; RP in RVW 1953).

—— (1935*a*). Letter to the Editor. *MMR* 65/766 (May), 90. Requests support for a memorial fund set up to establish a GH music room at Morley College.

—— (1935*b*). 'GH: dramatist!'. *College Pie* (*MCMag*) (Nov), 36. Recollections of two plays by H, in one of which he himself appeared.

—— (1937). 'The H music room'. *MCMag* 22/6 (Mar.), 12–13. Describes the music room at Morley College, providing a practical memorial to H.

—— (1938). [H]. In *The Orchestra Speaks* by Bernard Shore. Longmans, 218 pp. A short talk given as an introduction to a 1934 memorial broadcast.

—— (1949). 'H'. In *Dictionary of National Biography 1931–1940* ed. L. G. Wickham Legg. OUP, 968 pp. An account of his life and work.

—— (1953). *Some thoughts on Beethoven's Choral Symphony, with writings on other musical subjects.* OUP, 172 pp. Includes 'A Musical Autobiography' and RPs of RVW 1920 and 1934*b* (under title 'GH: an essay and a note').

—— (1954). 'GH: a great composer'. *Listener* 51/1318 (3 June), 965–6. A consideration of H's musical style and artistic stature (transcript of a talk broadcast in the BBC radio programme 'Music Magazine').

—— (1963). *National Music and other essays* (new edn.). OUP, 246 pp. Includes RP of RVW 1920.

VOCALIST (1902). [Editorial.] *Vocalist* 9 (Dec.), 258. A 'plug' for *Lied ohne Wörte* (H51), published in the same issue.

VOWLES, WILLIAM (1934). 'GH with the army: Salonica and Constantinople 1919'. *MTimes* 75/1099 (Sept.), 794–5. Anecdotes of H in the Near East, by one of his associates there.

W-Y, W. (1918). 'The Old Vic'. *MStnd* (26 Jan.). Report of a lecture by W. G. Whittaker on H's career and main works (summary RP in *MCMag* 27/5 (Feb.), 66–7).

WALKER, ERNEST (1930). 'H's harmonic methods'. *MMR* 60/716 (Aug.), 232–3. H's techniques as exemplified by the *Twelve Songs* (H174).

WALSH, STEPHEN (1967). 'Music last week'. *Listener* 77/1990 (18 May), 665. An assessment of *The Perfect Fool*.

WARBURTON, ANNIE O. 'Set works for O level, GCE. H: Mars and

Venus from *The Planets'. MTchr* 49/11 (Nov.), 13–14, 18. Technical descriptions of these two movements.

WARRACK, JOHN (1963). 'A new look at GH'. *MTimes* 104/1440 (Feb.), 100-3. H's compositional technique: his successes and failures.

—— (1974*a*). 'GH'. In *27th Aldeburgh Festival of Music and the Arts* (programme book), 5–6. Characteristic features of H's style.

—— (1974*b*). 'H and the linear principle'. *MTimes* 115/1579 (Sept.), 732–5. H's contrapuntal and harmonic techniques.

—— (1974*c*). 'Pioneer of the Planets'. *Observer Mag.* (22 Sept.) 57, 59, 61. Review of his life and work, and his current standing.

WESTERN, JOAN D. L. (1935). 'H music room'. *College Pie (MCMag)* (Nov.), 34. Outlines plans for the H memorial room at the College.

WHITE, R. T. (1924). 'The Perfect Fool'. *MTchr* 3/7 (July), 410, 412. Describes the plot of the opera, giving examples of some of the main themes.

WHITTAKER, WILLIAM G. (1914). 'The Cloud Messenger'. *Northerner*, 79–81. Origins and antecedents of the work and review of H's music.

—— (1917). 'Choral Society music'. *Northerner* 17/2 (Mar.), 34–6. Includes descriptions of the 2nd Group of *Choral Hymns from the Rig Veda, Ave Maria, Pastoral*, and *Tears, Idle Tears*.

—— (1918). 'Mr GvH'. *MHer* 844 (July), 199–202. Brief biographical details, with survey of work to date.

WHITTALL, ARNOLD (1974). 'Wagner, Schoenberg, H: a centenary essay'. *Soundings* 4, 87–99. Compares Schoenberg's and H's approach to composing music 'in the wake' of Wagner, with an analysis of *Egdon Heath*.

WILKINSON, FREDERICK (1974). 'GH as a friend'. *RCMMag* 52/2 (Summer), 54–7. Reminiscences of productions of H's works.

WILLIAMS, ALEXANDER W. (1934). 'GH and the critics: individuality of his work'. (Press-cutting from unidentified US journal; HBM). Discusses H's stature and individuality as a composer.

WILTSHIRE & GLOUCESTER STANDARD (1930). 'Cirencester hymn festival, conducted by Mr GH'. *WiltsGS* 94/4840 (26 July), 2. Report of the festival, with H's remarks on hymn-singing.

WIMBUSH, ROGER (1974). 'H'. *Gramophone* 52/616 (Sept.), 482. Brief review of a private recording of *The Vision of Dame Christian*.

WOOD, FREDERICK H. (1913). 'GvH: an appreciation'. *BlacknWT* 702 (15 Mar.), 9. An assessment of H's work as exemplified by a concert at Blackburn.

WOOD, RALPH W. (1938). 'The riddle of H'. *MOpin* 61/725 (Feb.), 401–2. Examines the reasons for the decline in interest in H's music after his death.

WOODWARD, DAPHNE (1985). *Essex Composers*. Essex Libraries, 32 pp. Includes a section on H and his work.

WORTHAM, H. E. (1924). *A Musical Odyssey*, Methuen, 199 pp. Contains a short chapter on H, considering his position in the development of English music.

—— (1927). 'Master craftsmen: 5. GH'. *M&Y* 7/1 (Jan.), 9–10. Assessment of his achievement, and main works to date.

YOUNG, PERCY M. (1939). *Pageant of England's Music*. Heffer, 166 pp. Includes a chapter on H and VW, describing their lives and music.

—— (1954). *A Critical Dictionary of Composers and their music.* Dobson, 381 pp. Includes an assessment of H's work, with suggestions of works for study.

—— (1967). *A History of British Music.* Benn, 641 pp. Includes a short section on H: his achievement as composer and teacher.

Index